Praise for THE OLIGARCHS

"In terms of sheer drama, it's an irresistible tale, and David Hoffman's new book . . . milks it for all it's worth . . . Many future readers will find themselves returning to Hoffman's book to find out what, exactly, makes Russia tick."

—*Newsweek*

"Hoffman brilliantly shows how seemingly halting and insignificant acts finally culminated in changes in a whole society."

—*Washington Post*

"Hoffman makes the tale of the men's rise and fall a masterful blend of adventure and serious, informed analysis."

—*Foreign Affairs*

"[Hoffman] offers one the most wide-ranging and sober of several recent descriptions of the oligarchs during the painful past decade of change in Russia."

—*Financial Times*

"Engagingly written . . . the most comprehensive and most fascinating account of the new Russia to date."

—*San Jose Mercury News*

"This sad story comes to life in David Hoffman's sprawling new book . . . for those interested in the future of this puzzled and puzzling country, Hoffman's book could not have come at a better time."

—*Washington Monthly*

"Hoffman's masterly account of this period . . . dispels any doubts that [the oligarchs] did call the shots . . . Without their efforts the Russian people would still be languishing under a hopelessly ineffective command economy. That is one view. The other is that these men were self-serving opportunists who carried out the biggest heist in history . . .

It is the success of Hoffman's compelling story that we come away convinced of both versions."

—*The London Sunday Times*
(Listed in 100 Best Books of the Year)

"Finally, a truly revelatory book about the men who remade Russia in the 1990s . . . experts will be astounded by Hoffman's great reporting, but any curious reader will be intrigued by the stories of these men's extraordinary lives."

—Robert G. Kaiser

"David Hoffman has produced a monumental book . . . *The Oligarchs* may be the last book ever written on the subject since it is hard to imagine anyone else trying to replicate let alone improve upon the quality of research, analysis, and prose contained in this book."

—Michael McFaul

THE OLIGARCHS

Wealth and Power in the New Russia

DAVID E. HOFFMAN

PublicAffairs New York

Published in the United States by PublicAffairs™,
a member of the Perseus Books Group.

 For information, address PublicAffairs, 250 West 57th Street, Suite 1321, New York NY 10107. PublicAffairs books are available at special discounts for bulk purchases in the U.S. by corporations, institutions, and other organizations. For more information, please contact the Special Markets Department at the Perseus Books Group, 11 Cambridge Center, Cambridge MA 02142, or call (617) 252–5298 or email special.markets@perseusbooks.com.

Book design by Mark McGarry, Texas Type & Book Works, Inc.
Set in Trump Mediaeval

Library of Congress Cataloging-in-Publication data
Hoffman, David E., 1953–
The oligarchs: wealth and power in the new Russia / David E. Hoffman.
p. cm.
Includes bibliographical references and index.
ISBN-13 978-1-58648-202-2 (pbk.) ISBN-10 1-58648-202-5 (pbk.)
1. Entrepreneurs—Russia (Federation)
2. Russia (Federation)—Economic conditions—1991–
3. Soviet Union—Economic conditions—1985–1991.
HC340.12 .H64 2001
338′.04′0947—dc21
2001048786

5 7 9 10 8 6

To Carole

Contents

Prologue

THE DEAD OF WINTER found the old man trapped in another brooding, dark season of discontent. Boris Yeltsin, the Russian president, had barely set foot in the Kremlin for two months after being hospitalized in December 1997 for an acute viral infection. In January he disappeared from view, far away from Moscow, at a wooded resort in Valdai, near the border with Finland. Yeltsin was capable of great spurts of activity, but now he was dormant. A year after recovering from heart surgery, his attention span grew short, and he seemed to fade in and out of discussions. In February he went to Italy for a state visit. He looked pale and stiff. At the Tomb of the Unknown Soldier in Rome, he broke protocol by failing to pay tribute to the Italian flag, despite frantic attempts by aides to stop him in front of it. He made a bizarre blunder by announcing that the UN secretary-general, Kofi Annan, would visit Iraq. Annan said he had no such plans. At a press conference, Yeltsin needed help answering simple questions. "I never said I would go to Iraq," he replied, befuddled.

To a small group of Russia's wealthiest businessmen, Yeltsin's behavior was deeply unsettling. Russia needed a strong political leader. With its president ailing, the country seemed adrift. The winds of the Asian financial crisis were already blowing into Russia, driving oil prices down and investors out. The businessmen had much to lose.

Just two years earlier, these tycoons had rescued Yeltsin from another of his dangerous winter hibernations. They offered Yeltsin their most talented political operatives, the enormous power of their television stations, and the front pages of their newspapers for his faltering 1996 reelection campaign. Yeltsin roused himself from a stupor, threw himself into the fight, and won. With the election victory, the tycoons and the president forged a bond—their wealth was grafted to his power. Neither they nor Yeltsin could let go of each other. As their power grew, the tycoons became known as simply the oligarchs, the men who owned and ruled the new Russia.

Now the oligarchs were restless, as their president once again drifted away. Boris Berezovsky was the most ambitious among them. He was a short man, with arching eyebrows and a soft, hurried voice. He had made his fortune exploiting the chaos of Russia's rapid transformation from Soviet socialism to market capitalism. He was fifty-two years old and indefatigable. His latest gambit was audacious—to replace the sitting Russian prime minister, Viktor Chernomyrdin, with someone else, preferably someone who would pay heed to the oligarchs. Berezovsky knew it was a huge decision: the prime minister was next in line of succession. Yeltsin was frequently ill. At any moment, his choice for prime minister could become the next president of Russia. Berezovsky and the other tycoons began to talk seriously about creating a "corporate government." They would become a shadow board of directors. With Yeltsin sick and distant, they would appoint ministers and they would informally run the country. They were Big Capital, and the state was feeble.

The tycoons gathered quietly at the headquarters of Yukos, Russia's second-largest oil company, which was run by one of the oligarchs, Mikhail Khodorkovsky. The shadow board of directors decided it was time for Chernomyrdin to go, and they discussed who would replace him. Berezovsky also met with Yeltsin's chief of staff, Valentin Yumashev, and the president's influential younger daughter, Tatyana Dyachenko.

On Saturday, March 21, 1998, at his country house outside of Moscow, Berezovsky gave a long, taped interview to *Itogi,* a television news program popular among the political elite. The program was carried on Russia's largest and most successful private television channel, NTV, founded by another of the oligarchs, Vladimir Gusinsky.

In the interview, Berezovsky declared pointedly that the campaign to succeed Yeltsin was already under way and that none of the leading candidates were "electable." He spoke vaguely about "immense opportunities to bring forward new people."

The interview was broadcast on Sunday evening. The next morning, Yeltsin fired Chernomyrdin.

This book is a chronicle of six men who helped lead Russia in one of the grandest, most arduous experiments ever attempted: to transform a vast country, in the grip of failed socialism, into an economy of free market capitalism. The story spans more than a decade and a half, from the dawn of Mikhail Gorbachev's *perestroika* and *glasnost* reforms in 1985 to the aftermath of Boris Yeltsin's resignation on December 31, 1999.

These six men became leaders of the new Russia, architects and apostles of a new order. By the end of the 1990s, they had tasted enormous political power or sizable wealth or both. Although their stories are different, the threads running through them are similar: they amassed and lost fortunes, took over the crown jewels of Russian industry, commanded private armies, played kingmaker in elections, and ruled the country and its citadel of finance, Moscow. They bought up the Russian mass media, especially television, and they seized not only factories but also the assets of the state itself, including the budget, the law enforcement system, and the Kremlin leadership. In their swaggering domination of early Russian capitalism, they were secretive, deceptive, and, at times, ruthlessly violent.

The new age that gave rise to these six men began on Sunday, March 10, 1985. Konstantin Chernenko, the Soviet general secretary, a sick man who had been in power only thirteen months, died, and the Kremlin physician, Yevgeny Chazov, telephoned Gorbachev, the youngest member of the ruling Politburo. Within hours black limousines were pulling into the Kremlin for the meeting that would put Gorbachev in power and eventually lead to the implosion of the Soviet Union. What Gorbachev began was revolutionary change that swept up every one of the six subjects of this book. Yet, at the outset, they were distant from the center of power. They were obscure scientists and academics, bureaucrats and students. Certainly, on the day Gorbachev became general secretary, it would have been impossible to pinpoint them as standard-bearers of the coming revolution.

In a second-floor kitchen of a modest Moscow apartment made of crumbling, prefabricated concrete slabs, a rangy, angry young man, a construction crew boss, sat grousing about life in "developed socialism." He was Alexander Smolensky, a thirty-year-old tough guy who drove a dump truck. He had grown up without a father. He was an outsider. His soul was filled with resentment at his lot.

At the Mendeleev Institute for Chemical Technology, a prestigious school for training chemical engineers, Mikhail Khodorkovsky, then twenty-one, was a year away from graduation. His boyish voice hid an inner drive and ambition. Khodorkovsky was already interested in economics—he collected the dues for the Komsomol, the Young Communist League, and was opening a youth café at the institute.

At a bastion of Soviet applied science, the Institute of Control Sciences, where mathematicians and theorists devised ways to control ballistic missiles and atomic power plants, Boris Berezovsky, thirty-nine years old, was a specialist in theories of human decisionmaking and headed his own laboratory, where he had lately been dreaming of winning a Nobel Prize.

Out on the highway to the international airport, a frustrated, skinny young man was at the wheel of his car, which he drove back and forth as an unofficial taxi. Vladimir Gusinsky, thirty-three, was drifting through life. Gusinsky was angry at the world. He had once dreamed of a career in the theater, where he had trained as a director, but he had failed to make it to the Moscow stage.

At the Moscow city council, Yuri Luzhkov sat in a sea of middle-aged Soviet bureaucrats and industrial managers. He did not stand out among the thousand members of the rubber-stamp city legislature. Luzhkov, then forty-eight, spoke the language of the managerial establishment. He was chauffeured around in a black, official Volga car.

At a backwater engineering and economics institute in Leningrad, a lanky redhead, Anatoly Chubais, thirty, displayed a certain stubborn, commanding presence. The son of an orthodox Communist who taught in the military academy, Chubais was losing his faith in the system.

Even if they had gathered in a room on the day of Gorbachev's ascension, these six men would hardly have known what to say to one another. They came from different walks of Soviet life, from the *nomenklatura* and sciences, from the shady world of street hustlers and the ranks of Soviet industrial managers. But what distinguished them was an ability to change. Every one of them learned to manipulate the old system while at the same time making an incredible leap out of it into the new world.

Four of them, Smolensky, Khodorkovsky, Berezovsky, and Gusinsky, became wealthy magnates over the next decade and a half, a coterie of financiers whose fortunes were made in the shadows of political power and who informally ruled the country in Yeltsin's time. Two of them, Luzhkov and Chubais, became powerful political figures. Luzhkov was twice elected mayor of Moscow. The city harbored the largest concentration of capital in Russia, and here Luzhkov built an empire of his own. Chubais was the longest-surviving economic reformer of the 1990s and architect of the largest transfer in history of state-owned assets to private hands. More than any other single individual, he was the father of the wild land grab that followed.

The six men and their country had little preparation and even less experience from history for such a momentous transformation. From where, and from whom, did they learn how to carry it out? In Soviet times, they found the keys to locked libraries and read the "restricted" books on Western economics and finance. They studied in Eastern Bloc countries such as Hungary and Yugoslavia, which were experimenting with more relaxed kinds of socialism, and they traveled to the West. They marveled at the brash heroes of Hollywood films, which were smuggled into Moscow on pirated videocassettes. Later, they were tutored personally at the knees of global tycoons and financiers such as Rupert Murdoch, George Soros, and many others from Wall Street, London, and private banking capitals from Geneva to Gibraltar. American and European investment bankers and lawyers flooded Russia after 1992, helping write Russia's mass privatization program, drafting the all-important laws governing companies, and setting up capital markets. International financial organizations—the World Bank, International Monetary Fund, European Bank for Reconstruction and Development, and others—brought Western templates and ideas to Russia's nascent capitalism in the 1990s.

The new Russian tycoons also borrowed amply from a rich history of plutocracy in Europe and the United States. Although the Russian fortunes were relatively small—the top four Russian commercial banks in 1995 would have ranked a little higher than thirtieth in Italy—they nonetheless adopted the style and methods of the great robber barons, emulating their brazen deals, steely self-confidence, daring gambits, and superrich fantasies. A resemblance to American capitalists of the early twentieth century was not entirely accidental. Theodore Dreiser's powerful novels *The Financier* and *An American Tragedy* were translated into Russian and widely read during the Soviet era because they provided such trenchant commentary on the underside of American capitalism. Many of the techniques of the first Russian financiers can be found in the deals made by Frank Cowperwood, the hero of *The Financier*, who exploited banks, the state, and investors, manipulated the whole stock market and gobbled up companies. The 1912 novel was based on the life of a real American magnate, Charles T. Yerkes.

But if they had Western models, these Russians were also unique. They inherited a country with a political and economic culture rooted in centuries of Russian obedience to authority, arbitrarily defined, from tsars to commissars. They inherited a society in which the simplest human instincts of individual initiative and entrepreneurship had been suppressed for seven decades, surviving only in the shadows. The Soviet mind-set lingered and could not be erased in the first years after the arrival of a market economy on alien soil.

Russia was also unique because of a critical choice made immediately after the Soviet Union collapsed. Yeltsin deployed a band of radical young reformers, including Chubais, who, believing they had little time, set out to wreck the old system at any cost. They chose to free prices and property first and to install rules and institutions of a market economy only later. The result was that Russian capitalism was born into an airless space, a vacuum without effective laws and a state so badly weakened it could not enforce laws that were on the books. Time and again, questions arose about the deals made by these six men: Were they legal? Were they criminal? But the questions were not easily answered because the players moved about in a world lacking the legal constraints or the moral compass of a mature Western society. In these early years, Russia was a state without the rule of law. Lying, stealing, and cheating were part of daily business, and violence, brutality, and coercion were often tools of the trade. It is not to excuse the contract killings, the blatant thefts, or greedy ambitions of those who led the Russian capitalist revolution to say that the entire experience occurred in a free fall, a zone of the unknown. One of the Russian magnates ruefully told me in the summer of 2000 that his once-cherished hopes in Soviet times about the magic of free markets, private property, and the rule of law had all turned out to be serious oversimplifications. "It's taken us much longer than we thought," he said, "and too many people were killed."

In the Western experience, tycoons often feasted off both the government and private capital. The Rothschilds were bankers to princes; J. P. Morgan was a bridge between British lenders and American railroads. But Russia's first tycoons drew their early sustenance almost entirely from one source: the state. They keenly saw, and exploited, its many weaknesses. They seized on the colossal imbalances in prices, property, and trade that were the legacy of the Soviet system—and made fortunes from it. With several notable exceptions, they built very little that was new on the ground in these early years. Rather, their first lessons were how to make easy money, which came to them so effortlessly that they seemed to grab it out of thin air.

In these early years of protocapitalism, the six men portrayed in this volume came to know each other well in business alliances, in friendship, and in hatred. Their troubled relations became a never ending public spectacle. At a private club on a hill overlooking Moscow's cityscape in September 1994, some of them signed a secret pact promising not to attack each other, a pledge they soon abandoned. They formed alliances and then destroyed them. They built empires and tried to wreck those of their competitors. They all agreed about the failure of the old system, but they held quite different visions of the new.

To understand how far the oligarchs came, it is necessary to begin where they began, with the Soviet years of stagnation, the shortage economy and shadow markets. All six men were shaped by this era of decaying socialism, a time when each of them began to think—and act—toward a new order. The first chapter of this book is set in the years of stagnation, a view from the street and from inside the dying system. The following six chapters probe more deeply the road each man followed in Gorbachev's era of restructuring, or *perestroika,* and into the first years of the new Russia. The remaining nine chapters, in Part II of the book, examine the tumultuous 1990s through the oligarchs' exploits and failures. It is the story of how a rapacious, unruly capitalism was born on the ashes of Soviet communism.

PART ONE

Chapter 1

Shadows and Shortages

IN THE SUMMER HEAT, the glass facade of Kursky Station loomed above the sweaty crowds. The train station hall was a monumental box of glass, concrete, and space; it was stark, modern, even utopian, and the design spoke of progress. Such progress! Reflected in the glass facade, the travelers and transients below were a bazaar of traders, strivers, hustlers, and survivors, trying to make the best of life in "developed socialism" in the Soviet Union. Pies? Beer? Ice cream? Live chicks? It was there, spread out before the glass wall and just beyond, in the open platform between the station and the rows of waiting trains. From here, the long-distance rail lines stretched toward far-off cities of the south, toward Baku, Tbilisi, and the Crimea. The commuter trains ran out of the capital toward small villages and country cottages, the dachas. On a summer day, the crowds surged out of Moscow on the commuter trains, the *elektrichkas*, to the villages of summer retreat, to the cool birches.

Most Moscow train stations were seedy terminals of despair. People slept on the floors, newspapers spread out under them; the waiting halls were zones of misery, reeking of drunks and stale smoke. But Kursky Station had been rebuilt in the 1970s, transformed into an architectural statement towering above the misery. It was a monument to a system that loved angular, concrete congratulations to itself. They were spread across the landscape of the Soviet Union, celebrations of ideology, great exclamation points—*to the achievements of the party and the people!*

But for most people who passed by them, these socialist monuments were no longer even noticeable, no more remarkable than a lamppost or a tree. The architectural style remained—massive and imposing—but the meaning was gone. The truth was that the people surging in and out of Kursky Station had stopped paying attention to the stale propaganda and the hollow modernism presented by the Soviet system. A chasm separated them from the state. They no longer believed in a bright Communist future. They knew that even as the system declared its greatness, it was stagnating, rotting from within. People spent half their lives in a struggle to overcome the most basic shortages, to lay their hands on a cut of meat or a pair of boots. They survived thanks to a vast, unofficial second economy—a shadow economy—that somehow provided a cushion against the harsh realities of life.

Irina Makarova knew both the reality and the lie. A bright young schoolteacher, with shoulder-length black hair worn in stylish curls, her face framed in aviator glasses, Irina made her way through the bustling crowd outside Kursky Station. She led her four-year-old daughter with one hand and gripped a bulging red rucksack with the other. It was a hot day in the summer of 1985, and she did not bother to notice the modernistic facade of Kursky Station. She did not pay attention to the declarations of the Party Congress or the latest five-year plan or the absurd television news broadcasts about peasants happily preparing for the harvest. It was all so distant from real life. At home, in the kitchen, they had been talking often about the new general secretary, about this younger man, Mikhail Gorbachev. But at this moment she did not stop to ponder politics or worry about the future; she worried about the water.

Irina clutched her young daughter's hand as they approached the small bustling square outside the train station. She stiffly resisted the pull toward a hulking, blue-gray vending machine, as big as a refrigerator, with the disgusting jar that everyone drank from. Long ago, the machine had boasted a real drinking glass and a separate, tiny nook in which you could rinse it, put your kopeks in the machine, and watch the sulphurous water pour down. But then the glass had been stolen. Someone replaced it with a jar, an old mayonnaise jar, with a grimy string tied about its neck. They all drank from the jar. She desperately hoped she could pass it without being tugged by her young daughter—who always wanted a drink—toward that jar with the dirty string.

Inside, the train station was cool and dark. She found the line for tickets to Kupavna, a small village of summer cottages beyond the oppressive metropolis of Moscow. Kupavna was their refuge, but it was never easy to flee the city. It meant struggling, shoving, pushing, and always hustling in small ways, grabbing what you could when you could. The line for the tickets on the *elektrichka* to Kupavna was the first hurdle. Children cried in the line, passengers pressed forward. People pressed so close that she could smell the soap—that brown, caked soap they used for everything—for the laundry, for the dishes.

The ticket windows were imposingly tall. Yet no one could look in or out. Each was closed off by a faded, dirty drawn blind that fell down to a tiny rabbit hole–sized sliding door at the bottom. The authorities did not want the angry crowds peering in, so they closed out the exhausted faces of the passengers with the impenetrable blind. Through the rabbit hole, Irina saw the hands, but not the face, of the clerk on the other side. Two tickets for Kupavna, fifteen kopeks each.

Then back to the doors. For all the vastness of the station hall, with its high ceiling and wall of glass and huge main floor, when it came to people, everything was constricted, as if a hand were reaching down and choking them at the throat. Four doors stood at the entrance to the tracks yet three of them were closed and locked, so people surged, pushed and shoved to get through the one door. Irina pushed out into the bright sunshine, toward the long, slinking green trains. Then, just as they turned toward the trains, she saw it.

Toilet paper!

A crowd was pressing shoulder to shoulder. Instinct and years of survival took over. Irina had long understood that to survive in this life, you grabbed what you could when you saw it. She saw they were selling toilet paper from an open box and didn't hesitate; she bought twenty rolls because it was there.

She had no free hand to carry the toilet paper. On one shoulder she carried the heavy red rucksack, packed with books and things for the dacha. With her other hand, she clung to her daughter. She dug into her bag and found a piece of string. She laced the rolls of toilet paper together and, without a moment's thought, she was wearing a toilet paper necklace. No one thought it unusual; it was life—she bought what came her way. When she wanted to go out and buy a chicken, she didn't. She bought toilet paper, and next time when she wanted toilet paper, she'd probably get a chicken.

They boarded the *elektrichka*. The wooden bench seats were three across, the wagons jammed full. A bicycle was parked in the aisle, dogs barked, fruit trees were bound in cloth bags, heavy suitcases piled on seats, children dodged and squirmed. It was stifling. The thick windows of the train were closed like vaults that trapped inside the smells of herring wrapped in paper, cheese, and cigarette smoke. The train lurched forward.

Despite the packed and stuffy cars, the heavy bag that cut a crease into her fingers, and the toilet paper rolls around her neck, something wonderful lifted her spirits when the train pulled out. The burden of Moscow slipped backward through the windows. It was true for all of them, the *dachniki*. They were escaping, running from the suffocating lives they led in the city to their own private reserves of fresh air.

As the train picked up speed and the city slipped away, the whine of the electric motors grew ever more shrill, then faded away. Hulking factories, fields of rusting cranes, and concrete skeletons of unfinished buildings passed solemnly by the window. It was a parade of decay.

Irina was a survivor and strove to do her best in a world of gross imperfection. She learned English and taught it at a special school, although she had never met anyone who spoke native English. She had always, loyally, put on that artificial face, that mask, at the meetings of the Komsomol, the party's youth organization, even though she knew the whole exercise was empty and meaningless. They implored her to be a true Komsomol member. To preach principles of the Komsomol builder! Yet she knew the system was creaking. Irina was thirty years old when Gorbachev came to power. She and her generation had come of age during the Brezhnev malaise of the 1970s and early 1980s. These were called the years of stagnation, the *gody zastoya*. But they were also called the period of senility—*marazm*.

The senility of Soviet socialism thrust its failure in their face every day. Often they dreamed of drinking a certain scarce tea with a yellow label. The leaves were finer and cut thinner, and when they brewed it, the tea was a rich reddish brown. The tea came in a yellow pack with an elephant on it. Supposedly it was from India. But there was a desperate shortage of this yellow-packeted tea. It was impossible to find and no one knew if it really came from India. But if you spotted it, you willingly stood in long lines for it, at any time.

Then there was the canned meat. The cans were discarded army rations, and everyone knew it. But fresh meat was nowhere to be found. In the provinces, people went for years without seeing fresh meat in the stores. The state dumped the tinned-meat army rations on them. If they saw twenty cans, they bought them on the spot. They hoarded it; they hoarded everything, just in case. Canned meat on spaghetti was a meal to savor. There weren't many kinds of pasta, either; the thick, long, grayish kind took forever to cook. They dreamed of the tea with the elephant, the stewed meat in cans, and perhaps real spaghetti. Sometimes they could obtain better pasta, like the finer types from Italy. They couldn't buy it, but they could—with great effort—get it. This was the story of their life; although the Russian language had a verb "to buy," they preferred to say "to get" or "to take." They would say, "I took a half kilo of butter." What you could "get" or "take" did not depend on money but on connections, on luck, on fate.

The Soviet state theoretically provided for almost everything—medical care, schooling, transportation, work. In the hulking gray headquarters on Marx Prospekt in central Moscow, Gosplan, the mammoth state central planning agency, arranged how to allocate every ton of steel, deliver every bolt, utilize every last gear in the administrative-command economy. Khrushchev had vowed that Communism would overtake capitalism by 1980. Yet in the mid-1980s, Irina's generation knew, felt, and tasted every day the hollowness of that long-ago promise. Soviet socialism provided less and less, and they struggled to survive with their own networks of friends and connections. They lived with a carnival of wants, always on the prowl.

The state stores never threw anything away. They just sold it to people. Irina had seen it many times: they wrapped up a package of outdated canned herring and stale bread, and one packet of the tea with the elephant. And, maybe, the pasta, in a fancy red cover. These packages were called *zakazy*, or orders, and every school, every factory, every kindergarten, and every institute offered them to workers, perhaps once a month. There was no choice: if you wanted to enjoy the Indian tea with the elephant, you had to take everything that went with it: the stale bread, the old herring.

Irina's generation lived their lives in long, slow cycles of shortages. The Soviet Union at the time was devoting massive resources to the arms race, but for its citizens there were toilet paper necklaces and outdated cans of herring. Every year, the shortages seemed to grow worse. At the beginning of the 1980s, there was cheese, one kind of sausage, milk, margarine, sugar, bread, and the basic necessities. Even so, back then, Irina and her family complained to each other that there was nothing in the stores. They would say it aloud, "there's nothing," and they meant that they wanted a bit of ham, but there was no ham. They wanted a beer but there was no beer. Sadly, they didn't really know what was coming; they could not imagine that there would *really* be nothing.

The shortages rubbed their emotions raw. Irina had seen the fire in people's eyes when suddenly bags of flour appeared in a store. Soon five hundred people were waiting, writing their place in line—their number—on their palms. The white-smocked counter lady was patient with the first hundred. Then she started snarling. She hated them. People would be begging. Please, give me two kilos of flour!

Once cans of condensed milk appeared, hundreds of blue cans, painstakingly arranged in a pattern on the counter. A year later, there was no sausage, only cheese and condensed milk. Then after another year, no cheese, only condensed milk. Then the condensed milk was gone!

There was bread and maybe sugar, but then the flour was gone. The shelves got more barren with each passing year, and one day the shelves filled up—with canned seaweed from the Far East, carefully arranged in delicate patterns, as the condensed milk had been. Although no one could eat it, the canned seaweed soon disappeared too.

Then there was the apple juice. Children always thirsted for something, but there was only apple juice, very poor quality, and even that was not always available. It came in three-liter jars with ugly labels haphazardly slapped on the outside. The juice tasted of iron because of the lid. A strong can opener was needed to pry off the lid, and very often the glass neck of the jar shattered in the process. The juice always had to be filtered through gauze to get the glass out of it.

One day Irina's sister-in-law called, shouted into the telephone, "Get dressed fast, Ira! Near the Sokol metro station, they have thrown out children's fur coats! Hurry!" She had used the verb "to throw out" but she meant put on sale. Irina's sister-in-law was 875th in line, and she put Irina down for 876. They rushed to the spot every day, for days, as the line dwindled. Three, four hours a day they stood in line, every day, no time left for anything else. It took all their energy. When their turn came, Irina bought several small fur coats and sewed two of them together to make one coat for herself.

When jeans arrived in the 1970s, Irina remembered how her generation went crazy. Clothes were important because as poor as they were, it was the only thing that differentiated them from each other. People would deny themselves food to buy something flashy or extravagant. They knew they could never afford to move to another apartment, but they could buy something to stand out in a crowd. Irina's monthly salary as a schoolteacher was 110 rubles, but she spent 100 rubles for a pair of winter boots. It was not enough—she still had no winter coat. When the boots wore out, she bought a coat but had no boots. When she had a brown skirt, she had no blouse to match it; when she finally had enough for a blouse, the skirt was worn out. People had one pair of shoes for all occasions.

Within the Soviet Union, consumers had developed tastes. They were hungry for goods, influenced by what they could learn and hear about the West. But the Soviet Union did not produce contemporary consumer goods to satisfy them, and jeans were the symbol of all they lacked. The Soviet planners had not, at first, made allowances for jeans and only later supplied cheaply made imitations of the Western ones. But real jeans could be had, from travelers or scalpers, or in the special shops where the Soviet elite spent their special hard-currency certificates. The younger generation—Irina and her friends—wore jeans to the theater, to the office, anywhere, for months at a time.

The years of *marazm* turned them all into a vast, informal human network of connections and friends that spread from family to family, from apartment landings to workplaces, from Moscow to the distant provinces, a chain of *svyazi*, or connections, that helped them survive when the system could not provide. This network was part of the vast second economy, a shadow system that existed alongside the official world of five-year plans. The shadow economy thrived in industry, in retail trade, in black markets and everywhere that people were struggling to make up for the failures of Soviet socialism. Irina knew a relative who was on the admissions committee for an institute, a much sought-after school. People fought to get in, and her relative took favors from the applicants. "Where would I get meat or sausage or medicine?"

she had asked Irina once. "How would I manage without my *svyazi*? I would be a helpless nobody." If you needed to see a doctor, you went there with a gift in your coat pocket, perhaps wrapped nicely in a treasured, brightly colored plastic bag. It wasn't bribery, but an accepted way of survival. To get Irina into a good hospital when her daughter was born, her sister-in-law had come up with several crystal vases and a couple of necklaces made of semiprecious stones for the head doctor.

The shadow economy nestled in the bosom of the official system. In the drive to shape a "new man," liberated somehow from greed and envy, the Soviet authorities had devoted enormous effort to wiping out the spirit of entrepreneurship. The system sought to eliminate all private property and quash private economic activity beyond control of the state. The official orthodoxy was strict and severe: people went to jail for economic "crimes," such as daring to buy and sell scarce goods or set up a small underground factory. The whole atmosphere, reinforced by decades of propaganda and penalties, created a cult of hatred toward those who made their own money. They were labeled speculators and criminals. Even so, the basic human instinct for entrepreneurship survived in this hostile climate. The desire to survive, to make the best of life, literally drove the shadow economy. The writer Andrei Sinyavsky, who served seven years in a prison camp for publishing his fiction abroad, recalled that in Soviet society all sorts of operations ran "on the left," or beyond the realm of the state, for personal gain. Theft at a factory or a collective farm became a way of life; underground "production" thrived despite the risks. Sinyavsky told a remarkable story about workers at a Moscow tram depot who, at their own risk and peril, revived an old tram, already consigned to the scrap heap, and put it back on track as their own private enterprise. "Outwardly, it looked like any other state tram," he recalled, "but inside, the driver and conductor were working not for the state, and the passengers' kopeks were not going to the state treasury. This was a private enterprise inside socialist city transport. Long after the crime was uncovered and the criminals imprisoned, people were still gleefully recalling the story of Moscow's private tram."[1]

Years later, Lev Timofeyev, an economist who frequently wrote about everyday life, recalled how the shadow economy spread through the official one. "A shadow beef filet is sold at a state-owned shop by a meat salesman, whom we know personally," he said. "Shadow wood grows in a state-owned forest. A physician renders shadow service to shadow patients in a state-owned hospital. Shadow goods are produced in the sphere of legal production. Shadow trades happen in the offices of official enterprises—both sellers and buyers of the shadow market occupy certain positions in the official administration. Even two soccer matches—a legal and a shadow one—take place simultaneously at the very same soccer field." This was a reference to an official match that, in the shadow world, was "fixed" beforehand for a bribe.[2]

No one ever thought they could get along without their own private networks, and decades before, a word had appeared in Russian, *blat*, which captured the basic dynamic of the shadow economy. It was once a faintly notorious word having distant connections to thieves, but the expression had evolved to refer simply to using friends and connections to get something. In the world of *blat* and *svyazi*, those who controlled the scarcity, those at the choke point of the shortage, like the butcher, held real power in people's lives. Although officially the Soviet authorities did not approve, the truth was that *blat* grew up because the Soviet system had failed—had created so many shortages and wants that people had found another way to satisfy them.[3]

Irina and her generation wanted more—much more—than the system could provide. The Soviet Union felt like a prison cell sometimes, the walls unyielding. The authorities strictly controlled travel abroad, monitored mail from outside, and put overseas publications under lock and key. They even saw evil in copy machines, which were locked up. Igor Primakov, a computer scientist, recalled how he would often cradle his shortwave radio on his lap and settle into his favorite easy chair, which could swivel in a 360-degree circle. At night during the 1970s, when Western radio broadcasts were jammed, he slowly, methodically, rotated the chair, exactly one degree right, two degrees left, three degrees right, until he could pick up the BBC or Radio Liberty. He learned English from the radio. Another force that broke down the walls of the Soviet Union was the Beatles. Against Soviet state ideology and mythology, the Beatles left an indelible mark on the youth of Irina's generation, who painstakingly copied down the stanzas of their songs, learning the English word by word.

By the early 1980s, the system had begun to weaken, and the way of life outside—including the often lavish capitalist lifestyles portrayed in American pop culture—increasingly seeped through. The most dramatic break was a technological invention: the videocassette recorder. When VCRs began to be smuggled in to the Soviet Union during the early 1980s, there was no stopping the flood tide of movies, and with the movies came a spellbinding glimpse of Western prosperity. The movies were easily circulated from hand to hand, and night after night, young people would stay up watching Western films, sometimes three in a row until dawn. They observed the other life closely: the clothes, the manners, the talk, and the meaning of money and wealth. They were awed when a Hollywood film character casually opened the refrigerator in his apartment: it was always full!

Primakov and his wife, Masha Volkenstein, a sociologist, recalled for me years later how they and their friends loved to play Monopoly, which someone had smuggled in from Spain. For a year, they stayed up late into the night in pursuit of Boardwalk and Park Place. It wasn't so much the money as the feeling of a Western casino, of freedom—it was Monte Carlo they were dreaming about.[4]

The day-to-day reality was a sullen struggle to survive, any way they could. The seemingly monolithic face of the Soviet centrally planned economy was in fact full of cracks, and they spent their lives squeezing between these cracks. When Irina's train stopped at Kupavna, she and her daughter rushed off, walking down the platform and across the tracks, down a path and toward the dacha. Kupavna was a poor village, and the local store offered only meager goods: fat in a huge bowl covered with flies, brown soap, cotton fabric in rolls, and vodka—an endless supply of vodka. Irina did not even bother to look inside. After leaving her things at the dacha, she walked through a small stand of birches to a forbidding wall, a barrier of prefabricated concrete slabs so high you couldn't see over it. And you were not supposed to go through it. The wall was the monolithic face of the system.

Beyond the wall lay a base for navy personnel, a military outpost. They called it the *gorodok*, little town. Irina had no idea what they did there and didn't care. She looked for a gap in the wall. The holes were patched over almost as quickly as people could find them. There—yes!—the slabs had separated. Irina slipped inside and made a beeline for a squat building near the main gate, Military Store 28. Officially, it was just for naval officers and their families, but no one noticed as Irina took a place in the line waiting for stuffed cabbages, sausage, and cheese. She had just found another crevice in the crazy world of the shortage economy.

Once again, for one more day, she had found a way to survive.[5]

*

From the time he was a boy, Vitaly Naishul knew that numbers could speak the truth. His father had been a mathematician who calculated orbits for Soviet space satellites. His mother also was a mathematician, and so was his sister. Naishul graduated from the mathematics faculty of Moscow State University. They were a family of the intelligentsia. His father held a sensitive, top-secret post, the details of which he was careful never to discuss at home, yet he also listened to the BBC and Voice of America on the radio. Naishul wanted to work as a mathematician too and kept his faith in numbers. He felt that they spoke logically, even powerfully—one thing you couldn't bend was the answer. There was truth in mathematics, and in the Soviet system of the 1970s it had not been ruined by ideology. Two plus two equaled four, and not even the system could change that. Or so it seemed.

Naishul was assigned a researcher's job in the Economic Research Institute of the State Planning Committee, or Gosplan, a citadel of the Soviet system. Naishul did not see himself as a builder of Communism. He wanted to be a mathematician, and took the job gladly.

Naishul sat in the very heart of a great beast, one that ruled the economic life of an empire, allocating the resources for everything from the titanium hulls of the world's largest nuclear submarine, the *Typhoon,* which were being built in the Northern Fleet shipyards, to the simple manufacture of a sundress from cotton and dyes in the provincial textile town of Ivanovo.

The empire was fabulously rich in resources, brimming with natural gas, oil, and vast quantities of timber, coal, and precious metals. It was also impossibly large, covering one-sixth of the Earth's landmass, stretching eleven time zones from east to west and straddling two continents, Europe and Asia. The monopoly on power over this gigantic country was held by the Communist Party in a top-down hierarchy, starting with the Politburo, then the general secretary, the Central Committee, and hundreds of thousands of party functionaries in republics, regions, cities, factories, theaters, offices, schools, and institutes. The party had a special personnel system, the *nomenklatura,* by which it kept track of this network of appointees, from the elite in Moscow to a distant factory director or infantry unit. All roads led back to Moscow and the central authorities. Not only did they command a globe-spanning military force, not only did they seek to control literature, art, theater, and culture, not only did they dominate the sciences and seek to rule a far-flung empire of satellite nations, but also from the center, from the corridors and balance sheets of Gosplan, they tried to control every important economic decision.

From his seat at Gosplan, Vitaly Naishul gradually began to see that something was wrong. Naishul's soft smile and black, wiry hair concealed a bit of revolutionary spirit. He did not openly display his suspicions and emotions, for that might have been risky. Instead, he began to secretly write about what he saw, and the result was a remarkable book in *samizdat* (or self-published) in dog-eared, carbon-paper copies. The book was titled *Another Life,* and it was a visionary tract.

To understand why Naishul's work—written at his kitchen table in the early 1980s—was so important, it is necessary to reach back in time to a momentous battle of ideas. Let's take a brief tour of this conflict, which was at the center of the Soviet economy and its collapse, before returning to Naishul.

In the Industrial Revolution of the mid-eighteenth century in Britain, automation and factories transformed rural, agricultural economies into urban, industrial ones. A new, more important economic actor was created, the industrialist, who pushed aside the early dominance of landholders, merchants, and traders. Adam Smith, the Scottish economist and philosopher, was the prophet of this new age. In his great work, *The Wealth of Nations,* Smith explained coherently how the central underlying motive in economic life is self-interest. In his most famous passage, he wrote: "It is not from the benevolence of the butcher, the brewer, or the baker, that we expect our dinner, but from their regard to their own interest. We address ourselves, not to their humanity, but to their self-love, and never talk to them of our own necessities but of their advantages." Smith said the individual "is in this, as in many other cases, led by an invisible hand to promote an end which was no part of his intention."

This observation marked a huge step forward in economic thinking. Smith made self-interest respectable. Central to Smith's argument was the concept of free trade and competition. His ideas were later refined by other European philosophers, who peered into the inner workings of early industrial capitalism and laid down a set of rules about the way the world worked. They believed that the basic relationship between employer and worker, or between land, capital, and labor, never changes. They stand in a state of "equilibrium." There could be changes in the supply of labor and capital, for example, but that only would only bring a new "equilibrium" that was profoundly stable.[6]

A relentless German revolutionary who lived a quiet, isolated life in London, Karl Marx mounted a mighty challenge to classical economics and the theory of stability. His long-time colleague, Friedrich Engels, said Marx was "before all else a revolutionist," because he saw the world not at rest in equilibrium but constantly changing. Marx believed that just as the new industrialists, the capitalists of his age, were displacing the landed, ruling classes, the capitalists would also pass. The system described by the classical economists would come to a spectacular end with a revolt of the working class. Marx saw capitalism as just a passing phase—although a necessary one—and believed that it would have to "ripen" fully before it would eventually consume itself.[7]

Marx and Engels gave full voice to their theory in *The Communist Manifesto*, published in 1848, in which they describe the world as splitting into "two great hostile camps," the capitalists or bourgeoisie on one side and the working class, or proletariat, on the other. Marx and Engels quite accurately observed that capitalism had unleashed enormous productive powers in the hundred years since the beginning of the Industrial Revolution. But they declared that capitalists had reduced everything in human relations to "naked self-interest." They saw the small shops and merchants of an earlier age turned into the "great factory of the industrial capitalist," where workers are "daily and hourly enslaved by the machine" and by the capitalist himself. They demanded the abolition of private property and predicted the demise of the bourgeoisie in a revolt by the working class.

Marx's ideology was enthroned in 1917, when Vladimir Lenin and the Bolsheviks seized power in Russia. But Lenin and his revolutionary cohorts did not seize a country with a ripe, developed capitalism of the kind that Marx had foreseen. Nor were they propelled to power by an abused working class. Instead, Lenin both sparked and led a revolt in a country where industry and capitalism were unevenly developed, the economy was predominately agricultural, and the people were disinclined to rise up against their economic masters. Lenin's accomplishment was to organize a coup d'état while giving the appearance of a workers' and peasants' revolt. Lenin shrewdly played on the peasants' hunger for land, but the Bolshevik revolution later proved a disastrous turn for the peasants. Lenin could not wait for capitalism to "ripen" as Marx had predicted and believed that the Russian revolution would touch off a worldwide socialist revolt. It did not, but in the years after the revolution, the Bolsheviks put into practice their ideas of what Marx intended, erratically and violently. It was the beginning of a seventy-four-year experiment to defy the laws of capitalism and suppress the basic instincts of human nature. It was an experiment that, however grim and ultimately disastrous, touched all of those described in this book, who attempted to lead Russia on a different path.

The experiment took twists and turns. The civil war was marked by chaos, anarchy, and a period of stringent economic measures known as War Communism. A relative easing began in 1921 under Lenin's New Economic Policy, which tolerated some market mechanisms in agriculture and trade. This short interlude was crushed by Joseph Stalin at the end of the 1920s. Stalin began to impose a massive command economy on the nation. He repeatedly tried to force prices downward, especially on grain and agricultural goods, with devastating results. Those who set their own prices, the private entrepreneurs, were accused of criminal "speculation." Stalin turned viciously against the stubbornly independent peasants, forcing them onto collective farms. In 1929 he attempted a forced "revolution from above," brutally collectivizing agriculture and creating a vast legacy of human misery—famine, death, and shortages.

One of Stalin's most important tools was central planning. The Bolsheviks had tried to get rid of money, to destroy free trade, to dictate prices—in short, to break the basic laws of capitalism. But now they went a step further, trying to coerce the behavior of the entire economy. Instead of leaving anything to choice and competition, to a multitude of accidental and self-interested transactions, the state seized all the levers of the economic machine through central planning. It adopted five-year plans intended to dictate how the economy would work; the first was approved in 1928. After a relatively good year, suddenly the targets were adjusted to accomplish the whole plan in four years. Later Stalin suggested maybe three years. Instead of the original goal to produce 35 million tons of coal over the period, the plan was revised to 75 million and then 95–105 million. "We are fifty or a hundred years behind the advanced countries," Stalin said in 1931. "We must make good this distance in ten years. Either we do so, or we shall go under."[8]

Any dissent was suppressed by fear, and central planning endured, along with legends of superhuman productivity. In September 1935, a coal miner, Alexei Stakhanov, supposedly achieved output fourteen times greater than the target and was hailed by the party as a hero; with this exploit the Stakhanovite movement was born, an idealistic symbol of the new society in the making.

Stalin's model heaved the Soviet Union into the industrial age, accomplishing in slightly over a decade what in other countries had taken more than a century. Gigantic factories were carved out of the wilderness; beyond the Ural Mountains, a colossal steelworks was built at Magnitogorsk that eventually churned out more steel than all of Canada. Stalin turned a backward country into a major industrial power at enormous human cost, as millions were sent to prison camps, including talented managers, engineers, technicians, and planners. Everywhere there were said to be spies, wreckers, and saboteurs. The burst of industrialization sucked labor from the villages into the cities, leading to misery and urban overcrowding. The Stalin model of central planning, directed at heavy industry and militarization, helped the Soviet Union through World War II and later was expanded to support a massive Cold War military machine. Virtually all other components of the economy were secondary, especially consumers.

By the 1970s, Brezhnev's era, the Soviet Union had become a global superpower, and yet the great economic leaps forward that Stalin had accomplished were no longer possible. The demands of a more complex economy made it especially difficult to set plans from above. Two attempts at reform—one by Nikita Khrushchev in the late 1950s and another under Alexei Kosygin in the mid-1960s—failed. The state kept its tight grip on property, prices, and trade; none of the attempts to breathe new life into the system worked. The oil price spikes of the 1970s and early 1980s had cushioned the decline by providing the Soviet Union with revenue from its vast reserves. But the West was beginning a new Industrial Revolution in high technology. The Soviet Union was entering the twilight years of the socialist experiment.

Now we return to Naishul, the mathematician sitting at Gosplan, the heart of the central planning machine. Naishul came to a profound conclusion in the early 1980s from his vantage point inside Gosplan: the system was sick. Supposedly, he knew, the Communist Party set down goals and instructions, which were passed down through Gosplan and then through the branches of government, the ministries, the factories. But the reality he witnessed was far different. One day, Naishul's boss went to the Kremlin, and when he came back to Gosplan, he told an amazing story of what he had just seen. The prime minister told the minister of metallurgy that the Soviet Union had to manufacture a new kind of steel in thin sheets. This was an order from the top, from the party, written into the party's guidelines for the five-year plan. And the minister of metallurgy said, without a pause, "No." But then he added, "Unless you give us the resources to build new factories and enterprises, we will not do it!" Naishul's boss just shook his head with amazement, for he thought the minister would be thrown out. Fired. Shot. But he wasn't. Nothing happened. That was a glimpse of how the system really functioned, and the system was sick.

Inside what was formally known as the administrative-command economy, there was a complex parade of input and output targets, goals and quotas, balances and controls, that marched up and down the ladders of authority. By the 1970s, the promenade of planning, an elaborate blizzard of paper, was nightmarishly complicated. Just the industrial supply and distribution plans created by Gosplan totaled seventy volumes of nearly twelve thousand pages and dealt with over thirty thousand commodities. The Gosplan mathematicians toiled over their models, but after a while, Naishul saw that his bosses took his mathematical work and, to his horror, they just *changed the answers* to fit whatever outcome they wanted or needed that day.

Naishul had a sudden insight. The system no longer was really commanded from the top. There was no dictator! Instead the whole bureaucratic planning system had become a strange, never ending, undisciplined bazaar. At the core there were no firm commands but bargaining. From below, factory directors made demands on the ministries and the ministries made demands on the central planners; all the tugging and pulling went up the ladder and then came tumbling back down again in the form of a cascade of decisions that never matched the initial demands. If the decision was to take away from one factory and give to another, the loser did not accept the decision and began to lobby others for what it wanted, sometimes not up the ladder but sideways, from other factories. The key players in these transactions were often not the central planners at all, but the factory managers, who gained more and more power as the system weakened.

Everyone, not just factories, was engaged in a wild crisscrossing web of demands, permissions, secret hoards, trade-offs, and shortages, and the planning system could hardly keep up, much less control it.

Naishul liked to tell of a Communist Party boss in a faraway region. The people in Moscow thought he was busily building socialism. But, the boss told Naishul, "My business, the first half of my day, is to exchange chickens from my region for eggs produced in another." The growth of these side deals meant that Gosplan gradually controlled less and less. In the 1920s, central planning had been born to grab the levers of power over the economy and jerk them sharply; now the levers were jerked back and forth and there was no result. The steering wheel was being turned, Naishul liked to say, and nothing was happening.

Naishul concluded that, surprisingly, the system had been infected by characteristics of the one great idea Marx and Lenin had sought to bury: capitalism. Gosplan resembled not so much the cathedral of Marx's hopes for a utopian workers' paradise, but rather a crude commodity exchange. The currency of this exchange could be many things, including the very stuff of the state machine—such as bureaucratic "approvals" or permissions. Anything of value in the hierarchy of Soviet life was traded: status, power, laws and the right to violate laws. Naishul discovered that even the official command economy operated on the principles of the shadow economy—the official world was rife with *blat* and *svyazi.* To Naishul it looked far more like a market than anyone wanted to admit. Naishul concluded that Soviet socialism was degenerating, slowly and agonizingly, because the great imperatives of the Stalin years, revolution and war, had long since vanished from the system.[9]

What's more, Naishul saw that there was no accountability. Factory managers took production goals seriously, but if they were producing something shoddy or unnecessary, the system imposed no penalty on them and they did not go out of business. As long as their product was in the plan, the state would provide them with new subsidies the next year. Naishul concluded that the vaunted totalitarian state was actually quite weak.

This weakness was evident in the statistical cover-ups that so angered Naishul. Virtually all statistical yearbooks, articles, and other material provided for open publication by the authorities had been scrubbed clean and altered to eliminate any negative information.[10] In most of Western Europe, life expectancy had continued to grow, but in the Soviet Union, during the years of stagnation, it leveled out, yet another sign that the system was in trouble. What did the bosses do? They made the statistics on life expectancy top secret. Demographers were told to work on "theoretical models" and were denied access to real data about the population.[11]

Perhaps the most audacious stretch of all was a series of mathematical calculations about supply and demand in the Soviet economy—the "balances." In a classic market system, supply and demand are balanced out by free prices: an excess of supply drives the price down, and an excess of demand drives it up. But the Soviet planners tried to break these basic laws and dictate supply, demand, and price. They decided that ten thousand automobiles would be manufactured, they decided how much iron, steel, and rubber had to be set aside to make them, and they set a final price for each car. The price was absurdly low, subsidized by the state without regard to the real costs of building the car. The result was that supply never could satisfy demand. Moreover, since individual initiative had been destroyed, laborers had no incentive to do a good job; the cars were shoddy and often missing parts the minute they came off the assembly line. The parts were stolen. The result was shortage—"deficit"—and a ten-year wait to buy a new car. The balances had become imbalances, and they were causing the whole system to wobble like a top.

Like massive tectonic plates under the Earth, out-of-control forces were grinding deep inside the Soviet economic system in the 1980s. The imbalances were surreal. Energy was cheap and was squandered; a ton of oil cost the same as a single pack of sought-after Marlboro cigarettes. The irony was that in Gosplan, the system lumbered on. Naishul saw, with alarm, that the great national "balances," which previously had been calculated once a year, were being recalculated more and more frequently—and frantically.

Naishul concluded that the Soviet system was in a deadly crisis. But he could not go out on the street and shout it, not in the early 1980s. Instead, he retreated to his private space, the kitchen, with two friends from Gosplan. In 1981, usually once a week, they gathered in his kitchen to talk—very privately—about what was wrong. Naishul discreetly began to write down his ideas. His friends told him to be careful—he could go to jail. But Naishul didn't stop. His ideas, which were remarkable for the time, spilled into the pages of the *samizdat* book.

"If nothing changes," he wrote to his readers in *Another Life*, "you and your children will continue to scurry around in shops, wear faded clothes and torn shoes, wait in a line for an apartment for ten years, curse the broken television or refrigerator, live and work in a decaying disorder." Naishul then went on to argue for change so profound that he still didn't dare utter it in public: he wanted to create a market economy with private property. He wanted to reward self-interest and competition. He offered his readers a farsighted description of how the vast property of the Soviet Union could be distributed to millions of people—private property—but those two words were officially unmentionable when Naishul dared to write them down. He promised a bit of a paradise would come out of privatization of the Soviet Union's vast property. "What enterprise would you like to own?" he asked in the text. "What shop? Food? Books? Clothes? Radio goods? Supermarket?" Wages would double, he promised; new shops and cafes would brighten their lives and they would enjoy a life without lines. Not only that, but the "window to Europe" that Peter the Great envisioned would reopen and they could travel the world and meet foreigners.

Then Naishul shifted his tone. Perhaps, he suggested, the reader would like to take a break from his description of "life in paradise" and go shopping. "You enter a food store to discover that there is still no milk, there has been no meat for a long time now, there is never any buckwheat. There is bread, but it is running out."

"You wished to buy a summer dress for your wife. There are no pretty ones for sale," he wrote. "Why?"

His answer vividly described how the Soviet system had become a tangled, unworkable mess. To fix the sundress shortage, he wrote, "the director of the clothes shop is worried by the absence of beautiful sundresses and turns to the garment factory. The director of the garment factory is horrified. 'I left our women without sundresses?' An order is issued immediately to sew sundresses of a new design made of bright fabric. There is no fabric to be found, so the director phones the textile plant. The plant, on learning that women are short of fancy sundresses, instantly orders better-quality cotton [be cultivated] in the vast spaces of Central Asia, and an improved dye made at the vast USSR chemical industry. When the director of a chemical factory learns that our dear women are naked, he starts producing new dyes, and for this he asks for different oil products and equipment."

Naishul noted that to fix one shortage, others were created. "To begin with, the garment factory, by decorating a sundress with several extra stitches, is now making less of other types of products ... of parachutes, for example, which led to interruption in the supply to the air assault troops. At another factory, for textiles, the care for women led to underproduction of some textile filters, as a result, some small branch of industry got clogged up. The chemical plant, carried away with the production of red dye for sundresses ... did not send enough of the red paint to the plastic industry, so a small plant making red alarm buttons began to produce them in green instead. . . ."

Naishul's secret manuscript was a glimpse into the tangled, atrophying Soviet economic system. By the time he finished writing *Another Life* in 1985, the troubles of the system were even greater than he had suspected. Economic growth had stalled; alcoholism, theft, and worker indifference were rampant; factories and enterprises stumbled from loss to loss; prices were set arbitrarily and remained hopelessly out of whack with reality.

Naishul did not know it then, but soon there *would* be another life, and it was not a life in Soviet socialism. The utopian experiment was coming to an end. As we shall see in the next six chapters, it was the economy of shortage and shadows, the chaos of central planning, and the driving force of self-interest that gave birth to the new capitalism—and the oligarchs of Russia.

Chapter 2

Alexander Smolensky

In the economy of chronic shortage that gripped the Soviet Union in the early 1980s, good books were a precious commodity, and books prohibited by the authorities were even more valuable. Although some books were banned as subversive, the Bible continued to exist in the officially atheist state. It could be found on private shelves, bought in shadow markets, obtained from foreign travelers, traded from hand to hand, and exchanged for something. As was true of everything else in short supply, the scarcity of Bibles gave them added value. On the black market, a Bible cost fifty rubles—nearly half a month's average salary.

The authorities had gone to great lengths to prohibit and inhibit the copying of printed matter, especially material considered a threat to official ideology. Even retyping forbidden manuscripts such as Mikhail Bulgakov's novel *Master and Margarita* could bring trouble from the KGB. A popular song lyric of the time referred to the East German–manufactured typewriter known as the Erika, and how it was used to make carbon copies of *samizdat* texts. "Erika can type four copies," went the song, "this is all, but this is enough."[1]

Using a copy machine in any office or institute required special permission, and most copiers were kept under lock and key. Alexander Smolensky had neither lock, key, nor special permission, but he had what in socialist lingo was known as the "means of production"—a printing press, ink, and paper. He worked in a state printing shop, and when the day was done, he took over the press and printed Bibles. He was a rebellious young man, with thin hair the color of wheat and a blond mustache, who had a certain intense street smarts, the product of life at the absolute bottom of Soviet society. For Smolensky, the end of socialism began with printing Bibles.

Smolensky had no higher education and few prospects for success in the years of stagnation. He was an outcast. His maternal grandfather had belonged to the Austrian Bund, a Jew who was a member of the Communist Party and fled from the Nazis to the Soviet Union before World War II. His mother grew up in Moscow, but the war brought suffering and misfortune to the family because of their Austrian origins. Pavel Smolensky, his father, was sent off to the Pacific Fleet when the war began, and his mother was resettled to a state farm in Siberia with a young daughter. They returned to Moscow after the war, where another daughter was born, followed by Alexander on July 6, 1954. His parents divorced when he was small.

Smolensky's youth was a painful one of "bread and water," he recalled. Hardship was common in the years after World War II, but it was aggravated for Smolensky because his mother, as an Austrian Jew, was barred from many jobs and was not admitted to an institute. She could not work, and they were poor. His father played absolutely no role in his life, he said, and he had no memory of him. Smolensky studied Hindi language for eight years, in hopes of finding a better life, but "I discovered that nobody needed it." He grew up in Moscow with his older sisters and his mother. A turning point came when it was time for Smolensky, then sixteen, to apply for his first internal Soviet passport, the key identification document for all citizens. Brimming with resentment, Smolensky came to the place on the form for nationality. He could enter either the nationality of his mother, who was born in Austria, or his father, who was Russian. Smolensky wrote "Austrian," and the entry only deepened his woes. As a Jew, Smolensky's career path was already limited; because he added Austrian, he was further stigmatized by the state as an outsider, excluded by the system from almost any upward path in life. "After that, I received everything that was due to me," Smolensky told me with a bittersweet half smile. "The state loves jokes like that."[2]

It was no joke. When Smolensky was drafted into the army, his documents included a long list of military districts in which he was prohibited from serving, including the most sought-after cities, Moscow and Leningrad. Smolensky was sent to faraway Tbilisi, the balmy capital of Soviet Georgia, an oriental city distant from Moscow in temperament and style. There Smolensky caught the attention of Eduard Krasnyansky, a twenty-six-year-old journalist who was serving out a deferred stint in the military. Krasnyansky recalled that when he first met Smolensky, the young man had eyes that sometimes were cheery and at other times burned like a laser. Smolensky was a *frondyor*, or rebel against the system. In the harsh world of Soviet army life, he could tolerate no slight, no insult, and was very much a loner. "A cat that walked by himself," Krasnyansky recalled, paraphrasing a Kipling poem. "Any kind of injustice, and we had many of them in our army, provoked him. He would never allow himself to be humiliated. He wouldn't allow the people around him to be humiliated. In the army, the older soldiers could get what they wanted. Some did it by humiliating the younger and weaker. Alexander Pavlovich wouldn't allow it." It was a common practice for the older soldiers to call the younger men by the more familiar address *Ty*, or you, as if they were children. But Smolensky wouldn't allow this small slight and insisted they address him with the more formal *Vy*.[3]

Krasnyansky knew the ways of Georgia, where he had grown up. He took Smolensky under his wing. They were quite different, Smolensky the angry kid who was so skinny his trousers were always sliding around his waist, and Krasnyansky the more knowledgeable and worldly older friend. When they needed cash, they came up with an idea. At the army newspaper, they had ink, paper, and a press. They started printing cheap business cards, teaching themselves how to set type. They sold one hundred cards for three rubles, undercutting the going rate of ten rubles. They sold most of them to Krasnyansky's friends and family contacts in Tbilisi. "We were cheaper, better, faster!" Krasnyansky recalled years later with a wide grin. They were soldier-businessmen, hustlers on the side. "We did all the typography," Krasnyansky told me. "A soldier had to live somehow."

Down to his last days in the army, Smolensky was a rebel. When the other soldiers were sent home at the end of their term, Smolensky was not given his release papers, a slight from a commanding officer for all the trouble Smolensky had caused him. One day, Krasnyansky and Smolensky went to see the officer, grabbed the papers off his desk, ran out of the office, climbed over a fence, and ran away, the release documents in hand. They got to the airport, but Smolensky had no ticket. Krasnyansky knew someone at the airport and fixed a ticket for his friend to fly back to Moscow.

On his return to the capital after two years in the army, Smolensky's prospects hadn't improved. The only thing he knew how to do was set type. Krasnyansky tried to get him admitted to the Polygraphic Institute, but Smolensky had two sisters and his mother to support, and instead of school, he went to work in a print shop. "I was an enemy of the people," Smolensky recalled, "or rather, son of enemies of the people. I couldn't find a decent job."

His bitterness deepening further, Smolensky proved a good hustler in the shadow economy. For three years after the army, he worked in the printing shop and then became a shop steward at the publishing house of a Soviet industrial ministry. His salary was 110 rubles a month.[4] He also moonlighted at a bakery. In theory, holding a second job was forbidden, but Smolensky got a laborer he knew to fake a permission slip. Smolensky earned another sixty rubles a month and gave ten to the laborer for the certificate.

Smolensky wore his first pair of jeans for a year. Like many of his generation, he spent hours complaining about his misery in the privacy of the kitchen. "The system was organized in such a way to make us think about food for half our life," he said, "and the second half was devoted to buying clothes to cover your ass."

To survive, Smolensky made good use of his press at night, printing Bibles in defiance of the system. It was his way of striking back. Smolensky said he was also trying to help the Church by printing the Bible "free of charge." The Russian Orthodox Church, he insisted, "was an institution that could help destroy everything that existed, the system." However, the church hierarchy was loyal to the state, so it is not clear why Smolensky thought he was striking back.

A more plausible explanation was profit. Smolensky found a crack in the system: there was a demand for Bibles and he had a means to print them. Alex Goldfarb, a biologist who was a key link between foreign journalists and dissidents at the time, had established his own channels for smuggling in books through diplomats and journalists. "The Bible was not only a thing of value in itself, but a major currency," he told me. "It was a way to support people. If you got a shipment, you gave them to families of people in prison, to support them." Smolensky may have easily reached the conclusion that fighting the system and making prohibited profits on the side were one and the same thing, Goldfarb explained. "Business activity was an act of political dissent," he said. "In those days, the system of values was different. People who stole printer's ink and printed Bibles were heroes; they were the good guys. The bad guys were the ones who informed for the KGB."[5]

Someone informed on Smolensky, and the KGB arrested him in 1981. It was the peak of the years of stagnation, and Smolensky was only twenty-seven years old. He was charged with "theft of state property," accused of stealing seven kilos of printer's ink and carrying out "individual commercial activity," which was prohibited. But Smolensky's case was treated as a minor one by the KGB. He recalled that they also tried to prove he stole the paper but could not. "Since there were no anti-Soviet leaflets, they said, 'Okay, we shall take pity on you.'" The case was turned over to the local police. Smolensky was sentenced in the Sokolnichesky Court in Moscow to two years on a prison construction brigade in the town of Kalinin, outside of Moscow. He was prohibited, by the court order, from holding any position for three years in which he would have a "material responsibility." In other words, the anticapitalists did not want Smolensky handling money. He had dared to engage in "individual commercial activity," and in 1981 that was still considered criminal.[6]

Smolensky's rebellious instincts were reinforced by the arrest. "All those procedures when the state thought they could tell me what was right and wrong," he told me later, his eyes still burning at the memory. "When it created conditions so I couldn't get a job anywhere, I couldn't earn money in an honest way, I couldn't enter a decent institute. They actually blocked all the ways for me! I couldn't go abroad. I just wanted to go as a tourist, and they said 'no, you can't.'" Smolensky said he was barred even from going to another country in the socialist bloc. "And I said, 'Do I have leprosy?' And they said, 'You are a dangerous element.'"

Smolensky found few open doors, but he was saved by the shortage economy. The Soviet central planners could never keep up with the demand for building construction in Moscow, and there was more than enough work. "In construction, you could always earn money," recalled Krasnyansky. Smolensky became a boss in a department of Remstroitrest, a state-owned apartment building and repair enterprise. He had a dump truck and a standard two-room, twenty-eight-square-meter apartment.

Moscow in those years was bursting with people, and the system had failed to provide them with enough housing. The wait for a new apartment lasted a decade or more. The state construction machine could not keep up with demand. Living space was in severe shortage, like everything else. Although the state had established the minimum housing space as nine square meters per person, nearly half the population of 9.5 million had even less than that.[7] The only safety valve was the wooded countryside—the villages of crudely built dachas that filled the forests outside the metropolis, where Muscovites escaped on warm summer evenings and where Smolensky would taste his first profits.

At the time, construction projects suffered from shoddy work and took years to complete. Massive, ugly apartment blocks were erected around the city out of prefabricated concrete slabs. There were no private construction companies. Factory construction also limped along, especially in those industries outside the favored military-industrial complex. In the last years of the Soviet Union, as factory managers gained more and more autonomy, many of them sought to plan their own projects. Often the only way to build something within a reasonable period of time was to hire small construction brigades that could work quickly, usually in the shadows.

In this world, the key skill Smolensky learned in construction was how to get his hands on scarce raw materials. If he needed nails or sand or cement blocks, he could not just go buy them. They could not be bought for any amount of money. They had to be procured, traded, or stolen—usually from some other project or site. Smolensky was good at getting.

Smolensky shared his generation's disgust with the doddering Soviet leadership. He was excited when a popular French rock group came to Moscow for a concert. Smolensky marveled at their shiny new equipment as it rolled out of the trucks and onto the stage. But Chernenko, the general secretary, then signed an article in a party newspaper saying that instead of subversive rock bands, the concerts should feature traditional Russian balalaika, accordion, and songs and dances, that "Western culture cannot come to our Soviet future." Smolensky groaned. "Oh God, no!" he thought. "It was such a bore, all over again."

His fears were unfounded. Chernenko's term was brief, and Gorbachev came to power. Smolensky, a small-time construction boss and rebellious *tolkatch*, or hustler, was uneducated yet shrewd. When the system began to change, he sensed it right away. He immediately saw something different in Gorbachev. Visiting Leningrad a month after taking office, Gorbachev spoke without written notes, which was unheard of for a Soviet leader. Gorbachev appeared with his wife, which was also extraordinary. He spoke freely. Smolensky was mesmerized; he recalled Gorbachev as the first Soviet leader he actually found appealing.

Yet, as Smolensky discovered, change was agonizingly slow. The Soviet Union was one of the hardest-drinking countries in the world. Vodka infused life and alcoholism gripped the population, taking a devastating toll on health and life expectancy. Moreover, the system encouraged the disease by providing enormous volumes of alcohol to the population as a way to make money for the state. In the shortage economy, there was always an ocean of vodka. One of Gorbachev's first moves was a campaign against excessive drinking. Smolensky said he was ordered by local party officials to take the reins of the antialcohol drive in his construction group, perhaps because he was known as a clever hustler who got results. But Smolensky immediately realized that it was a futile campaign. Every week, the party demanded that Smolensky bring them a report of how many drunks he had punished. How many? Well, he recalled later, for starters they could take all of the hundred construction workers in his outfit. Take them all—they worked in the open air, and Smolensky knew they started drinking in the morning and continued until they left in the evening. He could easily "punish" everyone working for him. Smolensky understood the scourge of alcoholism, and he knew how his workers burned themselves out on vodka. They even drank cheap cologne. The antialcohol campaign was ill-fated, he thought, just another absurd facade of the system and its endless propaganda campaigns, which no one believed. It was ridiculous: the state television broadcasts showed weddings of people with happy faces drinking juice. In real life, he knew, everyone kept drinking vodka. Despite his joy over

Gorbachev's ascension, the antialcohol campaign led Smolensky to wonder: would their life ever change?

On the economic front, Gorbachev's first two years were not promising. The young and energetic general secretary seemed to be groping for a way toward what he called "radical reform" of the socialist system, without breaking the grip of the Communist old guard. By his own later admission, Gorbachev wasted time.[8]

The summer of 1986 brought a bizarre backward step, the fight against "unearned income." The idea seemed to be to crack down on corruption, but the Politburo was unable to define "unearned income." In fact, the entire shadow economy pulsed with it, that vast network of *blat* and *svyazi* that had kept the country alive. Did you get "unearned income" by using your car for a taxi? Selling your homegrown cucumbers and tomatoes? The campaign was launched with vigor but spun out of control. In the Volgograd region, private tomato-growing hothouses were destroyed at the behest of the police and the militia. On the roads, police confiscated and destroyed the tomatoes. The newspaper *Literaturnaya Gazeta* published a long story about the affair headlined, "The Criminal Tomato."[9]

Later Gorbachev took two fundamental and far-reaching steps that began to unwind the socialist experiment. To help alleviate the shortage economy, and partly as a reaction to the misguided campaign against unearned income, a law was drawn up in 1986 allowing Soviet citizens to carry out "individual labor activity." The idea was to fill the gaps in the creaking, deficit-ridden economy by allowing people to become self-employed entrepreneurs. A large number of private activities soon became possible, including handicrafts and consumer services. A teacher could tutor students after school. Many teachers already were doing this, but the new law made their moonlighting legitimate; they no longer had anything to fear. Moreover, the law said nothing about prices—individuals could charge what they wanted. The law was a first tiptoe away from state controls. Still, there were strict limits. The new entrepreneurs could hire only family members; they could operate only where the socialist sector had failed, primarily in consumer shortages. The expense and difficulties of starting up were immense, and some activities were still forbidden, including all kinds of printing and printing presses.

Gorbachev's next step was even more profound. In a speech in 1986, he had drawn attention to the cooperatives, a type of quasi-private business that had its roots in the New Economic Policy of the 1920s. In English, the word "cooperative" has a socialist connotation, but in fact the cooperatives, as they were reinvented by Gorbachev, became the first private businesses in the Soviet Union. They marked a revolutionary departure from the decades of anticapitalism. Gorbachev's initial words were cautious, but their impact was far-reaching. The state began, gingerly, to allow these new autonomous businesses to take shape in 1987 in very narrow sections of the economy: recycling, baking, shoe repair, laundry services, and consumer goods. Although limited in scale, the cooperative movement seized public attention. The idea of private enterprises opening up amid a sea of socialist stagnation was a remarkable sight. One striking example was the appearance of pay toilets in central Moscow, operated by a cooperative. They were clean, played music, and offered rose-tinted toilet paper and new plumbing fixtures. Most people had never seen such a facility, certainly not in their own homes. Other enterprises soon followed, including youth discos and restaurants. When the formal Law on Cooperatives was adopted in 1988, many cooperatives were already well on their way to becoming private businesses. The threshold of a new age had been crossed.

The Law on Cooperatives contained a hidden time bomb set to explode the dreams of the Communists. One line in the text, little-noted until later, allowed the formation of financial or credit businesses as cooperatives; in other words, banks. Smolensky would eventually make a fortune from this small crack that had opened in decaying socialism.

The cooperatives sprouted up surrounded by many unknowns. Basic rules simply did not exist. Previously, Soviet planners had mapped out economic activity in the corridors of Gosplan. An enterprise simply was told to meet the goals dictated to it from above. But the cooperatives were allowed to make their own decisions and keep their gains. A most remarkable aspect of the Law on Cooperatives was a brand-new definition of personal freedom. The law said any activity not specifically prohibited would be permitted—a complete reversal of the decades of heavy-handed dictates of the state.[10]

Often the cooperatives simply brought into the open what was already going on in the shadow economy. Viktor Loshak, a soft-spoken, thoughtful journalist, was the economics editor of *Moscow News*, a newspaper that became a champion of *perestroika*, and he began to devote all his time to chronicling the growth of the new cooperatives. He wrote an influential series of articles from Armenia, where underground workshops, which had always existed in the Caucasus, now came into the open. He visited one cooperative making handkerchiefs.

"What made them happy most of all was that they could send their products by mail," he recalled. "At first, I didn't understand. But then I realized that when they were inside the shadow economy, the most difficult thing was the path from their production to distribution—because it was criminal. On any stage of that route, the police could catch them. And when they legalized themselves, they could send their products openly by mail. A lot of people were happy to tell others about what they had been doing secretly all their lives."[11]

The original idea was that cooperatives, given the new freedoms, would produce scarce goods such as the handkerchiefs or provide badly needed services like car repairs. But this rather quaint vision of small workshops humming with craftsmen was soon overtaken by more ambitious schemes. Some cooperatives found ways to get cheap or subsidized supplies, from the state or shadow markets, and sold them for fast profits. Somewhat later they pioneered importing scarce goods like computers and exporting natural resources for immense windfall profits. Cooperatives charged higher prices than the old state stores, spawning resentment in a population that was accustomed to a patriarchal state which supposedly gave them everything nearly for free and had regarded all private enterprise as immoral "speculation."

According to Anders Åslund, then a Swedish diplomat who served in Moscow, "A few bold entrepreneurs skimmed the market and did very well indeed because shortages were immense, competition and taxes were minimal, most regulations were unclear, and no one knew how long the feast would last." As it turned out, the feast was just beginning.

In 1987 Smolensky was summoned to the city party committee, the *gorkom*, where a functionary who supervised his construction unit, Remstroitrest, gave him an order: "Urgently establish a cooperative!" Ever the rebellious one, Smolensky, then thirty-three, replied, "Why me? Go yourself and do it!" But the *gorkom* threatened to fire him if he didn't follow instructions. This was a campaign by the party, and the word had come from the top: Smolensky must obey!

The problem was that Smolensky didn't have a clue what a cooperative was. "I was a state employee," he recalled. "All of us were state employees, and I had all kinds of plans, and directions and instructions, and it was like dropping me on the moon." Krasnyansky recalled later that Smolensky had been chosen precisely for his street smarts and hustle, which the party bosses had noticed. "Apparently, the party bosses were not idiots. They saw who was capable and who was not. They could have come to me a hundred times and I would never be able to do it. And they went instead to Smolensky. They saw that he had that fire, that he knew how to organize people, take risks."

Smolensky went to register as a cooperative at a small, barren office in central Moscow that had been set up to give permits to the new businessmen. There he was met by Yelena Baturina, a recent university graduate who was in charge of what was called "public catering," including bakeries, shoe repair shops, and hairdressers, among other things. Baturina was the assistant to a short, bullheaded official who had been put in charge of the cooperatives, Yuri Luzhkov, a veteran chemical industry manager who had become a deputy chairman of the Moscow city council. It was a chaotic time, and a motley crowd of hustlers spilled out into the hallways, struggling to fill out the proper forms to start their own business.[12]

Smolensky got his paperwork in order, but he felt completely out of place and was a little fearful of Luzhkov. He had trouble thinking up a name for his new cooperative. In Soviet times, state construction enterprises often just had a number, such "SU-6." Smolensky scribbled on the application the name of his proposed cooperative, Moskva. He came into the room where Luzhkov, in shirt sleeves, was sitting at a simple, empty table and submitted his documents.

Baturina scowled. "We already have Moskva, take away your documents!" She had a firm, no-nonsense voice. Smolensky wondered briefly if this was going to be like the antialcohol campaign and thought to himself, "Oh no, not all over again!" He paused and asked if he could name the cooperative Moskva-2.

"No!" she said. "We've already got Moskva-2."

Smolensky then pleaded. "Can it be Moskva-3?"

"Okay," Baturina relented. "Let it be Moskva-3." She wrote in the digit 3 next to Smolensky's handwritten Moskva.

On that day, Smolensky later recalled, "Communism was over for me."

Moskva-3 was a private enterprise, set up in Pervomaisky District, one of Moscow's thirty-three administrative areas, where Smolensky had worked at Remstroitrest. But he had precious little idea what he was supposed to do as a private entrepreneur. He had three thousand rubles saved up and wondered whether he was supposed to use his own money. He wondered where he would get supplies and what he would build. The party had ordered Smolensky to start a cooperative, but actually doing it came down to his own individual initiative. No one else had a clue.

Loshak, the *Moscow News* journalist, recalled that the very first cooperatives gathered scrap materials for resale. They tried to make crude kitchen furniture out of scrap lumber or flower boxes from used tires. Loshak said his first memory of Smolensky was collecting scrap materials. "He hired students, and they dismantled houses that were to be demolished and sorted out the door frames from the bricks. And they sold those things to people who were building country cottages."

Smolensky soon decided to make his own garages and small cottages, the dachas in the countryside. They were in high demand as Muscovites desperately sought refuge from the overcrowded city. Again, Smolensky saw a gap and filled it. The state construction enterprises would never build dachas; they couldn't even keep up with the demand for simple twenty-eight-square-meter apartments in the city.

But the immediate problem for Smolensky was the same one he had faced as a construction boss working for the state. In a universe of chronic shortages, raw materials were difficult to come by. There were no wholesalers who could sell him planks and nails. The state theoretically controlled all materials, but the practice was different. The competition for supplies was just another aspect of the vast, disorganized bazaar of Soviet socialism. The first private entrepreneurs had to rely on their wits—on *blat* and *svyazi*, on theft, bribes, and bargaining—to get supplies.

Alexander Panin, secretary of the city commission overseeing the cooperatives, recalled that the cooperatives started out desperate for the most basic things. "They needed a location to work from," he said. "They needed some stuff from which to sew things—cloth. Or if they wanted to make furniture, they needed to buy the wood or whatever—

planks. But the problem was the state distribution system existed. You couldn't buy a table, or wood, or planks, because everything was *distributed.*" The commission headed by Luzhkov tried to help the new entrepreneurs by demanding that state enterprises supply bricks or cement to a cooperative.[13]

It was not so simple. Smolensky recalled the bureaucrats in Moscow provided little help. "In those times, it was impossible to buy planks and nails in Moscow. It was just impossible. Not for money, not for anything." Money could not, by itself, purchase something in shortage. But Smolensky knew how to beg, bargain, and hustle in the socialist bazaar. He was soon sawing planks at an outdoor pavilion and building small structures—simple one- and two-room cottages, sheds, and garages in the countryside.

As an example of the new generation of cooperatives, Smolensky was selected one day to be a showcase for an American television news crew, in advance of President Reagan's summit meeting in Moscow. The film crew arrived at an open pavilion and watched as Smolensky's men hauled logs to a saw and then took the cut planks away, all of it by hand. The journalists quizzed Smolensky about why it was so primitive. They had no idea that what they were watching was a triumph for Smolensky—he was proud that it existed at all.

When I suggested to Smolensky years later that his early success was due to the imminent death of the Soviet state, he brought me up short. "We were not thinking about the death of the state," he said. Rather, they were worrying about their own fate. If Gorbachev were thrown out, would they be jailed and shot as speculators? Far from the death of the state, "we were thinking about *our* death!"

In the months that followed, Smolensky's cooperative became a booming success. The dachas were popular, and the Communist Party bosses again took notice. They pressed Smolensky to start a special waiting list for party chiefs to get dachas. Smolensky quickly complied; they may well have had some leverage over his lumber supply. "They started sort of putting their names on the list," Smolensky said of his new, elite customers, who were also curious about Smolensky's new business. Before long, the party would decide to experiment with private businesses too.

The cooperatives began on thin ice. The brief relaxation of the New Economic Policy in the early 1920s had lasted only two years; could the new Soviet cooperatives last longer? "These first people were just working within very rigid limits," Loshak recalled. "A step to the left, a step to the right, and they shoot." Yet a kind of deep-seated force was being released from the depths of the system, a trembling of the Earth so profound that it would provide an immense boost toward launching Russia on its way to a capitalist future. That force was money. In the shortage economy, when there was almost nothing to buy, when the decisions about allocating scarce goods were made arbitrarily without the forces of supply and demand, money had little significance. But on a sandy sawmill site, Smolensky, the angry young man, began to make money. He accumulated piles and piles of rubles—so much that he had no place to keep it all. He distrusted the state banks, so he kept his money in cash.

In the early Gorbachev years, the Soviet financial system was still run by the state. At the center of the banking system was one giant institution, Gosbank, which controlled the flow of money and credit. Smolensky was accumulating cash, but he knew that putting it in the bank would lead to unpleasant questions. Where had he earned so many hundreds of thousands of rubles? Why wasn't he paying more in taxes? The KGB was just waiting for Smolensky to walk into Gosbank. A second tier of five new Soviet state banks was not much better, but Smolensky was assigned, probably by the party, to use one of them, Promstroibank. He was required to use the bank for some transactions. He recalled that every time he wanted to make a small payment through the bank, he had to explain himself over and over to the bureaucrats. "My chief accountant was practically living there," he recalled. "She was an elderly woman, and she would go there with a bag full of chocolate, sausage, perfume. The system was the following: you had to visit several counters and put seals everywhere. You had to give something to each person. That was the system; otherwise nothing worked."

Moreover, the rigid Soviet financial system made it practically impossible for Smolensky to use his money as he wanted to, such as paying a supplier, without seeking permission from the state. "The state bank was so strong that it could destroy all the fruits of my labor with just one signature," Smolensky recalled. "I couldn't pay wages on time; I couldn't settle for goods; I had to bring all kinds of documents; I had to pay bribes; or maybe if not bribes, 'gifts.' I was fed up and felt it could not last."

One day in 1988, Smolensky decided to start his own bank, as some other cooperatives had recently done. He looked at the Law on Cooperatives, officially approved in May, and found the single line that allowed cooperatives to open their own banks. He went out and filed the papers, he recalled, "in order to stop the diktat of the state bank." Smolensky was again at the front lines of change. By the end of the year, forty-one new commercial banks had registered with Gosbank, and by the end of the next year, the number had risen to 225.[14] Bank Stolichny, which would become the core of Smolensky's business for the next decade, was registered on February 14, 1989, eight months before the Berlin Wall fell.

Just as he had plunged into the cooperatives, Smolensky began his quest to become a banker in total ignorance. "For several months I had a big desk and all my friends made jokes. On one side of my desk, I was chairman of this cooperative, Moskva-3. And on the other side I was director of a bank."

In 1989 the progressive newspaper, *Moscow News,* held the first ever roundtable discussion with the nascent commercial bankers, who were unknown to most of the public and deeply distrusted. A leading participant was Vladimir Vinogradov, one of the first commercial bankers, who was smooth and well tailored. It was rumored at the time that Vinogradov had made so much money so fast that he stashed it in his refrigerator. By contrast to the experienced Vinogradov, Smolensky was a rough-hewn construction boss who did not appear very wealthy. His manner was blunt. He demanded that the authorities leave the bankers alone. He was hardly the picture of a modern banker.

Alexander Bekker, then a journalist at *Moscow News,* remembered Smolensky telling him that Stolichny Bank was number sixty-four on the state registration list of commercial banks. "I am working for number sixty-four, and someday it will be working for me," Smolensky boasted. "I will have a credit history and a reputation."[15]

"I don't think he had a very clear-cut strategy at the time," Bekker recalled. "It was difficult to even know what a commercial bank should be." Smolensky's old army friend, Krasnyansky, said the key issue was avoiding the state. "The important thing was to find freedom for his money, so he could send it where he wanted without explanation," Krasnyansky said. "Only later did clients appear, and he saw that the bank could bring in a lot more money than sawing wood at the cooperative."

In the blossoming world of banking in the final years of Soviet socialism, much of the sustenance came from the state itself in the form of cheap credit. Many of the new banks were carved directly out of government ministries, industries, and special interests. The Ministry for Automobile Production created Avtobank; the Ministry of Oil and Chemical Engineering created its own Neftekhimbank; the state airline had Aeroflotbank. These banks and dozens of others were built to serve the state-owned industries behind them, and they could always count on a ready supply of subsidies. Big industries, regional governments, and the Communist Party and its many affiliates were the driving force in the explosion of the new banking sector, and their political clout and money dwarfed the more independent young cooperatives.

Smolensky, whose major asset a few years earlier had been his dump truck, was still the outcast. His bank had no government ministry at its back. Compared with the others, which had powerful patrons, the cooperative banks were small. Smolenksky's bank was not on the list of the twenty largest commercial banks in the Soviet Union in 1990.[16] Smolensky's overriding principle was that he wanted nothing to do with the state, except the freedom to do what he wanted. He insisted that none of his employees come from the state banks. He found young people to work for him who had no prior memory of Gosplan or Gosbank.

Smolensky was moving to a new level of business. He no longer wanted to saw logs. He closed down Moskva-3, his cooperative. A banker was born.

In the years after the American Civil War, huge quantities of British capital poured into the United States, chiefly as loans to the railroads. England, which had given birth to the Industrial Revolution and inspired the wisdom of Adam Smith, had become the world's financial center, flush with surplus capital that had to find a home. According to Ron Chernow, biographer of the great merchant banker J.P. Morgan, British investors were put off by the helter-skelter growth of the American railroads, and they feared the swindlers and fast-talkers who ran them. Morgan became a transatlantic intermediary between the source of capital in London and those who needed it in the United States. The London investors were often clueless and depended on Morgan's knowledge about the railroads. In the United States, the railroads were often in such a chaotic state that their only hope of attracting capital was through Morgan. As a journalist noted at the time, Morgan's great power came not from the millions of dollars he owned, but from the billions he commanded. He was one of the great middlemen of American history. The lore of American tycoons is often wrapped up in their role as masters over the railroads and steel trusts. But the key factor was the American hunger for capital; the capital itself had first come from England, as a result of successful commerce spawned by the Industrial Revolution.[17]

Consider the landscape that spread itself out before Alexander Smolensky in 1988. There were shortages of sausage in the state stores and the grim reality of a system in decay. No distant bankers hankered to invest their capital. Smolensky had seen the wounded dinosaurs of Soviet industry, primitive and ailing, and he also knew that centuries of authoritarianism had sapped the Russian population, which was passive and lethargic and would be difficult to revive.

In 1990 Gorbachev had toyed with a plan to turn the country into a market economy in five hundred days but discarded it. His economic policy zigzagged inconclusively back and forth. The chances for a huge infusion of private capital from abroad were not good. When one of the authors of the five-hundred-day plan, Grigory Yavlinsky, went to the United States seeking aid, he was snubbed by President George H. W. Bush. The West was not yet ready to risk money on the Soviet Union. The biggest source of capital—indeed, the only real source of wealth—was the state itself. The state possessed a sprawling network of oil fields, mines, factories, and pipelines. The state, through Gosbank, also controlled the money supply and credits, as well as all foreign trade. If there was money to be made, it would have to come from the state, either directly, as property and subsidies, or indirectly, by manipulating or exploiting the state's control over prices and trade.

In the late Soviet period, trading companies run by young hustlers and well-connected bureaucrats made quick fortunes this way. They bought oil cheap inside the country, paid bribes to get it across the border, sold it at world prices for hard currency, bought up personal computers from abroad, paid bribes to get the computers back inside the country, and sold them for fantastic profits, to be reinvested in the next lot of oil. The state created the conditions for this hustle by keeping oil prices low, by making the computers scarce, and by collecting the bribes.

For Smolensky, whose gut instinct was to distrust the state, the search for early capital was fraught with difficulty and danger. He had no hope of becoming an intermediary between borrowers and lenders in the Anglo-American tradition. The Soviet Union and later Russia were light-years away from the conditions that spawned the early American tycoons. Instead of becoming a Morgan or a Carnegie, Smolensky took what there was before him—the wild, unfettered, and warped Russian protocapitalism of the day.

Bekker, who had kept in touch with Smolensky, told me, "In Russia, there were only two ways to get seed capital for a bank. One was to service suspicious accounts and have the principle that 'I don't care what kind of money is in my bank. It's not my responsibility to check the passport of every depositor.' Another way was to work closely with the authorities and government officials and get budget accounts and profitable contracts." But Smolensky, he recalled, "didn't have *any* political contacts."

In the year before the Soviet Union collapsed, more than half of all the deposits in commercial banks were from the state.[18] The other half came from the cooperatives and other disparate organizations and nascent businesses. This is how Smolensky began to build his bank. He danced with those who would dance with him—Bank Stolichny ran with the fast-money men, including the entrepreneurs who began the first cooperatives and the hustlers. They were engaged almost entirely in high-stakes, quick-turnover deals that yielded obscene profits in cash. One method was generally known as arbitrage, taking advantage of the gaping price differentials that existed at the time between the heavily subsidized, fixed prices of the state-run economy and the free, higher prices of the market, both inside the country and abroad. Another lucrative business was currency speculation, taking advantage of hyperinflation. Between the collapse of the Soviet Union in 1991 and the end of 1994, the ruble exchange rate against the dollar dropped 95 percent. Smolensky and other bankers made enormous profits by essentially gambling on daily fluctuations in the ruble-dollar exchange rate.

When Smolensky was at the peak of his power in 1997, I asked him about these early years, and he acknowledged that much of his bank's money was wrapped up in currency speculation. Unlike a traditional Western banker, he simply did not make many loans. He remembered giving one loan to a watermelon farmer who grew his melons in

Uzbekistan and brought them to Russia for sale. He gave the melon grower a million rubles. Then ethnic clashes broke out near the farmer's land in Uzbekistan. The whole district was closed and he could not get the melons out to market. The authorities sent troops to the region. "Our guy was sitting on those watermelons, and I was having a heart attack!" Smolensky recalled. The loan was eventually repaid, Smolensky said, but lending seemed to him to be too risky.

"You couldn't give loans, in a normal sense, with such hyperinflation," he said. "We engaged in more speculative operations, that's true. Otherwise you couldn't survive. There was no real industrial production. So, who do you give loans to? They would go bankrupt the next day."

The young Russian bankers were intent on making a killing and at the same time were burying Soviet socialist ideology. The socialists had scorned financial manipulation as sheer greed. In the Soviet socialist economy, production and industry were king; money was just a tool for the larger goal of fulfilling the plan, for meeting the quotas. However, what Smolensky was doing had nothing to do with the plan. It was finance for its own sake, and that was a strange and utterly alien practice to the older Soviet generation, including many factory managers, bureaucrats, and KGB men. They did not inherit the new world of capitalism because they could not make this basic leap. The fleet-footed Smolensky and the boys on his currency trading floor danced right past the old guard.

In the last two years of the Soviet Union, currency transactions were still tightly controlled, theoretically. Smolensky's currency speculators had to be fast and invisible. By early 1990, Gosbank had only given two licenses to commercial banks for limited hard currency transactions, and the banks reported only a fraction of them to the authorities.[19]

Joel Hellman, a Columbia University doctoral student, was researching his thesis on the new Russian bankers in 1990 when he visited Smolensky. Hellman found that many of the bankers, as well as Gosbank officials, acknowledged that illegal hard currency transactions had blossomed well beyond the control of the authorities. Gosbank, which had once controlled all money and credit, was increasingly lost in the new environment. According to Hellman, Gosbank frequently threatened to fine the rambunctious banks—and did levy a $14 million fine against Smolensky—or freeze their accounts.

But the attitude of commercial bankers was cavalier. Smolensky told Hellman, "Our bank has outpaced events. We do something and official permission is granted after the fact. It would be impossible for us to wait for permission and then to act."[20]

Hellman recalled that when he first met Smolensky, he was struck by the newly remodeled, Western-style bank offices, with luxurious sofas. Smolensky's vice presidents all wore Armani suits. Smolensky later told me that he deliberately arranged it that way, but the young vice presidents never bought the suits on their own. When he went to Europe, Smolensky routinely bought two suits, two dress shirts, and two ties and carried them back to Moscow in his suitcase, distributing them to his young vice presidents so they would look Western and prosperous.

Smolensky's capital was small, and his operations secret. He did not publish periodic financial reports, and if he had, they could hardly have been honest. One of Smolensky's early assets was a "manuscript" that he claimed he had written about banking and was worth 200 million rubles. Smolensky said he simply wrote down everything he had learned and set the huge value of the document himself. "It was just the description of the system that I had created," he said. "How it works."

Presto! Instant capital.

Smolensky also participated in a web of cross-ownership with some of the other early banks. His bank owned shares in others, and they owned shares in his, and everyone grossly pumped up the value, as Smolensky had done with the manuscript. It was a paper trick, one of many used by the young commercial bankers who thrived in a world of fictions and facades.

When Hellman visited Smolensky in 1990, he noticed that the banker had spread out on his desk brochures promoting the big American mutual funds, such as Merrill Lynch and Fidelity.[21] Smolensky was looking for ways to ship cash overseas. It was a small glimpse of what, at that time, was already a torrent of capital fleeing Russia. Slowly at first, but later with more skill, the new Russian commercial banks built connections to the international financial system and discovered how to discreetly move cash into offshore zones. The goal was to avoid the risks of keeping money inside a turbulent and unstable country, and to dodge its confiscatory tax rates or keep the money away from partners, workers, or criminals. Smolensky, who was an outsider anyway, thought it was a rather logical response to the threats that always lurked inside the country for anyone who had money. "There were restrictions—now, I don't remember clearly," Smolensky said later when I asked if it had been difficult to transfer his money to Merrill Lynch. "Or actually, no restrictions. Anarchy." In its first published annual report, for 1992, Smolensky boasted that Stolichny was one of the first twenty Russian banks to be linked into the SWIFT international bank transfer system, and that Stolichny had thirty-four correspondent bank relationships abroad.

"People were bringing money, but we didn't know how to preserve it," Smolensky said. "We were looking for instruments to invest this money" in Russia, but "there were no instruments." So they sent the money abroad.

Smolensky's bank was the most closed and secretive of the new commercial banks, and he constantly attracted the attention of the suspicious KGB and Gosbank, which was later turned into the Central Bank of Russia. The authorities, who looked askance at the young banker, were forever curious about what was going on inside the walls of Stolichny Bank, but Smolensky stubbornly refused to tell them or let them inspect his bank. For years, the security services tried to show that criminals were among Smolensky's customers, but Smolensky was never arrested. Certainly, Smolensky's bank was a haven for the easy money of the early 1990s. A list of the major loans made by the bank in 1996 showed that half of them were either trading companies or oil and gas companies, both adventuresome businesses that survived by speed, secrecy, and a healthy disrespect for national boundaries and authority.[22] Among his colleagues, it was believed that Smolensky's Stolichny Bank had dealings with unsavory gangs and dirty money in its early years. A leading banker told me in 1998, "The main feature is being able to change. Smolensky is not what he was ten years ago. He is building a clear, open bank. Ten years ago, it was not. For sure, he had criminal elements—we all did. But I am sure no gangster can reach Smolensky, or even talk to him today."[23]

Smolensky spent years fighting one case. In 1992, the first year after the Soviet collapse, the banking system was still immature and crude. From the southern Russian republics of Dagestan and Chechnya the Central Bank received, by fax, a series of wire transfer orders known as "avisos." The avisos ordered the Central Bank to immediately transfer millions of dollars to various Moscow commercial bank accounts. The Central Bank, which at the time was still using the creaking teletype, complied—and the money flowed out, including about $30 million to Stolichny. Later, the Central Bank discovered that the avisos were faked, and it tried to recoup by taking the money back from reserve accounts maintained by Smolensky's bank in the Central Bank. A criminal investigation was opened against Smolensky. The whole affair was laced with questions that were never answered—such as why the Central Bank would give out so much money on the basis of a fax in the first place.

Smolensky told me he saw the case as a struggle between the new capitalists and the old guard, although it may have been a more mundane struggle over corruption and theft. Smolensky insisted he was wrongly targeted by the criminal investigation, which was closed in 1999 without charges. "It cost me a lot of blood," he recalled. After the case was closed, however, a Russian newspaper, *Sovershenno Sekretno,* which often had sources in the security services, published what it described as details of the case, alleging that Smolensky and another man had taken $32 million through the false aviso and stashed $25 million in a company in Austria owned by Smolensky's wife. Later, the newspaper said, Smolensky's bank acknowledged a "mistaken" borrowing of $4 million and repaid that sum.[24]

Throughout his career, Smolensky waged a bitter war with the state. The Central Bank chairman, Viktor Gerashchenko, was his nemesis. Smolensky complained Gerashchenko "deluged commercial banks" with "1928-model instructions," such as, "limit the issuing of cash." Or, Smolensky fumed, another Central Bank official sent a message, "I authorize the payment of wages." Smolensky retorted, "Don't my clients have the right to dispose of their own money?" Bekker told me that "the state hated Smolensky and his bank more than any other. He didn't bow to the KGB. He didn't bow to the bureaucrats. He didn't bow to the militia. Gerashchenko didn't like this independent and freewheeling banker."

Smolensky enjoyed unusual autonomy in the late Soviet period and the first few years of the new Russia. He fought back against the government, kicked out the Central Bank auditors, and refused to answer questions about his bank, and yet he survived. What was the source of his impunity? The answer is unclear. As we shall see later, the most successful tycoons often enjoyed mysterious, high-level protection, the details of which never became known. If he had it,

Smolensky still did not feel secure. Krasnyansky, Smolensky's old army pal, who eventually came to work at Stolichny Bank, recalled that he and Smolensky had their most candid conversations in the car. Smolensky was on his way to becoming one of the leading bankers in the new Russia. But one day, in the car, he turned to Krasnyansky. "Edik," he said, using an affectionate nickname, "we shouldn't be seduced by this. At any moment, even in our free Russia, they can still come and squash you like a bug."

Still, Smolensky had come a long way. In 1992 his bank earned 2.4 billion rubles on revenues of 6.1 billion. Not bad for a scrawny young man who started out printing Bibles at night, for a construction boss who was ordered to open one of the first cooperatives, for a dacha builder who filled a gap in the shortage economy.

Chapter 3

Yuri Luzhkov

IF THERE WAS a nightmare of the late Soviet years, a place that captured all the cumulative absurdity and folly of "developed socialism," it was the reeking, rat-infested vegetable warehouses of Moscow. These twenty-three mammoth storehouses were monuments to the Bolsheviks' peculiarly misguided distrust (and cruel oppression) of the Russian peasantry. From Lenin's early battles with the peasants to Stalin's forced collectivization, much of Soviet history was a war against the countryside to feed the cities. Although the mass violence ended after Stalin, the giant machine of central planning rolled on, confiscating the output of the peasants year after year and shipping it to the cities for storage until it was distributed. Huge quantities of vegetables and fruits—a year's supply—were brought from the farms into the Moscow warehouses just because of the state's monumental distrust of the peasants.

By the early days of *perestroika,* in the mid-1980s, these "vegetable bases" had become an organizational monster. The vegetables had to be brought in, sorted, stacked, packed, and preserved, sometimes for many months. The twenty-three warehouses, holding up to 1.5 million tons of fruits and vegetables, or enough provisions for a city of 10 million people, suffered all the symptoms of the shortage economy and all the underlying distortions of central planning. "Terminal filth, stench, mold, rats, flies, cockroaches—there was nothing so vile that it did not find its home in these warehouses," recalled Yuri Luzhkov, a seasoned Soviet industrial manager, after first visiting the warehouses.

Even the newer warehouses were stripped down and ruined by the workers, Luzhkov observed, "brought to such a degree of negligence that you could explain it only by some crazy idea, that the employees were obsessed with intentionally destroying everything, like an army retreating in the face of an attacking foe. Nothing should be left standing for the enemy."

The chain of rot began far away, on the farms. Stripped of any incentives, the 120,000 growers who served Moscow had long since stopped caring about the quality of the vegetables and fruits they shipped. They reluctantly brought their vegetables to a collection point, to be hauled away in a truck carrying a bill of loading that read simply "Moscow." By the time it got to the city, much of the cargo had begun to rot. The potatoes were infested with beetles. "The warehouses became dungeons whose contents were destroyed, not preserved," recalled Luzhkov. The rotting vegetables were then distributed to the state stores, where customers could only curse at black carrots, decaying greens, and moldering potatoes. There was a well-worn refrain by the store clerks as they handed out the rotting vegetables: "If you don't like it, don't eat it."

The vegetable bases, as they were known, were a triumph of collectivist labor. Everyone worked there, supposedly, for the "common good," and yet the reality was that no one did. The vegetable bases were run like army boot camp: every day twenty thousand Muscovites were drafted to re-sort, repack, and restack the spoiling, rotting produce. It was mandatory duty, dreaded for the filth and the rats. The hundreds of thousands of workers forced into the system simply stole what they could.

"The whole system was so deeply and pervasively corrupt that it made absolutely no sense to bother with any investigations," Luzhkov said. This was because the police were in on the deal. Financial controllers and inspectors just wrote off the losses, and party officials saw the mess as just another opportunity. They stole the best of what there was.

The stealing was so common and pervasive as to defy definition as criminal. "Here we are approaching the very core of socialism," Luzhkov observed. "To a certain degree, everybody was involved, and everybody participated—and under socialism, this means nobody. That was the crucial point, the most corrupting effect of the 'developed socialism.' Since everybody believed that they did not create this evil, coming home with bags stuffed with stolen products was not wrong."[1]

In December 1985, Gorbachev brought a new boss to Moscow, the rugged Sverdlovsk regional party chief, Boris Yeltsin. Soon Yeltsin began to take the city by storm in a very unconventional way—standing in line with average people, riding the trolley, poking into factories and stores unannounced, prodding the stale, atrophying socialist system. The growing shortages of food in the capital were a special concern to Yeltsin. Hearing there was veal at a butcher shop—exceedingly rare—he once went and stood in line for it. He insisted on a kilo of veal and was told the store had none. Yeltsin then forced himself behind the counter and, through a small window, spied the back room—where they were handing out chunks of veal to special clients.[2]

Yeltsin touched a populist nerve when he publicly criticized the system of *raspredelenie*, in which the party elites had access to special stores and quality goods that were denied to the general public. He became a genuinely well-liked figure among Muscovites, but populist rhetoric could not fix Moscow's ailing food distribution system. One after another, bureaucrats were given the job of straightening out the vegetable bases, and they were forced out in failure. In the summer of 1987, as the food situation in Moscow worsened, the fruit and vegetable bases were on the verge of collapse.

Yeltsin turned to Luzhkov, a stocky, bullet-headed industrial manager, who had been working as a senior-level administrator in the city government. Luzhkov was one of two deputies to the chairman of the Moscow city executive committee, the managers who dealt with the day-to-day affairs of the metropolis. He was the city official who handed out licenses for the first cooperatives.

The bureaucrat who previously headed the vegetable bases had just had a nervous breakdown. Yeltsin summoned Luzhkov. A mechanical engineer by training, Luzhkov did not want to take over the miserable vegetable bases, which he later recalled would be "an absolutely no-win situation." But when he met Yeltsin, he softened. "He didn't look at all the way I expected," Luzhkov said of Yeltsin. "He seemed tired, depressed." Yeltsin told Luzhkov the job would not be easy and then added, "I beg you."

Luzhkov knew the assignment could be the end of his career. But he said yes to Yeltsin and began his own voyage, a remarkable and tumultuous one, out of Soviet socialism.

When he was a nineteen-year-old engineering student in Moscow, Luzhkov was assigned to a temporary student work brigade in Siberia to help bring in the harvest. It was October 1955. The weather was generally warm during the day, when they gathered and dried the hay, but it turned unexpectedly cold at night, often dropping below zero. The students got stranded; someone had failed to arrange their transportation back to school. For several nights, they slept in hay, shivering, many of them becoming ill.

Then, by chance, a member of the Politburo showed up from Moscow. He was touring the harvest and made some perfunctory remarks, paying no attention to the complaints of the students. They asked to go home, saying they had no food, no medicine, no water.

Suddenly, out of the pack of students, Luzhkov rushed toward the Politburo member. Before anyone could stop him, the pugnacious young Luzhkov punched the party man on the shoulder. "You might go far in your career if nobody stops you—but you will definitely be stopped!" Luzhkov bellowed, then turned and ran.

"Luzhkov simply hit him on the shoulder," recalled his old friend, Alexander Vladislavlev, who was head of the work brigade. "That man yelled as if he had been stabbed with a knife."

The embarrassed, angry Politburo man demanded to know who was the boss of the brigade. Vladislavlev stepped forward. The party man signaled for Vladislavlev to get in his car and drove him twenty minutes across the barren Russian plain. A rain storm hit, and hail pelted the car under dark threatening clouds. Vladislavlev had no idea what was going to happen to him. Then, abruptly, the Politburo man told Vladislavlev to get out of the car, walk back in the hail, shirtless, and "finish the guy."

Vladislavlev didn't ask how to "finish" his friend Luzhkov. He just trudged back across the open fields, and when he returned to the camp, he recalled, he drank a bottle of vodka to keep himself from shivering to death. Soon the Politburo man called, "asking me what I had done to the guy. I said, 'I finished him!'" In fact, he did nothing.[3]

The truculent Luzhkov of that day was to become a leader of the new Russia. Luzhkov had suffered through a childhood of poverty.

Born September 21, 1936, he was the middle of three sons. His father was a carpenter and his mother a boiler room worker. The family lived on the first floor of a wooden barrack near the Paveletsky railroad station in Moscow. The three boys, their parents, and his father's mother all shared one drafty room without heat or running water. All three sons shared one coat that their father had brought back from the war. Luzhkov's memories were of constant hunger during the years of World War II and after. "I can't describe this," he recalled. "We always wanted to . . . not even eat, but to devour no matter what. Kids around us swelled and died from hunger." Once the boys were so desperate they ate—and salted—"white clay" they found along the railroad tracks and became dreadfully sick.

Luzhkov's most vivid memories revolved around the *dvor*, the courtyard, the center of his life as a youth. The courtyard was a world apart from the outside, "a small, self-organized community in opposition to the city and the state." In the space between the buildings, they set the rules, the ethics, and the morals. "There were intellectual courtyards, but there were sporty and even thievish courtyards as well," he recalled. "Ours was a hooligan courtyard, meaning that it provoked a special, risky mood—to get into a fight with somebody, to make yourself visible, to show some pluck." Luzhkov said his mother was so busy working—she took two, then three jobs—that she gave the boys "total freedom to secretly indulge our passion for dangerous games." Luzhkov was left to the "risky, reckless mood of the courtyard." They often disassembled artillery shells from the war front that they found on railway cars nearby. They would take out the gunpowder, make a fuse with a trail in the dirt, and set off a small firecracker-like explosion. Once Luzhkov had an idea: Why not set off the whole shell? He set the fuse and ran. A huge explosion followed, shattering windows. The police arrived, but the courtyard had its rules. No one gave him away. "The courtyard was as silent as the grave to the authorities," Luzhkov remembered.

Later Luzhkov enrolled at the Gubkin Institute of Oil and Gas, one of the premier training grounds for the rapidly industrializing Soviet Union. In the high-ceilinged halls and laboratories of the institute, the Gubkin students learned mechanical engineering, oil and gas geology, mining and refining from one hundred professors, including two prestigious academicians. Although the requisite Marxist-Leninist training was present, the curriculum was heavily weighted toward technical training. Overall, the school played a critical role—turning out specialists—and each student was given a very specific training over five years to fit into a given place in industry when they finished.[4]

Luzhkov graduated in 1958. He expected to go into the oil industry but was assigned to plastics. He protested loudly, to no avail. Nonetheless, Luzhkov did well. Plastics and petrochemicals came into greater demand in the 1960s, and he moved up the ranks. In 1974 he was appointed director of a design bureau in the Ministry of the Chemical Industry, and later he became director of Khimavtomatika, a maker of specialized equipment for chemical factories with twenty thousand workers. It was the largest single enterprise in the ministry and was divided between scientific research and factory work. It was here, as a top Soviet industrial manager, that Luzhkov took his first, tentative steps away from socialism, and it was a painful departure, seared into his memory.

In 1980, at the end of the Brezhnev period, Luzhkov proposed a somewhat unorthodox idea, that the science half of his enterprise be put on a very elementary self-financing scheme. "Self-financing" was a watchword of earlier attempts to reform the centrally planned economy, and it often went hand in glove with the growing independence of factory managers. Roughly speaking, it allowed factories to retain their own earnings. Luzhkov suggested selling the research results at Khimavtomatika as a commodity; when they developed a scientific process, they could peddle it and keep the profits. Luzhkov's proposal went to the top decisionmaking body of the ministry, the collegium, a group of senior managers who sat around a horseshoe-shaped table while an audience of 150 less senior workers looked on. Standing at a podium, Luzhkov outlined his plans. His idea was immediately and dramatically shot down by a representative of the Communist Party, who declared that Luzhkov wanted to violate the precepts of Marx and Engels. The party man opened up a volume of Marx and read aloud: science was the product of human thinking and could not be evaluated in monetary terms! Luzhkov was violating Marx!

That was the end of the idea. Luzhkov's minister had no desire to fight the party. What had been a modest step away from socialism had turned into a political hot potato. Luzhkov's idea was buried and forgotten. But he had marked himself as a man willing to experiment.[5]

At the beginning of *perestroika,* Luzhkov was fifty years old, but nothing at the time marked him as a political leader. By the same age, both Gorbachev and Yeltsin held high-ranking party posts.[6] Luzhkov had joined the party in 1968, but his preoccupation was Soviet industry and not ideology. Nevertheless, it was common that a top industrial manager would be drawn into city affairs. In 1975 Luzhkov was chosen to serve on a local district council, and two years later he became a member of the rubber-stamp Moscow city council, known as the Mossovet. Its size varied, but the Mossovet at this time had about a thousand members. The entire city was run by the party, and the Mossovet was an enormous, unwieldy legislature, a facade of authority that decided very little. Luzhkov accepted a part-time post as head of the city commission on consumer services. It was an important choice because it was here that the seeds of change would be planted in Gorbachev's early years of *perestroika.*[7]

In 1986 Luzhkov resigned from his industry post and moved full-time into the city administrative system. Yeltsin had arrived from Sverdlovsk and broke the news to Luzhkov personally; he had been made one of the deputy chairmen of the *ispolkom*, the city executive committee. His new duties included supervising the budding cooperatives in Moscow.

As already noted, the old party stalwarts of the time were suspicious; they saw the entrepreneurs in the cooperative movement as profiteers, speculators, and subversive enemies of socialism. When Luzhkov set up a commission to license the cooperatives in Moscow, the whole experiment stood on wobbly legs. "This was a mission, a very dangerous one," Luzhkov told me. No one knew if it could survive the dead hand of the old system, which had stifled so much individual initiative over the decades.

One unlikely champion of the cooperatives was a man who spoke in the dry, measured tones of a bureaucrat, Alexander Panin, a Leningrad management specialist who became Luzhkov's right-hand man in dealing with the cooperatives. Panin was among legions of experts who, in between endless cups of tea and idle hours in their institutes, were supposedly working to perfect socialist management techniques. Panin, who had been discreetly reading Western management texts, concluded that the most important thing was to unlock the brilliance and imagination of individuals. He took a courageous decision and wrote a letter to the Communist Party Central Committee in Moscow. His ideas flew in the face of decades of party doctrine. He was summoned to the Central Committee offices at Staraya Ploschad, or Old Square, and the party people listened, for a while. Panin told me that, by necessity, he had to dress up his notion of individual initiative with a lot of rhetoric, insisting that allowing individual initiative did not contradict socialist dogma. The party apparatchiks told Panin they could not help him, but they urged him to keep spreading his notions and approach the Communist Youth League, the Komsomol, which had a little more leeway for free thinking about such things. Amazed by their reaction, Panin kept up his campaign. He suggested a modest experiment in individual initiative—allowing people to start their own cooperatives, which would be very small private businesses, such as baking pies. Finally, the authorities agreed to let him try, and Panin became executive director of Luzhkov's Moscow committee on cooperatives—to oversee baking of the first pies of capitalism.[8]

Luzhkov and Panin began in a room as large as a dance hall on the sixth floor of the Mossovet building in central Moscow. Simple folding tables were brought in to one side of the room. The staff worked by day; then Luzhkov, in shirtsleeves, came in the evenings, usually after 7:00 P.M., often holding meetings with the new entrepreneurs until well beyond midnight. The new businessmen thronged the halls with their proposals, their paperwork, their questions, and their substantial problems, not the least of which were how to get supplies from the state-run economy and how to get a room or garage for their new venture. "Bearded, shaggy, and looking God-knows-how," Luzhkov later recalled of his impressions of the new businessmen, "but all of them were energetic, independent, and interested. One was offering to produce useful goods out of waste garbage. Another found consumer demand at a place where the state structures had no field of activity at all. Ingenuity, inventiveness, creativity—we saw so much of it in our room."

Luzhkov's young, stern aide was Yelena Baturina, whom he married after his first wife died of cancer in 1988. Baturina recalled how the people who came to the room were so different from the bureaucrats who worked in the Mossovet building, and how shocked the bureaucrats were to find the ragged entrepreneurs in their halls. "We were constantly transferred from room to room," she told me, "because neighbors complained that bearded, dirty people were sitting in the corridors and actually spoiled the image of the building!"[9]

Viktor Loshak, the *Moscow News* journalist who had been watching the drama unfold, recalled that Luzhkov had to defend the pioneering cooperative businessmen against bureaucrats who wanted to crush them. One group of bureaucrats were the fierce, large women who were official guardians of public health and safety. The bureaucrats had no idea that a new economy was being born in front of their eyes; they were supposed to uphold the dictates of the old system. "They resisted every microscopic step of the cooperative movement," Loshak told me.

"I was waiting for the first meeting of this commission. I remember the first woman who was going to be in private business—she was a theater specialist by profession. She had two or three children. She wanted to bake cakes for people for holidays, as a business.

"And Luzhkov said, 'Great!' And two or three others said 'Okay.' Then the opposite side started looking for reasons why they could refuse her. 'What is the size of your apartment?' they asked. And it turns out the apartment is big enough. 'Do you have a medical certificate?' She had a certificate. 'Will you be able to go on taking care of your children?' And it turned out her mother was in the same block of flats and could help.

"Then this bitch from the sanitary epidemiological service asked, 'Do you have secondary industrial ventilation in your apartment?' And this woman didn't even know what that woman was taking about. Nobody knew what it was, and I didn't know what it was. And that woman from the sanitary epidemiological service found some point number 3, article number 8, that when making cakes for sale there must be that industrial ventilation.

"Then Luzhkov said, 'Go—you know where! I'm chairman of this commission and this woman will start her business!'" Luzhkov won the vote and moved on to the next person, who wanted to open a bicycle repair shop.[10]

One evening in those early weeks, a party boss came and insisted that Luzhkov move "this entire public out of here." Luzhkov explained that the whole point was to let off the steam of public discontent. "The wave is rolling already," Luzhkov told the party man. "If we don't cope, we will find ourselves under this wave." At the same time, Luzhkov privately feared he was being set up for failure, that the cooperatives were going to be crushed and he would be blamed. "The future cooperators were eager to start business, but they were fearful of the future and they wanted to receive some kind of support from me. I cheered them up the way I knew how, but my heart was filled with anxiety and worry."[11]

Valery Saikin, chairman of the executive committee and Luzhkov's boss, told Luzhkov that the nascent private businessmen were subversive and fretted that they might come and demonstrate openly against the party chieftains. "Objectively, they are against the state economy. Against socialism," he said to Luzhkov. "I warn you: if they come to the Mossovet, you will be the one to go and meet them!"

"With pleasure," Luzhkov replied. "I will take my favorite cap, come to the balcony, and will wave to them like Lenin did when saying farewell to troops on the way to the civil war." Saikin was not amused.

Later, recalling those months of frenetic activity, Luzhkov said the evenings were not just bureaucratic work but offered a glimpse of the market economy—people anxious to work for themselves, not the state. "Dealing with the new people formed a new world outlook," he said. "I began understanding things that before I used to guess only vaguely. . . ."

But things were never clear-cut at the beginning. The first tiny steps toward a market economy were confused, inchoate, and shrouded in suspicion. Were the new businessmen taking bribes or paying bribes? Reaping windfall profits? Luzhkov heard the rumors. The confusion was partly justified; Panin noted that the pies made by the cooperatives cost seven or eight kopeks each, compared with five kopeks in the state store. To the people on the street, that seemed like profiteering. Sometimes they were better, sometimes not. The cooperatives began the long march toward the market saddled with great suspicion in a society that had known nothing like it.

The first cooperatives were dramatically different from the old state establishments. The cooperatives actually *cared* about their customers. "In the Soviet Union, the counter was like a barricade, with enemies on either side," Loshak recalled. "And suddenly they were not enemies. These people, the 'cooperators,' were interested in their clients, in having them buy something. When the first cooperative restaurant appeared, it differed drastically from all the others, from state restaurants."

David Remnick, a *Washington Post* correspondent, described the amazing scene at the first cooperative restaurant at 36 Kropotkinskaya Street. He said the menu included soup, suckling pig, salad, and coffee. "So attentive was the management to good service that it soon fired one waiter for being 'tactless.' The café was a sensation not only for the well-to-do Soviets and foreigners who could manage the dual feats of getting in the door and paying the check, but also for ordinary people who heard about it in the press. There were rumors of fantastic profits being made and charges of 'speculation.' The Communist Party newspaper Pravda asserted that the new system allowed some people to make 'significant sums that did not correspond to their expected labor.'"[12]

In this environment, Luzhkov was a curator of the new experiment who protected, nurtured, and monitored the cooperatives as they took hold. In his first four months, the number of Moscow cooperatives zoomed from four to more than a thousand. Luzhkov sponsored an exhibition of their work to mark the first hundred cooperatives and spread the idea. Yeltsin showed up to encourage him. A photograph shows Luzhkov admiring the exhibit stand of a cooperator making his own musical instruments. Baturina recalled, "The cooperatives worshiped Luzhkov because, out of all the official persons at that time, no one risked speaking out in their favor, in their defense." But Luzhkov, who in later years was famous for roaming city construction sites, rarely visited the cooperatives. Panin said Luzhkov was still cautious and saw himself as a "monitor" of the new businessmen. Neither the party bureaucrats nor the public was really prepared for what was being unleashed, he recalled. "It was a test, as usual, in the beginning," Panin told me. "You understand, if we hadn't monitored them, they could have poisoned people or used bad raw materials. And had they done that—we would have had a lot of problems ourselves. That would have been the end of the cooperatives."

As the cooperative movement blossomed, Luzhkov and Panin began to have their own private doubts. These ambitious new businessmen were rapidly overtaking the early concept of baking pies. They were branching out into work with Soviet industrial enterprises. They were experimenting with finance. The Law on Cooperatives had opened the door to private banks, and a few smart young men had figured out a way to launder government subsidies, intended for factories, into cash for themselves. They were obviously baking money, not pies. They were producing nothing useful for society, Luzhkov feared. "After the cooperative movement grew in scale and it became uncontrolled—then there was no stopping it," Panin told me. "All barriers were removed. They were allowed to do anything, and then masses of people poured into the movement without any control."

Loshak, the journalist, recalled that Luzhkov was outwardly still very much part of the system. He wore a black coat with a black fur collar and a fedora of the kind long favored by Communist Party ideologist Suslov. He was driven in an official black Volga car. But inwardly, Luzhkov sensed that the ground was trembling, even if he didn't fully understand why. Loshak got a glimpse of Luzhkov's changing mind-set one night in a long, soul-searching conversation with him. "We met after work; it was late at night, we sat together in his car. And we just drove around Moscow for a long time and talked. Our conversation was about down-to-earth things, about cooperatives and the people who came to the cooperative movement, about Moscow. We were beginning to understand something new in our life."

Loshak added, "If somebody asks you who is the father of capitalism in Russia, as a rule, there is always only one answer: It is Gorbachev. But in reality, one of the fathers of capitalism was Luzhkov."

Yet, Loshak added, Luzhkov never could have uttered those words at the time. Luzhkov did not imagine then that capitalism, markets, and private property might come to Russia. He was a "big boss," a product of the system itself, Loshak recalled. "But at the same time, he was a real person, which made him different from others. His eyes sparkled. I think that back then, he understood that somehow, people's interests must find a way out."

In the summer of 1987, Luzhkov accepted the supposedly suicidal mission of managing the vegetable warehouses. He felt doomed. "Nothing could save it from implosion," he recalled. In Moscow, discontent was growing over food shortages. One night, at a gala concert, the popular stand-up comedian Gennady Khazanov declared that Moscow "is the city of evergreen tomatoes." It was a play on words from old hackneyed slogans about the Soviet Union being a land of evergreen forests. When he made the crack about the tomatoes, Luzhkov, who was in the audience, felt the performer looked right at him—and the whole audience laughed.

For Luzhkov, it was a moment of acute humiliation, and right after the show he stormed over to the tomato warehouse. "I was horrified," he recalled. "I was pacing among the 'evergreen tomatoes,' squashed and rotting. I knew why they were like this." In the next few months, Luzhkov, as with the cooperatives, began to search for a few limited market solutions in a sea of socialist folly.

Every day, thousands of people were drafted from their regular jobs to work in the vegetable bases. The workers were drawn from schools, hospitals, laboratories, and institutes, which ordered them to go to the vegetable dungeons. The work was miserable, but they had no choice. "The chilled, humiliated, dirty librarians, engineers, and doctors were working under the supervision of regular warehouse workers, who appeared in their mink hats and sheepskin jackets like nobility and evaluated their efforts in order to inform the district party committee," Luzhkov recalled.

In a radical break with the past, Luzhkov decided to stop the forced march of ordinary Muscovites to the warehouses every day. He promised to save money by cutting back on waste and using the savings to pay his regular workers better salaries or hire part-timers. Luzhkov recalled the moment when a party official, standing at a large meeting, somewhat dryly announced that the city had stopped drafting people to work in the vegetable bases. It was just another line in the endlessly boring list of party "accomplishments." Suddenly, the audience erupted in cheers, an outpouring of enthusiasm unheard of in such a setting. The party man was stunned and embarrassed. He later telephoned Luzhkov and demanded to know if a trick had been played on him.

"Everything is true," Luzhkov reported. No warehouse in Moscow had a worker who was drafted.

Luzhkov figured that stealing in the warehouses was done by three different groups. Roughly one-third of the stealing was done by the workers, one-third by the truck drivers who delivered to the stores, and one-third in the stores. Luzhkov had an idea. If they lost fewer vegetables to spoilage, could they make more money and then pay people more—and perhaps reduce the stealing? It was a capitalist thought.

Luzhkov went to work on it. He asked his deputies for the official spoilage rate. The answer came back: 1 percent. "It was only then that I realized the pervasive cruelty of the system," he recalled. "With all the monstrous losses of up to 30 percent in the storage process, the system had the nerve to demand a loss of only 1 percent. It was a laughing matter, a myth, a caricature—but there it was. . . . The Soviet system formulated its laws on the premises of an ideal people living within an ideal social and natural environment. As a result, it did not matter how good you were or how well you worked—at the same time, it also meant that no one could meet the established quotas."

Luzhkov decided it was time for a change. He contracted a Moscow biologist's laboratory to give him realistic spoilage quotas for fruits and vegetables. Then he got the *ispolkom*—the city executive committee—to issue an ordinance ratifying these as the new quotas. With the new quotas in place, Luzhkov told the workers they could sell, for their own profit, half of what they saved from spoilage. "Not a third," Luzhkov intoned to the workers, "but half."

It worked. The spoilage was reduced, the quality of the produce was improved, and the workers were paid more.

But the higher authorities did not like it. In a reactionary spasm, Luzhkov was called before the committee of the people's control, a party watchdog commission. The committee accused Luzhkov of fiddling illegally with the spoilage rates. They accused Luzhkov of paying "huge bonuses" to a collective. A crime! But after a tense hearing, the committee backed down, and Luzhkov was let off.

Luzhkov had survived the suicide mission, but he never won the kind of popular approbation that Yeltsin enjoyed. The reason was that the vegetable bases went from grim to somewhat better, but the Soviet Union was coming unraveled at the same time. Luzhkov despaired when Yeltsin, who had been a source of support, was dumped as Moscow party chief in November 1987. The following year, he shook the hand of Yeltsin, then an outcast, at a Red Square holiday parade. They spoke for several hours, and Luzhkov expressed hope that they would work together again.[13]

The command system was growing weaker and getting tomatoes from Azerbaijan to Moscow became even more difficult, even if the vegetable bases were functioning. Despite Luzhkov's reforms, Moscow's food shortages worsened. Then another kind of hurricane approached and took Luzhkov with it.

The Gorbachev years of *perestroika* saw Moscow seething with dissatisfaction, but the deepest source of discontent was rotten leadership more than rotten vegetables. When he came to the city, Yeltsin touched a raw nerve with his populist campaigns against party privileges. The reaction went even deeper among the intelligentsia. They were sick and tired of the gray bureaucrats and the party apparatchiks telling them what lines in a script could be performed or what books could be read or what statistics about life expectancy could be published in a scientific journal (i.e., none).

Gorbachev's political liberalization unleashed a tidal wave of new thinking, and Moscow was awash in political clubs, interest groups, demonstrations, and ferment. What is striking about the rise of the "radical" democrats in Moscow is how randomly and even accidentally they all came together in a short period of time. The fall of the Berlin Wall in November 1989 had set the thinkers, artists, and professionals in Moscow afire.

Vladimir Bokser, a pediatrician who had also been an activist for an animal rights group, was one of the early democratic organizers. Bokser had the engaging manner of a friendly small-town doctor. But behind his calm demeanor lay a razor-sharp understanding of grassroots moods and politics. His primary interest was political freedom. He felt the intelligentsia was ripe for change. "Everyone came to understand that the leaders were not very honest people. They lie, they pretend," Bokser recalled. "That's what ended up uniting everyone. In a very precise way, at the end of the 1970s and in the beginning of the 1980s, a feeling of shame started rising." The intelligentsia revolted against the Communists, and they revolted first in Moscow. Bokser told me, "It was a revolution of the intelligentsia, purely cultural. There was no other revolution at that time. Before 1990, none of us had even thought about a market to any degree. In fact, people feared that. Most importantly, people didn't want these bureaucrats to sit there anymore, who decided everything for us, told us what films to watch; which books we ought to read. When people started watching what was happening outside the country, they wanted more openness. They wanted not only cultural openness but information openness. The first thing that happened was a revolution of openness, for an open society."[14]

One of the strongest voices came from a man with a very unremarkable appearance—short and slightly hunched over, with a full head of salt-and-pepper hair and a small mustache. Gavriil Popov, an economist who had once been dean of the economics department of Moscow State University, was then editor of a journal, *Questions of Economics*. Popov had doubts about the system in the late Brezhnev years, and as *perestroika* took off, he was a prominent voice leading society toward something new. Popov was a close ally of Yeltsin in the new elected parliament, the Congress of Peoples' Deputies, and he was constantly pushing Gorbachev to pursue more radical reforms.

The Moscow radical democrats were a loose group of political clubs, various associations for specific causes, human rights groups, and a host of curious and dissatisfied loners, many of them scientists. Under Popov, they came together to create a coalition, Democratic Russia. They decided to wage a campaign for the March 4, 1990, elections to the Mossovet, which had been reduced in size to 498 seats. This was a critical decision for the insurgent democrats—they decided to go local and make Moscow, not the national government, an engine for real change.

The democrats staged a noisy campaign: slogans blared from their megaphones in the subway underpasses, sound trucks roamed the streets. They had meetings in apartment houses, held two big street rallies, distributed thousands of mimeographed handbills, and put up posters in shops and the subways. They were the intellectual elite: among their candidates, 64.3 percent came from careers in higher education, science, engineering, the media, and arts.[15]

They scored a stunning victory, taking over the Moscow city government. They won 282 of the seats. On April 16, 1990, the newly empowered democrats assembled at the Mossovet and chose Popov as their chairman. The insurgents were ebullient to be capturing Moscow. They had shown they could compete with all those self-important men who had told them what to read and what to think. Ilya Zaslavsky, a chemical engineer who had been elected to the council, declared with boundless hope, "We will begin a new life."[16]

But as Popov and the other victors were soon to discover, a potential disaster was hurtling toward them. Food shortages were mounting. Hoarding and panic gripped the city; hundreds of thousands of people flooded into Moscow from the provinces looking for food. Lines sometimes blocked the big avenues. Each wave of rumors spread more panic: meat was running out! Bread was almost gone! Six weeks after taking office, Popov acknowledged that "the situation in the city is getting critical. There is a real danger of things spinning out of control. Hundreds of thousands of people are in the shops."[17] Bokser recalled, "Everyone was expecting there to be a famine in Moscow. Maybe it was exaggerated, but everyone expected it." A secret CIA analysis at the time reported the most probable outlook for the Soviet Union was "deterioration short of anarchy," and one thing that could push it toward total anarchy would be "massive consumer unrest." The CIA analysis said that any reactionary putsch, or takeover, would certainly target the radical democrats, including Popov.[18]

Popov's first major decision was to appoint a new chairman of the *ispolkom*, the city executive committee. Saikin, the previous boss, had gone on vacation. The head of the *ispolkom* would run the city, and if he ran it badly, the outcry would certainly wreck the reformers' chances of holding onto power.

None of those around Popov knew how to manage the sprawling metropolis. His inner circle included Bokser and Vasily Shakhnovsky, a one-time engineer who worked on thermonuclear synthesis at the Kurchatov Institute in Moscow. Shakhnovsky had been drawn into the blossoming world of debates, clubs, and elections in 1989, and he was elected to the Mossovet.[19] Another aide was Mikhail Shneider, a physicist at the Institute of Geomagnetism and the Ionosphere who had helped organize the elections with Bokser. Popov too was primarily a thinker. A common, albeit respectful jibe was that Popov needed to lie on the couch and think for several hours a day.[20] A theorist, even a bit of a romanticist, Popov did not think about potholes and streetlamps. He had no idea how many tons of vegetables were in the Moscow warehouses. He had no idea how to cope with the cigarette riots or the food shortages.

Popov feared that the radical democrats would be overwhelmed by their own lack of experience in governing. He was haunted by the idea that the whole experiment could fail; everything might collapse and they would be discredited, perhaps even jailed. It was just too heavy a test for the radicals, to make them run the whole city at the beginning. They were not ready. They needed a bridge to the old regime.

They also needed something from a long, deep tradition in Russian culture. They needed a real *khozyain*, a rich term in Russian that refers to the leader of a given social domain, a home, a village, an enterprise, or a country. The *khozyain* of a household, usually the oldest male, has responsibility for the welfare of the group. A real *khozyain* takes care of those in his domain. Russians tend to judge leaders on whether they give the impression of being a real *khozyain*—sometimes in appearance or in action. And a person who at least displays talents in this direction—who can manage the affairs of the day—is a *khozyaistvennik*.[21] Popov was in search of one because he clearly was not. Popov turned to Yeltsin.

The radicals met every morning for breakfast in a large room behind the stage at the Mossovet building to talk about their plans for the day. Popov toyed with the idea of bringing back Saikin, the old party man, to run the city, but the radical democrats wouldn't hear of it. He had other candidates from the old guard, but the radical democrats were dubious about them. Popov came to breakfast one day and reported that Yeltsin had suggested a candidate to manage the city—Luzhkov. But no one present knew Luzhkov.

"And we asked, who is this man?" recalled one of the democrats, Alexander Osovtsov.

The question hung in the air. Then someone recalled that the young cooperators, who were mingling with the new democrats, spoke highly of Luzhkov. Shneider recalled that he had just met Luzhkov. His first impression was vivid. "Soviet bureaucrat," he recalled. "Style of his speech, the choice of words, vocabulary, appearance, the way he talked to people—all of that spoke that he was a true Soviet bureaucrat. Just the way I had imagined a bureaucrat, because I had never dealt with bureaucrats before."[22]

Popov could not make up his mind. "Tomorrow, we have to make the decision," he told the radicals. "We must do it tomorrow."

Bokser went home distressed. The phone rang. It was an old acquaintance, a woman who was now a pensioner. Bokser told her how Popov was wavering on this critical decision, but Luzhkov was one of the finalists. The woman's voice brightened.

"That wouldn't be Yuri Mikhailovich?"

"Yuri Mikhailovich. How do you know him?"

"Wasn't he the head of Khimavtomatika?" This was the enterprise Luzhkov headed in the late 1970s in Moscow.

"Yes," Bokser replied, curiously.

"You know, I worked there ten years," she said. "I know him. I didn't know him well, but I heard that he always treated people well."

The next day, Bokser went right to Popov and recommended Luzhkov. "I heard that he treated people well," he said.

Luzhkov observed the democrats edgily, well aware that he was considered a member of the old guard, one of the apparatchiks whom the insurgents had vowed to throw out. He recalled that he was simmering with anger at the way the dissidents had blamed everything on the previous regime. He was "so enraged" by this that he decided to quit city government altogether. But then he went to the Marble Hall of the Mossovet to see the new politicians for himself. They didn't look like bureaucrats; they wore no ties. Luzhkov, who had once been energized by the cooperatives, took a similar liking to the rough-hewn new democrats. They had none of the "blind obedience" of the previous generation, he thought.

"You were dealing with intelligent, active, angry people, denouncing the idiocy of the old system and promising to fix everything fast," Luzhkov recalled. "These people greatly impressed me." But he knew—better than they—what a mess they had inherited. The supply lines that held the Soviet Union together were snapping, virtually every day. As Luzhkov mulled the future, his phone rang. It was Yeltsin, who had made his own comeback. On May 29, 1990, Yeltsin was elected chairman of the parliament in the Russian Republic, the largest Soviet republic, and was pressuring Gorbachev for still more radical reform.

"This is Yeltsin," the familiar voice boomed to Luzhkov. "Drop everything and get over here." At Yeltsin's urging, Popov chose Luzhkov to be city administrator and Luzhkov agreed. Popov told me years later that Luzhkov had several factors in his favor. He was never a top party boss. He had deftly managed the cooperatives, and Popov recalled that cooperative types had supported the radical democrats in their election campaign. Popov also knew Luzhkov had stopped the dirty, miserable work in the vegetable bases.[23]

Bokser went to see the radical democrats to ameliorate any concerns about the choice of Luzhkov. The first reaction was anger. "Betrayal!" the radicals shouted back at Bokser. "We want our own democrat!"

But the anger passed on the day Popov formally introduced Luzhkov as his choice before a meeting of the Mossovet. Luzhkov recalled that, at the moment of the introduction, Popov regarded him coolly. Popov made a curt introduction and then gave Luzhkov twelve minutes to explain himself. "I was shocked," Luzhkov recalled. How could he address the crisis gripping the city in just twelve minutes? The members bombarded Luzhkov with questions. One question came from a radical democrat.

"Tell us, what is your platform?" Luzhkov was asked. "Are you a democrat or a Communist?"

Luzhkov was flustered. Something welled up in him, and he blurted out an answer that resonated for years to come. "I always was and I am standing on one platform—that of *khozyaistvennik*," he said.

There was applause. The whole room broke into laughter. Luzhkov had unexpectedly disarmed the radicals and won them over. Shakhnovsky recalled that "this answer had a great influence on the democratic part of the Mossovet. This was a very bright answer." They voted for Luzhkov. Popov was the political leader, but Luzhkov the *khozyaistvennik*.

The year that followed brought more decline, as the Soviet Union careened toward its final months. Yeltsin, Popov, and Anatoly Sobchak of Leningrad, all leading democrats, walked out of the Soviet Communist party in July 1990 and turned in their cards. Life in Moscow grew ever more bleak. In the early autumn of 1990, as snow began to fall, a terrifying panic hit: the potato harvest was rotting in the fields.

Luzhkov looked to traditional command methods to cope with the chaos, imposing such measures as identity cards for Muscovites to buy food. As the shortages intensified, black markets sprang up outside the shops. Prices skyrocketed for what little was available. Osovtsov recalled that Luzhkov decided to use the militia to enforce rigid price controls. It was a totally Soviet response. Osovtsov spent hours attempting to persuade Luzhkov it would not work—in desperate times, the scarce goods would get whatever black market price was set for them. "I nearly lost my voice trying to show him these were completely meaningless measures," Osovtsov recalled. Rationing began in the major cities, including Moscow and Leningrad.[24]

In the end there was no famine, but shortages grew severe. In early April 1991, visiting a Moscow food store, my colleague Michael Dobbs ran into a man surveying the meat counter. "There wasn't anything here yesterday, and there isn't anything here today," the man said, gazing at counter, empty but for some ready-to-cook dinners of soggy sausage and congealed gravy. "I doubt very much there will be anything here tomorrow."[25]

The following summer, in 1991, both Moscow and St. Petersburg underwent a major political restructuring. The rubber-stamp legislature and a smaller, powerful *ispolkom*—both totally controlled by the party—were restructured into a more modern mayoralty. In Moscow, Popov ran for mayor and took Luzhkov as candidate for vice mayor. Popov had never shaken his reputation as a thinker and theoretician, and Soviet journalists referred to him by an affectionate nickname, "Hedgehog in a Fog," after a popular animated cartoon film. Popov seemed sensitive to the point. In a television appearance during the campaign, he said, "We need to use the personnel available now in our own country—including the staff from the old Communist apparat. Luzhkov, in my view, compensates for a lot of my shortcomings."[26]

The voters gave the Popov-Luzhkov team a huge endorsement. They won with 65.3 percent of the vote. Bokser observed a subtle change in Luzhkov. Before, Luzhkov had been a *khozyaistvennik*, a manager, while Popov played politics on the national stage with Yeltsin. But once elected as vice mayor, Bokser said, it was clear that Luzhkov was taking more and more power into his hands. After the election "it was as if he had become the heir of Popov, and he wasn't the heir before the election."

At 6:30 A.M. Moscow time on August 19, 1991, a group of discontented hard-liners, including the head of the KGB, tried to topple Gorbachev. They put him under house arrest at his dacha in the Crimea and called a general state of emergency. The KGB chief, Vladimir Kryuchkov, signed arrest warrants for seventy people, including Popov, Bokser, and Shneider. Popov was in Bishkek, Kirgizia, and would not be back until evening. Luzhkov, the acting mayor, got a telephone call at 8:00 A.M. from the city party boss, Yuri Prokofyev, who suggested that Luzhkov come to him "for instructions."

Luzhkov faced a choice—to go with the coup plotters or to join Yeltsin against them. According to Shakhnovsky, who was with Luzhkov at the time, Yeltsin called and asked Luzhkov to come to his dacha outside the city. Shakhnovsky recalled that Luzhkov was the leader of the city that day, and had he announced support for the putsch, things might have turned out differently. Instead, he got in a car and sped away toward Yeltsin. His name was added to the list of those to be arrested by the KGB.[27]

When he arrived at the dacha that morning, Yeltsin greeted him in an old T-shirt and slippers. He pointed to some apples on a windowsill and offered one to Luzhkov. "Moscow is with you," Luzhkov assured him. "Thanks," Yeltsin said. He urged Luzhkov to organize popular resistance to the coup. On the way back to the city, Luzhkov asked his driver to stop the car and change the license plates. They kept a spare set in the trunk. Just in case.[28]

Shortly after noon, Yeltsin denounced the coup at a press conference. At 1:00 P.M. Yeltsin climbed on top of tank 110 of the Taman Division and gave his famous speech protesting the coup. At 4:30 P.M. Luzhkov issued his own denunciation of the coup and called on Muscovites to join in a general strike.

"I realized the coup plotters were going to fail when I saw that Luzhkov was wholly against them," Bokser recalled later. "Why? Because Popov, for them, was a democrat and not one of them. But Luzhkov was a real *khozyain*. He had given so many people apartments, such as the head of the communications brigade, the pilot of the helicopters. All those people understood that in Moscow, the real *khozyain* was Luzhkov."

The real heroes of the August days were Yeltsin and the tens of thousands of Muscovites who turned out in the streets to defy the putsch. Luzhkov was not a public figure in the tense hours of confrontation. But he did play a role behind the scenes. Since most of the central newspapers and television had been shut down, he kept Moscow's telephone and radio channels open, especially Echo of Moscow, the radio station that helped antiputsch forces in the most critical hours. The Mossovet had been among the founders of Echo of Moscow because Popov liked the idea of an independent radio station. Soon after the coup began, the station sent a correspondent to remain at Luzhkov's side. Alexei Venediktov, the director, told me that the link to Luzhkov was critical—it gave hope to all those who opposed the coup. There were reports that Luzhkov was organizing a defense, deploying trucks and volunteers, and ordering huge cement barriers to be set up. Luzhkov was on the air only briefly three or four times, but just knowing that Luzhkov was against the coup was important. "Luzhkov was a party member, an apparatchik," Venediktov recalled. "If such an active member of the Communist Party as Luzhkov refused to join, that inspired hope." Four times in three days, Echo of Moscow was thrown off the air but each time found a way to get back on.[29]

Osovtsov recalled that Luzhkov remained cool and pragmatic, making lists of things that had to be done to defeat the coup plotters. "The conversation," Osovtsov recalled of a staff meeting the first day in Luzhkov's office, "was mainly about the building blocks to be delivered to the White House and Mossovet in order to circle the buildings; about cars with fresh drinking water for the crowds, about mobile toilets, and naturally about food and other similar things. The political aspect of the moment was clear."

But then Luzhkov stood up and walked to the window. His office was now in a high-rise building with windows that looked out to the White House, the Moscow River, and the Ukraine Hotel. A single armored personnel carrier was stationed in front of the hotel, a distinctive gothic tower, one of the seven Stalin built. Looking out the window, Luzhkov spoke, as if to no one in particular, although the staff was sitting right there in his office. "Between us," he said, "I will tell you. A coup is a colossal administrative undertaking." Referring to the Communist Party veterans who had staged the revolt, he predicted, "These Komsomol members will never cope with it—no way!"

He was right. The coup attempt collapsed.

Luzhkov came out of the failed coup with a wellspring of respect in Moscow. For the first time, he was seen as a politician, not just as an apparatchik. As the coup attempt fell apart, Luzhkov faced the crowds in the streets and successfully persuaded them not to go on a revengeful rampage through the Communist Party offices at Staraya Ploschad. When angry crowds threatened to topple the statue of infamous secret police chief Felix Dzerzhinsky, Luzhkov had it taken down carefully by a crane, realizing that the eighty-five-ton monument could wreck telephone cables and sewer lines underneath if carelessly felled.[30]

The coup had a debilitating effect on Popov. The collapse of the Soviet Union left him exhausted. When, after the coup, Yeltsin agreed to begin the rapid market reforms in Russia that came to be known as "shock therapy," Popov was skeptical. He was also disappointed that Yeltsin passed over him.

Popov also faced trouble in the city. He collided almost constantly with the Mossovet. There were strong suspicions that Popov was making his own business deals on the side. The food situation in Moscow and Leningrad was still deteriorating. Popov had never shaken his fear that everything they had done could fall apart, and he would be blamed.

In December 1991, just as the union fell apart, Popov told close associates he wanted to quit. They urged him not to. Shakhnovsky and Luzhkov went to see Yeltsin. It was the day the Soviet flag came down and Gorbachev relinquished the nuclear briefcase to Yeltsin. They asked Yeltsin to forestall Popov's resignation. He did. In January, Popov again told a wider group that he would resign, but at a meeting of Democratic Russia, he was again persuaded to remain.

Bokser recalled that Popov was ill and suffered from constant back pain as a result of a mountain-climbing accident many years earlier. Popov was also losing interest in Moscow. He longed to join Yeltsin on the federal level, but there was no place for him, and he increasingly disagreed with the Gaidar government. In the city, it was Luzhkov, not Popov, who held the actual levers of power. On June 6, 1992, Popov resigned, leaving Luzhkov the leader of a chaotic, hungry metropolis of 9 million people.

And the *khozyain* was not quite ready.

Chapter 4

Anatoly Chubais

IN THE VAST colonnaded Leningrad Public Library, with twenty-eight reading halls, 17 million books, 300,000 manuscripts, and 112,000 maps, Nina Oding knew the location of a special drawer where forbidden books were kept. Oding was a young assistant in the mammoth library in the late 1970s, and when no one was looking, she would curl up next to the special drawer and read the prohibited books. They were mostly Western books deemed subversive by the Soviet state. Stored in the *spetzkhran,* a separate locked room, the books were brought out to the special drawer periodically, on request by foreign readers. For everyone else, access to the books required endless forms and permissions, and even then, the books would often inexplicably disappear and be unavailable. "Sorry," the clerk would say, "the bindings are being repaired."[1]

Why were these particular works secreted away? The regime did not say. It was one of those unfathomable absurdities of "developed socialism" that the system gave loving care to books it wanted no one to read. The books were obviously not totally banned because a great library like this one, opened in 1814, could not acknowledge that they did not exist. Rather, in the twilight of the Brezhnev years, the regime simply decided to hide them, sort of.

The Publichka, as young scholars fondly called the library, was a space for free thinking at a time when Soviet thought control still inspired anxiety. In the high-ceilinged sociology and economics reading room—they called it "Sotz-Ek"—there were several bibliographers, young men who knew everything from Tibetan language to the entire writings of Solzhenitsyn. They were sympathetic toward the interested reader, and once a bond of trust was established, they would talk freely about anything. In those days, the readers called Publichka the "cemetery of brains," not because of the books but all the smart bibliographers, librarians, and readers who gathered there. There was a spirit of reading and debate in the air, especially in the smoking lounge and the cafeteria, a tiny place with just a few tables.[2]

Among those who gathered there were KGB agents and informers, but no one ever knew precisely the danger zone, the red line over which it was prohibited to step. The regime was old and sick, its fabled tentacles turning numb, its brain addled. Yet there was always a certain unpredictability that kept everyone from speaking out too loudly. Leningrad was known for an especially alert KGB division. Once a researcher came to the library and asked for forbidden books. He was told they did not exist. Then he came back—with the precise catalog numbers! He asked for them because he knew they were there, hidden away. The KGB began an investigation—where did he get the numbers?

Nina Oding was an acute observer of the crowds who surged in and out of the library. A short woman with a mane of curly auburn hair and mischievous eyes that could burst with enthusiasm or darken in seriousness, she possessed a splendid memory of the varied readers who came every day to the Sotz-Ek. She knew them by their faces and their ID numbers, which she easily memorized. Among them, she remembered a tall, handsome young man with striking strawberry-blond hair who was always hanging out, reading books on economics and politics. His name was Anatoly Chubais.

For the curious young academics of the time, Chubais and his generation, fear of the KGB was not an omnipresent dread, but it meant a certain cautious way of talking to each other in public. It became second nature. Everywhere around them was evidence that the system was slowing down, that the economy and industry were gradually becoming dysfunctional, that the leadership was corrupt and self-aggrandizing, but the young academics still spoke only in whispers and coded language. Their words about "perfection of the mechanism of production" were as gray as the stone face of the Leningrad Engineering Economic Institute at 9 Marat Street in the center of the city, where Chubais was an up-and-coming young professor.

Sometime after spotting Chubais at the library, Oding was assigned to a job at his institute. It was not by choice. She considered herself a freethinker, not a Communist Party member, and she believed that was why, after graduation from the university, the party bosses sent her to a dreary research institute for applied economics. "The economists at that time were these funny people," she recalled years later. "It seemed to me I had fallen into some kind of horror. They were all so woodenheaded. And ideological! And I was a progressive historian."

The institute was among hundreds where Soviet specialists were supposedly working on the colossal unsolved problem of the Brezhnev era: how to make socialism work better. In thousands of small cubicles, surrounded by identical blond wood cabinets, thin curtains, and green plastic-hooded desk lamps, in classrooms lined with chalkboards and half-empty cups of tea, Soviet researchers strove to find a "scientific" answer that would repair the ailing socialist machine. The researchers dutifully spent years examining the creaking cogs of Soviet industry, if only to find out how to nudge them forward or at least arrest the decay. They searched for "indicators," or clues, that would show how to stimulate a 2 percent improvement in labor productivity or 3 percent higher steel output. Every industry—machine building, coal mining, agriculture, metallurgy, and dozens more—had its own group of institutes going through the same motions. The one all-encompassing, great indicator of market capitalism, free prices, was not a possibility in Soviet socialism, so hundreds of thousands of researchers spent tedious years looking for other, inevitably artificial measurements of what was right or wrong, good or bad in economic life. Many of the researchers knew, or at least guessed, that their quest for the perfect "indicator" of socialist progress was futile.

Soon after her arrival at the institute, Oding was sent to the annual mandatory autumn pilgrimage to harvest potatoes on a collective farm. The entire institute went off to the eastern edge of the Leningrad region, a remote, depressed corner of the Soviet empire with rutted dirt roads passable only by tractor. The countryside offered a welcome break from the grind of seminars and endless discussions about perfecting socialism at the institute. They lived in old wooden barracks. By day, they banged together crude wooden crates and yanked potatoes from the ground, and by night they sang, drank, and talked. They were invigorated by the clean air, the soreness of tired muscles and the pain of sunburn, and by the influx of new friendships and the promise of romance.

They worked in shifts at the farm. Oding quickly recognized Chubais on the opposite shift. He was tall, with a long, handsome face and a complexion that quickly reddened when he grew emotional or angry. He came across as a very serious young man, dutiful, and a natural leader. He was correct, cautious, and sure of himself.

Back at the institute, he worked on the problem of "perfecting socialist research and development." Chubais was not an orthodox economist, Oding later recalled, but he was no dissident, either. He was, if anything, always diligent and a favorite of the older professors. He had been admitted to the Communist Party at a very early age, which was unusual. He would brush off the flirtatious girls with a soft unyielding smile, and they would turn away, proclaiming loudly, "He's hopeless!" But around friends he was engaging and good-humored. Like everyone in those years, Chubais was fond of the Beatles. He liked jazz, but you'd never find him listening to the Sex Pistols or Alice Cooper. He was a very upright young man.

At night, there was little to entertain them at the collective farm; a tractor would take hours to get to the nearest cinema. So they talked into the early morning. Here in the *glubinka,* or deep countryside, they were free of the KGB. On an October evening in 1979, Chubais and two friends from the institute began to argue about their seemingly endless search for socialist industrial perfection. One of the friends was Grigory Glazkov, a quiet, thoughtful specialist on the problems of industrial automation. The other was Yuri Yarmagaev, an emotional mathematician who generated ideas like the sparks from a welder's torch. Yarmagaev was an anti-Soviet radical, Glazkov a level-headed analyst who critiqued every idea, and Chubais an establishment man. Chubais was twenty-four years old, his friends both just a year older.[3] The long argument that night was the moment that changed their lives.

"It was a special year," Glazkov later remembered. "The Brezhnev era had a certain life cycle. It was very vigorous in the late 1960s, when Brezhnev took power. By 1975, it was the beginning of the end.

This was the turning point when the system began to fall apart. By the end of the 1970s, it was completely rotten. There was complete disbelief, complete disappointment in the existing Soviet system. Anybody with brains was very disappointed and very unhappy with the system. And in 1979, I think the system made one last attempt to fix itself."

The attempt came in an order from Brezhnev. The elusive search for "indicators" of socialist progress had gone nowhere. The economy of shortages grew worse. The factories made junk for consumers. So the scientific researchers in all the institutes were ordered to begin a new quest to improve the quality of the socialist industrial machine. And the blueprint for this new search was contained in Brezhnev's Decree 695. It was a huge, thick book of instructions. "It tried to be a system of measuring everything," Glazkov recalled. "Measuring economic success. Industrial success. Success in productivity and quality and so on. And that was the end, actually. The beginning of the very end of the system."

During the night at the *kolkhoz,* the three friends argued whether Decree 695 would work.

Yarmagaev was sure it was doomed. He had worked in a factory. He said socialist industrial perfection was utter nonsense. "Everything is lies. There is no such thing as a socialist economy. Everyone is stealing. Everything is plundered." When Chubais argued that there were "interests" in the socialist economy held by different groups, Yarmagaev shot back: "Let's take the director of the factory. He has one interest. His interest is in getting more money into his own pocket."

Chubais self-confidently and ardently defended Decree 695. He had once aspired to become a big factory director and he personally worked on the problems of measuring socialist industry. Glazkov recalled Chubais as a very tough debater. The Chubais approach was not to take an argument whole, but to take it apart, piece by piece. "Look," he said, according to Glazkov, "if we do this and that, and all this, and that, why is it not going to fly?"

When I asked Chubais about the debate more than two decades later, he remembered it clearly.[4] "I was really a supporter of the decree," he recalled. When Yarmagaev lambasted the document, Chubais felt his friend was being too emotional. He, by contrast, *knew* what was in the huge document, appreciated its complexity, its depth, all the professional effort that had gone into writing it. He grew exasperated. "How can he be saying all this is useless and purposeless?" he recalled thinking of Yarmagaev's tirade.

Glazkov turned to Chubais. He had trouble articulating what he wanted to say. He knew he could not win over the demanding Chubais with scientific arguments, because he didn't have any. "I just had a gut feeling that this thing is impossible," he recalled. He told Chubais that the whole Brezhnev decree was like a complex perpetual motion machine. They could debate all night about the various details, about the flywheels, gears, and pulleys. But, Glazkov said, the larger issue is that perpetual motion is impossible. It was a fruitless quest! It just won't work.

Then Glazkov came upon a simpler analogy. The Brezhnev decree was like a huge, sophisticated aircraft, he said. Imagine the complex structure of the wings, the cockpit, the whole interlinked set of hardware. It was all here in the blueprint of Decree 695. Just one problem with this beautiful design, Glazkov said.

There were no engines.

From that night, the three friends kept up their debate, and once they got back to Leningrad they decided to do something about it. Speaking out too loudly would be risky, probably useless. They decided to write an article together, trying to explain why all the searching for the "indicators" was a failure—why the perpetual motion machine could not really work. Chubais arranged to have the article published in an obscure journal.

They met in their kitchens or the dark, one-room communal flat where Chubais lived. On the last night before the deadline, Glazkov was still having difficulty putting their ideas down on paper. "We sat there till morning, and by morning he managed to finish it," Chubais recalled. What they had put on paper was a revolutionary idea, for them. They declared that the search for the fabled "indicators" of socialist industrial progress was essentially useless. All the struggle to measure factory output, labor, and production was in vain. Why? None of the hundreds of artificial "indicators" could possibly take into account what was happening across a vast economy with millions of decisionmakers. Only one powerful, single tool could take into account all those complex decisions: prices set by a free market. But at the time, in 1980, talk about free prices could bring trouble. Chubais and his friends had stumbled on a hugely important realization, at least for themselves, but what could they do with it?

*

The Chubais family kitchen echoed with arguments about Soviet power, economics, war, and dissent. The debates left a deep impression on Anatoly, youngest of two sons. His father, Boris, was a Soviet Army tank man whose unit had been surrounded on the Lithuanian border at the outbreak of World War II in 1941. Boris Chubais managed to break out of the blockade and survived the war, later serving as a commissar—a political indoctrinator of the troops. He was an unshakable believer in the Soviet system. "My father is one of those rare men who sincerely believed in Soviet power, in its ideas, in the Communist power, in Stalin," Anatoly recalled.[5]

His older brother, Igor, was born in Berlin in 1947, and Anatoly was born June 16, 1955, in Belarus. The family moved constantly, almost two dozen times, as Boris Chubais taught at military schools throughout the Soviet Union. Boris Chubais reared his sons with a military man's sense of basic decency. Igor Chubais recalled that his father took seriously the ideals offered by Communist propaganda. "I was formed on these ideas of honesty, justice, mutual help, solidarity, these kinds of things. But later on, I started to understand, they say one thing—and do another."[6]

Igor Chubais's doubts about the Soviet system were sealed on August 21, 1968, when Soviet troops rolled into Czechoslovakia to suppress a reformist movement. "In August 1968," he recalled, "it became clear to me that the authorities were lying. I didn't want to be deceived. And I concluded to myself, they are lying."

Igor, then twenty-one years old, was visiting a classmate on a summer holiday in Odessa and organized a one-man protest, carrying a Czech flag, in front of a statue of Lenin. "I was shouting, 'Get out, invaders!' and holding out this flag," he recalled. Nobody came, nobody saw it, and Igor was not arrested. But the spark of dissent against the system had been ignited. Back home in Leningrad, he wrote a mildly provocative article for the university wall newspaper (at that time one copy of a paper was simply hung on a wall for everyone to read) about the invasion. Igor choose his words carefully. The article created a stir. After the next class period, Igor saw all the students gathered around the article, reading it. Then he came back again after another class. "No wall newspaper. No paper! It had been taken away. So it actually hung for only twenty minutes."

A few months later, Igor's class received the results of their Lenin *zachyot,* a test to see how well they knew Lenin and other Communist dogma. At a ceremony to announce the results, the dean and the local party bosses were present.

They called the roll. Ivanov. "Passed." Petrov. "Passed." Sidorov. "Passed." Chubais. "No." A silence. When some students protested that Igor knew Lenin as well as they did, the party boss said the decision was final. Igor recalled that "I didn't want the Lenin *zachyot* anyway" but when he saw the party boss a few days later, he asked why it had been denied. The party man answered: "You are not only not going to get the credit, we are going to expel you from the university."

Igor's rebellion reverberated at home, where the intense arguments began. Anatoly was then fourteen years old. "At home, almost every day, active battles and disputes took place between my father and my brother—constantly and nonstop," Anatoly Chubais recalled. "Very long disputes, and I observed that process. Although there were two completely opposite approaches, there was one subject of conversation: the country, the history, the present times and the future." The arguments went well beyond Czechoslovakia—they fought over philosophy, economics, and the reasons for the Soviet economy of shortage. They once had a fight over why there was no sausage in the stores. When Boris Chubais's friends would come over, Igor would debate them too—it was that kind of home. The son could speak his mind, and Boris Chubais tried, openly, to persuade Igor he was wrong.

The thrust and parry of debate at home fascinated young Anatoly and left a lasting impression on him. After listening to his father and older brother—both graduates and specialists in philosophy—he decided that he preferred a more concrete discipline, economics. The philosophy debates were too abstract.

Boris managed to talk to the dean and Igor was not expelled. But the son's dissent caused his father a great deal of trouble. Boris Chubais was teaching at a military school of higher education. One day a general arrived from Moscow to lecture about the invasion of Czechoslovakia. The general waxed eloquent about how Soviet troops were "restoring socialism in Czechoslovakia." Igor Chubais, who had attended out of curiosity, could not contain himself. After the lecture he marched up to the general and declared bluntly, "I know another story. You are mistaken. Things are different."

The remark triggered a very unpleasant investigation by the Leningrad Military District headquarters of one of its most determined Communist Party ideologists, Boris Chubais. The turn of events was alarming, especially to his wife, Raisa. "My mother reacted to it very nervously," Igor recalled. "And I understood, and everybody at home understood, that my father could be dismissed, and then we would be left without any means of survival." Years later, Boris Chubais confessed to his elder son that a KGB man had come to him asking who Igor's friends were.

But the commission investigating Boris Chubais found out what the son already knew: he was committed to the system. "They only saw that he was quite an orthodox Communist," Igor later recalled. "And there was nothing to punish him for."

The episode showed Anatoly Chubais how the system reacted when it was challenged. He saw how the party tried to punish his father, a man born in the year of the Bolshevik revolution, who wrote a doctoral dissertation entitled "The Full and Final Victory of Socialism in the USSR" and devoted every day to advancing toward full Communism. The evidence suggests that, in his most formative years, the unspoken lesson for the young Chubais was that for new ideas to sprout, they needed protection. New voices also needed to be backed up by an iron will because they were always in danger of being silenced.

Anatoly Chubais loved the thrill of driving his own car. He drove fast and determinedly, always pushing his reactions to the edge. In Leningrad, he had a small yellow Zaporozhets, a rear-engine Soviet car made in Ukraine. "He drove at terrifying speed," recalled Oding, who was one of his oldest friends. "He would come to our house like that. The sound of the car was still whistling in his ears. It was as if it was a flying Mercedes. He loved that car, awfully." Another friend, Vladimir Korabelnikov, recalled that the car was dirty, "horrible," but gave Chubais more free time every day because he did not have to wait for a bus. Chubais would beg his friends to join him camping outdoors, and he drove the Zaporozhets to the forests outside of Leningrad, where they went hiking and rafting. What he loved more than anything else was whitewater rafting. They would build the square rafts on the spot, lashing together some logs and then steering them awkwardly in the rushing water and jagged rocks—it was sometimes dangerous, always a thrill.[7]

Chubais could also be terribly stubborn about ideas. Many of his friends recalled that Chubais needed to believe in an idea at all times.

Once he gripped a steering wheel, it would take enormous effort to pry his fingers off, to persuade him to change direction. He was extraordinarily determined. That was one of the great strengths of his character, but it created blind spots.

At the time of the debate on the farm, Anatoly was still very committed to improving the socialist system. In 1983 he defended his thesis at the Leningrad Institute. It was entitled "Research and Development of Methods of Planning, Improvement, and Management in Specialized Scientific Research Organizations."[8] Oding recalled she was going to skip the Chubais presentation because it seemed so predictable, but she changed her mind at the last minute. He defended the theme brilliantly, even emotionally, she recalled. He was articulate and well-spoken, and self-assured. For months afterward, "there were echoes" of that defense.

Privately, Chubais was beginning to shed his orthodoxy. Korabelnikov said one of his clearest memories was of Chubais telling him that he realized that economics ruled all, and that the only way to change the Soviet system was through economics. Others recall that Chubais eschewed Russian literature. He didn't have time: he was reading political economy.

After the debate on the collective farm, Chubais, Glazkov, and Yarmagaev were cautious. They knew they could not antagonize the system or alarm the KGB or the party by shouting that the search for indicators was futile. They had to move carefully, even secretly. There were very few people they could really share their ideas with. Yarmagaev knew another young researcher, Sergei Vasiliev, at the Leningrad Financial Economic Institute, which was somewhat more prestigious than theirs. One evening, about the time Chubais had defended his thesis, Glazkov invited Vasiliev to the Economics and Engineering Institute on Marat Street.

It was very late in the evening, Vasiliev told me, and the halls of the institute were quiet. Brezhnev had died the year before and Soviet leader Yuri Andropov, the one-time KGB chief, was signaling some desire to end the years of stagnation. The signals were faint—they had to be read between the lines of turgid essays in the official press—and it was not at all clear that Andropov knew a way out. But there was a hint that Andropov at least had a sense the system was failing.

Glazkov confided to Vasiliev that under Chubais they had created a secret team at the institute. It was "semiunderground," Vasiliev recalled.[9] He asked, what kind of team? "To change the system," Glazkov replied. "To change the economy through economic reform."

Vasiliev became the fourth member of the cadre, joining Glazkov, Yarmagaev, and Chubais, and he was regarded as the intellectual powerhouse in those early years. Chubais organized a low-key seminar on economic reform. A dozen or so people came to the meetings and gradually broached some of the progressive ideas they had been thinking about. Glazkov's role was to find the right kind of people and, very carefully, invite them, without raising suspicion. Yarmagaev was, as always, a fountain of ideas and energy who enjoyed a sharp debate. Vasiliev was the brains, the most highly educated and erudite.

Chubais became the curator; he organized the seminar, nurtured it, and protected it. He was not the leading economist or thinker, but he made space for new ideas in the otherwise stultifying political atmosphere of the time. He could get the required permissions and avoid trouble. He was, at twenty-eight, an up-and-coming researcher, albeit from a second-tier institute. Among his friends, Chubais forced the team into a certain discipline. "Without him, it would have just been talk in the kitchens," Glazkov said. "Nothing else. No seminar. No real work. No article, which the three of us wrote."

"He had a good reputation in the institute," Glazkov recalled. "Therefore, he had a good opportunity to arrange the seminars. It wasn't an easy thing at the time." The idea of organizing a seminar, for example, to study progressive reforms in Hungary could easily have brought trouble from the KGB. "Everything was ideological," Glazkov recalled. "The Communist Party is watching, and that's why you needed permission. It's not easy. But Chubais could get it. He was a Communist Party member! He could be trusted! That's how we did it."

"We knew that we were not free there," Glazkov recalled. "We knew that we had been watched, and that we couldn't allow revolutionary things there at all. The word 'market' was a dangerous word at the time."

As *perestroika* dawned with the arrival of Gorbachev in 1985, the topics at the Leningrad seminars grew more ambitious. The participants began to broach an altogether bold idea: introducing some aspects of the market to Soviet socialism. For a long time, they intensely debated whether the economy could be saved by such reform concepts as self-financing or by decentralization, which meant allowing factory directors to make more of their own decisions. Later, as the years went on, they concluded that the existing machine was probably doomed and would have to be massively restructured. Still later, they spent many days contemplating the prospect of a "transition" to some new kind of a system. Even the notion of a "transition" was a thrilling idea.

They were nurtured by the books at the Publichka, but they had other sources of inspiration as well. They had ample access to more radical texts in *samizdat,* the dog-eared, self-typed, or mimeographed manuscripts that were officially prohibited but widely distributed from hand to hand. "They would give you a photocopy and you could read it at night," Oding recalled, "and in the morning you had to give it back. And there was no guarantee that the person who gave it to you wouldn't tell on you."

Then came a sudden bolt of inspiration. They were profoundly inspired by a two-volume, 630-page book published in 1980 by a Hungarian economics professor, János Kornai. *The Economics of Shortage,* more than any other text, offered an insight into the failings of Soviet socialism. Hungary had been at the forefront of more market-oriented economic reform in the Eastern Bloc since 1968, and Kornai's groundbreaking work was almost entirely based on his observations about Hungary. But for the young scholars around Chubais, the work opened a window as no other Soviet or Western study had done on why the economy of shortage existed and how it functioned. Kornai examined the behavior of buyers, sellers, and producers in an absence of free prices, as well as the relationship between firms and the state under socialism and central planning.

Kornai asked his readers to imagine the economic relationship between a parent and child. He described this as five stages of "paternalism." In the first stage, which he called "grants in kind—passive acceptance," the infant cannot express his needs in words and receives all his nourishment and material needs from his parents. In the second, which he called "grants in kind—wishes actively expressed," the child lives with the family and gets everything for free, but there can be a certain amount of pleading and bargaining. The third phase he called "financial allowance," in which the child has grown up and moved away from home, say to college, but still depends on a defined stipend. The fourth phase, "self-supporting—assisted," Kornai defined as the child grown up and working for a living but being able to turn to the parents, if need be. And the last was called "self-supporting—left to himself," in which the child is grown and must rely entirely on himself.

Kornai pointed out that the ideal market economy was the last phase: the state did not bother to help or hinder firms and left them alone. But he concluded that the real root of the shortage economy was too much of the first kind of "paternalism," in which the state generously doled out subsidies to factories and enterprises, as a mother to a newborn. Kornai found that this led to unhealthy dependence, which he termed the "soft budget constraint," meaning that the firms never had to stop feeding; the more subsidies they wanted, the more they got. The point was that a factory which always got more regardless of how poorly it performed would never become accountable for its work—it would just go on producing shoddy goods because there was never any penalty for doing otherwise. Kornai concluded that the "softening" of discipline had led to the miseries of the shortage economy: the insatiable, unfulfilled demands of consumers, the hoarding, and the endless lines.[10]

The book first arrived in Leningrad as smuggled photocopies and instantly "became a Bible," Vasiliev recalled. "We had some ideas initially, but the book was kind of a catharsis. It pushed our thinking forward. You met a person and you said, 'Have you read Kornai? Yes?' And then it was a starting point for discussion."

Chubais recalled that Kornai showed him why the shortage economy persisted in socialism. Kornai demonstrated how the producers—the factories—always had first claim on subsidies and resources because they were fed them constantly by the paternalistic state. "He showed that the very distribution of resources happens in such a way that the producer always has a priority over the consumer, meaning that the consumer is always dissatisfied, there is always a shortage."

But Kornai alone did not lead the Chubais team out of socialism; he just helped them see it much more clearly. The other great inspiration of those years came from the Austrian economist Friedrich von Hayek, one of the most trenchant early critics of socialism, who was especially acute in his searing denunciation of central planning. Although Hayek's best-known work was *The Road to Serfdom*, a 1944 treatise about the dangers to individual liberty of socialism and central planning, Chubais took to heart a lesser-known economics text.[11] It was an article that Hayek had published in 1945, "The Use of Knowledge in Society."[12] The article articulated clearly what the Leningrad scholars had been groping toward since the debate at the collective farm: that free prices were the single most powerful "indicator" to measure all the millions of decisions in a large, complex economy.

Hayek used the example of a commodity, tin. In a free market, he said, if there was a shortage of tin, all the producers and users would adjust by producing more tin or using less or finding substitutes. Hayek pointed out that it was virtually impossible for a central planner to make these decisions for so many people, but that free prices could quickly and efficiently communicate the new situation to producers and consumers. As prices rose, some producers would make more tin or consumers might look for a different metal, and the effect would quickly cascade through the market economy, even if most participants did not precisely know why the adjustment was being made. Hayek said the freely set price for tin is like a high-speed network of information that works splendidly to allocate resources—just what an army of Soviet researchers had been hunting for all those years.

Hayek declared that the price system was a "marvel" which could free people from the "conscious control" of the central planners. At the time Chubais read this essay in Leningrad, the Soviet Union was the world's largest example of "conscious control," with rigid, fixed state prices set throughout the economy. Hayek, who won the 1974 Nobel Prize in economics for his work, had taken a battering ram to the underpinnings of Soviet socialism. Amazingly, his wisdom was smuggled past the KGB on those dog-eared photocopies, and it landed in the hands of an eager young generation of knowledge-hungry Leningrad academics.

Many years later, Chubais recalled the thrill of reading Hayek and instantly gave his own example of how Hayek's theory worked in practice in the United States. "One person is selling hamburgers somewhere in New York," he told me, "while another person is grazing cows somewhere in Arkansas to produce meat that will be used to make those hamburgers. But in order for that person in Arkansas to graze cows, there needs to be a price for meat, which tells him that he should graze cows."

"And the value of price," he said, "is absolutely universal, and absolutely fundamental."

The theories Chubais and his team were debating at their institute on Marat Street were also beginning to dawn on others in the Soviet Union. Even before the Gorbachev era, unorthodox thinking was fermenting in remote pockets. One was in Novosibirsk, Siberia, where an outspoken reformist economist, Abel Aganbegyan, had come up with a surprisingly candid and devastating critique of the ailing Soviet economy. Aganbegyan, director of the Institute of Economics and Management of the Siberian Academy of Sciences, was joined by a colleague, Tatyana Zaslavskaya, a sociologist. Zaslavskaya had prepared a landmark internal study challenging the entire structure of the Soviet economy, which was debated at a 1983 conference in Novosibirsk and later contributed to many of the ideas in Gorbachev's *perestroika*.

Chubais soon felt that he had to break out of the provincial world of the Leningrad institute and make contact with others, especially in Moscow. Although there were a few freethinkers in Leningrad, he knew that there must be dozens in the capital. Glazkov had taken a trip to Moscow and, through friends, brought to Chubais word of a bright, young economist there. He was Yegor Gaidar, who worked at the All-Union Institute for Systems Research, under the tutelage of a famous mathematical economist, Stanislav Shatalin. Like Chubais, Gaidar had also struggled with the grand quest for "indicators" and perfection in the Soviet industrial monster.[13]

But the difference was that Gaidar was in Moscow, at the center of the action, whereas Chubais was in a remote provincial institute. Gaidar was a child of the Soviet elite, grandson of a famous Red Army officer and author of beloved children's stories, and son of a Pravda journalist. When Andropov began to look for progressive ideas about economic reform, one of the young researchers who worked on the early drafts was Gaidar. The atmosphere in Shatalin's group was also more open than Chubais could ever afford to be in Leningrad, where the KGB was always watching. "Here you didn't have to cross your fingers behind your back when you talked," Gaidar recalled of Moscow's atmosphere.

Despite many appeals from Glazkov, Gaidar could not find the time to come to the Chubais seminars in Leningrad. "He was too busy to come to some tiny place, the Engineering Economic Institute," Glazkov recalled. "He was among the elite. He didn't care."

So Chubais went to Moscow and sought out Gaidar. Pyotr Aven, son of a leading mathematician, was working on econometrics in Gaidar's group and introduced the two men. He recalled that at their first meeting, Gaidar and Chubais understood that they shared the same ideas and fears.[14] Gaidar was by all accounts the smartest economist of his generation. "We were better prepared than Chubais. We were far ahead, and better educated," Aven recalled. But Gaidar was a product of the Soviet era and could be excruciatingly cautious about pushing the system too hard. Chubais shared that caution, yet he had that steely, whitewater-rafting determination and an absolutely unshakable self-confidence in whatever he was doing.

In the following years they were all reminded, once again, that the system was not yet ready for radical change. In early 1985, just as Gorbachev came to power, Gaidar's laboratory was given an assignment from the Politburo to study "improving economic mechanisms at the enterprise level," more of the same old nonsense from the past. But since the work was intended for the Politburo, Chubais and his team leaped at a chance to collaborate with Gaidar on the assignment. Working for the Politburo would give Chubais a bit of protection from the KGB, and for the first time he was working on something for the upper echelon of power, something more than abstract, what-if speculation.

"We started trying to think about real things, instead of all that bullshit we were engaged in during our formal jobs," Glazkov said. The Gaidar-Chubais group produced a 120-page report, adapting some of the Hungarian and Yugoslav reforms to the Soviet system. They called for abandoning planning dictates and permitting some free market mechanisms. When Gaidar's boss came back one day, he brought bad news: the plan had been rejected. "Which meant we were to give up our fruitless daydreaming" and come up with something "on a more mundane level," Gaidar recalled. But when Gaidar went home that day and turned on the television, he heard Gorbachev deliver a speech using some of the same terms they had put in the rejected report. It was a strange time; they had to constantly guess and read between the lines for opaque signals of change.[15]

Chubais had a personal brush with the KGB. In 1986 he attempted to attend a ten-month academic program abroad. Chubais recalled that it was in either Finland or Sweden. It would have been his first extensive exposure to the West, but he was denied permission to exit the Soviet Union by the KGB. Chubais said it was suggested that he not go to a capitalist country but rather study in a socialist country.[16] His brother, Igor, said the denial came because Chubais is Jewish on his mother's side. Chubais was deeply disappointed. It was a personal reminder that the authorities could crush you, if they wanted to.

The year 1986 was a critical turning point for Chubais and Gaidar. Chubais helped make arrangements for Glazkov to work in Moscow for a year. Glazkov was stationed at the Central Mathematical Institute, where he found, to his amazement, that researchers were openly toying with mathematical models of a market economy. At the end of August 1986, all the freethinkers in Moscow and Leningrad—about thirty economists—finally got together for days of debate at a rundown resort hotel, Snake Hill, in the forests outside of Leningrad. "It was the best time in our lives," Glazkov recalled. The forest was so isolated they felt free to talk without the KGB listening, and they trusted one another.

Glazkov recalled that Gaidar was the shining light of the group. He was the best informed and had the clearest vision of what was happening. "And it was clear that this system was not going to survive. So, the question became, what's going to happen when the system collapses? What are the scenarios?" Glazkov said that some of the participants wanted to debate the shape of a theoretical alternative economy for the Soviet Union, but Glazkov was more pragmatic; he wanted to focus the debate on the *actual* transition to a new economy. "I was only ready to raise the point," he recalled, "but wasn't ready to be specific. We were not ready. I was not ready. Nobody was ready!"

Gaidar recounted how at the end of the day they made campfires, sang, and told jokes. At the final seminar, he presented two satirical skits foreshadowing "the crisis to come." The first was titled "The Crest of the Wave," and it portrayed what each of them would do to reform the economy.[17] The second skit was called "Going Under," and it showed them all being sent to prison, stipulating the length of each sentence and the size of their food ration packets.

In the months that followed, Gorbachev's era of *glasnost* dawned. Taboos were being broken everywhere, Gaidar recalled, causing even more confusion. "The censors overseeing scholarly economics journals and publishing houses were tearing their hair out," he said. "They no longer knew what could be said and what couldn't."

When the progressive economists tried to organize another seminar outside Leningrad in 1987, under the auspices of Sergei Vasiliev's institute, the old guard struck back. Chubais said the agenda was officially approved by the party regional committee, which meant that it was certain to be a dead end. Gaidar, Chubais, and the whole crowd went to the resort but found the meetings so boring and regressive that they walked out of the cold conference hall and gathered in one of the lodges. There, in jeans and sweaters, they began a parallel seminar, talking more openly among themselves, as they had the year before. The group had grown somewhat since the previous year and now included Mikhail Dmitriev, a graduate student in regional economic studies at Vasiliev's institute who was well versed in Western economic theory.[18] Also invited from Moscow was former Gosplan mathematician Vitaly Naishul, who had written the underground text *Another Life* and was working with Glazkov at the Central Mathematical Institute. By this time, *Another Life*, still in typescript *samizdat*, had been widely circulated among the progressive economists. The reader may recall that in the first part of the text, Naishul had made a revolutionary argument that the property of the Soviet state must be turned into private property, literally distributed to the people.[19]

Standing before a stairwell at the informal seminar, Naishul made a rump presentation of his radical ideas. Spread out before him on the stairs were Gaidar, Chubais, and many of the other most progressive thinkers at the time. Naishul explained to them his concept of mass privatization in which every Soviet citizen would be given a check that could be used to purchase a bit of the enormous holdings of the Soviet state. The check would be worth 5,000 rubles and the result would be a daring leap toward the market.[20]

Naishul's remarks were received with sharp criticism. Both Gaidar and Chubais dismissed Naishul as too radical. They were pragmatic and wanted to try something that could actually work, not just get them in trouble with the KGB. Glazkov also thought that Naishul was jumping ahead too fast. "Look, there is a transition problem," Glazkov recalled saying. "What you are suggesting is too tough. The system will break. If you want to get down from a tall tree, you have to climb. What you are offering us is to jump. We will break our legs and our neck!"

Gaidar's objections, he told me later, were that private property would be "politically impossible" and that it was dangerous to introduce it when market institutions and property rights were not well developed. It was like trying to divide up the state's property on a roulette table, Gaidar said. The population would feel "cheated." As an economist, Gaidar was at the cutting edge of change. He was beginning work as economics editor of *Kommunist*, the once orthodox Communist Party theoretical journal. Gaidar used the journal to begin to break Soviet economic taboos, and he wrote about such once forbidden subjects as inflation, unemployment, deficits, and military spending. But Gaidar felt that Naishul had gone too far—it was just unrealistic to begin thinking about private property.

Chubais was also critical of Naishul's privatization plan. He said Naishul had adopted a "trivial" device—property checks for every person—to deal with what Chubais saw as a hugely complex transaction. "What was I criticizing Naishul for?" Chubais told me later. "I was criticizing him because when you try to solve a problem of such gigantic, immeasurable, supernatural complexity—as the problem of privatization was—in such a simple and stupid way as giving out 150 million vouchers to each citizen and then just giving him an opportunity to invest it wherever he wants, this is an extremely primitive technology, extremely primitive. The result would be gigantic disproportions. Millions of people would get something that is useless, while someone would get something fantastically valuable. Millions of people would be extremely dissatisfied, and disappointed, and so on. The disproportion between the complexity of the problem and the simplicity of the way to solve it was just way too big."

Even the discussion about private property could have brought trouble at the time, Chubais recalled. "Of course there was fear," he told me. "It was absolutely secret. We couldn't tell anyone from the outside that this discussion had taken place. Obviously, it wasn't part of any official program. If Naishul had given that speech at the official conference, it would have undoubtedly meant that all people who organized the conference would be fired, without a single doubt. That is 100 percent sure. The subject of the presentation was privatization—*private property!* It was far beyond the line of what was allowed at the time."

Somehow, word got back to the KGB that even the boring official conference had included anti-Soviet statements. An investigation was launched, and Chubais recalled the group being hauled before the KGB. "We were saying that we hadn't said anything of the kind, that we were simply studying the decisions of the party Congress and analyzing how to implement them better."

Dmitriev had been taking notes in an obscure type of shorthand that was not widely taught in the Soviet Union. He told me that after the conference, the rector at his institute demanded to know what was in his notes. Dmitriev typed up the minutes and in the process completely sanitized them, leaving out anything that was remotely controversial. He gave the rector the sanitized version. Satisfied that there were no anti-Soviet remarks at the conference, the KGB let it drop. They never found out about the far more radical ideas being debated on the stairwell.

Chubais lived modestly and seemed indifferent to wealth. His great luxury was listening to music on a cassette player in his Zaporozhets. He lived in a one-room communal apartment, extremely common in Leningrad, with a single large corridor and small rooms off to the side for each family. "He practically studied in the corridors," Oding remembered. "And there were a lot of neighbors. Everyone used the soap. There were problems about who took someone else's soap in the bath. You can imagine, right? Who took whose food? And he was almost never there—he was always at the library or the institute." Chubais had been waiting patiently on the "city line" for a municipal apartment, until some friends persuaded him that he would never get a private apartment that way and should go out and buy one, even if he had to borrow from friends. "He had certain limits, what one could do, and what one must not do," Oding recalled. "And he couldn't imagine that he could step over those limits and cross the boundaries, and allow more for himself. His personal demands were low. You live in a *kommunalka*, so you live there. It never entered into his head that he could take a step forward."

As Gorbachev's era of *glasnost* and *perestroika* accelerated, Chubais expanded his horizons. In 1988 he spent ten months studying in Hungary, which had carried out the most far-reaching economic reforms in the Soviet bloc. There the market was not an alien concept, and a visitor would have found the stores brimming with products. "It had a huge influence on him," Oding recalled. "He had made the Hungarian experience his own. He saw that within the framework of socialism, even within the Soviet Union, the Hungarian experience could be used. He even saw the insufficiencies of the Hungarian model."

After Hungary, Chubais seemed more relaxed and more curious than before. At the urging of friends, he made an attempt to become director of another institute but was defeated by more orthodox party members. He also visited the United States. "He was this rather correct person, who was maybe just one step ahead of the others, but not a kilometer," Oding recalled. "And suddenly, he started to work over new information. It seems to me that America had a great influence on him. He never doubted himself after that. He didn't have those socialist inclinations any more. After that, he had no more socialist illusions at all."

"His velocity changed," she added. "There are people who, when faced with new information, become paralyzed. But Chubais's mental processor leaped to some fifth generation. He worked it all over and ran more and more quickly." A hint of how far Chubais had come was a paper that he and Sergei Vasiliev delivered at a conference in Italy in September 1989. They concluded that the Soviet economy was basically doomed without massive change. Reform "turns out to be impossible with the existing structure of the economy," they declared.[21]

In the spring and summer of 1990, radical democrats swept into the Leningrad city council, just as they had in Moscow. Chubais self-confidently delivered a speech to them on "shock therapy" economic reform in Poland, and they installed him as chairman of a special committee on economic reform.[22] Chubais gathered around him many of the friends and allies he had made in the previous decade, and they began thinking about how to make the city a model for reform.

One of those on the team was Dmitri Vasiliev, a diminutive economist with thick glasses who talked in rapid-fire bursts. He had attended the famous Naishul debate on the stairs. Vasiliev, who was deeply interested in the idea of private business and property rights, came from a family that traced its Leningrad roots back six generations. He recalled this as a heady time. The Chubais team was suddenly thinking big and parceling out all the exciting new spheres of possible reform, such as land and currency regulation. The biggest idea of all was to prepare the city—or at least a part of it—to become a "free economic zone," sort of a demonstration project for radical economic reform inside the Soviet Union.

Vasiliev had been researching the newly emergent cooperatives, and he was given the task of privatizing small shops and businesses, which the others considered less exciting work than currency or land reform. Vasiliyev said that he saw that "the market economy was winning, and it was winning fast. For example, two hairdressers—one state, and one private—you couldn't even compare them. The private one was doing much better." Oding recalled that as Chubais and the team were drawing up their plans, out on the street the country was changing even faster—small kiosks and cooperatives were popping up everywhere.

Chubais was a champion of the free economic zone, but it was overtaken by events. The Soviet empire was inexorably disintegrating before their eyes. A free zone inside a collapsing country made less sense with every passing day. Then in 1991 the Leningrad council elected a new mayor, Anatoly Sobchak, a law professor who had been one of the most eloquent democrats of the Gorbachev era. Sobchak did not see the need for the Chubais experiment. He demoted Chubais from head of the economic reform agency to simply an "adviser," which effectively marked the end of the free economic zone. Characteristically, Chubais kept working on it long after the others had given up. "It lost all its meaning," Oding recalled, "because all of Russia become a free economic zone."

Then Gaidar called from Moscow in the summer of 1991. Boris Yeltsin had been elected president of Russia that summer. He was putting together a team for a truly radical attempt at economic reform in Russia, and Gaidar wanted Chubais to join them. Chubais drove his yellow Zaporozhets to Moscow and began working with the Gaidar brain trust. On November 9, 1991, he called Dmitry Vasiliev in St. Petersburg. Could he write a two-page program for mass privatization of all Russia?

And write it fast?

Chapter 5

Mikhail Khodorkovsky

Mikhail Khodorkovsky was a child of the last-ditch effort of the Soviet system to save itself. Desperate for a way out of stagnation, the Soviet leadership permitted a modest experiment in capitalism. It worked—and unleashed enormous, unexpected forces of change.

The experiment occurred in the Young Communist League (or Komsomol), the party's youth organization. Khodorkovsky was the deputy chief of Komsomol at his university. When the doors swung open to new opportunities, as they did repeatedly in the years of *perestroika*, Khodorkovsky rushed through, exploiting his connections with tireless determination and a surprisingly sophisticated understanding of loopholes and gaps in Soviet socialism. Was there a hidden force behind this unstoppable young man with the black hair, mustache, and distinctively high, soft voice? The accounts I heard from friends and colleagues suggested that there was not just one Communist Party boss who put his hand on Khodorkovsky's shoulder and said, "You will be our experimental capitalist, son." Rather, there were many patrons in high places, including the KGB. They anointed him, and Khodorkovsky anointed himself—with hard work and a gritty fortitude. "All the ventures that were started at this time succeeded only if they were sponsored by or had strong connections with high-ranking people," Khodorkovsky acknowledged in 1991. "It wasn't the money but the patronage. At the time, you had to have political sponsorship."[1] In the end, however, Khodorkovsky far outpaced his early sponsors. He was more ambitious and ruthless than the Communist Party apparatchiks who wanted to dabble in capitalism, and he was more clever than the KGB bosses in a position to help him. They never went as far as he did in the new world.

At a very young age, Khodorkovsky became one of the first titans of the new entrepreneurial age, a pioneering financier. But he could not have succeeded were it not for larger events. The first and most important was the disenchantment of youth with the painful shortcomings of Soviet socialism. This led to a profound shift in which the Communist Party decided to let some young people dabble in capitalism. Khodorkovsky seized the moment.

The disillusionment of the younger generation was brilliantly captured by Time Machine, a legendary rock band. A popular song, which often met huge applause in concerts, told of a ship piloted by an experienced captain who gets lost at sea in a storm. The song transparently hinted that this ship was the Soviet Union. In the end, after a shipwreck, the captain is lost but the passengers make it to a new land. The song ends with, "Those of us who have survived for different reasons, have forgotten the captain of that ship."

The lyrics were a powerful metaphor for the profound cynicism, disdain, and ambivalence that characterized the younger generation's attitude toward the Soviet leadership, the Communist Party, and all the official structures and boring propaganda that dominated their lives. They yearned to make it to some new land. They longed for the consumer goods, such as jeans, which the Soviet system could not give them, and rebelled by listening to rock music, which the Soviet system refused to give them. Many young people made their own tapes and crude records, which became treasured possessions.

The youth rebellion was a slow-moving but powerful tide for change, often expressed in later years with satire and rock lyrics that fell just short of confrontation with the system. Alexei Yurchak, manager of the Leningrad band Avia in the early 1980s who later became a professor of anthropology at the University of California–Berkeley, has chronicled the "last Soviet generation," young people born in the 1960s and 1970s, and how they cynically adapted to the demands of public life in the Soviet era—the empty promises—while privately rejecting them. They worshiped rock bands like Time Machine, which became popular in the early 1970s with romantic and lyrical music, and Avia, a late-Soviet band that was sharply cynical and funny. Yurchak told me that his band's lyrics were often a wild composite of different party slogans, which sounded hilarious to young listeners. In one case, Avia mimicked a famous Stalinist era song, "Wake Up and Sing," but with such a jumble of Soviet slogans that it sounded like, "Stop thinking about anything, just wake up and sing!" Avia's performances were themselves a massive theatrical satire on the Soviet system with a large troupe of performers. The girls were dressed in black stockings, black skirts, and white shirts, saluting and marching and forming human pyramids very much in the fashion of the Soviet 1920s—except they threw in a crazy, unexpected sexual twist, such as one of the girls bending over in front of the pyramid with her bottom to the audience. Off to the right side of the stage, there was always a huge podium covered with red velvet. Between songs, a man climbed atop it and shouted slogans that sounded Soviet but were really made up, and nonsensical. "Forward is not backward!" he shouted, "Hurray!"[2]

The younger audiences got the point and loved it. The humor was understated enough that Avia would not be banned by the system that it mocked. But there was always the feeling that someone was watching. Another rock band in Leningrad, Televizor, sang in the mid-1980s:

Okay, so they let us break dance,
Okay, so we can be happy sometimes.
But still standing behind the column
Is the man in the thin tie
With cement in his eyes.

The reference to the man with cement in his eyes was unmistakable—the party and its agents were watching and were in control. Ever since the Bolshevik revolution, the Communist Party leadership strove to keep the natural restiveness of youth in check. The primary mechanism was the Komsomol, an organization ubiquitous throughout the seven decades of Soviet history. "Whenever a group of teens or young adults gathered," wrote Steven L. Solnick, a professor at Columbia University who documented the demise of the Komsomol, "on factory floors and on battlefields, in barracks and in dormitories, during wartime and during harvests, at construction sites and on street corners—a Komsomol organizer loomed."[3] In a society in which the state tolerated no other voices but those of the party, there was little room for youth to find themselves in private associations. The Komsomol attempted to monopolize the lives of youth between the ages of fourteen and twenty-eight, although the leaders were often older.

For millions of youth, the main reason to join Komsomol was a cynical pragmatism: without it, a young person might fail to get into a university or get a good job. But by the late Brezhnev period, Komsomol had come to symbolize the same bleak, tired slogans as those of the party. The Komsomol leaders were widely viewed as ladder-climbing careerists, as apparatchiks with a certain obsequious character.

Gorbachev, who had once been a Komsomol activist, opened the floodgates to other organizations and other voices. He unleashed a surge in what became known as *neformalny*, or the informals: nonofficial associations, clubs, rock bands, and other groups that took shape outside the party and without official permission or regulation. During Gorbachev's era, an entire youth underground blossomed.[4] The youth movement was an open rebellion against the cultural orthodoxy of the past, and much of it was centered around a passion for rock music. In the 1960s and 1970s, Soviet authorities had tried to suppress rock, shutting it off radio and television. But the music spread anyway—on tapes recorded from Western broadcasts, on thin homemade plastic records, and through performances of thousands of unofficial bands that played in hidden cellars or, defying the authorities, in student and factory clubs. Black market trade thrived in record albums. The regime finally gave in and stopped attempts to suppress rock in the 1980s.

As the doors for freethinking opened up elsewhere, the Komsomol began to wither and suffered a drastic decline in membership. In Gorbachev's first three years, Komsomol membership fell by 4 million to 38 million in 1988. In earlier years, the problem of sustaining Komsomol membership had been so acute that figures were falsified. But even that could not mask the real crisis of the Komsomol in the mid-1980s. Membership dues—the lifeblood of the organization—were drying up. Viktor Mironenko, elected first secretary of the Komsomol in 1986, later acknowledged that he could not convince his oldest son to join.[5]

The Komsomol had to find a way to survive. Its leaders turned to the capitalist ferment on the street. By 1987, the cooperative movement was gathering steam, forming the first small businesses. The Komsomol chiefs, along with their elders in the Communist Party, decided to grab a piece of the action. They opened a door—and young Khodorkovsky breezed right through.

In the years before Gorbachev, one of the most popular ways to try and remedy the ills of the Soviet economy was "self-financing," or *khozraschyot*, the idea that a factory could retain its own earnings. When Luzhkov had proposed it in 1980, he was rebuffed, but later in the decade the concept took hold, especially as factory directors got more control over their own affairs. The Komsomol too began to apply self-financing to its myriad of local organizations, allowing them, for example, to decide for themselves how to use income from dues, as well as proceeds earned from the Komsomol's many tourism agencies and publishing houses. Given more fiscal autonomy, many local Komsomol groups simply went into business for themselves. The Komsomol became a Communist Party business school. Cafes, discos, bars, travel bureaus, printing houses, and other small enterprises sprang up, often with loans or subsidies from Komsomol budgets. These new enterprises were allowed to keep their own profits. Entrepreneurial zeal flourished. The Komsomol plunge into business marked an abrupt change of ideology, from decaying socialism to crude capitalism. But it also was a defining moment which suggested that the Communist Party, at the very highest levels, had sensed danger and roused itself for a controlled experiment in making profits. Olga Kryshtanovskaya, a sociologist who became one of Russia's most perceptive analysts of the new business elite, told me years later that the party hierarchy initially had doubts whether the youth experiment would work. It was, she said, "just a test." But then the test succeeded—beyond their wildest imagination.[6]

The experiment began with a bear of a young man, Konstantin Zatulin. In 1986 Zatulin, a postgraduate student at Moscow State University, was appointed an aide to Mironenko, the first secretary of the Komsomol. Zatulin was a specialist in industrial management and had studied earlier failed attempts to reform Soviet socialism, such as the Kosygin reforms of the 1960s. His first job was to draft a letter to the Politburo, suggesting new business directions for the Komsomol. The two-page letter took Zatulin six months to write because of enormous resistance, debate, and confusion inside the Komsomol apparatus. So many business concepts were alien to the old guard that it was extraordinarily difficult to put them on paper in a way that would win approval. Zatulin recalled that he fought with one high-level bureaucrat for weeks over the idea of establishing a company with shareholders who would be paid dividends. The bureaucrat could not grasp the concept of someone being paid who was not actually working on the factory floor. Zatulin persisted.[7]

He realized the importance of his assignment. Nothing less than the survival of the Komsomol was at stake. Among the ideas in Zatulin's letter was that the Komsomol take over the Soviet toy industry and that it finally abandon the decades-long practice of sending Komsomol youth out on grueling construction "work brigades." Both ideas were eventually approved. But perhaps the most far-reaching idea that Zatulin proposed was in science. In the 1960s, a youth organization called Fakel (Torch) had taken root in Novosibirsk, a center of Soviet scientific research in Siberia. The young people had found a way to earn money by helping technology-starved Soviet industry solve practical research problems, for additional pay. They were so effective that the party leadership became alarmed—and abruptly abolished Fakel. Zatulin proposed reviving the model. He suggested creating a series of "Centers for Scientific-Technical Creativity of Youth," which, in theory, would use young scientists to help Soviet industry solve technical problems. The idea was approved, ironically, by the lion of the Soviet old guard, Yegor Ligachev, who had often expressed strong views about banning rock music.

Ligachev had no idea that he had just approved a springboard to capitalism.

Khodorkovsky watched Komsomol membership rolls decline firsthand. He was deputy chief of the Komsomol at the Mendeleev Institute of Chemical Technology, one of Russia's oldest industrial schools, situated at Miusskaya Square in Moscow. Khodorkovsky graduated in June 1986, a year after Gorbachev took power. He had a chemistry degree and had also served on the institute's economics debating team.

The technical sciences were a breeding ground for many new capitalists because their studies included only a minimal amount of ideology and focused on practical questions of what worked and what did not. Alexander Khachaturov, who later became dean of economics at the Mendeleev Institute, told me that the chemists and scientists learned to sharpen their analytical skills and did not spend much time on Marx and Engels. "They entered the new life with ease," he recalled of the *perestroika* years. "They knew what *khozraschyot* was, what profits and profitability were." They also had an acute understanding of the country's political and economic failings. "Many felt that the country could not continue endlessly wasting its resources," he told me. "They sensed that the regime could not continue for a long time . . . with a leadership who could not put two words together."[8]

In the Komsomol, Khodorkovsky collected dues, a thankless task at a time when members were fleeing. "We often had to contribute our own money into it," Khodorkovsky told me.[9] "If someone didn't pay the Komsomol dues, then the deputy was reprimanded." He took a few fingers and rapped the back of his neck in a gesture of reprimand. Khodorkovsky recalled that he disliked the dues-collecting work and took the first chance that came along to do something else. He opened a youth café—one of the budding Komsomol businesses. "It didn't work out that well," he recalled. The café was in the wrong place. It was located inside the institute, but students fled each day for their dormitories—leaving the café empty. "That was my first experience, not quite happy," Khodorkovsky recalled. But the Komsomol beckoned with other, more lucrative possibilities.

One of these ideas was to prove crucial to Khodorkovsky's success. It was Zatulin's proposal for young scientists to make money by providing advice to factories and industry on technical issues. Factory managers had some discretionary funds to use as they liked. They often spent their money on contracts with institutes like Mendeleev for research and technical projects. To snare some of the money from such projects, Khodorkovsky started what he called the Foundation of Youth Initiative, a "youth club" that was in reality a nascent business under the protective umbrella of the Komsomol.

Khodorkovsky and his new venture soon reached a crossroads. It was the summer of 1987, just a year after graduation. Unexpectedly, he was forced to make a choice. His superiors told him either he could climb the ladder in the Komsomol, a decent career, or he would have to leave the institute to go off and continue what they called his "self-financing tricks." The term was a bit derogatory, since the more seasoned apparatchiks figured the capitalist experiments were just temporary. They demanded to know what Khodorkovsky would decide: stick with them and remain a dedicated Komsomol functionary, or go off on his "self-financing tricks"?

"So," Khodorkovsky recalled, "in a trembling voice, I said: *'self-financing tricks.'* At the institute they looked at me as if I was crazy."

"Many years later," he added, "I talked with people and asked them, why didn't you start doing the same thing? Why didn't you go into it? Because any head of an institute had more possibilities than I had, by an order of magnitude. They explained that they had all gone through the period—the Kosygin thaw—when the same self-financing system was allowed. And then, at best, people were unable to succeed in their career and, at worst, found themselves in jail. They were all sure that would be the case this time, and that is why they did not go into it. And I"—Khodorkovsky let out a big, broad laugh at the memory—"*I did not remember this!* I was too young! And I went for it."

One of Khodorkovsky's first targets for his business was a prestigious Soviet research facility. The Institute of High Temperatures spread out over seventy-five acres on the northern edge of Moscow, a vast complex of laboratories for the study of high-temperature physics, rocket propulsion, and lasers. This prominent institute played a role in the space race and the Cold War arms race, especially the final, futile quest for laser weapons. It was also an incubator for another more promising wave of the future: capitalism.

Founded in the 1960s, the Institute of High Temperatures grew rapidly and by the 1980s had four thousand workers. The leader was Alexander Sheindlin, an academician (the highest rank for a Soviet scholar) and one of the country's foremost experts in high-temperature physics. Sheindlin, a polite, easygoing man with large blue eyes, enjoyed not only stature at home but prestigious overseas contacts, which brought him valuable resources. "Our institute was a rich institute," he recalled.

One day, Khodorkovsky and one of his young associates arrived at the polished, laminated conference table at Sheindlin's office.[10] Sheindlin called them *rebyata*, an affectionate term for young fellows. "They were very young, I liked them a lot. I liked to see little sparks in their eyes," Sheindlin recalled. The young men were looking for scientific projects that they could carry out for his institute. They may not have used the words "self-financing tricks," but that was what they were interested in. "They were energetic people," Sheindlin recalled. "They were well-known Komsomol workers—they were refined, clean people, not petty thieves."

"They offered me nothing," he recalled. "They were good guys. They said, 'give us a little bit of money. We will look for something interesting. But we will work honestly.' There: *honestly,* they said." Sheindlin told me that Khodorkovsky wanted some "start-up capital," and Sheindlin quickly drew a comparison with the American industrialist David Packard, who started his business in a garage. Moreover, he said the bright young fellows had told him they had already received some help from the State Committee on Science and Technology, an influential government agency that oversaw scientific research—a calling card Sheindlin quickly recognized.

"Well, maybe I forget now," Sheindlin recalled, "but it seems to me I gave them 170,000 rubles." This was an enormous amount of money at the time. "We made an agreement," Sheindlin said, "that they had to do some kind of scientific research."

Sheindlin told me he never really expected them to do any scientific work for his institute. Perhaps he gave them the money because he expected simply to earn a profit from financial dealings, or perhaps Khodorkovsky's friends in high places had pressed Sheindlin into making the payment. The real reason is simply not known. When I asked Sheindlin, he acknowledged, "I knew that no kind of science was going to come from this. I knew that. I fully understood that they, realistically, could do nothing for my institute."[11]

For the next two years, Sheindlin did not hear a word from the bright young fellows. But he figured they were busy with his money. "To this day I don't know the details," Sheindlin told me. "They used this money to increase the money—many, many times. And the knowledge of working with money was not simple. All the laws that existed in the country! To work with lots of money, you had to know how to maneuver."

This was Khodorkovsky's secret: he knew. The episode at Sheindlin's institute was just one small window on a hugely important discovery that Khodorkovsky had made about the Soviet financial system. He discovered how to exploit the way money was controlled and used—and turn it into more money. And he was able to do it because the system let him experiment.

The Soviet financial system was a legacy of the Stalin years. In the command economy, money and finance were not the major factors in decisions made by factories and enterprises. Rather, factories strove to meet output targets set by central planners, and they received subsidies to do so. In the shortage economy, money alone could not always buy more supplies or lead to more output. What mattered was bargaining for scarce supplies and meeting the output quotas.

The Soviet system had two kinds of money. One was simple cash. This was real money that came in banknotes and coins. In the command economy, strict rules governed how enterprises and factories could use their cash, or *nalichnye*, which was used chiefly for wages. It was scarce, but a factory manager who could get some extra cash might also use it for something additional he needed, such as a truck or building a shed.

The Soviet system also had another kind of funds, known as noncash, or *beznalichnye.* This was not banknotes or coins, but a kind of virtual money that was widely distributed as government subsidies to factories. The *beznalichnye*, or noncash, existed only as an accounting unit. A factory would be transferred subsidies in *beznalichnye*, which it would record on its books and might use to pay another enterprise—but it was not something you could put in your wallet.

The key dilemma for a factory manager was that the system was rigid: mixing the two kinds of money was prohibited. The factory manager was not allowed to take the *beznalichnye* and turn it into real cash. Both kinds of money were controlled by Gosbank, the official state bank, and by the central planners.

However, factory managers almost always needed more cash than they could get out of the system. The supply of cash was tight, but the supply of *beznalichnye* was very plentiful—maybe because there was not much use for it. The result was an imbalance in the value of the two kinds of money. Cash was much more valuable and sought after. By some estimates, a cash ruble was worth ten times a noncash ruble.

This imbalance was an invitation to huge profits. Someone who figured out how to turn the *beznalichnye* into cash would make a fortune. The planners' greatest nightmare was that someone would do this and pump the relatively worthless state subsidies into real cash rubles.

Khodorkovsky figured it out. Starting in 1987, he began to churn the relatively useless *beznalichnye* into sought-after cash and, even better, into even more valuable hard currency. The full story, even a decade later, is a bit of a mystery, and I discovered that many of those who participated in Khodorkovsky's money machine were reluctant to talk about it. The process obviously was trial and error, but for Khodorkovsky it was far more lucrative than the youth café.

The crack in the system started with the Komsomol, which was looking for a way to stay afloat and wrangled a special privilege for its businesses, including the cafés and discos. On December 28, 1987, the central committee of the Komsomol gave its local organizations a new set of financial rules, allowing them to raise and spend money as they pleased and set up their own bank accounts. This was in keeping with the spirit of self-financing. One of the rules was extremely significant: Komsomol organizations could, in certain cases, mix the *nalichnye* and *beznalichnye*. (It is possible that the new rule came out after the practice had already begun that year.) The youth groups could do what no factory director dared: turn the useless noncash into cash and pay more people with it or build a nice dacha in the woods outside of Moscow. This opened up new horizons for making money—and making it virtually out of nothing. All that was needed was the right permits, and perhaps payoffs for the proper authorities, and suddenly a small privilege turned into something very valuable indeed: cranking the state subsidies into cash.[12]

At approximately the same time, Zatulin's idea of students doing work for factories became a reality with the opening of a new kind of business known as Centers for Scientific-Technical Creativity of Youth, or NTTMs by the Russian acronym. Khodorkovsky in 1987 transformed his youth club into an NTTM, which operated, broadly, under the auspices of the Komsomol. The NTTM was supposed to perform scientific and technical research. But the real core—the attraction that brought the young researchers to Khodorkovsky's door—was money.

Khodorkovsky worked from a small, shabby office, set just slightly below street level on 1st Tverskaya-Yamskaya Street in central Moscow. At the time, a Komsomol activist was supposed to look like a good party man and dress nicely. But Khodorkovsky did not fit the party mold.[13] He was always uncomfortable in suits and ties and more commonly appeared in jeans and a sweater; he had worked jobs sometimes as a freight loader and carpenter, and recalled that his childhood ambition was to become director of a big Soviet factory. His father, who worked at a high-precision machine tools plant, was Jewish, which meant Khodorkovsky was probably barred from ever obtaining a high-level party position, even though he held a junior post in the Komsomol at Mendeleev. After the Mendeleev Institute, he studied at the law institute for a few years, telling friends that it was necessary to be able to understand and exploit decrees issued by the government.

The youth science centers were sprinkled throughout Moscow's thirty-three districts. Khodorkovsky found a home in the Frunze District, a prestigious central area, because he had a good connection there.[14]

What kind of business did the youth science center carry out? The key was churning noncash into cash. Spread across the Soviet Union was a vast archipelago of research institutes—many, but not all of them part of the Cold War military machine—which had a lot of extra noncash. Khodorkovsky, using the privileges of a Komsomol man, could set up what were called "temporary creative collectives." These were simply a group of workers, often the same workers who were already inside the institute or enterprise or sometimes a truly temporary group from outside. The key advantage was that the "temporary creative collective" could legally be paid in cash. Then Khodorkovsky, again because of his Komsomol affiliation, could draw up contracts for the collective to perform some kind of research project, write software, or build something for the institute. Sometimes it was just a pro forma arrangement to work on a project on which they already labored, sometimes it was a new project. The important point was the money machine: Khodorkovsky could take the noncash from the institute and turn it into cash to pay the "temporary creative collective." This was not just peanuts, but real money churning from idle state subsidies into hard cash.

Khodorkovsky probably received special permission at the bank—special patronage was important at every turn—to transfer the noncash into cash. In reality, the cash he got was spread around: to the workers, to the institute and its director, to Khodorkovsky's science center, and a percentage rebated to the Komsomol. The tightly regimented control of cash had just sprung a leak, but it was not some wild-eyed radical who had breached it. Rather, it was a zealous child of the Soviet system.

An early recruit to Khodorkovsky's youth science center was Leonid

Nevzlin, a computer programmer. Nevzlin told me that he spotted a newspaper advertisement for Khodorkovsky's science center and went to investigate. He arrived there in November 1987, when the operation was just a few small rooms—being hastily repaired—and a dozen people. Nevzlin, with hair brushed across his forehead and large green eyes that gave him rock-star good looks, was working in a state geological research institute, drawing the usual meager state salary. However, he had written a computer program to help enterprises keep track of accounting and deliveries. After he signed up for Khodorkovsky's science center, Nevzlin began to "sell" the software—which he already had created—over and over again to various institutes and factories. He was using Khodorkovsky's process to churn the relatively worthless noncash held by the factories and institutes into cold, hard cash.

The alluring alchemy of Khodorkovsky's system was that he shared the cash with the participants such as Nevzlin—many times more money than any of them had earned before in their official jobs. After a few months of this, Nevzlin recalled, he felt wealthy.[15] Dozens of hungry young researchers began showing up at Khodorkovsky's door.

The directors of enterprises and institutes who used Khodorkovsky's services were also grateful—Khodorkovsky had a magic channel that could give them added cash too, since they usually got a slice of the proceeds. For the factory bosses, the risks were minimal because Khodorkovsky came with a seal of approval from the system itself.

Kryshtanovskaya, the sociologist who studied the Russian elite, told me that the industrial directors who cooperated with Khodorkovsky knew "that they were working with the authorities, that it wasn't con artists." In this case, the transaction was a breeze, a simple bank transfer, which would have been difficult or impossible if not for Khodorkovsky's good connections. "There is an institute. The institute has an account at the bank," Kryshtanovskaya told me. "There is an NTTM. It has an account at the bank. So money from bank number one is transferred to bank number two. And the NTTM, they take money from that bank." She added, "The process of privatization had begun—the first kind of privatization was that of money itself."

Kryshtanovskaya recalled that the possibilities multiplied as the bright young fellows came up with new self-financing tricks. "They started to think, 'How can we get money?' That is, you had to convince the director of the enterprise that he *had* to do some kind of work. And these teams were created around people like Khodorkovsky and others who were very young and cynical, who offered to the directors, 'We will bring you this groundbreaking research!' Or 'we'll put some kind of business plan in place!' They used a sort of intellectual preemptive strike. They foisted it on people. And very often they would take that so-called 'research' and sell it to many enterprises for profit. And practically all of them became very rich people."

Khodorkovsky was making money from thin air. No manufacturing was involved; no widgets rolled off assembly lines. Andrei Gorodetsky, who worked with Khodorkovsky in the early days and later headed the trading desk at a Russian bank, told me that the science centers often did not pay the institutes or factories for use of the equipment, laboratories, or space where the work was done. "In reality, these NTTM were making money while using state property. But the state generally closed its eyes to this." He added, "All these centers did not really produce anything. They were middlemen. We simply worked as middlemen. There was no business—purchase and sale did not exist."[16]

By 1990 there were forty-seven youth science centers in Moscow. The same techniques were being applied to other Komsomol activities—rock concerts and beauty contests were a favorite way to churn noncash into cash. Any group of people could be turned into a "temporary creative collective" and used to funnel the useless noncash into real money.

Khodorkovsky went farther and faster than many others, constantly hustling to think up new avenues for making easy money. But he needed help. "The money didn't do the trick," Khodorkovsky once said. "Old friendships did the trick."[17] Khodorkovsky's hunting ground was the upper echelons of Soviet industry and science. In 1994 Khodorkovsky told an interviewer, "I invented several financial methods that were broadly used and that in the best days allowed me to conduct up to five hundred contracts for scientific research simultaneously. Five thousand people were working there."[18]

Later I asked Khodorkovsky what had been his big breakthrough, because clearly he had zoomed ahead of his generation. I had spoken to dozens of people who worked with Khodorkovsky, but the kernel of his success was always elusive. Khodorkovsky was a workaholic, they said. He was well-connected. He hustled, he shared his rewards, he was never flashy.

Many of those who came to the youth science center recalled that

Khodorkovsky multiplied their income for doing the same work as before. But Khodorkovsky's own account revealed a moneymaking machine that was more ambitious and audacious than I had imagined. He told me he had turned the noncash not only into ruble cash but also into hard currency—into dollars.

"A separate breakthrough for us, in comparison with all the other NTTMs, was that, all the others said, what do we need this *beznalichnye* for? And they were trying to increase the share of cash. And to do a little work, trying to maximize the share of cash, through many things, and get them in the form of wages. Our real breakthrough was that, we said, okay, all the cash will be given to the working labor collectives. And we collect the *beznalichnye.*"

What did Khodorkovsky do with it? "We were saving the *beznalichnye,*" he told me. "People just didn't care about the *beznalichnye,* they were not interested, because nothing could be done with it." The reader is reminded that Khodorkovsky was already a world apart from many other young men of his generation. At twenty-four years of age, he possessed a bulging supply of Soviet government noncash rubles. "I was saving it," he said. "I knew for sure that we would be able to come up with something. We saved, accumulated a lot of it." Since the *beznalichnye* was a virtual money that existed on ledgers only, Khodorkovsky must have had permission to keep it in an account or perhaps got control of someone else's account. It was not the kind of money that could be kept in a shoebox.

In the next stage, Khodorkovsky went on, he found some enterprises that would exchange the noncash for valuable foreign hard currency. These were export companies—primarily in timber—that had plenty of hard currency. "We went to the Far East, and we bought a lot from timber people," Khodorkovsky said. "It took us a year to save the money and get this idea." Although Khodorkovsky left it unsaid, the process was obviously immensely lucrative: he was trading relatively worthless noncash for very valuable hard currency. Since the Soviet Union had rigid exchange rates and restrictions on hard currency, Khodorkovsky was probably offering the timber companies a hugely advantageous rate that allowed them to get more for their hard currency than if they had to trade it at the official rate. The fact that Khodorkovsky was dealing in hard currency was a clue that his money machine was accelerating to new levels and that he had patrons in high places.

All along the chain, Khodorkovsky had protection from above. Even though he decided not to become a Komsomol careerist, the Komsomol was critical to his early gains. Moreover, the Komsomol affiliation functioned as an umbrella, offering Khodorkovsky legitimacy and access at a time when many young, hustling businessmen feared that at any minute the KGB would take them away. The cooperatives were just beginning, and they faced many of the same uncertainties, without the benefit of Komsomol protection.

Another source of Khodorkovsky's support was the imprimatur of the State Committee on Science and Technology, which was, in theory, cosponsor of the youth science centers. This powerful agency was a conduit between the Communist Party and the state scientific research institutes, and it had enormous influence over Soviet science and how scientists worked. Just mentioning that he had support from the State Committee opened doors for Khodorkovsky. "I could always refer to it," he told me. Several earlier accounts by journalists suggested that Khodorkovsky received money from the State Committee. Khodorkovsky told me that he did not, saying that the officials there had made promises but were too high up in the Soviet system to worry about some young *rebyata* playing capitalist games. But Khodorkovsky acknowledged that on one occasion he got valuable protection from the committee. "Our law enforcement agencies at that time did not quite understand what *perestroika* was," Khodorkovsky recalled. Under Soviet law, entrepreneurship was criminal, and the law had not been repealed, even as entrepreneurship was gradually being spawned by the system. The law was not widely enforced but could be a pretext for harassment. "The militia came to us," Khodorkovsky recalled, "and started inquiring how we got our profit." Khodorkovsky said he appealed to the chairman of the State Committee. "I told him in detail what we did and what we were doing, and he called some militia boss and asked him to leave the NTTM alone." That kept the authorities off his back for two years, he recalled. Those were the two most important years of his fledgling money machine.

Khodorkovsky told Peter Slevin, then a reporter for the *Miami Herald,* that at one time he had enthusiastically embraced all the old Communist Party ideology; he "totally believed that capitalism was decaying, that Lenin was right and that the future lay in Communism." But then Khodorkovsky said he went through a "total rethink" and emerged a full-blooded capitalist. This rethinking happened in the years when Khodorkovsky was discovering how to turn the relatively useless *beznalichnye* into real money. It completely changed his views, he said. "The people who had known me before the change didn't recognize me after." He added, with a bit of hyperbole, "If the old Mikhail had met the new one, he would have shot him."[19]

While most of the world was asking in the late 1980s whether Gorbachev's *glasnost* and *perestroika* reforms were irreversible, at the street level change was unfolding with incredible swiftness. Within a few months of starting the science center, Khodorkovsky decided to transform it yet again, this time into a cooperative, the quasi-independent businesses that could set their own prices. The cooperatives were already emerging as the next wave, and they were another step removed from his original Komsomol sponsors. Moreover, as Smolensky had discovered, a small provision in the law on cooperatives permitted them to start their own banks.

But first Khodorkovsky had to register the cooperative with the city authorities. He visited the Mossovet building, where licenses for cooperatives were being given out by the stolid Luzhkov, who rejected his first application. The cooperatives were generally, until that time, engaged in concrete activities such as construction, pie baking, or car repairs. They were not engaged in amorphous "scientific-technical" work. Luzhkov had doubts about the scheme, according to Panin, Luzhkov's staff assistant on the cooperative licensing commission. Luzhkov had spent his entire career in the chemical industry and knew the Soviet system from the inside out. But that experience only added to his worry about Khodorkovsky. Luzhkov recognized that behind the scientific research, Khodorkovsky was churning noncash into cash. "Luzhkov sensed it very well, like no one else, because he had been director of an enterprise, and he said these two systems, noncash and cash systems, must not be combined," Panin recalled.[20]

Khodorkovsky was persistent, however, and despite Luzhkov's misgivings, he received permission to start a cooperative in a few months. How he overcame Luzhkov's doubts is not known. But Khodorkovsky clearly was not one to be intimidated by roadblocks. He just jumped—or was lifted with an invisible hand—right over them. He had gone very far, very fast in eighteen months, from graduation in the summer of 1986 to running the youth science center and its financial network in late 1987 and establishing a cooperative after that. His pace did not slow down—he had a wheelbarrow full of money and needed to do something with it. The "self-financing tricks" were working, but they were not enough.

When he was invited to go abroad on a business trip in 1988, Igor Primakov, a scientist living in Moscow, pondered what to bring back from the West: shirts? jeans? Primakov, a specialist in using computers to predict earthquakes, finally decided to bring back a personal computer, which he knew could be resold in Moscow at a huge profit. By scrimping and saving up his travel allowance, he managed to buy an Amstrad 286 desktop computer for about $3,000 in Italy. Once home, Primakov sold the computer for 70,000 rubles. "It was my salary for forty-eight years!" he recalled.

Why did Primakov's computer bring such a high price? The Soviet Union was caught in a time warp. The economy stagnated in the late 1970s and early 1980s, precisely at the moment when the West was going through the silicon chip revolution. While personal computers blossomed in the West, they barely existed inside the Soviet Union. The demand for them was enormous.

Primakov sold the computer through a cooperative to an institute. Once again, noncash was turned into cash. The institute had an abundance of noncash to purchase the computer with, and the cooperative acted as the middleman, turning the non-cash into real rubles to pay Primakov. He recalled nervously going to the state savings bank to collect his payment. The bank office closed for an hour just to count out the 70,000 rubles, which he took home in a bag. "When I did it once," Primakov told me, "I had no plan to go back there and buy two or three computers, make the same profitable deal again and again. But I know now that dozens of people made these deals, one or two years before me. When they did it once, they understood there was a window of opportunity, that you can buy one, two, then eight."[21]

Khodorkovsky was always on the lookout for new opportunity, and, flush with money-machine profits, he plunged into trade in personal computers, spending his hard currency to buy them abroad, importing them, selling them for *beznalichnye,* and changing the noncash back into cash or hard currency again. "We started circulating money very fast, especially when the computers started," Khodorkovsky recalled. The financial chain had grown longer, and delays or interruptions could break it. There were constant uncertainties about getting the computers into the country and changing the money. But Khodorkovsky was calm. According to a young man who worked with him on the computers, "Khodorkovsky could think, more than talk. He could listen to ideas."[22] Khodorkovsky was a closed, almost secretive person about his business but attentive to the winds of capitalism swirling around him. He read every decree and announcement carefully, looking for loopholes, and he knew about the unwritten loopholes too. "It is possible to find loopholes in every law, and I will use them without an instant of hesitation," he once boasted.[23] Personal computers were one of the most profitable means of arbitrage—taking advantage of the enormous differences in prices inside the Soviet Union and outside it. Khodorkovsky had added a new dimension to his money machine. He was now trading in not only cash but goods—in this case computers that were as good as gold.

Khodorkovsky recalled that at some point his money-and-trade machine was growing so fast that its finances began to fray. He was stretched thin because of the long chain of conversion and transfers, from noncash to cash to hard currency to computers and back again. "We needed someone who could sell the hard currency, pay them the rubles, get the currency, again buy the computers. As you see, the cycle was quite long."[24] The cycle also included other commodities that could be profitably traded. At the time, arbitrage was such a simple way to make money that a multitude of commodity exchanges opened their doors in Moscow. Yulia Latynina, a hard-digging journalist and novelist who delighted in exposing skullduggery in Russian finance and industry, recalled that Khodorkovsky's early years were characterized by rumors of all kinds of deals for scarce goods. They included importing fake Napoleon brandy and bogus Swiss vodka bottled in Poland, as well as stonewashed jeans, which were in huge demand, and laundering Communist Party money. Of all the myths, Latynina recalled, Khodorkovsky and his team would later admit only to the work of their science center and the computers. But, Latynina recalled, she had been told by Nevzlin that they also brought in the fake cognac: "'Okay,' Khodorkovsky's deputy Leonid Nevzlin waves his hand. 'We financed the cognac. No one, ultimately, was poisoned by it.'"[25]

Khodorkovsky's next move was into banking. At the time, the all-pervasive Gosbank, the main bank of the Soviet centrally planned economy, had split off five new specialist banks, known as the *spetsbanks,* for agriculture, industry and construction, foreign trade, retail savings, and the fifth, Zhiltsotsbank, for financing social needs, such as housing. Khodorkovsky showed up one day at Zhiltsotsbank, which was in his district, and asked for a loan. "I heard such things could happen!" he laughed years later, recalling the audacity of the request. The bank didn't throw him out. Bank officials explained that they could only give a loan to a state enterprise operating under the official state plan, and Khodorkovsky was not a state enterprise and was not under the plan. They also told him that if he was a bank they could give him a credit—but, at that moment, he was not a bank either. At the time, the very first commercial banks were being permitted, many of them taking advantage of the Law on Cooperatives.

It was another of those breakthrough moments when Khodorkovsky was anointed or anointed himself. The management of Zhiltsotsbank agreeably helped Khodorkovsky set up his own commercial bank and then made him loans to finance the computer deals.[26] Zhiltsotsbank signed on as founders of the new bank, but Khodorkovsky recalled they did not contribute any capital. He said the bank's original capital included 2.5 million rubles from the science center's profits. Khodorkovsky's bank went through several name changes and was formally registered as Bank Menatep at the end of 1988.[27] "We were meeting practically no obstacles from the state structures," he commented. "A rare occurrence of circumstances."[28]

Rare indeed, but not for a favorite son of the system.

Two years after first visiting the Institute of High Temperatures, Khodorkovsky called on Sheindlin at home. Sheindlin told me that Khodorkovsky informed him that he had come into a lot of money and wanted to create a bank. But Khodorkovsky was worried about status and connections—he needed some high-level sponsors. "They were young kids," Sheindlin recalled. "I took them in warmly. We drank good wine and vodka together. I listened and I said, 'You are great, kids! Tell me, and any way I can help, I will.'"

Sheindlin agreed to sit on the board of the new Bank Menatep. At the infrequent meetings, he recalled, "We sat together and drank tea for two or three hours, and spoke about the situation in the country. So, that was for them, for the kids, very important."

The "kids" were no longer kids. They were beginning to set up offshore accounts and move hard currency in and out of the Soviet

Union, where the old underground economy was rapidly becoming the primary economy. Although private property had not yet appeared, Khodorkovsky was at the forefront of the rapidly emerging world of banking and finance, at the cutting edge of proto-capitalism. Joel Hellman, a Columbia University graduate student who came to Moscow to research a doctorate on the new Russian banks, found that Menatep was low-key and inscrutable, compared with some of the other flashy new commercial banks that blossomed in 1989. "No one spoke English, no one had Western suits," Hellman recalled of Menatep. "They didn't rush to fancy offices. They kept it low-key."[29] But Khodorkovsky was undeniably among the leaders of his generation. When Gorbachev invited a group of politicians, scholars, and journalists (the word "businessmen" was not used) to the Kremlin to talk about reform in 1990, Khodorkovsky was among them.[30]

As the "kids" were feeling their way to riches, they also sensed danger. What if the whole experiment collapsed? Would they have any allies to defend them? Nevzlin, who had become a partner and confidant of Khodorkovsky, was extroverted, whereas Khodorkovsky was reclusive. Nevzlin had an idea: they needed to explain themselves because on the street, and in the public mind, there were many doubts about their business. What was a commercial bank? What was Menatep? Rumors swirled that it was a front for the Komsomol or the Communist Party or the KGB; the same rumors dogged almost all the young commercial banks at that time.[31]

Nevzlin proposed that they explain themselves in a small book, an explanatory tract. Khodorkovsky went along because Nevzlin urged him to do so. They had become close partners. Nevzlin recalled that they were living in a country house outside of Moscow, he on the first floor and Khodorkovsky upstairs. In 1991, the last year of the Soviet Union, they dictated their thoughts into a tape recorder and then published *Chelovek s Rublyom* (Man with a ruble), mimicking a famous Soviet play about Lenin, *Man with a Gun*. The book jacket featured dollars and rubles. Their company Menatep-Inform printed fifty thousand copies.[32]

The book was fifty thousand shouts at the system. Khodorkovsky and Nevzlin screamed, Get rich! Like us! The entire treatise has the tone of brazen teenagers taunting their parents. It has only one idea: getting rich is not evil. The exuberant writing is quite a contrast to the low-key Khodorkovsky, a shy banker in jeans and flannel shirts. I think the book was a crude attempt by the pair at public relations. The book is so filled with exhortations and clichés that it is almost unreadable. "Our compass is profit," they wrote. "Our idol is his financial majesty the capital." Their goal: "to become billionaires." They asked, "What is a good leader? It seems to us that it must first of all be someone who brings profit." They invoked Henry Ford as one of their heroes. "A man who can turn an invested dollar into a billion is a genius."

In their rambling discourse, punctuated by headings such as "Menatep: A Way to Being Wealthy," Khodorkovsky and Nevzlin celebrated greed, which may explain why they felt compelled to write it: they feared envy, jealousy, and misunderstanding. Their fears were not unfounded. Suspicion of capitalism, wealth, and property, a feature of Soviet propaganda, was a deeply held belief in Russian culture, one that would linger, especially in the older generation, for years after the demise of Soviet Communism. The "kids" did not know what was coming and sought to justify their extravagant new status. "Ourselves for ourselves," they declared of their philosophy. "Being wealthy is a norm of being." They ebulliently recalled a lavish business presentation they had made at the Moscow Commercial Club, a favorite watering hole of the newly rich, with fireworks, food, drink, and entertainment for four hundred guests. "Glasses were filled with twenty brands of cognac, whiskey, champagne, gin, all kinds of wines, liqueurs, more than fifty kinds of drinks for all tastes. We did not begrudge the expense of arranging the party." They described their lavish hospitality as "the highest form of ethics." But the point of describing their glittering party was not so much to brag as to defend and justify. "We, Menatep, can afford not to fear the results of our own work, can afford to show off what we have earned," they insisted. Whereas Lenin's formula was equality in poverty, "we are advocates of equality in the right to be rich."

Charles Ryan, a Harvard graduate who came to the Soviet Union in its final year to work for the European Bank for Reconstruction and Development, got off a train one day in St. Petersburg, where he had been sent to give advice to some young reformers, including Anatoly Chubais. Ryan recalled walking across the square looking for a bus, thinking that he was anxious to quit being an adviser and participate in the "hunt and kill" of the emerging capitalism. He spotted a man wearing a sandwich board advertisement, two strings, and a sign that read: "Buy Shares of Bank Menatep."

"I say to myself, this is funny, I gotta see this one!" recalled Ryan, who had spent some time on Wall Street before coming to St. Petersburg and knew a few things about shares. "A bank? So, the guy is standing there. He's got a greasy handful of these little scraps of paper that say Menatep Bank shares. I bought a couple. I whipped out a couple of those twenty-five ruble notes with Lenin's face on them and I bought myself a little fistful. I got in a taxi, and I am cracking up at the idea that you can just buy these bearer notes, you know, shares on the street. I am thinking, this has got to be a pyramid scheme.

"I get to the hotel and click on the television. You know, back then the television ads in Russia, there was no picture. Just a line of the name of the company and a phone number."

"Surprise: there's a face! And it's Mikhail Khodorkovsky. And there he is, waving a fist at the television and saying, 'My name is Mikhail Khodorkovsky and I am urging you to guarantee your future and *buy shares* in Bank Menatep! It's a commercial bank.'" Ryan was amazed. "It was couched in the usual sort of Soviet language, but the bottom line was, buy these damn things and you're going to get rich. Which was weird, and interesting, I thought. It's interesting that they are appealing to people's desire to make money."

The significance of the Menatep shares, one of the first such stock offerings, was that once again Khodorkovsky was at the head of the pack, relentlessly looking for new avenues and directions in which to expand. Despite his penchant for secretiveness, Khodorkovsky decided that he wanted to make Menatep into a household name and turned to Vladislav Surkov, a wiry, chain-smoking young man whom he first met at the youth science center. Surkov had made his first money by using a state press to print reproductions of a famous painting, which he then sold for a huge profit on the street outside an art exhibition where the original was hanging. "I liked Khodorkovsky at first glance," Surkov recalled, "because he immediately took a sheet of paper and started drawing circles and arrows, and he said that in several years we're going to have an empire."[33]

"I knew that many people, the majority of people, were very skeptical about Khodorkovsky's ideas," he added. "Everybody thought that the Communists just gave young people a chance to play for about two or three years, and that they would never give us a chance to go further." But Surkov said he believed in Khodorkovsky's dream of an empire, however distant it may have seemed from the shabby beginnings in the youth science center. "I wanted to be like a hero in the movie *Pretty Woman*. I wanted to be a big businessman who's sitting in a big hotel, supervising big events."

Surkov became Khodorkovsky's marketing man. He hired some journalists he knew, and together they sat down for a brainstorming session, thinking about how to create an advertising campaign. Instead of long, boring Soviet-style television appearances, Surkov came up with snappy, attention-getting ads. He thought up a four-second flash on the television screen that said simply, "Bank Menatep," and he got the bank's name posted in a corner of the television screen during the weather broadcast on *Vremya*, the main nightly news broadcast, which was rigidly controlled by the party. "People remembered it," he recalled of the weather advertisement, "but we had to coordinate it with the party central committee." Surkov also cajoled famous Russian actors into appearing in Menatep television spots, encouraging them to give testimonials using any words that came to mind, and he negotiated appearances by Khodorkovsky on popular television talk shows, including *Moment Istiny* and *Tema*, a popular program that often broke Soviet-era taboos.

Although they were advertising in public, Menatep was not really interested in the public. The bank was a largely closed financial nerve center for Khodorkovsky's trading and currency operations. The point of the advertising and shares campaigns was political insurance against a crackdown by the authorities. If the Communist Party had started the whole experiment, it could also shut it down. There were dark clouds of retreat in 1990, as Gorbachev hesitated with *glasnost* and *perestroika*. "We wanted many thousands of shareholders in our company because we expected that the authorities would say at any time, 'Enough!' When they came to our bank to disperse it, we wanted them to encounter the resistance of many shareholders," Surkov recalled.

Within the bank, Khodorkovsky was creating a money machine that would tower above the first modest transactions with *beznalichnye*. He realized that the really large sums to be found in Russia were not in the private sector, which was still in its infancy. Khodorkovsky and Nevzlin decided to go for the big money—to milk the state, the largest source of capital, more directly than before. They began roaming the increasingly chaotic corridors of power. The Soviet Union was already coming unglued, and a new power center had emerged with Yeltsin at the head of a separate Russian government. Khodorkovsky became an adviser to Yeltsin's prime minister, Ivan Silayev. What he did in this post is not known precisely, but it must have given him an ideal vantage point for identifying new sources of cash.

Meanwhile, the Soviet government was cranking out huge amounts of credits to enterprises in a vain effort to keep them from falling apart. Menatep became an authorized bank, one of the chosen commercial banks that served as an intermediary to transfer government money to enterprises. The rate of return for working with the government money was, on the face of it, not very lucrative, Khodorkovsky told me. But Khodorkovsky could parlay the state credits—which came practically free, like water from a tap—into good profits. He took the state credits, used them for his own purposes, and paid the state back much later. It was free capital. Khodorkovsky told me that in 1990 and 1991, the computers and hard currency earnings began to play a secondary role in his bottom line. "The main thing was credits" from the state, he recalled. "Basically, we took money from the state, gave it to state enterprises, and then took money from state enterprises and returned it to the state." The turnover was tremendously profitable in part because neither the state enterprises nor the low-paid bureaucrats fully understood the time value of money; Khodorkovsky could earn his profits by holding their cash and using it. Latynina wrote that Khodorkovsky was also very skillful at manipulating the bureaucrats. "He was one of the first to understand the advantages of investments in government officials," she wrote. "Receptions for high-level guests at the bank's country cottages on Rublevskoye Highway . . . would be returned in income a thousandfold."[34] In other words, Khodorkovsky and Nevzlin realized the value of connections—that a bureaucrat, properly entertained, could sign over a big account to their bank, and they could make millions of dollars just playing with the money of the state.

Khodorkovsky's machine was moving into overdrive. His network of connections began to stretch far abroad to such confidential offshore banking havens as Switzerland and Gibraltar, as well as the

United States. The Soviet government maintained tight restrictions on hard currency, but the young commercial banks, including Menatep, began to routinely ignore them.[35] The gradually collapsing Soviet state had no way to keep track of the fleet-footed easy money boys. Khodorkovsky's early offshore network extended to Geneva, and a private investment bank known as Riggs Valmet. The firm had offices in Gibraltar, Cyprus, the Isle of Man and other financial centers known to cater to wealthy individuals and companies seeking ways to avoid taxes and move money offshore. After the Berlin Wall fell in 1989, Riggs National Bank of Washington had purchased a 51 percent stake in Valmet as part of a plan to expand into Eastern Europe and Russia.[36] Khodorkovsky was not yet thirty years old—and only a few years earlier had tried unsuccessfully to open a youth café in Moscow—when he first became a client of the exclusive Geneva investment bank. At the lavish party Khodorkovsky threw in 1991 at the Moscow Commercial Club, where a jazz band played softly and Mercedes Benzes and BMWs filled every available parking space outside, a representative of Riggs Valmet told a reporter that Khodorkovsky had already been a client for two years. "They are the most sophisticated in Moscow," he said of Khodorkovsky's team. Also, Platon Lebedev, who was then Menatep's financial director, called Riggs "our teachers" and added, "Their Swiss branch is our second home."[37]

Five days after the August 1991 coup attempt against Gorbachev, Nikolai Kruchina, the Communist Party treasurer, threw himself out of a window. Six weeks later, his predecessor, Georgi Pavlov, fell to his death the same way. They took with them one of the great secrets of the Soviet denouement: what happened to the billions of dollars held by the party? The missing cash and gold of the Communist hierarchy became an enduring and unsolved mystery, one that even a decade later could arouse the most intense arguments and speculation among Moscow bankers and politicians. No one knows for sure how much money was involved or where it went, but the speculation often pointed to the "kids" of the Komsomol, the most successful of whom was Mikhail Khodorkovsky. Was it possible that this bright young fellow, who found his first wealth as the system scrambled to rescue itself, became the Communist Party's life raft as well, helping the party bosses or KGB transfer riches safely away to foreign bank accounts? Khodorkovsky already had the skills, the network, and the foreign contacts.

Khodorkovsky has denied a role in saving the party's money. But he made an ambiguous statement about it in the early 1990s. "A bank is like a waiter," he said. "Its business is to cater to the clients independently of their political beliefs or affiliation with this or that camp. Its job is to take or give money to someone, registering the deal. So it is not clear to me, what is the fault of those banks that kept the Communist Party money on their accounts? Had I been offered to keep them in my bank, I would also have considered it as an honor. Then all of a sudden the Communist Party was declared a criminal organization, and the banks servicing it became if not criminals then some kind of accomplices. It should not be this way."[38]

Yegor Gaidar, who was Yeltsin's first prime minister, told me that the only people in Russia who could really help find the Communist Party money were the KGB—and they had probably taken the money out. Gaidar turned instead to the international private detective firm, Kroll Associates, to help find the party money.[39] Gaidar authorized a fee of $900,000 for three months. By May 1992, the probe had produced a lot of paperwork, but the Russian security service was not cooperating, and Gaidar concluded the investigators were coming up with nothing useful. He stopped the search.

At the same time, Fritz Ermarth, a top CIA official, heard about the investigation from a retired CIA colleague. The retired colleague told Ermarth that the new Russian government wanted to find "the vast sums essentially stolen by the KGB on behalf of itself and the CPSU and deposited abroad in bank accounts and front companies." Ermarth said his former colleague wanted to know if the U.S. intelligence community could help the Russian reformers get the money back?[40]

Ermarth said that U.S. intelligence could help find the money. But should it? A high-level White House group was convened to decide. But the answer came back: no. Ermarth said the rationale was "capital flight is capital flight. We can no more help Russia retrieve such money than we can help Brazil or Argentina."

The case was closed, and the money never found.

Chapter 6

Boris Berezovsky

On languid summer days, Leonid Boguslavsky took his small skiff, powered by a cranky motor, and zoomed out over the shimmering flat surface of the lake outside of Moscow. When the motor broke down, as it often did, Boguslavsky spent weeks searching for spare parts. Then he devoted hours taking it apart and then reassembling it, tenderly coaxing it back to life. A computer specialist, Boguslavsky was curious about how things worked. He had a feel for the motor. He knew when it could run and when it would not.

On a summer weekend in 1974, Boguslavsky planned an outing with a dozen acquaintances, including one of his closest friends, Boris Berezovsky. Both he and Berezovsky were young researchers at the Institute of Control Sciences, a prestigious think tank for applied mathematics, automation, and the emerging computer sciences. Boguslavsky, then twenty-three years old, was reserved, while his friend Berezovsky, five years older, was irrepressible. Berezovsky had a full head of black, wiry hair and longish sideburns. He spoke rapidly because he thought rapidly. Sunday? Sure. The lakeside party was set.

On Saturday, the motor died. Boguslavsky knew it was impossible to get spare parts before Sunday, maybe not for days or weeks. When Berezovsky and the others arrived on Sunday, he told them the bad news. He suggested they play football and forget about the boat. The others agreed, but Berezovsky refused to believe the motor was dead.

"Leonid," he implored, "let's try to fix it."

"Boris," he replied, "there is no way to fix it. What do you know about engines?"

"I know nothing about engines, but we have to try! We have been *dreaming* about water skiing, it will be a great thing if we can fix it!" Berezovsky said, his speech picking up speed as it did when he got excited.

"Okay," Boguslavsky relented, confronted with his older friend's considerable powers of persuasion. "I bet you—it's just impossible. I know this engine. Something has happened, and we just can't fix it."

While their friends went to the beach and lit a bonfire, Boguslavsky and Berezovsky headed off to the dock to try to repair the motor. Boguslavsky did the work, while Berezovsky talked and talked and talked. Boguslavsky thought to himself: Berezovsky can't even use a screwdriver, but he sure can talk! Three hours later, they had taken apart and reassembled the motor. It was still dead. They had missed most of the party, yet Berezovsky insisted they *had* to keep trying. "We tried this and that," Boguslavsky recalled. Berezovsky would not give up. The sun was going down, their friends were tired, and Berezovsky finally acknowledged that Boguslavsky had been right all along, the motor could not be fixed.

Berezovsky was like that. He always raised the bar to the highest notch and went for it. He was always in motion, always racing toward the goal, never knowing or fearing obstacles. Even if no one else believed it was possible, Berezovsky had to try, and he would only abandon his quest at the very end, at the very last minute, if it became absolutely and unassailably clear that the goal could not be reached.

There was one other reason he might give up, and that was that Berezovsky's mind was restless, his emotions ever changing, and he sometimes lost interest in what he had started. But as long as he wanted something, he did not relax, not for a minute. "He has this attitude," Boguslavsky recalled many years later, when both of them had become successful businessmen, "never stop attacking."[1]

Moscow is a flat city of broad boulevards, crisscrossed by a lazy river and its tributaries, strewn with a hodgepodge of buildings, from elegant stone prerevolutionary apartment houses to ugly concrete prefab high-rises and Soviet-era utopian monstrosities. A few gentle hills rise on this flat plain of diversity, and one of them lifts Profsoyuznaya Street as it extends outward from the center of the city. Perched on a slope at 65 Profsoyuznaya Street is the Institute of Control Sciences, a sleek box of an office building fronted by a pond. It is an island of seeming calm isolated from the metropolis. Huddled in their tiny closetlike offices or drinking tea in the high-ceilinged classrooms with picture windows overlooking the city, the scientists and researchers here formed the brain center of Soviet technology. Founded in 1939, the institute had originally been an outgrowth of Stalin's drive for rapid industrialization. After World War II, a whole new family of mechanical beasts had arrived, requiring ever more sophisticated controls such as intercontinental ballistic missiles and atomic power stations and jet fighter planes. The scientists wrote the algorithms that guided these rockets and jet planes. They toyed with the flow of giant oil refineries and searched endlessly for the perfect automation for a thousand assembly lines. On their chalkboards were scratched mathematical formulas for controlling anything that moved, from the orbit of a supersecret satellite to a scheme for sorting the mail. As the Soviet Union forever struggled to keep up with Western technology, the institute became an elite and prestigious scientific center encompassing everything from cybernetics to pneumatics to the study of decisionmaking. One of the most famous accomplishments was the algorithm of professor Mark Aizerman, who figured out how to keep a tank's gun locked on a target while the tank itself was in jerky motion.

But the institute was more than chalkboards, theorems, and assembly lines. It was a freethinking cauldron of intellectual ferment, a club for nonstop debates about literature, theater, philosophy, *perestroika, glasnost,* auto parts, sausage, the shortage economy, and whatever else could be chewed over. Science was their purpose but life was their diet. Most of the scientists wrote their papers at home on the kitchen table and spent their days at the institute in these discussions. Vladimir Grodsky, who worked in the institute at the time, recalled it was very much like the mythical Institute of Research into Magical Processes described in the famous 1966 Russian novel, *Monday Begins on Saturday*, by the brothers Arkady and Boris Strugatsky. "It was a science fiction novel in which all the intellectual elite, a lot of really intelligent and talented people, got together in one particular place."[2]

In the halls of the Institute of Control Sciences strolled gifted mathematicians and theorists, who worked with their formulas and enjoyed the luxury of time to think. They were grateful for a small place to scratch out their ideas, a decent salary, a seminar where they could brainstorm, a cup of tea, and the intellectual room to thrive. But they did not make their own space; it was provided to them by others, who found the money and the means.

Berezovsky was one of those who found the means. He streaked through these halls like a comet. He was a compressed ball of energy. Constantly in motion, he was burning with plans, ambitions, ideas, and, most of all, connections to make them happen. He was also restless, always racing down the long hallways, always calling on the phone from halfway across Moscow. His colleagues liked to say he was distributed over time: he was always in several places at once. Somehow, with an insistent, gentle charm, and a fierce underlying desire, Berezovsky got what he wanted.

Berezovsky was the only child of a Jewish construction engineer and a pediatric nurse. His father had come to Moscow in the 1930s from the Siberian city of Tomsk. Berezovsky's father worked his entire life building factories in bricks and stone. Berezovsky was an only child, born January 23, 1946, just after the war, and enjoyed what he called a "very happy Soviet childhood." He attended a forestry institute before coming to the prestigious Institute of Control Sciences as a young researcher January 23, 1969.[3] As a Jew, Berezovsky faced hurdles. There were tacit, unspoken limits on how many Jews could hold senior posts, defend dissertations, enjoy the status of a laboratory chief, or win a prestigious prize. Everything required five times greater effort for a Jew; anti-Semitism was a Soviet state policy. "For me, there was no political future," Berezovsky told me. "I wasn't a member of the political elite. I am a Jew. There were massive limitations. I understood that perfectly well."[4] Yet the Institute of Control Sciences became one of the safe harbors for Jews. Many Jews had been inclined toward science to avoid serving the Soviet regime directly and to find professional satisfaction. The best and brightest Jewish scientists gathered at the institute. "It was a surprising place," recalled Alexander Oslon, who came to the institute in the 1970s as a part-time student. "Surprising in the quantity of unusual people—by their energy, their intellect, their originality. There was an extremely rich intellectual life at the institute, both scientific and humanitarian. It was a phenomenon. In the sphere of Soviet life, these were the brightest people who had come together. It was, to a meaningful degree, a Jewish institute."[5]

In the world of late Soviet socialism, a scientist could hardly dream of accumulating great property and wealth. But status in one's field, even worldwide recognition and fame, was extraordinarily important and could lead to material gains. Berezovsky labored at applied mathematics, but, by his own account, he was not a brilliant scientist. What he was talented at—what everyone remembers from his two decades at the institute—was a flair for making things happen in a world of lassitude and false pretenses. Although impulsive in his desires, Berezovsky thrived on inventing tactics to achieve them. He had an analytical mind, along with enormous energy and willpower. The years at the institute were a precursor for all that was to come, for Berezovsky's transformation into one of the most wealthy and influential men in Russia. In the halls of the Institute of Control Sciences, the comet burned brightly.

Aizerman, the famous professor at the institute who had solved the tank gun problem and also pioneered research in imaging and pneumatics, believed that a scientist should break into a new direction every five years. He began to champion scientific study of decisionmaking. At the institute, the basic research unit was a laboratory, which was not a room filled with test tubes but a grouping of researchers around a theory or an idea. Berezovsky eventually headed his own laboratory devoted to the theory of decisionmaking, using applied mathematics to study the processes of how choices are made.[6] In the Soviet system, certain scientific research, especially mathematics, could be one step removed from the ever present heavy-handed ideology. For example, mathematicians worked for years on models of a market economy—this was permitted because they were *models*—while surrounded by the obvious failures of Soviet socialism. The market models were useful to the mathematicians because they learned about Western methods and read the Western literature, but they could not apply what they learned to what they saw on the street. Likewise, the study of decisionmaking was an abstract pursuit that may have had little influence on decaying Soviet socialism. Mark Levin, a professor of economics who did graduate work at the institute and knew Berezovsky in the early days, recalled that Aizerman was a visionary who didn't care precisely where the field would lead him. "We are pioneers," was Aizerman's outlook, Levin told me. "Our task is a new frontier. And we can't allow ourselves to work out the details. Others will do that. Our task is to create various directions. To work out what we can. And then go forward. And let other people take care of the details."[7]

What was remarkable about Berezovsky was not so much the science as the method. "He was a generator of ideas," recalled Grodsky, who worked in Berezovsky's laboratory at the time and later became a leading Russian specialist on public opinion and polls. "He expressed everything that appeared in his head. Half of it could be nonsense, but the other half was genius." Oslon recalled Berezovsky, for all his determination, was not a very good administrator, and his laboratory often failed at simple paperwork or housekeeping tasks. "They were burning all the time," he told me. "They were always in the midst of creative surges." Berezovsky was too busy to be bothered with mundane tasks. "He was so active that you couldn't catch him," Oslon recalled. "He was in one place one minute, and in another the next. He had a million phone calls. A million places where he was late to arrive. Another million places where he promised to arrive but never went."

If there was a method to his madness, Berezovsky was constantly marshaling whatever resources his incessant networking could unlock. "It was pure business," Grodsky told me. "The possibility of organizing seminars, conducting seminars, organizing trips abroad, receiving delegations from other universities, traveling there, making speeches there—not everybody had that. Boris knew how to build relations with people. He could basically find a common language with anyone."

The hustling and networking was not confined to academic pursuits. The head of a laboratory was expected to be a provider for his people, a hunter and forager for his extended family. Even though they were the elite of Soviet science, the traditions of *blat* and *svyazi* were alive and well. Berezovsky's days were filled with the hassles of not only organizing a seminar but also finding an apartment for a colleague. He took care of his researchers, and a place in his laboratory was a coveted privilege.

For many who aspired to succeed in the Soviet industrial and scientific system, a higher academic degree was essential. "A dissertation was currency," Grodsky recalled. "What mattered was whether you were a doctor of science or a candidate of science, a member of the party or not a member. It was a completely different social hierarchy. And that is why, often times, graduate studies and scientific degrees served as a kind of currency of exchange. 'I take you as my graduate student, and you allow me to buy a Zhiguli car without having to stand in line.' It was a funny exchange, but it did take place. This is how these relations were built."[8]

Berezovsky's recollections of his years at the institute support the suggestion made by many that science was not at the center of his days. "I worked at science with pleasure," he told me. "But I felt that this wasn't 'mine.' That is, I wrote a hundred articles and three monographs. I did something in my field, something meaningful, I think. But I managed it with great difficulty. I had to keep myself within very strict limits. Because I didn't have any supertalents, *right*? In mathematics. And I simply had to control myself all the time. And—how can I put this?—I will tell you a funny thing. It's hard to believe now because I am seen today as a person who is in many places at the same time. But three years of my life—*three years of my life*—I dedicated myself to proving one theorem. Day and night. Because everything I do, I do to an absolutely maximum degree. If I am working on something, I will work only very seriously, eighteen or twenty hours a day. I proved that theorem and defended my dissertation. And when I defended it, when they confirmed me as a candidate of science, one of my friends showed me that there was a mistake in my proof. I spent *two more years* dedicated to fixing that mistake."

Berezovsky took in talented, unemployed mathematicians, just to feel the satisfaction that they were working near him. "There were a few prominent mathematicians whom Boris simply watched out for," recalled Oslon. "To a large extent they had no relationship to the practical activity of the laboratory. They worked on high, pure mathematics. He simply created a few tranquil places for them so they could work normally. One of them had no work, just odd jobs—for example, he cleared snow from rooftops. Borya took him on.

"That was, for Boris, a kind of a weakness. A sort of special sympathy. Maybe his desire to help mathematicians was some subliminal thing. . . . He also wanted to be a mathematician. He had an inclination to do pure mathematics. Maybe he dreamed of doing 'high' mathematics. On the other hand, the strength of his character was that he was always a very practical person."[9]

Berezovsky's interests would blossom and then suddenly fade. He sometimes could not sustain interest in his own projects. Once, Grodsky recalled, political fever swept the institute as they began to hold elections for an internal council. Berezovsky "also became enthusiastic and started playing. And then he suddenly lost interest. He said, 'Come on guys, quit this. Who cares? This is all rubbish. We won't be doing this!'"

Yet Berezovsky was constantly climbing his own ladder to higher status. His charm, sincerity, cunning, and energy were valuable assets. Oslon said, "There are different levels of status: candidate of science, doctor of science, senior lecturer, professor; then there are awards, Lenin Komsomol Award, State Award, Lenin Award. A person who is motivated to climb up this ladder must possess them all. Like a king who possesses a crown and a throne, these are symbols. You had to spend a lot of time for those symbols, but once you got them you could start thinking about the next step."

Levin said that even the process of earning a doctorate was more a lobbying campaign than a scholarly quest. "In those years, it was less of a scientific process and more a political process. And it has to be said that the political process—Berezovsky did that brilliantly."[10]

Berezovsky turned his attention to winning prestigious prizes; he set out for the first level, the Lenin Komsomol prize, and won it. Then he set out to win the far more difficult State Prize, which was awarded by a jury. To win the prize, he had to actively hustle for it; the art of convincing was as important as the science itself. Boguslavsky told me that Berezovsky threw his energy into seeking the honor, "building relations with people, getting references, getting all kinds of very important documentation to support the case." But, he recalled, Berezovsky failed to win the prize. "There was much more competition."

Berezovsky was undeterred. He told Boguslavsky that he had already decided on the next step: the Nobel Prize.

"His real goal was the Nobel Prize," Boguslavsky recalled. "He put the bar at that level, and he was really thinking how to approach this as a goal, this summit. He spent a hell of a lot of time, and did a good job, recruiting young, talented kids from the university, building his scientific team, building his muscles, brainstorming. He wasn't a real scientist in terms of doing particular work, like using techniques and methods. He wasn't good at that. But he was quite creative with certain ideas, using talented kids for the routine work. He was good at deciding what subject to attack and how to get a certain solution that could be applicable for the Nobel Prize. It was not a joke. It was an absolutely real thought."

"You know what stopped him?" Boguslavsky recalled. "*Perestroika.* It opened up another opportunity. If *perestroika* had not brought the commercial side, he would have been going after the Nobel Prize until he died."[11]

Berezovsky's path to wealth began with a simple want—a car. In the early 1980s, a personal car in Moscow was a rare possession. Boguslavsky had an old, battered red Zhiguli. Berezovsky coveted that car.

The Zhiguli model was a modified compact Fiat. It had been manufactured since 1970 at a colossal assembly line in the Volga River town of Togliatti, named after the Italian Communist leader. The Volga automobile factory, known as Avtovaz, was an entire Fiat assembly line, imported from Italy. From his work at the institute, Berezovsky had connections with Avtovaz and proposed a deal to Boguslavsky. He would send the old red Zhiguli to Togliatti and get it completely renovated—an almost unimaginable dream, since auto parts were extremely scarce. Berezovsky's deal was this: if he arranged the renovation, they would share the car.

"I said okay, fine," Boguslavsky told me. "I didn't like this shitty car, which broke down every day, because it was too old. It would be like a new car. And I remember, I asked him, who will deliver the car from Moscow to Togliatti?"

Berezovsky, who had just received his driver's license, replied that he would just drive the 634 miles to the auto factory. Boguslavsky was incredulous. "How can you? Two days ago you just got a license! How can you drive there?" Boguslavsky insisted that before taking the car, Berezovsky would have to demonstrate that he really knew how to drive. They set up a test. Boguslavsky parked the car on a ramp, setting the hand brake. He challenged Berezovsky to get in, start the car, and drive it forward without rolling back.

Berezovsky flunked—the car rolled backward. But then he turned on his charm. "He is very pushy when he wants to get to the target," Boguslavsky recalled. "He said, 'Leonid, don't worry. Everything will be just fine! Let me drive to Togliatti!" And Boguslavsky relented.

When the car came back, good as new, Boguslavsky didn't ask any questions. They shared the car; one week Boguslavsky drove it, the next week, Berezovsky. Soon Boguslavsky noticed: Each week, he drove five hundred kilometers and Berezovsky drove three thousand kilometers. The comet was unstoppable. "I cannot tell you how happy I was," Berezovsky recalled.[12]

As Soviet socialism degenerated, the authorities placed great faith in the idea that scientific research could rescue it. The central planners and party ideologues nurtured hope that science—empirical data, mathematical formulas, the best minds—could cure the long, slow economic stagnation. The Institute of Control Sciences was tightly interlocked with Soviet factories, as every researcher endeavored to "prove" that his science had reaped practical rewards in the economy. There is a Russian word that described this complex relationship, *vnedrenie*, literally introduction or inculcation. It meant that everything in science must be shown to be useful and practical.

"All theories, all formulas, all experiments ultimately had to have some kind of *vnedrenie,*" Oslon told me. "Any kind of technical discipline, including applied mathematics, mechanics, physics—all of this had to be 'inculcated.' What did inculcation mean? Every dissertation consisted of some practical part, in which the methods of application were described. How the scientists' theory is applied in practice: for a factory, for an institute, for a transportation system." The scientist sent the results to the factory, which then provided a document, known as an *akt,* to certify that the research had indeed been useful.

"Moreover, that it is not simply useful, but that it had an economic effect. So, there would be a note where it was written that, 'As a result of inculcation of the development of applicant for the degree of candidate of technical sciences, Mr. Ivanov, a savings of 10,000 rubles was obtained.' Signature, seal. That is why all the scientist-organizers, who had graduate students, collaborators and co-researchers, strove toward establishing connections with practical organizations." The *akt* would be followed by contracts for ongoing research, which in turn became a source of revenue for the institute.

Berezovsky's laboratory earned its *vnedrenie* from the Avtovaz plant in Togliatti. The plant was one of the largest industrial undertakings in the Soviet Union. It churned out hundreds of thousands of the little Zhigulis and accounted for over 1 percent of the entire economy. Oslon recalled the institute would typically have a plan: "Laboratory of Berezovsky. Client: the factory Avtovaz. Theme: development of the system of designing of automobiles." The laboratory wrote reports, the institute sent them to the factory, the factory paid the institute and sometimes the researchers.

But in the late Soviet years, everyone knew that *vnedrenie* had become a shell game, part of the business of jockeying for resources inside an economy of scarcity. No amount of scientific research was going to save the dinosaur of developed socialism, but the subsidies for research kept coming and the researchers kept insisting they were actually making industry better. "We had a foolish system," said Grodsky. "There existed a whole bunch of methods, calculations of how this formula had influenced the process of producing cars, whatever. It was very funny. It was kind of a game, and everybody was playing." He added, "Boris was a genius in the sense that he was one of the first people at the institute who established very profitable contacts between his lab and Avtovaz. It was money that people could live and work on."[13]

But Berezovsky had far greater visions than small-time favors and pocket change. He knew that the boxy little Zhiguli cars were the dream of Everyman. Avtovaz to him was more than a factory. It was a gold mine.

"I understood one important thing," Berezovsky told me. "At that time, an enormous number of people wanted to buy cars. It didn't matter if they lacked an apartment. It didn't matter if they lacked clothes. *But if only there would be a car!*"

Berezovsky paused. He was sitting in the nineteenth-century mansion he had transformed into a business club wearing a pressed white business shirt and an elegant maroon silk tie, sipping from a glass of red wine. He savored the memory, as if it had rushed back to him again through all the years, of how desperately people wanted a car of their own, a dream that he too had shared.

"Possessed," he told me, pausing again. "I remember myself. My first car appeared when I was forty years old. Half a car. One week mine, the other week his. And we didn't argue about it once. Not once."

The Volga automobile factory was built in the spirit of the triumph of socialism. In 1967 young Komsomol construction brigades from three hundred cities and towns converged on a barren site near the Volga River to erect what would become the largest automobile factory in the Soviet Union. They began excavating not just a mammoth factory but a whole factory city, including blocks of apartments to house

150,000 future autoworkers. For three and a half years, every day, forty-five thousand workers, two hundred bulldozers, five hundred construction cranes, one hundred excavators, and two thousand dump trucks labored to erect the new industrial metropolis.[14] The plant itself was a gigantic building, fourteen kilometers around the perimeter with twenty-one entrances. On April 19, 1970, the first car rolled off the assembly line, the VAZ 2101, a modified Fiat 124 with a tiny 1.2 liter engine and trademark squared-off nose and round headlamps. It was called the Zhiguli, named after the rolling hills on the west bank of the Volga River. Just three years later, the millionth Zhiguli was produced, and by 1974 the plant reached full production on three massive assembly lines, each with a capacity of 220,000 cars a year.

The scale of the factory was immense, but so was the demand for cars, just one of many consumer goods that had fallen into shortage.[15] In the late 1970s and early 1980s, the factory began to run afoul of the larger malfunctioning of central planning. Shortages of parts and bad workmanship plagued the little Zhiguli. By the years of *perestroika* in the late 1980s, the factory was rotting from within. Soon the vultures came to pick over the carcass.

The central planners created a car distribution system that had no relation to the market. Prices didn't really matter; color was irrelevant, a guarantee useless. The idea of kicking the tires and slamming the doors was ludicrous. The distribution was based on party, privilege, and connections: cars were sent to various groups, such as unions or enterprises or Komsomol, based on *svyazi*, and the groups decided who would get the prized vehicles. At issue was not whether you could buy a Zhiguli but whether you could get one after ten years of waiting on the list, and whether, if you got one, you would keep it or resell it immediately at a huge profit.

To make matters worse, the simple Zhiguli was not a breadbox, although it looked like one. It was a moderately complex piece of machinery that needed maintenance and spare parts, and they too slipped into the shadow economy. Like the cars, spare parts were distributed by the planners and not the market. Soon, as millions of Zhigulis began to wear out brake pads and foul spark plugs, as fenders were crunched and headlamps shattered, spare parts became a valuable second currency. They were tradable, portable, and always in demand. As the shortages grew, so did the value of the parts. It was a classic example of the socialist economic crack-up in slow motion. A

Zhiguli owner removed the windshield wiper blades from his car every time it was parked so they would not be stolen. The shortages grew more and more severe in the 1980s; at one point there were special gangs with giant suction cup devices. They would spot a clean, uncracked windshield, and, when no one was looking, stick the suction cups on it, pop it out, and steal it in a flash. Adding to the despair of car owners, the network of service stations were also chronically short of spare parts, and any kind of serious repair demanded not only a mechanic but spare parts. The 1,033 service centers could hardly cope, and during the period of Gorbachev's reforms, the black hole of auto spare parts became a gaping abyss.

Avtovaz was suffering not only because of the overall crisis of Soviet socialism. The factory was being destroyed from within by theft. Crude laws of supply and demand existed in the black markets. If something was in shortage, and was badly needed, the demand was met by stealing. If cars and spare parts were currency, then Avtovaz was an enormous treasure chest. The factory was theoretically owned and run by the state, but as state control weakened, others began to rob the treasure. So strong was the black market demand for spare parts that whole containers of them were brazenly stolen off the factory floor by criminals, causing the assembly line to grind to a halt. As criminals grew even more daring, they stood on the assembly line and chose which finished cars they would take. Moreover, the factory depended on a network of suppliers that was growing weaker as the Soviet Union itself was spinning apart. Cars right off the assembly line were traded to suppliers for desperately needed parts, which were being stolen anyway. The fences around Avtovaz became famous as a twenty-four-hour black market in parts and whole cars. Avtovaz, a company with 4 billion rubles in sales and $670 million a year in hard-currency earnings from exports, a vast warehouse of windshield wipers and carburetors that were extremely valuable, a phalanx of assembly lines producing modest but desperately sought automobiles, was being turned into an extremely lucrative bazaar. The managers of the factory knew that their plant was being dismembered, and they joined in the festival of theft. Everything was for the taking.

Berezovsky was losing his interest in science. His restless mind was wandering. "I have always done only what I loved," he told me years later. "I have never 'gone to work.' Right? I do only that which I love." Berezovsky also claimed that he had an acute sensitivity to the change going on around him. "You must look at the world through the eyes of a child," he said. He saw in 1988 that the Soviet Union was undergoing a profound transformation. Gorbachev had flung open the doors of opportunity; the cooperatives were springing to life; the first banks were opening. The long socialist experiment in collectivism was ending, and the advantage would fall to individuals who seized the moment, who could think for themselves. Berezovsky envisioned himself among them.

"Speaking bluntly, the tragedy for the majority of people was the state had taken care of them, and the state had cast them aside," Berezovsky recalled. "That is, overnight the state ceased to care about them, right? Millions of people ended up without social protection, couldn't go to the health clinic. People thought that someone was supposed to take care of them. The state, right? I didn't think that way. Maybe more quickly than others, I understood that this was the beginning of a new era."

Berezovsky leaped into the business world. By his account, his first deal was software. "We simply used the knowledge that I had gained professionally, from the institute, and the work we had done at the institute, and started to sell that work." Berezovsky was no Willy Loman, going door to door peddling his wares. He worked at a state institute and sold the software to the State Committee on Science and Technology, the powerful government agency that was a conduit between the Communist Party and the Soviet scientific establishment. Berezovsky said he "absolutely vulgarly lobbied our project" with the agency. "We convinced them that it was a good product, and we sold tens of thousands of copies of this software. And those were the first millions of rubles that we earned, and a million rubles at that time was a whole lot."[16]

Berezovsky was a relentless charmer. His friend Boguslavsky recalled that Berezovsky—the compressed ball of energy—could also display a certain studied patience when it suited his needs. He thought nothing of waiting on a doorstep to personally buttonhole someone for a favor. "There were not a few occasions when Boris needed something from me," Boguslavsky recalled, "and in the morning I would be walking downstairs, and I would see Boris at the entrance, just waiting for me. He was waiting because he wanted to fix something with me, and my phone was busy or turned off, and he wanted to do it right then—so he would just sit and wait at the entrance." The same scene—Berezovsky waiting patiently in a Kremlin anteroom, waiting in a television studio outer lobby, looking for a favor or a deal—would reappear over and over in the years to come.

The intrepid Berezovsky used the same patience and resolve to good advantage with one of the executives at Avtovaz, Vladimir Tikhonov, who often came to Moscow on business trips. According to Boguslavsky, when Tikhonov arrived in Moscow for meetings, Berezovsky, for whom no task was too humble, would volunteer to be his chauffeur. Tikhonov often met in Moscow with Italian auto industry chiefs and specialists who had designed the Togliatti plant. As they were shuttled around Moscow, their driver, Berezovsky, absorbed every word.

"Boris was never shy," Boguslavsky recalled, "if he needed something."

In January 1989 Gorbachev's economic reforms were still a matter of great uncertainty in the West. At the end of the previous year, a secret national intelligence estimate prepared by the CIA and other U.S. intelligence agencies opened with a declaration that "Gorbachev's efforts at reviving the Soviet economy will produce no substantial improvement over the next five years." There is "some chance that Gorbachev's economic programs may not survive."[17]

In the end, Gorbachev survived in office only three more years. But 1989 turned out to be a remarkable political turning point toward the end of the Cold War. The Soviet Union pulled its last troops out of Afghanistan; the Communist Party began to lose its monopoly on power; the Berlin Wall fell; and in the spring, the Congress of People's Deputies became the first popularly elected legislature in Soviet history. Despite pessimism about Gorbachev's future in the U.S. intelligence community, the economic revolution he had unleashed was unfolding on the streets and in the cooperatives. One very small glimpse of it could be seen in a café on Moscow's Leninsky Prospekt, where the first roots of Berezovsky's capitalist empire were sunk into the earth.

The café was called Adriatica, and in January 1989 Berezovsky, Boguslavsky, and Pyotr Aven, a mathematician-economist who had worked with Gaidar in Moscow, as well as some other friends, gathered there to start a business. They didn't have a clear idea. They were just being carried along by the times; everyone around them was going into business, and they were already a little bit late. Boguslavsky said the idea was to set up a legal "shell," into which each of them could bring their own deals. They rented a small room and put up a chalkboard on which they wrote ideas for the fledgling business. A detailed account of those years was written by Yuli Dubov, who became a deputy to Berezovsky. He has called the book a novel—he changed the names of the participants and added some unrelated events to spice up the story—but he has also said, "I painted what I saw." Many people I spoke with who knew Berezovsky in those years described the book, *Bolshaya Paika*, as the most precise account of the period, although it is sometimes overly generous in its portrayal of Berezovsky.[18] Dubov listed the ideas that the novice businessmen wrote on the board:

> We need our own bank.
>
> At least we need to organize normal conditions here! We spend days here, and there is nothing to guzzle!
>
> I suggest we get seriously involved in medicine.
>
> We need normal phones. And at least one Xerox machine.

What would the business do? In some cases, they threw in existing individual projects, such a computer networking contract that Boguslavsky had in Czechoslovakia. It brought in early cash. While his friends were casting about, Berezovsky had a vision. He wanted to start a big business, nothing like the small cooperatives then dotting Moscow street corners. He decided to form a joint venture with a foreign partner, which would be more solid than a cooperative and could be useful in getting money out of the country. Aven told me that Berezovsky always had the largest ambitions of anyone in the group. "Berezovsky always wanted to have a billion dollars," he said. "He always would take higher risks."

From his days as a driver for Tikhonov, and from his expanding contacts at the factory, Berezovsky learned of an Italian company, Logosystem SpA, a systems integrator based in Turin and a Fiat supplier. The specialists from Logosystem frequently flew to the Soviet Union to fix the assembly line at Avtovaz. When Western businessmen came to the Soviet Union, they were often bewildered by an array of problems and inconveniences. Berezovsky knew he could smooth out their troubles. Berezovsky offered to become an intermediary for the Italians, giving them a base in Moscow for their work with Avtovaz. They agreed. In May 1989, Berezovsky founded Logovaz—borrowing half the name from the Italian Logosystem and half from Avtovaz.

For Berezovsky, the sprawling Avtovaz plant in Togliatti was fertile ground for his human networking talents. "When he got to Avtovaz, he started to search," Aven told me. "What did the executives need? They needed connections in Moscow, and they didn't have them. They wanted to go abroad with an Academy of Sciences delegation, and he could help them."

His first major break came with Alexander Zibarev, who was then a deputy general director of the factory in charge of spare parts. Berezovsky made a classic connection: he brought Zibarev to the institute to work on a dissertation, which was essential for any up-and-coming Soviet industrial manager. In 1987 Zibarev received a candidate of science degree from the institute based on his thesis, "Perfecting the Centralized Mechanism of the Distribution of Spare Parts for Automobiles," using Avtovaz as an example. Zibarev later defended his doctoral dissertation too. Berezovsky told me that he took a "very active part in the work on that dissertation."

Zibarev "wanted to be respected," Berezovsky recalled. "And to defend a candidate's dissertation, that means respect." Berezovsky insisted that Zibarev wrote the dissertation himself, although "he discussed very many things with me."

In turn, Zibarev helped Berezovsky, bringing him to the executive suites of Avtovaz, where Berezovsky met Vladimir Kadannikov, the head of the enterprise. Kadannikov was considered part of a new generation of *perestroika* industrial managers and had become director in 1986. Berezovsky wanted the factory to serve as one of the founders, as well as a client, of his new company, Logovaz. According to Boguslavsky, the powerful Kadannikov at first didn't see the point—why did he need an intermediary with the Italians? But finally, Boguslavsky said, Kadannikov agreed to give Berezovsky money just to get him out of his hair. "Initially, he was very skeptical," recalled Boguslavsky, who became deputy director of Logovaz. Later Kadannikov became more enthusiastic.

Dubov, the author, told me that Berezovsky came across to the Avtovaz executives as someone who could think big, as they did. "He simply understood that, of course, you could first create a cooperative, a small one, and then come to Avtovaz and say, 'I have a small cooperative, let's work.' But you could also come to Avtovaz and say, 'Let's create an enterprise together.' What sense did it make to come to Avtovaz with another cooperative? Some fifty cooperatives would have already been there, and he would have been the fifty-first. But he was the only one to come and say, 'Let's work together.'" Both Zibarev and Kadannikov eventually became part of Logovaz while keeping their positions at the factory. Kadannikov proved key in making deals that were profitable for Logovaz at the expense of his own factory, Avtovaz. But this awkward position was not unusual for the times—most top executives were scrambling for a piece of the action on the side.

In his novel, Dubov described the first meeting with Kadannikov as a seminal moment. The director "didn't retain in his memory any details of the meeting and failed to feel anything important about it. But he should have. Precisely at that moment a small knot was tied, and a tiny thread began to stretch. And this thread was to develop into a net, sometimes visible, sometimes not, but a very solid one, that would later seize the fate of the country, that of the factory, and the fate of many people, including the director himself. And very likely some of these people, having a more fine intuition, would have flinched at that minute and looked at their watches. Because the first brick was laid in the foundation of the financial empire." That empire, in real life, was called Logovaz.

With the Logovaz structure in place, Berezovsky began to build an automobile empire. "In the first stage," Berezovsky told me, "everything that Logovaz did, I tried to do myself. That is, I wanted to see how it worked." For example, Berezovsky planned to sell secondhand imported cars. He went to Germany, bought a Mercedes, and drove it back to Moscow, where the car could be resold at a fantastic profit.[19] He made the trip to Germany and back ten times.[20]

The future tycoon discovered that business required guts and risk taking. But he retained his early impulsiveness. Without much advance planning, he decided to import a fleet of 846 small Fiats. Berezovsky recalled that he persuaded Avtovaz to give him a loan of $5 million to buy the Fiats. How he got the loan is not clear, but Berezovsky had connections with the company's top brass, including Kadannikov. What sounds like a simple transaction—importing foreign cars—was not at all simple in Soviet times. Berezovsky said he brought in the cars "absolutely officially, put them through customs, and organized their transportation" from Europe to Moscow. "Brought them to Moscow, sold them, and we at that time earned more or less

$3 million. At that time, this was colossal money. That was the first real business that I had done except for software."

Boguslavsky said the Fiat deal originated with Berezovsky's joint venture partner, Logosystem, in Turin. "It really was a hell of a job; it was so risky!" Boguslavsky recalled. "And this was one story that shows Berezovsky's mentality. Basically, other people would probably spend months just checking everything, trying to understand if they would fail or not." But Berezovsky "jumped on the opportunity immediately." Boguslavsky recalled that "a real crisis" ensued because Logovaz was not prepared to receive the cars, which were obsolete by Western standards and had been parked in a lot in Scandinavia for a year. Boguslavsky's memory was that Logovaz got a bad deal with the Fiats and earned no profit, only "three million dollars of experience rather than three million dollars of cash."

Dubov described a far more colorful account of the Fiat deal in *Bolshaya Paika*, although it may be slightly exaggerated. The cars were approaching the Russian border, he wrote, when someone noticed a government rule that such cars could not be imported for retail sale; they could only be imported for "internal use" by an authorized importer, of which there were only one or two—and Logovaz was not among them. The Berezovsky character in Dubov's account was in Italy, and when the Logovaz office called from Moscow to tell him of the snafu, he replied, "Stay cool, guys." The next day, the Berezovsky character discovered a state enterprise next door to the institute that was authorized to import cars, and he called the director.

"It was Friday," Dubov wrote, "and so for two days and two nights, they wined and dined the director and two of his deputies, called up girls for them from the Metropol Hotel, gave them gifts, and by Sunday evening they signed documents" allowing the cars to be imported.

Boguslavsky said the deal for the Fiats whetted their appetite for the real gold mine: becoming a nationwide dealer for the sought-after Zhigulis. To Berezovsky the cars were a symbol of potential riches. He did not have good connections in other industries, but he had built them in the auto factory. "For him, the car business was always associated with big business," Boguslavsky recalled.

Once the pride of young Komsomol construction workers with a glint of socialist idealism in their eyes, the factory was literally coming apart at the seams in the last year of the Soviet Union. The managers began to form their own companies, taking advantage of their connections. They bought the cars cheaply off the assembly line or the rail cars and resold them for quick superprofits, often out of lots elsewhere in Togliatti. They were nothing more than middlemen, and the trade was so lucrative that they found themselves jockeying with criminal gangs for the right to claim the cars still coming off the assembly line every day. The old system of distribution by *svyazi* was falling apart and the new system was chaotic, violent, and exceedingly lucrative. "In Togliatti, they started growing like mushrooms," recalled Yuri Tselikov, a midlevel Avtovaz executive, referring to the middlemen and a wave of crime and violence that swept through the factory city in those days. "Cars were given to them, and they started to stuff their pockets."[21]

The factory was a state enterprise that had been built by the state and received state subsidies. The Zhigulis came out of the gate with artificially low, subsidized state prices. Then they were sold at a huge markup. The traders were effectively sucking the value out of Avtovaz, but they were doing it with the permission of the managers inside. In some cases, they *were* the managers. Valery Ivanov, a tall, dark-haired, harried, and courageous journalist for a local weekly newspaper, the *Togliatti Review,* documented the many ways in which the factory began to fall apart in the 1990s. The result of his probing articles was a spate of angry threats. He recalled that the mushrooming private firms arranged a deal with Avtovaz management. They would take a batch of cars—one hundred or two hundred—on "consignment," meaning that they could take the cars now for a small sum and pay the rest back later, or not at all. "It was a theft scheme, crudely put," Ivanov recalled. The bureaucrats who worked in the factory took bribes to grease the way for the deals, which were measured in a special code: the height in centimeters of a stack of dollars. "And so they would say, for that contract, well, five centimeters of dollars."[22]

Thuggery and theft erupted at Avtovaz in other ways as well. When criminal groups stood on the assembly line and claimed the cars as they rolled off, anyone who interfered would suffer; violence spread. Anatoly Ivanov, a union leader and an electronic technician at the factory, told me how he spoke out once in a newspaper interview against a scheme, which was widely used, of false exports of Zhiguli cars. Since markets in Eastern Europe were growing more competitive, Avtovaz often shipped cars there and sold them at a loss. The official explanation was that Avtovaz was cutting prices in an attempt to hold on to its share of the market. But Ivanov and many others suspected that the scheme was designed to suck the lifeblood out of the factory. He believed that the cars were not really exported. The documents were taken over the border and stamped, but the actual cars were resold on the domestic market at a huge markup. Ivanov asked, "If the factory has no money, why are we sending these cars out to export, an export where the cars don't even arrive?" A week after these remarks were published, Ivanov was leaving for work before dawn. A hired killer lurked at the entrance to his apartment. The gunman fired and wounded Ivanov in the leg. Ivanov later was elected to the Russian parliament from Togliatti.[23]

Dubov, in *Bolshaya Paika,* offered a graphic description of the chaos at the factory. He wrote that the police no longer needed to cultivate sources to learn about the Russian criminal world. "It was enough to spend just one week at the factory. Without hiding, representatives of all criminal groups wandered about the factory."

"The cars were distributed among them at the assembly line," he went on. "An agreement had been made not to carry out *razborki* (violent showdowns) on the factory premises; that is why everybody behaved quietly, closely observing their competitors' actions. Meanwhile, outside the factory, explosions and shots rang out. The big automobile war invaded half the country."

"The chronicle of actions was horrifying. In Moscow . . . a real battle took place, with no fewer than fifty people involved. Result: six people killed, unknown number of wounded, three cars burned, and a police car blown up from a grenade launcher. . . . A series of explosions in 'pocket banks' that were providing services to this or that criminal group. People disappearing. Raids on saunas and restaurants where the leaders of the criminal world were celebrating automobile deals. It smelled of blood and gunpowder."[24]

The suppliers were also caught in the web of violence and coercion. "The director of one tire factory, who didn't sense the situation right away, was put on the window sill and asked whether he knew on what floor his office was located, and how long was the distance to the pavement. The director flinched and immediately signed approval for a shipment of train cars with tires, not even asking how and when they would be paid for."

As the factory sank into the mire of lawlessness, the methods used to drain value out of the enterprise multiplied. One of the most common was the reexport scheme. Ivanov and others have suggested that Berezovsky was part of this scheme. Berezovsky insisted to me that it "was never done" by Logovaz. But it was one of the most common methods of making a fortune from the factory in the years Berezovsky was associated with Avtovaz.

Berezovsky described for me his own ambitious plan. He struck a deal with Avtovaz and Kadannikov that would multiply his capital many times over and launch him on the path to becoming one of Russia's richest men. Instead of small consignments of one hundred or two hundred cars, Berezovsky persuaded the factory to give Logovaz a huge fleet of cars on consignment—tens of thousands. Ivanov put the first batch at thirty-five thousand Zhigulis. Berezovsky told me the terms were 10 percent down and the remainder to be paid two and a half years later.

The hidden trick in the deal was that Berezovsky was going to repay Avtovaz in rubles—and hyperinflation was just around the corner. The hyperinflation meant that he would pay back for the cars in rubles that were worth far less than they had been when he bought the cars.

For example, in January 1993, the wholesale price of a basic Zhiguli, the model VAZ 2104, was 1.9 million rubles, or about $3,321.[25] The Logovaz retail price for this car, also in January 1993, was $4,590, or a markup of $1,269 per car.[26] Over the next two and a half years of inflation, the ruble went from 527 to the dollar, when Berezovsky made the deal, to 4,726 to the dollar.[27] The deal meant that Berezovsky was getting the cars for a song and paying for them in currency that was rapidly turning to toilet paper. (Another way to look at the deal was this: after the down payment, he agreed to pay the ruble equivalent of $2,989 later for each car, but in fact, after two and a half years of inflation, he would pay back only the ruble equivalent of $360 for each car.) He knew what he was doing. If he took a consignment of thirty-five thousand cars and made, conservatively, $3,000 on each—between the markup and the currency margin—that was a $105 million deal.

"Of course, we would return the money as late as we could, because the value of the money was falling," Berezovsky told me. "We understood that a powerful process of inflation was going on. The devaluation of the ruble. The economists at Avtovaz didn't understand this."

"We were considering things that those on the other side were not considering," Berezovsky said. While chaos reigned outside the factory gates and criminals lurked on the assembly line, Berezovsky described Logovaz, which created a network of dealerships, as above the fray. The smaller gangsters who took the cars on "consignment" didn't pay the factory back at all.

"We were the first in Russia to create a market, a real market for cars," Berezovsky claimed. "Before, it existed only like this: the government price is this, and the 'black price' is this. And we created a real market. Any person could come officially to a store and buy a car. That is a market, isn't it?" Years later, Kadannikov was asked if he regretted giving the cars to Berezovsky. "I cannot regret it," he replied. "It was clear to me why we were giving them the automobiles for sale, because before it was not sales we had, but 'distribution.' Then everything collapsed. Our grounds can keep no more than ten thousand automobiles, which is three days' work. We needed to find a place for others in order to keep the plant in production. Logovaz came to us with a dealer network." In fact, Kadannikov was almost giving away the cars, allowing Avtovaz to be further drained of its lifeblood.

But even as he became the largest Zhiguli dealer, Berezovsky was still restless. In a philosophical mood, he had once quoted the great physicist and human rights advocate Andrei Sakharov as saying "the meaning of all life is expansion." Berezovsky was looking for expansion. Dubov observed in *Bolshaya Paika* that the "wild outburst of uncontrolled business" at Avtovaz was "a serious threat. It was obvious that it couldn't continue this way. But it was also obvious that the factory's leadership, stuck under the various bandit 'roofs,' was unable to undertake any constructive action."

The factory itself was a valuable prize. In 1991 the Wall Street firm of Bear Stearns was commissioned to do a study of Avtovaz for potential foreign investors. Its report said nothing about gangsters at the gates but underscored the assets: a factory three times the size of the average U.S. automobile plant, with four assembly lines, capacity to produce 740,000 cars a year, and a country of people who were hungry, absolutely desperate to fulfill the dream of owning a car. In the Soviet Union there was one car for every 22.8 people, compared with one for every 1.7 in the United States.[28] There was a fortune waiting to be had. According to Dubov, Berezovsky "decided to stake his all."

"To take the factory for himself."[29]

Chapter 7

Vladimir Gusinsky

THE DAWN OF *perestroika* found Vladimir Gusinsky at a dead end. An easily insulted young man with outsized emotions, Gusinsky had trained as a stage director but failed to find a place in the world of Moscow theater. He was a Jew, and he believed that anti-Semitism was the unspoken reason why doors slammed in his face. Jewish directors had made it in the Soviet theater, but not Gusinsky. He had dabbled in staging public concerts and cultural events, and he even helped produce the entertainment for the Goodwill Games in 1986. But those days had turned sour when he got in trouble with Moscow's Communist Party committee for a harmless prank. He told them to go to hell.

In the mid-1980s, Gusinsky was going nowhere. He drove his car as an unofficial taxi, carrying passengers to and from the new international airport, earning cash to support his wife and young son, and hoping to restart his life.

Late one evening, Gusinsky, who was skinny and wore a leather jacket, stepped out of his car to smoke a cigarette. By chance, he had stopped near an electric streetcar depot. He glanced at a back lot where they kept the big electric transformers.

"I turned around and suddenly I saw a vein of gold," he recalled. "What was it? A huge wooden reel, two meters tall, wound with copper cable—copper cable that was used for the transformer of the streetcar. It was long, pure copper. And I realized, here it is, the gold mine!"

The gold mine was copper bracelets, which had become a craze at the time. They had a faintly oriental appeal, and people wore them to fend off illnesses or evil spirits. Gusinsky took one look at the wooden spool of copper wire, officially state property, and finagled three reels for next to nothing. He found an idle state factory with a metal-stamping machine on the edge of Moscow. For some cash on the side, he arranged for high-quality metal-stamping molds to be fashioned at a closed military factory. Soon the six stamping machines were working overtime.

Gusinsky started a cooperative and quickly became king of copper bracelets in the Soviet Union. The simple bracelets carried an imprint of two tiny dragons and were imprinted with the word "Metal," the name of Gusinsky's fledgling business. The stamping machines worked around the clock in three shifts, each machine capable of six strikes per minute. Soon the cooperative was stamping out 51,840 bracelets a day. The bracelets cost him three kopeks to make and he sold them for five rubles apiece. In a single day, his revenues were 259,200 rubles, more than five hundred times the monthly salary of a doctor of science at a leading institute. "In those days," he recalled, "it was gigantic profit." Gusinsky had made his first fortune and restarted his life.[1]

He was born October 2, 1952, an only child, into one of the millions of Soviet families that had known the pain of repression. Gusinsky's maternal grandfather was shot during Stalin's purges. His grandmother had spent ten years in the gulag and after World War II was ordered to live at least one hundred kilometers from the center of Moscow as part of the sentence. Gusinsky's mother and her sister had nonetheless entered Moscow undetected and lived with friends. His mother even attended the Gubkin Institute for Oil and Gas without being caught. Gusinsky's father, Alexander, was a simple man without any higher education. He had served in the Red Army during the war and worked at a factory making custom cutting tools.

Gusinsky and his parents lived in one room, an eighteen-square-meter flat in a working-class neighborhood. As a boy, he often felt resentment welling up in him. "I was a youngster and I knew already that the word 'Yid' was an insult," Gusinsky told me. "Just like all the boys, I was very afraid of fighting at the beginning. I used to think that for sure if I hit my adversary hard and hurt him, he would certainly hit me back and I would be hurt even more—so I was scared. And then it so happened that some guys a bit older than me drove me into a corner in the courtyard and started pestering and insulting me. And I remember this strange feeling, a sudden complete sense of freedom: it did not matter to me what they were going to do to me." That time, Gusinsky struck back, thinking he must fight back "while I still can."

"I was never scared to fight, one street against another, courtyard versus courtyard," he recalled. Once, a group of older men were drinking vodka and playing dominoes after work in the courtyard. Gusinsky was ten or eleven years old, and as he came home after school on a warm afternoon, the older men chided, "Here comes the little Yid." Gusinsky erupted with rage. He seized an iron pipe and flailed at the tormentors, who ran from him, frightened that he had gone mad. "I was in tears and I was chasing them with a pipe around the whole courtyard," Gusinsky recalled. "I was in tears from fury and insult, not from fear."

Gusinsky grew up "on the street," as he later put it. "I am a product of the street. I was born in the street and learned to defend myself in the street."

After studying mathematics in high school, he felt the sting of prejudice again when he tried to enroll in the theoretical physics department at the Moscow Physics-Engineering Institute. It was a prestigious school that prepared specialists for the Soviet military-industrial complex. Jews were unwanted. "I really knew mathematics and physics well. I was absolutely confident. Everybody was telling me: they don't take Jews there." Gusinsky said he ignored their advice. He applied—and was rejected. He was offended, and angry.

Gusinsky enrolled instead at the Gubkin Institute of Oil and Gas because his mother had studied there. Gusinsky was a bad student at the school that students fondly called Kerosinka. "I was not interested," he acknowledged. "I took offense at everyone, almost against the whole world." Gusinsky did not finish his studies at Gubkin. By his own account he dabbled in the black market, working as a *fartzovschik*—daring young traders who dealt in imported jeans and audiocassettes and changed money for foreign tourists. Gusinsky recalled that he couldn't get the hang of being a so-called speculator. "I bought several pairs of jeans, then I tried to sell them and it turned out I sold them cheaper than I bought them," he told me ruefully. Gusinsky often joked that he was not cut out to be a street trader. However, in later years, he showed a knack for entrepreneurship that far overshadowed his lack of skills as a jeans trader.

Having failed his classes at the institute, Gusinsky went into the army in 1973, where he was trained as a junior sergeant in the chemical intelligence troops. These units would enter the battle zone after a chemical or biological weapons attack. But Gusinsky's strongest memory of the army was that he had to stand his ground. "I had perfect relations with everybody in the army except for complete idiots and scoundrels," he recalled. "I only lost several teeth in the army, so nothing horrible was going on—these were the usual fistfights; it happens. In two years in the army, I learned only one thing, the ability to fight for myself."

After the military, he was adrift back in Moscow. A friend urged him to enroll in another prestigious school, the State Institute for the Study of Theatrical Arts. Gusinsky replied that he had not read Stanislavsky or Shakespeare or Molière. But with two months before the entrance exams, he decided to try. He spent nights poring over books. His friend reassured him, "Piece of cake—you'll make it," but Gusinsky feared that Jews were not welcome at the institute; the theater, like film, was under strict Communist Party control.

The oral exams were given by a renowned director, Boris Ravenskikh, chief stage director of Moscow's Maly Theater. At the time of the exams, Gusinsky, still thin as a rail and angry at the world, came before Ravenskikh for the required interview. Behind Gusinsky was Valery Belyakovich, another drama student.

Ravenskikh asked Gusinsky, "Why are you going to study stage directing?"

"I want to understand life," he replied. "A lot in this life surprises me."

"What surprises you most?" Ravenskikh asked.

"Lack of communication between people," Gusinsky responded. "People have lost the ability to understand each other."[2]

Ravenskikh immediately took an interest in the intense young man, who was the only one in the class with no drama experience.

"He believed very much in the idea that a stage director is a person with life experience," Gusinsky recalled. "He was selecting people by intuition. And he told me, 'I'll take you.'"

But Gusinsky again felt touched by anti-Semitism. Ravenskikh was warned by a party official: "What are you doing? Out of fifteen people for this year, you are taking three Jews!" According to Gusinsky, Ravenskikh did not like to be pressured. Ravenskikh stubbornly insisted that he remain in the class.

At the institute, Gusinsky was always brimming with jokes and running in a dozen directions. Despite shortages everywhere, Gusinsky found scarce white paint to spruce up the theater at the institute. He found a pair of speakers and wired up a sound system. He put his hands on a tape recorder when his class needed one. He brought scarce or banned LPs to his friends. "He gave me a record of Krokus, it was Polish!" Belyakovich recalled. "It was banned—a very expensive gift, because it was impossible to get even a Polish LP. I had no other LPs." At the lunch hour at the institute, Gusinsky often took five friends, packed them into his tiny car—he was the only one with a car—and they dashed away from the campus for a break.

Gusinsky "was always taking us to theaters; he had connections everywhere," Belyakovich remembered. "In those days it was hard to get tickets; it was always difficult." It was practically impossible to get into Moscow's famous Lenkom Theater, but Gusinsky managed to do it for a preview of *Yunona and Avos,* a hugely popular rock musical that blazed new trails in the theater at the time because it lacked ideology. Gusinsky told his classmates to show up at the Lenkom at 10:30 A.M. and instructed them to wait for him outside until he gave the signal: "And then I whistle, and you follow me!"

Soon Gusinsky had them inside for a rehearsal right behind the director. The first part of Gusinsky's last name means goose in Russian, and that was his nickname. "He was swimming like this all the time," Belyakovich said, "and we would ask him, '*Gus,* can you get us tickets for this?' And he would say, 'Wait,' he had a lot of acquaintances. He was different because of his communicativeness and networks. But bringing twelve people in was very top class! He introduced us as stage directors, claiming that we had to be there."

His teacher, Ravenskikh, left an impression on Gusinsky. Ravenskikh refused to be pushed around and was willing to experiment even within the regimented, ideological realm of Soviet theater. Ravenskikh once was ordered to stage Brezhnev's sugary ghost-written war memoir, *Malaya Zemlya,* at the Kremlin Palace of Congresses. The book describes Brezhnev's role in a 1943 battle in which the Eighteenth Army captured and held a piece of land, Malaya Zemlya, on the Black Sea for 225 days. The role of the battle was played up after Brezhnev came to power, but Brezhnev had done nothing out of the ordinary. Ravenskikh went to the scene of the battle to ponder his assignment. He did not want to do it, but refusing would be risky. He then returned to Moscow and declared that he could not do the play and would not: Brezhnev's role had been overstated.

Under Ravenskikh's tutelage at the institute, students pushed the boundaries of what was permissible. They could breathe more freely at the institute than on the formal stage. Gusinsky and his class read and staged a part of Nicholai Erdman's play *The Suicide,* a black comedy about an ordinary Soviet citizen who is driven by despair to attempt suicide but is finally too cowardly to carry it out. The play had been banned in 1932 and was never officially staged in the Soviet Union.

For graduation, students were required to stage a play in a real theater, not at the institute. Moscow was the center of theatrical life, yet it was nearly impossible for students to stage their diploma plays in the capital, and it was quite common to look for a stage in the provinces. For his diploma work, the equivalent of his graduate thesis, Gusinsky went to Tula, a hardscrabble industrial town south of Moscow. At the Tula State Dramatic Theater during the 1979–1980 winter season, the ever enthusiastic, ever thin, ever emotional Gusinsky staged *Tartuffe,* by Jean-Baptist Molière, the seventeenth-century French playwright. The show was billed as a comedy, an experimental one-act play by students. Importantly, it borrowed fragments from a work on Molière by the twentieth-century Russian writer and playwright Mikhail Bulgakov, which Bulgakov wrote in the second half of 1929.[3] As Gusinsky was well aware, Bulgakov had focused on the relationship between the artist and power, between Molière and Louis XIV. The tense relationship between artist and dictator was one that Bulgakov knew well through his own great heartache and pain in the early Stalin years. His play about Molière was rehearsed for four years—but banned after only seven performances.

By 1979 Bulgakov was no longer totally prohibited but was still informally proscribed. Gusinsky's performance in Tula gained a popular following in part because it also was slightly beyond what was usually permitted by the authorities. The audience entered the theater to guitar music or a band. Alexander Minkin, a lively, bearded drama critic who later became a well-known Moscow journalist, had studied at the theater institute at the same time as Gusinsky. Minkin concentrated on theory and criticism, while Gusinsky's training was practical as a stage director. Minkin told me that Gusinsky implored him to come to Tula to see the premiere—to take an *elektrichka,* a commuter train, four hours to Tula!—but he refused. "I thought in advance that it was going to be horrible, it was going to be rubbish," Minkin recalled. "I didn't think he was a good director." Moreover, he added, "Moliere is always very boring. He is a classic, but a boring one. That is why I believed neither in Gusinsky nor in the fact that he could stage Moliere."[4]

But Minkin changed his mind and went to Tula, and Gusinsky's production turned out to be a popular hit. "I laughed so much, my stomach ached," Minkin recalled. "It was done with such taste, with such humor!" According to the *Moscow News*, the house was full every night, and Tula youth talked about nothing other than *Tartuffe*.[5] Gusinsky was the heart and soul of his company, working with them late at night, driving them home in his car, bringing them gifts of sausage from Moscow.

Gusinsky had been lucky in Tula; the authorities allowed him to stage a play that was slightly off-key to the trained ear of the Soviet propagandist. Moreover, Gusinsky had added sonnets from Shakespeare, including a strongly antiauthoritarian sonnet at the close.

"It was not against Soviet power, it was about a rebellion of a man, an artist, against any power," Gusinsky remembered. "And it was not anti-Soviet; it was just that they are all crazy, all our fucking Soviet power, all those Communists—they believe that anything going beyond certain boundaries is aimed against them." Gusinsky took his play to Kiev, where it was closed down by the party city committee for being anti-Soviet after a few performances. The party bosses wrote a complaint to the Central Committee in Moscow. "It was probably then that I learned that I could not march in formation," Gusinsky recalled, referring to the rigid conformity demanded by the party.

Gusinsky "stubbornly wanted to stage the next play in Moscow," Minkin told me. "Year after year, he went and bowed from the waist to everybody—to the Culture Ministry of the USSR, to the Culture Ministry of the Russian Republic, to the Cultural Department of

Moscow. He went everywhere, including all the theaters. He asked them to give him a stage. He asked head directors, theatrical leaders—nothing. And every week he hoped, because someone had promised him something. And he waited, waited, and waited. And another six months passed, and nothing again. He started anew, and he was given some promise anew, and he waited again. But that was horrible. He wasn't doing anything! There was energy in him like an atomic bomb, but there was no way out."

The Moscow theater world was crowded and competitive, and it would have been painstakingly difficult for Gusinsky to break into it under any circumstances. He had good connections, having studied under Ravenskikh and the renowned Yuri Lyubimov, director of the Taganka Theater. But he still could not break down the barriers and get a play to the stage in Moscow. Gusinsky believed the reason was anti-Semitism, and perhaps his lack of talent. "I am a Jew. It was prohibited. Plus, in fact, I was not a very talented stage director."

Through the early 1980s, Gusinsky searched in vain for a place in the theater. His quest was a long and frustrating one. "Many times he told me, 'This is my last attempt,'" Minkin remembered. "'If they deceive me once more, if they don't let me stage a play, I will go into business. I won't take it any longer.'"

He found work organizing public events such as concerts and sports. As stage director for Ted Turner's Goodwill Games in 1986, he organized the opening and closing ceremony, setting up performances at the Kremlin Palace of Congresses for the foreign participants. He enjoyed good connections with the Komsomol and the KGB. But when I asked him about it years later, he said it was dreary. "I was simply earning money," he said.

Minkin was more blunt. "That was shit," he recalled of the events Gusinsky organized. "For a theater director to be involved in that was horrible. Is this real work for a director—to stage how girls walk and throw those stupid sticks? No, that's impossible." Minkin recalled that Gusinsky was still dreaming of a break into the theater at the beginning of *perestroika,* hoping that changes in the political mood might leave him an opening. But one day his organizing of public events took a turn for the worse because of a stretch of black ribbon.

In the early days of *perestroika,* Gusinsky organized a Day of the Theater, sponsored by the Komsomol city committee. On the broad main avenue in Moscow then known as Kalininsky Prospekt, Gusinsky set up a string of small outdoor cafés with special themes: one for writers, one for artists, one for musicians. "All was well because this was a day of culture, and I took very earnestly everything that Gorbachev was saying—here, it started, freedom came." But one thing had not changed: the party tightly controlled public space, especially open squares and buildings. Kalininsky Prospekt was a special street, the route that party leaders and others took to the Kremlin. Some of the artists who were helping Gusinsky decided to *change* the way Kalininsky Prospekt looked, and they laced the trees with black ribbon. It was a harmless gesture, but some low-level KGB men took offense. Gorbachev might see it as his limousine sped toward the Kremlin! They hauled Gusinsky before the Komsomol city committee and accused him of anti-Soviet activity. As he had many times before, Gusinsky got his back up. He lashed out. He argued with the Komsomol chiefs as they demanded he change this, change that, hew to the party line. And they insisted that he apologize to everyone in the Gorkom, the city Communist Party committee.

Gusinsky erupted. He shouted that they were fools, that their parents had been fools, that they would die fools. He slammed the door and walked out. The Day of the Theater was to be held in two days. They canceled some of the events and flooded the rest with uniformed and plainclothes security men, a tactic designed to throw a wet blanket on any public event. The local KGB men wanted to lock up this impertinent young man, Gusinsky, and throw away the key, but Gusinsky told me years later they did not succeed. They "were prevented from eating me up, let's put it this way," he recalled. "I was not staging any more mass performances; this was the last one. But they were not given the chance to finish me off."

The episode proved a valuable lesson for Gusinsky. He realized that he had to work on maintaining good relations with people in power, even if he despised them. At the time, he was quietly protected by a high-ranking party official, Yuri Voronov, who was deputy head of the Culture Department of the Central Committee. There was another episode too. According to a close friend, Gusinsky in this period was also caught trading hard currency, which was forbidden. No charges were ever brought against Gusinsky, the friend said, but as a result of the brush with the authorities, Gusinsky established close ties with some KGB officers. Gusinsky came to the attention of Filipp Bobkov, a deputy KGB director who headed the notorious Fifth Main

Directorate, which waged war on dissidents. Bobkov, whose job included keeping tabs on the intelligentsia, may have found Gusinsky a valuable source of information about what was happening in the theater. Many years later, Bobkov became part of Gusinsky's corporate high command. Gusinsky was learning how to cultivate friends in high places.[6]

The world of the early cooperatives in Moscow was wild and unpredictable. The whole idea of entrepreneurship had been labeled criminal in Soviet times, and the first businessmen were often regarded with deep suspicion, as hustlers at the edge of society, a ragtag bunch of experimenters and gamblers. In 1988 and 1989, Gusinsky fit in among them perfectly—he had the imagination and the guts. His almost instant success with the copper bracelets showed him how to make money fast, and his experience with the black ribbon scandal had pointed toward another essential ingredient of success: connections. The Communist Party was still all-pervasive; authority and power were something that had to be bought. To make money, Gusinsky realized, he needed connections. An aspiring businessman could not simply close his door and keep to himself; he needed to succor bureaucrats and politicians, to have friends in the KGB and the police. Gusinsky was an early and avid student of the nexus between wealth and power. He practiced cultivating politicians and security men, harboring them and exploiting them.

At first, the draw of power, the absolute beauty of making money by your own ingenuity and someone else's permission slip or signature, was appallingly simple. After the bracelets bonanza, Gusinsky opened a new cooperative that made cheap figurines, copies of famous Russian artworks from molded plaster. They were covered with a microthin layer of copper, using special chemical baths. As with the bracelets, the costs were minimal, the profits fantastic, and the copies were beautiful—as long as you did not notice the plaster core. Hood ornaments for foreign-made cars were very popular too; he made a mint with imitation Jaguar hood ornaments. But to duplicate Russian art he needed protection. He wanted to formally export the fake figurines, which would mean handling hard currency, and that was another reason he needed protection. Moreover, Gusinsky's cooperative was officially registered as part of the Soviet Cultural Foundation, of which Raisa Gorbachev was a board member. This government foundation was prohibited by Soviet law from engaging in commercial activities; if he flaunted the law, there could be trouble. Again Gusinsky found a way out by using his connections. He turned to Voronov, the Central Committee man who had protected him during the black ribbon scandal, and managed to get a letter of permission from the Soviet prime minister, Nicholai Ryzhkov, allowing him to export his fake figurines for hard currency. It is not clear precisely why the party man helped Gusinsky. But for Gusinsky, it was a fantastic mix: plaster, permission, and hard currency. Gusinsky told me it was his first big political success, and it led to more.

"I realized then there are ways of working with the authorities," Gusinsky said. At some lower levels, it was as simple as bribes. But Voronov and bureaucrats in the Central Committee were above this petty corruption, Gusinsky realized. He discovered that at higher levels, the trick was to establish good relations with officials. Finally, he learned somewhat later that it was also possible to influence the very highest officials, but the approach, the delicate dance, must be handled with great care. The key was to offer something the official needed to advance his career. Then bribes weren't even necessary, not even a good personal relationship, Gusinsky discovered. The official would almost always help, out of self-interest. "So it was always important for me to understand, what does this boss need?"

The most important boss Gusinsky would befriend in these years was Yuri Luzhkov, the stout, strong-willed bureaucrat who had been put in charge of Moscow's chaotic vegetable bases and also licensed the cooperatives. Gusinsky and Luzhkov had their quarrels and differences, but their paths were intertwined for more than a decade.

In the late 1980s, Gusinsky recalled, Luzhkov would meet well into the early morning hours with the young entrepreneurs of the cooperatives. Luzhkov listened patiently to their problems. It was foolish to go to Luzhkov's office before midnight because that's when he *began* working with the new businessmen, often not finishing before dawn. For Gusinsky, it was amazing: the average person in Moscow might wait on line for a week to see a local bureaucrat, but here was a man who was deputy head of the Moscow city executive committee who would see every single cooperative businessman in his waiting room before going home.

Luzhkov was a widower in those years, and late one evening he invited Gusinsky to his home. "A lonely man, he was not old then, but perfectly lonely," Gusinsky recalled. "He said, 'What shall we have, let's have tea.' I said, 'Let's drink tea.' Now, what have we got for tea? Out of his refrigerator he took a piece of stale, moldering rye bread. This I remember distinctly. He had nothing at home because he didn't live there. He would sometimes sleep there, but very often he simply spent the night at his office. Strange person. My relations with him then grew very warm."

In 1988 Gusinsky opened a cooperative, named Infeks, as a consulting company to help Western investors fathom the complexity of doing business in the Soviet Union. He was still a skinny young man wearing outsized eyeglasses and a big smile. For a fee, Gusinsky served as a fixer and provided legal advice and crude marketing data. He was working out of a cramped, windowless office on the far outskirts of Moscow, hardly a financial kingpin, but he was increasingly a man with connections who knew his way around the corridors of power.

Gusinsky's horizons were rapidly expanding beyond Moscow. In 1988 a group of American businesspeople came to Moscow looking for investment opportunities, among them Margery Kraus of APCO, a consulting firm owned by Arnold & Porter, then Washington's largest law firm. Kraus and Gusinsky quickly found that they understood each other and on December 13, 1988, announced plans for a joint venture partnership to bring business prospects to Moscow. When Western clients came to the capital, Gusinsky would help them navigate the often obscure world of the bureaucracy.[7] Kraus took Gusinsky to dinner one evening in Washington. She needed some cash afterward and walked with Gusinsky to an automatic teller machine to get the money. Gusinsky was wide-eyed. He had never seen such a thing. The machine was part of an electronic banking network called MOST, which was written on the ATM. Gusinsky adopted the name for his new joint venture and eventually for his Moscow bank. In Russian, the word "most" means bridge. Gusinsky said the new business would be his bridge to the outside. He told Kraus, "For us it will be a hard currency machine."

Boris Khait, then Gusinsky's deputy, recalled that APCO asked them to carry out a study of the food market because a midsize American fruit wholesaler wanted to know about the demand for fresh fruit. Gusinsky carried out a market "survey" by sending out students to question foreigners in the city, who, it was thought, would pay in hard currency. They were asked what kinds of fruit they wanted to buy in Moscow. Khait was puzzled to learn that the greatest demand was for something called "kiwi." Khait had been deputy director of a medical technology institute and considered himself a relatively well educated man. But he had never heard of a kiwi.[8]

Gusinsky took Luzhkov to the United States on a tour arranged by Kraus, his partner in Washington. Luzhkov, who still had crude ideas about economics, wanted to start a huge, centralized food manufacturing business in Moscow. He asked Gusinsky about creating "an immense enterprise that would manufacture everything" the city needed. Gusinsky was skeptical; at this time, Luzhkov was still "a Soviet bureaucrat with no idea about how the market worked—that the main point is to allow everybody to produce everything, and then there will be no problem of food supply." Luzhkov still thought in terms of massive, centralized, state-run factories, and he persisted. "Do you know anybody in America?" he asked Gusinsky.

The tour was an eye-opening experience for both of them, Kraus recalled. No one was interested in Luzhkov's plan for a giant centralized food factory in Moscow, but Gusinsky and Luzhkov found themselves flying on private jets. They were featured guests of corporate giants Phillip Morris and ConAgra Foods. They also visited Lehman Brothers on Wall Street. Kraus recalled one remarkable afternoon when, after meeting ConAgra officials in Omaha, Nebraska, the two Russians toured a local supermarket. Luzhkov asked a constant stream of questions and insisted on seeing the back of the store where the meat was cut. "Luzhkov was just blown away," Kraus recalled of the goods-laden store they inspected. Another time, Kraus was driving them to an appointment and pulled in to a Kentucky Fried Chicken drive-in for lunch. When their order came down a chute and through the car window, the two Russians were amazed. They had never seen such a thing. Gusinsky and Luzhkov were a funny pair, two men not widely known outside the Soviet capital, a hustling cooperative pioneer and a Moscow administrator exploring superprosperous America like virtual time travelers in a strange land. In New York City, they were shown an overstuffed candy store. They insisted that a driver take them to a dozen more stores to satisfy themselves that the first one was not just set up for their visit. Soon they realized there really was one on every corner. Luzhkov lost his luggage and Kraus bought him new clothes. He traveled with two pair of socks, which he washed in the hotel room. Gusinsky absorbed the lessons well and one night was sitting in Kraus's kitchen, pondering his future. "He drew on a napkin his vision for a conglomerate," Kraus recalled. "He wanted to talk about *everything!*"

Back in Moscow, Gusinsky's faith in political connections proved critical to his next big leap, into construction and real estate. Earlier, in his Metal cooperative, he had built small, stand-alone shell-shaped garages out of corrugated metal, which sprang up around the dreary apartment blocks of Moscow. In the cooperative days, it was enough to make things people wanted and sell them. But now Gusinsky wanted to repair and reconstruct old buildings. Moscow was littered with long-forgotten, dilapidated structures, and the lethargic state construction firms did not want to bother with small jobs. Gusinsky realized that he could make a small fortune by fixing up buildings and selling them on Moscow's increasingly high-priced real estate market, where rents for good offices and luxury apartments were approaching New York and Tokyo levels, pushed up by burgeoning demand among the new rich.

But first Gusinsky had to get a bargain on the old buildings. He needed Luzhkov. As a city official, Luzhkov could, with a stroke of the pen, parcel out city buildings. But Gusinsky knew that Luzhkov had to benefit in some way as a result. This was not a matter of crude bribery. What Luzhkov needed was career-enhancing results. Mikhail Leontiev, a journalist who knew both Luzhkov and Gusinsky at the time and later worked for Gusinsky, told me, "Luzhkov is a workaholic. He likes to have a result. Gusinsky is very energetic too. They complemented each other very well."

Luzhkov desperately wanted to expand Moscow's overburdened housing supply. Gusinsky and Luzhkov struck a deal: Luzhkov would give Gusinsky the rights to an old building, absolutely free. Gusinsky would then reconstruct the building and give half or even 75 percent of it back to the city. For Gusinsky, it was still enormously profitable to sell the remaining part, and for Luzhkov, who controlled the building permission slips but had no other resources at his disposal, it was an effortless way to gain valuable, freshly repaired housing and office space for the city. Later, the scheme became the backbone of Luzhkov's method for rapidly increasing residential housing in Moscow; hundreds of thousands of square meters of housing space were built by contractors with similar deals.

Moscow in the early 1990s was just beginning to blossom into the money-soaked, anything-goes Russian boom town that it later became, where corruption was rife and there were no clear boundaries between private and public interests. To get something done in the city, you needed money and influence, guts and bribery, and the whole environment was one of secrecy and deception. Even the smallest city department blithely demanded some kind of bribe or payoff, and big projects were always accompanied by hefty corruption. This was the world in which Gusinsky made his early fortune.

Yuri Schekochikhin, a crusading investigative journalist and democratic reform politician, wrote despairingly that criminal structures were coming to power in the city, taking advantage of the triumph of the reformers in 1990 and 1991. In a lengthy article published in June 1992 in the newspaper *Literaturnaya Gazeta,* which he entitled simply "Fear," Scheckochikhin said his sources were so fearful that they insisted on answering questions about Moscow corruption on hastily scribbled bits of paper, which they then burned. The criminal structures "have already divided among themselves the spheres of influence in Moscow," he wrote. "They have already sold out to each other Moscow's tasty morsels."

"Who governs Moscow today?" he asked. "Those who took into their hands Moscow's assets—its land, its buildings, and whole districts." Schekochikhin said the real power in the city was reserved not for small businessmen who got started after Communism collapsed nor the "real criminal businesses" that took advantage of "chaos in the country," but rather a shadowy "third group" close to the city government. He noted how Luzhkov had given a building to Gusinsky's company, Most. "I have information that Most has bought up virtually for nothing over one hundred buildings in Moscow already and there is no law that can prevent it from doing this," he wrote, saying that it was not the elected leaders who were running the city but the tycoons close to power. These were the "real masters of Moscow."[9]

Gusinsky was getting into big money, far more than he had ever known before. Tens of millions of dollars were running through his hands. His life was a blur of long nights and weekends with never a day off.

Danger lurked where money accumulated. When he first started stamping out bracelets, Gusinsky came face-to-face with small-time gangsters. The criminal gangs that had existed below the surface of

Soviet life—and under the heel of Soviet authority—became brazen during *perestroika,* just as the cooperatives blossomed. The bandits would be at the door as soon as they smelled money. At first, Gusinsky simply puffed up and tried to scare them off with the same volcanic anger he had once summoned up as a boy on the courtyard. "You would take something heavy in your hand and scare them away," he recalled. But soon he was hiring his own security force to keep out the gangsters who demanded money for protection. Gusinsky knew he lived in a lawless vacuum and it was no use turning to the police. He had to make his own rules, since he was probably operating outside the Soviet-era laws that made entrepreneurship a crime. "We had two options," he said, "to either pay the bandits or to keep the security service on the payroll." Later, as his businesses grew, especially as he built an empire in construction and banking, Gusinsky kept the bandits at bay with his own thousand-man security service. Bobkov, the former high-ranking KGB general who had been in charge of persecuting dissidents, became a key member of Gusinsky's corporate high command. Bobkov was described by Gusinsky as an analyst, but he was really concerned with all aspects of Gusinsky's security. In Gusinsky's empire, as in others, private in-house security services oversaw many different aspects of defending the company, from bodyguards to "analysis" of competitors to links with the state security organs. Gusinsky was a pioneer in creating these private services, which drew from elite Soviet military units and the KGB. For years, Gusinsky brushed off criticism of his security operation, saying it was necessary to keep out the criminals and guard his construction sites and bank branches. "Bandits, bandits, bandits!" he moaned when I asked him about the dangers he felt. When criticized for Bobkov's presence in his organization, Gusinsky declared that he would "hire the Devil himself if he could provide us with security."[10]

Gusinsky's financial center, Most Bank, which began as little more than an accounting department, expanded with the patronage of Luzhkov. The bank snared the city's main accounts in the early 1990s, a privileged status that allowed Gusinsky to play with municipal deposits, earning handsome profits for himself while he paid a small percentage back to the city. Gusinsky set up his offices in the same high-rise building where Luzhkov administered the city, next door to the Russian White House. Gusinsky's own automatic teller machines were stationed in the hallways, and the elite in Moscow were using his Most Bank credit cards. As he famously put it at the time, it was possible to make money from thin air.

What did it take to survive? As he looked out from his high-rise office at the sprawling city below him, Gusinsky pondered his success. You had to have some kind of inner drive, some kind of inner fuel that forced people like him to want to be first. It was a very small group of people, willing to take risks, desperate to succeed.

In the days of Gorbachev's *perestroika* and *glasnost* reforms, and later during the radical change of the early Yeltsin years, journalists became beacons of hope for Russian society. Especially after the Soviet collapse, journalists were admired and respected. "They were rulers of the minds," Oleg Dobrodeyev, a prominent television editor and executive, recalled in an interview many years later.[11] "In the first Supreme Soviet of Russia, one-tenth of its members were journalists. Their popularity and their authority in those years after August 1991 was fantastic!" It was not unusual for journalists to participate openly in politics. Dobrodeyev remembered that the journalists became the eyes and ears of the intelligentsia, the banner carriers for reform and democracy; sometimes he was even invited to participate in closed government meetings. "People who were the base of reforms—the engineering and technical intelligentsia, doctors, teachers, those who sincerely wanted changes—looked to journalists as their brightest representatives, and spokesmen of their aspirations."

In contrast to the gray, obedient Soviet-era press, brash new publications sprang up, such as the newspaper *Kommersant,* which became the bible of the early cooperative movement. The editor, Vladimir Yakovlev, recruited young reporters who were open-minded about a whole new language of commerce, capitalism, and money, a vocabulary that simply did not exist in the staid world of Soviet journalism. One of this generation was Mikhail Leontiev, who was a friend of the early cooperative businessmen. He got his start with the first issue of *Kommersant* in 1989. Leontiev later moved on to another prominent reform paper, *Nezavisimaya Gazeta,* which had been created by the democratic reformers who triumphed in Moscow city politics. The name meant "independent newspaper." The office was spread out on an old factory floor, and it attracted many of the most talented journalists of the day with the idea that it would remain truly independent.

But Leontiev felt dissatisfied. The salaries at the newspaper, while larger than others, were still relatively paltry. And as time went by, the paper's early romanticism was dulled somewhat by immutable laws of market economics: a newspaper that lost money inevitably faced commercial pressures. "We had to buy newsprint at market prices," Leontiev told me. "There was very little advertising, naturally. And the main source of money was sponsors." Leontiev began to quarrel with Vitaly Tretyakov, the editor of *Nezavisimaya Gazeta,* saying that "it was unfair to drag money from sponsors and consider ourselves independent." Leontiev added, "It was mainly I who found sponsors. Not all of them were honest people, and we had to take it into account. We made them feel happy for giving us the money. This was the system."[12]

Soon Leontiev and other journalists were thinking of leaving *Nezavisimaya Gazeta* and creating their own paper. Their idealism was tempered by the reality that they needed to find an owner, rather than beg for periodic injections of cash from publicity hungry sponsors. They knew that a Moscow banker would have his own desires and demands, but it seemed far more comfortable to have a single, known investor than to constantly search for, and pander to, outside sponsors. Leontiev met Gusinsky in the cooperative movement and introduced Gusinsky to his circle of friends. He quit *Nezavisimaya Gazeta* and began to press Gusinsky to bankroll a new paper. "You could become a media magnate yourself," Leontiev told Gusinsky, and they talked about the project for months, starting in 1992, the first year of post-Soviet Russia.

Leontiev recalled that Gusinsky was entranced with the idea from the start. "He is a very ambitious person. I think that I hit the bull's-eye. He may have thought about it before. I don't claim I gave him this idea, but I was pressing on him to make the decision. The idea was to create a professional paper. At that time, bankers had a great deal of very cheap money. It didn't cost anything. It was impossible to find a liquid use for it. At that time, everybody began to support different papers."

Sergei Zverev, a bearded, sandy-haired, hardened political operative who worked for Gusinsky through much of the 1990s, recalled that Gusinsky had been upset by newspapers criticizing his business activities in the city.[13] Gusinsky soon grasped that he could protect and defend himself and his public image. Leontiev agreed. "Volodya cared about this image very much," and it would be enhanced as the publisher of a reputable paper.

Gusinsky told me he listened to Leontiev's proposal from a different perspective. The truth was that he hardly understood the ideals and romantic notions of journalists like Leontiev and Dobrodeyev, people who saw their mission as leading society. "I did not perceive mass media as mass media. I could not even understand what it was," Gusinsky told me. Rather, Gusinsky was searching for a tool for influence and power. He had played the game, like all the businessmen of his generation, by paying bribes when necessary, deploying his security service when called for, and flattering top politicians with his plans and ambitions. But Gusinsky said the pettiness of the influence-peddling game sometimes left him feeling empty; bribery was a dead end because ultimately anyone with enough money could pay a larger bribe. The increasingly costly and intense competition to buy influence seemed to be outrunning itself.

Bribery "is humiliating for me," Gusinsky told me. "It means that either I am doing something that I cannot spell out in public—that I'm a rascal—or that money is being extorted from me by force. In which case, it means I am afraid, that's why I buy him."

"I gave bribes, no secret. To live in Russia, to live in the Soviet Union, and not to give bribes is absurd. But I was trying to do it as seldom as possible." Gusinsky wondered, instead of endlessly competing to buy influence, was there a way to exert greater, more systematic power? And then it dawned on him. "A newspaper!"

"When I started the newspaper, I will say it directly as it was: it was nothing but an instrument of influence," Gusinsky said. "One hundred percent—influence over officials and over society. I was creating the newspaper exactly for this aim." He added, "If an official turned bad, I would attack him with a newspaper and tell the truth that he demanded money, extorted it, or accepted conditions dishonestly."

Leontiev had no illusions. Gusinsky, he realized, was "trying to develop a system of promoting himself, of self-defense through the press." Gusinsky hired professional lobbyists such as Zverev. "The main aim for Russian public relations was not about creating an opinion about a firm in society," said Leontiev. "The society plays a secondary role here. The main thing is those who make decisions: the power structures, the Kremlin, and the cabinet. The aim was to get this or that signature."

When Gusinsky's newspaper *Sevodnya* appeared in February 1993, it was a respected liberal organ that soon attracted many of Moscow's most talented journalists. It was born out of an inchoate and incompatible mix of the journalists' ideals and Gusinsky's desire for power and influence. "If anybody tells you that we clearly understood what we were doing, it was not so," recalled Zverev. Originally, Gusinsky and two partners, one of whom was Smolensky, invested $6 million. But the partners dropped out; they could not take the heat when the newspaper came under fire or went on the offensive. Gusinsky acknowledged that it was often a difficult choice for him too, because there were so many people who could be wounded by a newspaper article. Despite the torrent of complaints and competing pressures, "I stayed on, deciding: let me try."

Sevodnya had a small circulation, forty thousand copies, was entirely in Moscow, and ran little advertising, but it earned a niche among Moscow's elite. Gusinsky ran the newspaper as a hobby. One day, Leontiev asked him to appoint a manager, since no one seemed to be running the paper. Gusinsky didn't want to bother wasting a good manager on the newspaper. In other businesses, Gusinsky explained, a good manager could earn $100 million a year. "If I ask him to work with the paper, he will only be able to cover its losses, which are $6 million. For me, it is better if he earns the $100 million and I give $6 million to you, and keep $94 million!"

Despite Gusinsky's ambivalence about the newspaper, it was the seed of what would become his grandest project. When *Sevodnya* began publishing, a group of disgruntled journalists at the state-run Ostankino television station took notice. Until then, no one had associated Gusinsky with the news media. But his new paper was smart, progressive, and privately owned. It was a signpost. They followed it.

On television, Yevgeny Kiselyov was a voice of authority. He spoke slowly, thoughtfully, and deliberately, with resonant, deep tones. His handsome, rugged, square-jawed face was almost always set in an expression of sobriety. He had a healthy shock of brown hair and a prominent mustache. But what made Kiselyov so powerful as a television personality was a voice that never hurried and often paused for effect.

Kiselyov had once been a Persian translator with the Soviet Army in Afghanistan and later taught Persian at the KGB academy. He was unhappy there and jumped at a chance to start a journalism career at Radio Moscow's Persian-language service. Later he moved to television, and in the first days after the collapse of the Soviet Union in January 1992, he went on the air at the state-run Ostankino channel with a new weekly analytical program, *Itogi,* or summing up, which quickly became a success, driven by Kiselyov's authoritative personal style.[14]

But as 1992 wore on and Yeltsin came under increasing fire from parliament, Kiselyov noticed that the Kremlin was hankering to impose more control on Ostankino to bolster Yeltsin's position. Igor Malashenko, who had once worked for Gorbachev's press service and later became director of Ostankino, abruptly resigned, complaining about growing political pressures. Through a series of ominous personnel shifts, Kiselyov felt a chill through the hallways—and feared that soon he would be asked to take direct orders from Yeltsin's henchmen. "I sensed that the clouds were becoming darker and darker," he recalled.[15]

Kiselyov knew that Gusinsky had invested big money in a daily newspaper and wondered whether he would consider bankrolling a television show. Kiselyov talked over the situation with Dobrodeyev, who was producer of *Itogi,* and suggested they approach Gusinsky together. Kiselyov telephoned an old friend, Zverev, who had begun working for Gusinsky's companies.

Zverev was immediately enthusiastic. The call from Kiselyov came in the morning, and a meeting was arranged to take place later in the day. Kiselyov and Dobrodeyev took the elevator to the offices of Gusinsky's companies, the Most Group, on the twenty-first floor of the high-rise building where Luzhkov's offices were also located. Dobrodeyev recalled that the offices of the Most Group looked "extremely serious."

In Zverev's office, Kiselyov presented his idea. He wanted to find an independent financier for his program *Itogi.* They would leave state-run Ostankino. They wanted journalistic freedom and they wanted to make more money as well. "Journalists were living almost in poverty, including myself," Kiselyov recalled. "We wanted to go independent because we wanted to produce what we really wanted to produce. We wanted to attract new, young, talented people, offer them good money for the job, and earn something for ourselves."

Surprisingly, Zverev jumped out of his chair and hustled down to

Gusinsky's office. He returned a few minutes later and invited the astonished Kiselyov and Dobrodeyev to see Gusinsky—*immediately.*

They walked down the hallway to Gusinsky's office, which, although it had a fabulous view, was furnished rather darkly. Gusinsky was no longer the skinny boy who slipped his friends into the Lenkom theater. He had put on some weight, and he wore aviator-style glasses and a rumpled white shirt and tie. But his face retained an extraordinary ability to reflect his boundless, ever-changing emotions. His eyebrows rose and fell, and his sentences burst out as soon as a thought occurred to him. When Kiselyov walked in, Gusinsky was enormously excited. He had never met Kiselyov before but admired the newsman greatly. Gusinsky was little known in public, but Kiselyov was a household name, the Russian Walter Cronkite.

"Imagine!" Gusinsky recalled. "Kiselyov in the flesh, at my office. How can this be? This is Kiselyov himself. As if we were sitting here and Margaret Thatcher walked through the door. God Almighty! It's like this!"

Kiselyov and Dobrodeyev laid out their plan, asking Gusinsky if he could finance the production of *Itogi.* But Gusinsky's brain was already in overdrive. Yes, he said immediately, he would finance their show, but why stop there? "This is a small project," he said. "I think the big project is to start an independent television company, broadcasting twenty-four hours a day; that's what I am really thinking of."

The guests were speechless. No such independent television existed in the new Russia, only state television inherited from the Soviet Union. Kiselyov reminded Gusinsky that a channel would require a frequency to broadcast on—and they had none. But Gusinsky was way ahead of them. He quickly pointed out the sorry state of Channel 4, a government station that was a dumping ground for unwanted programming by the two main state channels, Ostankino and Russian Television, which had Channel 1 and Channel 2, respectively. Channel 4 was a disaster; no one watched it or cared about it, and Gusinsky was already plotting to lobby the Kremlin for a decree signed by President Boris Yeltsin giving him Channel 4.

Within a few hours, Kiselyov, Dobrodeyev, and Gusinsky were surrounded by lawyers and financial experts, and they were deep into planning their new project. Such were the times that dreams were unlimited and enthusiasm contagious. "Gusinsky was a very dynamic person; he moved very rapidly across his huge office," Dobrodeyev recalled. "The whole situation was in keeping with the times in Russia, when things appeared out of nothing, and it happened very, very rapidly. Grandiose projects appeared. Banks appeared. A television company appeared. The negotiations weren't long. We are going to create television. Money wasn't a problem. Other resources, connections—not a problem! Back then, the will, the desire, the drive solved absolutely everything."

Dobrodeyev recalled that he had no idea whether the new television channel could succeed commercially. "I think most people had great doubts about the commercial side of the matter," he said. "It was a matter of status. The best years of very many newspapers, really good newspapers, of various television programs, were precisely those years when the owners treated them as if they were standing next to a masterpiece. It was like, 'And I have a newspaper. I have a *good* newspaper.'"

Gusinsky approached Malashenko about being manager of the new channel. Malashenko recalled that Gusinsky treated his newspaper as just a hobby. "It was a status symbol. . . . So very quickly I realized that for him a TV company would be another—how to say it—architectural detail, an ornament on his façade." Nonetheless, Malashenko agreed to become the new boss of the Gusinsky channel. Malashenko had his own reasons: he was humiliated when he resigned from Ostankino. He wanted to get back at his tormentors by starting a rival independent channel. "I wanted revenge," he remembered.[16]

Gusinsky also had a score to settle. He had an ongoing personal feud with Mikhail Poltoranin, the press minister in Yeltsin's government, whom Gusinsky regarded as an anti-Semite. Poltoranin had insulted Gusinsky at some point in recent years, and "I had a strong desire to have a fight with him," Gusinsky recalled. "I even drove to his office twice especially to run into him and punch him in the nose." Starting a television station outside the control of the state was sweet revenge, Gusinsky felt, but that was not all. "I just wanted to be number one," he recalled of his early enthusiasm for television. "I think I started it because I had to be the first, because no one else had his own television channel, and I would have one."

Gusinsky was also thinking about money. In the United States, someone had mentioned to him that a minute of advertising on television sold for millions of dollars. "I seized the meaning," he recalled. "Here it is, the gold mine, yet again. I understood that it was 100 percent possible to make money."

The first year was exhilarating. Malashenko hastily drew up a plan which predicted they would need $30 million for the first fifteen months, and Gusinsky found the money with other investors, including Smolensky. They bought cameras, equipment, and office space, and they kept a wary eye on the news. Russia was heading into a mammoth political crisis, a face-off between Yeltsin and hard-liners in parliament. They were not yet on the air, but building a new, private channel was exciting. "It was a great time," Kiselyov recalled later. "We were doing something for *ourselves,* we had complete freedom, we traveled a lot, and we felt that we were doing something significant, probably the most significant project of our lives." When Kiselyov and Dobrodeyev left Ostankino, they took dozens of the best television people with them to the new, private channel, including announcers Tatyana Mitkova and Mikhail Osokin.

The Gusinsky high command could not decide what to call the new channel. Malashenko suggested NTV for Novoe Televidenie, or New Television. The others winced. It sounded awful, they thought. Then someone said, how about Nezavisimoe Televidenie, or Independent Television. No, that didn't work either. According to Malashenko, they decided to call it NTV and leave it at that. There was no official name, but Malashenko thought up a slogan. In Soviet times, he had spent years studying the United States and was fond of an old Strategic Air Command slogan: "Peace Is Our Profession." He adapted it to NTV: "News Is Our Profession."

NTV went on the air October 10, 1993, a week after the confrontation between Yeltsin and parliament turned violent. At first, the nascent station had only an hour a day of programming on a weak St. Petersburg channel. In the midst of Yeltsin's war with parliament, which was unfolding virtually across the street from Gusinsky's offices in the mayor's building, Malashenko sat in his car, a battered old Moskvich, and used his mobile telephone to try and make appointments in Cannes, where the television film and miniseries market was opening. As televisions screens flickered around the globe with the scenes of tanks bombarding the White House, Malashenko was trying to shout over the din, persuading people that a new television station in Russia wanted to buy their films. He then flew to Cannes and frantically tried to buy more programming. "People didn't want to sell," he recalled. "It was incredible to believe that a guy would come from Moscow, where parliament is being shelled, to buy movies."

For six months, Zverev lobbied for a decree from the Kremlin that would give NTV the cherished Channel 4 airtime. Zverev argued that an independent channel would be a valuable source of support for Yeltsin, but he was lobbying for an idea that no one could grasp. "Nobody understood what independent, private television would be like," Zverev recalled of his difficult and exhausting effort to win the presidential decree. Someone was blocking it, and Zverev could not figure out who. Once, by chance, he took Kiselyov to see Yeltsin's tennis coach, Shamil Tarpischev, a member of the president's inner circle, who had an office in the Kremlin. Zverev discovered the source of his troubles: Tarpischev was blocking the decree because he wanted Channel 4 to be a sports channel. Zverev persuaded him that NTV would broadcast sports, and his resistance ended.[17] Yeltsin signed the decree in December, and in January, NTV went on the air six hours a day, starting at 6 P.M.

Malashenko was still harried: he had managed to buy only two weeks' worth of programming. As tapes arrived in Russia, they were immediately dubbed and thrown on the air. It was chaos, but they were having the time of their lives.

The highest aspirations of the new television pioneers was to exist beyond the grip of the state, to produce what they called "normal" television. One of them had suggested half-jokingly that NTV should stand for "Normalnoye Televidenie." Gusinsky loved movies, especially those from the West, and dreamed simply of a television channel broadcasting movies and news bulletins.

Gusinsky had started his newspaper with the idea of broadening his influence. Later he would relentlessly use his television channel as a political tool as well, and it would lead to endless troubles. But at the outset, the participants told me, they had not fully understood the risks. They had not even dreamed, back then, of turning their channel against Yeltsin, a friend and guarantor of the free press, whose own signature on the decree had given them the right to broadcast.

Gusinsky was now more than just a Moscow businessman who had connections. With NTV television and the newspaper *Sevodnya,* he had become a pillar of the new Russia.

His rivals had already begun plotting how to tear him down.

PART TWO

Chapter 8

Unlocking the Treasure

THE REVOLUTIONARIES were young men in their thirties, self-confident, hopeful, untested in power, and confronted with a task far beyond their imagination or practical experience. For years, as assistant professors and little-known specialists, they had been dreaming about marginal, incremental changes to the stagnant Soviet system. They had satisfied themselves studying the slightly more progressive examples of economic experimentation in socialist Hungary and the Latin American transformations. Now, as they gathered in a government guest house, dacha 15, in Archangelskoe, a village west of Moscow, they were facing an entirely new world. The Soviet Union was in its death throes. They were being called not to save it but to bury it.

After the failed August 1991 coup attempt, Mikhail Gorbachev remained in office four months longer in a vain attempt to keep the Soviet Union from disintegrating. The final blow came in early December, when Boris Yeltsin and the leaders of Ukraine and Belarus, meeting at Belavezhskaya Pushcha, a hunting resort outside Brest, declared their own union, defying Gorbachev. The Soviet flag was lowered from the Kremlin three weeks later, on December 25, 1991, just after Gorbachev announced his resignation.

In the months before the final collapse, Yeltsin had begun to assemble a parallel regime that would take the radical economic measures Gorbachev had never made. Yeltsin passed over the older, well-known economists of the Gorbachev years and settled on thirty-two-year-old Yegor Gaidar, author of some of the best Soviet analyses of the economy in the party's journal of ideology, *Kommunist*.[1] Yeltsin recalled that Gaidar led a team of "arrogant young upstarts" who were "independent thinkers raring to go." Instinctive and intuitive, Yeltsin ruled by feeling rather than by policy; he liked the simple directness of Gaidar's proposal for a "big bang," a sudden jump to the free market modeled on Poland's experience after the fall of the Berlin Wall. Yeltsin was infected with Gaidar's enthusiasm for economic shock therapy. "I couldn't force people to wait once again," Yeltsin recalled, "to drag out the main events and processes for years. If our minds were made up, we had to get going!"[2] Yeltsin wanted to make sure he totally destroyed Soviet Communism. Pyotr Aven, who worked alongside Gaidar, remembered that "Yeltsin was interested only in power. He wanted a team that would be very aggressive in throwing out all the old bureaucrats. He also understood that, to us, Yeltsin was a god, and we would follow him."[3]

In September-October 1991, Gaidar closeted himself with other young economists at dacha 15 to begin drawing up the details of Yeltsin's radical economic reform. Everyone who had worked with Gaidar knew he was a gradualist by temperament, a cautious reformer, ever respectful of the existing powers. For years, he had insisted on trying to accomplish modest, realistic steps rather than risk a giant leap that would never stand a chance. Aven had suggested to Gaidar in Soviet times that they study Sweden, a Western social democracy, as a model, but Gaidar knocked down the idea as too radical; he instead suggested Hungary, which was safely within the Soviet bloc. Gaidar had a very strong intellect; he was the best and brightest of his generation, yet he also had a tendency to ponder the data, to see different sides of an argument.

Among those Gaidar put on his team at the dacha was Anatoly Chubais, fresh from St. Petersburg and less well known than Gaidar at the time. Chubais too had been a gradualist in earlier years, but now he heartily embraced the need for radical change. While Gaidar had a slightly professorial, diffident air, Chubais was determined and self-assured. Of all those at the dacha, Chubais became the reformer who survived the longest, remaining in high-ranking posts throughout the 1990s. He was resolute and unyielding. It was his greatest asset, as well as a source of aggravation to those around him, that Chubais did not budge from a position once he had made up his mind. Gaidar was a trailblazing intellect but not a politician; Chubais was not an original thinker but a skilled, steely executor and political warrior. In the next few years, the two of them—Gaidar, short and stocky, a Pooh bear with a large, welcoming face, and Chubais, tall and lean, with a shock of sandy red hair and a complexion that flushed brightly whenever he became emotional—were transformed from obscure academics into the chief engineers of Yeltsin's economic revolution. They set out to accomplish nothing less than wreck the old system—smash the entire complex of planning, thinking, and behavior inherited from Lenin, Stalin, and their successors.

They each scored a singular, huge accomplishment toward that goal and left an equally disturbing legacy. Gaidar's most important contribution was to free prices from state control, crippling an oppressive tool of the centrally planned economy. But Gaidar's legacy was a tidal wave of hyperinflation that washed over Russia once prices were free, and it was far more destructive and persistent than Gaidar had imagined possible. It eroded the life savings of the population, disenchanting them for years to come.

Chubais's most important act was to break the state monopoly on property, putting the enormous industrial wealth of the country into private hands. The whole fate of the new Russia as a free market economy lay in whether these new, private owners would eventually prove more effective in running factories than the failed Communists. But Chubais did not pay heed, or care, to whom the riches of Russia were distributed, as long as they were private owners, free of the state. He figured that after several generations, the market would sort out the best from the worst. Surely, the worst would go broke by their own ineptitude and the best would enjoy the fruits of their labors. It was that simple: classical market theory. The reality would prove not so elegant.

Furthermore, both Chubais and Gaidar left a dangerous vacuum—the great breakthroughs toward free prices and private property were made without first building the key institutions of a market. In the chaotic dawn of Russia's post-Soviet statehood, the economy was a wild, uncontrolled jungle without rules of the game and those who enforced them. In a mature market economy, competitors can pursue their disputes in forums with defined rules. They are like boxers in a ring. The contest is settled by the rules—either through the courts or in capital markets, where winners and losers are sorted out based on performance. But Russia did not have these forums, nor a strong state to create them, and this vacuum undermined the very aspirations and accomplishments of the revolution. How could Chubais possibly realize his dream of creating "effective owners" if there was no mechanism to reward the good and punish the bad? What good were free prices if no one was sure about their rights to property and profits? Gaidar regularly acknowledged that they were haunted by these unknowns. Was it better to unleash the boxers first or build the boxing ring for them to fight in? In the heady onrush of events in 1991 and 1992, Gaidar and Chubais decided: the boxers first; someone else, later, would take care of the rest. Chubais was certain that the players themselves would inevitably build the ring, once they saw it was necessary.

They were driven by urgency. They believed they could not put the revolution on hold for the years it would take to build up the institutions. But there was another, deeper reason—often unspoken but clearly evident—why Yeltsin, Chubais, and Gaidar did not immediately see the need for a stronger state. The Soviet state had been powerful and overweening; in their experience, authoritarianism had been a central, defining source of evil. They were thinking about destroying the old system, not recreating it.

As the autumn of 1991 set in, Gaidar and his brain trust feverishly prepared for Yeltsin's major economic speech to the Russian parliament at the end of October. A sense of unreality filled the air as the Gaidar team set out on a mission unlike any in their lives; it was at once exhilarating, frightening, and unimaginable. Mikhail Berger, then the economics editor of the newspaper *Izvestia*, who was respected by the young reformers and witnessed the Gaidar team firsthand, recalled that dacha 15 was brimming with expectation. In their banter and debate, it was as if they were on another weekend retreat like the two seminars of 1986 and 1987 outside of St. Petersburg, except this time the stakes were enormous, and real. "The atmosphere was as if the young people went on a hike somewhere to the mountains or just out of town," recalled Berger. "It was the atmosphere of a club, and a game. In fact, everybody felt as if it were not for real."[4]

"Imagine, they sat discussing things and then someone might ask,

'And who is going to be transportation minister?' They started laughing. 'Here we are, fresh from the institute, discussing who is going to be transportation minister!' They treated it as some kind of game, not serious enough. They argued for a long time about who was going to be prime minister. None of them wanted to. Pure Kafka. Kids, sitting at the dacha, writing a program and trying to form a government. Of course, later it would change. But at that moment, it looked like a fairy tale about some kind of magic cave where they said 'take as much treasure as you can carry on your back.' It was a cave of power. They tried to take as much power as they were able to carry."

But for all the revelry, the Gaidar crew brought to dacha 15 some profound shared assumptions, forged in Soviet times when they were little-known mathematicians, economists, and professors. They were saddled with the baggage of their past experience, and they were not quite prepared for the entirely different challenges of a new economic and political system.

Just the fact that the Gaidar brain trust isolated itself at the dacha reflected the insular method they had adopted in the Soviet years. When Chubais first created his small cadre of freethinking economists in Leningrad, it was done in great secrecy to avoid attracting the attention of the KGB. The same mood prevailed when they retreated to a stairwell to debate Naishul's radical ideas. The Soviet system had forced them to be conspirators; it crushed those who did not conform. Mikhail Dmitriev, the young economist who had been called on the carpet for the notes he took at the 1987 seminar, told me that Gaidar and Chubais had learned everything about politics under a regime that would immediately destroy any far-reaching new ideas. "By definition they were successful because they were conspirators, they were not open, they were mainly acting in a very narrow circle," he said. "And all these habits couldn't be changed quickly because by the end of the 1980s both Gaidar and Chubais were already in their mid-thirties, and people don't change easily in this respect."[5]

Another legacy of their past was their shared disdain for politics. In the 1980s, Gorbachev had unleashed freedom but lagged behind on economic change. They were determined to avoid Gorbachev's quagmire of politics—endless plans that went nowhere, such as the five-hundred-day plan to turn the Soviet Union into a market economy, which was never adopted. Instead, they thought of themselves as technocrats, pure economists who would find the right thing to do and smash through the old barriers to getting it done. They believed, Soviet-style, that they only needed to please one man, the boss at the top, Boris Yeltsin.[6] They also believed that the problem of the old system was too much political interference; certainly, a more purely economic approach would be more successful.[7]

Although their economic ideas were modern, capitalist, and radical, their political tactics were often arrogant and naive. They bypassed the parliament, which grew alienated, and Gaidar was especially poor at communicating with the public. The more determined and cunning Chubais turned out to be a sharper political operative, but both of them, along with Yeltsin, neglected from the outset to lay a grassroots base for their revolution. Gaidar later acknowledged it was a serious miscalculation that left them at sea and vulnerable. It might have been impossible to build such a popular base anyway, given the excruciating pain they were about to inflict on Russian society, but Gaidar told me they saw themselves as economic professionals, not politicians. "We had Yeltsin, who was an extremely efficient politician at the time, very popular and very active and a strong Russian politician," he said.[8] But Yeltsin was not enough, considering the enormity of their revolution.

Yet another fundamental belief among the Gaidar brain trust was that Russia, despite its backwardness and terrible history of autocracy, would be fertile soil for a market economic system. Russia, they believed, was not an exception to the basic rules of human behavior. Gaidar and Chubais were certain that if they created free choice, people would take advantage of it and respond to incentives. They hoped that all the collectivism, passivity, paternalism, and destruction of initiative and entrepreneurship that was a legacy of Russian and Soviet history would melt away as a beachhead of free markets, free trade, private property, and free prices was established. This assumption—that Western market economics could take root in Russia despite its peculiar cultural and historical experience—was one of the most fateful and daring of their time. It was a gamble. A decade later, the validity of this idea was still vigorously debated.

The Gaidar team also realized that no one would be building monuments to them for the transformation they intended to impose on their country. They often described themselves as kamikaze pilots, because they would certainly destroy themselves in trying to tear down so many entrenched interests. Not only would they battle old-school bureaucrats, party bosses, the military and security establishments; they were setting out to destroy the mindset of millions of Russians who knew no other political or economic life other than what they had experienced during Soviet Communism. The kamikaze idea emboldened them because they had no careers, no promotions to worry about. But it also weakened them because it gave their opponents the idea that it would only be a matter of time until the reformers disappeared from the scene.

Gaidar and his brain trust knew that time was not on their side. The Soviet legacy was formidible: dozens of government ministries lorded over branches of industry; within them, the bureaucrats wanted to preserve their bastions of power. In the factories, the powerful "red directors" stood to lose their prominent status and sprawling empires. They all wanted to stop the radical reformers. The special interests insisted: why not restructure industry more slowly, factory by factory? Why not wait until a reliable legal and financial system was established? Why not free prices later, after private property rights are guaranteed, and after the huge Soviet monopolies are dismembered?

But Gaidar and Chubais believed that gradualism was akin to death; it would strengthen the vested interests and doom any real chance at reform. Chubais said it was only an illusion that change could be done "gently, slowly, and painlessly, so that everybody should be happy."[9] Gaidar and Chubais had no intention to be gentle, slow, or painless. Later they would be criticized over and over again by those who said there was another way—if only they had taken more time, if only they had been more careful, if only they had rebuilt industry case by case, if only they had taken care to build institutions first. Many of these arguments were correct in a theoretical sense but were far removed from the real world that Gaidar and Chubais confronted. The reformers feared they did not have more time—to wait was to fail. I think their fears were not imagined. All around them were signs of utter collapse. At any minute, they could be history too.

In the final months of its existence, the Soviet Union slid into utter economic chaos. After the failed August coup, the country was rife with predictions of famine, catastrophe, and collapse. Grain deliveries to the state dropped by a factor of four. "People simply weren't hauling it to the elevators," Gaidar recalled. "Why should they? To get some piece of paper that, out of habit, everyone still calls money?" Both Gaidar and Chubais were haunted by what they saw on the streets of Moscow: the worst shortages ever. "Moscow in December

1991 is one of my most painful memories," Gaidar said later. "Grim food lines, even without their usual squabbles and scenes. Pristinely empty stores. Women rushing about in search of some food, any food, for sale. . . . Expectations of disaster were in the air."[10]

The chaos deepened as the Soviet state itself—the vast chain of commands and controls that stretched from Moscow to the most distant province—seemed to tear apart. The military and security organizations were in a "state of shock," Gaidar recalled, while the republics went their separate ways. Yeltsin was a popular leader, but in the final months of the Soviet Union, he had "no levers of control."[11]

Gaidar was strongly influenced by the example of Poland, which had launched shock therapy on January 1, 1990, by freeing prices and trade. Poland's "big bang" was led by a reform economist, Leszek Balcerowicz, and it bore immediate dividends; consumer shortages gave way to brimming street markets, and the initial burst of inflation was relatively short.[12] Poland's shock therapy was in part the handiwork of the Harvard economist Jeffrey Sachs, who, along with a group of other Westerners, urged Russia to take the same route. The role of the Westerners—both individuals and governments—in Russia's transformation later was hotly debated. But the most important actor was Yeltsin himself, who made the first big leap. According to Berger, Gaidar and his brain trust drafted a speech for Yeltsin in which they deliberately did not name a day when prices would be freed. They feared a specific date would lead to hoarding and panic, which they could hardly afford. Yeltsin sent back a draft in which he had scrawled that prices would be freed by year's end. "Everybody was shocked, that was something that could not be announced beforehand," Berger recalled. "They kind of persuaded Yeltsin to cross it out." But when he gave the address on October 28, 1991, Yeltsin reinstated the remark. He declared plans for a "one-off unfreezing of prices in the current year." That meant before January 1, 1992, just two months away. The Gaidar brain trust could do nothing more. "Yeltsin just pulled the lever," Berger told me.

In this landmark speech, Yeltsin fully embraced shock therapy. "A large-scale reformist breakthrough is needed," he declared, promising that "we shall finally begin, in reality and not just in words, to haul ourselves out of the quagmire that is sucking us in deeper and deeper." Yeltsin endorsed the basic Gaidar plan for free prices, free trade, and mass privatization. He optimistically—even foolishly—promised that "people's lives will gradually get better" by the next autumn.

When his father stopped by the dacha, Gaidar mentioned that he might join the Yeltsin government. His father blanched, Gaidar recalled, "an expression of stark fear on his face." Timur Gaidar knew the job was political suicide but urged his son to go ahead. The following week, Yeltsin formally appointed Gaidar a deputy prime minister to lead the revolution.[13]

Late one night, Gaidar took Chubais aside. Gaidar worried about money, prices, finance, and the looming prospects of panic buying, hunger, and a devastating winter. He would lead the first wave of radical reform, but he knew that if they made it to spring, there would be a second wave that would be far more difficult. The goal of the second wave was to profoundly change the underlying structure of the economy. It would involve carrying out the largest transfer of property to private hands ever attempted in modern times. Privatization was going badly in Poland and Hungary, and Gaidar needed someone who would see it to the end. He asked Chubais.

"Yegor," Chubais replied, with a deep sigh. "Do you understand that regardless of what the result will be, I will be hated for the rest of my life because I was the person who sold off Russia?" Gaidar replied that they would all "have to drink from that poisoned chalice."

In earlier years, Chubais had paid little attention to privatization, which he found more of a dull organizational chore than an economics challenge. There wasn't a single economics textbook he had seen about privatization, and few members of his team were interested in a field that had been nonexistent in Soviet times.[14] One of the most basic tenets of Soviet Communism was the nationalization of all means of production except for individual labor; the very words "private property" came to the fore only in the final years of Gorbachev, and few of the young academicians really understood its implications. In the brief period in St. Petersburg city government, among those on the Chubais team, only Dmitri Vasiliev had worked on privatization, and he had focused on small businesses.

Once he was given the assignment of carrying out the grand transfer of property, however, Chubais characteristically turned it into an intense crusade. He championed private ownership as the equivalent of personal freedom. "We need to free the economy from the state," he declared. "To free the country from socialism. To shake off the terrible chains of that gigantic, all-pervading, bureaucratic, ruinous, and ineffective state."[15]

The first thing Chubais discovered was that someone else was already feasting at the table. Property was being grabbed, stolen, and gobbled up by the old guard, factory managers, and party elite, who were taking advantage of chaos in the country. Chubais called it "spontaneous privatization," and it was out of control. As the reins of central authority were loosened in Gorbachev's years, factory managers gained ever more power over their own domain and lined their own pockets. Using cooperatives and joint ventures, and later shell companies and offshore havens, they leeched the cash or raw materials out of state enterprises. Their overlords, bureaucrats in the government ministries, were also carving up the spoils for themselves. It was common for a state enterprise, such as a steel factory, to give birth to a small "pocket" bank, perhaps on the factory grounds. Then the bank would give birth to a trading company, which would take over the sale of the factory's output—state property—and the profits would disappear into the offshore accounts of the director and his friends, perhaps using the pocket bank. There was nothing to stop it. In his landmark October speech, Yeltsin had noted that while the reformers debated privatization, "the party and state elite, meanwhile, were actively engaged in their own type of privatization. The extent of it, and the enterprise and hypocrisy, are simply amazing. Privatization in Russia has long been under way, but wildly, spontaneously, and not infrequently on a criminal basis."

"In reality, it was theft of state property," Chubais recalled, "but was not illegal because there was no legal basis for the transfer of property into private hands."[16] The result of spontaneous privatization was a spoils system that rewarded the factory managers and political bosses and left out everyone else. Chubais was offended at the rude, defiant way the old guard was going about it. The essence was that "if you are cheeky, daring, and resolute you will get everything," he recalled. "If you are not very cheeky and not very daring, just sit quietly."

Chubais had caught wind of something. Theft, insider dealing, and hidden money flows characterized the entire first decade of Russian capitalism, but in that early period it seemed to be the particular skill of the old guard, the party, and managerial elite. Later, many others would learn the benefits of being daring and cheeky.

In 1992, Chubais uncovered a good example of how spontaneous privatization worked. A group of party bigwigs set up a dummy corporation called Kolo Ltd. to take over Energia, a huge Soviet-era rocket engine and satellite manufacturer, a crown jewel of the military-industrial complex, at a fraction of its real value. The founders contributed their "intellectual property" (their ideas), which they arbitrarily valued at millions of rubles, and then tried to grab not only the massive rocket company but a military airfield as well. Chubais recalled that the thieves had created an "absolutely impregnable scheme," and "the interesting thing about such deals is that we cannot untangle them." When the rip-off was finally discovered, Chubais stopped it and fired one of his own deputies for approving it. But he was only beginning to think about how to halt the orgy of stealing already under way.[17]

When Chubais first got the privatization assignment from Gaidar in November 1991, Vasiliev wrote him a simple, three-page memo based on his St. Petersburg experience with the small businesses. Vasiliev told Chubais privatization of property should be "maximally wide," or involving as much property as possible, and that the best way to carry it out was through competitive auctions, selling property for cash.[18] In the months that followed, as small-scale privatization of bakeries and hair salons and other businesses was getting under way, Chubais embraced cash auctions, thinking it was the best example of a free market at work—open and competitive.

On April 4, 1992, Chubais and Gaidar flew to Nizhny Novgorod, 250 miles east of Moscow on the Volga River, to witness one of the first auctions, hoping to turn it into a political event. They faced growing resistance in Moscow and needed a symbolic boost. In Nizhny they were greeted by hundreds of demonstrators outside the former House of Literacy, many of whom were shop workers, fearful and envious of those who would buy their shops at cash auctions. Although Chubais and Gaidar believed that openly selling small enterprises to the highest bidder was the only fair and uncorrupted method, there was a chorus of demands that shops should be given to their workers, an emotional pull that ran strong after seven decades of socialism. The workers held placards, "Gaidar and Chubais! Find another city for your experiments."

"Democrats!" spat out an middle-aged grocery clerk. "Speculators, the lot of them!"

As they arrived at a back entrance of the hall, the two reformers were confronted by shouting, hissing, and screaming crowds. Chubais lost his cool and got into a shoving match with some of them as he and Gaidar tried to break through toward the door. "The whole situation got to us," he recalled. "Gaidar and I understood that what we came here for had to be done at any cost." Gaidar recalled that all the Russian elite was hoping the experiment would fail. "All of them were saying, 'Auctions, what auctions? In Russia? Are you from another country? Do you not understand that it will not work?'" They had to demonstrate it would work, or they would be overrun by the vested interests.[19]

Fortunately, inside the hall, it did work. An auctioneer wearing a red bow tie and white silk shirt mopped his brow, slicked back his hair, and announced that Sewing Shop 38 on Yamskaya Street was up for grabs. The auctioneer, Arseny Labanov, called out the rising bids—100,000 rubles, then 500,000 and 2 million—and the store was sold for 3.6 million rubles, or about $36,000. The rest of the day brought the cash auctions of twenty-one cafés, hair salons, cheese shops, and other retail outlets, with the state reaping the proceeds. Chubais was in a fighting mood when he got inside the hall, but the elegance and simplicity of the auction calmed him. The auctioneer was "a real pro, an artist," he recalled. "He had a natural gift for it."

"It was quite a sight," Chubais went on. "We had just emerged from the Soviet system. It was the early market period, the early democratic period, when the mere word 'auction' was taken as something anti-Soviet. And here we were watching the real procedure! With real live winners who were purchasing a bakery or a store." Chubais recalled witnessing open auctions "based on competition, instead of doubtful tête-à-tête deals where bribes are discussed." He and Gaidar sat together during the auction, Chubais marveling to himself how far they had come. "A mere five months ago we were writing all kinds of drafts. And now we were here, the official representatives of power, who succeeded in getting things done. It was a moment of happiness."

Gaidar also had his moment when it all seemed to fall into place. The shortage economy had existed in the Soviet Union for as long as he could remember. In the final years of Soviet socialism, the shortage of goods had created an ominous monetary "overhang," a huge surplus of rubles, since there was nothing to buy with them. A few days after price liberalization, Gaidar heard amazing news. Truck drivers were protesting. Not because of shortage, but the opposite—the stores would no longer accept any more cream! For Gaidar, it was a fleeting but wonderful sign—a reinforcing signal that shortages would end with free prices. Money and goods would come into rough balance. "For the person who lived in the realities of the end of 1991, when the shops were absolutely empty, and everybody knew nothing would appear there," Gaidar told me, it was unimaginable "that there could be a situation when they would not accept any more cream because they did not *want* any more cream."[20] In fact, the example was premature: it took many months for shortages to disappear, but they did.

Gaidar persuaded Yeltsin to sign a decree liberalizing all kinds of trade in early 1992. Street trade was an illicit, criminal offense in Soviet times. Just after Yeltsin approved the document, Gaidar was driving through Lubyanka Square, past the famous children's department store Detsky Mir, when he spotted a long line twisting around the block. At first, he thought it was just another symptom of shortages—"probably something just appeared on the shelves." But he was amazed to look closer: the line was not desperate shoppers. It was desperate sellers. "Clutching a few packs of cigarettes, a couple of cans of food, or a bottle of vodka, wool stockings, mittens, or a child's sweater, people with the 'Decree on free trade' newspaper clipping pinned to their coats were offering various little items for sale."[21] The scene was a first, tangible sign of their gamble that Russia was not exceptional—give people incentives, and the market will come.

"We need millions of owners, not hundreds of millionaires," Yeltsin declared in a speech to the Congress of People's Deputies on April 7, 1992, coining a populist slogan for mass privatization. He won applause with the line, but the truth was that privatization was heading in exactly the opposite direction, toward creating just a few hundred millionaires. In a speech to the Congress of People's Deputies in April, Chubais acknowledged the mounting criticism that "auctions are only for the rich." Privately, he and Vasiliev were having second thoughts about the auctions. They realized that cash auctions were not suitable for the colossal task of privatizing all of Russian industry. They worried that the angry shop workers in Nizhny Novgorod had a good point: what if all the property was bought up in auctions by a tiny percentage of the population? The rest of the country would be left behind, and that could spark a political time bomb of envy and resentment. "Gradually, we came to understand that society simply cannot absorb the idea of selling property for money," Vasiliev recalled. "It would lead to people thinking that everything was bought by bandits and those who had stolen money."[22]

In a series of concessions and tactical maneuvers, Chubais put privatization on a new track in the next year and kept it from being derailed. Despite fierce opposition, he was able to keep privatization moving ahead, and there was much still to be done: privatization of 5,603 large enterprises with a combined workforce of 15 million. Chubais earned his reputation in this period as a feared manager and fearless infighter. His stubbornness paid off, but so did another personal characteristic—he would sometimes compromise and cut corners in pursuit of his larger goal.

In a clever organizational move, he created a new agency, the State Property Committee, within Russia's hidebound bureaucracy. At first, committee members worked in bare, unheated offices in the grubby high-rise towers along Novy Arbat, the grim socialist-realist avenue of utopian architecture in the center of Moscow. Later, they moved to a drafty ministry building near Red Square. In the early months, they churned out ideas and documents day and night. "We had no heat, no Xerox, no fax, no food," recalled Jonathan Hay, one of the Americans who came to help. "The first time I came there, I saw just Dmitri Vasiliev and thirty people sitting in a huge hall, just this small man in big glasses, and they were all around him, in a heated discussion, talking about small-scale privatization." By his own account, Chubais was overwhelmed, with heaps of papers on his desk, phone calls streaming in, and crowds of people in the reception area demanding his attention. But Chubais enjoyed what Berger called a clean slate—he started from scratch and could build privatization from the ground up.

To a far greater extent than other reformers, Chubais attracted Westerners to help with privatization. The international financial organizations saw the young reformers as the best hope of Russia and provided money for technical assistance. Lawyers, economists, public relations people, investment bankers, and government officials—they all trouped through the shabby offices of the State Property Committee.[23]

By the time he got organized, Chubais faced a virtual tug-of-war. The industrial property in theory belonged to the state, but in practice different groups laid claim to the treasure. Managers felt they knew the factory best; workers felt entitled since they had put so many years on the assembly line; the local governor and politicians saw the juicy plums and wanted the right to distribute them. These were "stakeholders" whose demands would have to be dealt with. The likelihood of meeting all their demands was zero. Meanwhile, a fourth group, the party nomenklatura, was already helping itself. "There hasn't been a fair privatization in the history of mankind; this has to be accepted," Berger recalled of the choices facing Chubais. "Chubais had one main goal: to destroy the monopoly of the state on property. At any cost."

Chubais believed that outsiders—the new generation of private owners, perhaps even foreign investors—who had never had a stake in the factory would be the best ones to eventually restructure it. At least theoretically, he thought, they were the ones who would become the most "effective owners." Cold-eyed outsiders would be more inclined to strip away the inefficient equipment and the excessive spending on kindergartens and resorts that were part of every socialist enterprise and retool it with new investment and a view toward longer-term profit.

But Chubais could not afford to ignore the insiders: the workers and managers. They were powerful stakeholders, and in his original speech, Yeltsin promised to split the state property with the workers. The idea was immensely popular because of the legacy of socialism and the ideology of a workers' paradise. Larisa Piyasheva, a privatization expert working for the Moscow city government, had campaigned to turn everything over to the workers all at once. Chubais was vehemently against it, seeing that the workers, in reality, had little control over a business. When it came to key decisions of ownership, the workers were under the thumb of the all-powerful managers. Both workers and managers were insiders, and insiders would be the least likely to break with the socialist past.

At first, Chubais did not want to resolve this conflict in the Supreme Soviet, a parliament largely elected in Soviet times and dominated by old-style former party officials and the so-called red directors, the Soviet-era factory managers. But he could not delay forever; he needed a legal basis for privatization. In March 1992 Chubais proposed a privatization law. He offered to give workers and managers—the insiders—40 percent of the shares of an enterprise, with the rest to be sold off to outsiders. But the overture to the insiders was not enough. In the first months of shock therapy, factory production plunged and the red directors struck back in the Supreme Soviet, where they had a strong advocate in Arkady Volsky, an imposing former Communist Party apparatchik and adviser to several Soviet leaders. Volsky had built up a lobby of the old-guard economic elite. The red directors also had a sympathetic ear in Ruslan Khasbulatov, the chairman of the Supreme Soviet. Although originally chosen by Yeltsin, Khasbulatov was increasingly outspoken against the youthful Gaidar government, and within two years he would be leading an open rebellion against Yeltsin.

The general notion of privatization was still popular, but the insider-dominated parliament wanted more than Chubais offered. They came up with a second plan, known as Option 2, which turned over 51 percent of each enterprise to the insiders, with the rest to be sold off to outsiders or held by the state. Chubais was dead set against this, fearing that the insiders would preserve the status quo. If the whole idea was to forge a new generation of effective owners, how could they be created out of the same old, tired Soviet factory managers?

But in the end, faced with certain defeat, Chubais gave in to the factory bosses. "We understood there would be no privatization if the directors didn't support it," Chubais recalled later.[24] The bosses were still strong, and the government weak. To defeat the insiders would have required more willpower than Chubais or Yeltsin could summon, more than the system could stand. "We would have had to put all the directors and all the bosses in jail," Chubais later recalled. "Or at least half of them, in the hope if you put half in jail, the other half will shut up." Neither Chubais nor Yeltsin were ready for that.[25]

On June 11, 1992, the Supreme Soviet approved the privatization law.[26] It was the last time parliament approved privatization; after that, opposition intensified, and Chubais relied solely on Yeltsin's decrees. This was a seminal moment for Chubais. For all his steely self-confidence and determination, he decided to make a crucial trade. He gave up one of his most cherished ideas at the time, the importance of outside owners, to achieve his larger goal of transferring the property out of the hands of the state. The deal was a precursor of what was to become a trademark Chubais method, one that led to a corrosive weakening of his own principles later on.

Still, at this point, Chubais was single-minded. "Every enterprise ripped out of the state and transferred to the hands of a private owner was a way of destroying Communism in Russia," he told me. "This is how we understood the situation, without any exaggeration. And every extra day we worked, we could privatize another ten, twenty, or thirty enterprises. And at that stage, it didn't matter at all to whom these enterprises went, who was getting the property. It was absolutely unimportant whether that person was ready for it."

In *Another Life,* his visionary *samizdat* text in the early 1980s, Vitaly Naishul had described the key role the *nomenklatura* and factory managers played in the Soviet industrial empire. They were the "guiding nucleus" of its success, he acknowledged, and could not be ignored, even in a shift to the market. But Naishul speculated, with remarkable prescience, that it was possible to redistribute—very widely—the entire property of the Soviet state, so it would not just wind up in the hands of the directors and the elite. He proposed that every person in the country would be given five thousand "special personal investment rubles" which they could then invest in factories, stores, and enterprises, possibly chosen from a list published in the newspaper. Naishul's underground manuscript described mass privatization with a dreamy romanticism, trying to popularize the idea of creating millions of shareholders, the equivalent of a class of stock hounds watching their dividends. "Your enterprise will function, sell and buy," he wrote. "You and other owners will get the profit and split it among yourselves, and mind the enterprise like your personal belonging." Naishul was years ahead of his time.

Chubais and Gaidar had once poured scorn on Naishul's privatization plan, saying his ideas were too complex, entirely unworkable, and too radical. But in the summer of 1992, the environment had changed dramatically, and Chubais found a new enthusiasm for Naishul's vision. Mass privatization was a political weapon that Chubais could use to blunt the land grab by the nomenklatura and the factory directors. Moreover, he could create at least the impression that millions of people had become property owners—he could coopt the angry shop workers they had seen in Nizhny Novgorod, putting a share of stock in their hands instead of a placard.

Inspired by the popularity of a privatization scheme being used in Czechoslovakia at the time, the Chubais team decided to give away property to the whole country—all at once—in 148 million checks, or vouchers, which could then be traded at auctions for shares of companies.[27] Critics later called them "worthless candy wrappers," and Chubais never lived down his absurd promise that a voucher would be worth enough to buy two Volga automobiles.[28] In fact, the vouchers themselves were less an economic tool than a political gambit by Chubais to make all people feel they were getting a piece of the pie. The Chubais agenda was simply to win popular support for privatization and thereby make it irreversible.

The vouchers were handsomely printed in a rich brown to look like currency, with an etching of the Russian White House by the Moscow River, which then housed parliament. They were called "privatization checks" because Yeltsin hated the word "voucher." At cabinet meetings, Yeltsin forbade officials from using "voucher" because he thought the English word was vulgar, but it stuck nonetheless. Each voucher had a face value of ten thousand rubles and could be picked up at the local bank for twenty-five rubles, or about ten cents. They could be traded for an employee's shares of his company, deposited in mutual funds, or simply sold or exchanged. "The share is a real right to property . . . a sort of ticket to a free economy for every one of us," Yeltsin promised when he announced the voucher scheme on August 19, 1992, a year after the failed coup against Gorbachev. From October until the following January, 144 million vouchers, or almost 98 percent of the total, were picked up.

The voucher was a forced redistribution of property, designed to forever end state control and halt spontaneous privatization by the elite. Chubais was boldly creating a new group of stakeholders: the general population. The voucher scheme "signifies the death of the command economy and the political system that was built on the basis of total state property ownership," Chubais told reporters.[29] Later he recalled that "the beginning of mass privatization—privatization based on the 'rules'—meant the end of stealing state property by the high and mighty."[30]

However, the voucher was just an interim step in the redistribution of property, a way station en route to a new class of owners. How long it would take to reach the goal, who those owners would be, and whether they would be "effective owners" was still uncertain. Private companies would be created out of the voucher auctions, and those companies would issue shares that would be bought and sold freely. That was a goal in and of itself, Vasiliev told me. But what came next? He said it was obvious that "the effective owner would appear only after the property was redistributed, after some serious period of time."[31]

As the opposition rallied in the Supreme Soviet, Chubais began a political counteroffensive for the voucher phase of mass privatization. Paul Bograd, a political consultant then working for Sawyer-Miller, a Boston firm, came to Moscow in August to help Chubais engineer a public relations and advertising campaign for the vouchers. Bograd immediately got a taste of what he was up against. He suggested a television advertisement for vouchers featuring Chubais. An older, Soviet-era bureaucrat told Bograd that advertising by the state was always anonymous. Chubais couldn't do it *personally*!

"Chubais listened," Bograd recalled. "He said, I will take responsibility for this. Failure, good or bad, someone has to own it."[32]

On the day the commercial was filmed, Bograd's heart sank: Chubais was sitting behind a desk with a flag behind him, looking like a stale Soviet *apparatchik*. "I said, try it a different way, maybe without your coat on? Or maybe standing, or leaning on your desk?" recalled Bograd, who wanted to put a little flair into Chubais. "People have had years of watching Soviet officials sitting behind their desk with their jacket on, flag and all! They have been completely discredited."

"Okay," Chubais said, "I will stand." He stood. "But I am not taking my jacket off!" Chubais felt that he had to talk to people in their own language, and that meant talking to millions who were shaped by the Soviet mind-set.[33] He was also sensitive about appearing too Western. He got ready to start his speech. Then he looked back at Bograd, smiled, and unbuttoned the jacket.

As a political gambit, the vouchers galvanized the population and became the single most important symbol of the reform years. Although experts suggested the voucher be denominated in abstract "points" rather than money, Chubais insisted they must have a monetary face value, since the whole point was to make vouchers look like a gift to the public.[34] "They seized the nation's imagination," recalled Leonid Rozhetskin, a Wall Street lawyer and Russian émigré who arrived in Moscow in 1992 to begin working with Chubais and Vasiliev. "It was at the time an absolute public relations boon to the reforms. Every newscaster, every channel was asking people on the street five or six times a day, 'What are you going to do with your voucher?' And for a period of time, the voucher may have been the most liquid form of security in the world. It could be bought and sold at every street corner kiosk and metro station from Vladivostok to St. Petersburg."[35]

The vouchers were traded by the bushel at Moscow's nascent commodity exchanges. On the largest floor, the Russian Raw Materials and Commodity Exchange, a scruffy bus station–like hall in central Moscow that traded commodities in the morning and vouchers in the afternoon, volume reached 60,000 to 100,000 vouchers a day, or about $1 million. At the end of the process, the volume reached $10 million. Traders hauling shopping bags and suitcases stuffed with vouchers often roamed the hall.

In the twenty months of the voucher program, the price gyrated widely, reaching a high of $20 and a low of $4, largely depending on the wild shifts in Russian politics. In metro stations, people lined the walls with signs pinned to their coats: "I will buy vouchers." Or, written on the flip side: "I will sell vouchers." The vouchers were freely tradable, and many millions were immediately exchanged for a bottle of vodka or sold for a song. Brokers began scouring the country for vouchers, which they stuffed in suitcases and took on overnight trains to Moscow for trading and speculating, since the street price often varied from place to place.

For the reformers, the public reaction to vouchers reaffirmed their basic assumption: Russians would respond to market incentives, and they would adopt the new ideas of shares and property ownership. Chubais later boasted, "You can ask a *babushka* in the Smolensk region what dividends are, and I think she will reasonably explain to you what they are. You would agree, that a year or a year and a half ago, the same *babushka* might have told the questioner to pack it."[36] Some enterprising businessmen were soon setting up voucher mutual funds. Chubais and Vasiliev were euphoric. "There was a feeling, this is our victory!" Chubais recalled. The hope was that investment funds would collect vouchers from the population, invest them in companies, demand good management and profits, and distribute dividends to the investors. Chubais predicted the investment funds would be ideal for "people who just want to make a reliable investment and receive a return on it." Chubais recalled how strange and sudden it all was. Even in frozen Yakutia, in the far northeastern corner of Siberia, thousands of miles from Moscow, there was a voucher mutual fund! When first told about voucher funds, an official there was puzzled. "It took me six months to run around the tundra trying to distribute the vouchers." Then he asked Chubais, "Now, should I run back to collect them?"[37]

The early euphoria faded when Chubais realized that he had liberated an unpredictable, voracious monster. Over the coming months, dozens and then hundreds of voucher funds sprung up, with loud and insistent advertising. Many of the voucher funds were just covert attempts by companies to buy up their own shares. But others were independent and aggressive; the largest Moscow fund, First Voucher, collected 4 million vouchers.[38] Soon the funds got out of control. They were completely unregulated, and Chubais failed to anticipate how fast they would proliferate. In the end, about six hundred voucher funds collected 45 million vouchers. The market that had started without institutions had become a jungle. Unscrupulous funds promised outrageous dividends, took vouchers, and never returned anything to investors, just selling the vouchers and stealing the proceeds. The managers of one fund, Neftalmazinvest, which had promised to invest in oil and diamonds, made off with about 900,000 vouchers. In the end, ninety-nine of the voucher funds disappeared without a trace.[39] People felt deceived, and they were.[40] It was just the beginning.

The voucher program was launched in October 1992 under enormous pressure. The Congress of People's Deputies, the broader legislature that met twice yearly, was set to reconvene on December 1, 1992. A new avalanche of criticism was certain, and Chubais did not yet have a single actual sale of a factory to show for it. He was desperate to complete a showcase sale before the congress began and urgently sought help from Western investment bankers.

One of them was Hans-Joerg Rudloff, president of Credit Suisse First Boston, who was a visionary financier. Rudloff had taken his firm into huge gambles as Communism collapsed, making deals with the struggling new states of Eastern Europe. He was accustomed to being wooed by prime ministers and to making fateful decisions about their ability to borrow on world markets. Rudloff, son of a German leather manufacturer who had memories of rebuilding the family factory after World War II, had sharply conflicting feelings about the chaos he saw in post-Soviet Russia. Rudloff clearly understood the lingering legacy of Soviet Communism. He knew the absolute power that the Communist Party had once held over the country, the fear that it had sometimes instilled, and the vacuum that was created when it disappeared. Who would seize the enormous inventory of factories, mines, shops, and warehouses that were up for grabs? Rudloff had grave doubts that it could be done rationally, but he was also drawn by the prospect of making a fortune.[41] His first encounter with the young Russian reformers, in early 1992, had gone badly; they seemed arrogant and turned down his offer of help. He left thinking they were hopelessly naive and vowed not to come back. But come back he did, believing that "we can't miss the biggest emerging market in history."

Through an acquaintance, Rudloff recruited a young finance specialist, Boris Jordan, who came from a family of fiercely anti-Communist Russian émigrés in New York. Jordan, a pink-cheeked, baby-faced young man, then twenty-five years old, was an incredible hustler, whose grandfather fought against the Bolsheviks with the White Army. Jordan longed for a chance to go to Russia. He grew up speaking Russian at home and passed the Foreign Service examination, but the State Department said he would never be sent to Russia as a diplomat. At the time, he was making airplane finance deals in Latin America. "I loved the deal-making environment," Jordan recalled. "But wouldn't it be better to do it somewhere I actually speak the language?"[42]

Rudloff hired Jordan and sent him to Moscow. "I smell change," he told Jordan. "Go there and find out."

Jordan was paired with Steven Jennings, a tall, square-jawed New Zealander, then thirty-two, who was as calm as Jordan was excitable. Jennings, a policy wonk who made his mark in New Zealand's 1980s privatization, had been working on a World Bank project to restructure Hungary's banking system when Rudloff recruited him for Russia. "When I walked into the office the first time, Steven had books everywhere," Jordan told me, recalling their first meeting in London. "He wrote books about privatization, and he loved the stuff. I wasn't interested in it. I was interested in how to make money."

Yet Jordan's first impressions of Moscow on his exploratory trips were discouraging. There were no markets yet. "Steven," he told Jennings, "unless this country creates markets I am not going to have anything to do here."

Once they moved to Moscow, Jordan and Jennings were familiar faces in the cold, empty offices of the State Property Committee. They brought the needy Russian staff office supplies, coffee, and ideas. "We had a lot of lazy, arrogant investment bankers come and offer to work for money," recalled a Westerner who witnessed the early months. But Jordan and Jennings seemed different: they were always hanging around. Credit Suisse First Boston became a support branch of the privatization agency. The Westerner remembered of Jordan and Jennings: "They were six foot three, in your face, and ready to go."

The pair went to Chubais and made a deal: they would help advise on the first auctions for free, which was Rudloff's idea. "Don't take any money from anybody," Rudloff told his young charges. "If we are going to risk this thing, which has a 20 percent chance of success, we might as well not take any money. So they can't accuse us of profiting off a failed program." Rudloff recalled, "We said we can't miss the biggest emerging market in history, but we can't go in saying we are going to make money. We will see what comes out of it in two or three years. I told them, don't worry about profits."[43]

Chubais took them on. Jennings was amazed when he got to Moscow and saw that all of Russia was about to be sold off by a "tiny group of people with these tiny shreds of legislation." It was "like the first step walking up Mount Everest, that's what it felt like."[44]

Their goal was to organize the first sale of a factory, the venerable Bolshevik Biscuit Company in Moscow. Founded in 1855 by a Swiss baker and later nationalized by the Soviets, the factory was well known for its elaborate cakes and cookies. Jordan and Jennings spent a month working around the clock trying to indoctrinate and cajole the management and workers. Over endless cups of tea and cookies, Jordan explained the basic concepts such as equity and the meaning of outside ownership. In this first sale, management and workers kept 51 percent of the company and the remaining 49 percent was offered to the public for vouchers. Jordan and Jennings set up an exhibition hall on the Moscow River for the big event, expecting thousands. They were not trampled, but hundreds came on the first day, offering their vouchers in a bid for shares. In a back room, Jennings and Jordan watched apprehensively as a computer tallied the auction. They could not believe what they saw. Jennings had earlier worked on a sale of an almost identical cookie company in Eastern Europe, which was sold to Pepsi for about $80 million.

Bolshevik Biscuit had just sold for $654,000.

Jordan recalled, "We looked at each other and said, 'We are on the wrong side of this deal. We shouldn't be representing the government. We should be buying the stuff!'"

"We quit!" they said to each other.

What Jordan and Jennings had seen was the dawn of Russia's transformation. Not only was the enormous stock of factories, mines, and smelters about to be sold, but judging by any comparison around the rest of the world, it was to be sold dirt cheap. Chubais didn't care; to him, the important fact was the process of redistribution. But soon the smell of money lured all kinds of investors—mega-moneyed foreigners, sharks, vultures, and gamblers—to the scene.

Gaidar, the "kamikaze" reformer who thought he would only last a few months, was ousted under pressure from the Congress of People's Deputies in December 1992, after less than a year in office, just as Chubais was selling off Bolshevik Biscuit. To appease the industrial lobby, Yeltsin replaced Gaidar with the stolid Viktor Chernomyrdin, the one-time Soviet natural gas minister who transformed his monopoly into Gazprom, Russia's largest company. For the young reformers, the appointment seemed ominous. Chernomyrdin's first words stunned them: "I am in favor of reforms, of a real market," he said, "but not of a bazaar."[45]

Even worse, Gaidar's nightmare scenario, hyperinflation—when prices zoom upward—was fast becoming a reality. The inflation was fueled by massive subsidized credits that the Russian Central Bank was pumping into the economy, at the behest of the "red directors," the Soviet-era factory bosses, and their patrons in the Supreme Soviet. The parliament had installed Viktor Gerashchenko as chairman of the Central Bank in the summer, and the former Soviet banker cheerfully opened the sluice gates to new credits. The Central Bank was giving out credits to factories at 10 or 25 percent a year while inflation was raging at 25 percent *a month*.[46] The flood of credits did little to revitalize industry but had a perverse effect on the economy, triggering inflation that became political poison as people saw their money evaporate. Berger recalled trying to persuade Gaidar to show some sympathy for people who suffered. Gaidar insisted that from an economics point of view, the ruble savings were just figures on paper; in fact, they had long ago been used up by the Soviet Union on the arms race. The money was just a "line on people's accounts."

"Yegor," Berger insisted, "we need to at least promise people that in five or seven years, you will pay them back. Not you, but others, it does not matter."

Gaidar refused to make the pledge, saying he could not deceive people.

"Don't deceive, but use a little populism!" Berger implored Gaidar, with growing exasperation. "Say, 'Yes, we will return it later, the red bandits stole it all.'"

"No," Gaidar replied somberly, "I know we won't be able to return it later. I cannot deceive the people."

"PROMISE IT!" Berger shouted. "Or you won't be able to work."

"No," Gaidar said. "We have no right to do it."[47]

Gaidar's departure left Chubais vulnerable and worried about the deepening opposition to reform. Chubais had briefly pondered quitting with Gaidar but agreed to stay on to finish the job he had begun.[48] The Supreme Soviet was considering a bill that would totally stymie privatization. Yeltsin had warned in December that reform was in "serious danger," and the danger seemed to only grow deeper as Yeltsin squared off against his Communist and nationalist critics in parliament. Those critics were led by Khasbulatov and Yeltsin's vice president, Alexander Rutskoi, the Afghan war veteran and former general who derided the young Gaidar government as "little boys in pink shorts." Yeltsin called for a referendum on reforms, and Chubais poured himself into making it a success. By the winter of 1992, Chubais had launched the privatization of small shops but had not yet sold off the factories. The process was not yet irreversible; "it can be strangled in the cradle yet," he said.[49]

Tensions between Yeltsin and the parliament ran high. Vladimir Shumeiko, then first deputy prime minister, showed Chubais a gun that he was carrying around with him. "He said he got it recently and if Khasbulatov tried to arrest him, he would shoot and he would definitely kill five or ten people," Chubais recalled. "And while on the one hand it was nonsense, on the other hand I think it was the truth; he would have really shot and killed about five people. The situation was rather hot."[50]

The referendum on Yeltsin's reforms was set for April 25, 1993, and became a turning point. The voters were asked four questions: (1) do you support Yeltsin, (2) do you support Yeltsin's economic policy, (3) do you want early elections for president, and (4) do you want early elections for parliament? The whole idea of a referendum was risky: had Yeltsin lost, it would have been a defeat for all he stood for. The Yeltsin team campaigned with a snappy string of answers to the referendum questions: "Da, Da, Nyet, Da" (yes, yes, no, and yes). Chubais portrayed the referendum as a case of the people against the politicians. "Our main support is the people," he insisted at a press conference four days before the vote. "The people who have become stockholders at their own enterprises, the people who have swapped their privatization vouchers for stocks of enterprises, the people who have won contests to buy shops or restaurants."

Chubais was sure that if they lost the referendum, his privatization struggle would be in vain. In the weeks before the vote, he had fought tooth-and-nail against bills and resolutions in the Supreme Soviet that would bottle up privatization. At one point, without telling Yeltsin or Chernomyrdin, he secretly wrote up an order to abruptly cancel the whole privatization program and took it in his pocket to parliament, where, if necessary, he was ready to blow up his entire project and let the blame fall on Khasbulatov. He never carried out the stunt, but no tactics were off-limits for Chubais. When Communists in Chelyabinsk, in the Urals, tried to start a regional revolt against privatization, Chubais immediately flew there and publicly challenged them. What the public did not see was a four-hour long harangue against the Chelyabinsk governor back in Moscow. Chubais threatened to block the governor at every turn. "I will simply strangle you," Chubais threatened him.[51]

Chubais never let it be told, but he had deployed a secret weapon to help Yeltsin win the April referendum. Chubais privately met with George Soros, the Hungarian-born superfinancier and philanthropist, who was in Moscow to launch a program to help scientists. Soros agreed to bankroll the pro-Yeltsin referendum campaign, the first but not the last time he would come to the rescue of the reformers. A Chubais representative, a Westerner, went to Switzerland and made the financial arrangements for a $1 million transfer from Soros to off-shore accounts that Chubais could draw on for the campaign. The money helped the Yeltsin forces buy advertising to drown out the voices of the opposition.[52]

Chubais was no longer on speaking terms with Khasbulatov. In the halls of parliament, "they talked openly about prison cells being readied for us." Chubais told me that on April 24, the night before the vote, "I was sitting in my ministers' office, destroying documents, because I understood if Yeltsin were to lose the election, Khasbulatov would not pity his opponents."

As it turned out, Yeltsin won the referendum, with 58 percent expressing confidence in him and 52 percent approving of economic reform. The threats to privatization eased. The referendum provided Yeltsin some political breathing space before his confrontation with parliament turned violent in October. By then, however, much of Russian industry was already on its way to being sold. There was no turning back.

"If the problem is only that the rich will buy up the property," Chubais mused at one point, "I am sure that is the way it must be."[53] The privatization slogan had been to create millions of shareholders, and indeed the voucher plan had touched millions. But in the next step, the ownership of Russia's property was reshuffled once again, this time into fewer hands, including a few millionaires. These were men who had daring and smarts, who had come to the same realization that struck Jordan and Jennings on the day Bolshevik Biscuit was privatized—that Russia held incredible treasure and Chubais was practically giving away the keys to anyone who was farsighted enough to take them.

William Browder was one of them. He was the grandson of Earl Browder, leader of the American Communist Party (1932–1945). Bill Browder yearned to see the Russia of his family roots, and after Stanford Business School and a stint working privatization in Poland, he joined the Eastern Europe team of Salomon Brothers in London to specialize in Russia. Browder, who has a wry but incisive sense of humor and a sharp eye for finance, found it lonely work: no one believed there was any business in Russia. The boss threw some expense account sheets at him and told him to go to Russia and see what he could find.

Browder snared an assignment to advise the trawler fleet in the northern port city of Murmansk on privatization. The manager of the fleet told him there were one hundred ships, and each cost $20 million new. But management was entitled to buy its 51 percent of the company for the equivalent of just $2.5 million. Browder took out a sheet of blank white paper and did some quick calculations. His scratch-pad math practically screamed off the page: huge assets were for sale, cheap. "I thought to myself at that moment," Browder recalled, "I cannot make a lot of money as an investment banker in Russia, but I can make a lot of money as an investor in Russia." Browder went back and started to sketch out the value of other companies, especially in the oil industry. "Sure enough, the same thing in oil!"[54]

Browder eventually built up the largest private investment fund in Russia. But in these early days, the picture of riches in Russia was hazy, the prospects dim. Companies had no open financial data, managers were distrustful, marketing or business plans did not exist. The risks were imponderably large. Back in London, Browder at first met with skepticism and disbelief. "I was running around Salomon Brothers trying to find someone who would listen that this was going to be the most unbelievable investment opportunity there ever was," he told me. Eventually, he got permission to invest $25 million, a tiny sum for one of the world's largest investment houses, but a large commitment for Russia at the time. Browder bought as many vouchers as he could, and then bought shares in little-known companies.

Browder had an advantage. He knew an oil trader in Moscow who had rudimentary information about the companies that were being privatized, especially in oil. "At the time, just knowing the names of the companies and roughly what the production and reserves were was huge, valuable information," Browder recalled. He had the facts on a spreadsheet but was careful not to show it to anyone. He had the first crack at the best investments, since everyone else was in the dark.

At the time, not everyone could see through the fog of despair that blanketed the Russian economy. There were almost daily stories of factories failing, workers without wages, idled assembly lines, and industrial misery. Who wanted to buy an old Soviet factory with no competitive markets, aging equipment, no serious accounting, and thousands of dependent workers? It was not a pretty sight. Rutskoi, the rebellious Yeltsin vice president, declared that the reformers had "turned Russia into an economic dump."

Indeed, the big money was not in property, but in finance. Currency speculation, trading in gold and precious metals, arbitrage in oil—these were the new gushers of the first post-Soviet years. Smolensky, devoting himself to his banking business, was distinctly uninterested in Russian factories. He was making a mint running dollar-ruble speculation, changing money back and forth every day and gambling on tomorrow's exchange rate. Gusinsky was cementing his alliance with Luzhkov, making money from real estate and using the city government deposits in his bank.

But some Russians had a clue of what lurked behind the door Chubais was opening. Khodorkovsky bought up a huge quantity of vouchers. His Bank Menatep was a major player in the voucher market, even though Khodorkovsky knew Russian industry was in deep distress. "Idealism," Khodorkovsky recalled of his decision to buy vouchers. "Since my childhood I wanted to be director of a plant. My parents worked at a plant their whole lives. I was sure and I am still sure that the most important thing is industry." But like many others, Khodorkovsky was shooting in the dark. He could not figure out which factories were potentially lucrative, so he bought many. Using his connections, he was able to pick up many factories in so-called investment tenders, in which the winner promised to make investments later on but rarely did. The journalist Yulia Latynina said Khodorkovsky turned Menatep into the first Russian investment bank, with fierce determination. "No other bank dug up industry with such rage and omnivorousness," she recalled.[55] Khodorkovsky purchased large blocks of shares in timber, titanium, pipe, copper smelting, and other industries, more than one hundred companies in all. Khodorkovsky told me that he hired Andersen Consulting to survey the crazy-quilt industry he had assembled, and the management consultants told him he had gathered up the equivalent of a South Korean conglomerate. They described for Khodorkovsky how it could work, like Samsung. The comparison did not appeal to him. "When it was done," Khodorkovsky recalled, "I said, this cannot work." He would soon decide to go after the richest single treasure, oil.

Behind the shuttered factory gates, a mammoth fire sale was getting under way. Judging by the number of vouchers and their street price, the total value of Russian industry was under $12 billion. In other words, the equity of all Russian factories, including oil, gas, some transportation, and most of manufacturing, was worth less than that of Kellogg or Anheuser-Busch. In a privatization carried out with special restrictions against foreigners and outsiders, Gazprom came out of the voucher auction with a value of under $228 million, or about one-thousandth of the value put on it by foreign investment banks. The market value of Zil, the famous truck and limousine maker with 100,000 workers, was $16 million. The market value of the giant Gorky Automobile Works, known as GAZ, which manufactures the Volga car, was $27 million. Indeed, the auto factory was so lucrative that the managers used state credits to buy up 1.8 million vouchers through dummy firms and then tried to grab the factory for themselves, but they were stopped when the scheme was uncovered. The market value of two household names in Russian manufacturing,

Uralmash and Perm Motors, were $4 million and $6 million respectively. Whereas American firms typically have market values of $100,000 per employee, Russian firms obtained voucher auction values of between $100 and $500 per worker, or two hundred times less.[56]

Jordan was scouring Russia for vouchers, which he bought every day from a small circle of Russian brokers and then sold to foreign investors at a giant markup. Even though he had spotted the ludicrously low factory values, Jordan never invested in factories, instead working frenetically as a middleman speculating in vouchers, for which there was often a sudden demand before a big auction. Jordan had trouble finding a safe place to store the mountains of vouchers and eventually settled on a vaultlike room in the tall high-rise building across from the Russian White House. This distinctive building in Soviet times had housed the Socialist bloc economic association, the Council on Mutual Economic Assistance. It was the same building where Luzhkov and Gusinsky had set up their offices. Every night, after buying up vouchers, brokers would take the risk of delivering them to the underground room, and Jordan would go there to inspect the paperwork. With hundreds of thousands of vouchers, the process was a logistical nightmare. One evening Jordan noticed the clerks slicing up condoms with scissors and then using them to bundle the vouchers. They had no rubber bands.

For a few sweaty hours during the violent October 1993 confrontation between Yeltsin and hard-liners at the Russian parliament, Jordan and the Chubais staff suffered a terrible scare—they feared the rebellious nationalists and hard-liners, led by Rutskoi and Khasbulatov, might storm the room where the vouchers were stored, just across the street. Tens of millions of dollars worth of vouchers were lying there—the guts of the whole privatization program!—and in one moment they could have gone up in smoke. But the anti-Yeltsin forces at the White House never discovered it. The voucher vault was safe.[57]

At the beginning of 1994 came a dawning realization in the West that Russian industry was going to be a new Klondike. Yeltsin won a new constitution that gave him broad powers and a new legislature. The old Supreme Soviet was history. Jordan recalled that he had tried, in vain, in March 1993, before Yeltsin won the referendum, to interest foreign investors in the vouchers. "I would go out and tell people about Russia, and no one would let me into their office," he recalled. "Nobody cared. All around the world I went for three weeks. And in

November, I went on another roadshow. Then people started to open their doors to me. And in March 1994, every person in the world wanted to know who I was."

Between December 1993 and June 1994, when the voucher phase ended, Jordan and Jennings had traded 16,346,070 vouchers—more than 10 percent of the total. Foreign investors were hungry for Russian stocks, even though they often knew nothing about the companies they were buying. Even an oil major like Lukoil had barely one page of financial data to share with investors.

A turning point came in May 1994 with the publication of an article in the *Economist* titled "Sale of the Century," which laid out the stark math: Russian assets were very, very cheap compared with similar property elsewhere in the world. The article noted that shares in Bolshevik Biscuit were trading at $53 each, or three times the price at the 1992 privatization. Still, Bolshevik's market value per ton of output was $9, while a Polish biscuit maker, Wedel, was valued by its stock market then at $850 a ton.[58]

Right after the *Economist* article appeared, Browder recalled a flood of interest in Russia among his colleagues in London, who earlier would not give him the time of day. "I was sitting on the trading floor and all of a sudden all the managing directors are around my desk. 'Bill,' they said, 'Interesting stuff you are doing there. Can you get us some Lukoil?'"

Despite two years of political crisis, Chubais had delivered on his core promise to put state property into private hands. About fourteen thousand firms went through voucher auctions in twenty months, and thousands more small shops and businesses were privatized; all told, about 70 percent of the economy was put into a new private sector.

Would the new owners prove more effective than the Soviet masters? At the end of the period of mass privatization, in mid-1994, there were plenty of danger signs. Rozhetskin traveled the back roads of Russia, looking at factories, and many of the owners he encountered were not interested in building the businesses they had purchased cheaply. Instead, they were just stripping the assets and sucking out the cash flow. The whole idea of corporate management skills, boardroom discipline, and effective ownership seemed distant, the concepts inchoate.

But Chubais was not concerned with that. The lessons of management and ownership would come later. If the owners were bad, they would fail. "That's all there is to it," he said. "And if the second owner is bad also, he will go broke. If he is good, he won't."[59]

In late 1994, Chubais was ebullient about the future of the property he had freed from the state. "Everything that we've done already has convinced me that our country is on the doorstep of an investment boom," he said. "And these are not my fantasies."

One day after mass privatization was complete, Rudloff found himself sitting across the table from Chubais. Ever the gruff skeptic, Rudloff looked at Chubais and asked him point-blank, "What have you really done for Russia?"

Chubais, who had steely nerves and an unshakable sense of mission, replied, "I have privatized power. I finished off the Communist system."

Rudloff was speechless, because what Chubais said was both breathtaking and true.

Chapter 9

Easy Money

BORIS BEREZOVSKY, full of plans, came to the Russian Finance Ministry several times in 1993. He wanted to see Bella Zlatkis, a career bureaucrat, a stocky woman of Latvian descent, with short, black hair and an authoritative tone. In the early 1990s, Zlatkis had been appointed to head a new department in the ministry. It was called the Department of Securities and Financial Markets, although no one really knew much about securities and the financial markets were just beginning to take shape.

Berezovsky was a fountain of ideas, she recalled, and ever so insistent. In her small office, Zlatkis listened as Berezovsky described his latest dream. He wanted to construct a new auto factory, to create a "people's car" like the Volkswagen. Berezovsky's company, Logovaz, was already Russia's leading car dealer, taking thousands of Zhiguli cars from the Avtovaz factory in Togliatti and paying for them much later, in deflated rubles. Now Berezovsky was proposing to go further. He told Zlatkis he needed to raise $2 billion to build a factory to manufacture the people's car. Imagine how Russians would flock to the showrooms! A car was the dream of the Russian Everyman, and Berezovsky had a financial plan to match his imagination.

The privatization voucher had blazed a trail through the consciousness of the Russian people. On the streets, vouchers were ubiquitous; the exchanges hummed with voucher trading. The public was learning fast about shares, pieces of paper with a real value. Voucher funds, promising lucrative returns, spread like wildfire, beckoning new investors.

A thought occurred to Berezovsky: if the state could issue securities—the vouchers—then why couldn't he? The people would finance the "people's car." They would buy shares.

The Avtovaz factory in Togliatti was troubled, overrun by petty criminals and robbed blind by its managers. But the director, Vladimir Kadannikov, stood behind Berezovsky's dream. The sandy-haired Kadannikov, who had taken the helm of Avtovaz in 1986 at the beginning of *perestroika,* was one of the country's most prominent industrial generals, and he lent an air of authority to Berezovsky's scheme. Kadannikov recalled how Volkswagen—the German people's car—had also gotten started with small individual investments before World War II.[1]

"What's good for Avtovaz is good for Russia," Kaddanikov had boasted, borrowing a famous slogan of American capitalism.[2] The boast came, oddly, as Kadannikov's own manufacturing kingdom was being dismembered and was collapsing under the weight of theft, violence, and hyperinflation.

Zlatkis was skeptical about Berezovsky raising the money from shares to build his dream factory. The Russian financial markets were still inchoate, a grab bag of small commodity exchanges, without controls, selling vouchers and a handful of company shares in between tons of steel pipe. They were growing faster than the rules, the government, or the laws could keep up. Zlatkis was being thrust onto the frontier of wild capitalism, the kind without institutions or rules. Berezovsky was proposing to create a new, private financial instrument, with certain unique features that would make it behave like real money. He implored Zlatkis to approve it. The new security would be a huge precedent, a leap into the unknown. It was so new, Zlatkis concluded, that there were no laws governing it.

"I saw the flaws of the investment project," Zlatkis later told me. "They needed $2 billion to establish what they wanted. But the financial market can give just so much. They could collect $100 million; they couldn't possibly have collected more. But with that money, they couldn't build anything. Maybe a garment factory, but not anything in auto manufacturing that would be interesting."

Berezovsky would not give up. "He was sure that he would be able to collect $2 billion in Russia," Zlatkis recalled. Berezovsky wanted to sell shares. At the mention of the word, Zlatkis recalled a snowy night back in December 1991 when she had just taken the job in the Finance Ministry. The Soviet Union was collapsing and Yeltsin was coming to power at the beginning of shock therapy. Zlatkis was heading home from her office at 11:00 P.M. on a winter night; the streets were dark and the sidewalks icy. As Zlatkis shivered, her driver took the wheel of the unheated, aging Zaporozhets and rounded a dark corner near Red Square. Zlatkis saw a familiar sight: in the cold, a long line of people, just standing and waiting, under a single lamp. She told the driver to stop. She got out to see what might be at the end of the line. She saw mostly elderly women, bundled against the cold.

She heard them talking about "shares." They were standing in line to buy a piece of paper that promised huge returns in a year. The shares were issued by Bank Menatep. "We have been here for several days, standing in line to buy shares," Zlatkis was told by the first woman she met. "They are selling shares. They are going to pay a big interest on them. We are investing a thousand rubles. And they promise that in a year, they are going to pay ten thousand rubles." The women were waiting for easy money.

Zlatkis did not dare mention that she was chief of a Finance Ministry department for securities. But she could not remain quiet. She tried to persuade the women that it was all a mistake, a rip-off. They would never see the money again. Her driver tugged at her coat, saying it was useless to persuade them all by herself. But Zlatkis persisted, despite the cold air and the hostile looks. Sadly, they were being deceived. The shares were not legal. They would lose the money. Couldn't they see?

The women huddled closer, closing their circle against her entreaties. They told Zlatkis to get lost. They would not listen to her. They glanced anxiously over their shoulders as she begged them to realize that the shares were worthless. "They were very angry," Zlatkis remembered. "They just drove me away. I couldn't do anything. I was talking to people who were absolutely not ready to hear me, to understand me."[3] Soon the scene in the snow would come back to haunt her—and them.

*

The great inflation of the early 1990s did not subside in Russia as it had in Poland. Every month in 1992 and 1993, the ruble's value fell as the Central Bank recklessly pumped billions in fresh credits into the system. A full year after Gaidar had set prices free, consumer inflation in Russia was still galloping ahead at 25 percent a month.[4] By the end of 1994, consumer prices were 2,000 percent higher than they had been in December 1990.[5] Viktor Gerashchenko, chairman of the Russian Central Bank, thought in Soviet fashion that pumping more money into the economy would save it. Instead, he was wrecking it.

Gaidar was not completely blind to the damage to the economy, even though he had trouble displaying sympathy for the population. "Hyperinflation is the most terrible monetary catastrophe of all," he recalled years later. "It occurs when the public has lost all faith in its own national currency and rushes to get rid of it, buying up whatever comes to hand."[6]

That is precisely what happened in Russia. Hyperinflation destabilized the economy and wiped out the savings of a population. It was cruel and unusual punishment. A scientist, whose salary in Soviet times may have been two hundred rubles a month, who may have saved five thousand rubles over a career, saw the value of his entire life savings shrink to a loaf of bread. But for the most cunning and daring businessmen, the wave of inflation was an incredible opportunity. It heralded an age of fantastically easy money, of fortunes spun out of thin air. The lure was especially strong for those who already had connections, such as the cooperative businessmen, nascent bankers, Komsomol activists and ex-KGB agents, and those who had guts, including intrepid university students who had never known the Soviet system.

Russia was a broken country that needed to attract investment, build confidence in its currency, and establish the basic institutions of the market. The wave of easy money was enormously destructive to all these goals. It taught all the wrong lessons, and the damage lingered throughout the 1990s. The mind-set of these years was that it was far more profitable to wheel and deal with finance, to leverage money, and to exploit the distortions of inflation than to build a business brick by brick. The profits were astounding for Russia, but so were the costs—easy money put off the hard work until later.

In the Soviet system, money played a secondary role in the economy. In the years after the revolution, a few Bolsheviks even fantasized that money would disappear altogether in the workers' paradise. Soviet industry was geared first and foremost toward meeting production targets and plans, and money was not generally critical to success or failure. If the goods from a factory were shoddy or unneeded, the factory still got subsidies. A whole panoply of notions about money and its relation to private ownership—profit, loss, debt, interest, shares and dividends—did not exist. Moreover, for consumers as well as factories, goods in the shortage economy existed beyond the reach of money; the key factor was access or privilege, not cash.

When it came to money, Russians harbored a deep and abiding distrust of their rulers. Soviet leaders had periodically confiscated people's savings to soak up the so-called monetary overhang, the excess rubles that accumulated because there was nothing to buy. The last confiscation was still fresh in public memory, inflicted by Prime Minister Valentin Pavlov, who suddenly withdrew fifty and one hundred ruble banknotes from circulation in 1991.

When Yeltsin launched shock therapy by freeing most prices, his central goal was to ensure that money and prices, and not the dictates of central planning, would play the leading role in the complex drama of economic life. For the Yeltsin revolution to work, it had to impart a profound new meaning to the definition of money, to infuse the ruble with value and bury the Soviet legacy. In theory, money and prices would become the chief indicators of success or failure, separating good from bad.

But when shock therapy began, the first results did little to establish faith in the currency. The initial surge of inflation heightened mistrust of the ruble. In 1992–1994, the Russian people showed they were indeed rational actors in response to economic change: they got rid of their rubles as fast as possible. The dollar became king. Primitive barter trade took hold, as refrigerators were traded for pickles and coal for flour, and nothing for rubles. Those who had the means sent their money abroad, creating a river of "capital flight" out of Russia that continued for years. But most ordinary people just looked for somewhere else to put their money—perhaps in dollars under the mattress.

Just as hyperinflation began to roll through the economy, just as people began to think about getting rid of their rubles as fast as possible, Chubais opened the door for an alternative place for their money—the voucher and voucher mutual funds. The voucher funds soon evolved into all manner of get-rich-quick temptations and climaxed in 1994 in a wave of popular but destructive financial pyramid schemes. If the voucher was a legal financial instrument, given to everyone as a gift by the state, it was not such a big leap to imagine that other pieces of investment paper could be legal too and satisfy the hunger for quick rewards in a time of runaway inflation. Gaidar feared at the outset that the vouchers would lead to massive speculation—the gambling kind. He was absolutely right. The voucher funds soon began to play on people's expectations for easy money, sprinkling their names with the words "diamonds" and "oil" and offering annual returns over 500 percent.

The voucher had opened a door, and beyond it was a wonderland of unregulated securities, surrogate money, and wild finance, a period that was a perfect illustration of what happens when the market has no rules. A population that for seven decades had been lectured about the ills of bourgeois capitalism was suddenly told, "Get rich quick!" They were not just invited but exhorted to get rich. The exhortations were carried by ads in the newspapers and on television, followed by an army of people to help make the dreams come true. Voucher traders became brokers, speculators, and in some cases thieves. Yevgeny Myslovsky, a veteran Soviet-era prosecutor who later investigated many of the dubious financial schemes of the early 1990s, chronicled a typical rip-off by one voucher fund, Astron. The director collected a thousand vouchers from 254 people between December 1992 and March 1993. He then sold them for 5 million rubles, of which he spent 1 million on himself and paid out some of the remaining money to lure more investors. But he invested in nothing—it was strictly a trick.[7]

Psychologically, Russians were totally unprepared to resist the new temptations of wealth. They knew practically nothing about real money or investment; many had never seen a personal check or stock certificate. Alexander Oslon, a leading pollster, described the first post-Soviet years as similar to a man released from prison. When the prisoner first gets out, he is overwhelmed by the blinding light, the fresh air, the euphoric freedom, and the sense of being weak-kneed and naive in a strange new world. The Russian people went through the same transformation. "They emancipated themselves from censorship; they freed themselves from the pressure of the authorities; they emancipated themselves from economic monotony," Oslon explained.[8] "Their initiatives and their desires, which were always imprisoned, were set free." But they didn't know how to handle it.

"In that time, elements of a new language appeared," Oslon recalled. "Words like 'business,' 'limited,' 'joint stock company,' 'funds market,' 'dollar exchange rate.'" The new language was followed by alluring, stark, and unrealistic ideas of how the market economy would function. "At the beginning of the period was a fairy-tale concept of capitalism, 'a field of miracles,'" Oslon told me. He remembered that millions of people were captivated by a television advertisement for one investment fund in which a father and son are sitting, fishing. The son says, "Papa, we are sitting here, and the money is coming!" The message: you can sit and do nothing, and money springs up on its own accord. This yearning for a miracle, for dreams to come true, was fertile ground for the man with big ideas, Berezovsky.

Berezovsky's brainchild was the All-Russian Automobile Alliance, known by its Russian acronym, AVVA. The alliance was an ingenious scheme that would both tap into public anxiety about high inflation and exploit the pent-up desire of millions of people to own their own car. Berezovsky was general director of the alliance, and the handsome certificates he would sell to the public were signed on the reverse by Kadannikov, director of the huge Avtovaz factory in Togliatti, who became the new chairman of AVVA.

One day after the December 13, 1993, election, in which Yeltsin won approval of the new Russian constitution and a new parliament, the securities went on sale in the vast exhibition hall on Manezh Square next to the Kremlin.[9] The certificates were printed in Switzerland on paper fine enough for any national currency, with special protection against counterfeiting. Each one was engraved with a portrait of a famous prerevolutionary Russian industrialist, such as Savva Mamontov, a patron of the arts and literature, iron magnate, and the largest shareholder of the Moscow-Yaroslavl-Archangelsk railroad. The certificates were specially flown to Moscow from Zurich in heavy wooden crates and stored under tight security.

The certificates said quite clearly on the front side: "One Share." The nominal face value was ten thousand rubles, and each certificate carried eight perforated coupons attached to the bottom, labeled

"Check to Receive Dividends." Berezovsky promised that the first dividends would be paid in 1995, even though the new auto factory would not go into operation for a few years.

But the back of the certificate held a clue that not everything was as it seemed. The certificate was not a share of stock in the legal or traditional sense. Rather, it was a new kind of security, a hybrid called a "bearer certificate." The bearer certificate gave the person who held it only one right: to exchange it for one genuine share of AVVA. However, trading in the bearer certificate was very difficult, and all the shares not claimed (meaning most of them) would be controlled by AVVA itself. In other words, AVVA was selling papers that said "One Share" on the front but said they were not a share on the back. The certificate holder had no voting rights. Real control rested with the founders of AVVA, a series of companies and banks close to Berezovsky and Kadannikov.[10]

Berezovsky added a special twist to discourage people from trading in their certificates. With much hype, AVVA promised to give away 100,000 Avtovaz cars and big discounts on car purchases in a lottery for those who held the certificates. Berezovsky personally announced the first lottery on February 18, 1994, saying 6,500 cars were being offered—every tenth car for free, and the others with 25 percent and 50 percent discounts.[11] But the rules of the lottery were that only people who did *not* trade in their certificates could participate. In the end, the car giveaway lotteries were held just three times. The gambit worked: most people did not trade in their certificates and just stashed them in a drawer. This was good for Berezovsky because it meant he could keep the money and keep control of AVVA too.

There was another trick. The AVVA papers were not imprinted with the name of the bearer, as required by law for a real share of stock. This made the papers, like privatization vouchers, easier to trade on the street. But consequently there would never be a proper list of those who bought them because there were no names. Thus it would be extremely difficult to pay dividends, as promised.

In public, Berezovsky's ambition was sky-high. The "people's car" project, he announced, would build a new factory in Togliatti to manufacture 300,000 cars a year. The project was estimated to cost between $1.5 billion and $3 billion, although Berezovsky initially hoped to raise about $300 million from selling the AVVA certificates and the rest from a foreign investor, who was portrayed as just around the corner. Kadannikov frequently and prominently suggested the possibility of a joint venture with General Motors. A team of industrial and factory specialists at AVVA worked out dozens of different scenarios for the envisioned factory and visited auto parts suppliers all over Russia.[12] Zlatkis recalled that Berezovsky "was planning to become a Ford," a pillar of the Russian auto industry. "It was his favorite topic to talk about. I'm convinced he was planning to build it." President Yeltsin signed a decree in late December 1993 awarding AVVA substantial tax breaks over the next three years.

Berezovsky's public declarations about the "people's car," however, were not the whole story. As early as 1994, Berezovsky was also planning, with Kadannikov, to buy a sizable chunk—perhaps all—of the Avtovaz factory, which was being privatized.[13] Berezovsky shrewdly realized that Avtovaz was an industrial crown jewel of Russia but would be sold cheaply in the privatization giveaway. So he and Kaddanikov essentially created a scheme to raise the necessary money from people on the street, and they used it to buy shares in Avtovaz.

Yuli Dubov, author of the thinly disguised novel about Berezovsky, *Bolshaya Paika,* wrote that the takeover had to be plotted in secret, "so that the people in the factory wouldn't understand" the real intention, "and so that the poor Russian people, intended to be the main source of the operation's financing, would head for the cash collection points."

Dubov's novel contains some remarkably precise details about the AVVA scheme that are supported by other evidence. Berezovsky deliberately created the hybrid security so he could sell as many certificates as possible while bypassing laws that required shares to be registered in someone's name. "We won't be selling shares, we'll be selling securities," the Berezovsky character says in Dubov's book. "Did you get that? The law doesn't say a word about that sort of paper!" When the operation was over, "the only shareholders will be us, ourselves, and we," he added. "And we will be making all the decisions. And meanwhile, the rest of the people will be sitting with their wrap papers. And it will be even better if they keep their papers to themselves, for good."[14]

At the Finance Ministry, the responsibility for registration of a new security fell to Zlatkis. Berezovsky lobbied her for permission to sell the AVVA certificates. Zlatkis knew that the new security was not covered by existing law. "The lawyers, who saw that issuance, said it was legal," Zlatkis told me. "It was in accord with Russian legislation at that time." The law didn't even mention these new types of securities, known as bearer certificates. Berezovsky drove right through the gap.

He then lured two of Zlatkis's deputies to come to AVVA and made her a tempting offer. Zlatkis said her salary at the time was the equivalent of $30 a month. Berezovsky offered her a job at $15,000 a month. "I couldn't even imagine such a salary could exist," she told me. "Had I believed in all those things, in all those projects, I would have taken the offer. And for a long time I had doubts." But Zlatkis told me she ultimately turned Berezovsky down because she thought AVVA's financial plan would never work—they could never collect the kind of money Berezovsky dreamed of.

At first, Berezovsky's plan looked like a winner. Outside the Manezh exhibition hall, right next to the Kremlin, long lines formed to buy the certificates; AVVA also accepted vouchers in payment. "Let's go!" implored the AVVA television advertising. The AVVA certificates soon became some of the most traded papers in the Moscow commodity exchanges. The venture reaped about $50 million between December 1993 and mid-1994. All together, 2.6 million people gave their money and vouchers for a piece of paper that did not even have their name written on it. Then Lyonya Golubkov took to the airwaves, and Berezovsky's automobile alliance ran out of gas.

Golubkov was the name of a character in a television commercial. He was slightly pudgy, with unkempt, greasy black hair and a dull metal tooth. Unassuming and disheveled yet brimming with enthusiasm, Golubkov became the prophet of the easy money age. Supposedly he had once been a tractor driver, but his life changed overnight when he bought shares in a company called MMM and struck it rich. He bought a pair of boots for his wife, then a fur coat, and finally splurged on a trip to San Francisco to watch Russia play in the World Cup. Golubkov's fictional adventures were the centerpiece of a phenomenally successful television advertising campaign that took Russia by storm in the spring of 1994. Golubkov sold dreams, and the weary Russian people bought them, spending billions of rubles to purchase certificates in MMM promising instant wealth at 3,000 percent interest a year. Golubkov played on Russian television screens night after night for months—2,666 ads aired on Russian television in March, April, and May alone—in spots that always featured the same sprightly music, a simple white backdrop, and a slapstick style and usually ended with the ubiquitous MMM logo.[15]

Behind the curtains of MMM was a reclusive former mathematician, Sergei Mavrodi, who traded in jeans, records, and other goods in the Soviet days and later started a cooperative in the *perestroika* years, selling computers. Mavrodi was a quiet figure; when his apartment was later searched, police found it relatively modest, filled with butterfly collections and a stuffed bat on the wall. In 1993, when vouchers appeared, Mavrodi moved into the world of securities, and his voucher investment fund, MMM-Invest, became one of the largest and loudest in Russia. "MMM Invest turns your vouchers into gold!" promised the television commercials.[16] However, Mavrodi was to make a far greater contribution to Russian capitalism than just speculating in vouchers. He showed an entire country how to make money out of thin air.

On June 11 and June 16, 1993, Mavrodi officially registered the MMM joint stock company, with 991,000 authorized shares at a nominal price of a thousand rubles each. In the following months, Mavrodi then spun a web of associated companies—named after jewels, such as Diamond and Sapphire—which would trade in hybrid securities, the same "bearer certificates" that Berezovsky had used in setting up AVVA. Although the government had approved the issuance of 991,000 MMM shares, Mavrodi really sold millions of these bearer certificates, each of which was not actually a share but a claim on a bit of a share.

At least Berezovsky promoted his partnership with a famous industrialist, Kadannikov. Berezovsky had a tangible, if unrealistic, goal of building a factory, with the promise of dividends sometime in the future. By contrast, Mavrodi produced nothing but the lure of quick riches. In one memorable advertisement, Golubkov and his older brother Ivan are in San Francisco for the soccer match. Ivan sits in the stands, his head in his hands. He moans despairingly: I worked my whole life and got nothing! And Lyonya, this little brat, did nothing, and he's rich.

Mavrodi's company opened branch offices where investors could buy the certificates. In a few weeks, or even days, a purchaser could trade in the certificates for cash at the MMM central office at 26 Varshavskoye Shosse in Moscow. The redemption price was set by

Mavrodi, who was making a market in his own securities and sent the price higher and higher. The securities soared from 1,600 rubles, or the equivalent of a dollar at the prevailing exchange rate, in February to 105,600 rubles, or $50, in late July 1994. It was a classic pyramid scheme, in which money from the new investors was used to pay off earlier investors.

Mavrodi was imitating a famous American con artist, Charles Ponzi, a dapper rogue who in 1920 collected an estimated $15 million in eight months by persuading tens of thousands of Bostonians that he had unlocked the secret to easy wealth. Ponzi claimed to have found a way to profit by speculating in international postal reply coupons, a form of prepaid return postage for use in foreign correspondence. After he had paid off his first round of investors—he had paid 50 percent interest in ninety days—new money was rolling in. He was simply reshuffling the money from new investors to old ones, which came to be known as a Ponzi scheme. Ponzi snared forty thousand investors before the scheme crashed.[17]

In Mavrodi's case, the visible payout was a key part of the marketing trick. Myslovsky, the prosecutor who later investigated the scheme, pinpointed the central deception of Mavrodi: he alone controlled the market in MMM certificates. The company created wild demand for the certificates but "kept silent about the fact that it had a right to stop buying the papers any minute or drastically cut down the quotes," Myslovsky said. For those who got the huge payouts, the game was lucrative, but there was always a big risk that the music would stop suddenly and everyone holding the certificates would be cheated.

While the price soared, Mavrodi was secretive about how he was able to generate such handsome returns, and it appeared that millions of people did not want to know the truth. They lined up—sometimes by the hundreds—to buy the certificates. The government too was passive and mystified. Zlatkis told a journalist at the time that the returns were amazing, but she saw nothing illegal. "They must be working really hard with their securities and the money every day to manage it," she said.[18] Another time, she declared, "There will always be a financial product offered to the market. We cannot ban this process."[19]

What Mavrodi had really mastered was marketing. His television advertising was created by Bakhyt Kilibayev, a thirty-six-year-old Kazakh film director who touched the raw nerves of post-Soviet Russia. The advertisements were brief and rather crudely produced but poignant in message; they offered a powerful antidote to the prevailing cynicism, pessimism, and worry about daily life. The advertising also dealt head-on with ignorance and naïveté about finance and securities. In one of the initial spots, an elderly man is seen buying an MMM certificate for the first time. "Indeed, a strange piece of paper," acknowledges the cheerful announcer, as the old man peers through his broken eyeglasses at the document. Later, eyeglasses repaired, he collects his cash. In another spot, newlyweds Igor and Julia, both students, quarrel over their meager budget. "Not a simple solution, but a decision is taken," intones the announcer as they slap their cash on the counter at MMM. When they return three weeks later to collect, Julia's eyes light up and they embrace. "It's better than a stipend!" exults Igor. In another commercial, a lonely single woman, Marina Sergeyevna, believes in no one, says the announcer. But then she collects her cash at MMM and declares, "They did not fool me!" She later gets a boyfriend on the strength of her winnings. "Here, we don't fool people," declares the announcer. The message was clear: MMM paper is strange but worth real money. It is better than government stipends, and we won't fool you as Prime Minister Pavlov did.

But the most powerful television huckster was Golubkov himself, the erstwhile construction worker now living the high life.[20] In one of the early advertisements, he is shown dressed in an ill-fitting suit, holding a pointer, and motioning toward a chart, plotting the ever rising path of the family's fortune and acquisitions: boots, fur coat, furniture, and a car next month. At the top of the chart: a house.

"House in Paris?" inquires his wife, Rita, sitting in her housecoat in an overstuffed chair and munching chocolates.

"Why not?" says the announcer, as Golubkov looks up dreamily at the ceiling.

In yet another spot, Lyonya and his older brother, Ivan, who is a tattooed coal miner, argue at a kitchen table, a bottle of vodka and pickled cucumbers between them. Ivan declares that Lyonya is a freeloader, a *khaliavschik*. "You blockhead!" Ivan declares. "Don't you remember what our parents taught us? To work honestly. And here you are running around and making a fuss buying stocks. You're a *khaliavschik!*"

Lyonya answers slowly. "You're wrong, brother. I'm not a *khaliavschik*, brother. I earn money honestly, with my excavator. And I buy shares that bring profit to me. You wanted to build a factory. You can't build it on your own. But if we all chip in, we can build one that will bring profit to us and feed us. I'm not a *khaliavschik*, I'm a partner."

The announcer then intones, "That's true, Lyonya, we're partners. MMM." Lyonya's explanation was completely false—there was no factory—but it contained a kernel of Mavrodi's philosophy, which was to get everyone to "chip in." Another spot showed the family at the kitchen table as Lyonya's wife, Rita, cheerfully draws a diagram on a piece of paper to explain MMM—a large square—and then arrows pointing inward. "Like a huge pool!" exclaims Ivan. "And it is always full." Everyone chips in! It was the essence of a pyramid scam.

The advertising was so successful only because the real economy was such a mess. As hyperinflation destroyed savings, as factories closed down and workers went unpaid for months or even years at a time, the Lyonya saga, broadcast day after day, beckoned viewers to new heights of optimism and prosperity. It was no contest—the sorry Russian people could hardly resist the fantasy offered by Mavrodi, and the Russian state was too weak to do anything about it.

Once Mavrodi and Berezovsky began, others followed and Russia turned into a bazaar of easy money temptations. One widespread scheme, Russky Dom Selenga, carried as its motto: "Every grain of sand of your deposit, we turn into a pearl."[21] On a typical day of advertising in the popular *Moskovsky Komsomolets* newspaper, the First Financial Construction Company offered "up to 1,600 percent in rubles." Another, ALD Trust, promised investors 500 percent on rubles, or 60 percent annual return on dollars. In a Moscow weekly free newspaper, *Extra-M,* the Mosimportbank offered 30,000 percent interest on five-year ruble deposits, although it was later pointed out the sum was a math trick taking advantage of the difference between simple and compound interest.[22]

The proliferation of easy money traps and lures crept into every corner of life. Soon shares of pyramid schemes were being traded in the Finance Ministry cafeteria, the very institution that was supposed to be policing them. In the cafeteria, employees could buy certificates for "Tibet," AVVA or MMM. No one could dampen the frenzy; the ministry workers were caught up in Lyonya's dreams. Zlatkis said, "As soon as I emerged from my office, someone would catch me in the corridor, I mean some ministry official or employee, and would start asking me: 'Bella, tell me honestly, what do you think, if I sell my apartment and invest all the money in Tibet, will I be later able to buy an apartment for my daughter?' I began to explain that you will lose your apartment. But the woman said, 'You don't want to help us!'" Zlatkis only slowly—too slowly—began to realize the frenzy had become an epidemic. Even the esteemed halls of the Russian Constitutional Court were not immune; court justices bought paper in an outrageous pyramid called Vlastilina. The mastermind was Valentina Solovyova, a one-time barbershop cashier who created her pyramid without any advertising at all, just word of mouth. She promised returns of 100 percent a month, a Zhiguli car for half the market price in the same period, or a Mercedes at one-third the price over three months. A river of cash began arriving at her offices. She used the cash to reward the first depositors in order to attract more. Yevgeny Kovrov, who later investigated the case and headed a government commission to represent the victims, told me that Solovyova's word-of-mouth approach was as evocative and phenomenally successful as Mavrodi's massive advertising. "The rumor about this firm spread all over Russia," he recalled. The first car giveaway ignited a burst of enthusiasm. One person told a friend, and the friend came running. Vlastilina seemed to be especially attractive to the elite—pop star Alla Pugachova reportedly lost $1.7 million. Solovyova set a minimum deposit of 50 million rubles, and still people came. "People got that money together from entire factories," Kovrov recalled, "and transported it there in bags. And, judging by the accounts of witnesses, they would sleep in front of her offices, making campfires."[23] Solovyova was convicted in 1999 and sentenced to seven years in prison for taking the ruble equivalent of $130 million from 16,500 victims, although no one knows where the money went and the investors got nothing back.

Zlatkis recalled that the frenzy finally seeped in to her own home. One day her husband asked her about the pyramids. "He couldn't understand why everybody around us was getting rich, and he was not."

In July 1994, the Russian authorities began to raise questions about MMM. "Lyonya is getting on my nerves," Yeltsin grumbled. The State Antimonopoly Committee asked television stations to stop broadcasting MMM commercials, to no avail. Then the tax inspectorate said one of Mavrodi's subsidiaries, Invest-Consulting, owed 49.9 billion rubles in taxes, payable immediately. Prime Minister Chernomyrdin weighed in, saying, "We must warn those like Lyonya Golubkov and Marina Sergeyevna, the opportunities for easy money in the market will soon disappear." But the voice of Chernomyrdin, who had presided over a growing backlog of wage arrears in the real economy, was faint in comparison with the wonderland of riches offered by MMM. On July 27, Mavrodi fired back in a newspaper advertisement: "So, the authorities do not like Lyonya Golubkov and Marina Sergeyevna. But do Lyonya Golubkov and Marina Sergeyevna like the authorities? No one's asked about that. Yet."

The next day, the pyramid collapsed. The MMM certificates had been trading at over 100,000 rubles, but at 11:00 A.M., Mavrodi announced that the new price—which he alone set—was only 1,000 rubles. Thousands of angry shareholders blocked the Varshavskoye Shosse, the wide boulevard where MMM was located, and riot police were called out to control the crowds. Mavrodi issued a reassuring statement that investors need not worry, the share price would climb back up to 125,000 in a few months. He urged everyone to hold onto their papers. "We, unlike the state, have never deceived you," Mavrodi declared. "And never will." Many people were still prepared to believe Mavrodi. "The papers are saying MMM are charlatans, but I trust them over President Boris Yeltsin and his government any day," a pensioner, Maria Vasilievna, told a reporter. "What has the government ever done for us, except trick us with their money reforms?"[24] Days later, Mavrodi began to issue a new security, MMM "tickets," which were emblazoned with Mavrodi's portrait. Hundreds of investors returned, hoping that the bubble had not really burst. They too were fooled. Mavrodi had been authorized to sell 991,000 shares, but in the end he deceived between 5 and 10 million people. He was later arrested for tax evasion in a high-profile police raid and was held two months. But he was released after he won an off-year election to parliament and thus received immunity from prosecution. He disappeared and was never prosecuted for the pyramid scheme; six years later Russian authorities said he was still being sought.[25]

The collapse of MMM threw into sharp relief the near total passivity of the state. Yeltsin and his reformers had let capitalism run untethered, and it had gone berserk. "The government had absolutely nothing to do with it, gave no guarantees, and will not interfere at all," Yeltsin said after the crash of MMM. Zlatkis was overwhelmed and complained in June that proliferating pyramids were "out of control" and "coming down on our heads like an avalanche."[26] Zlatkis told me the government didn't really have a clue what was going on; in the ministry, some of her aides even asked if she wanted help in getting one of Vlastilina's cars at half price. "No one understood anything, not even in one of the divisions of my department," she recalled. Myslovsky recalled that he saw huge files on the cases, but the general prosecutor was ordered by someone in power at the time not to proceed. "The main slogan at the time was 'get rich,'" he recalled. "The legislative base was very unclear. These companies were conducting very aggressive advertising, they had a lot of money, and the state reaction was weak, toothless."[27] Vyacheslav Mavrodi, Sergei's brother and partner in MMM, later told a television interviewer, "If the law enforcement bodies thought I was a swindler, why did they let me do it?"[28] Zlatkis recalled, "I had a feeling of helplessness all the time. I knew perfectly well how it was going to end, and I couldn't do anything about it."

Dmitri Vasiliev, the Chubais deputy, saw the episode in much darker terms. The reformers had neglected to build the institutions of a market, and as a result chaos was spreading. Vasiliev believed the Finance Ministry had "totally failed" to control the pyramids and was unable to regulate the financial markets. The derivatives used by Mavrodi were no more than "lottery tickets," he told reporters the week after the collapse, "these scraps of paper are not securities." Vasiliev warned that without stronger government regulation, "scandals will snowball." As early as 1992, the reformers had discussed whether to build an independent securities commission, but no one had been interested. Now the wreckage of unbridled capitalism was strewn across the landscape. In the autumn of 1994, Chernomyrdin agreed to set up a securities commission, with Vasiliev as its chairman, to regulate the market. Mavrodi, Vasiliev later recalled, was "the mother of our commission."

After Mavrodi ran into trouble, his top lieutenants from MMM came to see Zlatkis, demanding approval of a huge new share issue, knowing full well the proposal would be rejected. It was a trick—if the share issue was denied, Mavrodi would try to shift blame for his troubles to the government. Zlatkis saw through the ruse and stalled, saying that the papers were not in order. She asked one of the visitors, "Are you a lawyer or an economist?"

He replied threateningly: "Neither. I am an athlete. Target shooting is my line."

The collapse of Mavrodi's pyramid destroyed confidence in Berezovsky's automobile alliance, but the real damage had begun earlier, in the spring of 1994. Mavrodi was a better huckster than Berezovsky. Promising instant returns, Mavrodi siphoned off the easy money, as did the other high-yielding schemes, and sales of the AVVA certificates fell off. Still, Berezovsky had done quite handsomely in the year of the pyramids; according to financial records that were made public later, AVVA had collected 25.3 billion rubles from selling its certificates in 1994, or about $15 million. Kadannikov and Berezovsky later put the total raised at $50 million, although that appears to include interest and profits from reinvestments. In effect, AVVA used the cash it gathered and immediately recycled it, speculating in privatization vouchers, high-yielding bank certificates, and other quick-money schemes, doubling and tripling the winnings. Easy money was easy.

Although the public may have believed during 1994 that it was seeing the birth of a "people's car," in fact Berezovsky put the money elsewhere: in buying up partial control of the Avtovaz factory. Financial reports show that AVVA spent 6.1 billion rubles, or about $3.1 million, to buy a third of Russia's largest car factory, an astoundingly tiny payment for such a huge industrial asset. Berezovsky used two separate methods. First, AVVA used vouchers to buy shares in the factory. Second, AVVA was the winner of an August 8, 1994, investment tender for Avtovaz. The tenders were supposed to be competitions in which the winner made sizable investments in the future in the enterprise, but one official told me later that AVVA was the only bidder.[29] At some point, Avtovaz then issued new stock, and a further chunk was given to AVVA. After all this, AVVA owned 34 percent of the factory. On July 23, just seven months after AVVA had been launched at the exhibition hall in Moscow, Berezovsky was placed on the eleven-member board of Avtovaz. The people's money had helped put him there. It was the perfect plot: he collected money from the public and used it to bootstrap himself and Kadannikov into private ownership of the factory. According to Yuri Zektser, who later became general director of AVVA, inside the company it was absolutely clear by the late summer of 1994 that the Berezovsky scheme had not collected enough money to build an auto factory. Moreover, negotiations with General Motors were bogging down because it feared the political risks of investing in Russia. (Also, there were signs of a war looming in Chechnya, and Russia went through a one-day currency panic in

October.) Kadannikov hinted at the difficulties on November 2, 1994, in a newspaper interview, suggesting that General Motors had proposed a tiny project to make twenty thousand cars a year, which "doesn't suit us." However, he reassured people that "the anticipated absence of the foreign participation won't disturb the realization of the AVVA project."[30]

What Kadannikov didn't say was that months earlier Berezovsky and he had used the people's money to buy Avtovaz shares, and there wasn't going to be a "people's car" any time soon. Then, in mid-January 1995, Kadannikov publicly acknowledged a delay, saying the project would be scaled down; in mid-February, he said it was impossible to start building the factory and that AVVA had raised only $50 million out of a planned $300 million. The final acknowledgment that the project was dead came in a May newspaper announcement that AVVA had held its annual meeting on April 7, 1995. The announcement blamed "negative tendencies in the economy and social sphere in the middle of 1994" for the "unfavorable investment climate."[31]

The people's car would have to remain the people's dream. But the people certainly would not get their money back. Berezovsky's scheme had been structured so carefully that, in the end, neither he nor the buyers of his certificates had a list of who held the papers. That was the idea—no list, no refunds, no problems. The certificates were worthless unless the bearer could find the right place and time to exchange them for a genuine share of AVVA. At the 1995 annual meeting, and at every subsequent meeting, it was also decided not to pay dividends. In fact, in the following six years, AVVA never once paid dividends, despite the millions of tiny coupons it had distributed attached to the certificates. The dividends were as much an illusion as the "people's car." The promised 100,000-car lottery was stopped after three offerings and 14,000 cars.

The promises that AVVA made to the people who gave their money were broken, repeatedly. The real winners were Berezovsky and Kadannikov.[32] In 1996, when asked what happened to the people's money and to AVVA, Berezovsky replied, "It has lived up to every promise it gave. We collected about $50 million, then we made this money work, and at least it did not melt down. . . . We succeeded in preserving the money, we did not spend it on our needs, on entertainment and pleasure."[33] Instead, they spent it on buying their own car factory.

*

The saga of the All-Russian Automobile Alliance offers a glimpse of the easy money years but does not tell the whole story. Easy money could be plucked from the hands of bureaucrats, found on the rudimentary commodity exchanges, or reaped by streetwise youths in seedy currency exchange booths. Easy money was an era, a culture, an experience—and for some with exceptional guts and savvy, a defining moment.

Andrei Melnichenko was one of them. He progressed nicely through the best schools—he was a champion of the Olympiads, Soviet-era academic contests—and enrolled in physics at the prestigious Moscow State University. Tall and a bit awkward, with a soft complexion and straight hair parted down the middle, Melnichenko, often dressed in jeans and T-shirts, had the innocent looks of a teenager but the wits and cunning of a financier. In the final years of the Soviet Union, from his dormitory room in the dark labyrinth of the university building, Melnichenko became a youthful trailblazer in the era of easy money.

In his second year, 1991, as the Soviet system disintegrated, the school turned into an informal commodity exchange. The hallways and courtyard buzzed with people selling a ton of copper or oil, usually stored in a state-run factory or warehouse. But everything was traded for cash, and the traders needed a secure, swift, and mobile source of currency. Melnichenko became their man—the premier moneychanger of the Moscow university traders, helping them switch from dollars to rubles and back again, often within hours. Melnichenko and two friends worked out of their dorm room, where they kept a single paper notebook to record the transactions and a large wooden box to store the money. "The university dorm no longer looked like a place where students lived, studied, and did homework, but it resembled a stock exchange," Melnichenko recalled. "All over the place there were announcements, people buying and selling things. There was a big turnover of commodities and goods—automobiles, trucks, sugar, metals—whatever you wanted." For three years, Melnichenko paid little attention to his studies but devoted all his energy to hustling rubles and dollars. At first, the day brought in as little as $100 profit, perhaps $2,000 on a very good day. But within a year, the business exploded, and the three students were handling $100,000 a day.

The great inflation of 1992–1994 was like an escalator. Every day, relentlessly, the ruble's value declined against the dollar. Melnichenko and his friends discovered how to use the escalator to make a fortune.

The trick was to take rubles, change them into dollars for a short period, and then pay back the same amount of rubles, which were now worth less, and pocket the profit. The rubles could be borrowed for 10–13 percent a year, but inflation was eroding their value at 25 percent a month. Money fell into their hands out of thin air. All they needed was the guts—and sometimes it required steel nerves—to be a trader. Melnichenko told me that trainloads of commodities were being bought and sold at the university. Because buyer and seller often did not trust each other, they arranged for a deposit in cash. Melnichenko collected these deposits too, and his capital soared. He didn't even have a safe for storing the cash, but the dorm room had a heavy door, which he locked very carefully. The boys in jeans and T-shirts started to think about life after graduation.

Melnichenko and his friends followed their clients when they moved off campus to nascent city commodity exchanges. Melnichenko opened a tiny office in a shabby two-room apartment and put a two-line advertisement in *Moskovsky Komsomolets,* a popular broadsheet newspaper: "We buy currency. We sell currency." The phones never stopped ringing. Customers arrived in the first room with bags of cash, and the deals were closed in the second room, where Melnichenko installed a money-counting machine and a real safe. The boys started to get rich. "We all rented very nice apartments, bought ourselves cars, and lived decently," Melnichenko remembered.

When the laws changed and they needed a formal license in 1992, Melnichenko found a minuscule one-room bank, Premier Bank, and struck a deal with the owner. He would function under the protection of their license, paying a fee while expanding his money exchange points in the city. For a brief time, he also traded in vouchers and in cigarettes, which were in such demand that cartons of them or whole truckloads could be substituted for currency. When I met Melnichenko years later, I asked him if he recalled having any hobbies or pastimes in those years. He could remember none: just hours and hours on the phone, checking rates, changing money.

Melnichenko's most important commodity was information. He and his team started each day counting their cash and then deciding what direction the ruble-dollar exchange rate would probably take. They called competitors to see what rates they were offering. There were no computer networks, no exchange floors or flashing tickers, only the telephone. Then clients began calling; a factory needed to change $100,000 in earnings from a shipment of titanium into rubles—fast. For several years in the early 1990s, all such deals were made in cash, which was a boon to Melnichenko. As the rate gyrated during the day, they worked swiftly, constantly telephoning, counting banknotes, buying and selling. "From dawn till dusk," Melnichenko said. "And often at night as well, because there were night flights, people coming here from the regions, and they needed to catch a flight back home." They soon reached several hundred thousand dollars a day in trades and hardly ever suffered a loss. The mechanism was as good as a printing press: it cranked out profits all the time. No messy factories to bother with, no aging equipment to replace, no troublesome socialist legacy or red directors to worry about. "To lose was quite difficult," he recalled. Melnichenko, who was thirteen years old when Gorbachev launched *perestroika,* started wearing a tie.

Melnichenko had set up a currency exchange in Moscow, United Currency House. On October 11, 1994, known later as "Black Tuesday," the ruble exchange rate plunged from 3,081 per dollar to 3,926. Melnichenko told me that one day before the crash, "we foresaw that it could happen the next day. We bought a lot at the exchange." Then when the ruble took a nosedive, Melnichenko moved in for the kill. "We sold at maximum," he recalled. "On that day we made more than $10 million."

Melnichenko's secret was not his alone. Ruble-dollar speculation became a mainstay of the easy money era in the early 1990s.[34] The incentives were stark: industry was flat on its back and would require massive amounts of capital investment, but currency speculation involved low overhead, high profits, and no property. Who could resist? "Good money was earned on speculation. It was easy money, easy capital," recalled Alexander Smolensky, who in those days was running ruble-dollar operations with cash from Moscow retail clients. Smolensky collected rubles and changed them to dollars, and back to rubles again. "You give money in the morning and collect earnings in the evening," he said. "It required whoever was the fastest. We spent whole days in the bank—it was like a race, like a machine that was printing money. Every day, it brought more and more money. The most important thing was not to make a mistake. God took mercy. Converting, trading, earning, converting, trading, earning—it was like that every day."[35]

The profits from currency speculation were not the only way to make easy money. The combination of a weak government and high inflation spawned other schemes to score a quick fortune, especially for those with political connections, including the early cooperative businessmen, veterans of the party and Komsomol, and their patrons in the former KGB. These were the cream of the elite and, their pipeline for easy money came directly from the government.

In the early 1990s, Russia had no central treasury and came to rely on "authorized" commercial banks for deposits and disbursement of the state's money. The system was corrupt from the outset but lingered on for years. The banks cozied up to underpaid bureaucrats to snare the lucrative business, with bribery and coercion. The bureaucrats looked the other way as huge sums were "deposited" with the financiers. The bankers then did not disburse the money as they were supposed to, but used it instead for their own purposes. They often repaid the money to the state much later, or not at all. The fleet-footed bankers exploited a simple premise: money has value over time. The corrupt government officials willingly ignored this concept, allowing the financiers to feast on the state's riches.

The authorized bank system is another example of how the easy money years distorted the formative years of Russian capitalism. Why would banks want to get involved in the risky business of lending to troubled Russian factories or wobbly new businesses if they could simply feed at the trough of the Russian state? They were spoiled by free money from the government, which postponed the day when they—and all the others in the easy money generation—would have to learn how to invest in the real economy and earn profits the hard way.

The impact of easy money lingered through the 1990s. Sergei Yegorov, the chairman of the Association of Russian Banks, offered a revealing look at the distortions in early 1997. He reported that of $21 billion in banking credits issued in 1996, only 1.2 percent were long-term loans to businesses, while 90 percent were disbursed for short-term transactions on government debt, and the rest went to import-export operations. In other words, the commercial banks were barely making any loans at all in the real economy. They were little more than casinos, thriving on easy money.[36] One study found that from 1994 to 1996, half of the banks' profits were generated from easy money. Almost no one got big loans, and the longest term for a loan was one year.[37]

Smolensky, Khodorkovsky, Gusinsky, and Berezovsky all capitalized in the early 1990s on the system of "authorized" banks. Gusinsky, with support from Luzhkov, dominated the burgeoning Moscow municipal accounts for several years. Smolensky serviced accounts for the Kremlin administration, among others. Berezovsky used the same tactics to garner the cash flow of the national airline, Aeroflot.

Khodorkovsky had once boasted that his bank, Menatep, could survive under any regime, and a former vice president of Menatep told me why: the bank was structured to parallel the government. Khodorkovsky and his lieutenants all had direct lobbying links to key ministers, and their deputies to the deputy ministers. The bank thrived on a web of government lending programs, ranging from defense spending to food purchases; the Russian Finance Ministry was one of its major clients and loans for the state made up more than half of Menatep's lending activity in 1995.[38] The former Menatep vice president tried his hand at Western-style investment banking but later concluded, in frustration, that it was futile when the bank earned millions of dollars in profit for doing nothing as an "authorized" bank. "There was just no point" in the painstaking work of investment banking, he said, "when you could go have a *banya* session with your buddy at the Finance Ministry and they would put in $600 million."

"The Ministry of Finance would put that money on deposit in Menatep Bank and then instruct them to disburse it to the regions. What Menatep would do was take that $600 million, not pay the ministry anything, and they would delay the start of payment to the regions. When the people came to get the money, they would just delay it for three weeks. Then they would issue not cash but promissory notes—Menatep promissory notes—instead of cash!"[39] During the interval, Menatep put the money into high-yielding investments, reaping millions of dollars in easy profits for which they had done absolutely nothing except willfully ignore the government's instructions. No one was caught, no one was punished.

"The thing was that the crazy money was being made on special relations with the government," Vladimir Vinogradov, the founder of Inkombank and one of the leading commercial bankers of the 1990s, told me years later after his financial empire had collapsed. "For example, money was taken from the government to finance some programs. Those programs were not financed or were financed just one-tenth of what had to be paid. And the money was invested into vouchers, and they were changed for shares."[40] Presto! Easy money was turned into private property.

In the early 1990s, one of the Westerners who got a ringside seat in the age of easy money was Victor Huaco, a one-time Citibank expert on the Latin American debt crisis, who ran his own ruble-dollar currency business in Moscow. He later helped large Western investors navigate the murky world of Russian banking and investments. Huaco, an immaculately dressed financier who saw many parallels between the Russian chaos and the Latin economic upheavals of the 1980s, told me that one of the enduring mysteries was who really picked the winners and losers in the age of easy money. Huaco said he always sensed that there was a "magic hand" behind every deal, that politicians and bureaucrats helped their friends drain the lifeblood of the state itself. The "magic hand" was another sign of what would become the single most destructive phenomenon of the first decade of Russian capitalism, the corruption of power by wealth. The seeds were planted in Soviet times, in the shortage economy and the traditions of *blat* and *svyazi*. But the trend accelerated in the years of easy money, when the Russian state was so weak and so bereft of rules and institutions that it was blown away by the forces of wild capitalism that it had unleashed. Later a coterie of financiers became so powerful that they nearly took over the state itself.

Huaco told me that the "magic hand" of power was often hidden from view. The pyramid schemes had stolen from people with great fanfare, and the currency traders were in the open, but the authorized banks worked in secret. The winners got special insider information, which they used to strike it rich. According to the journalist Yulia Latynina, a deputy minister of finance once announced that bonds from a state bank would not be paid. The price plunged. Khodorkovsky then bought them up. Several days later, the deputy minister announced that, in fact, they would be paid. The price surged.[41]

"For me, the question always was, where did this magic hand come from?" Huaco asked. "The magic hand came with money, and these people utilized the money to make ten times more by having access to information or deals. When the magic hand picked them, it did not only give them money, it gave them information. They knew certain things and placed their bets accordingly." In one case, Huaco helped a Russian government agency borrow money from a Western lender. The loan was guaranteed by Russia, transferred to Moscow, and deposited in a Russian bank. A while later, the government agency that was supposed to get the proceeds from the loan complained about never receiving it. Huaco tracked it down. "The Russian bank had just churned it into their own investments," he said. The magic hand was at work again.[42]

Periodically, the government would announce with great solemnity that the days of easy money were over. Alexander Livshitz, an economic adviser to Yeltsin, declared after the MMM disaster, "The time of easy money is passing."[43] He could not have been more wrong.

The age of easy money, the roaring 1990s, masked a dark side of the new Russia. The oxygen of freedom was exhilarating, yet many took it as an invitation for brazen abuse. There was freedom to skirt the law, cheat the state, steal from the population, and get away with it. Coal miners, pensioners, teachers, and nurses went without pay because the "authorized" bankers—the tycoons—who were supposed to distribute their pay on behalf of the state used the money instead to make a quick windfall. Russia offered the spectacle of an elite in Moscow that had become stronger than the state, protected by their own private armies, strong-arming the government into relinquishing its riches, threatening and coercing anyone who stood in their way.

Boris Yeltsin and the liberal reformers around him had spent their best years destroying the symbols of Soviet power, and they did not want to revive the big state; it was a danger still fresh in their memory. In a decision that would have profound consequences for the early years of Russian capitalism, the liberal reformers choose to provide maximum freedom first and rules later. Into this vacuum rushed chaotic forces of evil—the cheaters and charlatans, the hooligans, criminal gangs, corrupt politicians, bureaucrats, natural resource barons, Mafia kingpins, ambitious tycoons, and former KGB bosses. Sadly, in the enfeebled condition of the new Russian state, which could barely muster a pauper's salary for militiamen and bureaucrats, money bought power. The very essence of the state—authority to set the rules of the game—was simply privatized by the new capitalism. The sequence was unmistakable: the wave of money came first, starting with early opportunities to sell oil and computers for superprofits. The easy money was followed later by privatization of gigantic factories and natural resource treasures. Money and property invariably brought competition and conflict. And conflict needed a place to settle its disputes, but since the rules were still not drawn—the laws not enforced, the courts not effective—the new money and property interests created their own rules outside the law, using bribery and corruption, using violence and coercion, all of which could be easily purchased. The cycle was complete: money ruled.

In the excitement of the easy money years, a profound fact was often overlooked: from the tsars to the Soviet Communist Party, Russia simply never had a tradition of the rule of law. Russians have spent centuries appealing to individuals—a concrete person with whims, a tsar, a party boss—rather than to an abstract law that has no personality, that exists above individual discretion.

When Soviet power was demolished, a lid was lifted; the weight of arbitrary Communist Party rule ceased to exist overnight. This was a moment of great danger that no one fully understood. No one thought to put anything in place of the heavy lid. Russia was suddenly thrust into a void.[44] Slowly, new laws were written and a new constitution was adopted on the heels of the violent shelling of parliament in 1993. But the utterly painful reality of the 1990s was that Russia remained in a vacuum, a free fall, a place of arbitrary power, individual whims, and private score settling. It extended from a simple street corner, where a traffic policeman spent his day taking petty bribes, to ghastly shoot-outs between gangs of thugs, to the highest echelons of the Russian state itself, where money, that mighty symbol of onrushing capitalism, was a potent, caustic force.

The astonishing corruption of post-Soviet Russia was hardly new; the culture and practice were centuries old. Bribery flourished in the time of Peter the Great, who hanged a Siberian governor, Gagarin, for corruption and three years later hanged Nesterov, the man who exposed the governor, for bribery. Throughout the entire reign of the Romanov dynasty, corruption remained a source of income for both petty government employees and high officials. In Soviet times, the definitions changed: the authorities persecuted and prosecuted the perceived enemies of socialism, including those with entrepreneurial instincts. But old-fashioned corruption remained below the surface, in the shadow economy; it was frequently the only possible way to carry out market transactions in a planned economy.

A powerful legacy of the Soviet era—the hostile ideology toward entrepreneurship and capitalism—persisted in the new Russia. The cops on the beat during Russia's first taste of wild capitalism were the same ones inculcated with the Soviet notions that all businessmen were criminals for the mere fact of doing business. They were the same ones who grew up on a Soviet legal code that criminalized all kinds of market transactions. These law enforcement officials never absorbed the radically new idea that their job was to protect business. Once I asked a Russian police academy instructor about a string of unsolved murders of bankers. He grew indignant and began shouting at me, pushing his chair away from the table, standing, and glowering. "If a banker gets killed, it's because he did not have a strong enough security service!" he declared. He did not see protecting a banker as police work.

In many oppressive regimes, there is a powerful link between a weak state, corruption, and authoritarianism. If the laws are unenforceable or nonexistent, then just about anyone can be found at fault. This greatly enhances the power of selective prosecution: the rulers can decide arbitrarily who will be caught and punished. Here was the core of Russia's troubles in the 1990s. The archaic tax laws, for example, were impossible to obey. A small businessman once told me that the total official tax bill on his business was 110 percent of the profits, a refrain that I heard time and time again. The laws made almost every businessman and taxpayer a lawbreaker—and thus a potential criminal and thus a willing supplicant to power and, finally, a briber. Alexander Gurov, the head of an Interior Ministry training institute, once candidly acknowledged that this mentality had become embedded in the Russian people. "Of one hundred people stopped by the traffic police," he said, "95 percent were offering bribes even before the policeman opened his mouth."[45]

Chapter 10

The Man Who Rebuilt Moscow

THE CATHEDRAL was as grand as the military victory it commemorated. After Russia's army turned back Napoleon in 1812, Tsar Alexander I ordered the construction of a mammoth temple to mark the triumph. The Cathedral of Christ the Savior was started in 1839 and completed forty-four years later, a colossal thirty-story structure of 40 million bricks, with walls more than three meters thick, sheathed on the outside with slabs of marble and granite and crowned with a gigantic cupola, covered in copper weighing 176 tons. At the summit stood a cross three stories high. The main cupola was surrounded by four belfries in which hung fourteen bells with a combined weight of sixty-five tons. Twelve doors sculpted in bronze led to the interior of the grand cathedral, which was both a religious shrine and a war memorial. "Tsars came and went, old generations died off and new ones populated the earth, Russia threw herself into the chaos of wars and conquests, suffered recurring waves of famine and epidemic, and yet nothing interrupted the effort to complete this extraordinary structure," one historian wrote. The finished temple, consecrated on May 26, 1883, was a signature structure of Moscow.

In 1931 Joseph Stalin ordered the magnificent cathedral blown up.

After four months of scavenging the edifice for every scrap of gold, prying off the marble and copper and weakening the bricks with small dynamite blasts, workers toppled the structure in a series of explosions on the cold morning of December 5, leaving behind a tall, smoking mound of rubble. "A terrifying silence reigned in this place," a witness noted.[1] Stalin wanted to build an even larger "palace of soviets," a high-rise taller than the Empire State Building, with a gargantuan statue of Lenin on top. Architectural competitions for the new skyscraper went on for years, but the project was abandoned after Stalin's death. In Nikita Khrushchev's time, a large, heated outdoor public swimming pool was built on the site. The cathedral was officially wiped from the history books, but not from memory.

In 1989, when Mikhail Gorbachev permitted more openness about the past, Vladimir Mokrousov constructed a small plaster-and-cardboard model of the cathedral, working from an old photograph of the original cathedral that a friend had given him. Like all who dared defy official ideology, Mokrousov was cautious and indirect, at first. A prolific sculptor with a lined forehead, gray eyes, long, gray hair, and shaggy beard, Mokrousov worked out of a drafty, aging two-floor studio in Moscow with creaky floorboards. He created a mock-up of the original cathedral, working quietly. He had to hide the model because the Union of Artists still had a charter prohibiting members from working on religious subjects. The cathedral was at least officially a forbidden topic, and Mokrousov did not want to take the risk of attracting the attention of the KGB.

In 1989 a competition was announced for a World War II war memorial in Moscow. The entries were displayed at the Manezh exhibition hall next to the Kremlin, and Mokrousov, in a flash of rebelliousness, decided to submit his model cathedral to "correct the mistake" that Stalin had made.[2] It was just one of four hundred entries—many of them bearing the hammer and sickle—but Mokrousov's particular model caused a stir. It was on display for two weeks and then suddenly disappeared. Mokrousov said the KGB seized it and put it in a vault. But the KGB was too late. Mokrousov's model sparked interest in the idea of resurrecting the church. In addition to a newspaper article about it, a small grassroots movement was born, the members gathering periodically in Mokrousov's studio. They called themselves the Obschina, a Russian word that means a local religious or ethnic community. In the next few years, the Obschina activists stood on street corners across the country seeking signatures and small contributions for restoration of the grand cathedral. Their dream was strictly a street-level affair; the Russian Orthodox Church and the Russian state paid them little heed.[3] On December 5, 1990, to mark the anniversary of the destruction of the cathedral, a stone was laid near the spot, and the following March, a two-meter-high plaster cross, sculpted by Mokrousov, was erected; people gathered around it and prayed. They were a mixture of nationalists and religious believers at first, but later, after the August 1991 coup, they were joined by some of Russia's democrats, who saw the cathedral's rebuilding as a symbolic spike through the heart of Communism. In 1991, on the sixtieth anniversary of the cathedral's destruction, Boris Yeltsin declared that "this unprecedented act of vandalism was committed not by foreign invaders but by people blinded by false ideas and motivated by hatred toward everything good and saintly."[4]

Yeltsin appointed Yuri Luzhkov mayor of Moscow after Gavriil Popov unexpectedly resigned on June 6, 1992. Luzhkov inherited a confused and worried citizenry facing grim shortages and deep uncertainty. He recognized that he needed to inspire hope, but he was not a charismatic figure. He was a pragmatic man, a Soviet-era administrator and engineer with a limited understanding of politics. Certainly he had no idea what kind of politics would inspire people in the brand-new state that was unfolding. Vasily Shakhnovsky, who was a senior aide to both Popov and Luzhkov during this time, told me that Luzhkov took office suddenly, unexpectedly, without a grand plan or strategy. Shakhnovsky recalled, "He found himself in a very difficult situation because he didn't have a ready, thought-out program." Shakhnovsky said Luzhkov followed his instincts.[5]

"The most important thing now is to survive this moment," Luzhkov told a Moscow government meeting at the time he took office, launching a massive and ambitious construction plan for the city, which he hoped would provide jobs—and take the edge off popular discontent, fueled by unemployment and despair.

On the streets, the Obschina was collecting contributions with growing vigor, the members standing in subway stations and posting notices on light poles seeking support. The Obschina won official government recognition, allowing it to register as a legal group and open a bank account. Activists presented tens of thousands of signatures to the authorities, petitioning for reconstruction of the cathedral. A small bank was even started in the name of reconstruction of the church. But no matter how hard the grassroots campaigners tried, they were amateurs, and the chances of their dream becoming a reality remained slim. They raised only paltry sums from their public solicitations. Mokrousov's wife, Valentina, who had become treasurer of the Obschina, began to wonder if they would ever succeed; members were asking why nothing was happening. "There was very little money, but we needed to do something, at least start something," she said.[6]

Luzhkov took notice. His parents had told him the story of the cathedral, he recalled, and he had seen photographs of it and heard legends of great craftsmen who worked on the original structure.[7] According to Mokrousov, Luzhkov personally signed an order turning over to the Obschina the 6.7 hectares of land on which the cathedral had once stood, so that they could build a small chapel. At the time, the chapel seemed like a modest but practical goal. The Mokrousovs then discovered that the land was occupied by a Chechen used-car dealer. In a daring gambit, Valentina went to the dealer and demanded payment for use of the land. To her utter surprise, he immediately paid her 3.5 million rubles, the equivalent of several thousand dollars, in cash. With this money, the Obschina erected a fence and commissioned some blueprints, but their dream was still elusive. Yeltsin put reconstruction of the cathedral on a list of big projects to be built in the new Russia—someday.

In 1994 a leader of the Russian Orthodox Church patriarchate took Valentina aside. "Soon everything will be fine for you," he told her. "Soon the cathedral will begin to be built."

"And who, can I ask, is going to do it?" she inquired.

"Yuri Mikhailovich is taking this job upon himself. He is serious. Luzhkov is not Yeltsin. If he says he will do it, he will."

On February 23, 1994, the Moscow architecture council approved a new, enlarged plan to reconstruct the cathedral. It was far more ambitious than anything Mokrousov had ever dreamed of—a full-fledged reconstruction, not just a model or a small chapel.

Mokrousov's grassroots campaign was overtaken by a far more powerful force: Luzhkov. Mokrousov and his wife were privately somewhat bitter that their own hard work, painstaking years of standing on street corners seeking signatures and donations, had been abruptly tossed aside. They resigned from the Obschina, which was soon abolished by a formal notification from the patriarchate, and the land for the cathedral was taken back by the city. Luzhkov took over the financial side of rebuilding the cathedral too. In September, an official Moscow city fund for reconstruction of the cathedral was announced, and on January 7, 1995, the cornerstone was laid. Luzhkov said he wanted to complete the new cathedral's shell in time for the commemoration of Moscow's 850th anniversary in 1997. Yeltsin granted a federal tax break for contributions to the effort.

What occurred in the next year was nothing short of remarkable for a city where, in Soviet times, ambitious building projects had often languished, unfinished, for many years, a city struggling with unmet needs in housing, health care, schooling, and roads. Luzhkov sent into battle an army of 2,500 construction workers who labored around the clock, pouring a mountain of concrete to meet blueprints that were fresh off the drawing boards. The workers were forced to pause several times, waiting for the designers to finish the plans. The poured concrete was warmed with electric heaters in winter to keep it from freezing. Luzhkov agreed to a method of construction that would use 10 million bricks instead of 40 million. Twice or three times a week, Luzhkov arrived on the site, promising the workers an endless supply of *kvas,* the sweet Russian soft drink made from fermented bread.

A forest of construction cranes rose by the Moscow River, as well as a chorus of doubts. Would it not be better, critics asked, to rebuild one hundred smaller churches, which were also destroyed by the Communists, or ten new hospitals? Wasn't the symbolism of the cathedral a throwback to the age of Russian imperialism? Why such a brazen, mammoth structure at a time of so many other troubles and desperate needs? Luzhkov did not heed these complaints. He built.

On the outside, the cathedral, 335 feet high, resembled the original, but inside, in addition to the chapels, it was a modern headquarters for the patriarchate, with garages, elevators, conference rooms, video systems, modern ventilation, and cafes. In place of the swimming pool built over the original building site, a gigantic gray, granite-covered base stretched for a city block, housing the Church of the Transfiguration and a museum of the history of the cathedral. The southern side held a massive twelve-hundred-seat Hall of Church Councils, five refectories, and a kitchen capable of feeding fifteen hundred people.[8]

Luzhkov devoted attention to every detail. By one account, it was calculated that less gold could be used to gild the cathedral's domes—just twenty kilos instead of the original 312.6 kilos—by spraying a fine layer of golden lacquer that included only microscopic particles of gold between a layer of titanium nitrate, as a base, and a graphite overlay. Luzhkov, wanting to check whether this would look real, supposedly went to the patriarch of Moscow and all Russia, Alexy II, with two samples, one the cheaper version and one real gold leaf. Without disclosing which sample was real, he asked the patriarch to choose which one looked better. The patriarch choose the cheaper variant, which was used.[9]

After years of lassitude and shortages, and despite criticism and economic chaos all around him, Luzhkov's reconstruction of the cathedral made a powerful, symbolic statement at the dawn of the new Russia. The structure itself was an imposing castle by the Moscow River, with a fairy-tale look that shimmered from a distance. As a religious shrine and architectural monument, the cathedral was unquestionably a potent symbol. But I think it had a broader message as well. The reconstruction was an antidote to all the uncertainty and doubt of those first tumultuous years of change. Luzhkov's message was, It can be done.

But how? Six years after it was begun, the project, originally estimated between $150 million and $300 million, had cost $700 million. Luzhkov and Yeltsin offered only vague explanations about how the cathedral was financed, but the riddle was partly answered on January 6, 1996, when a large marble plaque was erected outside the lower cathedral. In gold leaf, the plaque declared: "These were the first to contribute selflessly," and then listed well-known and lesser-known bastions of finance and industry. Among the first on the list was Alexander Smolensky's Stolichny Bank of Savings, which donated fifty-three kilos of gold for the cupolas of the cathedral. The natural gas monopoly Gazprom donated 10 billion rubles for marble to clad the walls. Inkombank gave $1.5 million and two dozen icons. The Moscow Interbank Currency Exchange donated $1 million. In the next four years, the lists of donors grew, and new tablets were erected. The donors included the biggest Moscow utilities and city-affiliated businesses, such as the telephone and electric companies, prominent banks, restaurants, retailers, food traders, oil exporters, a famous chocolate company, and dozens of other factories and firms, powerhouses of the new capitalism and the new Moscow.

The donors were not entirely altruistic. The truth was that their contributions were as much a tribute to Luzhkov as to the cathedral. Luzhkov created a political machine in which power and property—his own formidable rule and his control over Moscow's enormous resources—were leveraged into rebuilding the city. In Luzhkov's realm, the laws of the market and the law of the land were not nearly as strong as the hand of the mayor. When Luzhkov made demands, businesses leaped to attention; without Luzhkov's support, they could not survive. The financiers, traders, industrialists, and restaurateurs all paid up, and were rewarded in return. As soon as Smolensky contributed the gold ingots, the patriarchate deposited its accounts in Stolichny Bank of Savings. Mikhail Ogorodnikov, spokesman for the city's cathedral rebuilding fund, explained: "Luzhkov was able to understand and combine this wish for economic freedom with economic diktat. Eighty percent of the money for the cathedral was donated by banks and corporations. How is it possible to make them work for the city? Luzhkov got them to understand: if you do nothing for the city, you will not find it comfortable here, you will not survive without the support of the city." Unlike others who tried to coax Russia's new rich to give money, Luzhkov was more direct. Ogorodnikov described Luzhkov's approach this way: "You live in this city. You are making money in this city. Pay the city its due. Otherwise, you will not be here."[10]

What Luzhkov reconstructed was not just the cathedral that Stalin demolished, not just a gleaming symbol of post-Soviet Russian renaissance. The cathedral was also a concrete demonstration of a new model of capitalism that Luzhkov muscled onto the Russian stage in the 1990s, a model that mixed public and private interests, blended power and money, spawned corruption and massive new public works, all with one central figure, Luzhkov, at the helm.

The Luzhkov model—Moscow Inc.—was not what the reformers had in mind. Anatoly Chubais and Yegor Gaidar were dreaming of building a Western-style model of capitalism, with underlying principles of competition and openness and a separation of business and the state, and they wanted to leave it to the market to choose the winners and losers. By contrast, Luzhkov intended to choose the winners and losers himself. Instead of a Western approach, his model was more in the inscrutable traditions of the East, centered on the whims of a potentate rather than profit and loss. Luzhkov's model was called, by some, "state capitalism" because the city itself became a major participant in business. Luzhkov did not object to the label "state capitalism." Critics also called it "crony capitalism" because it benefited Luzhkov's pals.

In Moscow, Luzhkov had the instincts of a populist, the organizing skills of a machine politician, and the ambitions of a builder. He borrowed from both Chicago's Mayor Richard Daley and New York's master builder Robert Moses. He did not see building—and grand architecture—as an end in itself, but as something that a politician does for people. He was not a towering designer who looked down from great monuments, but a street-level pol who understood the power of looking up at them.

Luzhkov's empire had a seamy side—corruption and his own heavy-handed style—but he was immensely popular, especially in the years of frenetic building in the mid-1990s. Muscovites twice elected him mayor by large margins, 89.6 percent in 1996 and 70 percent in 1999. He had no serious competition in 1996, but in 1999 was challenged by a well-known, liberal former prime minister, Sergei Kiriyenko. Nonetheless, Kiriyenko's campaign flopped. Muscovites seemed to approve an implicit trade-off Luzhkov represented: he would take from the new rich and give to the city. Galina Starovoitova, a progressive member of parliament from St. Petersburg who was murdered in 1998, told me once that Luzhkov won popular approbation, rather than scorn, for squeezing money out of banks and businesses. "A lot of ordinary people think these new rich, these new Russians, should share their wealth with the city," she said, "and this is a way to cut, a little bit, their superprofits."

The rise of Luzhkov's empire in Moscow was not inconsequential for all of Russia. It appeared in the early, inchoate years as the country was groping out of the darkness of Soviet socialism, when it was not clear how to build markets in a country that had no experience with capitalism since early in the century. Soon it became evident that not just one but several paths could be taken on the road to a market economy. One was the Chubais-Gaidar liberalism, in which market forces ruled. A second was rapacious, winner-take-all, oligarchic capitalism, which will be more fully detailed in the next chapters. The third type was Luzhkov's boss-ruled city machine.

These differing approaches did not mean that Luzhkov and Chubais politely debated each other in front of a chalkboard in an economics classroom. It was real-time trial and error, a zigzag of thrust and retreat. Luzhkov, who rose to power somewhat by chance with Popov's departure, was not the type to waste time with theory. He was a doer, shaped by the old Soviet-era managerial experience but also animated with a contemporary alacrity, seizing on his good fortune to lead the most prosperous metropolis in the country. In the end, Luzhkov put into practice an enormous, functioning example of what he thought the new Russia should be.

Larisa Piyasheva had her own vision of capitalist Moscow. An ultraliberal economist, Piyasheva had been recruited by Popov in November 1991 to carry out rapid privatization of business and industry. Previously, the city had practically given away apartments to their current inhabitants. The next stage was to privatize small businesses. Piyasheva wanted to give all the stores, cafeterias, restaurants, beauty salons, auto repair garages, and shoe repair shops of Moscow to the workers, and all at once. It was called "avalanche" privatization, a simple, bold, and far-reaching idea. Piyasheva saw it as entirely free market, and also very populist. "An enterprise would be given to the employees for free," Piyasheva told me of her plan. "They became the owners. My idea was that property should be given away. It used to be state-owned property; now it would become private property." Like the other liberals, Piyasheva figured that eventually the good owners and the bad would be weeded out by market forces, but she did not want to waste time sorting it out at the beginning. In her "avalanche" idea, a week was all that would be needed to approve the privatization of any enterprise. Presto: the hairdressers would own the salon, the mechanics would own the garage. "Some become rich, others lose," she said. "But this stage of competition is not under state control."[11]

Piyasheva's idea never had a chance, however. One reason was that Popov, who had brought her into the city government, was growing weak politically, constantly quarreling with the Mossovet, the city council. Piyasheva's privatization plan was announced in November 1991, but barely a month later, on December 19, Popov made his first attempt to resign, saying he felt reforms were being frustrated by the city council.[12] He was out of office six months later.

One of the first things Luzhkov did on becoming Popov's successor was to fire Piyasheva and bury her liberal ideas. "He just got rid of the whole department," she recalled, "and he took everything into his hands." Piyasheva saw—accurately—the side of Luzhkov's character and mentality that wanted to be a *khozyain*, the evocative Russian term for the leader of a given social domain, a home, a village, an enterprise, or a country. Luzhkov was a *khozyain* who wanted to extract a price from the city's businesses. Through leases, contracts, and rent obligations, every player in the Moscow economy would be captive to Luzhkov. "Their concept was directly opposite to mine," Piyasheva told me. "When I was talking about fast privatization, Luzhkov would say it was impossible to give property to people just like that. Don't give anything for free! Everything should be managed. Luzhkov is the owner. He can close down any restaurant and any hotel—he can change an owner. He has the authority. He is the *khozyain*. And as the *khozyain*, he manages his household. If something dissatisfies him, he changes it. And he keeps full order. It is a feudal way of organizing things."

After disposing of Piyasheva's radical ideas, Luzhkov's next move was to take on Chubais and block mass privatization in the capital. In the summer of 1993, Chubais, who was then trying to get his legislation through the recalcitrant Supreme Soviet, came to Luzhkov's office. They drank tea. In appearance, they were contrasting figures: Chubais, tall, with his gangly posture and youthful self-assuredness; Luzhkov, short, pugnacious, with a bald cannonball of a head and rugby-players' build. Both men had, once, accepted the Soviet system and then found their own path out of it; both were at the time supporters of Yeltsin, who was facing an increasingly tense revolt in parliament. Quietly, Luzhkov told Chubais that, although they had been allies in the past, he could not support mass privatization. There was no money in the country, so the factories would be sold for nothing, he complained. Besides, I think that Luzhkov may have had an unstated reason for opposing voucher privatization: he wanted to pick the new owners of property in Moscow, not leave it to the winners of a voucher auction, beyond his control. "Let's agree that privatization cannot be conducted this way—property cannot be sold that cheaply," Luzhkov appealed to Chubais. "We will get a speculator instead of a *khozyain*."

Chubais was not impressed. He wanted to break the grip of the *nomenklatura* on property, and Luzhkov symbolized that grip. They agreed on nothing, Luzhkov recalled.[13]

Luzhkov supported Yeltsin during the events of October 3–4, 1993, when Yeltsin violently faced off against the rebellious parliament, shelling the White House where his nationalist and conservative critics were holed up, accompanied with armed hoodlums. The confrontation left 145 dead. Luzhkov sat in on Yeltsin's crisis meetings and cut off water, telephones, and electricity to the besieged White House during the confrontation. Just as Yeltsin used the events to write a new constitution giving him broad powers, Luzhkov too used the crisis to impose a new political structure on the city, which was confirmed by voters in the December elections. Instead of the unwieldy 498-member city council, Luzhkov, with Yeltsin's backing, created a new thirty-five-member city Duma, or legislature, which proved almost totally compliant in the years ahead.

After the October events, Luzhkov again appealed to Chubais to stop mass privatization. Chubais refused. Luzhkov declared war. "From now on, you are my ideological enemy and I am going to fight you and the methods you are instilling in the country with all possible means," he said.[14] Privatization of large enterprises in Moscow then began to slow, and Luzhkov bent the city to his own will. He simply refused to follow the national privatization program. He went to Yeltsin on November 24, 1993, and argued that Chubais was selling off the country "for a song."[15]

Luzhkov was no stranger to the failures of the Soviet system and saw himself as an advocate of the market. But Luzhkov's understanding of the market, and of private property, was that it had to be managed by a *khozyain;* property was earned by hard work, not received for a token price. When it came to putting property into private hands, Luzhkov wanted to know the capabilities of his new owner first, while Chubais wanted to give away the property first and let the market sort out the effective owner later on. This went to the heart of their vastly different models of capitalism for Russia. Luzhkov said that "a man works with initiative not because he has property but exactly because he does not have property, yet has the right to earn it with productive labor." Luzhkov scorned the new owners that Chubais created as "parasitic capital"—people who didn't know the first thing about factories and manufacturing but put their money in Swiss bank accounts or into "foreign villas, yachts, cars, and other pleasures." In Luzhkov's world, these were never going to be good owners, they would never meet his definition of a *khozyain.* "Do you think such people—whose wealth fell on their heads—could turn into effective owners, organizers of industrial production? Of course not," Luzhkov said. "They felt they were 'caliphs for an hour' and were trying to exploit this hour to the maximum, pressing everything possible out of their new property."[16]

Luzhkov still believed in some aspects of the old system, including state subsidies, and he was not allergic to state ownership of industry, whereas Chubais sought to raze the command economy to the ground. Years later, Luzhkov continued to pump subsidies into the ailing Zil truck factory to keep it alive, but over time this approach did not work. Luzhkov abhorred the suddenness and seeming haste of shock therapy; it offended his sense of order. "Chubais is a radical," Luzhkov said. "He thinks in extremes. One moment, he opens the lid of the coffin, the next he is hammering the last nail into it. In his life everything is like this—the last blow on something or someone. I prefer to move by steps and not by revolutionary, radical leaps and bounds."[17]

Most importantly, although he did not talk about it openly, Luzhkov did not want to lose control of the money. As he built his empire, every storefront and every factory was a potential source of revenue. And if the property was to be doled out by the murky, ad hoc decisions of city hall bureaucrats, rather than in open auctions, the possibilities for corruption were greater.

The confrontation with Chubais gathered steam in the spring. At a press conference on February 11, 1994, Luzhkov vowed not to allow the national privatization program to be carried out in Moscow and blasted Chubais, saying that he had privatized Russia "the way a drunkard sells off all his possessions in the street in order to buy booze." The "drunkard" phrase stung. Chubais replied that Moscow had the worst privatization record in Russia, with only 2 percent of the large businesses privatized. Chubais fumed: "This is bureaucratic lawlessness that is a violation of the rights of the simple person." Privatization, Chubais added, takes "from the hands of the high-level bureaucrat the property that he truly does not want to let go of, the property that was the foundation of his power for decades." On March 23, 1994, Chubais announced that he would order fifty factories in Moscow auctioned off despite Luzhkov's objections.[18] Then on April 1, Luzhkov struck back, suspending the registration of enterprises as joint stock companies, a critical prelude to privatization. Chubais accused the mayor of breaking the law. He appealed to the general prosecutor, demanding that Luzhkov be charged with criminal negligence. Luzhkov refused to budge. Prime Minister Chernomyrdin ordered Luzhkov to fall in line with the national program, and Luzhkov still refused. The quarrel was settled on June 10, 1994, when Yeltsin announced that Luzhkov had won. Yeltsin said at a news conference that efforts to reconcile the two had failed, so he ordered the government "to leave Moscow alone."[19] The move was widely seen as expressing Yeltsin's gratitude for Luzhkov's support during the battle with parliament the previous October. A bitter Chubais washed his hands of the capital. "In Moscow we see so many breaches of the law, so many breaches of the constitution, so much corruption that I can have nothing to do with it," he said.[20]

The decision was a critical victory for Luzhkov on the path toward building his own municipal empire. Taking control of the city's property—storefronts, office buildings, factories, parking lots, hotels, theaters, schools, and more—gave Luzhkov an important source of revenues and power.

In the days of hyperinflation, cash lost its value rapidly, so Luzhkov found other currency with which to make deals. He leveraged, bartered, and traded his real estate for the things he needed for the city. These informal trade-offs were not necessarily wrong or illegal. The idea had been tested in Luzhkov's early dealings with Gusinsky, in which the city gave away buildings in exchange for renovation and a return "gift" of half the real estate. The trade-off gambit became standard procedure. For example, in the mid-1990s, Inkombank had grown to be Russia's third largest bank, and its largest commercial bank. The president, Vladimir Vinogradov, wanted to set up his corporate headquarters in a rundown prerevolutionary building near the Kremlin. The city simply gave the building to Inkombank in exchange for a promise to restore it and a long-term lease. Two years later, when I visited, the headquarters building gleamed with an elegant, turn-of-the-century look. Luzhkov came to the ribbon cutting. A small fifteenth-century church in the square, just in front of the bank, was also restored, at a cost of several million dollars, by Inkombank. Vinogradov, who had been among the early leaders of the cooperative movement, became a Luzhkov backer and donated twenty-four restored icons from the seventeenth and eighteenth centuries to the cathedral project. Luzhkov bestowed Vinogradov with a city award. Vinogradov contributed to Luzhkov's pet project to build apartments for Russians living in Sevastopol. The bank won city accounts and financed city projects, such as demolishing the unsightly five-story Khrushchev-era apartment blocks.[21]

This cozy relationship was reenacted over and over, especially with Vladimir Gusinsky, who became the most prominent of the bankers allied with Luzhkov. Luzhkov described Gusinsky as a business "partner" in this period.[22] Gusinsky located his headquarters in the mayor's high-rise; city workers were paid from Gusinsky's Most Bank and withdrew cash from automatic teller machines placed in the lobby of a building housing city offices. In 1994 Gusinsky's bank held a significant portion of the city's revenues, including deposits of the departments of municipal housing, licensing, education, architecture, finance, international relations, traffic police, and city militia, among others.[23]

Luzhkov's city government leased out property for a nominal sum, but then the city bosses made unwritten demands not in the lease: to plant trees, rebuild a hospital, pave a highway, set up a kindergarten. The side deals were more important than cash. In 1994 Luzhkov was anxious to clean up an old toxic dump, which he called an ulcer on the city. Wastes had been accumulating there for decades and the dump was described by one specialist as an ocean of contamination. Luzhkov turned to a privatized dump truck company, Moscow Mechanized Construction Number 5, which agreed to take on the hazardous task of removing the poisonous eyesore. The company removed 2.6 million cubic yards of soil and replaced it with clean sand and earth, working around the clock for two years. But the company, which primarily worked on city housing construction sites, also needed Luzhkov's help. It had bought a $10 million fleet of new dump trucks from Volvo but still owed $3 million, which it could not pay. Luzhkov came to the rescue, arranging a loan at 4 percent interest from a Moscow bank, when market interest rates were far higher, so the firm could settle the debt. When the toxic waste dump was cleaned up, Luzhkov held a ceremony to mark the accomplishment and handed some workers keys to new Zhiguli cars and new apartments as prizes.[24]

Mikhail Moskvin-Tarkhanov, a member of the city Duma who had been among the Moscow reform democrats in the early 1990s and later became a Luzhkov loyalist, said the mayor essentially invented his own substitute for the Soviet command economy. Moskvin-

Tarkhanov described it as "soft administration and strong economic regulation." He explained: "That is, we have a soft administrative system when we can first say what we want, then propose, then force, and finally punish."[25] Pavel Bunich, an adviser to Luzhkov who had worked with him in the Soviet years on the idea of self-financing for factories, made no secret of the fact that Luzhkov had figured out how to squeeze Moscow's new businessmen. "Luzhkov knows how to 'sweat' sponsors, but he also knows how to thank them. All bankers and entrepreneurs know: money in the morning, and in the evening they can get privileges on rent, city orders, credits, or loans."[26] Bunich added: "Luzhkov has certain levers that make it possible for him to thank sponsors. If you are a businessman, it would certainly be better to have an office in the center near the Kremlin. Luzhkov can do it for you. Luzhkov can establish rent from zero—skywards."[27]

Alexei Kara-Murza, a liberal philosopher and politician in Moscow, told me once, "The problem does not lie in the fact that Luzhkov is so unique, but that Moscow is so unique in Russia." The city floated on rivers of capital that simply did not exist anywhere else in Russia. In 1997, five years after Luzhkov became mayor, the city reaped 25 to 30 percent of the taxes of the whole country but had only 6 percent of the population. Of Russia's twenty-five hundred banks, seventeen hundred of them were in Moscow; of the top twenty-five banks, all but one were in the capital, and they held 80 percent of the deposits. Eighty percent of nationwide television advertising originated in Moscow. Muscovites were twice as likely as city dwellers on the whole in Russia to travel abroad, and more than twice as likely to own a telephone, a personal computer, a microwave, or a credit card. Moscow was the citadel of Russian capital, and the rush of riches became so strong that even St. Petersburg, Russia's second-largest city, seemed a sleepy backwater by comparison.[28]

Gaidar later called attention to just one of the many ways Luzhkov exploited Moscow's unique position. Russian law required companies to pay taxes where they were officially registered. The far-flung national monopoly networks all registered in Moscow. Rostelecom was in charge of telephones over all of Russia, but it paid taxes to Moscow. Unified Energy Systems, the electricity monopoly, generated power and distributed it over all Russia, but it paid taxes to Moscow. The same was true of Gazprom, the mammoth natural gas monopoly, and Transneft, the oil pipeline company, both of which spanned not only Russia but parts of Europe. They too paid taxes in Moscow.[29] "Moscow happens to sit next to a fountain spouting gold," Gaidar declared. It's a city with "money to burn."[30]

When I asked Luzhkov about this, he took issue with the claim and insisted that the big companies brought no more than 12–15 percent of the city budget. Luzhkov said the Moscow miracle was not the result of its status as the capital, but the way he managed it. He was a pragmatic *khozyain* with the riches he inherited. He paid the doctors and teachers on time, and pensioners rode city transport for free. "We say that we are going to build 3 million square meters of housing, and we do," Luzhkov insisted. "We say that 5 million square meters of roads will be repaired, and we do the repairing." And the best evidence, Luzhkov recalled, was that business flooded the capital. If he had been a bad *khozyain*, business would have fled.[31]

Wearing his trademark leather cap, Luzhkov jaunted about the city on Saturdays, touring construction sites, trailing journalists, aides, and petitioners, demanding explanations, poking into blueprints, and dressing down his lieutenants. Luzhkov's visits never provoked soaring rhetoric, just a staccato of short, sparse, blunt sentences, not unlike the bricks and mortar around him. Luzhkov was not a philosopher king; he spoke the language of construction, engineering, and chemistry. He thought in terms of goals set, approached, and achieved, and, if not achieved, he angrily demanded to know why. He resembled, more than any Russian politician of the age, the visionary Robert Moses, who built the great complex of parks, beaches, apartment houses, bridges, parkways, and roads of modern New York City. Like Moses strolling through Central Park or Coney Island, Luzhkov roamed his domain, dreaming of public works large and small. He meddled in everything from the largest covered stadium in Europe to the tiny details of a fast-food menu.

In these years, Moscow was a city of 8.6 million people, although by some estimates there were another million or more unofficial residents or visitors at any moment. The city, spread out over 1,091 square kilometers, suffered from aging and decrepit infrastructure. The most dramatic examples came very suddenly on a cold winter day when the massive underground heating pipes melted the frozen ground above, and grotesque chasms opened up—swallowing cars and people. Everywhere, the city was hurting from years of neglect: roads with enormous potholes, chipped and slippery steps, invisible traffic lights, trees choking from pollution, streets groaning with auto gridlock, and always those smelly, dark, forbidding entrances to residential apartment blocks.

But in Luzhkov's day, the city became cleaner, and more functional, than at any time in memory. Luzhkov opened new subway stations, paved rutted roads, created outdoor markets, built playgrounds, installed public fountains, and, most importantly, alleviated the pent-up demand for housing. He built between 3.0 and 3.4 million square meters of new apartment space each year. He sold apartments to the rich and used the proceeds to pay for fresh housing for tens of thousands of families who had been on municipal waiting lists for years. To his credit, whenever there was a city emergency, a bridge collapsed, or some other disaster erupted, Luzhkov showed up and took charge.

But at some point Luzhkov hungered for more. Vladimir Yevtushenkov, a one-time plastics engineer who was a close friend of Luzhkov and became one of Russia's richest men, told me that Luzhkov grew restless and hankered for something more creative than building apartment blocks and paving roads. "He wanted to try things of a larger scale," Yevtushenkov said.[32] Luzhkov's wife, Yelena Baturina, recalled that he saw construction as an ideology, a beacon that could inspire people, keep them from losing faith. Luzhkov "understood the most important thing," she said, "that at such destructive times, it was important to find an idea that would unite people. In Moscow, building became an idea that united Muscovites."[33] On Luzhkov's birthday one year, his wife was wondering what to give him. She spotted an excavator by the roadside. She had the shovel filled with roses and delivered it to Luzhkov. The perfect present for The Builder.[34]

When I interviewed Luzhkov, after a long wait, I wanted to know: what was his great vision or inspiration as a builder? I had long assumed that Luzhkov's ambition was defined and expressed by construction—the new city squares, the parks and highways, the towering new apartment buildings that were his trademark. But his answer was less visionary than I had expected. Luzhkov told me his real "ideology" was not so much construction for its own sake but making the city more livable. This was a street-level, populist perspective, not quite the soaring motive that I had once assumed. "In 1995 I couldn't speak about it because life in Moscow was so revolting," he said. "Moscow was so dirty that if I had spoken about comfort, I would have been told, you are mad, you are crazy. Now I say it fearlessly and openly and frequently: we must make our city more comfortable." Luzhkov's definition of comfort was broad, embracing symbols of "spirituality," such as the cathedral, as well as more mundane affairs like the Ring Road.[35]

The Ring Road was a Luzhkov project that virtually reshaped the city. A beltway encircling Moscow, the 109-kilometer road was known in Soviet times as a dangerous, rock-strewn, potholed mess. Over five years, at a cost of 18 billion rubles, Luzhkov rebuilt the entire route into a eight-lane superhighway, complete with on-ramps, rest stops, pedestrian overpasses, gas stations, and radar speed traps. Luzhkov also dreamed of turning Moscow into a year-round sports capital. Once a week, Luzhkov played soccer with his staff at the Luzhniki stadium along the Moscow River, and he also played tennis there with his wife. Soon, tall construction cranes hoisted into place a 10,000-ton steel ring supporting a 140-foot-high, 12-acre sliding roof of glass-reinforced plastic, making it Europe's largest domed stadium. The $230 million renovation included replacement of the seats. Luzhkov's wife, Yelena Baturina, won a contract to replace old wooden benches in the 85,000-seat stadium with new plastic seats that met European standards for matches to be held there.[36]

One of the great pieces of unfinished business of the Soviet era was Poklonnaya Gora, or the Bowing Hill, a historic site that derived its name from an old tradition in which travelers coming to Moscow bowed to the capital. It was also said that by tradition soldiers departed for war from the hill, and to it they returned victorious. From here, Field Marshall Mikhail Kutuzov yielded Moscow to Napoleon in 1812, vowing not to lose Russia. After World War II, a sporadic effort was made to build a war memorial on the hill, and in the 1980s the chosen design was a central monument of red granite, cast in the shape of a massive curling banner topped with a star. During *perestroika,* the design became bogged down in debate and protests, and when Luzhkov became mayor, it was unfinished, although a spacious war museum behind the monument was partly complete. Luzhkov retooled the project and, in a crash construction effort, finished it in 1995, in time for celebration of the fiftieth anniversary of the victory over Germany. Luzhkov constructed a Russian Orthodox chapel, a synagogue, and a mosque on the grounds of the park. He was widely known for encouraging religious tolerance and revival, except for Chechens, who suffered on the streets of his city. Near the park, Luzhkov began construction of a giant international business and trade center with a pedestrian bridge spanning the Moscow River.

When Yeltsin was worried in 1993 about demonstrations outside the Kremlin walls in Manezh Square, Luzhkov threw up fences around the spot, which kept all the demonstrators away. The fences were ostensibly for a construction project. But only later did Luzhkov actually come up with the project—to build an underground shopping mall. The mall would be three stories deep, with 23,408 square meters of retail space. Typically, Luzhkov set stiff deadlines and demanded round-the-clock construction but then disrupted the plans with his own personal whims. According to one engineer, three months before the opening, Luzhkov ordered drywall ceilings to be replaced with brass strips. Mistakes by the architect resulted in part of the mall being unrentable. In the early years, the mall was a commercial disaster: the rents were so high that it was mostly vacant. The Manezh turned into a $110 million white elephant.[37]

Luzhkov preferred, and imposed, a kitschy, baroque aesthetic on his Moscow monuments and buildings. Sometimes it was no more than an extra frill, such as functionless turrets atop a modern glass-facade office building to spice it up.[38] Other times, it was more profound, especially when the aesthetic decision was left to Luzhkov's friend and prolific sculptor Zurab Tsereteli, a Georgian-born artist whose impact on the cityscape rivaled that of Luzhkov. The gregarious Tsereteli had a penchant for Soviet monumentalism, but his style was sentimental and sugary. Tsereteli, president of the Russian Academy of Art, received a large portion of municipal art commissions in the Luzhkov years, and his flamboyant work left an indelible impression. For the Manezh shopping mall, Tsereteli designed a simulated voyage through Russian centuries, set in marble, chrome, and brass. Outside, he arranged a fountain decorated with bronzes of animals from Russian fairy tales. At the Moscow Zoo, Tsereteli designed a cavelike fantasy entrance with a waterfall and clock. Instead of the Soviet red granite banner on Poklonnaya Gora, Tsereteli designed a 141.8-meter-high obelisk that supported a 24-ton likeness of the Greek goddess Nika, accompanied by two trumpeting angels. Critics called it a "grasshopper on a stick." My own impression is that the sculpture was peculiar, but the park itself, with a broad promenade, forest, and a small hill for sledding, was a city dwellers' delight, an example of how Luzhkov understood that a population packed into tiny apartments needed functional, pleasant outdoor spaces. In the afternoon and evening, from early spring through late autumn, the park was often full, despite the artistic oddities.

The mayor patiently tolerated criticism of Tsereteli's style. Writer Alexander Solzhenitsyn fumed that "Moscow is being recklessly disfigured" and dismissed Tsereteli's works as "massive and third-rate memorials." One grim, bulky Tsereteli sculpture about genocide, titled *Tragedy of the Peoples*—a monument showing a line of starved, naked figures collapsing into a cluster of tombstones—was originally placed at the opening of Poklonnaya Hill. After complaints that it was too depressing, mobile cranes came one day and hauled it away to a spot behind the museum.

Tsereteli sparked his greatest outcry with a 165-foot-high, $15 million statue of Peter the Great erected on the Moscow River, not far from the cathedral, in 1997. The very idea of the sculpture is absurd: Peter the Great, founder of the Russian navy, moved the Russian capital to St. Petersburg to escape Moscow's dark intrigues. But what really triggered protests was the actual sculpture itself, which depicts an awkward tsar astride a galleon, holding a golden map, as little metallic flags flutter in the breeze. Critics said the proportions were wrong; the statue looked like a big toy soldier. Despite protests, Luzhkov backed Tsereteli, and the monument remained. A visitor cruising down the Moscow River in a tour boat would see, in short order, Gorky Park and a model of the discarded Soviet space shuttle; Tsereteli's Peter the Great; and the Cathedral of Christ the Savior. At times Moscow could seem like a very strange post-Soviet Disneyland.

But it was also true that Tsereteli played a serious role in the painstaking, complex job of duplicating the original paintings inside the cathedral. He oversaw 360 painters working intensely over an eight-month period—often 200 of them at any one time were on the scaffolding—using computer-enhanced images to visualize depth and dimension from old photographs.[39]

Of all the buildings, parks, and monuments, the cathedral became Luzhkov's most famous contribution to the city skyline. Ogorodnikov recalled the storied history of the original structure—Tsar Alexander I blessed it, three more Russian emperors took forty-four years to erect it. "And Luzhkov did it in five years," he said. "It was important for his career. He built a monument to himself."

I remember my own first impressions of Moscow in the winter of 1990: a dark and closeted city slumbering under a gray fog. The barren high-rise apartment blocks were forbidding towers in the night, their entrances threatening and foul-smelling. Grimy store windows featured faded cardboard cutouts of nonexistent groceries. Moscow was described once as a "dysfunctional dystopia that somehow kept on barely functioning."[40] But the Moscow I came to know in the Luzhkov years fairly crackled with light and an energetic if superficial brashness. It became a city of extremes, of generous and garish gestures, of wealth gained and spent obscenely, of casinos, discos, restaurants, electronics, gastronomes, mobile phones, billboards, boutiques, and a nascent middle class. A real estate boom sent prime office rents to levels higher than the most prestigious buildings in New York and Tokyo. More than 150 casinos, nearly half of them unlicensed, opened in the mid-1990s. At the Cherry Casino on the New Arbat, my *Washington Post* colleague Lee Hockstader found hundreds of Russians thronging to the blackjack and roulette tables on weekend nights, but the slot machines were practically ignored. The manager was quick to explain. "You can't show off to a slot machine," he said. "These people don't just come to gamble. They come to show off their money, flash it around. And a slot machine doesn't care if you have a big roll of $100 bills in your pocket."[41]

A rich young Muscovite spent hundreds of thousands of dollars to plaster billboards all over town with a close-up image of his exquisite wife and an inscription, "I love you." For weeks, the billboards were a mystery. No one could figure out who had put them up or why. When the story was finally told, many people deemed it a shining and chivalrous act—not ostentatious in the least.[42] Hockstader recalled that Luzhkov and eighty close associates dropped by the swanky Maxim's restaurant a few weeks after it opened in 1995. "There were spit-and-polish waiters, Tiffany lamps, Belle Epoque paintings, soft music, terrific wine, sublime food—and a check that ran more than $20,000," he reported. "The mayor's party paid cash. In dollars, of course."

The new luxury and excess in these boom years often lay awkwardly juxtaposed against the reality that poverty was still widespread, even in Luzhkov's city. Only a thin layer of the elite and the newly rich could really afford the sleek cocktail dresses, jewels, and furs displayed in Moscow's boutique windows.

Emotions were often rubbed raw in the contrasts between freshly minted wealth and aching poverty. When Yeltsin was preparing for heart surgery in October 1996, I decided to try and find out what it was like for an average Russian who needed the same heart operation. In the courtyard of the Bakulev Cardiovascular Surgery Institute, I found Nina Dyomina, a lonely figure dabbing tears from her eyes with a soiled handkerchief. "Money, money for everything," she cried softly. "The only word you hear is 'money!'" In a hospital ward, her husband, Viktor Dyomin, then fifty-eight years old, lay in need of heart surgery. Although the operation was theoretically free, Dyomina, who had come from a provincial town, needed money to pay for medicines and care, and even then she might have to wait years for her husband's operation. The formula was simple: no money, no surgery. Those who could pay for private care got it. Those without money, forced to depend on the aging Moscow city health care system, could wait forever. Despite all the money lavished on the cathedral and the Manezh shopping mall, the number of hospital beds in Moscow did not grow in the 1990s, and two health care systems existed: one for the haves and another for the have-nots. For many of the most unfortunate city dwellers, the homeless, Luzhkov offered the boot. Police rounded them up from railway stations and vegetable markets and put them on trains, forcibly deporting them to villages or makeshift camps far beyond the city limits. Nor was it pleasant to be dark-skinned in Luzhkov's city. Those with darker complexions who were thought to be from the North Caucasus—especially from Chechnya—were often unceremoniously rounded up on city streets after the Chechen war began.

Luzhkov regarded Moscow as a fortress and he fought for years to keep the gates closed to outsiders. Defying the courts, he enforced a Soviet-era residence permit, known as a *propiska,* for everyone living in the city. In the Soviet era, people were told where to work and live by the Communist Party. The 1993 Russian constitution attempted to bury this legacy. It promised that all Russians "shall have the right to freedom of movement and to choose their place of stay and their residence." But the constitution was only paper; in practice, Luzhkov was stronger. The old Soviet procedures were kept alive. Luzhkov feared a wave of immigrants that would overtax the city and compete for its resources. The *propiska* stood, although it was later called a fee for residency. Obtaining one in the mid-1990s required a payment of about $7,000, far beyond the means of most people living in the provinces.[43]

Despite the gaps between wealth and poverty in post-Soviet Moscow, Luzhkov was not just a mayor for the rich. He was attentive to the needs of the pensioners, the middle class, and the poor and was popular among them. He was far more public than any other politician of the time, plunging into the cold Moscow River for a swim, fit as a fiddle, or singing a song on stage at a local theater.

Luzhkov tried to ease tensions brought on by unemployment and the humiliation many felt as the old verities of the Soviet system disappeared. He became the champion of a grimy, sweaty army of traders who carried goods on their backs, into Russia from overseas and back and forth between Moscow and the provinces. Known as shuttle traders or *chelnoki,* after the Russian word for the shuttle in a weaving loom, which rapidly carries thread back and forth, they numbered a million or more in the mid-1990s, hauling suitcases, duffel bags, boxes, and crates for endless hours on planes, buses, trains, and cars, often under exhausting and miserable conditions—including frequent demands from militiamen for bribes—just to earn small profit margins. Luzhkov provided a king-sized crossroads for shuttle traders at Moscow's Luzhniki stadium. Outside the arena, under a statue of Lenin, spread over dozens of acres, he established a bazaar that rivaled Middle Eastern souks. Every day, thousands of people came to buy and sell, many arriving at dawn after overnight bus rides from the provinces and departing again before sunset, carrying their goods home for peddling on a distant street corner. The shuttle traders were often teachers, nurses, and military officers, moonlighting to eke out a living. When the buses pulled out from Luzhniki, they left behind mountains of empty boxes, remnants of the shoes and video machines that the traders had unpacked in order to squeeze more into each nook and cranny of the bus. The market itself was a chaotic sea of bargain hunters, gawking at leather coats and wolfing down sausages and potatoes. The goods—imported coats, rugs, watches, shoes, hair dyes, sweaters, tapes, and more—were hoisted on rickety metal frames reaching high into the trees. "This kind of business," Luzhkov declared, "has become a way of survival for millions of Russians." The markets also became havens for criminal gangs that extracted protection money from the merchants.

As Moscow's mayor, Luzhkov was a micromanager when it suited him. On holidays, he often would dictate the kind of signs and lights storefronts could display. He once signed a decree banishing certain English words and insisting that Russian words be used instead, to be chosen from a list provided by—Luzhkov. Thus "minimarket" became "gastronom." Those who dared defy the mayor were subject to fines up to $700.[44]

Luzhkov fussed over the smallest details. He personally selected the caricature of a nineteenth-century Russian cossack officer as the mascot for a new chain of fast-food restaurants in the city, Russkoye Bistro. He chose the smart orange uniforms, the borscht and tea, and scrutinized every item on the menu, including such Russian traditional foods as hot *pirozhok* pies and the drink *kvas*. "Everything we sell was tasted by the mayor himself," boasted Vladimir Pivovarov, the deputy general director. The restaurants were part of the Moscow city commercial empire, often described as "state capitalism," in which the city was the direct owner of the business. By 1997 Moscow Inc. included fifteen hundred businesses, mostly former Soviet enterprises, and the city was a partner with outside investors in another three hundred firms. The businesses included hotels, construction outfits, bakeries, publishing houses, banking, aviation and communications firms, beauty salons, an oil refinery, and a pair of venerable, troubled auto factories. Luzhkov was in position to give city businesses a huge advantage over competitors. In the case of Russkoye Bistro, the city contributed choice spots for the restaurants, cheap utilities, and bank loans at low interest rates. The system captured perfectly Luzhkov's vision of the *khozyain*, but it hardly fit the Chubais notion of a new generation of private owners competing in the marketplace. Arkady Murashev, a former Moscow police chief who led a liberal opposition campaign for city council, infuriated the powerful mayor once when he said Luzhkov had become "the biggest entrepreneur in the city, having taken control of everything."

But Luzhkov's brand of state capitalism failed when it came to a far more ambitious commercial venture, rescuing the moribund Zil truck factory. Once a crown jewel of Soviet industry, Zil built the four-ton bulletproof limousines enjoyed by Communist Party leaders. The factory fell on hard times after it was privatized. The first private owners used some questionable financial schemes to nearly wreck the company. The city took a controlling stake in a bailout in late 1996. A factory that once churned out 200,000 vehicles a year was making only 17,000 that year and sinking into loss and debt. "Comrade Zilites, I think that you steal!" Luzhkov thundered to the assembled management of Zil one day, after the city assumed responsibility for the faltering plant. Luzhkov, with typical brusqueness, declared later: "They say to me, you are crazy. The factory has already died. Nothing of the sort. Give me half a year, and Zil will be standing quite seriously on its feet."[45]

He was wrong. Luzhkov funneled enough cash into the factory to keep it afloat, in part by guaranteeing a loan from commercial banks. He forced municipal departments to order Zil trucks. But the trucks Zil made were uncompetitive on the open market—a far more popular model was made by the rival Gaz factory in Nizhny Novgorod—and Zil was, in true Soviet fashion, cranking out a product for which there was no market. Four years after Luzhkov's promise to put Zil back on its feet, the company was still running in the red, with no end in sight. Luzhkov fared just as poorly with the other big Moscow auto factory, Moskvich, for the same reasons. State capitalism simply could not substitute for a real market.

The dark side of Luzhkov's empire was endemic, uncontrolled corruption, fueled by the passions of the new money that flooded Moscow. The city was rife with protection rackets—virtually every business had to employ a *krysha*, or roof, for protection in the early 1990s—and several large organized crime gangs thrived. Bribery, kickbacks, and secret overseas bank accounts were common, and disputes were settled with car bombs and contract murders. In this respect, Moscow was not unique, but a more concentrated example of the corruption sickness that befell all Russia. When the government itself was a major breeding ground for corruption, when city bosses and federal ministers were routinely on the take, the law enforcement authorities alone could not have cleaned up the mess. They were just as much a part of the corrupt network as the ministers and bureaucrats. The issue was much more profound: Russia had not become a state with the rule of law, and its rulers were often indifferent to, and sometimes complicit in, the chaos.

Luzhkov told me he struggled with the crime wave in Moscow, but he laid blame for it on the way Russia's economy was built in the early

1990s, when the "shadow economy" turned into big business. "Representatives of the criminal world penetrated both business and law enforcement bodies," he said, "and they imported their rules." He insisted that the level of corruption in Moscow was lower than in other cities.[46]

But it was impossible to do business in Luzhkov's Moscow without being harassed for bribes by inspectors, police, and bureaucrats. To get a street-level view, one day I visited a typical bakery and candy store near Moscow State University, Bread Store 185. In the back of the store, I listened to Vera Trusova, a pleasant woman in a boldly striped sweater who was once an engineer, describe the trials endured by small businesses in Luzhkov's city. She cupped her hands in a begging sign of helplessness as she recounted how the latest city inspector, who was checking price stickers, imposed fines on her that were equal to a month's pay. The petty corruption—demands for bribes were made by anyone with a badge—were wrecking her business. "If she comes right now, I am still going to bow down before her," Trusova said of the latest inspector. "And I am going to say, 'Yes, how much?'" Trusova wrote a letter to fellow small business owners, in which she recalled how a team of inspectors was "driving by the store, and a lamp was not burning in the window. A fine. They approach the store, and there's a cigarette butt lying on the ground. A fine. The salesperson was not wearing a cap. A fine. And they found dust on the lamp in the storage room, a fine. They wrote out a pile of fines and walked out of the store, happy!"

A more ominous shadow was cast over Luzhkov's empire on a gray Sunday afternoon, November 3, 1996. At about 5:00 P.M., an American businessman, Paul Tatum, left the Radisson-Slavyanskaya, a 430-room hotel he had helped convert into one of the first Western-style hotels in the city. Tatum, a flashy, eccentric forty-one-year-old Oklahoman who was among the early wave of enthusiasts about the rise of capitalism in Moscow, walked with two bodyguards toward the Kievskaya Metro stop, just beyond the hotel. As he descended down the worn stone steps of an underpass, a lone gunman opened fire from the parapet around the stairway. Twenty shots rang out, eleven of them hitting Tatum, who died shortly after being shot. The killer escaped, leaving behind the murder weapon, a Kalashnikov free of fingerprints and wrapped in a plastic bag.

At the time, Tatum was locked in a nasty business dispute over the hotel. Tatum's company owned 40 percent, the Minneapolis-based Radisson Hotel chain owned 10 percent, and Luzhkov's city held the other 50 percent. Tatum's fight pitted him against Umar Dzhabrailov, an ethnic Chechen, a slight man with shoulder-length hair, always impeccably tailored, who swooped up and down the main hallway of the hotel surrounded by a flying wedge of bodyguards. Dzhabrailov was the city representative of the joint venture that was running the hotel, as well as other properties. Tatum had been sharply and openly critical of Dzhabrailov—saying he was part of the Chechen mafia in Moscow—and their arguments spilled into the newspapers and television. Tatum said he was being pushed out of the hotel venture; Dzhabrailov said Tatum failed to pay his debts. Tatum arrived at the hotel one day in June 1994 and was blocked by armed guards. He held a news conference in the hotel parking lot to denounce his Russian partners. A week and a half later, accompanied by a dozen bodyguards and wearing a bulletproof vest, he bullied his way back into the hotel.[47]

Dzhabrailov denied any role in Tatum's killing, but questions haunted him. Less than a month after the assassination, the United States revoked Dzhabrailov's visa after a journalist for *USA Today* reported to the embassy that his life had been threatened by Dzhabrailov during an interview about Tatum's murder.[48]

Luzhkov remained silent about the murder for a long time. Inexplicably, he kept Dzhabrailov in place and later promoted him to manage the Manezh shopping mall. Still later, Dzhabrailov campaigned for president of Russia, plastering central Moscow with his smiling face on billboards.[49] Luzhkov later told a reporter, "If the American side has sound evidence of his involvement in this horrible murder and terrorist act, I am ready to draw the most radical conclusions—I mean to stop all contact with him, business or personal. If not, we will take the decision on whom to deal with on our own, without any pressure or instructions from America."[50] Luzhkov said in response to my question about Tatum: "There was no decisive reaction to this murder from your side either. And I have as little to do with this murder as you do."[51]

Tatum's killer was never found by Moscow's homicide detectives. That was not unusual: in the city that year they found the killer and the person who ordered the killing in only three of 152 murders believed to be contract killings.[52] Nor did the Moscow newspapers and central television stations raise the issue at the time.

Luzhkov was almost never criticized by the press, in part because he provided a financial lifeline to many newspapers and television stations in the form of subsidized rents. One journalist told me that his entire apartment building, occupied by the newspaper's reporters, was given to them cheaply by Luzhkov. They believed he could take it away, and they were careful not to offend him. Luzhkov was a king in his own realm, and he reveled in the fact that no one could challenge him. "For long years, Yuri Mikhailovich lived in an environment, in an atmosphere of being everybody's favorite," his friend Yevtushenkov told me. "He was a sacred cow whom nobody dared criticize much."[53]

When Luzhkov was offended by an article or a broadcast, he regularly sued for slander in the city courts—which he also subsidized—and won almost every case. But this insular cocoon later proved costly to Luzhkov.

In a speech that was reprinted in *Moscow News*, an independent weekly newspaper, Yegor Gaidar said, "The economic life in Moscow is terribly bureaucratized and full of regulations, which results in widespread corruption. Everybody who has to deal with the Moscow municipal structures knows it perfectly well. And, regrettably, the process here is growing bigger, not smaller."[54] Luzhkov filed suit against Gaidar, saying the city's reputation had been hurt. Gaidar took the case seriously. His lawyers provided evidence of bribe taking in the city, but, after an initial victory in the lower court, Luzhkov won on appeal. The judge gave no reason.[55] Yet the obvious truth of Gaidar's claim was illustrated once again in November 2000, when police arrested Vladimir Kochetkov, who was head of a municipal housing and construction authority, after he tried to extract a $827 bribe for signing a contract for street lights. They found that Kochetkov had a $700,000 Swiss bank account, and they discovered $67,000 in a plastic bag behind a radiator in his house.[56]

The first years of the new Russia were a perplexing time for Luzhkov as a political leader. The country declared itself a democracy and market economy, but the laws, traditions, and mind-set of the earlier era lingered. There was no handbook for this twilight zone between the Soviet experience and the new capitalism. One of the most difficult questions was the relationship between public and private interests. The old system was ruled by arbitrary party diktat, and private business interests did not exist or were banished to the shadows. Then, practically overnight, the party was gone and replaced with a new electoral-based democracy. The new political leaders, among them Luzhkov, were just as suddenly faced with a plethora of hungry new private business interests. These business interests, no longer relegated to the shadows, were powerful. In the passage from the old world to the new one, the lines between public interest and private gain were blurred. The private interests helped themselves to the public treasure, and the new leaders of Russia—including Luzhkov—let them at it.

The mixture of public interest and private business was foreshadowed in a brief controversy involving Luzhkov's role in a company called Orgkomitet, which had somehow secured the monopoly privilege to sell city-owned housing to private owners. In 1991 Luzhkov, then vice mayor under Popov, became head of Orgkomitet. As a city official, he transferred the rights to two valuable buildings to Orgkomitet, which was an apparent conflict of interest.[57] After press criticism and pressure from a prosecutor, Luzhkov resigned from the company on April 22, 1992. One of Luzhkov's assistants told me that Orgkomitet was one among many shady, quasi-private companies that began to feed off the city in the 1990s, and Luzhkov got involved by "accident." Luzhkov later said, "Orgkomitet was created along with a huge number of new market structures at a time of pervasive uncertainty. As soon as we saw what it was, we immediately liquidated it."[58]

But Orgkomitet was an early precursor of Luzhkov's basic system, which combined public and private interests. This approach came into full view in the 1990s with the birth of a corporate giant headed by Luzhkov's close personal friend, Yevtushenkov, the one-time plastics engineer, a quiet and cautious man with wire-rim glasses and a very low-key style that belied his influential position at Luzhkov's side.

Yevtushenkov's path to wealth began at a small backwater of the municipal bureaucracy, the Moscow City Committee on Science and Technology. It was a marginal department, and Yevtushenkov, the director, found that his budget subsidies had dried up. In 1993, the year after Luzhkov became mayor, Yevtushenkov went commercial. He simply transformed his small city department into a private company. The original idea, he said, was to generate profit for the committee to substitute for lost state subsidies. "I was experimenting, as everyone was," Yevtushenkov explained. His experiments became very profitable indeed, leading to the creation of a sprawling conglomerate with holdings in telephones, electronics, insurance, tourism, and other businesses. The company was called Systema.

Yevtushenkov told me that he was a friend of the Luzhkov family but insisted that he did not use his friendship to speak with Luzhkov about business ventures.[59] Another Luzhkov assistant said that Yevtushenkov was closer to Luzhkov than anyone else except Luzhkov's wife, Yelena Baturina. Yevtushenkov had been best man at their wedding. Luzhkov's wife was president of a plastics company, Inteko, which Luzhkov had described as his chief source of family income. At one point Yevtushenkov sold his 24 percent interest in another plastics factory, Almeko, to Baturina's firm, which she ran with her brother Viktor.[60]

The source of early capital for the Systema conglomerate is not known. One version came from Yevgeny Novitsky, president of Systema, who said the conglomerate grew out of a group of import-export companies making easy money in the early 1990s selling Russian oil abroad and importing computers. "We took loans, purchased oil, sold this oil to the West. Then we bought computer goods, televisions, computers, food products, sold them in the market here, and on account of this, a large profit market developed. In 1993 it was possible to make 100 percent in one operation. Buy something for a dollar, sell it for two." The story sounded typical of the quick-riches tales of the era, but it did not account for the advantage that Yevtushenkov enjoyed as a pal of the mayor.

That advantage came in the early days of privatization. According to its own reports, Systema's assets multiplied almost sixfold between 1994 and 1996, to more than $1 billion. One of the most revealing acquisitions was the Moscow telephone monopoly, the fifth-largest phone system in the world, with 4 million lines. It was a notoriously creaky network, and one exchange, 231, had been in service since 1930.[61] But it was still a potentially lucrative company, since the demand was strong for more and better phones. If telephone rates could be raised—and that was a decision Luzhkov would have to take—the phone company could be profitable. "Quite by chance," Yevtushenkov recalled, "I found myself in a field that began to develop very fast—telecommunications."

When Luzhkov's government decided to privatize 33 percent of the telephone company in 1995, Yevtushenkov went for it. He just created a new version of his old city government committee. The name was slightly changed, however, from Moscow City on Science and Technology to Moscow City on Science and Technology and Company. The "and Company" was a group of firms mostly controlled or owned by Systema. His new firm was declared the winner of the Moscow City Property Fund investment tender for the Moscow phone company on April 21, 1995. The price was $136 million, of which $100 million could be provided in equipment; the price was a fraction of the company's market capitalization at the time of $2 billion.[62]

When the privatization results were announced, the winner was identified only as the "Moscow Committee on Science and Technology and Company." The Systema conglomerate, the real force behind the deal, was not mentioned. The privatization was an insider deal. It was exactly the kind of cheap sell-off that Luzhkov was publicly denouncing in his fight with Chubais, but his own city was engaged in the same practice, benefiting his friend Yevtushenkov.[63] When I asked the Moscow property committee for details of the tender, all I received was a fax listing the conditions before the tender, and a second page, a short list of investment tender winners for the week. No prices, no terms, no details.[64]

Systema was a very private, almost hidden company. In the mid-1990s, when Yevtushenkov was expanding, Systema was not well-known and received less attention than the financial and industrial empires of Gusinsky, Smolensky, Berezovsky, and Khodorkovsky. Even the smart financial analysts in Moscow seemed confused about Systema. As late as 1998, stock brokers who issued research bulletins to foreign investors about the telephone company often failed to note that the "Moscow Committee on Science and Technology and Company" was linked to Systema. Nor was it clear who really owned the Systema conglomerate. The company issued no detailed reports on its ownership and only skimpy financial documents. Novitsky told me the parent company was 100 percent owned by another firm, Systema-invest, which in turn is 40 percent owned by a Luxembourg investment company, and the remainder in the hands of individuals, including Yevtushenkov. Luzhkov denied that Systema was "a spare pocket for the mayor."[65]

As Moscow boomed, Yevtushenkov's conglomerate became ever more deeply woven into the fabric of the city's financial flows. The Moscow Bank for Reconstruction and Development, part of Systema, became one of Moscow's "authorized" banks, with the lucrative privilege of distributing city money, such as the subsidies to Zil. Systema's insurance company insured the Moscow subway. Systema-Neft operated a chain of Moscow gas stations. Systema-Gals was a major real estate developer in the center of Moscow. Systema Telecommunications had interests in two Moscow cellular phone companies, one of which became a market leader. Systema also owned Detski Mir, the famous, sprawling children's store, the Intourist travel agency, and a group of electronics factories. Yevtushenkov wore many different hats all at once: Luzhkov's friend and adviser, the boss of Systema, and other posts such as chairman of the council of the Moscow Stock Exchange. He moved effortlessly back and forth between public interest and private business.

Alexei Ulyukaev, a reformist member of the city council and the deputy director of Gaidar's institute, described this as typical of the Luzhkov method. "In the Moscow network, it's important to have two legs—one in business, the other in the administration," he told me. Luzhkov created a system in which it was not unusual for a city department to be linked to a private business. "On the one hand, they manage budget money," Ulyukaev said, "but then they are, on the other hand, making money. And third, the city oversees it all. They are supply, demand, and administration." Ulyukaev called it "commercialization" of the government. "Virtually every structure of the city has its own off-budget fund," he said, used for collecting profits from its businesses. The profits were often hidden. In a prospectus written for overseas investors in 1997, the city admitted that all of its off-budget funds amounted to a fifth of the entire $9.9 billion in revenues, and many experts said the actual amount was far greater. Ulyukaev said the details remained undisclosed to the city council as well.[66]

What would be considered conflict of interest in a Western economy was standard procedure in Moscow. When the city borrowed $500 million on global capital markets in 1997, it decided to make loans from the proceeds to encourage investment. Yevtushenkov had a seat on the twenty-four-member council that decided on the loans. Who got the money? Systema did—at least three loans: $16.5 million for a downtown real estate project, $16.5 million for a factory making television sets, and $15 million for a plant making digital telephone exchanges. Yevtushenkov told me he wasn't present when the loans were discussed, but a city official said he was present and sat silently.

The rise of Systema is not just a story about wealth or about Luzhkov's blatant mixture of power and money. At the time Systema began to take shape, the new Russian economy was becoming a tribal, clannish system. It was giving birth to conglomerates (politely called financial-industrial groups) that were in fact small empires in the making, often allied with a political leader. Luzhkov, the boss of a sprawling, increasingly prosperous metropolis, needed his own alliance with a financial-industrial group. In the early years, it had been Gusinsky, and later it became Systema and Yevtushenkov.

Luzhkov began to think about new horizons. Reporters were already badgering him about whether he would run for president. Yeltsin, then sliding into sickness, would not be president forever. "I am tired of repeating that I do not intend to run," Luzhkov replied in 1995. "This is not my cup of tea." He then added, "But even if I decided to run for president, is it a crime, an illegal act?"[67]

In fact, Yevtushenkov and Luzhkov, who vacationed together and spent hours on weekends in long discussions, began to speculate privately about what it would take for Luzhkov to run for president, after Yeltsin. In the end, Luzhkov supported the Russian president during the 1996 elections, but the discussions went on long after that. Yevtushenkov believed that Luzhkov had one very powerful argument: he could change the country in the same way he had rebuilt Moscow. Yevtushenkov felt that Luzhkov had a chance to make history.

It was a daring thought, but there was one problem that would only show itself later: Luzhkov was not ready. He was at heart a *khozyain*, a manager, a Soviet man who had adapted to the new economy. He was still a creature of Moscow's unique situation, and his experience in politics was forged within the protected cocoon of Moscow. The bustling city-state was a world apart from the rest of Russia.

Chapter 11

The Club on Sparrow Hills

IN ALL OF MOSCOW, few vantage points are as spectacular as Sparrow Hills, a forested, sloping rise perched above the Moscow River where it makes a lazy turn toward the Kremlin. On summer afternoons, the woods offer a cool refuge from the city. Riverboats and barges ply the waterway. The hill is commanded by the imposing thirty-five-story tower of the Moscow State University building. A broad promenade at the top of the hill overlooks the river and offers a panoramic overview of the city horizon, from the Luzhniki stadium in the foreground to the needle-like Ostankino television tower in the distance. Down each side of the hill from the university runs Kosygin Street, one of Moscow's most placid, tree-lined boulevards. This is a prestigious neighborhood, home to the university, the Institute of Chemical Physics, and Mosfilm, once the heart of the Soviet movie industry. Sparrow Hills is also the fictional point at which Woland, the devil, alights on his steed and flies heavenward in the final scenes of Mikhail Bulgakov's classic novel, *The Master and Margarita*.[1]

It was on the crest of the hill that a few wealthy Russian businessmen gathered at a private villa overlooking the river in September 1994. They were mostly young, and their fortunes were even younger. Mikhail Khodorkovsky, then thirty, had only seven years earlier tried to start his youth café at the Mendeleev Institute. Alexander Smolensky, then thirty-nine, had been building dachas from logs seven years earlier. Boris Berezovsky, at forty-seven the oldest in the group, had founded Logovaz in a café barely five years earlier. They were joined by several others: Vladimir Vinogradov, thirty-nine, a pioneer among the early cooperative businessmen who became president of Inkombank, one of the biggest of the new commercial banks; Vladimir Potanin, thirty-two, a son of the *nomenklatura* whose bank was expanding very rapidly; and Mikhail Friedman, thirty, who made his first money in a cooperative—washing windows—but was now also head of a fast-growing bank. Two others were quite prominent at the time but later faded from view: Oleg Boiko, thirty, a financier who had supported Yegor Gaidar's party in the early years, and Alexander Yefanov, thirty-eight, president of Mikrodin, a company that invested in heavy industry but was later absorbed into Potanin's empire. As a group, these onetime hustlers and jeans traders were blossoming as tycoons.

They came to the club at the urging of Vasily Shakhnovsky, then thirty-seven, one of Yuri Luzhkov's top aides. Shakhnovsky, who had steely gray-blue eyes that crinkled at the edges, receding, wiry hair, and a brownish beard speckled with gray, was one of their generation. Only five years earlier, Shakhnovsky had been drawn into the ferment of the democracy movement in Moscow city politics. He worked for Gavriil Popov and then Luzhkov, holding a top position on the mayor's staff. From his perch at city hall, Shakhnovsky saw that Russian political and business life was increasingly chaotic. The years of upheaval—the August 1991 coup attempt, the 1992 Yeltsin economic revolution, the October 1993 violent confrontation with parliament—left businessmen without established rules of the game. It was a time when the young financiers and industrialists knew quite well how to get what they wanted from politicians or bureaucrats, but they had only a faint notion of their collective power. They could bribe their way to an export permit but had no idea how to change export policy. Shakhnovsky called the group *bolshoi kapital,* or big capital, but they were adrift, without a voice. The businessmen said they wanted a "normal country," with normal laws and a normal government and a normal economy, but they didn't have one, nor a clue about how to get there. Most of them had been working so intensely on their own businesses, they had not looked at the big picture.

Moreover, Shakhnovsky saw that the young tycoons dealt with the government in one crude way: bribery and coercion. It was an all-or-nothing environment, and every businessman faced a stark choice, as was often said: "annihilate or be annihilated."

There were no rules. "If one was playing soccer and another was playing rugby, there was no game; it led to a fistfight without rules," Shakhnovsky recalled. Increasingly, Shakhnovsky saw that the businessmen settled their scores on the street. "At that time in particular, there were no rules at all." Worried about the disorder, Shakhnovsky decided on his own to do something about it. "Bribes cannot be given forever," he said. "Sooner or later, there is an end to everything."

Shakhnovsky recruited the businessmen to join an exclusive, secret club of their own. In Shaknovsky's mind, the club was to be a protected place where they could be free to talk, argue, and hopefully coalesce around their common interests. Shakhnovsky told me he did not want to create a salon of deal making. He wanted his guests to think broadly: how *bolshoi kapital* could make an impact on the newly emergent Russian democracy and economy. He wanted them to come up with ideas about how to lobby the government in a civilized way—how to create good public relations for themselves—as was done in every normal country.

The club took shape, but not in the way Shakhnovsky had envisioned. The businessmen were far too concerned with their own problems to see the big picture. Two years later, in 1996, they finally came together as a single, powerful group, when they felt their wealth and property were threatened. But at the beginning, they had pressing parochial worries. They wanted protection—from each other. The first order of business at the club was to create "civilized rules of the game with each other," Shakhnovsky said. They drafted a charter. The essence was that they would not attack each other. They pledged not to bribe the law enforcement authorities to go after each other, or use newspapers and television to smear each other. At the time, all of them were building up their own private corporate armies and intelligence agencies for doing just that. Many of them had hired ex-KGB chiefs for the task. One purpose of these well-paid, well-equipped spies was to dig up dirt and compromising materials, known as *kompromat*, to use against rivals or the government. *Kompromat* could be purchased, easily, from the official security services and agencies, including the ones that had been part of the KGB and still had access to its mountains of files. Or, if not bought, *kompromat* could be manufactured—using forged documents—and it would be just as effective. Moreover, it was not difficult to spread. To deploy a war of *kompro-*

mat against enemies, a banker did not need to own a newspaper or television station or radio station. It was enough to pay a relatively small sum, even a few hundred dollars, to a desperate journalist. Not all journalists were corrupt, but some were, and they would publish or broadcast just about anything for money.

In their charter the tycoons agreed: no *kompromat* against each other. "Maybe a bit utopian, a bit of a childish idea, but at that early stage, they agreed to it, and had some success in somehow channeling the process," Shakhnovsky told me later.[2]

It was the nature of their informal, exclusive club that no one quite remembered years later whether the charter was written or oral, and whether they had signed it or not. Leonid Nevzlin, who was Khodorkovsky's partner, recalled that it was an oral agreement. "It was discussed, but not put on paper," he told me. Khodorkovsky could not remember attending the meetings at all. Vinogradov said, "I don't remember whether we actually put our signatures on it." Smolensky said, "There was no document, there was an oral agreement. We agreed not to bite each other, not to resort to the mass media in order to settle our relations, not to use law enforcement to settle our commercial problems."[3]

Shakhnovsky told me the document was written down, drafted and redrafted; the language was kept very general. "It was being corrected, some would sign it, some would add corrections," he recalled. "There was a document all right, but since this was a very amorphous creation, it cannot be said that all accepted it and all began to follow it. It was signed."

"I think the minute they walked out of the gates of the building," Vinogradov recalled, "they immediately broke the agreement." He was right, and the following years brought every one of them into fierce conflict with each other. They broke their promises and used the law enforcement agencies and the mass media to attack each other.

Yet Shakhnovsky had indeed started something. The members of the club on Sparrow Hills multiplied their millions, and their quiet little club later blossomed into much more than the debating society envisioned by Shakhnovsky. It was the beginning of a daring attempt, far more audacious than Shakhnovsky could have imagined at first, to take over the country.

•

The club on Sparrow Hills met regularly, every other week, at the villa overlooking the river. Nestled among the trees, the villa was set back from the street by a long driveway, completely shielded from view by an imposing stone wall. It was a perfect hideaway, behind a guarded gate, part of a sprawling network of city-owned buildings. The businessmen arrived at 7:00 P.M. for drinks and then dined around a table. They talked late into the night, until the city horizon stretched out before them in a twinkling sea of lights. They met for the first time in September 1994 and for the last time in the autumn of 1995, but the club revived itself, in other places and other times, for another two years after that.

From the first meetings, the businessmen were frustrated in their search for a political patron. Yeltsin's Kremlin was split by competing factions. Chernomyrdin, the jowly, inarticulate prime minister, was the epitome of the old Soviet factory directors, hardly a promising candidate. None of the young economic reformers such as Gaidar and Chubais were prominent, experienced, or powerful enough to lead the ambitious new elite. The view from Sparrow Hills, as one participant later recalled, was "completely disillusioned."[4]

One evening Shakhnovsky invited Luzhkov to meet them. According to Shakhnovsky, the club was pondering whether Luzhkov could be their standard-bearer. "These people were prepared to put their stake on him," he said, "and were ready to perceive him as a man who would move their interests forward among political circles." But the effort failed. In the first meeting, it was evident they simply did not speak the same language. Luzhkov, then fifty-eight, had traveled part of the way toward the market economy, but he was suspicious of the young businessmen, who seemed to represent the speculative, gambling side of what he called "parasitic" capitalism. He retained the instincts of his training as a Soviet-era manager; he was a *khozyain.* By contrast, the young banker-industrialists, most of them two decades younger than Luzhkov, were cynical and ambitious. They, unlike Luzhkov, had never run a factory, but they knew more than he did about how to gamble on the ruble-dollar exchange rate and move their winnings offshore. At least two of the young tycoons, Smolensky and Khodorkovsky, long ago, during *perestroika,* applied to Luzhkov for a license for their cooperatives. They may have shared some common ideas back then, but no longer.

Smolensky recalled that Luzhkov immediately alienated the tycoons by bringing along two of his lieutenants, Vladimir Resin and Boris Nikolsky. Smolensky saw Luzhkov's men as cut from the same cloth as the mayor, old-school guys out of sync with the fleet-footed financiers. "Nonliquid stuff," Smolensky scoffed at the memory. Smolensky remembered that one of the young businessmen said to Luzhkov, "Yuri Mikhailovich, you want us to invest in Moscow? You are digging a hole in Manezh Square" (the excavation had just begun). "We think this is not a valid project." In other words, it was a money loser.

Luzhkov stubbornly replied, "I dug, and will keep on digging! And you are not to give orders to me, and I won't take your advice on that."

"Fine," the businessman said. "It's your decision, Yuri Mikhailovich."

The young bankers felt themselves to be newly minted Masters of the Universe. They did not want to be bossed around. Luzhkov, however, could have it no other way. He *was* the boss. He would decide where to dig, even if he had started digging for no reason at all except to stop a protest rally. His entire mind-set was that of digging, and his model of capitalism revolved around his own central role.

"Luzhkov arrived to this meeting as, above all, a *khozyain* who considered himself much wiser and more farsighted than the people sitting around the table," Shakhnovsky recalled. "And he was not talking with these people as partners. No. This was a conversation looking very much down, very much so. He was lecturing them some, he was giving them advice some, but it was not a conversation."

Berezovsky was appalled at what Luzhkov told the tycoons. Berezovsky believed Big Capital should tell the government what to do, and not the other way around. "We just scattered away from him," Smolensky recalled of Luzhkov after that meeting. "We were the Moscow bankers, and he just lost us."

Although Shakhnovsky wanted to keep the club's attention on the big picture, he was undone by Berezovsky, who soon brought to the club just the kind of deal making that Shakhnovsky hoped to avoid. Berezovsky remained the compressed ball of energy his friends had described in earlier years. In the autumn of 1994, he launched himself into a new orbit of dreams and plans. While other members of the club were still debating who in politics could become the patron of Big Capital, Berezovsky was already out recruiting. He didn't start small: Berezovsky wanted Boris Yeltsin.

The auto business proved lucrative and dangerous for Berezovsky. By the time the club began to meet in 1994, Logovaz was not just Russia's largest Zhiguli dealer but was also selling Mercedes, Honda, Chevrolet, Chrysler, and Volvo vehicles and was planning to feature Daewoo cars as well. Towering billboards with the Logovaz white and blue symbol were erected on the major arteries leading into Moscow. A Logovaz report describing the company's marketing strategy boasted that although in 1993 only seven out of ten people knew what Logovaz was, by 1994, ten out of ten knew the company's reputation in the car business. Logovaz spent $1.2 million for advertising and public relations in the year that ended in mid-1994. The firm's big attention-getter was Moscow's annual August auto show. Berezovsky also sponsored an annual $100,000 Triumph charity arts prize.[5]

But the car dealerships had a dark underside—the business was a magnet for criminal gangs. Moscow became a playground for rival underworld mobs, who saw the car dealerships as a prize. At one point in late 1993 Berezovsky fled Moscow for Israel, where he received citizenship.[6] He apparently had been targeted by the gangs. In Moscow, two warring mobs, one led by Chechens, who were known for their ferocity, and the other by the Solntsevo gang, a Slavic mob named after a district in southwestern Moscow, were competing for control of the auto dealerships. In September 1993, Berezovksy's Logovaz car parks were attacked three times, and his showrooms bombed with grenades.[7]

On Novokuznetskaya Street, an old Moscow avenue with a creaky tram line, Berezovsky's command center was the Logovaz Club, a restored early nineteenth-century Smirnov family mansion. From the outside, the Logovaz Club is an unmarked, low-lying gray building. But inside it is an old world–style salon, lavishly gilded and ornately decorated. The room I remember most was the spacious anteroom where I waited before appointments with Berezovsky: soft yellow walls, a red rose painted on the ceiling arch, tinkling glasses at the bar, a battalion of red wine bottles, blond wood chairs arranged in front of small round Parisian-café tables, an illuminated aquarium against one wall, and always a crowd of people shifting in their chairs, waiting to see Berezovsky. He would come breezing through, hands in his suit pockets, stride up to you, and beg your pardon. He was running late—always running late. He would be back, he promised, and he usually was. Meanwhile, the anteroom stirred, cellular telephones hummed, buzzed, and screeched, and the soft colors were broken by the latest news bulletins from a jarring, oversized, wide-screen television mounted on one wall.

At 5:00 P.M. on June 7, 1994, Berezovsky walked out the door of his club and climbed into the backseat of his Mercedes 600 sedan, behind the driver. In the front, next to the driver, sat his bodyguard. At the peak of rush hour, Berezovsky's Mercedes wheeled out of the courtyard and onto the street, passing a parked Opel. A remotely controlled bomb, concealed in the Opel, exploded with enormous power, ripping apart the front of Berezovsky's Mercedes, sending thousands of small, deadly metal pellets flying through the air. Berezovsky's driver was decapitated, his bodyguard lost an eye, seven pedestrians waiting for the tram were injured, and windows in a building a block away were shattered. Climbing out of the bloody, smoking wreckage, Berezovsky was burned and badly shaken. Logovaz issued an angry statement that "this tragedy shows beyond a doubt that there are forces in society that are actively trying, by barbarically criminal means, to keep civilized entrepreneurship from developing in our country." No names were named.

It was a fearsome time: police said fifty-two bombs had gone off in the city by June of that year, compared with sixty-one for all of 1993. The bomb set for Berezovsky was the most powerful of them all. Vladimir Kadannikov, Berezovsky's partner and director of Avtovaz, offered a $1 million reward for information leading to identification of the "initiators and perpetrators of the terrorist act" against Berezovsky. They were never found.

Berezovsky told me that four days after the bombing, still in bandages, he attended a reception held by Yeltsin to mark a Russian holiday. "Yeltsin saw me and he was surprised and asked what happened. I told him." According to Berezovsky, Yeltsin motioned to his security ministers. "Do you see what happened to him?" he said of Berezovsky. "I am giving you one month to find out who did it."[8] They never did find out. Berezovsky flew to Switzerland for medical attention.

When he returned to Moscow, he was burning with ambition. He wanted to be more than Russia's biggest car dealer. Leonid Boguslavsky, his friend from early years at the institute, recalled that Berezovsky was thinking as early as 1992 about television, especially powerful Channel 1, with a broadcasting signal that reached almost every household in the former Soviet Union. The Soviet authorities had invested in expensive satellites to make sure Channel 1 blanketed nearly 200 million people. The Logovaz business was "just a tool," the Logovaz clubhouse was "just a tool," Berezovsky told his friend Boguslavsky. "The most important tool will be Channel 1."[9]

Channel 1 and the related transmission and production facilities—including the 1,771-foot broadcasting tower in Moscow, Europe's tallest structure—were once supported by the state, but the government no longer shelled out the lavish subsidies of the Soviet years. Moreover, Channel 1, or Ostankino as it was also known, was riddled with theft. While the government continued to provide enough support to keep the powerful signal on the air, advertising money was diverted by individual production companies, very little of it finding its way back to the channel as a whole. The situation was similar to the assembly line in Togliatti, where cars rolled off practically for free, and middlemen sold them for a small fortune. In television, the state kept the "factory" going by subsidizing the broadcasting signal, but others reaped the cash from advertising. While Channel 1 claimed it ran only nineteen minutes of advertising a day in mid-1993, a study of programming found it broadcast one hundred minutes a day. Thus, even at the lowest rates, the revenue flow was 60 to 75 billion rubles a year, but a government audit found only about 11.2 billion rubles actually reached the station.[10]

Igor Malashenko, who resigned in early 1993 after a brief stint as director of Ostankino, told me: "Commercially, it was an absolute disaster. It started in a very simple way: you know, when advertising was introduced, nobody knew how to sell it. And managers of Ostankino were just these old-time Soviet bureaucrats. Suddenly they found that they didn't have money to buy programs because state financing virtually stopped. And then imagine, some young producer would come to them and say, 'Okay, I will provide you with programs. I just need to barter with you. I don't need any money from you. Just give me a certain amount of advertising time. I will sell it myself, it's my risk.' These idiots were absolutely happy—but economically they destroyed Ostankino."[11]

Sergei Lisovsky, a concert promoter and entertainment mogul who became one of Russia's leading advertising tycoons, told me that in the early years Channel 1 merely sold off the errant blank spots between programs—the thirty-second or sometimes five-minute holes that were the result of sloppy scheduling. Later, as big advertising money flowed in to Russia, the various producers and programs began freelancing, selling their own advertising. To advertisers, especially Western consumer goods companies like Proctor & Gamble, this was bedlam. If they bought time, they had no idea what was being shown and no guarantee that it would be film, sports, or soap opera.

Moreover, the state continued to underwrite the costs of broadcasting the signal—electricity, satellites, and all the other expenses of Channel 1—although there was less money than in the old days. The carcass of a state-owned television network remained, while the lifeblood, advertising revenue, disappeared into the hands of the independent producers.

Berezovsky knew where the money lay. He had his own inside line to Channel 1 through a company called Reklama Holding. The word *reklama* means advertising in Russian, and Reklama Holding was formed to try and monopolize the advertising time on Channel 1. Berezovsky's advertising agency, Logovaz Press, had been among the founders of Reklama Holding. Lisovsky was the power behind Reklama Holding. The plan was that the company would be an intermediary, selling time on Channel 1 to advertisers and then buying it in wholesale blocks from the channel, cutting out other middlemen and gaining more control. Lisovsky and Berezovsky, as well as others involved in Reklama Holding, were making themselves the middlemen, while turning over a slice of their profits to Channel 1.[12] Berezovsky's ad agency, Logovaz Press, earned $1 million in profit in 1993–1994, according to the annual report.[13] One reason for the profits was that Logovaz Press was enjoying an 80 percent discount on advertising time. Once again, Berezovsky was getting something practically for free—the airtime—and reselling it for a small fortune.

Meanwhile, the television audience was burgeoning. After decades of dry programming, Russian viewers were entranced with films and soap operas from the West. Programs like the Mexican serial *The Rich Also Cry* and the American-made *Santa Barbara* drew enormous audiences. For advertisers, Channel 1 could deliver tens of millions of potential consumers who had a pent-up demand for Western goods like toothpaste and breakfast cereal. The cost of advertising in Russia per viewer was ridiculously cheap compared with the West. It cost about $1 to reach a thousand viewers in Russia, compared to about $15 per thousand viewers in the United States.[14] Channel 1 had much broader reach in 1994 than Gusinsky's smaller, private NTV, although Gusinsky's channel was attracting attention with popular movies and talented news broadcasters. Channel 1 bridged the vast distances of Russia through transponders and satellites erected and supported by the state.

In the early meetings of the club on Sparrow Hills, Berezovsky launched an idea that catapulted him from a car dealer to a kingmaker for the remainder of the decade. He wanted the political influence, as well as the profits, that would come from commanding a television channel. He told the other businessmen he was putting together a plan to privatize Channel 1. Was it a business deal or a political deal? "Both," Berezovsky declared. By cutting out all the other thieving middlemen, Berezovsky could make a fortune. By dictating the news coverage, Berezovsky could become a power broker.[15]

Simultaneously, he was working his way into Yeltsin's inner circle. The restless Berezovsky could demonstrate an unexpected humility, and patience, when it served his ends. He had waited at the door for his friend Boguslavsky on those long-ago mornings; he had patiently played chauffeur to the Italians to learn more about their business with Avtovaz. Now he was applying the same tactics with the Kremlin and Yeltsin's family. He patiently infiltrated Yeltsin's inner circle.

Berezovsky had been introduced to the Kremlin crowd by Valentin Yumashev, a fresh-faced young journalist who had ghost-written Yeltsin's memoirs. Yumashev had been close to Yeltsin since the days of *perestroika,* and he was an editor at the popular weekly magazine, *Ogonyok,* which Berezovsky began to support financially. How did Berezovsky first meet Yumashev? The intermediary was Pyotr Aven, whose father was a mathematician at Berezovsky's institute. Aven had worked alongside Gaidar during *perestroika,* was foreign trade minister in Gaidar's government, and had been present at the café when Logovaz was formed.[16]

A key witness to these events is Alexander Korzhakov, Yeltsin's beefy longtime bodyguard, who stood loyally at Yeltsin's side in the 1980s when Yeltsin was cast out of the Communist Party. Korzhakov, who had been assigned to protect Yeltsin by the KGB's Ninth Directorate, remained Yeltsin's friend and sidekick. They drank together and traveled together when Yeltsin was out of favor. Korzhakov was rewarded when Yeltsin came to power. Korzhakov built himself a small army in the early 1990s as head of the Kremlin's presidential security service. By some accounts, Korzhakov's army contained several thousand men, including the crack Alpha antiterrorist troops. Korzhakov's recollections are valuable because he had a firsthand view of events, but they are colored by his bitterness at being fired by Yeltsin in 1996 and his deep suspicions of the new capitalists, chiefly Berezovsky, who helped get him fired. Korzhakov comes across as a reactionary who saw no need for democracy or capitalism, a one-time

Photo by David E. Hoffman

Boris Berezovksy

Photo by Dmitry Azarov/Kommersant

Vladimir Gusinsky

Photo by David E. Hoffman

ANATOLY CHUBAIS

Photo by David E. Hoffman

ALEXANDER SMOLENSKY

Photo by Pavel Kassin/Kommersant

Mikhail Khodorkovsky

Photo by Dmitry Azarov/Kommersant

Yuri Luzhkov

Photo by Nikolai Moshkov/Itar-Tass

THE SHORTAGE ECONOMY: A STORE IN NIZHNY NOVGOROD, 1991.

Photo by Boris Kavashkin/Itar-Tass

THE CATHEDRAL OF CHRIST THE SAVIOUR, REFLECTED IN THE MOSCOW RIVER.

Photo by Valentin Sobolev/Itar-Tass

CHUBAIS INTRODUCES THE PRIVATIZATION VOUCHER IN 1992.

THE PRIVATIZATION VOUCHER

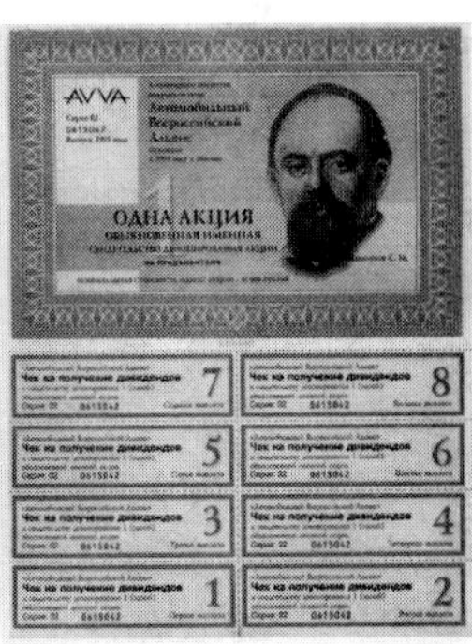

THE CERTIFICATE FOR THE ALL-RUSSIAN AUTOMOBILE ALLIANCE

Photo by Irakly Chokhonelidze/Itar-Tass

BUYING AND SELLING MMM SHARES IN MOSCOW, 1994

Photo by Lucian Perkins/The Washington Post

Yeltsin on the campaign trail in 1996.

Photo by Alexander Chumichev and Alexander Sentsov/Itar-Tass

President Yeltsin meets with the feuding oligarchs on September 15, 1997, during the bankers' war. Valentin Yumashev is to Yeltsin's right. The oligarchs are, from left to right: Mikhail Khodorkovsky, Vladimir Gusinsky, Alexander Smolensky, Vladimir Potanin, Vladimir Vinogradov, and Mikhail Friedman.

Photo by Lyudmila Pakhomova/Itar-Tass

Demonstrators gathered outside NTV in April, 2001 to protest the take-over of Gusinsky's independent television channel.

Photo by Dmitry Azarov/Kommersant

President Vladimir Putin

Photo by Pavel Smertin/Kommersant

A woman begs for money in a Moscow underpass a decade after the Soviet collapse. For many, the change from communism to capitalism meant impoverishment.

Photo by Lucien Perkins/The Washington Post

A couple in Red Square at a rally for Yeltsin at the end of the 1996 campaign. The younger generations found it easier to adapt to the changes of the 1990s.

factotum who rose beyond his abilities but had a front row seat at the time Berezovsky arrived in the Kremlin.[17]

Korzhakov said it was Yumashev who first brought Berezovsky into the Yeltsin inner circle, just after Yumashev finished writing up Yeltsin's second memoir, published in Russian as *Notes of the President.* It was late 1993, after the violent October clash with parliament. Yumashev had penned the book quickly, but the Kremlin did not have a good idea how to get it published. "Now I understand that if we had organized an open tender, there would have been a line of publishers," Korzhakov recalled. "But Valentin presented the whole business of publishing the book as a feat, a courageous act, implying that only Boris Abramovich Berezovsky was capable of such an act." Yumashev invited Berezovsky to the Kremlin and introduced him to Yeltsin. Berezovsky supposedly arranged for a million copies of the book to be published in Finland. The publisher was Ogonyok. Berezovsky brought the royalties to the Yeltsin family, Korzhakov recalled. He claimed a London bank account was opened to accept Yeltsin's royalties.[18] "That is how this businessman found himself in Yeltsin's grace," Korzhakov said.[19]

Berezovsky was soon invited to join the Presidential Club, an exclusive Moscow sports enclave Yeltsin had set up for his closest cronies. But instead of playing tennis there, Berezovsky set about lobbying for the television channel with a clever line that played to Yeltsin's political instincts. The Russian president was under attack from all sides. The new channel would be Yeltsin's instrument, Berezovsky promised; it would be the "president's channel." Berezovsky was aided in his lobbying efforts by Yumashev, who had Yeltsin's trust.[20] The charm offensive worked, and on November 29, 1994, Yeltsin signed a decree, number 2133, which effectively privatized the enormous television channel without an auction as required by law. The new owners' founding capital was $2.2 million.[21] The name of the new organization was Russian Public Television—ORT in the Russian acronym. The idea of "public" television, which would not be state television, was a novelty, and no one knew precisely what it would become. The government retained 51 percent of the shares of ORT, but the rest were divided among a group of wealthy bankers and a smattering of industrialists. An ORT oversight board was created with Yeltsin as chairman, but Korzhakov later said it never met. Berezovsky was the driving force behind the new channel; the state was sure to be an absentee landlord.[22]

Berezovsky drew his partners from the Sparrow Hills club of businessmen. The new shareholders included Berezovsky, Khodorkovsky, Friedman, Smolensky, and a few others. Khodorkovsky recalled that Berezovsky simply telephoned him to ask if he would take 5 percent. "I fully trust him; he created his own deal, which successfully developed," Khodorkovsky said.[23] Berezovsky later consolidated most of the shares in his own hands.

Berezovsky said that when he began to take over the television channel, costs were running at $250 million a year while advertising revenues were only $40 million.[24] He said a large amount of advertising revenues were being siphoned off by the independent producers. He slashed spending and came up with a plan to recapture the advertising market.

The new owners were preparing to take control in April. The channel's new executive director was to be a popular television personality, Vladislav Listyev. With his handlebar mustache and probing, brazen style, Listyev, thirty-eight, was perhaps the best-known television star of his generation. His broadcasts had broken public taboos on topics such as sex and money in the late Soviet years, and his *Field of Miracles,* a sort of *Wheel of Fortune* game show, was a hit. Listyev was not only an on-air host; like other independent producers, he owned an advertising agency, Inter-Vid, which had been a participant in Reklama Holding.

Berezovsky decided the only way to regain control over advertising was to stop everything and start over. He proposed a three-month moratorium on advertising on the new channel. "This was my personal idea," he said. "This caused wild surprise." Berezovsky said Listyev was originally against it but eventually agreed.

On February 20, 1995, Listyev announced a moratorium on advertising on Channel 1, a risky move designed to give the new channel time to cut out the cancer of corruption and theft. Malashenko later told me that Listyev and Berezovsky had no choice if they were taking control of Channel 1. "You could not reform Ostankino," Malashenko said. "The only thing you can do is you start a new entity, transfer the license, and take anything you need from Ostankino, and just destroy this piece of shit entirely. And it was done."

Millions of dollars were at stake. Listyev's announcement meant losses for those who had already booked time or wanted to sell time in these months on the station, including the independent producers. At least in theory, those who would suffer losses also included Lisovsky,

Berezovsky, and Listyev himself. Lisovsky, the advertising mogul, tried to get Berezovsky to negotiate a new contract. Berezovsky refused and demanded a moratorium on all advertising. "We calculated how much we were going to lose" without commercials, Berezovsky recalled, "but how much more we were going to gain later," once they controlled the advertising. The moratorium was a bold move—and one that potentially could create many enemies.

On March 1, 1995, a month before he was to take over a revamped ORT, Listyev was gunned down by two unknown assailants in the entranceway of his apartment. The murder shocked the country. Yeltsin came to the Ostankino station and denounced the "cowardly and evil murder of a very talented world television journalist." Yeltsin sacked the Moscow prosecutor and police chief and blamed Luzhkov, whom he accused of "turning a blind eye to the mafiosi" in the city.[25] It was a gesture meant to underscore the Kremlin's distrust of Luzhkov, which, as we shall see, was deepening.

No one was ever accused of the Listyev murder, and the investigation eventually ran cold. The case was entangled in speculation and intrigue; the truth seems to have long vanished.[26] Yevgeny Kiselyov, the prominent NTV journalist who had left Channel 1 to work for Gusinsky, told me he did not accept the theory that Listyev was killed because of the conflict over advertising. "I am quite convinced he had nothing to do with advertising," Kiselyov said. "All the financial matters, concerning advertising—to stop advertising—they weren't his decision. Other people were responsible. He was just in charge of programming. . . . He was a creative person."

Others also agreed that the moratorium, which lasted four months, was decided by Berezovsky, not Listyev. As Lisovsky said to me, "Everyone knew perfectly well that from the moment ORT was created, it was Boris Berezovsky who managed all the issues concerned with advertising. Solely Berezovsky. Because Berezovsky said from the very start that money is to be discussed only with him, and only he will make the decision."

Another television figure who was close to Berezovsky at the time told me, "Everyone knows that Berezovsky controlled all the finances. Lisovsky and Listyev came to see *him* about money." Although this source said no one really knows who killed Listyev, he believes the assassins were shadowy security services, or their hired guns, seeking to prevent the channel from being passed to Berezovsky.[27]

Later, in taking over the channel, Berezovsky set up a new monopoly advertising system. In this arrangement, the channel sold blocks of airtime to Lisovsky's agency, Premier SV, which was the sole agency reselling the time to advertisers. Berezovsky said the moratorium had worked, and the contract with Lisovsky was on favorable terms. "We dictated the conditions," he said.[28] Berezovsky also controlled the news decisions at ORT, and the Logovaz waiting room was often full of television officials coming to him for their instructions.

"We prevented the ruin of the main national channel. We blocked the rivers of theft," Berezovsky said.[29] He made a similar claim about the way he handled the assembly line in Togliatti. There Berezovsky became a big player who displaced all the small-scale operators. He had created a "civilized car market," as he liked to say. Likewise, in television, he took over the advertising market. He took control of the money—blocking out all the small-scale rip-offs. "Berezovsky, it's another one of his traits," Lisovsky recalled. "When he comes to a place, he controls all financial flows himself. That is his strict rule."

Berezovsky had reached his goal, taking over Channel 1, but the way he went about it injected a sour note into the club on Sparrow Hills. Shakhnovsky recalled the businessmen "were supposed to communicate there and work out some common approaches, while business should have remained outside."

"What destroyed it? If we look back, it was Berezovsky's position that destroyed this idea. When concrete business was introduced to this club's work, it actually ruined it."

In the summer and early autumn of 1994, Vladimir Gusinsky was doing well. His new television station, NTV, was bristling with the best talent and had been given coveted additional time on Channel 4 for broadcasting. His alliance with Luzhkov was in full swing, and it was helping them both. He had thriving businesses in construction and banking, as well as an expanding news media empire that included the newspaper *Sevodnya* and a radio station, Echo of Moscow. When a public relations company, Vox Populi, came up with a list of Russia's wealthiest and most influential bankers that summer, Gusinsky was ranked first among the richest and second among the most powerful. By contrast, Berezovsky was seventeenth among the wealthiest and thirteenth among the most powerful.[30]

Yet Gusinsky was not invited to Sparrow Hills, and it was no accident. Shakhnovsky told me as he met the businessmen that summer, trying to organize the club, Gusinsky was blacklisted by the others. "Everybody spoke against it because Gusinsky had a conflict with practically every one of the participants," Shakhnovsky recalled.

In the months that followed, Gusinsky sailed into a storm. The dark clouds were the result of a combination of factors that suddenly came together like a hurricane, an unpredictable mix of high winds and choppy seas. One reason for the storm was the frenetic energy of Berezovsky, who was ruthlessly expanding—and colliding with Gusinsky. Another was Yeltsin. Forever guarding his own political supremacy, plagued by paranoia and weakened by illness, Yeltsin was especially nervous about Luzhkov's growing popularity in Moscow. With the fears about Luzhkov came paranoia about Gusinsky. Moreover, the Kremlin was stumbling into a dirty little war in Chechnya, the horrors of which were magnified many times—and for the first time—by Gusinsky's television station, NTV.

Berezovsky was indefatigable. He liked to say that in Russia, the first treasure to be privatized would be profit, then property, and finally debt. Berezovsky meant that the first thing he wanted to take in a company was its cash flow, and only later would he be interested in owning it, and perhaps never. It was in pursuit of such cash flow that he ran headlong into Gusinsky over a lucrative business deal. At the time, Gusinsky's Most Bank and Avtovaz Bank, which was under Berezovsky's control, were competing for the right to handle hundreds of millions of dollars in overseas ticket sales from the Russian national airline, Aeroflot. At the time, Aeroflot often ran short of fuel, and pilots went unpaid for months. Aging planes—beached dinosaurs with droopy wings, punched-out windscreens, doors open forlornly to the winds—could be seen on tarmacs scattered across the country, missing engines and parts that were scavenged to keep other planes in the air. The decrepit, huge, erratically scheduled airline was another vivid example of post-Soviet theft. The government paid for the fuel and salaries, sometimes, but the cash from ticket sales, especially tickets bought with hard currency overseas, just disappeared. Just as the auto factory and television station gave rise to corrupt middlemen, so too Aeroflot spawned theft. The cash from ticket sales, instead of flowing back to the airline, was being siphoned off to hundreds of secret foreign bank accounts. Nikolai Glushkov, one of Berezovsky's partners, later claimed that Aeroflot was a treasury for the Russian secret services abroad.[31]

Sergei Zverev, who was a lobbyist for Gusinsky then, told me that Most Bank planned to take over the Aeroflot accounts, which they were sure contained hidden treasure. "We knew that if we could command the financial flows in the right way, we would be able to find additional tens of millions of dollars inside the company, or even hundreds of millions," he recalled.[32] But Berezovsky had the same idea. Ownership of shares in Aeroflot was not an issue—the company had been privatized but the majority of the block of shares remained state-owned. The trick was to get control of the huge cash flow, which Glushkov estimated at between $80 million to $220 million at any one moment.

In the corridors of the Kremlin and at the exclusive Yeltsin sports club, Berezovsky spread tantalizingly poisonous gossip about his rival, Gusinsky. According to Korzhakov, Berezovsky "would regularly report what and where Gusinsky said about the president, how he cursed him, what name he called him, how he wanted to deceive him." Berezovsky came to the Kremlin with real or imagined bits of intelligence, what Korzhakov called "new ominous details." For example, according to Korzhakov, Berezovsky claimed "Gusinsky was sitting in a bunker with Luzhkov and drinking. And making a toast to Yuri Mikhailovich as the president." Berezovsky then supposedly told Korzhakov that Gusinsky sent a little package every Thursday to the Moscow government, with a specific sum of cash for each person, from five hundred to several thousand dollars, depending on how useful they have been. It is impossible to know who is more creative in this tale: a vengeful Korzhakov, who later turned against Berezovsky, or Berezovsky himself, devilishly competitive, who was trying to discredit Gusinsky and Luzhkov simultaneously.

Korzhakov claimed that Berezovsky turned to Yeltsin's younger daughter, Tatyana Dyachenko, when Korzhakov would no longer carry Berezovsky's tales to Yeltsin. Why Korzhakov stopped being the courier is not clear. Korzhakov claims Berezovsky lavished gifts on the president's daughter, including a Russian-made Niva jeep and a Chevrolet Blazer, which Dyachenko later denied.

Gusinsky knew that Berezovsky was feeding the growing hostility toward him. But he told me in retrospect, "Let's not demonize Berezovsky. Everybody says, Berezovsky arranged it. But it was not Berezovsky—Yeltsin did it. What does Berezovsky have to do with it? Certainly, Berezovsky was stirring things up, since he wanted to get this, to do that. Yes, this is true. But if there were no Berezovsky, there would be some Sidorov—so, what's the difference?" When I pressed Gusinsky, however, he acknowledged the conflict with Berezovsky was real. "Of course, a hundred percent, a war was on, more than this, a very tough confrontation about Aeroflot and many things. Berezovsky was very envious that there was NTV."[33] The war between them was just the first in what became almost constant internecine combat among the tycoons and their various financial empires in the years ahead.

Yeltsin's inner circle was hardening in the autumn of 1994 around a hawkish group known informally by critics as "the party of war," with Korzhakov in the center. They were directly responsible for the onset of the Chechen war and, two years later, came very close to persuading Yeltsin to cancel elections. Korzhakov became so powerful that, at one point, he attempted to dictate oil export policy to Chernomyrdin.[34] The "party of war" dominated the Kremlin just as Yeltsin's grip was weakening. On August 31, Yeltsin was in Berlin attending a ceremony marking the withdrawal of troops from Germany. He appeared drunk, grabbed the baton of a band leader, and tried to conduct the orchestra, a bit of unbecoming clownishness seen around the world on television. Some of Yeltsin's more liberal aides wrote him a letter complaining about his behavior, and they were sidelined. When Yeltsin flew back from the United States on September 30, he failed to get off the plane in Ireland to see the waiting prime minister. Many assumed he was drunk. Deputy Prime Minister Oleg Soskovyets, another in the "party of war" who eventually met the Irish prime minister, was quoted by *Tass* as saying: "Boris Yeltsin is healthy." This was a lie. Korzhakov later admitted Yeltsin had suffered a heart attack on the plane.[35]

In Moscow, fast-paced crises kept the Kremlin reeling. On October 11 came the unexpected "Black Tuesday," when the ruble lost 27 percent of its value. On October 17, Dmitri Kholodov, an investigative reporter for the mass-circulation daily *Moskovsky Komsomolets* who was probing military corruption, was killed in a bomb blast. Many journalists and politicians were outraged at the brazen murder of the young reporter.

Yeltsin, isolated and ill, was told that his enemies were everywhere. Korzhakov claims Berezovsky brought him *kompromat* about Gusinsky. Berezovsky had lit a fuse, and it was burning inside the Kremlin. He was using Korzhakov and Yeltsin for his own goals, to crush a rival.

One day at a Kremlin lunch with Korzhakov, Yeltsin asked, "Why can't you deal with what's-his-name, with Gusinsky?" According to Korzhakov's account, Yeltsin then complained about Gusinsky's car cutting off his wife and family on the highway into town. "How many times did it happen when Tanya and Naina were driving somewhere and the road was blocked to make way for Gusinsky? His NTV has gotten out of control; it behaves imprudently. I order you, deal with him!"

Korzhakov claims he protested that they had no legal grounds. "Find something," Yeltsin steamed, according to Korzhakov's recollection. "Follow him around everywhere, give him no peace. Make the ground burn under his feet!"

The ground soon began to burn. One of the first signs came on the morning of November 19, 1994, with an article in *Rossiiskaya Gazeta*, a pro-Kremlin state-owned newspaper. The article was headlined, "The Snow Is Falling." It quoted unnamed sources with dark hints that a shadowy Moscow financier—Gusinsky—was preparing to make Luzhkov president. The article reflected the depths of the Kremlin's paranoia about the Moscow mayor and Gusinsky, who was blamed for the October ruble crash and depicted as a diabolical powerbroker, buying up the mass media. The Most empire, the article said, "is planning to force its way to power."[36] Gusinsky read the article knowing that it was a threat. "The first political hunt had begun," he recalled. He was the prey.

Gusinsky's troubles also had their origins in the Chechnya misadventure that Yeltsin, Korzhakov, and the "party of war" were soon to embark upon. The Chechen republic, in southern Russia, was increasingly coming under the control of separatist leader Dzhokhar Dudayev, and the Moscow authorities, isolated and blind, were sliding toward war. The first stage came in mid-November, when Russian intelligence services secretly arranged an assault by forty-seven tank crews, under the cover of an attack by an "opposition" to Dudayev. The "opposition" were really untrained Russian troops, recruited just days before from Moscow's Interior Ministry forces, the Kantemirov and Taman Tank Divisions. The youthful soldiers were not even told where they were going or why. The tank offensive was begun on

November 26, but as they rolled into the capital, Grozny, the poorly prepared troops were slaughtered by a fusillade of rocket-propelled grenades fired by the Dudayev forces. The whole covert operation turned into a bloody debacle for which the Kremlin was slow to admit responsibility. Twenty-one soldiers were captured by Dudayev's forces and shown on television. The head of the Kantemirov division, General Boris Polyakov, resigned, saying the assault had been arranged behind his back.[37] What made these tense days even more dangerous for Gusinsky was the sudden, amplified power of television. Polyakov's resignation had been broadcast on NTV, which infuriated the Kremlin. "When these guys decided to start the war, they started to think about media coverage, and it made them extremely nervous," Malashenko recalled. They were nervous because there was one channel, NTV, that they could not control. One day in November, just before the tank debacle, Malashenko, then president of NTV, met a top official from the security services while waiting for an appointment in the Kremlin. The man was intimately involved in the tank assault. He was an old friend of Malashenko. "Igor!" he implored Malashenko. "Can you forget about Chechnya for just two weeks? In two weeks, we'll finish the whole operation and I personally will go on NTV and tell you the whole story." Malashenko was stunned. Was he crazy? "Do you sincerely believe you can wind up this problem in two weeks?" Malashenko refused to stop the coverage.

Just as the tank debacle was unfolding in Grozny, Gusinsky was summoned to the Kremlin by Korzhakov's deputy, Georgi Rogozin. "He started a soul-searching discourse about how one should be in love with the authorities," Gusinsky told me, "and what one is to do."[38]

On the morning of December 2, black-masked men wearing fatigues without any insignia and carrying automatic rifles pulled up to Gusinsky's home outside Moscow and tried to start a fight with his security detail. The masked men left, but they returned to tail Gusinsky on the highway as Gusinsky was driven from his country house to the center of the city. They followed him all the way to his offices in the high-rise building on Novy Arbat. The high-rise also housed offices of Luzhkov's city government. Gusinsky had no idea who the armed, masked men were, but in fact they had been sent by Korzhakov, who later chortled, "The bankers' security guards were nervous, and Gusinsky himself was scared to death." When Gusinsky reached the high-rise, he scurried inside and up to his twenty-first-floor offices, while Korzhakov's goons began to gruffly interrogate Gusinsky's security guards in the parking lot. Up in the windowed tower, Gusinsky began madly calling for help. The goons left, and at 5:30, another group of masked, armed men arrived in crisp fatigues with weapons. They bore no markings, no insignia, just menacing masks and guns. They roughed up Gusinsky's security guards in the parking lot and forced several of them to lie in the snow for several hours. An agitated, panicked Gusinsky then called a friend, Yevgeny Savostyanov, head of the Moscow branch of another federal security service.[39] Savostyanov was a liberal, a bearded academic who participated in the pro-democracy movement during *perestroika* and had been close to Gavriil Popov. Savostyanov sent a team of agents to the high-rise tower.

Korzhakov's Kremlin goons were suddenly nose-to-nose with Savostyanov's Moscow agents, and a fight broke out. Korzhakov claims that Savostyanov's men were slightly drunk. Shots were fired, one of which grazed the leather jacket of one of Korzhakov's men. Another bullet hit a car. Just when the situation was about to explode, one of Savostyanov's men recognized one of Korzhakov's, with whom he used to work. The Savostyanov team realized they were up against the elite presidential security service and retreated.

Korzhakov recalled that when he heard about the episode, he went immediately to Yeltsin, who signed a decree firing Savostyanov. Then Korzhakov sent a small unit of rapid-reaction troops to Gusinsky's parking lot. They blocked the entrances to the building and began checking all the cars in Gusinsky's fleet. "The driver of Gusinsky's armored Mercedes locked himself inside the car," Korzhakov recalled. "When he was asked to get out, he refused. Then a grenade was put on top of the car. He immediately jumped out." It was typical of Korzhakov's swaggering style. He claimed the grenade didn't even have a fuse.

Meanwhile, Gusinsky summoned Moscow's press corps to the scene. The Korzhakov goons were captured by two dozen television news crews, with the Gusinsky men still facedown in the snow. The episode was known long after as "faces in the snow." The reasons for the confrontation remained unclear to the outside world that night. Certainly, the Kremlin's anger at Gusinsky over coverage of Chechnya was one plausible reason for the assault, but it was not evident precisely who had sent the goons. After the confrontation in the parking lot, Gusinsky realized who he was up against, and he was furious.

Gusinsky later reflected on the events: "If back then these morons at the Kremlin were smarter, they would have called me and said, 'Volod, we beg you, please give us your support here.' I probably would have tried to. But they decided to intimidate me. And I'm an idiot, a ram from childhood. If you are going to threaten me, get lost!"[40]

On December 5, Gusinsky was again invited to see Korzhakov's deputy, Rogozin. He decided to disarm all his bodyguards, so there would be no question about shooting back if another confrontation erupted. He also decided to send his wife, Lena, and his young son to London. As he was headed for the Kremlin, Gusinsky got a call from his security chief that three blue Volvos, unmarked, were trailing his wife on the way to the airport. "There are men with machine guns sitting inside," the security man said.

"Got it," Gusinsky replied, curtly.

At the table with Rogozin, Gusinsky broached the idea of a compromise. What would it take?

"Chechnya, *Kukly,*" said the Korzhakov deputy, suggesting that Gusinsky's television station needed to fall into line. He was referring to *Kukly,* a brand-new television satire program, based on puppets, which often made fun of Yeltsin and his men.

"I am not going to discuss it," Gusinsky cut him off. He would not give up the station.

Rogozin replied, "Something needs to be done; the emotional temperature needs to be lowered."

"Are you letting my wife fly out today, by any chance?" Gusinsky asked.

"Judging by your behavior," Rogozin replied cagily.

Gusinsky had a sudden flashback. He was in the courtyard as a small boy. He was picking up the pipe in his hands to smash the man who had called him a Yid. He looked Rogozin in the eyes. "I told him that I would personally kill him, if anything happened to my wife and child," Gusinsky recalled. "This was an unpleasant incident for me. I told him, 'I don't need any security. I will personally strike you dead, I'll strike you dead myself.' Probably this is wrong, uncivilized, but I had no choice. Had something happened to my wife and child at that point, I would have killed him in his office with something heavy, an ash tray, anything."

Gusinsky's wife flew out of the country. But the pressure on Gusinsky did not let up. Korzhakov boasted in a newspaper interview a few days later that "hunting geese is an old hobby of mine." The Russian word for goose—*gus*—is a play on Gusinsky's name, and a favorite nickname for Gusinsky.

In mid-December, Kiselyov got a telephone call from the Kremlin. The warning was blunt. "You are in great danger," said Viktor Ilyushin, Yeltsin's chief of staff, who had dialed Kiselyov directly, not even through a secretary. Kiselyov went to the Kremlin to meet Ilyushin for a formal interview, in which Ilyushin said nothing. But after the interview, Ilyushin took the television anchor aside, and said, "You have big problems, guys." Just a year before, Yeltsin had signed the decree giving NTV the expanded airtime on Channel 4. Now Yeltsin's wife, Naina, could hardly watch the channel, Ilyushin reported. "Why did you do that terrible story?" Ilyushin demanded to know.

"What terrible story?" Kiselyov asked.

Ilyushin said the Yeltsin family was distraught over an NTV feature about how Yeltsin was deeply unpopular even in the village where he was born. The story reflected a sad truth: Yeltsin's public approval ratings were sliding into single digits because of the strains of reform and the shadow of war.[41]

Gusinsky too was feeling more and more pressure. "They summoned me to the Kremlin and they told me, if you continue showing Chechnya, we will strip you of NTV and kill you," Gusinsky recalled. "It felt scary. But I could not agree to it, of course. I grew up on the street, didn't I? I don't like to be threatened. I am deeply scared, of course I am, but I cannot show to anybody that I am afraid, can I? I said, fuck off—all of you."

If his tormentors thought they had defeated Gusinsky, they were wrong. They saved him. The beginning of the Chechen war in December 1994 changed Gusinsky's life forever. It forged a new, popular, private television channel, NTV, which soon posed a serious challenge to Yeltsin's authority.

NTV not only brought home the horrors of the war but became a sort of alternative power center, telling the stories that the government would not admit. Night after night, NTV broadcast in a way that television in Russia had never done before. When a Russian helicopter was downed, NTV showed the bodies, but government officials said nothing. When Russians were taken prisoner in mid-December, NTV showed them; the government said there were no prisoners. When Yeltsin said the bombing of the presidential palace in Grozny had stopped, NTV showed the bombs still falling.

Kiselyov told me that in 1994, even before the war began, "We were permanently in Chechnya from late spring, throughout the summer, into the fall." More than any other television channel, NTV was prepared when the war broke out, and broadcast footage of the troop concentrations, the mobile field hospitals, and the war itself. Gusinsky recalled, "Thanks to our honesty in covering that war, we became the NTV company. We were honest. We were showing what we had to show. It was exactly at that point that I realized what public service was. Exactly at that point."

Fearing arrest, Gusinsky left Russia on December 18 and remained in London for six months. The pressure, the threatening phone calls, and the vows to shut down NTV continued into the spring as the war turned into a quagmire for Yeltsin. Kiselyov told me that after all the tumult he and his colleagues had been through in recent years, when the Chechen war began, they knew exactly what to do. They did not debate how to cover the war—they went and did it. "We had a good understanding that information was a powerful tool in our hands, to fight back," he said. The reporting was impassioned, at times sickening in its unblinking treatment of the war's ghastly, bloody victims. My colleague Lee Hockstader, who covered the war at great risk and with enormous personal intensity, wrote of NTV: "Mangled limbs, agonized death throes, eviscerated corpses, all of it was fair game for the evening news. The tone of some of the coverage became overtly antiwar." Oleg Dobrodeyev, who had founded the channel with Gusinsky and Kiselyov, led the day-to-day coverage. His rule was that if correspondents saw it, they aired it. "I remember myself sitting and watching all those reports, making decision about what would and would not be put on the air," Dobrodeyev told me. "I broadcast everything," he said, because the footage spoke for itself—powerfully. The pathos of war on television, which Americans had discovered a generation earlier in Vietnam, proved gripping to Russian viewers, who had never seen anything like it.[42] NTV enjoyed a surge of public trust. Television became the chief source of information about the war; newspapers and magazines were far behind. Vsevolod Vilchek, a longtime public opinion specialist for Channel 1 and later for NTV, reported that when people were asked at the outbreak of the war if they were following events, 80 percent said yes. The audience for television was expanding, but the share of the new viewers that went to Channel 1 was tiny, just a few percent. The second channel, RTR, did better, but NTV got an astounding 70 percent of the new audience.[43] NTV doubled its total viewers and at the peak of the war NTV audience in Moscow was 48 percent—nearly half of all the televisions turned on at that time.[44] Those early months of the Chechen war transformed NTV into Russia's most professional television channel, and people noticed. So did Yeltsin.

On July 8, 1995, NTV aired another segment of its regular weekly satire program, *Kukly,* which featured life-sized puppets and was written by a wicked humorist, Viktor Shenderovich. *Kukly* had been launched just as the Chechen war was getting under way, and it unexpectedly became another thorn in Yeltsin's side. The show that evening depicted government leaders as tramps who could not subsist on the government's minimum wage. Yeltsin was shown wandering through a passenger train, begging for change, dragging his security chief, Korzhakov, along as a baby. Yeltsin had a thick skin after years in politics, but Gusinsky believed *Kukly* provoked him into fits of rage. After the train episode, the general prosecutor launched a criminal investigation of *Kukly,* which brought the show even more attention. Nothing ever came of the probe, but Gusinsky realized the penetrating influence of his television channel. "Yeltsin had quiet hatred reserved for me," Gusinsky said. Yeltsin once called Luzhkov personally and implored him to ask Gusinsky to stop the puppet show.

"They humiliate me!" Yeltsin begged. But the show went on.

The Kremlin attack on Gusinsky had one major consequence: it drove a wedge between Gusinsky and Luzhkov. The Moscow mayor felt the pressure from the Kremlin and wanted to keep his head down. Gusinsky's Most Bank depended on the "authorized" accounts of the city, but those accounts were shifted to the new Bank of Moscow. Gusinsky's relationship with Luzhkov cooled. At some point the two men, who had been so close to each other since their days in the cooperative movement, stopped talking to each other. Gusinsky also lost the Aeroflot business to Berezovsky, a decision taken in the Kremlin as punishment for his opposition to the war.

"It was a very difficult time for the whole group," Malashenko recalled of Gusinsky's team, "because people in the bank were of course extremely upset. For them, it was the death of their business.

But I told them, listen guys, we don't have much choice. We are not going to sacrifice NTV."

Gusinsky had reached a crossroads. He decided that his future lay not in banking and not in construction, but in media, as a mogul. A one-minute advertisement on NTV cost about $10,000. It was a tremendously valuable enterprise, both for business and for politics. He had built it up from almost nothing. Gusinsky was proud of this: his assets were not "ready-made" Soviet-era enterprises like Berezovsky's Avtovaz or Ostankino. Gusinsky was an entrepreneur, perhaps because he had to be—he built from zero. He had no reservations about lobbying the government, as he had done to win the license for NTV, but the station itself was created by him. It was not a Soviet leftover. It was his ticket to the future.

The view from the club on Sparrow Hills was different. The other tycoons were just beginning to look over a thick book from the State Property Committee. It was a list of ready-made Soviet-era factories and other industrial assets that would soon be theirs for the asking. They didn't want to start something from scratch, as Gusinsky had, when there were such lucrative properties just waiting to be plucked—the best mines and oil refineries in all of Russia.

Chapter 12

The Embrace of Wealth and Power

CHARLES RYAN, who delighted in buying a fistful of Menatep Bank shares on a street corner in 1991, became an adviser to the privatization team working with Anatoly Chubais. One of his first acquaintances was Alfred Kokh, a sharp-tongued, bullheaded young man, deputy head of the Leningrad privatization office in those early days. Later both of them came to Moscow. Ryan cofounded United Financial Group, an investment bank. In 1995 Kokh was appointed acting director of the State Property Committee, in charge of continuing the sell-off of industry begun by Anatoly Chubais, who became one of two deputy prime ministers.

It was a difficult time for the Chubais team; the privatization of state property had stalled, Boris Yeltsin was weak, and the Communists were gaining strength in polls for the December 1995 parliamentary elections. On Saturdays, Kokh was often in his office, and the door was open. Ryan liked to wander in and shoot the breeze on these quiet afternoons with Kokh, who was known for his earthy language and short temper. One day in late summer of 1995, as they were talking, Kokh asked Ryan casually, "What do you think about Uneximbank and Menatep?"

Ryan discovered that Kokh was working on a privatization deal that would change Russian capitalism and politics forever. On his desk was a scheme in which Russia would give away its industrial crown jewels—the most lucrative oil companies and richest metal mines—to a coterie of tycoons, all of them from the Sparrow Hills club. Vladimir Potanin of Uneximbank was first in line, followed by Mikhail Khodorkovsky of Menatep. From the beginning, Kokh had handpicked the winners, Ryan recalled. According to the plan, shares in the factories were to be given to the tycoons for safekeeping, in exchange for a loan to the government. Everyone knew the deficit-ridden government would not repay the loan. Then the tycoons would sell the shares, as repayment of the loans. But there was a twist. The tycoons would probably sell the shares to themselves, very cheaply, through hidden offshore companies. That way, they would get the valuable assets for next to nothing. It looked to Ryan suspiciously like a backdoor giveaway, a loan to the government in exchange for colossal oil and mineral riches. The scheme was called "loans for shares," and Ryan told Kokh: "This loans for shares thing really stinks."

"What do you mean?" Kokh asked.

"You know Alfred, the funny thing is that you are going to get hosed. You are going to be the scapegoat for all this. You are the one signing all the orders."

"That's not true," protested Kokh. "Everything I have done has been approved by Anatoly."

"Alfred, you're such a joker. In four years, Chubais is going to have some great job, and you're going to be the sucker."

Kokh grew furious and shouted at Ryan, "Fuck you!" Ryan later recalled, "I told him where he could stick it. And this loans for shares thing was pretty much the end of my friendship with those guys."[1]

In feasting on easy money, Khodorkovsky tasted every delicious morsel. His bank, Menatep, generated handsome profits with ruble-dollar speculation, plunged into voucher trading, and was a leader in the superlucrative "authorized" banking for the federal and Moscow governments. But in the summer of 1995, one of the most rewarding easy money schemes, ruble-dollar speculation, finally dried up. The Russian Central Bank, struggling to bring inflation under control, imposed a new exchange rate "corridor," a narrow range in which the ruble would be allowed to rise and fall against the dollar. The banks could no longer gamble on wild swings in the exchange rate. The Central Bank would use its reserves to enforce the limits. Chubais declared that the era of easy money was over. For banks that were speculating on the exchange rate, he said, "buying and selling dollars is an avenue that is now closed."[2] Chubais hoped that getting control of the currency would finally dampen the raging hyperinflation that had begun in 1992 and lead to the first real stability in the economy since the beginning of shock therapy.

Soon it became evident that the days of easy money were not yet over. Other fast-money games abounded, and new ones were being invented. A short-term government bond, with a maximum term of three months, was paying amazingly high annual interest rates, sometimes climbing over 200 percent.[3] The sizzling bond was easy money with the added benefit of low risk: it had Russian government guarantees. The new bonds were called GKOs, and they would eventually lead the Russian government to disaster. But in the early years they were incredibly profitable: just sit back and watch your money grow by leaps and bounds.

Despite this and other easy money temptations, Khodorkovsky did not want to live out his life as a banker; he longed to be a captain of industry. During mass privatization, Khodorkovsky snapped up many industrial firms, bidding with nothing more than a promise to make future investment. In September 1995, he created a financial-industrial conglomerate, Rosprom, to control his twenty-nine industrial companies in oil, metallurgy, chemicals, food processing, textiles, wood pulp, and paper.[4] Still, Khodorkovsky was not satisfied with the grab bag assortment of factories he had assembled. When international consultants Arthur Andersen suggested that he model himself after Samsung, one of the Korean *chaebol*, or industrial conglomerates, Khodorkovsky immediately dismissed the idea, thinking it could not possibly work in Russia, and decided to pour his energy into "one branch" of industry. That branch was oil.[5]

Away from Moscow, on the other side of the Ural Mountains, in the broad basin of western Siberia, the Soviet Union had opened up huge new fields of oil and gas in the 1960s and 1970s. The deposits stretched across the West Siberian basin, which is drained by the Ob River, Russia's third largest, as it wanders 3,650 kilometers from Altai in the south to the Kara Sea in the north, largely fed by spring thaws and melting snow. The river's course is a road map to mammoth underground reserves of oil and gas, but unstable bogs and harsh weather conditions discouraged exploration until the 1970s. Then, in the late 1970s and 1980s, the giant fields were recklessly and wildly exploited in a frantic effort to prop up the failing Soviet economy with revenues from oil exports. At the time of the Soviet collapse, oil extraction in Russia was sliding downward, from a peak of 591 million tons in 1987 to 303 million tons in 1998.[6]

The Soviet oil industry was a vast archipelago of outdated, state-run "production associations," oil enterprises based largely on the location of their fields. More than anyone else, Vagit Alekperov, an ethnic Azeri who was director of a production association in Kogalym, led the way in transforming post-Soviet Russia's industry into modern Western-style companies. In 1991 and 1992, huge volumes of oil were being illicitly exported to take advantage of the large gap between domestic and export prices; a ton of oil sold for export would fetch $100 or more but could get only a fraction of that price on the domestic market. In this time of terrible flux and wholesale theft, Alekperov created his own Western-style oil company, Lukoil, out of three Siberian production associations, two refineries, and a trading company. Lukoil was Russia's first vertically integrated oil company, handling everything from exploration and drilling to refining, distribution, and sales, very much like modern Western oil companies. Alekperov, who took the initiative at a time when the economy was in chaos, set an example that the Russian government under Yeltsin then followed for the rest of the industry. The idea was to reassemble the oil fields and refineries of the far-flung Soviet system into a dozen large private companies, building a new, market-oriented oil industry. By contrast, the natural gas behemoth Gazprom was left largely as it had been in Soviet times, as an inefficient and hidebound monopoly. On November 17, 1992, Yeltsin signed a decree establishing the first three vertically integrated oil companies, including Lukoil, and ordered the industry restructured.[7]

Khodorkovsky saw the prize he wanted, but it took him several years to reach it. Shrewd and calculating, he found an inside track. During the first year of the Yeltsin government, Khodorkovsky became an adviser to Vladimir Lopukhin, Gaidar's minister of fuel and energy. The Gaidar cabinet was in office for less than a year, and the carving up of the oil industry had just begun, amid much uncertainty.

When Khodorkovsky took the job with Lopukhin, he did not want to leave Menatep Bank, so Lopukhin created an informal position, with the rank of deputy minister, putting Khodorkovsky in charge of the energy ministry's "investment fund." What this really involved is not clear. However, it must have given Khodorkovsky an excellent source of intelligence about the oil industry. Nevzlin, Khodorkovsky's long-time partner, told me that "the only plus I remember" from Khodorkovsky's appointment "was that he managed to get acquainted" with the powerful Soviet-era directors of the production associations, known as the "oil generals." At the time, few outsiders knew what was really going on in the oil production associations, and the oil generals were secretive, but Khodorkovsky got a glimpse of their closed world.[8]

What he found was that Alekperov had created his own empire in Lukoil. Another oil general, Vladimir Bogdanov, the strong-willed boss of the production association in Surgut, along the northern bank of the Ob River, created a similar kingdom of his own, Surgutneftegaz. Khodorkovsky was a Moscow financier, not an oil general, but had ambitions to stand shoulder to shoulder with Alekperov and Bogdanov. He set his sights on the new vertically integrated holding company that would eventually become Russia's second largest oil giant. It was called Yukos, and the core was a production association, Yuganskneftegaz, on the southern bank of the Ob River. (A second production association, Samaraneftegaz, was also added to Yukos.) The boss of Yuganskneftegaz was Sergei Muravlenko, whose father was a legendary Siberian oilman. Muravlenko became just the kind of contact Khodorkovsky later needed for his takeover. Yuganskneftegaz had enormous potential; it was extracting 33 million tons of oil a year in 1993, nearly 15 percent of all western Siberia's output. Yuganskneftegaz also had some of the largest reserves in Russia, including the biggest single undeveloped field, Priobskoye.[9] Nonetheless, like most Russian enterprises, Yuganskneftegaz was not an ideal company—it had big tax debts and wage arrears, and it suffered losses by selling oil at Russia's artificially low domestic prices.[10]

Khodorkovsky was not the only one to spot an opportunity in Siberian oil. Foreign investors who came to the nascent Russian stock market avidly sought out shares in oil companies. It was said in the early 1990s that the cheapest place in the world to drill for oil and gas was on the Russian stock market. These stock market investors did not really care about sloppy management, overdue taxes, and crazy prices; in fact, most never even visited the companies in which they invested. They just bought the stocks and hoped to make a killing. The investors, many of them really just sophisticated gamblers, were lured by cheap assets, and that meant oil reserves in the ground, of which Yuganskneftegaz had plenty. The former production associations, which I will call the oil field extraction companies, did the real work of the industry, bringing the oil out of the ground. On the Russian stock market, it was possible to buy large blocks of shares in these oil field extraction companies. Yuganskneftegaz was one such alluring stock. It was the equivalent of a midsized international oil company such as Amoco.[11] The shares of Yuganskneftegaz started trading in the summer of 1994, and they were featured in research reports by Moscow's small but growing legion of stock brokers.[12]

Even for gamblers, there were risks in buying shares in oil field extraction companies like Yuganskneftegaz. First, there was the theft. Russian oil industry managers, local politicians, criminal groups, and assorted sharks and financiers discovered ingenious ways to leach the wealth out of the extraction companies. Buying the stock did not guarantee that you would get the oil wealth. The managers, for example, could easily siphon off the profits into an offshore private "trading company" and leave you with the debts and wage arrears. A common technique was called "transfer pricing." An extraction company sold oil to another company at an artificially low price, say, $2 a barrel. The second company then sold it for export abroad at a much higher price, say, $18 a barrel. The result was that the extraction company, with all the drills, wells, fields, and workers, lost money, while the second company made a handsome profit. The wealth was transferred from one company to the other, often in secret using shell companies and offshore havens.

The second risk was ownership. For the hungry investors who bought up stocks of the oil field extraction companies, there was the prospect that they, in turn, would be swallowed up by one of the new holding companies that the Russian government was creating in the early 1990s. These holding companies became corporate energy giants practically overnight and ranked among major international oil firms. The holding companies were fattened up by the state, which awarded them lucrative stakes in the oil field extraction companies. In general, the Russian government gave the holding company at least 51 percent of the voting shares in the extraction companies—enough to ensure the that holding companies got control. The government then planned to sell off its part of the holding companies after three years, reaping a nice chunk of cash.

The risk for investors in the extraction company was that, when the holding company took over, the new bosses could easily siphon off the oil wealth for themselves. The holding company could use transfer pricing, asset stripping, and other means to redirect the profits. The shareholders in the oil field extraction company would be robbed. They would have lots of stock certificates, but none of the profits. The situation was ripe for conflict. The holding companies, which had a majority of shares in the extraction companies, would naturally want to exercise their clout. The extraction companies had their own minority shareholders, who could be prickly and rebellious if they saw they were being ripped off.

The collision between oil field extraction company and holding company is exactly what happened at Yukos. A reclusive American investor, Kenneth Dart, heir to a foam cup fortune, bought tens of millions of dollars worth of stock in two extraction companies, Yuganskneftegaz and Samaraneftegaz, in those early years, figuring that, despite all the problems, they had cheap assets—oil in the ground. Dart's purchase was secret at first, but later led to a bitter public fight with Khodorkovsky, master of the Yukos holding company.[13]

Yukos was created as a holding company in 1992, incorporating Yuganskneftegaz, Samaraneftegaz, and refineries. Yukos was offered for sale three years later, in 1995. Khodorkovsky recalled that he doubted whether the government, having created the oil holding companies, would ever sell them off. "I could never believe that the state would sell oil," he said, insisting that he did not contemplate becoming an oil general in 1992, while he held the informal post in the fuel and energy ministry. Only in early 1995, Khodorkovsky said, did he begin to believe it was possible to buy Yukos.

Why? Something Potanin had cooked up called "loans for shares."

Vladimir Potanin was a member of the Sparrow Hills club but a latecomer to the world of the young Russian tycoons. He arrived on the scene long after the others had suffered the hard knocks of the cooperatives and their nascent business ventures. During the tumultuous years of *perestroika,* when Mikhail Khodorkovsky was transforming worthless noncash into cash, when Boris Berezovsky was setting his sights on Avtovaz, and when Alexander Smolensky was building dachas, Potanin was a low-level bureaucrat in the Soviet Foreign Trade Ministry, where his father also worked. He started his first business in 1990, and he reaped his first fortune only after the Soviet Union vanished. Yet this pugnacious young man with thinning hair and a gravelly voice became ringleader of all the tycoons in 1995 in their greatest single property grab. He came on suddenly, out of nowhere, helping them and helping himself, enormously.

As a child, Potanin did not know lines and shortages. His family enjoyed access to special privileges, including well-stocked food stores and frequent travel abroad. When he was very young, Potanin lived in Yemen; later he spent four years in Turkey. When he was a teenager, his father was the Soviet trade representative in New Zealand. In Moscow, Potanin grew up in a tree-shaded neighborhood known as Matveevskoye, not far from where Stalin and later Brezhnev had their dachas. Alexei Mitrofanov, a childhood friend, recalled that they would often play in a nearby wood, hiding behind the trees and watching the Soviet bosses drive up to the dachas in their limousines.[14] When I talked to Potanin's teachers at School 58, I got the impression of an independent young man who was surrounded by elite trappings. His classmates were sons and daughters of Soviet diplomats and KGB agents who often spent months or years abroad. "When they came back from their summers abroad, they gave a report about the country in which they had lived," the head teacher, Nina Yermakova, told me over tea and cookies as she brought out well-worn class scrapbooks. "We are talking about the broad horizon that these kids had," she said, pointing to a photo of earnest young Potanin, who scored top marks for an essay on Tolstoy.[15]

Potanin was admitted to the Moscow State Institute of International Relations, a training ground for the cream of Soviet officialdom, especially future diplomats, trade officials, and KGB agents. He graduated in 1983. "The school taught us how to behave in the corridors of power," Mitrofanov said. "How to build relationships with people in power, what to say and what not to say." These were the young men and women whom the Soviet Union wanted to send abroad, the future grain merchants, spies, and arms traders. Although surrounded by the ever present ideology, a certain pragmatism was the order of the day.

The future envoys had to know how to be clever in dealing with the capitalists they would meet. Oleg Churilov, a classmate of Potanin, told me "the emphasis was always on the practical issues" in their training, such as finance and currency, which Potanin studied in the International Economic Relations faculty.[16] Potanin's textbooks included titles such as *International Currency-Financial Organization of Capitalist Countries, Currency-Credit Relations in World Trade,* and *Finances of the Capitalist States.* Soviet socialism was troubled within, but for Potanin and his classmates, the important lessons were about the capitalists outside.

His friends suggest Potanin saw clearly the real world outside, but not the Soviet Union's rot from within. His years at the institute were the final ones of the Brezhnev period, but in his crowd it was not certain, or even evident, that Soviet socialism was headed for a crack-up. "All of the students at that time did not think the period was a stagnation period," Churilov recalled. "We did not think that the country was in a state of decline or that the economy was going through difficulty."

After graduation, Potanin landed in the Foreign Trade Ministry, where his father had made a career. He was assigned to Soyuzpromexport, a Soviet state export company, first as an "engineer," which was a clerk's position, and later as an "expert," which meant a senior clerk. Oleg Klimov, who was Potanin's boss then, recalled the young man's enthusiasm. But his task was dreary—selling fertilizer abroad: nitrogen, potash, and phosphate. Potanin was a Soviet phosphate fertilizer salesman-bureaucrat.[17] The job provided one clue to Potanin's future fortune, however: he traveled to the Far North, such as the Kola Peninsula, where the Soviet Union had a huge potash mine. In the same division of the Trade Ministry, there was also an ore section. In his visits to the North, and in the ore section, Potanin learned firsthand about a Soviet metals colossus that had been excavated out of the Arctic tundra, Norilsk Nickel. Founded in Stalin's era of industrialization, Norilsk was originally hacked out of the ice by prison camp labor. Later it became a major producer of nickel for the war effort. At the time of the Soviet collapse, Norilsk produced 98 percent of Russia's valuable platinum-group metals and 90 percent of its nickel.[18]

Potanin was just beginning to dabble in private business when the Soviet Union fell apart. Growing bored after seven years at the Trade Ministry, Potanin saw that many of his friends were going into business—the state trade monopoly was disintegrating and quick fortunes were awaiting those who could master private trade deals, exporting cheap domestic oil, timber, and minerals to markets abroad and importing consumer goods like computers. In March 1990, Potanin prodded twenty small trade organizations, most of them state-owned Soviet agencies hankering to make deals, to give him about $10,000 in start-up money for his new trading company, Interros. Soon thereafter, Potanin realized the trade organizations really needed a bank, and in 1992 he set up one for them. This is when Potanin got his biggest break. For a young man who had done nothing exceptional in the *perestroika* years, Potanin exploded out of the blocks. As the Soviet trade bloc in Eastern Europe collapsed, a Soviet state-run bank, the International Bank for Economic Cooperation, was in financial trouble. The Eastern European states that had loans from the bank could not repay them. In 1992 the bank's management sent out letters quietly urging some of the bank's customers within Russia to shift their money to Potanin's bank. The suggestion was that this would save them from difficulties. How these letters came about is not clear, but it was one of those moments when Potanin most likely had a little help from the "magic hand" of power. Potanin appears to have effectively taken the deposits and assets away from the troubled state bank, while leaving behind the debts. Potanin inherited a $300 million windfall over a six-month period. He seems to have done nothing to earn the money other than offer a safe harbor. Almost overnight, Potanin's bank had become a major Russian financial institution. By comparison, Menatep Bank, which had been started several years earlier, had assets of $835 million.[19]

In April 1993, Potanin, still on a roll, created the United Export-Import bank, known as Uneximbank, which also enjoyed explosive growth. Potanin's license for Uneximbank was approved with unprecedented speed by the Russian government and Central Bank, with support from the reformist finance minister at the time, Boris Fyodorov. Potanin clearly had friends in high places. The early founders of Uneximbank included Potanin and his business partner Mikhail Prokhorov, who had been a foreign trade official in Soviet times and was also a son of the *nomenklatura.* Prokhorov also worked at the failed state bank from which Potanin got his $300 million. They put together about forty major Russian exporters and foreign trade organizations. One of them was Techmashimport, a state-owned oil and chemicals import-export firm. When I asked Gari Titarenko, vice president, how he had come to join Potanin's bank, he recalled, "Potanin himself was always a very humble and smart boy. He was very respectful; during meetings he always paid a lot of attention to Techmashimport." Why? "He wanted all our money to go through Uneximbank."

Soon the smart boy demonstrated that his real talent was in the easy money scheme of "authorized" banking. Potanin once said Uneximbank was a "commercial bank with a state mentality," and the state mentality meant the state's cash flow. While the others were no slouches at milking the state, Potanin seemed to have a golden touch. In the summer of 1994, when he was invited to the club on Sparrow Hills, Potanin was rapidly burrowing into one of the richest lodes of the government, the State Customs Committee. The customs service was bulging with cash it had accumulated from import duties. Potanin somehow persuaded the customs service to put the cash in his bank, in return for creating a system to ease shipments by importers and exporters through customs—by paying duties in advance on their goods. If they sent Potanin money before their goods reached the border, Potanin could switch the money quickly to the customs service accounts to pay the duty. This wasn't very difficult because the customs service accounts were in his own bank. Potanin provided the Customs service with computers too, so they could keep track of the incoming payments. It was convenient, especially for Potanin, since the crossroads of all the money was in Uneximbank. Potanin's balance sheet swelled further as authorized bank for the Finance Ministry, the tax service, the arms control export agency, the City of Moscow and others. Potanin was also serving the accounts of Norilsk Nickel, which became a shareholder in Uneximbank. In 1994 Uneximbank began the year with $322 million in assets, and it ended the year with $2.1 billion.[20] Potanin was rocketing to the top of the banking charts and by December and had his eyes on Norilsk Nickel itself, a lucrative industrial prize. But how to get it?

Potanin went to Boris Jordan, the whiz kid who had shouted for joy in the first voucher auction when he realized how cheaply Bolshevik Biscuit had been sold. Jordan was setting up his own firm, Renaissance Capital, with partner Steven Jennings in early 1995. They left Credit Suisse First Boston to make their own fortunes as stock brokers in the Russian market.

"I have this idea," Potanin told Jordan one day. The Russian government was desperate for cash to pay overdue wages and pensions. Potanin had the cash, although much of it was actually the government's own deposits. Potanin suggested, to Jordan, making the government a deal: give it a loan and take some factories as collateral. "He needed someone to write it up," Jordan told me. Jordan and Jennings, who had played a key role in launching voucher auctions and had made a small fortune as voucher speculators, were once again on the ground floor of Russia's great sell-off. "Steven and I sat down and started thinking," Jordan recalled. One late night in Jennings's apartment, they sketched out the plan. In this early version, they proposed that banks loan money to the state and take the shares as collateral. If the government failed to pay back the loans, they could sell the shares for a very handsome commission. The plan called for a 30 percent fee, which was generous indeed. "Don't forget our background," Jordan said when we talked about it years later. "We were brokers!" They thought getting a fee for selling the shares would be the point of the whole scheme. "I always thought that I am going to do something and earn my fee," Jordan said. "We never perceived it as a vehicle to take the companies for *themselves,*" he said of the tycoons. "At least I didn't."

Potanin had another idea.

For a few more days, Jordan and Jennings hammered out their plan and wrote up a white paper for Potanin. They put no names on it. Jennings claimed there was a "certain logic" to the scheme from the Russian government's point of view, since it would bring badly needed cash to the budget to pay pensions and teachers. Moreover, the young Russian stock market had gone through its first major decline in late 1994. Share prices were way down. Under the Jordan-Jennings plan, the government could hope to fetch a higher price for the factories later on, when presumably share prices would again be higher. Also, it was possible that top managers from the private sector would be brought in to improve the performance of the factories. But Jennings told me he insisted that the deals must be completely transparent and open to international competition. If not, he said, "it will be a disaster." Jordan gave the white paper to Potanin. "This is how you do it," he said.[21]

But what happened next did not follow Jordan's script. Potanin took their paper but "destroyed the concept," Jordan said. In the end, the process was not open to foreigners, was not transparent, and turned out to be rigged. It also had one profound consequence that they did not foresee: the white paper was the beginning of a merger between the Russian tycoons and the government. The tycoons found their political patron, an answer to their search on the Sparrow Hills. He was Boris Yeltsin, and they were about to graft their wealth to his power.

In the 1990s, no other civil servant, no other reformer, oil general, red director, or politician had quite the same survival skills as Chubais. He exhibited extraordinary determination under fire, and he believed the ends justified the means. But Chubais was a survivor for another reason as well. He would push, drive, and force his way forward, but then he usually spotted the moment for a compromise. This was the secret to his success in mass privatization. The famous compromise with the Supreme Soviet, allowing insiders to control the newly privatized companies, served the larger goal of getting property out of the hands of the state.

Now Chubais, one of the two deputy prime ministers, was on the verge of another remarkable demonstration of his iron will. He was going to harness the power of the tycoons to that of the ailing Russian president and try to save them both. Once again, he was willing to pay a price, for it meant subverting his own ideals in pursuit of the larger goal. He did it without evident hesitation.

Chubais was quite certain of those ideals in the early years of mass privatization, when he and Yeltsin championed a populist slogan: "We do not need hundreds of millionaires, but millions of property owners." Chubais was a crusader out to break the grip of the old *nomenklatura* and halt the wild, "spontaneous" privatization by the factory directors. He was dead certain that the way forward lay in the magic of the market. It was the market that would choose winners and losers; it was the market that would determine who would become an "effective" owner of the new property taken from the state. The market was the boxing ring that would sift out those who deserved to survive, by dint of their ingenuity, and those who should go broke. For Chubais and the reformers, the lesson of Soviet socialism had been that no single politician or bureaucrat, acting arbitrarily, can be as effective at making decisions as the collective wisdom of the marketplace. Chubais and his generation of reformers believed the overly politicized decisions of the Communist Party had proven totally ineffective. The way out lay in rigorous market competition, and to be competitive the market had to be open. This is why Chubais was so enamored of the small business auctions he and Gaidar had witnessed in Nizhny Novgorod: it was pure, elementary competition.

On March 30, 1995, Potanin appeared before the Russian cabinet. Down both sides of a long, horseshoe-shaped table, cabinet members sat shoulder to shoulder, small bottles of mineral water, note pads, and sharpened pencils neatly arrayed before them. The prime minister sat at one end, his voice amplified by a microphone, while aides and visitors were seated in an open section of the room at the opposite end. Potanin had prepared carefully for the meeting. He outlined an early version of his loans for shares plan, drawn from the Jordan-Jennings white paper. In a session that lasted four hours, Potanin, joined by Khodorkovsky and Smolensky, told the ministers that a consortium of commercial banks was prepared to loan the government 9.1 trillion rubles, or $1.8 billion, in exchange for collateral in shares of some of Russia's largest enterprises. This was no small change. The budget called for raising 8.7 trillion rubles from privatization during the year, but so far the State Property Committee had taken in a paltry 143 billion rubles.[22] Wages and pensions were going unpaid across the land. The bankers were offering the government a plan to reap the whole year's privatization revenue in one fell swoop.

Among the forty-four companies that the bankers wanted, it was no accident that both Norilsk Nickel and Yukos were on the list: Potanin had put them there. Just the day before, Potanin had been carefully going over the details of his plan with Kokh, the blunt-spoken privatization chief. Potanin already had the support of deputy prime minister Soskovyets, whose realm included heavy industry and who was part of the reactionary group around Korzhakov, Yeltsin's security chief and leader of the so-called party of war. But the question remained, What about Chubais, the other deputy prime minister?

The young reformers on the Chubais team were privately disgusted by the obvious corruption in the loans for shares scheme. Dmitry Vasiliev was Chubais's original deputy at the State Property Committee and in 1995 was chief of the Russian federal securities commission. He told me that Jordan came to him one day with an early draft of the loans for shares white paper. "I said I think this scheme is corrupt," Vasiliev recalled. "What actually happened was even worse than we ever expected."[23]

Everything about loans for shares was the opposite of what the reformers had once stood for. It reeked of picking winners and losers arbitrarily instead of letting the market decide. It meant that the new owners were being selected, once again, by politicians, not by market competition and not by the testing of strength in the "boxing ring." And the loans for shares deals were carried out not in the open but largely in secret, by offshore shell companies and hidden accounts. Even the auctions were corrupt: the auctioneer himself, in most cases, turned out to be the winning bidder. The auctions were rigged, and Chubais let it happen.

If Chubais had any doubts, they were fleeting. On the day of Potanin's presentation to the cabinet, Chubais recalled, "I understood immediately that I was going to support this idea at any cost."[24] Sergei Belyaev, another Chubais recruit from St. Petersburg, told me that Chubais's only concern was whether the banks were really serious about coming up with so much money. Chubais wasn't questioning the plan, just whether the tycoons would pay. "He saw a certain danger here that the banks would deceive us," Belyaev told me. "They would take the packets of shares and won't give any money."[25]

But evidently Chubais swallowed those doubts quickly because in the autumn of 1995, another threat loomed—loss of the whole privatization drive. The political atmosphere had turned gloomy. Yeltsin suffered two heart ailments during the year, the Chechen war was dragging on, and Yeltsin seemed to have lost his way as a champion of the democratic movement. The polls showed that every week the Communist Party was coming closer to a victory in the December elections for the lower house of parliament, the State Duma. The Russian Communists were led by Gennady Zyuganov, a one-time Soviet party propagandist. Zyuganov liked to present himself to Westerners as a modern social democrat, but at home he was an ideologue who sounded harsher themes of nationalism. Zyuganov's positions on the economy were hazy; he talked about renationalizing some banks but also declared his support for "mixed" forms of property ownership. When Zyuganov said he would reverse privatization, Chubais took the threat seriously.

Chubais, who became extraordinarily unpopular among Russian voters in these years, felt increasingly isolated in his post as deputy prime minister. He was marginalized under Chernomyrdin; there was a "complete blockage" of his goals by the other deputy, Oleg Soskovyets. Chubais told me he felt Chernomyrdin had 50 percent of the government in his hands, Soskovyets had 40 percent, and he had only 10 percent. "Privatization was practically stopped," Chubais recalled. The Russian reformers had envisioned a second phase of privatization, after vouchers, in which state-owned factories, refineries, and mines would be sold for cash to the highest bidders. Chubais saw the failure to get this phase of privatization off the ground as a major setback, not only for the budget but for his larger hopes of creating a new class of private owners. At the time, he recalled, "There was no consolidation, no political force standing behind private property."[26]

Jordan and Jennings traveled constantly around Russia, poking their noses into aging factories and debating how to best sell off shipyards and mines. They always stopped in the office of the factory director. They kept track of what they half jokingly called the "Lenin index," a tally of how many pictures of Lenin they saw still hanging in the general directors' offices. One might assume, with the collapse of the Soviet Union, that the "Lenin index" would decline. But in fact, they discovered, it did not. One reason was that in mass privatization, Chubais had compromised by giving insiders, the Soviet factory directors, a chance to keep control of their factories. The pictures of Lenin remained in place. The "red directors" still ruled Russian industry. This, coupled with public discontent, was what made Zyuganov a powerful figure and worried Chubais.

Then Potanin made a potent argument to Chubais. He suggested that loans for shares would correct the earlier compromise, which had prolonged the reign of the red directors. Potanin especially wanted to torpedo Andrei Filatov, a giant of a man who was the red director of Norilsk Nickel. His legendary influence reached all the way from the tundra to the Kremlin. "During the loans for shares auctions, it was not possible to declare this at the time because it was politically unacceptable," Potanin admitted later. "But the real reason was to bring normal management to sizable companies and to break the red directors' lobby. It was the most important thing."[27] What Potanin did not say, was that the "normal management" he had in mind was to be the inexperienced financiers like himself and Khodorkovsky. Could they manage better than the old factory bosses? Chubais knew that the factory directors, siphoning off the profits into their own pockets, were poison for the market, but there was no way to know whether Khodorkovsky, Potanin, or Berezovsky would be any better, or why. Nonetheless, he saw the tycoons as the epitome of modern Russia and the factory directors as crusty symbols of past failures. Paul Bograd, the political consultant who had grown close to the Chubais team, recalled that Chubais believed the young tycoons would bring "some semblance of competent corporate management, as opposed to doing nothing and allowing these places to be looted. Which, given the state of management then, was likely to happen."[28]

Khodorkovsky recalled that in early 1995 "a situation arose when it became clear to everyone that big industry remained in the hands of the red directors, and if nothing happened, then they would bring the Communists back to power."[29] Chubais had many motives, but this one was at the core: to defeat Zyuganov and the Communists—forever. If Zyuganov did well in the December elections, it was already clear that he would become the leading challenger to Yeltsin in the 1996 election. Chubais knew that Yeltsin was weak physically and could see from polls that he was weak politically. He feared a Zyuganov victory would lead Russia backward. Chubais never advertised it publicly—he attempted to keep the goal obscure so as not to alarm the opposition—but loans for shares should really have been called "tycoons for Yeltsin." Chubais was willing to hand over the property without competition, without openness, and, as it turned out, for a bargain price, but in a way that would keep the businessmen at Yeltsin's side in the 1996 reelection campaign.

I personally had my doubts at the time about whether Chubais was this farsighted, and it was hard to even imagine Yeltsin running for president again. But in retrospect, I was wrong about Chubais and Yeltsin. Loans for shares was the first phase in Yeltsin's reelection campaign. It was the weld between the tycoons and the Kremlin, the embrace of wealth and power. Chubais later acknowledged the tradeoff. "The fact that these would be the forces supporting their own private property, that they would defend their private property, and that in the political process they would be, by definition, against Communists and pro-reform—that was 100 percent sure," Chubais told me. "And that is what happened."

Gaidar, who remained a confidant of Chubais, although he was not in government at the time, acknowledged, "It was not the most pleasant choice. I would rather not be in a position to make this choice. But I really think that if Yeltsin, Chernomyrdin, and Chubais had not gone to this loans for shares scheme, which radically changed the composition of forces in the economic elite, I think that Zyuganov's chances of winning the elections would have been substantially better, and maybe he would have been unbeatable."[30]

Jordan explained, "You have to remember that every year until Yeltsin got reelected, everyone in this country, including me, was worried that the Communists were going to come back. I don't believe they were thinking much further than, the Communist risk must be taken out of the game. And that's what they were thinking about—they *weren't* thinking about the economy!"

On August 30, 1995, Yeltsin signed a decree putting loans for shares in motion. But the plan was already changing in ways that made it even more appealing to the tycoons who were lobbying for it. When Jennings originally wrote the white paper, he had insisted on international competition—foreign oil companies would be welcome to compete for Russia's riches. However, the door was slammed shut on foreigners in the autumn, in part thanks to the efforts of Khodorkovsky and one of his deputies, Konstantin Kagalovsky, a shrewd former Russian representative to the International Monetary Fund and World Bank. Kagalovsky, who had been among those helping Gaidar at the dacha in 1991, waged a campaign to exclude foreigners from the Yukos auction by making the rules ambiguous enough to create doubts among investors about whether they could legally keep the properties if they won. Scaring away foreign investors had a larger purpose as well—the tycoons were not so rich that they could outbid foreign oil companies in an open competition. Khodorkovsky did not want to have to face British Petroleum in a bidding war for Yukos. By slamming the door on foreigners, he was making sure that the price of the properties would be as low as possible.

Chubais also had a cunning plan to ensure the loyalty of the tycoons. He created a dual key system, in which the first key for each factory would be given out before the 1996 presidential election, but the second key—the one that allowed the businessmen to lock up and keep their property—would be distributed only after the 1996 election. Thus the magnates would have an interest in seeing Yeltsin reelected because if Zyuganov came to power, they could kiss their factories and oil fields good-bye.

As it was hammered out in September 1995, the loans for shares plan called for the State Property Committee to hold auctions in which the banks could bid for state shares in the enterprises by offering low-interest loans to the government. The shares were to be held as collateral. Until the loans were repaid, the banks were allowed, indeed encouraged, to take the factories under control and to manage them. Then, if the government later defaulted on the loans, as everyone expected, the banks could sell the shares in a second phase, paying back the loans but keeping 30 percent of the proceeds as a commission. The sell-off was set for September 1996, but the elections were held earlier, in June and July.[31]

In a key procedural twist that enormously helped the tycoons rig the auctions, they were allowed to bid on their choice property while also being the auctioneer. For example, Menatep Bank was the official "organizer" of the auction for Yukos as well as the chief suitor. This was a glaring conflict of interest, but increasingly it was the businessmen who dictated the terms to the government and not the other way around. They picked the companies they wanted, they picked the terms, and they picked the outcome. In the next few years, this became the kernel of how the businessmen dealt with the state. Joel Hellman, an economist for the European Bank for Reconstruction and Development, later termed it "state capture," meaning that businessmen and vested interests turned around and "captured" the government.[32] This was not an abstract idea in the Russia of the 1990s. It was the credo of Berezovsky: big capital should talk and politicians listen.

Amazingly, both Chubais and Kokh maintained a public facade at the outset of the loans for shares auctions that all was going normally. Kokh told reporters that the auctioneer was "largely a technical function and does not give any additional advantage" to the bidders. Chubais was even more brazen. "As you may know," he told journalists on September 25, "we don't predetermine the buyer." The procedures for the auctions "will be free and competitive." This was sheer nonsense. The reality was that Chubais and Kokh handpicked the winners: Potanin, Khodorkovsky, and Berezovsky won their prizes in quick succession. Just as the tycoons demanded, foreign bidders were excluded, again with the support of Chubais and Kokh. "Russian capital cannot yet compete with foreign capital," said Kokh, parroting the Khodorkovsky line.

On September 25, Yeltsin approved a list of forty-four companies that were going to be offered for the loans, but two weeks later it was narrowed down to twenty-nine. In the final version published October 17, 1995, there were only sixteen enterprises. Four more were not auctioned due to lack of bids. Of the dozen loans for shares auctions that took place between November 3 and December 28, 1995, the overwhelming majority went to the banks that acted as organizers of the auction, their secret shell companies, or affiliates of the enterprises themselves. The deals were rigged.[33]

On November 17, Potanin seized his prize, a 38 percent stake in the metals giant Norilsk Nickel. The initial offering price had been $170 million, and Potanin won by offering just $100,000 more. This was a mere pittance for a company that reported 1995 revenues of $3.3 billion and profits of $1.2 billion. Although the truth of the company's financial condition was murky, it was clear Norilsk had enormous potential, borne out in the next few years when the company generated billions of dollars in profits. There were four bids that day, three of them from Potanin and his affiliates. The fourth came from another Moscow bank, Rossiisky Kredit, through a front company, Kont. This bid was for $355 million, far more than Potanin had offered. But Kokh "smelled a rat," and he disqualified the bid on the narrow technical grounds that the bidders did not possess a reliable bank guarantee for the capital they were offering, while the capital of the other bidders, all Potanin affiliates, "seemed credible."[34] One reason why Potanin's capital was so "credible" is that the government was filling up his bank with its own money. An Interior Ministry investigator, whose probe into the Norilsk case was later closed without charges, ferreted out one interesting footnote to Potanin's victory: one of his front companies, Reola, lacked the same bank guarantees, but Kokh didn't seem to take notice.[35]

Khodorkovsky's prize, Yukos, came with somewhat more difficulty and drama but demonstrated anew Chubais's determination to remain on the path he had chosen. It also showed that Khodorkovsky could be ruthless. At stake in the December 8 auction was 45 percent of the shares of Yukos in a loans for shares deal, as well as another 33 percent in an investment tender. The starting price was a $150 million loan for the shares, and $150 million for the investment tender, with the winner required to promise another $200 million investment in the company. Khodorkovsky's bank, Menatep, was organizing the auction. Khodorkovsky was bidding through one of his front companies, Laguna.

However, another group of three banks was preparing a serious bid for Yukos. This troika of prominent tycoons was made up of Vladimir Vinogradov of Inkombank, Mikhail Friedman's Alfa Bank, and Valery Malkin's Rossiisky Kredit, which had lost out weeks earlier on

Norilsk. The three bankers objected immediately to Menatep's demand that all the deposits for the auction be put in Menatep, and this time Kokh listened. He agreed that all the money would instead be deposited at the Central Bank.

However, the three bankers didn't really have enough money. They needed a $350 million deposit and sent out feelers to foreign investors, but without much luck. One of the investors they approached was California billionaire oilman Martin S. Davis. What the three bankers did not know is that Khodorkovsky was playing hardball. Khodorkovsky dispatched one of his top lieutenants to the United States to deliver a blunt message to Davis that the laws in Russia on foreign investment in loans for shares were at best vague (as Khodorkovsky had earlier ensured they would be) and at worst could cost him everything if tested in court. The Russian told Davis that if he invested in the rival consortium bidding for Yukos, he would lose all his money. "You put at risk $300 million," the Russian said. Davis decided not to invest, although Khodorkovsky's rivals never knew of the secret mission.[36] When I asked Khodorkovsky about it, he brushed it aside. "They spoke about it," he said of his rivals, "but I didn't believe that a foreigner would give money. Because on my side I was trying to raise foreign capital also—nothing!"

Instead of cash, the three bankers offered the equivalent of $370.2 million in short-term government bonds, the high-flying GKOs, and said they would put $82 million in cash into the Central Bank. But Kokh rejected the GKOs, as did Chubais. Only cash would do. They were saying, in effect, the Russian government would not accept its own bonds as a deposit for the auction. This meant that the three bankers were out of the running. "We had cash," one of Khodorkovsky's vice presidents later told me. "We were quite sure our competition did not have cash."

Even without knowing about the secret mission to discourage their investor, the three bankers were furious at Khodorkovsky. They knew Menatep was organizing the auction and bidding at the same time, which was bad enough. But they also suspected Menatep was able to cough up the cash thanks to its close ties to the state and to Yukos itself. They knew that Khodorkovsky had mammoth loans and deposits from the Finance Ministry; the federal government was Khodorkovsky's largest single client. In a rare public attack on a fellow tycoon, the three bankers demanded that the Yukos auction be postponed and fired off a fusillade of complaints at Khodorkovsky. They even threatened to dump all their GKOs and disrupt the government securities market.[37] But Chubais was determined not to be derailed. "Nothing doing," he insisted. Chubais later suggested the three banks were making so much noise because they were just angling for a deal with Khodorkovsky for a piece of the action.[38]

Years later, a top executive at one of the three banks told me that "Khodorkovsky was buying Yukos with the money of Yukos. They didn't pay their taxes and decided to accumulate the money, and the deal was, later on they would decide what to do with the taxes. That's what made us so angry—no, I would say, mad. They stole the company."

At some point, Pyotr Aven, president of Alfa Bank, went to see Chubais. They were old acquaintances. Aven had been present when Chubais first met Gaidar, and he had been a minister in Gaidar's government. Despite Aven's appeals, Chubais would not budge on the issue of using the GKOs for the deposit. The three bankers were out of luck. Chubais and Aven ruined their friendship over the Yukos auction. Chubais told me later that his chief concern at the time was getting cash for the budget. He added, "One can make claims that Khodorkovsky wasn't using the right money, that he was using Yukos' own money, and one can say he was using some of his deposits which the Ministry of Finance had placed with him, and that his sources had been formed in a wrong way. But my criteria was simple: besides all the political thoughts, I desperately needed money for the budget."

Chubais got the money, but where did Khodorkovsky find it? The answer is unknown. Khodorkovsky by this time had a financial and political network that stretched across Russia and abroad. He was on good terms with Muravlenko, the president of Yukos, before the auction, and Muravlenko had helped Khodorkovsky lobby the government against foreign investors. But it is not clear whether Yukos had such cash—the movement of large amounts of money is often hidden in shell companies and not evident from official annual reports and audits. Khodorkovsky said he borrowed money from other tycoons. "Smolensky gave us money, Most Bank gave us money," he said, adding that Menatep also borrowed from several defense factories which it had worked with in the past.[39] "Yukos at that moment had wage debts, six months' wage arrears, they didn't have any money at all," he claimed.

Kokh later hinted that Khodorkovsky had indeed exploited his connection with Yukos to raise the cash to buy Yukos. He suggested Khodorkovsky pledged future oil deliveries for loans. The three other bankers "could not collect as much money as Yukos and Menatep could obtain, for instance, against oil futures," Kokh wrote. "All sorts of things become possible when such an oil company joins forces with a large bank. This made people angry, and they started repeating angry mantras like 'if we could only separate Yukos from Menatep' and the like. But strategic alliances are legal and play a positive role."

On December 8, Khodorkovsky walked away with his prize. His Laguna front company paid $159 million, just $9 million over the starting price, for the block of 45 percent of Yukos shares. He won the investment tender for the 33 percent block of shares by offering just $125,000 more than the starting price of $150 million.

On the same day as the Yukos auction, Potanin snapped up another oil company, Sidanco, winning 51 percent of the shares for $130 million. The two oil generals, Alekperov and Bogdanov, also won loans-for-shares auctions for pieces of their companies, Lukoil and Surgutneftegaz respectively. The Surgut auction was an especially graphic example of how the Chubais ideals of openness and competition were ignored in practice. Outsiders were warned in advance by the the Surgut management not to make a bid, and the airport in Surgut was closed that day, so other bidders could not fly in to buy part of the company. They did not.[40]

The final oil prize of the year was claimed, at the last minute, by Berezovsky. In the summer of 1995, he abruptly parted ways with Kadannikov, the Avtovaz factory director who had been his partner in AVVA and in the Zhiguli deals. Kadannikov, facing a growing tide of debt and backlog of wages at the factory, unexpectedly demanded a huge repayment from Logovaz for an earlier shipment of thousands of cars. Berezovsky didn't flinch. He needed to raise $4 million overnight and he found it, selling off part of Logovaz and paying the factory on June 22, 1995. By this time, Berezovsky had already put himself into a higher orbit. He had taken on the Aeroflot accounts and taken over the ORT television channel, and now he was hankering for a piece of the oil industry sell-off.

Yuli Dubov, the author of *Bolshaya Paika,* the roman à clef about Berezovsky, told me once that Berezovsky only really functioned in a crisis environment. Berezovsky habitually waited until ten minutes after a deadline to even begin to think about how to act. "He is one of those people who can exist calmly and comfortably only in extreme situations, in which not a single other person would feel comfortable," Dubov told me. He described Berezovsky as among those who never rest, who change things by the sheer force of their energy, who "constantly have a nail in their chair."[41] It was this Berezovsky who, in late summer and early autumn 1995, rushed into the loans for shares giveaway.

He lobbied the Kremlin to hastily slice off a new vertically integrated oil company, Sibneft, which included Russia's largest, most modern refinery in Omsk, and a Siberian production association, Noyabrskneftegaz. Korzhakov recalled that Berezovsky's pitch was that he needed oil revenues to support the television channel. Korzhakov said, "I am not very good at economics" and gave his approval. He and a top Yeltsin aide called a regional governor and the minister of energy to "put in a word for Berezovsky," Korzhakov said.[42] If he did not know much about economics, Korzhakov was clearly drunk on power. "Berezovsky needed my okay, for if I had been told he was founding an oil company without my knowledge, I would have instantly made short work of him," Korzhakov later said.[43] Yeltsin signed the decree creating Sibneft on September 29, 1995, making it Russia's sixth-largest oil company. With Kokh's help (he drafted a key document for Berezovsky in the middle of the night to meet the next day's deadline), the controlling block of shares in Sibneft was hastily thrown into the loans for shares auctions. It was scheduled for December 28, 1995, to be the last. The starting price was $100 million.

Like the other tycoons, however, Berezovsky didn't have that kind of money, nor did he have much time. He had met the superfinancier George Soros, who was already spending hundreds of millions of dollars on philanthropy inside Russia, supporting civil society and helping Russian scientists, writers, and teachers through the difficult early years after the Soviet collapse. Alex Goldfarb, the biologist who had once been a link between dissidents and foreign correspondents, was close to Soros and also knew Berezovsky. Desperate to raise money, Berezovsky visited Japan, Germany, and New York, looking for loans to help him buy Sibneft. But he ran into a wall of refusal. Goldfarb, who attended Berezovsky's presentation to Wall Street money men, recalled, "Investors were afraid it could all fall apart. At that time, Berezovsky was no one."

After Berezovsky left New York, Goldfarb helped him pass along a thick file of documents about Sibneft, some of them crudely sketched and typed, to the Soros financial team in New York. Berezovsky later told me he had been seeking $50 million from foreigners for the purchase of Sibneft.[44] He had asked Soros for $10 million to $15 million.[45] Goldfarb told me that word came back in a few days from New York: no thanks. Soros was not even willing to put in a million because he felt "the risk was too great," Berezovsky said. Berezovsky recalled that Soros told him "I cannot give you even one dollar" because he was worried that Zyuganov, the Communist Party leader, would be elected president and then renationalize private property. Berezovsky eventually found the money for Sibneft with help from Smolensky.[46] On the day of the auction, Berezovsky won with a bid just $300,000 over the starting price of $100 million. A few years later, the company had a market capitalization over $1 billion.

Throughout 1995 there were hints of what the tycoons were up to, but never a full picture. Perhaps a full picture was impossible, since the always secretive magnates were never a cohesive group. Their overlapping alliances and frequent conflicts subdivided and recombined them into several amorphous groups. The clans of Russian capitalism were just beginning to coalesce in 1994–1995, laying the groundwork for what would later become a full-fledged system of rival tribes—powerful and well-financed groups of politicians, factory directors, moneymen, journalists, and corporate secret agents.

Lumbering out of the fog of confusion and chaos in the first years, a new capitalist leviathan was visible, but its true nature was hard to discern. Just two weeks before Potanin's cabinet appearance in March to pitch loans for shares, one member of the Sparrow Hills club, Oleg Boiko, spoke publicly about some aspects of the tycoons' private discussions. Boiko described creation of a "big eight" of financial-industrial giants who were contemplating a greater role in politics. Boiko named companies, not people: Logovaz (Berezovsky), Menatep (Khodorkovsky), Stolichny Bank (Smolensky), Alfa Bank (Friedman), Mikrodin (Yefanov), and several others associated with Gazprom. Boiko, however, did not include the fast-rising Potanin or Vinogradov. Without mentioning their weekly meetings on the Sparrow Hills, Boiko accurately described the early political mood among the tycoons—that they lacked a clear-cut political patron, and they were nervous about further upheavals. They wanted normalcy. But Boiko's comments, which stirred much talk about the "Magnificent Eight," failed to point to the loans for shares grab just around the corner. Boiko did not participate in loans for shares and later slipped from prominence.[47]

The most prescient of those who discovered the rising clan structure of Russian capitalism in 1995 was Olga Kryshtanovskaya. Usually wearing her hair pulled back in a bun and evincing a patient, tutoring manner, Kryshtanovskaya often resembled a very proper schoolteacher. But in fact she was a laser-smart sociologist. She made a specialty out of studying the Russian elite, and she was perfectly positioned to see the leviathan coming out of the fog. In the early 1990s, she carried out her research by going from person to person, trying to understand the business practices, finances, and mores of the "new millionaires." Kryshtanovskaya and her band of student researchers conducted long interviews with dozens of businessmen. They were invited by some into luxurious marble palaces and by others to meet on a park bench. She found one future industrialist, Kakha Benzukidze, living in a one-room apartment and sleeping on a cot. Kryshtanovskaya painstakingly traced how they had made their first money and how they had made it grow. She compiled lists of the wealthiest businessmen and lists of the biggest banks, and then she made cross-checks and diagrams, trying to piece together companies and empires. Then she carried out still more interviews to find out how they worked. Kryshtanovskaya spotted the emerging clan structure and wrote a penetrating piece about it, brilliantly summarizing the history of the late 1980s and early 1990s. The essay appeared in *Izvestia* in January 1996 under the headline, "The Financial Oligarchy in Russia." It was a turning point that brought the tycoons' actions into focus. More than just wealth, they were amassing political clout. Kryshtanovskaya pioneered the idea that the tycoons were becoming an oligarchy—a small group men who possessed both wealth and power. She spotted the rise of Potanin's Uneximbank, the power of Khodorkovsky's Menatep, and the significance of Gusinsky in Luzhkov's realm, although Berezovsky did not appear on her list.

Much of what the outside world knew about Russia in the early 1990s was focused on Yeltsin and his power struggles, which dominated the headlines. But two diplomats stationed in Moscow, both veterans of the Soviet period, also spotted the rise of the clans in the summer and autumn of 1995. Glenn Waller, a shrewd Australian diplomat who had spent nearly a decade in the former Soviet Union and Russia, wrote a lengthy and perceptive cable in May on Russia's "financial-industrial elite" that captured virtually all the key players of the Sparrow Hills club. Moreover, Waller nailed down the marriage of wealth and power, the merger of financial and political interests, which was at the core of how Potanin, Khodorkovsky, and Berezovsky were functioning at the time. He warned that although privatization had given the new tycoons fabulous wealth, they should not be regarded as resembling Western titans of capitalism. "The relationship between business and government in Russia remains very close," he wrote, "indeed incestuous. Even the 'new' business elite grew out of the Soviet system—most (if not all) of the private financial groups made their first capital through their privileged access to party and Komsomol funds or through political contacts (in Russian: *blat)* in government ministries. Today, they continue to rely on government favors. . . . Big business in Russia continues to coalesce around powerful political leaders."[48]

A hard-nosed skeptic, American diplomat Thomas E. Graham was back in Moscow for his second tour of duty in the summer of 1995. Graham was trying to explain to himself—and to policymakers in Washington—how Russian capitalism was morphing into rival clans and warring financial-industrial groups. What Graham saw did not neatly fit into the Washington idea of brave reformers led by Yeltsin and Chubais fighting off the Communists.

One day, the word came back from Washington: please don't use the word "clan" anymore. The State Department bureaucrats didn't like it; "they said 'clan' has an anthropological meaning; you can't apply it to Russian politics," Graham recalled. So he fixed the language in his cables to read "elite groups often referred to in Russia as clans," and in the summer of 1995 he began to dig deeper. In the autumn, he asked for permission from Washington to publish an article in Russia spelling out his unvarnished views on what was happening. Graham told me he did not expect approval because a diplomat was supposed to be discreet; it was not very often that a political counselor was permitted to publish strong views of his own in the country where he was serving. Public statements were for presidents and secretaries of state. But the approval came and Graham wrote, without the usual diplomatic niceties, about what he saw happening around him. The essay was published on November 23, 1995, in the newspaper *Nezavisimaya Gazeta*, which had recently started receiving financial backing from Berezovsky. Graham declared that "a new regime has emerged in Russia" characterized by a stable, but vigorous, contest between rival clans. The essay, which filled an entire page of the newspaper, was the talk of Moscow for days. Graham argued that the real balance of power in Russia was not Boris Yeltsin against parliament, not reform against revanche, but the noisy pushing and shoving of the clans. And he used the word "clan" without hesitation. Graham outlined five major clans, including Chernomyrdin's energy lobby, Luzhkov's Moscow group, the Korzhakov "party of war," and Chubais together with the tycoons; he told me years later that he erred by including the hapless Agrarian Party as fifth. But in retrospect, the essay precisely captured the emerging structure, mechanics, and methods of financial and political tribes.

The publication triggered an angry reaction by both governments. The Russians lodged an official protest with the U.S. embassy, mortified not by Graham's conclusions but by his public candor. Back at the State Department, Graham's essay hit like a thunderclap because of the unspoken message that the Clinton focus on Yeltsin and the young reformers was misguided, that other power brokers were rising, and that they were not necessarily committed to Western-style democracy. It was not the message the U.S. government wanted to hear. Graham told me he braced himself for trouble in Moscow after the dustup over his article, fearing that Russian sources would stop talking to him.

Instead, the opposite happened. The tycoons did not flinch from the image Graham had described. Vitaly Tretyakov, editor of *Nezavisimaya Gazeta,* who had published the article, gave a copy of it to Berezovsky, who liked it so much he invited Graham for a chat at the Logovaz Club.[49]

At the end of December 1995, the magnates of Russia had reached a turning point. Potanin, Khodorkovsky, and Berezovsky had pocketed their first keys to industry, as the loans for shares auctions came to an end. Gusinsky had returned to Moscow over the summer.[50] Gusinsky was expanding his media empire.

Meanwhile, the political mood in the country was grim. In the parliamentary elections, the Communists won the largest single bloc of seats in the next Duma. Their leader, Zyuganov, was well positioned to run for president the next summer. In January, the Chechen war spilled over into neighboring Dagestan in a terrible, bloody battle between Russian troops and a small band of Chechen separatists holed up in a border village, Pervomaiskoye. Inside the Kremlin, Yeltsin was in the grip of the reactionary Korzhakov and his "party of war." Then on January 16, Yeltsin abruptly fired Chubais from his post as deputy prime minister. Chubais had weathered more than four years in the cockpit of privatization and economic reform, but he had become a hated symbol of all the tumult and pain Russians had endured. "He sold off big industry for next to nothing," Yeltsin told reporters. "We cannot forgive this."

But Chubais would soon be back because the embrace of wealth and power had just begun. The tycoons had taken their share of property, but soon they would be called on to return the favor. They would be asked to help their troubled patron, Boris Yeltsin, and once again help themselves.

Chapter 13

Saving Boris Yeltsin

In Davos, a tiny Swiss Alpine ski resort, Gennady Zyuganov, the Russian Communist leader, stopped in the lobby of the Sun Star Park Hotel to give another autograph. Mikhail Berger, the economics editor of *Izvestia*, watched with a sense of alarm as a swarm of Western business executives hovered around Zyuganov, hanging on his every word and pumping his hand, their eyes expectantly surveying the possible next president of Russia. Zyuganov, fresh from his triumph in the December parliamentary elections, purred pleasantly to his Western suitors. He gave about twenty interviews a day to the press. He rubbed shoulders with the world's financial and political elite at the annual conference of the World Economic Forum in the first week of February 1996. Amid the tinkling of champagne glasses, the unceasing corridor chatter, and the crush of a standing room only press conference, Zyuganov stole the show in Davos, presenting himself as a kinder, gentler Communist who would respect democracy and some kinds of private property. Leading the early polls in the campaign for the Russian presidency, Zyuganov called himself "the most peaceful man on the planet" and insisted he would not undertake wholesale renationalization. "We understand that if we start taking factories back, there's going to be shooting from Murmansk to Vladivostok," he declared. Berger, who had been close to the reformers since the early days, reported from Davos that Zyuganov—a beefy, muscular man with a high forehead and thinning, pale hair—was the center of attention among Western moneymen. "The impression was that the West was already prepared to recognize him as the next president," Berger reported.[1]

The Zyuganov appearance in Davos led to a quiet drama that was to change Russia's course once again. Anatoly Chubais, Boris Berezovsky, Vladimir Gusinsky, Mikhail Khodorkovsky, and Yuri Luzhkov all attended the conference and watched Zyuganov's appearance with varying degrees of alarm and anxiety. They knew him better than the corporate mavens who crowded around him in the hotel lobby. Led by Berezovsky, they decided on the spot to try and save Boris Yeltsin.

Ousted by Yeltsin and unsure of his own future, Chubais cut a lonely figure at Davos in 1996. It was the fifth time he had been invited to the World Economic Forum, and he personally knew many of the captains of Western industry. They had once regarded him as the greatest hope for Russian reform. But now Chubais was out of office, and Zyuganov was on the rise. The adulation for Zyuganov stunned Chubais. He told me that in Davos, "I saw many of my good friends, presidents of major American companies, European companies, who were simply dancing around Zyuganov, trying to catch his eye, peering at him. These were the world's most powerful businessmen, with world-famous names, who with their entire appearance demonstrated that they were seeking support of the future president of Russia, because it was clear to everyone that Zyuganov was going to be the future president of Russia, and now they needed to build a relationship with him. So, this shook me up!"[2]

Chubais called back to Moscow and spoke to Arkady Yevstafiev, then deputy director of ORT television, who had been his press spokesman and adviser in the early days of privatization. Chubais asked for copies of the Russian Communist Party platform and other Zyuganov statements, which Yevstafiev quickly faxed to Davos.[3] On the closing day in Davos, Chubais called a press conference in which he denounced Zyuganov for "a classic Communist lie," presenting himself as a moderate to the Westerners while saying something quite different at home. "There are two Zyuganovs, one for foreign and one for domestic consumption," Chubais said, reading from a Communist

Party text that called for nationalization of energy and banking and reversal of privatization. If the Communists return to power, Chubais insisted, "the first move will be to forbid the free press." Then Zyuganov will "put in prison all his political enemies." He warned darkly, "My judgment is that this kind of policy will inevitably lead to big bloodshed in Russia."[4]

Gusinsky was also alarmed by Zyuganov's appearance in Davos. Gusinsky recalled that earlier, in Moscow, he held long discussions with Zyuganov, urging him to become a social democrat, as other former Communists had done in Eastern Europe, saying that if Zyuganov would cast himself simply as a champion of the downtrodden, he would enjoy a long political career. "Stop being a Communist, put the label away, don't scream about private property," Gusinsky urged Zyuganov. "This is normal, so turn normal!"[5]

But in Davos, Gusinsky realized Zyuganov would not change. "I was present at the meeting between Zyuganov and Swiss bankers. It was very important for me to see how he was going to behave. And when I saw that he was looking into their eyes and lying to them, that he was saying exactly what they wanted to hear, a typical Soviet Communist KGB trick, I knew it! They will close us down. The minute he wins, he'll shut us down. I was frightened."

Zyuganov's silky words to the Western businessmen also gave Berezovsky a start. "Zyuganov was a danger to us, and to Russia," he told me later that year.[6] The compressed ball of energy went into action. For nearly a year, Berezovsky had been at odds with Gusinsky, but in Davos he picked up the phone in his hotel room and called him. They quickly agreed to meet. Both set aside their differences, which went back to the 1994 fight over Aeroflot and the faces in the snow episode. "We didn't waste time finding a common language," Berezovsky recalled. "We both understood that the threat of a return to Communism required a joint counter-attack."[7] Gusinsky recalled later that Berezovsky came to him and said, "I think it is time for a truce. The country is at a crossroads, to the left or to the right. These are not the elections, but almost a civil war—without shots being fired."

"I completely agreed with him," Gusinsky told me. "I believe that if it had not been for Berezovsky at that time, Yeltsin would not be the president of Russia, and most likely history would have been different."

Berezovsky also got a warning in Davos from the financier George Soros, who feared Zyuganov would defeat Yeltsin. Soros recalled telling Berezovsky that if the Communist leader were elected, the tycoon would "hang from a lamppost."[8] Berezovsky's recollection of the conversation was that Soros told him Zyuganov was a sure winner and Berezovsky should leave the country to save himself.

Berezovsky would have none of it. "George, I think that we will manage to defeat Zyuganov," Berezovsky confidently told Soros. Then "I had the impression that he looked at me as if I were mad."

"Boris," Soros replied, "you are wrong."[9]

Berezovsky next talked to Chubais, alone. Berezovsky suggested that Chubais bring together a group of tycoons to back Yeltsin. Then he and Gusinsky attended the Chubais press conference with Berger, the journalist, sitting between them, and they loved every word of Chubais's attack on Zyuganov.[10] Berezovsky then went to Mikhail Khodorkovsky, Vladimir Vinogradov, who was also in Davos, and even to Luzhkov, seeking support for an alliance to save Yeltsin. Their alliance became known as the Davos Pact. Although Luzhkov did not formally join the businessmen, he decided to throw his weight behind Yeltsin, setting aside the strains of 1994–1995.

Berezovsky and Gusinsky were wealthy men, but the "Davos Pact" was not only about wealth. The two tycoons now controlled two of the three major television channels in Russia. They could sway public opinion, and that, for Yeltsin, was the most valuable currency of all.

Back in Moscow, Berezovsky hurled himself into the new project. With Gusinsky, Khodorkovsky, and Vinogradov already on board, he recruited Alexander Smolensky, Vladimir Potanin, and Mikhail Friedman, the Alfa Group chief, accompanied by Pyotr Aven, his politically astute partner. This "group of seven" (Berezovsky, Gusinsky, Khodorkovsky, Potanin, Vinogradov, Smolensky, and Friedman-Aven) made up the core of the financial-political oligarchy. Most had been at the club on Sparrow Hills, most had participated in loans for shares. Now they set about trying to save Yeltsin.

The oligarchs agreed that Chubais, the steely, resolute architect of mass privatization and loans for shares, was the logical choice to manage Yeltsin's reelection campaign. The determination Chubais had shown over the last four years was just what the group of seven magnates were looking for. Less than six months after they had benefited so handsomely at the loans for shares auctions, and still awaiting the "second key" to their industrial treasures, they simply hired Chubais, who had been out of government since Yeltsin fired him in January. The tycoons paid him a handsome salary for his services.

Chubais created a private fund, the Center for Protection of Private Property, and told the tycoons he needed $5 million to do the job. "You give $5 million to me, not for me but for me to create a structure to which I will attract the best people," Chubais said he told the tycoons. "Within five days, the credit was extended and received." Chubais described the money as a no-interest loan. He set up the fund and then invested the money in the superprofitable bonds, known as GKOs, which were paying ever higher annual yields at the time because of uncertainty over Yeltsin's future. The GKO yields in May-June 1996 topped 100 percent. Chubais said he paid staff salaries out of the GKO profits. His own salary was $50,000 a month. Chubais said he paid taxes on a $300,000 income that year.[11]

The money that went to Chubais hinted at the much larger role the oligarchs would later play in financing Yeltsin's campaign. It was also a sign of how Chubais was drawing closer to the businessmen. He had become *their* agent. "We didn't have any doubts about his decency," Berezovsky recalled. "Plus his brains, strength, and organizational abilities." Chubais was also impressed by the tycoons and their willingness to unite behind Yeltsin. "The fact that big capital turned to Yeltsin," Chubais told me, "had a very serious impact on all the business elite, directors of enterprises, governors, and ministers. This had a very serious impact on all of the political elite of the country, a psychological impact."[12]

But before Chubais and the oligarchs could help Yeltsin defeat Zyuganov, they had to save Yeltsin from himself. The old man was brooding about his troubles and misfortunes. Winter was always the cruelest season for Yeltsin, bringing new illness and isolation. He had suffered a heart attack in October and had been all but invisible during the autumn 1995 parliamentary campaign. For the first time in his life, he felt politically isolated, and his poll ratings were almost zero. "At that time my whole life seemed under assault," Yeltsin wrote of the dark winter days, "battered about by all sorts of storms and strife. I stayed on my feet but was almost knocked over by the gusts and blows. . . . It seemed as if all were lost."[13] Yeltsin's deteriorating health remained largely hidden from view. Yeltsin acknowledged in his memoir that the Kremlin doctors wrote a letter expressing concern about "the catastrophic state" of his heart, although the letter was shown to him much later. They warned that frequent travel and stress were "a real threat to the health and life of the president."

His political life was also draining away. On January 11, a team of top Yeltsin advisers, led by the Kremlin political strategist Georgy Satarov, sat down together to plan for the campaign. The election would be held in six months, and the outlook was as grim as it had ever been. Yeltsin stood at 3–4 percent in the polls, while Zyuganov was leading the pack with 20 percent. "At the meeting there was total pessimism, a total absence of hope," one participant, Igor Mintusov, recalled later.[14] "Of ten people who spoke, nine said it was senseless, a lost cause." Nonetheless, the Satarov group pushed ahead, looking for a strategy that could save Yeltsin.

Reacting to the December setback in the parliamentary voting, Yeltsin had fired three people who were closely associated with the early democracy and reform movements: Chubais, Foreign Minister Andrei Kozyrev, and his chief of staff, Sergei Filatov. Chubais was replaced with Vladimir Kadannikov, Berezovsky's one-time partner from Avtovaz and AVVA. Kozyrev was replaced by Yevgeny Primakov, then head of foreign intelligence and a representative of the old Soviet *nomenklatura,* who was no friend of the West. The new look of Yeltsin's team was nationalist and regressive, and the oligarchs worried that Alexander Korzhakov's clan was gaining ground in the Kremlin.

Despite his standing at the bottom of polls, Yeltsin decided to run for reelection. He said his motive was to stop the Communists from returning to power. Yeltsin appointed Deputy Prime Minister Oleg Soskovets to head the campaign. Soskovets was put in charge of collecting the 1 million signatures necessary to put Yeltsin's name on the ballot. What should have been a relatively easy organizational problem turned into a disaster. Soskovets, a product of the Soviet era, was woefully unprepared for running a real campaign. He ordered the Russian railroad ministry workers to be coerced into signing pledges for Yeltsin. Yeltsin said he heard that railroad workers were being forced to sign up when they got paid. "They were sent to two windows, one to get their pay packet, and the other to support President Yeltsin. I asked that the story be checked out, and it turned out to be true." Arkady Yevstafiev, the Chubais lieutenant, told me that he and Yeltsin's daughter Tatyana Dyachenko (who would play a large role in the campaign in the coming months) went to the Ministry of Railways and took samples of the signatures gathered there. Yevstafiev then had the samples checked. In four days he got a response. "Fifty percent of them were fake," he said.[15] Yeltsin said of Soskovets, "My campaign manager had 'forgotten' that we were already living in another country and not the old Soviet Union, where politicians could buy voters so crudely."[16]

When Yeltsin finally made his announcement speech on February 15 in Yekaterinburg, where he had once been Communist Party boss, a number of his closest advisers stood in the wings and cried. Some of them feared they were witnessing Yeltsin's last hurrah. Most major polls put Yeltsin in fourth or fifth place in the presidential race. It was a frigid, damp day and Yeltsin's normally booming baritone was reduced to an unhealthy rasp. "We were standing behind the curtains, and several of the president's aides—their eyes welled up with tears," recalled Mintusov. "Here was this elderly president with his hoarse voice who was showing this tremendous determination. It was an emotional moment."

"At key points in his life, Yeltsin wakes up," Berezovsky told me of Yeltsin's revival in the spring of 1996. Yeltsin shrugged off ill health, depression, and drink. He literally climbed out of his hibernation, a great political animal if there ever was one. "He was born with a sense of power," Gusinsky marveled. "You have two hands, two feet, and a head, and so do I, but Yeltsin was also born with a sense of power." Yeltsin roused himself for the sake of keeping this power, but he needed help.

"We realized that the first problem was to get information to Yeltsin," Berezovsky said. "We had to break down the walls that had been built around him. We agreed to stop fighting among ourselves, and to try and connect with the president's team and tell them."[17] Berezovsky went to Viktor Ilyushin, an old Sverdlovsk hand in the Kremlin, a low-profile, silver-haired, quiet Yeltsin man who had warned Yevgeny Kiselyov about the Yeltsin family's unhappiness with NTV. Ilyushin arranged a meeting with Yeltsin, Chubais, and the oligarchs.

In the intensifying romance between wealth and power, between the tycoons and their patron, the meeting was a turning point. Yeltsin knew most of those at the table, but, isolated in his hospital bed and protected by Korzhakov, he had not seen them in a long while. He recalled that he at first regarded them "rather cautiously," feeling that "they had nowhere to go, that they had to support me, and I thought that the conversation would probably be about the funding of my campaign."[18]

But the oligarchs had a different plan. Before the meeting, they agreed that someone would try to deliver the raw truth to Yeltsin that he was no longer popular, a painful realization that, according to Ilyushin, the president had not absorbed. "We agreed that we were going to tell the truth to Yeltsin, that his popularity was 3 percent," Gusinsky said, "because his KGB men . . . were telling him stories that it was not less than 98 percent."

Smolensky recalled that Chubais arrived carrying a briefcase. Despite the elegant Kremlin lunch, Chubais plopped his briefcase on the table and took out some papers. Chubais, fearless in the face of power, abruptly fired off the bad news. "Boris Nikolayevich, the situation is not simple. Your rating is 5 percent!"

Chubais showed some of the papers to Yeltsin. The president glanced at them and tossed them aside. "This is all rubbish," Yeltsin said.

"Yeltsin grew tense and red," Gusinsky recalled. Speaking very slowly, Yeltsin said, "Anatoly Borisovich, we have to figure out who prepared those ratings. I think this is not true." Yeltsin emphasized the last words, *not true*.

Chubais then turned scarlet. There was a long pause. Gusinsky spoke up. "Boris Nikolayevich, everything that your people say to you, your circle, is all lies."

"He turns to me, he gazes," Gusinsky recalled. Gusinsky felt that Yeltsin strongly disliked him, that he was only allowed to set foot in the Kremlin because Yeltsin now needed him and the bankers to hold on to power—such a cynical man, Yeltsin.

"And how do you know what my men are telling me?" Yeltsin inquired of Gusinsky, again speaking slowly.

"Boris Nikolayevich," Gusinsky replied, "because you act foolishly. That's why. I see it—you act foolishly because they give you this sort of information."

Another long pause, as Gusinsky remembered it. Both Smolensky, who was seated next to Yeltsin, and Gusinsky, who was across from him, remembered that Yeltsin was figuratively looking around for a heavy plate to throw at Gusinsky.

"Somehow we moved on," Gusinsky added. "Keep in mind," he told Yeltsin sympathetically, "if the Communists come back to power, you will be held personally responsible. All of us are here for this reason: to prevent them from coming back."

Yeltsin's recollection was that the businessmen also expressed their own fear of Zyuganov. "The Communists will hang us from the lampposts," he quotes them saying as a group. "If we don't turn this situation around drastically, in a month it will be too late."

Throughout the meal, Yeltsin largely remained silent. The bankers suggested Yeltsin put Chubais in charge of his campaign. Yeltsin, who had only recently fired Chubais, later said this suggestion "amazed me most," although he acknowledged his own growing dissatisfaction with Soskovets. The bankers left and shook hands with Yeltsin, not really knowing if they had gotten through to him or not.

Before the meeting, Berezovsky had quietly approached Yeltsin's wife, Naina. He had asked her to help arrange a ten-minute tête-à-tête with the president after the lunch. Berezovsky reminded Yeltsin of his request as the other tycoons were leaving, and Yeltsin gave him an approving look. When they were alone, Berezovsky recalled, he told Yeltsin that trouble was brewing. He told Yeltsin that Korzhakov wanted to call off the elections because Yeltsin's standing was so low. "Boris Nikolayevich, you cannot use force to solve the problem," Berezovsky said. "If we follow this route we may get into a civil war."

Yeltsin looked down at Berezovsky. "Is this all you have to say?"

"Yes," said Berezovsky.

"I left with a heavy feeling," Berezovsky recalled. "Everybody felt that he failed to understand, that he did not understand."

"The very next day," Berezovsky recalled, "he gave the order to reorganize the headquarters." In a method familiar to all, Yeltsin maintained his power by balancing competing groups. He was the arbiter, the great circus master, who kept his lions and tigers jumping through hoops with a long whip. Yeltsin did not immediately close down the Soskovets campaign operation but created a rival, a campaign council chaired by himself and attached to it an all-important new analytical center headed by Chubais. The analytical center became a second campaign headquarters; the money came from the oligarchs.

The key figure at the analytical center was Yeltsin's youngest daughter, Tatyana Dyachenko, who stepped into politics for the first time as her father's eyes and ears in the campaign organization. She was a short woman, shy, with her father's eyes and loose bangs over her forehead. Dyachenko had studied to be a systems programmer and worked at a defense-related bureau on space trajectories. She was not a public figure, and little was known about her at the time. She had no experience in politics, but she could speak to her father in a way no one else dared. The oligarchs saw her as a detour around Korzhakov to get information to Yeltsin.

"She had a lot of the features of her father," Berezovsky recalled. "She worked twenty hours a day." She was stubborn, like the president, he said, but she would listen. Yeltsin recalled that before she joined the campaign he feared "I was going to break down" under the stress, but she offered him a glint of optimism. Valentin Yumashev, who was Yeltsin's ghostwriter and had introduced Berezovsky to the Kremlin inner circle, joined Dyachenko on many political missions. Chubais quickly realized the value of Dyachenko's presence, especially in bypassing Korzhakov. Soon Dyachenko and Yumashev were traveling all over Moscow, recruiting advertising men and political consultants to come to Yeltsin's rescue.

On March 4, Dyachenko and Yumashev came to see Igor Malashenko, the president of NTV, and appealed to him to take on one of the most important jobs in the campaign—media and public relations. It was an extraordinary gesture to a leader of the Gusinsky camp. Malashenko, who has the short-cropped hair of a drill sergeant as well as finely honed political skills, told them he believed Yeltsin had "an enormous hidden support because the nation is basically non-Communist." And, he said, "the only thing he needs is a real election campaign: to make news every day, to make stories that look good on television." Malashenko regaled them with Reagan campaign techniques he had heard about, such as visiting a flag factory.

But Malashenko worried that Korzhakov and his pals did not want to go ahead with a real campaign. Malashenko was "not full of joy" about working for the Kremlin, Gusinsky said. There were obvious drawbacks. One was that Yeltsin's political standing was so low that Malashenko might not be able to turn it around. And there was the ever worrisome threat of Korzhakov, who had masterminded the faces in the snow attack on Gusinsky in 1994. Finally, there was the biggest risk of all—the move could compromise NTV's cherished reputation for independence, earned during the Chechen war.

"Igor, I beg you to take the job at the Kremlin," Gusinsky recalled telling Malashenko. "This is a team decision. This is a team game. We are defending ourselves from the Communists."

"You lay me bare," Malashenko protested, according to Gusinsky.

"Yes," Gusinsky said, "I lay you bare. But I am exposing myself too, believe it or not. I am not concealing that this is our team decision. We must prevent the Communists from coming to power."

Malashenko soon thereafter met with Yeltsin. He was blunt. "Listen," he told Yeltsin, "you cannot just use the media as a propaganda tool of the Soviet times. It doesn't work; you need to get elected. You need to work a lot. You should go all over the country, make news, make speeches, meet people, and so on." Malashenko advised Yeltsin: run a modern, Western-style campaign in a country that had never really known one.

"On a visceral level," Malashenko told me, "he got it."

Touching a sensitive subject, Malashenko reminded Yeltsin that he was one of Gusinsky's partners. He asked Yeltsin to stand by him in case of another attack from Korzhakov. According to Malashenko, Yeltsin understood and agreed. Gusinsky later attributed Yeltsin's acquiescence to his sense of power—Yeltsin knew he needed Malashenko, regardless of what had gone before. "For the sake of this sense of power," Gusinsky said, "Yeltsin was prepared to love his enemies, betray friends—it was all the same to him. The goal was to hold on to power."

Chubais recruited the best and brightest political operatives from the financial clans. "From each of them, I took their strongest people," Chubais said. Among them were Shakhnovsky, Luzhkov's senior aide, who had organized the Sparrow Hills club, and Sergei Zverev, another Gusinsky man who was a superlobbyist. Others included Yevstafiev, the Chubais aide who had recently been working at Berezovsky's television channel; Alexander Oslon, the leading commercial pollster; Vyacheslav Nikonov, a former member of the lower house of parliament; and Satarov, who was Yeltsin's political adviser. Many others worked as freelancers on the side, such as Sergei Lisovsky, the entertainment and advertising magnate. The team was just getting organized in March when the campaign nearly went off a cliff.

The art and science of public opinion polling was still crude in 1996. Instead of telephone surveys, pollsters relied on an army of foot soldiers who went door to door with clipboards and questionnaires, often having doors slammed in their face. But it was possible, with enough pluck and care, to build a picture of the electorate. Oslon's polls charted this picture. Months-long backlogs in paying wages spread across the country, feeding discontent. The Chechen war was deeply unpopular. The January battle in Pervomaiskoye was especially humiliating for Yeltsin. He had demonstrated before television cameras—by moving his head back and forth like a sharpshooter through a scope—how thirty-eight crack Russian snipers were watching every move of the rebels and predicted they would be defeated in a single day. Instead, they escaped. Yeltsin looked totally disconnected from the bloody reality of the war. Oslon told me back then, "Chechnya is the fundamental question. There's nothing left for him to do but end the war in Chechnya." Yet another factor was Yeltsin's isolation "behind the Kremlin walls," Oslon said. Russians felt they had lost touch with their leader, a one-time streetcar populist who had inexplicably become a distant caricature of himself.[19]

Yet the polls also showed that Yeltsin had a store of popular support, if he could unlock it. For all his mistakes, Yeltsin's ratings went up as voters began to think about where the country was going next, rather than about the past. Instead of capitalizing on his strength, Yeltsin came close to discarding it.

What Berezovsky had told Yeltsin was true: Korzhakov was hoping to call off the election rather than risk defeat. In late February, Soskovets secretly hired a group of American political consultants to analyze the trends in public opinion. On February 27 Soskovets told one of the consultants, Richard Dresner, that "one of your tasks is to advise us, a month from the election, about whether we should call it off if you determine that we're going to lose."[20] Korzhakov tried to persuade Yeltsin to abandon the elections. "It is senseless to struggle when you have a 3 percent approval rating, Boris Nikolayevich," Korzhakov said, according to Yeltsin's account. "If we lose time with all these electoral games, then what?"

Korzhakov later offered his own explanation, saying, "It was clear to me whom we were going to elect: either Zyuganov or a sick president. That is why I was suggesting to postpone the elections by two years."[21]

Dyachenko later recalled that Korzhakov wanted to "preserve his influence" on Yeltsin and surrounded him with "a tight circle of his men." Soon "Papa got encircled by people who were all saying as one: why do we need this most difficult campaign? You shall stay on for two more years .... later we will hold the elections calmly. All the democratic values will be preserved."[22] Korzhakov knew what others did not: Yeltsin was seriously ill. But the full weight of the idea to postpone the elections cannot be placed on Korzhakov's shoulders alone. At some point, it became Yeltsin's idea. He pushed forward a plan, in violation of the constitution, to dissolve the State Duma, the lower house of parliament, ban the Communist Party, and postpone the elections. "I had to take a radical step," Yeltsin said in his memoir, without really explaining why. "After the ban, the Communist Party would be finished forever in Russia," he recalled thinking at the time. But Yeltsin would undoubtedly be finished too, and his account leaves many questions unanswered about why he went so far with such a risky scheme. "I don't know whose crazy idea it was exactly," Berezovsky recalled, "but Korzhakov and the gang were very actively trying to bring it to life."[23]

On March 15, a Friday, the State Duma voted 250 to 98 for a nonbinding resolution to repeal the 1991 agreement at Belovezhskaya Pushcha. This was the agreement, after the failed coup, between Yeltsin and the leaders of Ukraine and Belarus. Meeting at a hunting resort outside Brest, they declared their own union, defying Gorbachev and triggering the end of the Soviet Union three weeks later. The Duma vote was a political statement, a bit of grandstanding by the newly elected Communists and nationalists. But to Korzhakov and his party of war, the vote was a perfect pretext to trigger dissolution of the Duma. Over the next two days, a hidden drama of extraordinary significance unfolded in the Kremlin. It was so secret that most journalists, including myself, had only a vague clue, until long after it was over, what had happened. I should have paid more attention to Yeltsin's reaction to the vote on Saturday. Yeltsin said the Duma had called into doubt its own legitimacy, as well as "the possibility of holding presidential elections." I didn't realize it at the time, but Yeltsin meant every word.

Early on Saturday morning, Yeltsin summoned Anatoly Kulikov, the interior minister, to the Kremlin. The barrel-chested Kulikov, inscrutable behind glasses with thick, tinted lenses, was an architect of the Chechen war and presided over a far-flung national police force, riddled with corruption. When he got to Yeltsin's office, he saw the Russian president "excited and agitated," he recalled. As soon as Kulikov sat down, Yeltsin told him he had decided to dissolve the Duma, ban the Communists, and put off the election. "I'm not going to tolerate it any more," Yeltsin said. "I need two years." Kulikov recalled that Yeltsin kept repeating, "I need two years." Yeltsin said the decree would be sent out in the afternoon.[24]

Kulikov, while promising to follow orders, asked for time to consider Yeltsin's plan. He said he would come back to Yeltsin at 5:00 P.M. He then had a cognac with Korzhakov and Soskovets, at Korzhakov's invitation, and realized, as they spoke "passionately," that they were architects of the idea to put off the elections. When Kulikov called around to the general prosecutor, Yuri Skuratov, and the chairman of the Constitutional Court, Vladimir Tumanov, he discovered Yeltsin had told each of them, untruthfully, that the other ones approved of his plan. Kulikov entered Yeltsin's study again at 5:00 P.M. and found the Russian president "morose, his face sallow." Kulikov expressed grave doubts about the plan, warning Yeltsin that if he went ahead it could lead to a "social explosion" in Russia, "and we did not have forces to manage the situation." For Yeltsin, this must have been an ominous warning, that the army and interior troops would not support him. Yeltsin, undeterred, ordered aides to prepare the decrees. Kulikov went to the Kremlin office where they were drafting the documents. He walked up to a window overlooking Red Square, which at about 6:00 P.M. was full of people strolling on the cobblestones.

"Don't you dare prepare this decree," Kulikov implored the aides. "See these people walking around? Tomorrow, after the decree is signed, fires will be burning here. And I don't know at what other places in Moscow, how many around the country. We don't have forces to keep the situation under control. This is the path to civil war."

Kulikov was summoned back to Yeltsin's study on Sunday morning at 6:00 A.M. He found Yeltsin even more somber, and tormented. To Kulikov's surprise, Yeltsin had also summoned the heads of the Moscow city and regional interior troops, who would have to handle any riots. One of them told Yeltsin that sixteen thousand troops were ready but another ten thousand to twelve thousand were needed. Kulikov noticed Yeltsin had a decree on his desk firing him. Unbowed, he protested once again that Yeltsin would ignite a civil war if he went ahead with his plan. Kulikov said the army might not stand behind Yeltsin; the prosecutor and chairman of the Constitutional Court also opposed the plan. Then Kulikov asked a question. Yeltsin wanted to ban the Communist Party. "Does anyone know where their headquarters is located?"

Yeltsin looked at the two Moscow interior chiefs. He asked the first one, then the second one, "Do you know where?"

"No," they admitted.

"I know where," said Mikhail Barsukov, head of the Federal Security Service and a crony of Korzhakov. Barsukov shuffled through some papers. "1 Okhotny Ryad," he announced. "The State Duma." Kulikov thought it was Barsukov's way of breaking the tension, a joke.

A long pause. "No one looked up; all sat silent," Kulikov recalled. "This was a very difficult period." He expected to be fired by Yeltsin at any minute. But after a long silence, Yeltsin said, "Right, certainly, they must be dispersed. I need two more years." Yeltsin also said, "Of course the only obstacle is the constitution." He then gave a signal, a hint, of uncertainty, Kulikov noticed. He said he would consult with others, including Luzhkov.

That morning at home, Yeltsin had also heard protests from his daughter, Dyachenko. "I told him that no one was going to understand him, that this meant losing everything that had been achieved with so much effort. But he was not taking my words seriously," she recalled.[25]

Berezovsky and Gusinsky had also picked up word of the plan through Kremlin leaks. "When we learned what was being prepared, we felt that the moment had arrived when we must try to prevent the situation through the mass media," Berezovsky said, "to make it public in order to oppose it." On Sunday, there were still hours to go before the evening broadcasts. Ilyushin, Yeltsin's loyal aide, had started leaking word of the dramatic plan to call off the elections to Gusinsky's NTV television channel. "We were getting information virtually live," Malashenko recalled. "Ilyushin was a very secretive guy, so, you know, to leak the information, it would mean the situation was disastrous, just disastrous. And he was leaking information to us."

Sergei Karaganov, deputy director of the Institute of Europe, also played a small role. Karaganov was one of the leading foreign policy analysts in Moscow. He served on the President's Council, a nearly defunct advisory panel to Yeltsin. The president paid heed when Karaganov wrote him a personal letter, warning that the West would not understand if he called off the election. Yeltsin would be isolated and cut off from the world.[26]

Finally, Dyachenko saw her father was "in the mood to take the final decision—a dangerous one, I fear." She called the one man who was fearless in the face of Yeltsin's immense power—Chubais, head of the analytical center and agent of the tycoons. She met Chubais at the Kremlin, took him into the president's reception room, and demanded a meeting with Papa. While Chubais waited outside, she went in and beseeched her father to listen to Chubais. "Papa said he did not want to listen to anyone. But he did not say that he had taken the final decision. I never kneeled in front of anybody, but here I was ready to fall to my knees and beg. Perhaps he sensed it," she recalled. Yeltsin agreed to see Chubais, who entered the room, and Dyachenko left. Later she recalled hearing shouting through the door. Yeltsin recalled that Chubais was red-faced.

"Boris Nikolayevich," Chubais began, "this is not 1993," when Yeltsin had faced off against a violent, rebellious parliament. "The difference between that moment and now is that now, the one who goes beyond the constitutional boundaries will fail first. It doesn't matter that the Communists were the ones to go out of bounds back in 1993. It's a crazy idea to get rid of the Communists in this way. The Communist ideology is in people's heads. A presidential decree can't put new heads on people. When we build a normal, strong, wealthy country, only then will we put an end to Communism. The elections cannot be postponed."

Yeltsin recalled they spoke for an hour. "I practically shouted, something I rarely do," he said. "And finally, I reversed a decision I had *almost* made."[27]

Chubais later recalled that at the end of the very heated argument, Yeltsin finally admitted it was wrong to postpone the elections. He turned to Chubais and said, "And you, Chubais, made many mistakes in privatization."[28]

At about 5:00 P.M. on Sunday, a bomb threat was ostensibly made against the Duma. The building was evacuated and surrounded by interior troops. This was the first cue in the plan to dissolve the Duma by force. But just as they had come, the troops left. The order came: Pull back to the barracks. Yeltsin did not pull the trigger. He later attributed his decision to the arguments of Chubais and his daughter. Now he had to fight for reelection and for that, his friends, the oligarchs, were still at his side. But it would also mean that, as Malashenko had warned him, he would have to work for it.

*

Yeltsin had to break out of the "Kremlin Wall" syndrome. He had to persuade voters that he was not a distant tsar. A trip to Krasnodar in southern Russia, set up by the Soskovets campaign group, was, typically, a public relations disaster. Yeltsin barely got close to any voters and was surrounded by cordons of security men and local *chinnovniki*, the bureaucrats.

Although Yeltsin did not know it, Shakhnovsky, now working for the Chubais analytical center, had secretly sent photographers to Krasnodar. They captured the sight of Yeltsin, miles away from the voters. Shakhnovsky told me he compared the photos with earlier pictures shot in 1991, showing Yeltsin plunging into welcoming crowds. When Malashenko showed Yeltsin the two sets of photographs, the president got the message. "I almost yelped in pain," Yeltsin said. "It made a strong impression on me. It had only been five years ago. I remembered how I felt back then when I met people and everything fell into place."[29]

Yeltsin realized he needed to wage a "real" campaign and get closer to the voters. The first thing he did was remove Soskovets from the campaign and put Chubais in control. Shakhnovsky took over the scheduling and Yeltsin hit the road, visiting two dozen cities in four months. In a scene that became part of the campaign lore, Yeltsin, energized by applause from young people at a rock concert in Rostov-on-Don, playfully danced onstage.

Yeltsin tried to edge aside Grigory Yavlinsky, the centrist leader of the Yabloko party, who was also running.[30] Yavlinsky refused to leave the race, but Yeltsin seized pride of place as the only real democratic and reform alternative to Zyuganov. Yeltsin's poll ratings began to climb into the teens in March, and by late April he was coming close to a neck-and-neck race with Zyuganov, who had crisscrossed the country with a droning, gloomy stump speech. On April 2 Yeltsin announced he was ordering the withdrawal of Russian troops from Chechnya, and soon he signed an agreement in the Kremlin with Chechen resistance leader Zelimkhan Yandarbiev. Yeltsin also made a quick visit to an airfield near Grozny. Although his actions did not stop the fighting, they gave Yeltsin a public relations boost.

The tycoons injected a strange twist to the campaign on April 27 in an open letter published in Russian newspapers. The letter, expressing alarm about a schism in Russian society, appealed to the military, businessmen, politicians, and opinion makers "to pool their efforts in searching for a political compromise," although Yeltsin and Zyuganov were not specifically mentioned. The letter, written in cautious and even obfuscatory terms, was largely critical of the Communists and in retrospect appears to be a tactical warning from the tycoons to Zyuganov not to rip Russian society apart, even as they were ripping him apart. The implicit message to Zyuganov was to keep things calm or else. The letter was signed by thirteen financiers and industrialists, Berezovsky first, including the rest of the group of seven, who were committed Yeltsin backers. "It was a kind of warning to Zyuganov and Korzhakov," Smolensky said. "We tried to get across the message that we shall slap anyone's hands if they try to break the democracy." In other words, this is our election, don't mess with it.

Yeltsin's political operatives had Zyuganov in their sights, but first they had to sell Yeltsin himself, and that was extraordinarily difficult. Paul Bograd, a political consultant, prepared a detailed look at the polls, which he submitted on April 25 to Chubais. Drawing on eighteen months of data, Bograd found the voters in a foul mood. "Sixty-five percent of all voters want to vote against President Yeltsin," he reported. "Sixty-five percent of voters do not want to vote for Zyuganov." He added, "The winner will be the candidate whom voters do not vote against."[31] Put simply, this political math meant that Yeltsin's campaign had to make him the lesser of two evils by discrediting Zyuganov. They had to create a black-and-white choice, which was not simple given the strong negative feelings about Yeltsin. Oslon, the Yeltsin campaign pollster, told me that an added danger zone for Yeltsin was his health—if people saw he was frail, his support would crumble.

The kinder, gentler campaign for Yeltsin was born in a brainstorming session at Video International, one of the two major television advertising firms in Moscow at the time. The leader of the team was Mikhail Margelov, a strapping, worldly, ambitious young man who came from a family of military and intelligence officers. Margelov taught Arabic language at the KGB's Higher School, a training academy for spies, and later worked for the official news agency Tass. But in the 1990s he plunged into the capitalist pursuits of advertising and public relations. Video International made a pitch to the Chubais team on how to sell Boris Yeltsin to the skeptical Russian public. Margelov recalled, "Our starting point was, Yeltsin is president. He is ruling the country. He has made very many mistakes. People who loved him in 1989–1990 do not love him now."[32] The result was a nationwide television advertising blitz in which Yeltsin did not appear, except in the very last spot. Instead, elderly people, veterans, and working-class voters offered soft and fuzzy testimonials for the Russian leader. Most of the subjects in the ads were closer to the profile of Communist supporters but said they were voting for Yeltsin. The theme of the spots was "Choose with Your Heart," an attempt to open the door to votes for Yeltsin while sidestepping economics, crime, ideology, and thorny issues that might remind voters of why they disliked Yeltsin. Margelov recalled that he made one commercial showing a sailor promising to vote for Yeltsin, despite the fact he had not been paid in months. But the commercial was discarded at the last minute—no one would believe it.

Yeltsin was above the fray in his advertising, cast as the guarantor of stability, a father figure. "Maybe it sounds even idiotic to the Western mentality," Margelov said of the "Choose with Your Heart" campaign slogan, "but for the Russian mentality it sounds quite natural." Dyachenko brought Margelov a box of Yeltsin family photos. He selected some of the best, and they became the centerpiece of the final commercial in the set: Yeltsin narrating his own family history. Against sentimental music in the background, Yeltsin's voice reminisced about his mother's hotcakes, and the photos showed him as a young man, trim, with a thick pompadour of black hair—an athlete, a rebel, a father and grandfather. Finally, an older, puffy Yeltsin, seated in a beige chair and wearing an open-necked white shirt, came before the camera and offered sympathy for the pain his countrymen had felt in recent years. "Not a person in the country has had it easy," he said. The closing slogan was, "We Trust, We Believe, We Hope."

Alexei Levinson, a specialist in Western-style "focus groups," using test groups to evaluate products or ads, told me such powerful television advertising appeared in Russia for the first time during the 1996 campaign. "For many Russians, advertising is a new thing, only two or three years old. There's hardly a kid who—like you in America—knew advertising from childhood. And for adults it is still something they are not accustomed to.

"Those who were least likely to vote for Yeltsin were over fifty, but they were also the most affected by commercials," he said. "They were the most vulnerable to the commercials. They also hated them the most. It wasn't simple. The trick in the commercials was that the people in them were 100 percent Zyuganov-type voters. You look at a person talking about the hardships of life, not necessarily linked to Communist rule, and all of a sudden he says, 'Let's vote for Yeltsin.' It made a mishmash of their brains."[33]

In Moscow, which had one of the most proreform electorates in the country, Luzhkov was a powerful engine for Yeltsin's reelection campaign. Luzhkov appeared on thousands of billboards around the city, shaking Yeltsin's hand in endorsement. He stood shoulder to shoulder with Yeltsin at a final concert in Red Square before the vote, leading the cheers. Yeltsin's natural base was among young people, and Lisovsky, who had begun his career staging concerts in Soviet times, approached MTV about an appearance by Yeltsin similar to the one President Clinton made in 1992. Back then, MTV staged a highly successful youth get-out-the-vote campaign called "Choose or Lose." Clinton's appearance on MTV was rewarded by a strong showing among young voters. But this time MTV was nervous about Yeltsin's apparent weakness and refused to cooperate, giving Lisovsky three videocassettes of the Clinton appearance and telling him they wanted nothing to do with Yeltsin. Lisovsky modeled "Vote or Lose," Yeltsin's youth campaign, on the MTV idea, including dozens of concerts across the country that spring. But the Yeltsin campaign concluded it was not enough to recast Yeltsin in soft focus. It was not enough for Yeltsin to dance on stage.

They had to destroy Zyuganov.

The front page of the newspaper held a startling photograph. Rations of sausage were curled on newspapers and set out on the floor. Everyone who saw the picture instantly recognized the scene from the past—the scramble for a piece of sausage, the lines, the shortages, the Soviet life. It was the sixth issue of a newspaper with a circulation of 10 million—more than twice that of Russia's best-selling weekly *Argumenty i Fakty*—that materialized in mailboxes and at public gathering places across Russia in April, May, and June 1996. In bold letters across the top, the newspaper was called *Ne Dai Bog!* (God forbid!), and it was one of the most successful tools in Yeltsin's negative campaign against Zyuganov. *Ne Dai Bog!* was an unrelenting, cleverly written crusade against Communism, and it was especially aimed at the provinces outside of Moscow, where Zyuganov was running stronger than Yeltsin, and where the transition to the market economy had been the most difficult. Every issue of the paper carried biting articles, lavish color photos, and illustrations to drive home the message that Zyuganov would take the country backward. In the sixth issue, the front page carried a faked transcript of a supposed secret Communist Party meeting. "We blurted it out!" read the headline. "We will not be able to give the people anything that we promised." In an earlier edition, featuring a children's essay contest, one child wrote: "Russia is my home, my fortress. But if Communists come to power—my coffin."

The newspaper was secretly created and published by Yeltsin's campaign. It was among the many different "black" propaganda ploys—disinformation, dirty tricks, paid newspaper articles, unsigned advertising, falsified documents—used to carry out the attack on Zyuganov. In another example, a million small posters were printed showing a glowering, threatening Zyuganov and the words: "Buy food—It could be your last chance!" The posters were adhesive backed and difficult to remove. They were stuck on food store windows all across Russia, a blatant scare tactic. The Yeltsin campaign never admitted they were behind it, but they were.

The campaign also mixed the technology of black propaganda with the reach and credibility of the mainstream news media. Journalists told my colleague Lee Hockstader that the Yeltsin campaign lavished hundreds of thousands of dollars on them for favorable coverage, mostly to drive home the anti-Communist attack on Zyuganov. The payoffs ranged from thousands of dollars a month for a top reporter to just a hundred dollars to a freelance journalist. The bribes and payoffs were especially welcome at struggling newspapers and media outlets, where salaries were low.

Even without the dirty tricks and bribes, Yeltsin reaped a huge wave of support among Russian journalists in the campaign against Zyuganov. Many honest and reputable reporters threw themselves into the task of defeating Zyuganov out of genuine fear about the return of Communism. They completely shared Berezovsky's views, expressed to me right after the election. "It's not an election as normal," Berezovsky said. "It's not an election of the kind you have in the United States. It's not Republicans versus Democrats. It was a situation where we had to choose between two systems."

Berezovsky and Gusinsky devoted their powerful television channels to reelecting Yeltsin, and the third channel, RTR, was state-owned and easily manipulated by the Kremlin. The result was blanket coverage favorable to Yeltsin. In the five weeks before the June 16 first-round vote, Yeltsin received three times more airtime on prime-time news programs than his rival.[34]

The pro-Yeltsin bias came not only because the oligarchs ordered it, but also because journalists willingly joined them in the crusade. Yeltsin went so far in his memoirs as to claim that Malashenko "created a firm vertical chain of command for work with the television reporters and journalists." In reality, this did not happen because it wasn't necessary—the journalists willingly entered the Kremlin corral.

Among the television channels, ORT was sympathetic to Yeltsin, as Berezovsky had promised it would be. But Gusinsky's NTV, born in the crucible of the Chechen war the previous year, earned a reputation for standing up to the Kremlin. Now, in a different situation, NTV shifted and went over to Yeltsin's side. Dobrodeyev, who with Kiselyov and Gusinsky had founded the channel, recalled later that he backed Yeltsin instinctively, without hesitation, because of his memories of the Soviet years. "For people of my generation, it was a matter of principle," he said.

Kiselyov had also been in Davos and shared the anxiety of the tycoons when he saw Western businessmen rubbing elbows with Zyuganov. The election "wasn't a choice of supporting George Bush or Al Gore. It was a different choice, in a politicized society in transition, with an economic crisis that was not yet over, and with all the problems including Chechnya that we had." In the months before the election, Kiselyov found that "rank-and-file correspondents, producers, reporters, news readers, all of them were enthusiastically and wholeheartedly supporting Yeltsin, with all the drawbacks, with all the understanding of his illness, his drinking habits, of his personality deteriorating, all of us understood that—we thought he was a better choice than Zyuganov."

After the fact, Gusinsky concluded that he had made a fundamental mistake in cooperating so closely with Yeltsin in 1996 because the Kremlin got the idea that the news media—including his cherished NTV—could be treated like an obedient puppy. The flirtation with power took an immense toll on Gusinsky later on. But at the time, it seemed the right thing to do. "The fact is, we stirred hysteria and scared ourselves," Gusinsky recalled. "We had no political experience.

And we all decided that we had a mission to prevent the arrival of the Communists. And journalists decided that if the Communists came, that would be the end. They were defending themselves, you see. They were not electing Yeltsin; they were defending themselves and their right to do their job."

"The people who worked for the mass media, 90 percent were democrats. It was not paid for!" Berezovsky insisted. "It was their own opinions."

In this atmosphere, the news media became a tool of the Yeltsin campaign. Even the worst of the "black" propaganda made it into the mainstream press. An example came just days before the first round of the election. On June 8, *Nezavisimaya Gazeta,* Berezovsky's newspaper, published a lengthy, alarmist article asserting that the Communists would not accept defeat peacefully. The article was a fabrication from the "black" side of the Yeltsin campaign. It claimed to reveal top-secret intelligence reports that Zyuganov was "losing control." It claimed that radicals inside the party were preparing, through an elaborate eight-step plan, to seize power after the election, since they could no longer win it through democracy. The whole document was intended to raise fears about Zyuganov, and publication in *Nezavisimaya Gazeta* was just the first step. Next it became presidential ammunition.

Yeltsin gave a preelection interview to Kiselyov. The interview, broadcast on June 9, was taped earlier in a spacious, imperial-style room in the Kremlin, with Yeltsin in a dark gray suit, his hair brilliant white, sitting close to a round table in a pink-upholstered, gilded chair. "Boris Nicholayevich," Kiselyov asked in his slow, trademark voice, "tell me please, there is only one week left to the elections. Do you have fears that there can be some unexpected unpleasantness, provocations, attempts to do something to disrupt the elections?"

Yeltsin replied that he just happened to read an article about that in the newspaper. "When an enemy, or a rival to be precise, loses confidence—and he is losing confidence now . . . you must expect that he will attempt to stir up the situation," he said. The message was that Zyuganov equals instability. The fabricated memo was now transformed by Yeltsin into something real.

In the final weeks of the campaign, the oligarchs also lent a hand to Alexander Lebed, the gruff, deep-voiced, charismatic former general who was also running for president. The Lebed gambit was intended to help Yeltsin by further eroding Zyuganov's support. Berezovsky's television channel aired a five-minute video portraying Lebed as a born leader, "one of us," like Yeltsin. Berezovsky told me he also held long talks with Lebed, who "reflects the problems and doubts" of ordinary Russians. Vinogradov said his bank, Inkombank, took it upon itself to finance Lebed's campaign but coordinated it with the Chubais headquarters. "Lebed did everything we told him to," Vinogradov said. Vinogradov estimated he spent $10 million to support Lebed's campaign.[35]

The Yeltsin campaign had an official budget of $3 million under campaign rules. But it spent many millions—perhaps $100 million or more—for the "black" propaganda, for the printing of *Ne Dai Bog!*, for the "Buy Food" posters, for payoffs to journalists, for personalized letters sent through the mail to every veteran of World War II, and for many other hidden campaign activities. The campaign headquarters was awash in cash. A friend of mine stumbled onto a youth campaign workers' conference at the Hotel Orlyonok, near Sparrow Hills. During the three-day affair, youth leaders were called one by one to a separate suite used by the chairman. There they were each handed a sack of cash.

Who paid for it all? Every journalist has a moment when his cumulative experience becomes a blindfold—mine came on the issue of the campaign financing. After years of watching American politics, where businessmen always make hefty contributions to candidates, it seemed perfectly natural to me to assume that the Russian tycoons bankrolled Yeltsin's campaign. My impressions were reinforced by the details I already knew of the tycoons' interest-free loan to Chubais.

But the deep, dark, dirty secret of the 1996 Yeltsin campaign was different. As I should have known, the tycoons didn't pay, they got paid. They delivered to Yeltsin their best brains and their airwaves, and they bankrolled Chubais. But when it came to big money, to the tens of millions of dollars needed to stage Yeltsin's reelection campaign, the flow of money was not from the oligarchs to Yeltsin, but from the state to the oligarchs.

They did not use government money directly. Rather, with help from the campaign headquarters, they created a hidden scheme in which they obtained government bonds cheaply. The bonds were deliberately sold to the tycoons' banks at a deep discount. Then the banks could resell the bonds at a market price, raising quick cash, which they were then supposed to spend for campaign activities. How much they actually spent for Yeltsin and how much they pocketed will never be known. The details were so secret that even five years after the fact, many people still refused to talk about it, but I am confident that the scheme existed. A top campaign official told me that the oligarchs could not spare tens of millions of dollars at the time. Instead, they laundered cash by buying and reselling the government's own bonds. Precisely how they got the bonds is a mystery. Another source who directly participated said: "It goes without saying that no one was giving away money for nothing. That is all I want to say on this subject. Do you understand? Your information is correct." The most likely source of the river of laundered money was the government's dollar-denominated bonds known as MinFins, because they were issued by the Ministry of Finance. In May 1996, the Ministry of Finance issued the sixth in a series of MinFin bonds, $1.75 billion worth of financial certificates. Financial specialists told me it would not have been difficult for the government to parcel out some the bonds to favored banks.[36] The scheme had a certain elegance because the tycoons were not sucking money directly from the budget. Rather, they were finagling an asset cheaply—the government bonds—and selling them dearly. It was just like their past deals, importing computers, exporting oil, and speculating on the ruble-dollar exchange rate. The Yeltsin reelection campaign was financed with easy money. Satarov, the Yeltsin aide, later said in an NTV documentary about the election, "Let us not be naive, let us understand that black cash is turned over in our elections all the time, by everybody."[37]

Vinogradov, who had been at Davos and attended the meeting with Yeltsin in March, nonetheless was something of an outsider among the tycoons. He refused to participate in the ORT consortium and did not win any loans for shares auctions. He claimed that he also got left out when the MinFin loot was distributed. "When the register was written, who was to get what at MinFin, they didn't write anything next to our bank," he said. Vinogradov said $100 million was spent from the scheme on Yeltsin's campaign and $200 million stolen, although precise figures are hard to find. "This was a very large business, black business," he said. "After the election there were informal lists of who stole how much. It was written there how much Smolensky stole, how much Khodorkovsky stole, how much Berezovsky got. He got the largest share."[38]

Chubais oversaw the campaign's treasury, other campaign workers told me. When I asked him about it, he immediately recalled happily discovering a stack of *Ne Dai Bog!* newspapers at home, years later, reading them over again with great pleasure. "But it wasn't for free," he said. "It cost money, serious money." When I pressed him where the money came from, Chubais dodged the question. "Whether there had been some financial schemes, giving them an opportunity to receive certain privileges, or whether there had been no such schemes, I am not ready to answer," he said. "I am not ready to either confirm or deny it."

Konstantin Kagalovsky, a well-informed political operative who helped Khodorkovsky win the loans for shares auction for Yukos, wrote a newspaper article several years later expressing chagrin at the financing of Yeltsin's reelection campaign. Kagalovsky said no one in Russia believed the oligarchs used their own money to finance the Yeltsin campaign. Rather, they were used for their "technical" abilities—a reference, I think, to the scheme for reprocessing the bonds. Then Kagalovsky added, "Such a mechanism for financing the elections is called 'corruption in defense of democracy.'" Chubais, he said, "can deservedly be considered the founder of this system of 'corruption in defense of democracy.'" He added that it became the norm under Yeltsin in the following years. "Once you try it, you like it," Kagalovsky wrote.[39]

It is an oversimplification to say that Yeltsin won the election because of *Ne Dai Bog!* or because of the overwhelming support of journalists or secret deals by bankers. No amount of campaign dirty tricks, advertising, and airtime can change the fact that Yeltsin won the election because of a profound choice Russian voters faced. For all their flaws, Yeltsin and Zyuganov represented two opposing visions of Russia's future. Zyuganov did not really understand, nor want to take, the path of market capitalism, which was still fragile in Russia. Yeltsin was barely capable of building that capitalism, but he was committed to the notion of it. Russian voters were only four years away from the memory of empty store shelves. My own travels at the time suggested that the best way to understand why Yeltsin won was to ask voters whether, and how, they had adapted to the new life of the 1990s, especially the economy. Millions of pensioners and elderly had not adapted—and voted for Zyuganov. But millions of younger people had adapted, and I think there was just barely a critical mass of them by June 16, 1996. One day during the campaign, in the Volga River city of Nizhny Novgorod, I interviewed a bright young banker, Sergei Kiriyenko, who was then thirty-four years old. He told me, "We are in the middle of raging river rapids. We can go back. Or we can stubbornly go ahead. In the worst case, if we go back, we will lose everything we have already gained." Yeltsin, he added, "is going to the other shore, where I want to go."

To get to the other shore, Yeltsin also needed the oligarchs—he needed their March "wake-up call," their media bullhorns, their talented staff, and their money-laundering abilities. They helped amplify his message, discredit Zyuganov, and bring off a victory. The oligarchs saved Yeltsin to save themselves, and he allowed them to do it. Both also believed they were saving Russian capitalism, and they were. Yeltsin won 35.28 percent of the first-round vote, to 32.03 for Zyuganov, 14.52 percent for Lebed, and 7.34 percent for Yavlinsky. The results forced Yeltsin and Zyuganov into a second-round runoff. Yeltsin fired his unpopular defense minister and gave a new Kremlin post to Lebed in order to attract more voters to his side. The campaign staff began planning for a vigorous final assault that included a heavy schedule for Yeltsin. Then Yeltsin's roller-coaster ride of 1996 took another terrifying nosedive.

Four days after the vote, two campaign officials left the Russian White House at about 5:20 P.M. The first to walk out was Lisovsky, the entertainment and advertising mogul, who was carrying a Xerox box wrapped in white twine. He was stopped at guardhouse 2, a small structure through which visitors enter and exit the fenced compound. The guards asked Lisovsky if he had a pass for the box. He did not. They asked to see the box.

At that moment, a final, climactic confrontation between Chubais and Korzhakov began. For months, ever since Yeltsin had decided to go ahead with the elections, Korzhakov had been growing increasingly restive. In early May, Korzhakov admitted to a reporter for the *Observer* of London that he wanted to call off the elections, and Yeltsin quickly put him in his place.[40] Yeltsin said Korzhakov would stick to his duties as a bodyguard, and the campaign would go on.

Korzhakov knew the Chubais team was carrying big money around in gym bags and suitcases; in fact, his presidential guards were also ferrying around cash, "driving money around the whole country in suitcases."[41] The argument with Chubais was, in fact, about more than campaign money. Korzhakov said he saw himself as a champion of "Russia and the state," and his rivals as "a camp of those who wanted to sell and rob this Russia." The Chubais group saw the opposite: Korzhakov as a power-crazed reactionary who did not understand democracy or capitalism.

Korzhakov set a trap for the Chubais group. The details of the trap remain partly obscure, but the existence of a trap is not in dispute. Korzhakov and one of his deputies, Valery Streletsky, later boasted they had engineered the net. Streletsky has claimed he bugged the room where Chubais aides kept the cash in the Russian White House and lay in wait for someone to come for it.[42] Lisovsky told me that Korzhakov's team had been planning the trap for two months.[43] Yeltsin said in his memoir it was Korzhakov's "final counterstrike." The chief of the presidential bodyguards "had been spoiling for a scandal, and now he had found one."

The box contained $500,000 in neatly wrapped U.S. dollars. Minutes after Lisovsky was arrested, Yevstafiev, the Chubais aide, walked out of the White House and into the same guardhouse. "I saw people standing with Sergei [Lisovsky] with guns," he recalled. Yevstafiev added that he heard someone tell Lisovsky to take the box, that Lisovsky was bending over and Yevstafiev warned him not to touch it. Yevstafiev was also detained. Both men were taken to closed rooms, their mobile telephones were taken away, and Streletsky's men began to interrogate them.

When both Yevstafiev and Lisovsky disappeared, the campaign headquarters started looking for them. Yevstafiev had left word with his office that he was going to the White House and would be back in an hour. When he failed to return, they grew worried. They found him under armed guard—by Korzhakov's men. "The men with guns had the order to shoot if necessary," Yevstafiev recalled. They offered to give him an injection for "high blood pressure," which he firmly refused, suspecting it was something else.

About an hour later, a third man, Boris Lavrov, a commercial banker, was found in the room with the safe by the Korzhakov guards and was questioned also. He had another $38,850 in his briefcase. He told interrogators that Lisovsky had come to the room with Yevstafiev, and that Lisovsky took the box with the $500,000 and signed a receipt for it.[44]

The tycoons and campaign staff were already gathering for a previously scheduled meeting at Berezovsky's Logovaz Club that evening. But as they pulled up to the building on Novokuznetskaya Street, they were under a watchful eye. Korzhakov had put the building under conspicuous surveillance from unmarked cars and rooftops. Zverev, the Gusinsky lobbyist, recalled that the campaign constantly worried about Korzhakov. "We had the impression something was going to happen," he said.[45] Still, Chubais wasn't sure Korzhakov would go so far as to arrest his campaign staff. "Until the last moment, I couldn't believe that Yevstafiev was arrested," he recalled later. "It seemed absolutely impossible to me."

Once again, Chubais exhibited nerves of steel. From Berezovsky's elegantly appointed mansion, he picked up the phone. It was now late in the evening. He could not reach Korzhakov, and Yeltsin was asleep and could not be awakened. His anger rising by the minute, Chubais finally reached Barsukov, the head of the Federal Security Service. Barsukov was a weak figure who had been overpromoted by his pal, Korzhakov.

"I told him I would destroy him," Chubais said. "I promised him that. I would destroy him if a single hair fell from Yevstafiev's head." Unexpectedly, Barsukov quickly backpedaled. "He was saying, 'It was no big deal, we are holding him temporarily, another thirty minutes, then everything will be all right. Just don't worry.'"[46]

Kiselyov, the NTV founder and anchor, got a call at home and was told by Malashenko to rush to the television studio and "be prepared to stay on the air throughout the night." Malashenko was both Kiselyov's colleague as president of NTV and Yeltsin's campaign media boss. NTV went on the air after midnight with news of the arrest, portraying it as a trap set by Korzhakov. Kiselyov appeared, announcing an "emergency" news bulletin, and reminded viewers that Korzhakov had admitted in May he wanted to call off the elections. "It looks like the country is on the brink of a political catastrophe," Kiselyov said. "I would like to wish you a good night, but I cannot."[47]

The final countdown had begun: one group or the other was going to be sacked in the morning. Kiselyov then went to the Logovaz Club, where he found anxiety rising. Gusinsky, Berezovsky, Chubais, Zverev, Yumashev, Dyachenko, and the liberal governor of Nizhny Novgorod, Boris Nemtsov, all milled about. Zverev said, "I went away to destroy some documents because there could be some arrests that night."

"Everyone understood," Kiselyov said, "that tomorrow morning,

Korzhakov would go to Yeltsin and say, 'Look, Boris Nikolayevich, these guys whom you trust so much are crooks. They are stealing money, in cash, from under your nose. They are just bringing it in empty Xerox boxes from the very building where the government sits, and you have to decide, finally, who you trust."[48] That was, in fact, exactly the Korzhakov plan.

"Everybody was very frightened," Kiselyov recalled. "It's not as if people were trembling—no one said it openly, no one confessed—but I had a feeling that some of the people gathered in the Logovaz mansion were afraid to leave. They were thinking, I could be arrested." Kiselyov said that Dyachenko's presence through the night gave them confidence that they were safe, inside the Logovaz Club at least. "Korzhakov would not dare" storm the building with Dyachenko inside, he assumed.

But even as they waited anxiously in the Logovaz Club, Gusinsky and Berezovsky had in their hands a weapon more powerful than Korzhakov's presidential guards. Their television station broadcasts in the middle of the night had electrified the political elite in Moscow and underscored how close the oligarchs had bound themselves to Chubais and Yeltsin. The campaign staff, the businessmen, and the broadcasters were all on the same team.

At 1:00 A.M., after Chubais reached him by phone, Lebed tried to call Korzhakov and Barsukov on a special top-secret Kremlin phone system, S-1 and S-2. No answer. Lebed then deployed his cannon-sized voice and vivid vocabulary on behalf of the Chubais team in a televised statement. "Attempts are being made to wreck the second round; that is my first impression," Lebed said. "Any mutiny will be crushed and crushed with extreme severity. Those who want to throw the country into the abyss of bloody chaos deserve no mercy at all." Lisovsky and Yevstafiev were released about 3:00 A.M., after ten hours of interrogation. Their captors were unnerved by the television broadcasts. Chubais later told me that television proved to be the key element in the whole affair.

The race was on to get to Yeltsin, but he slept through the night, hearing about the confrontation only in the morning from his daughter. Bleary-eyed, the Chubais team gathered at an office in the tower where Gusinsky had his corporate headquarters. Just outside was the parking lot where Korzhakov had forced Gusinsky's men to lie facedown in the snow. It was decided that only Chubais could persuade

Yeltsin to save them, just as Chubais had talked Yeltsin out of canceling the election two months earlier. Chubais had reached Yeltsin in the morning on a phone with a direct line to the Kremlin.

"When I talked to him on the phone, he said nothing terrible had happened," Chubais remembered, "that people had tried to steal money, but everything was in order now. 'We won't allow anyone to steal money. Don't worry. Everything is all right.' I told him that no, it wasn't all right, that the situation was absolutely catastrophic, and I absolutely had to meet with him. He really didn't like that. Nevertheless, he set up a time."

Edgy and exhausted, the Chubais team felt the outcome was wildly unpredictable. Quite possibly, they were losing out to Korzhakov. They would be fired from the campaign, arrested, and jailed. But they were cheered up when Yumashev made a surprising guess about what Yeltsin would do. "Boris Nikolayevich is going to fire Korzhakov," he predicted. "I don't know why, but I have known Yeltsin for a long time." The others were startled. "Many of us were so tired that we were not quite aware of what was happening around us," Kiselyov recalled, but Yumashev's statement made an impression on everyone. Zverev told me, "Yumashev whispered, 'He's going to fire them.' We were shocked. No one believed him because we were sure that *we* were going to be fired."

Chubais went to see Chernomyrdin, who had cautiously kept his distance from the warring camps. Chubais came out with all guns blazing. This was a do-or-die situation, he screamed at the Russian prime minister. Chernomyrdin kept very quiet. "I simply told him that the time had come to say his word," Chubais recalled. "He had kept quiet for five years, and now it was, either say everything in an hour, or you will be destroyed tonight. There was no middle ground left, no middle whatsoever. You have two hours. If after this you don't go to the president, and don't say it is either 'me or them,' you are a piece of shit. You don't exist any longer."

Chubais next bumped into Chernomyrdin a few hours later in the anteroom of Yeltsin's office. Chernomyrdin looked at Chubais and reported, "I've said it all to him."

When he entered Yeltsin's office, Chubais felt weak-kneed. "I felt that I wouldn't be able to convince him, and that the situation was almost hopeless; there were no chances." He feared Yeltsin would brush off the conflict as a small misunderstanding, as he had earlier in the day.

It is not known what happened in the meeting, but the result was that Yeltsin decided to fire Korzhakov, Barsukov, and Soskovets, the entire "party of war." Yeltsin went before the television cameras to make the announcement. "All the time I am being reproached for Barsukov, Korzhakov, and Soskovets," Yeltsin said in a somber monotone. "Does the president work for them? They began to take too much on themselves and give too little."

"It was a stunning episode," Kiselyov recalled. After making his statement, the gray-faced Yeltsin looked at the assembled journalists and beamed broadly. "So what? Why are you staying? You should be rushing to the telephones to announce the breaking news!" Kiselyov saw a flash of the spunky old Yeltsin.

Chubais, triumphant, immediately called a news conference at the Radisson-Slavyanskaya Hotel. He denounced the arrests the night before at the White House as an attempt to wreck the campaign. When asked about the box of money, Chubais threw up a smoke screen. "I am firmly convinced," he said, "that the so-called box of money is one of the traditional elements in a traditional KGB, Soviet-style provocation, of which we have very great experience in our country." Chubais suggested the money had been planted. "We are well aware of how foreign currency, money, used to be planted on Russian dissidents and not just on them, and recently we saw a similar situation when drugs were planted. It is, unfortunately, a demonstration of the methods that have become almost commonplace again for Barsukov and Korzhakov, and I am sure this provocation, this falsification, will soon be completely dispelled officially by the bodies of law and order." Chubais was not asked further about the money.[49] In an interview with Chubais that evening on NTV, Kiselyov did not once inquire about the box of money.

Five days later, disaster struck Yeltsin again.

At Video International, preparing for an intense second-round campaign, Mikhail Margelov recalled that the company's president, Mikhail Lesin, returned from a meeting of the campaign headquarters with bad news. "It seems that we will have to work during the second round in a difficult situation," he said.

"What do you mean?" Margelov inquired.

"We will work with the absence of the client," Lesin said.

"Can we ask more questions?" Margelov said.

"No."

Yeltsin's busy travel schedule was canceled. His aides said he had a cold. "The president is in good form," said his press secretary, Sergei Medvedev.

On June 26, Yeltsin had come home at about 5:00 P.M. While resting briefly in an armchair, he suffered a major heart attack. His doctor was nearby and he was treated immediately. Yeltsin recalled in his memoir how the Kremlin doctors had been trailing him throughout the campaign, warning of the consequences of his intensive activity. Now the stress and strain had caught up with him. "The pain sliced through me, an enormous crushing pain," he recalled.

The heart attack posed an extremely delicate problem for the campaign. Oslon's polls showed that if the public knew Yeltsin was in ill health, he would lose support. The polls showed Yeltsin's poll rating was slipping one-half to one percentage point each day. The campaign staff had prepared a huge finale of Yeltsin appearances across the country, and all the events would have to be canceled.

"We also had to try to prevent any leaks about my illness and hold back information from everyone," Yeltsin recalled. On the weekend before the July 3 vote, Yeltsin taped a preelection address to the country. A camera crew came to Barvikha, the presidential rest home just outside Moscow. Then the tape was brought back to Video International for editing. One of the cameramen told Margelov to be prepared for a shock. The old man was in very bad shape.

"It was quite obvious that it was very difficult for Yeltsin to speak," Margelov said of the tape, which he saw in its raw form. "He was sweating all the time. It was difficult even to pronounce words. Sometimes he couldn't finish the sentence. Sometimes it was difficult for him to even breathe."

The video specialists then carried out an amazing reconstruction. Using digital editing technology, they spliced and retouched the entire short speech. "It was serious work to make it look nice," Margelov told me. "Not many people could see that something was wrong." The precarious health of the president was covered up on the eve of the vote. My own impression of the tape, the night I saw it on television, was that Yeltsin seemed wooden, and the tape was jerky. But to millions of people, that was hardly a clue that he had just suffered a major heart attack.

"We were absolutely sure we were doing the right thing," Margelov said. "No, there were no moral questions during the second round: are we deceiving somebody or not? Because I think the goal was quite obvious. Not one of us wanted the Communists back." Then the tycoons delivered their final election gift to Yeltsin: they broadcast the doctored tape and didn't say a word about Yeltsin's heart attack. Malashenko was present when the videotape was made. "What could I do?" Malashenko said. "He was very sick at the moment. The only thing I did to protect my conscience, I didn't tell anything to my colleagues. The sin was fully on me. Journalists were never aware" of it. "And I just had to do my job as a member of the election campaign. And my position was very simple. I made the statement publicly more than once that I prefer Yeltsin's corpse to Zyuganov. Unfortunately. That was my choice."

The deception continued on Election Day. Yeltsin cast his ballot at a polling place in Barvikha. Kremlin video cameras showed Yeltsin standing and at one point flashing his familiar wry smile. But the videotape was edited—to delete the two white-coated doctors standing nearby. That would have been a clue that something was amiss, a risk that Yeltsin and his campaign did not want to take.

On July 3, Yeltsin was elected with 53.82 percent of the vote to 40.31 percent for Zyuganov, and 4.83 percent "against all." The Davos Pact succeeded, and Chubais was euphoric. In a press conference on July 5, Chubais compared Yeltsin to Peter the Great, Russia's foremost westernizer, and announced that Russia's post-Communist path was irrevocable. "Irrevocable. Russian democracy is irrevocable; private ownership in Russia is irrevocable; market reforms in the Russian state are irrevocable."

Berezovsky was also feeling expansive. Just after the election, he made a single comment that came to crystallize the power and reach of the Russian oligarchy. In a postelection interview, Berezovsky told the *Financial Times* that the seven tycoons controlled about 50 percent of the Russian economy. Berezovsky overstated their economic prowess, but he was more than correct about their political influence. They had arrived at the definition of an oligarchy—they were rich and powerful kingmakers.

The seven met after the election to decide which of them should go into the government. Chubais said they could appoint one of their own as a deputy prime minister under Chernomyrdin. The embrace of wealth and power was now complete, and it was time to sort out the loot.

In earlier years, when the moguls gathered to talk or make deals, when they dined in the villa on Sparrow Hills, or when they entered the Kremlin to warn Yeltsin, they were largely hidden from public view. But in the autumn of 1996, it was no longer possible to conceal their ambition and their presence in the highest councils of the state. They worried, among themselves, about a backlash. Five of them had parents, either one or both, who were Jewish: Gusinsky, Berezovsky, Friedman, Smolensky, and Khodorkovsky. Gusinsky was elected president of the Russian Jewish Congress in January 1996 and was making business deals in Israel. Individually, some of them had brushed up against anti-Semitism in earlier years, but now, as a group, they began to fret about the possibility of a public reaction to the "Jewish bankers." The spiteful words were already on the lips of some nationalists and reactionaries. Berezovsky told me at the time, "Of course anti-Semitism exists today in Russia. And it exists today not only in closed form, as it existed in the Soviet Union, but in open form as well." The earthy Smolensky said the oligarchs knew they fanned resentment and envy, recalling a popular saying, "If there is no water in your faucet, it is the Jews who have drunk it."

Partly out of fear of stirring up more public emotions, the group settled on Potanin as their man in government because he was not Jewish. Soon, however, Berezovsky went into government as well. On October 29, he was appointed deputy secretary of the Kremlin Security Council and given responsibility for working out a settlement in Chechnya. The appointment was followed by the disclosure in *Izvestia* that Berezovsky held an Israeli passport. Under Russian law, he could not hold dual citizenship and work in a sensitive government post, and the news triggered howls of protest from nationalists and Communists in parliament. Berezovsky responded to the disclosure with clumsy explanations. He said he had only visited Israel twice, once for three days and once for six days, and the last time was in 1994. He feigned ignorance of whether he had formally been given Israeli citizenship. "I started the formalities; I did not bring the process to the end," he said in a television interview with Kiselyov. "When the question arose of my citizenship, the hitch was that I did not know what the situation actually was."[50] In fact, he was an Israeli citizen, and he had his citizenship annulled to take the Security Council post.

The Davos Pact solidified Berezovsky's convictions that wealth should dictate to power. In his view, the tycoons were the best and brightest of their generation. Just as they had made fortunes in the new system through skill and foresight, he said, they also proved brilliant political kingmakers in the election. The people who served in government should listen carefully. "Strong capital—strong country," Berezovsky declared.

"From my point of view, in general, power and capital are inseparable," Berezovsky told me in December. Then he paused. Berezovsky, in a business suit and crisp white shirt and tie, was speaking in a small hideaway office at the Logovaz Club. He rethought what he had just said and offered a modification. "I think that two types of power are possible," he said. "Either a power of ideology or a power of capital. Ideology is now dead." The new power was capital. "I think that if something is advantageous to capital, it goes without saying that it is advantageous to the nation." In other words, the oligarchs would show Russia the way.

Berezovsky swiveled in his chair slightly, and an aide brought a cellular telephone for a quick conversation. He resumed the interview in a philosophical mood that reflected the thrill of the election victory, a sense that he had done everything right, a feeling of enormous satisfaction at the rise of the oligarchs. He had lived through a revolutionary time, Berezovsky reflected; Russia was passing through a stormy, violent upheaval in which public property was passing into private hands. All revolutions were unavoidably painful, filled with jealousy and envy. Even among the tycoons, he said, those who won the greatest prizes were still greedy for more, and those who lost out were not happy. Society too was deeply divided, he admitted, and the poor were embittered. "I know that in the United States and Western Europe, very rich people are also not really liked," Berezovsky said. "And I can tell you that in today's Russia, this feeling of dislike for the rich is a hundred times greater than in the West. But I'm certain, this is a matter of time. And I'm certain that in time, society will to a larger extent understand that the rich are not those to whom suddenly, unexpectedly, wealth fell on their heads, but that the rich are those who, first of all—there are exceptions—but the rich are those who first of all are more capable, more talented, and more hardworking than others."

Berezovsky was correct that the tycoons were talented and hard-working. But it was also true that many of them did have sudden wealth fall on their heads. Berezovsky might also have added that they were the most ruthless and relentless of their generation. His own empire was still expanding and included the Logovaz car dealerships; Sibneft, the oil company; Aeroflot, where he was profiting from the cash flow of overseas ticket sales; ORT, the television channel; Transaero, an upstart Russian airline; and a number of media properties, including *Nezavisimaya Gazeta*. But now, in his moment of victory, Berezovsky yearned for respect, for himself and for the oligarchs.[51]

This desire grew stronger as the tycoons began a romance with foreign capital after the 1996 election. A turning point came in November, when the Russian government floated a $1 billion Eurobond, the first such borrowing on global capital markets since the 1917 revolution. The successful flotation opened doors to relatively cheap foreign capital for the tycoons, if they could pass muster with Wall Street and in the financial capitals of London and Frankfurt. The oligarchs began to draw from a vast new reservoir of cash.

But first they had a very important series of transactions to complete at home. After September 1, 1996, it was time to collect the "second key" from the loans for shares auctions. As planned, the winners of the first auctions were given permission to sell off the shares they had taken as collateral for the loans to the government. And as Ryan had predicted, they sold the shares to themselves.

Khodorkovsky proved the most cunning. Amid the tumult of 1996, he finagled a deal allowing him to take control of Yukos early. Khodorkovsky got Yeltsin to sign a decree that allowed him to issue new shares in Yukos to pay off the debts of the subsidiaries. This meant, simply, that there would be one-third more shares outstanding than before. The effect of issuing the new shares was to reduce the size of the block that Khodorkovsky was holding for the government. It fell from 45 percent to 33 percent. Then Khodorkovsky appeared again, on the other side of the counter, to buy the new shares. This time, he bought most of the new shares for what a source told me was $100 million. Recall that Khodorkovsky also had purchased a block of shares in 1995 at an investment tender. When the new shares were combined with those he bought at the investment tender, Khodorkovsky controlled more than 51 percent of the company. The point was that no one could take it away from him—Khodorkovsky had grabbed the "second key" even before the official ceremony.

Khodorkovsky originally loaned the state $159 million for the 45 percent stake in 1995. A year later, he sold the stake to himself, using a shell company, for $160.1 million. The state's profit on the deal was almost zero. The state gained little more than it had in 1995, and Khodorkovsky got an oil company. In the original concept of loans for shares, there was a hope that when the shares were sold, the state would reap a higher price. But in fact once the oligarchs began selling the companies to themselves, the prices remained rock bottom.

Potanin then sold the 51 percent of Sidanco, the oil company, for which he loaned the government $130 million. The winner of the stake: Potanin (again). He paid $129.8 million. Within a year, Potanin sold just 10 percent of Sidanco to British Petroleum for $571 million! Later in 1997, he sold the 38 percent of Norilsk Nickel to himself, for $250 million, an improvement over the $170 million he had loaned the government, but a pittance considering the billions of dollars in revenues Norilsk was to produce annually in the next few years.

Berezovsky got the key to Sibneft without spending too much. He had loaned the government $100.1 million for 51 percent of the company in 1995 and sold it eighteen months later to himself for $110 million.

Gusinsky never got a chance to play in loans for shares, but after the election, he too was rewarded. The state natural gas monopoly, Gazprom, purchased 30 percent of NTV, providing Gusinsky with badly needed capital for expansion.[52] Yeltsin also signed a decree giving Gusinsky twenty-four-hour access to the airwaves on Channel 4, an important concession that allowed Gusinsky more time to broadcast commercials as well as news and films.

Smolensky eschewed loans for shares, except to serve as a financier for Berezovsky. But Smolensky also reaped rich rewards for his role in the election. He had increasingly set his sights on becoming Russia's largest private commercial bank, and his prize came late in 1996. The formerly state-owned Agroprombank, one of Russia's largest banks with 1,254 branches, was failing due to poor management and the stagnation of Russian agriculture. A Central Bank official told me at the time that Agroprombank was within six to eight weeks of being closed. The government couldn't afford a bailout, nor could it close the bank, which had branches in the farm belt where the Communist and Agrarian Parties dominated. So the state announced a competitive tender, but only two banks submitted bids. Smolensky walked away with the bank for $24 million, defeating Bank Imperial, which was backed by Gazprom. "I was 99 percent sure I would win," Smolensky acknowledged. He pledged to provide $180 million in loans to farmers at low interest rates over the next five years. But the prize for Smolensky was the branch network—it would help him make a giant leap toward becoming the largest private retail bank in Russia. I was told by another banker that properly constructing a new bank branch in Moscow required about $2 million. Smolensky had just purchased 1,254 new branches for the equivalent of one for every $19,000 of his investment. The only bank with more branches would be Sberbank, the old state savings bank. Smolensky renamed his bank SBS-Agro.

The Davos Pact had another unexpected impact. It demonstrated that television commanded enormous political influence in the new Russia. The great pioneer was Gusinsky, who had tasted this power of television in 1994–1995 with NTV's critical coverage of the Chechen war. But the election had made it even more vivid: the television channels could create and destroy. Their next victim was General Lebed, whom Yeltsin appointed to head the Security Council. He had signed an important cease-fire deal with the Chechens in August but grew outspoken and insulting as Yeltsin's heart surgery loomed. Sensing a power vacuum in the Kremlin, Lebed was speaking about Yeltsin as if he were already gone. Having been built up as a serious candidate by ORT and NTV, Lebed was unceremoniously crushed by the same channels, which now broadcast unflattering stories about him. NTV aired videotape, some of it admittedly eighteen months old, showing an extreme nationalist and fascist group known as the Russian Legion marching in St. Petersburg and suggested that these were Lebed's forces. Lebed was fired by Yeltsin on October 17. Andrei Richter, who taught journalism at Moscow State University and headed a media law center there, said the television networks had served as the Kremlin's attack dogs. "There is a word, *Fas!* when you have a dog and you let it attack someone," he said. "It means, 'Go ahead, kill! Bite!'"[53]

Berezovsky had no qualms about this; political influence was his main benefit from ORT. But Gusinsky began to feel doubts that matured in later years into full-fledged regret. When I asked him to look back at the events of 1996, he said his support of Yeltsin was "a conscious decision—a wrong decision."

"I think we were learning as a society," he said, "and I was learning together with the rest. We were learning that no noble aims can be reached by dirty means. I am certain of this today."

After the euphoria of the summer campaign, Chubais ended the year on a difficult note. Yeltsin admitted openly for the first time that he needed heart surgery, which was scheduled for November. Chubais desperately wanted to work outside of government but "to my biggest sorrow" was pressed into becoming Yeltsin's top aide in the Kremlin. "I was appointed head of the presidential administration, but there was no real president," Chubais recalled. "Physically, there was no president." No one knew if Yeltsin would survive the surgery. Instead of a fast start to Yeltsin's second term, Russia went into a long winter period of stagnation. The old man hibernated again.

Chubais began to think that maybe it was time to change the rules of the game.

Chapter 14

The Bankers' War

THE WINTER MELTED into a spring season of promise in early 1997, and once again Boris Yeltsin rose from adversity. After risky heart surgery in which his rib cage was opened and five arteries were replaced, Yeltsin spent months recovering away from the Kremlin. Anatoly Chubais, chief of the presidential administration, was effectively the acting president, surmising what Yeltsin might do but with no way to ask, no one at the other end of the phone. His critics mocked him as "regent," a civil servant behind the throne, which is exactly what he was. The throne was empty. "It is monstrously difficult to run the president's administration in his absence, a very unpleasant occupation," Chubais confessed.[1]

Yeltsin had lost fifty-seven pounds by the time he officially returned to the Kremlin on December 24. "Good morning," he greeted the guard in a slow, breathless voice. "I'm in a good mood, in good health, ready for the fray." But he spoke too soon. Yeltsin fell ill with pneumonia and his return was delayed nearly two months. Finally, he launched his second term in March, appointing Chubais first deputy prime minister and giving him broad authority over the economy, including the powerful portfolio of finance minister. Yeltsin then sent his influential daughter Tatyana Dyachenko to Nizhny Novgorod to persuade the young reformist governor there, Boris Nemtsov, to accept a post as deputy prime minister in Moscow, alongside Chubais.[2]

Nemtsov had caught Yeltsin's attention years earlier when, as a young physicist, he led demonstrations against a nuclear power plant during *perestroika.* After Yeltsin appointed him governor of the region, which was heavily dependent on the defense industry, Nemtsov earned a reputation as an economic reformer. He quickly privatized small business and experimented with change on the hidebound Soviet-era collective farms. Tall and exuberant, with a perpetually youthful manner, Nemtsov was never afraid to speak his mind. He once told me that Russia desperately needed young people in leadership. "We need to get rid of the drunk old men at the top," he said.[3]

Nemtsov took up Yeltsin's offer to become a deputy prime minister in Moscow in March 1997. He and Chubais, dubbed the "young reformers," heralded a new activism, a fresh start for Yeltsin's second term. They were emboldened by signs the economy was perking up after so many years of decline. The sky-high interest rates on short-term government bonds, the superlucrative GKOs, had subsided to reasonable levels after the election. The gates to foreign capital were open, not only for the government but also for Russian companies. The spring brought a Russian stock market boom, which in turn gave rise to a young, prosperous, and lively new class of Moscow professionals in the brokerages and exchanges. Chubais was especially proud that hyperinflation had finally been quenched. "Let it be etched on my gravestone as one of the most impressive achievements of my life," he said.[4] But intractable problems remained; millions of people were still paid months late. In many parts of Russia outside of Moscow, real money had disappeared, and a medieval economy of barter had taken its place.

From the outset, Nemtsov declared that his goal was to vanquish "bandit capitalism." Nemtsov often, and gleefully, declared, "I am for people's capitalism." In his first months in office, he tried to show what he had in mind. He ripped up an outrageous sweetheart deal giving huge rewards to the management of the natural gas monopoly, Gazprom, which was partially owned by the state, and demanded better terms. In a bit of showmanship, Nemtsov got Yeltsin to sign a decree ordering government bureaucrats to give up their cushy foreign-made limousines and drive Russian cars such as the Volga, a chunky sedan manufactured in Nizhny. Yeltsin, proud of his young protégé, gave up his Mercedes for a while and rode in a Zil limo used for Soviet Politburo members. But eventually he went back to the Mercedes. Nemtsov also pushed through a measure calling for high-ranking government officials to disclose their income, a novelty for a political elite nurtured on secret payoffs and offshore bank accounts. Nemtsov and Chubais promised to junk the system of "authorized banks" that the tycoons had exploited for easy money. They also promised to end wasted subsidies on housing and to reform the mammoth energy monopolies. Nemtsov's showy, populist initiatives attracted wide attention, and his poll ratings zoomed upward. He was often mentioned as a possible successor to Yeltsin. However, the "young reformers," Nemtsov and Chubais, took criticism from their own ranks that their agenda was shallow. Dmitri Vasiliev, the Chubais privatization deputy who became head of the federal securities commission, privately argued to Chubais that the second term was a golden opportunity to strengthen those vital institutions—rule of law and market regulation—that they had neglected at the outset of "shock therapy." But Vasiliev's voice went unheard.[5]

In April, Nemtsov met individually with the oligarchs. "I explained my intention . . . to establish new rules," he said—from now on, the government would be open, transparent, and competitive. No more rigged auctions. There would be open tenders for everything, even provision of army rations. What's more, he told the bankers that he and Chubais wanted to focus on creating a new middle class. The bankers replied enthusiastically that they would support him, especially in his desire to create open, above-board rules of the game. Nemtsov recalled the oligarchs' lament that their previous wars—the *kompromat* and media combat, violence, theft, and deception—were a waste and they wanted to leave those days behind.[6]

It was all nice talk. In fact, Nemtsov was suggesting nothing less than dismantling the system of oligarchic capitalism that had taken shape under Chubais, Yeltsin, and the tycoons. The system had at its core a quick-profit, no-tomorrow ethos that was forged in *perestroika* with the explosion of cooperatives and banks, reached full strength in the frenzy of vouchers and easy money, and ripened into enormous property grabs in the loans for shares auctions. Nemtsov didn't stand a chance against this system with words alone.

At the time, the oligarchs were given a popular moniker, the *semi-*

bankirshchina, or rule of the seven bankers. It was a play on words from the label given to a group of seven boyars who ran Russia in the seventeenth century during a brief period between tsars. The *semi-bankirshchina* ruled even when Yeltsin was in the Kremlin.

The model of oligarchic capitalism, centered in Moscow, spread quickly throughout Russia's regions, as local barons copied what they learned from the tycoons. They grabbed control of factory complexes, glued themselves to regional governors, and sought fortunes with the same audacity that had rewarded the Moscow tycoons. Even in the capital, the ruling oligarchy extended beyond the seven to include dozens of other magnates who were less well known. For example, Vladimir Yevtushenkov, president of the conglomerate Systema and longtime friend of Yuri Luzhkov, was an influential tycoon in his own right who had assembled, with help from the city, a $1 billion group in mobile telephones, electronics, hotels, tourism, insurance, oil, and other properties.

While Nemtsov played for the television cameras, Chubais quietly underwent a fundamental rethinking of his own experience over the last few years. He reached a conclusion that had far-reaching consequences. Chubais decided that he had to break the incestuous relationship between wealth and power, a bond he had done so much to forge. Perhaps loans for shares had been necessary in 1995 to sell off the factories to younger managers, crimp the red directors, and raise money for the budget. That was worth it. Perhaps it had been necessary in 1996 to get Yeltsin reelected and destroy Zyuganov. That trade-off too was worth it. But in early 1997, Chubais was troubled by the merger of wealth and power. Chubais never denounced "bandit capitalism" because in fact it was *his* capitalism; more than anyone else, he had designed, nurtured, and protected it. In fact, he admired some of the tycoons, whom he considered modern capitalists. But he nonetheless decided the rules would have to change; he could no longer dish out the goodies as he had before.[7]

Chubais seethed in anger at Boris Berezovsky's statements that the businessmen would run the country like a board of directors. When Chubais accepted this arrangement for the sake of the 1996 election, he certainly did not see it as permanent, as Berezovsky did.[8] Chubais told me that before 1996 he was totally preoccupied with defeating the Communists. "There was nothing more important than this," he said. "We could sacrifice a lot for this goal." After Yeltsin was reelected, however, his outlook changed. He did not want to become a tool of Berezovsky, and he figured there was no better time to free himself than at the beginning of Yeltsin's second term. "Yeltsin was president, but this was a different president," he said. "This was Yeltsin elected anew, and if from the very beginning we didn't start a new life with a different president, later on it would surely be impossible to do so."[9]

Chubais had often demonstrated his preferred tactic for achieving change. He drove hard, then compromised, then came back again seeking to repair the earlier mistakes. For example, he made a huge bargain during mass privatization by allowing the red directors to keep control of their companies. Then he tried to compensate later by shifting property to the tycoons in loans for shares. Now he set about trying to fix the errors of loans for shares. One of the mistakes had been the rigged auctions. He decided the days of rigged auctions were over. Regardless of what had gone before, the market would now pick winners and losers. According to Yeltsin, Chubais declared it was time to show the oligarchs who was boss. "We need to sock them in the teeth for once in our lives!" Chubais said. "We won't achieve anything if we don't do this."[10]

Chubais told Vladimir Gusinsky about his change of heart in late 1996 or early 1997. Gusinsky was preparing for the next big wave of privatization. At stake was an enormous telephone and communications company, which Gusinsky wanted badly. "You should keep in mind," Chubais told him, "this will be an auction, and the person who wins will be the one who pays the most." Chubais was unusually insistent. "Do you understand, Vladimir Alexandrovich?" Chubais asked Gusinsky.

"Of course, of course," Gusinsky said, according to Chubais. "I clearly understand that."[11]

In fact, Gusinsky and Berezovsky did not understand. They heard what Chubais said but did not take him seriously. In their view, the rules of the game could not be switched off like a light. They thought it was just rhetoric, like Nemtsov's "bandit capitalism" slogans. Besides, everyone knew that it was not so simple. Was Chubais really changing the rules or just finding a new label for the same old game? One hint that nothing had changed came when Gusinsky was appointed as consultant to organize the telephone company sale, a role that in the past had been reserved for the prearranged winner. Gusinsky and Berezovsky simply assumed that the oligarchs would continue to carve up the country for themselves, with Chubais as their handmaiden.

Soon they were all headed for disaster. Although the tycoons told Nemtsov they were fed up with the dirty little wars of Russian capitalism, they were plunging straight into the most vicious, destructive feud of the decade.

In the spring of 1997, the capital market boom was in full swing. Russia had opened itself to the outside world, and a torrent of investment in stocks and bonds flooded into its nascent exchanges. Planeloads of investors were shuttled into town and given tours of Red Square, the Bolshoi Theater, and the Kremlin; they bought billions of dollars in Russian equity and debt. Dana F. McGinnis, a Texas fund manager, recalled the atmosphere of his early visits, which eventually led him to invest more than $200 million in Russia. "There was great optimism that there would be an end to the arms race and that some 250 million people would be brought into the capitalist fold," McGinnis told my colleague Steven Mufson. "There was a buzz in the air. The country was evolving by the hour. You could feel it."[12] By 1997, the reelection of Yeltsin seemed to have opened the spigots all the way. Russia was awash in speculative portfolio investment. Foreigners, who never visited the factories or refineries they were investing in or asked who ran them, plunked down billions of dollars for stocks and bonds. Foreign portfolio investment—the purchase of stocks and bonds—rose from $8.9 billion in 1996 to an incredible $45.6 billion in 1997, equaling 10 percent of the Russian economy.[13] William Browder, who had come to Russia in the early days of privatization and discovered the Murmansk ship bargain as well as dozens of other undervalued companies, later set up his own fund, Hermitage, which became one of the best-performing funds in Russia in 1997, with a mammoth $1.2 billion in Russian equities under management. The savvy Browder, who was then thirty-three years old, was just one of many who rode the boom to new heights.

The allure of stocks was the "two-cent kilowatt." A Moscow fund manager explained it to me this way: shares in a Russian electricity monopoly were selling at the equivalent of two cents per kilowatt per line, while a Brazilian electric company sold at fifty cents; in the

United States it was five dollars. The two-cent kilowatt looked pretty cheap if you figured Russia would be stable and grow in the years ahead. "It was clear skies as far as the eye can see," recalled James Fenkner, a bald, acerbic analyst for Troika Dialog, one of the largest brokerage firms in Moscow. Fenkner was a hardened, well-informed veteran of the crazy 1997 boom. "Toward the end, everyone was after everything," he said. "All you had to do is say a Russian word, and if the Russian word had 'share' attached to it, you could sell it."[14] The Russian Trading System, an over-the-counter electronic stock market, soared nonstop for months. The index became the best performing emerging market in the world during 1997. The Moscow brokerages opened spacious new trading floors with flickering computer screens, frantic traders entwined in telephones, and a vocabulary of "blue chips" and "second-tier stocks" that glossed over the underlying problems. It had an aura of Western modernity, but underneath it was cutthroat.

In securities, dirty dealing was widespread, and practices that would land a broker in jail in the West went unregulated in Russia. Insider trading was common, as were techniques like "front-running," when a local broker would exploit the rise in a stock price created by his own client's large order, or "ramping," which meant trying to run up a stock price by issuing glowing—and usually misleading—research reports. Brokers often made side deals for their own accounts while trading in the same stocks for clients, a conflict of interest that the investors never knew about.[15] Russia had the markets but not the rule of law or the business culture of a mature market economy, which would deter cheating and theft. Dmitri Vasiliev, then the securities commission chairman, told me he spent most of 1997 trying to enact regulations to bring order to the unruly market. It was a nearly impossible task. Russia's companies beckoned with cheap kilowatts, and in that summer of frenzied activity, Moscow became a gold rush town. It was easy to conclude that Russia had climbed out of the post-Soviet economic quagmire for the first time. Leonid Gozman, a political adviser to Chubais, marveled, "If this is not success, what is success?" Every stock deal, every loan offering had a shimmering story to go with it. I got a taste of this when Alexander Smolensky stepped out onto the stage of world finance.

Smolensky had come a long way from his days as a typesetter. His bank, SBS-Agro, was one of the largest commercial banks in Russia, with $5.2 billion in assets, forty-three thousand employees, and the most admired corporate art collection in the country. His plastic credit cards were used by members of parliament and his automatic teller machines were located inside the Kremlin. His conference room was hung with nineteenth-century Russian and German portraits and decorated with sculpted elephants, to which he had taken a liking. Smolensky never lost his earthy, streetwise manner, but he now was at the pinnacle of Russian business. He no longer needed to bring a few extra suits in his suitcase for his vice presidents. They could buy their own.[16]

In July 1997 Standard & Poors issued its first ratings of four Russian commercial banks, including Smolensky's SBS-Agro, which soon became the first to tap into global capital.[17] Smolensky floated a $250 million Eurobond at 10.25 percent, which was just 4.25 points over U.S. Treasury bonds.[18] Xavier Jordan, a vice president of J.P. Morgan, lead managers for the loan, explained to me later the way he had pitched the Smolensky loan to investors. Russians had an enormous storehouse of savings under their mattresses, he said, perhaps 30–40 percent of the economy. They didn't trust banks, which held only a tiny fraction of the country's savings. Smolensky was building a retail banking empire that people could trust, he said. "If you assume Russia is going to converge into the real world," he added, Smolensky would capture those mattress savings. "That's a license to print money."[19] It was a wonderfully simple story: Smolensky, the onetime dump truck driver, builds the Russian equivalent of the Bank of America. Imagine: Smolensky, whose "risk" was just a shade greater than U.S. Treasury bills, could pull all those wads of dollar bills out from under the soggy mattresses! The story lasted about a year.

In the rush for black gold, Gusinsky was left out. He never got a chance to grab a Siberian oil company, and he never participated in loans for shares. Gusinsky often boasted that he did not dirty his hands in old Soviet factories.[20] Perhaps it was just as well because the failed theater director did not understand factories and refineries, conveyor belts and pipelines. Rather, after the Yeltsin election, Gusinsky hunted for his own black gold. He wanted to make big money, but not from mining nickel or hydrocarbons. Gusinsky sought wealth in the television airwaves, the silent digits of computer transmissions, the tiny pulses of electricity that carried phone conversations. He wanted to become Russia's king of communications. His black gold shimmered with silicon chips, fiber-optic cables, satellite beams, and electronic pixels.

For Gusinsky, the key lesson of Russian business in the early 1990s was to think big. Nothing was impossible if you could imagine it vividly enough and then work like a dog. Finances and business plans, lawyers and accountants—these were mere details. His experience in founding NTV was a good example. When Yevgeny Kiselyov and Oleg Dobrodeyev came to him seeking money for a single program, Gusinsky expansively proposed building a whole channel. They did not hesitate over viewer demographics, broadcast signals, or licenses. They dreamed of a television channel, threw themselves into it, and now NTV was an impressive reality. The same boundless energy still motivated Gusinsky in the spring of 1997. His enormous ambition *was* his business plan.

At the core of Gusinsky's dream was an incredibly optimistic vision of Russia. He believed in the birth of a new middle class. If it developed, the middle class would fuel demand for consumer goods, for washing machines and soft drinks, and the advertising would be carried by NTV. The middle class would also desire high-class movies and hard-hitting news and analysis that NTV offered. With more discretionary income, the middle class would go to restaurants, buy personal computers, and rent telephone lines. They would drive new cars, use mobile phones, and listen to the radio on their way to work. They would travel and hunger for information about the outside world. At every turn, Gusinsky would be there.

In January 1997, Gusinsky left his post at Most Bank and devoted himself full-time to building a communications empire under the new conglomerate name, Media-Most. Sergei Parkhomenko, one of the most respected newspaper journalists of the day, and Masha Lipman, an exceptional editor who once worked in our bureau at the *Washington Post*, designed and built from scratch a glossy, informative newsmagazine, *Itogi*, which Gusinsky launched in 1996.[21] Alexei Venediktov and other radio journalists who had started the popular Echo of Moscow radio station sold it to Gusinsky in 1994, and it thrived. A slick television magazine, *Seven Days*, rocketed to a half million weekly circulation. Gusinsky spent long hours with media giant Rupert Murdoch, whom he greatly respected, and embarked on a major new venture,

NTV-Plus, to blanket Russia with pay satellite television. "There was this terrible enthusiasm, when there was an expectation of the booming economy, that it's going to expand very, very quickly," Igor Malashenko recalled of the plans for NTV-Plus. Gusinsky financed the first stage of NTV-Plus with the capital from the sale of 30 percent of NTV to Gazprom.[22] Gusinsky said marketing studies showed he had a potential audience of 10 million subscribers for NTV-Plus. To fulfill his dreams, Gusinsky planned to launch a new, expensive satellite. He also needed good programming. He only had to imagine and to build, and the viewers would come. It might eventually cost billions, but Gusinsky never put finance first. They would find the money.

Another vision of electronic black gold that Gusinky harbored was telephones and communications. In the mid-1990s, Russia had only nineteen telephone lines for one hundred people, compared to fifty-eight for the United States and forty-nine for Great Britain. Once modernized and privatized, the telephone networks could be a source of colossal profits. Like oil reserves, the phone lines represented a concrete, tangible asset: add up the number of subscribers and multiply by the payments, throw in new equipment and a growing middle class, and you get a machine that prints money. Gusinsky saw telephones as a communications business that dovetailed with his knack for television. However, in Gusinsky's circle, there were doubts about this. Malashenko told me he worried Gusinsky was going too far. Whatever the future of telecommunications, the existing telephone enterprises were creaky old Soviet outfits of the kind Gusinsky had so far avoided.

To privatize the phone system, the Russian government created a new holding company, Svyazinvest. The word *svyaz* in Russian means a link, connection, or communication. The philosophy was the same as with oil: the state created a holding company out of thin air, gave it control over valuable state-owned enterprises, wrapped it in a pretty bow, and sold it off. The new holding company was given controlling stakes in Russia's eighty-eight regional telephone companies, with 22 million phone lines. The promise of Svyazinvest was large, but so were the problems. The owner would have to get control over dozens of independent telephone companies and a maddening patchwork of tariffs, old technology, and political cross-currents. It might take years, as well as serious investment by a company with real experience in telephones, to straighten out Svyazinvest. Moreover, the phone system had a silent watchdog. The military and security services viewed the telephone lines as their sphere of influence. When the Soviet KGB was broken up, several divisions—the Eighth Division, which dealt with ciphering, and the Sixteenth Division, which dealt with deciphering and electronic surveillance—were turned into a new stand-alone security service, the Federal Agency for Government Communications and Information, directly under the Russian president.[23] The military also had a strong interest in the telephone system, on which it relied for its communications.

The Russian government failed to sell 25 percent of Svyazinvest in 1995. The Italian state-owned telephone company, Stet, had offered $640 million for the stake plus a promise to invest $754 million over two years. But the deal fell apart. The publicly stated reason was that the Italians made certain last-minute financial demands, but the real reason was objections from the military and security services to a foreigner buying up Russia's telephone lines.[24]

After the 1996 elections, Gusinsky set his sights on winning Svyazinvest. He went to Alfred Kokh, the blunt-spoken director of the federal property agency, who was a Chubais man. Gusinsky wanted to organize another attempt to privatize Svyazinvest. He suggested making Svyazinvest a stronger company by combining it with Rostelecom, the Russian long-distance provider. Then, Gusinsky told Kokh, he would try to persuade the generals and security agencies to approve the sale. Gusinsky told me that Kokh let him go ahead because Kokh thought the military would never agree to the deal. Naturally, Gusinsky also knew that if he organized the privatization—as the presale "consultant"—he could expect to have the inside track on winning the company. Those were the rules of the game the oligarchs had already established. Vladimir Potanin had organized Norilsk and won; Mikhail Khodorkovsky had organized Yukos and won. Why couldn't he?

Gusinsky contributed only a small portion of the finances behind the deal. He brought in a foreign strategic investor, the Spanish telephone giant Telefonica SA, the investment bank Credit Suisse First Boston, and Mikhail Friedman's Alfa Group. One of the big private investors in Gusinsky's group was Benny Steinmetz, an Israeli financier and diamond tycoon. Gusinsky's role was to lead the political charge for the deal—to be the influential point man for a consortium of investors. If they won the Svyazinvest auction, the actual day-to-day work of running the company would be in the hands of Telefonica.

Gusinsky worked hard at his role. He drank vodka with the generals and gently persuaded them that the Spanish telephone company would not threaten their prerogatives. It was certainly not a disadvantage that Filipp Bobkov, the former KGB general, was now on Gusinsky's corporate team. Soon Russia's military and security agencies signed off.

Gusinsky's real worry was not the military but the other oligarchs. He constantly fretted about Potanin. In the early months of his preparations, Gusinsky pressed Chubais to keep Potanin's fast-growing bank, Uneximbank, out of the bidding for the phone company while Potanin was first deputy prime minister. Chubais agreed and went to Potanin, asking him to remove himself from the competition. Potanin consented, but he revoked the pledge as soon as he quit the government on March 17. He wanted to play, and he said the promise to stay out was good only as long as he was a government official.[25]

The atmosphere among the oligarchs grew tense. Malashenko told me at the time: "It's funny when people talk about the seven bankers ruling the country; they *hate* each other. They have conflicting interests. When they sit together, around the same table, you can feel the tension in the air."[26]

Gusinsky nervously watched Potanin's money. He believed he could compete against rational outside investors for Svyazinvest because they would take a cold-eyed look at the company based on its assets and the potential value of the telephone lines. But he feared it was hopeless to compete against someone like Potanin, who commanded so much cash he could practically throw it at the deal. He knew Potanin's bank held an enormous deposit, more than $1 billion, from the federal customs service. Gusinsky also believed that Potanin had obtained, through a leak, Gusinsky's complete documentation about the Svyazinvest deal. That documentation would give Potanin a big advantage.

Gusinsky and Friedman went to see Chubais again, privately. According to Gusinsky, they told Chubais that they believed Kokh, the privatization chief, was taking money from Potanin. Chubais defended his man, saying Kokh was honest. The disagreement was the first dark hint of the explosion to come.[27]

Gusinsky's anxiety about Potanin was well founded. In addition to sitting atop a mountain of cash, he had access to even more money through Boris Jordan, the hyperactive young financier and broker who scored big in vouchers and later helped conceive loans for shares. Jordan recruited superfinancier and philanthropist George Soros into Potanin's deal for buying Svyazinvest.[28] Potanin did not meet Soros until much later; the Svyazinvest deal was the result of Jordan's hustle. "I sold him on the business deal," Jordan recalled of Soros. "But I know what sold him on Russia—it was Nemtsov."[29]

Soros was deeply ambivalent about investing in Russia. As a rule, he did not like to invest in countries where he was a philanthropist. His contributions to Russia were substantial. Among other things, he singlehandedly helped publish new, honest history textbooks for Russian schoolchildren, provided stipends for scholars and scientists, and rescued the "thick journals," a rich tradition of Russian literary magazines such as *Novy Mir* whose circulation had plummeted. Soros also displayed an acute understanding of the importance and difficulties of building civil society in the post-Soviet world. Soros shunned Berezovsky's solicitation for Sibneft in 1995, fearing the political risks. But two years later he was ready to sink real investment into Russia. When I met Soros for breakfast in Moscow at the Metropol Hotel one morning in June 1997, I was fascinated to hear his analysis of the Russian economy; Soros had earned billions making the right calls at the right time. Russia, he said, "moved from the excesses of the Soviet system to the excesses of laissez-faire capitalism, or, more appropriately here, robber capitalism." The oligarchs? "They are pretty crude and pretty rapacious."

Nonetheless, Soros was greatly encouraged by the appointment of Nemtsov. The young reformer persuaded Soros that the time had come to invest in Russia. "I can see the path by which robber capitalism can turn into legitimate capitalism," Soros said.[30] Although I didn't know it at the time, a few days after our breakfast, Soros personally extended a helping hand to the cash-strapped Russian government. Chubais and Nemtsov had pledged to pay off government workers' back wages by July 1, but they were short of funds. Kokh called Jordan, saying the government was desperate. Jordan then called Soros in New York—but his office said he was in Moscow at the Metropol. Jordan went to the hotel and talked Soros into making a quick personal loan of several hundred million dollars between June 25 and July 3, until Russia received the proceeds of a Eurobond issue.[31] Another secret I didn't discover at the breakfast was that Soros was also making a large investment with one of the robber barons he denounced, putting $980 million into Potanin's bid for Svyazinvest. The stock market boom made every investment seem like a sure thing. Soros later disclosed that his total investment in Russia was $2.5 billion, making him by far the largest Western portfolio investor in Russia at the time.[32] He too was chasing black gold.

Potanin's investment consortium for Svyazinvest was, typically, an offshore web of shell companies. The chain of transactions flowed from a company called Bidco, based in Cyprus, through another company, Investco, in the British Virgin Islands, which was a front for another company, Svyaz Finance Ltd.; then to another company, IFCI (Cyprus) Ltd., based in Cyprus. It also included Mustcom Ltd. in Cyprus. Russia's economy may have been on an upswing, but when it came to big money, investors still wanted to remain in the relative safety of offshore havens.[33]

Potanin claimed that Svyazinvest was a "strategic investment," but his preparations spoke otherwise. Potanin was a speculator. He was putting in only about $200 million of his own cash. Jordan contributed another $200 million from Renaissance. The rest was raised from outside investors, including Soros. Ultimately, Potanin was gambling on quickly reselling the company to someone else who might pay twice as much for it. "It was getting something for nothing," one of Potanin's investors told me later. "If he spent $1.5 billion, he could sell it a year later for $5 billion." The premise was not outrageous in the superheated boom of that summer.[34]

Potanin, like Gusinsky, staked everything on his own sway as an oligarch. According to documents that he gave to investors, Potanin's game plan was a gutsy one, built entirely on his own clout. After winning the first 25 percent of Svyazinvest, he promised he would elbow into the management suite and assume control over sale of the next 24 percent, which was going to be offered within nine months. Potanin told his investors that he could appoint managers, get the company's books, and sell off the next chunk of Svyazinvest to a strategic investor.[35] The unspoken calculation was that this would fatten up the price of his own stake. It all depended on Potanin's ability to move quickly into the company. "We never thought we would buy that second stake," Jordan told me. "It was always in the plans to sell that second stake to a strategic investor, which would have boosted the value of our stake." He added, "Let's be honest, George Soros is no long-term investor. He never held anything longer than a week! He's a trader. George Soros was going to trade that baby out to a strategic investor right after the next deal." Potanin surely would have liked to do the same. Potanin promised to hold the shares for two years, but I think he would have gladly sold them sooner.

Gusinsky also longed to make a killing on Svyazinvest. Only days before the auction, a friend of mine recalled, Gusinsky was openly talking about the billion dollars he was going to make on the deal. Gusinsky differed from Potanin in that he had already brought in Telefonica, an experienced phone company that intended to actually build telecommunications in Russia, whereas Potanin was playing for casino profits.

In a real competition, the winner isn't chosen before the race begins. But in the crude culture of Russian capitalism in the 1990s, the winner was usually chosen in advance by the participants. The Svyazinvest auction was set for July 25. The Kremlin was jittery about deepening tensions among the oligarchs. Yeltsin sent Yumashev, his chief of staff, who had replaced Chubais, to suggest to the tycoons that they solve the issue "peacefully, without the news wars and without planting bombs under the government." Amazingly, Yeltsin's own man did not suggest a fair competition. Rather, as "a last resort," the two sides should divide up the spoils fifty-fifty, among themselves. This was a remarkable glimpse of how oligarchic capitalism had entrenched itself in 1997—the president himself wanted the boys to share the loot, quietly. They refused.[36]

Russian law required a minimum of two bidders for an auction to be legal, but many auctions were rigged anyway. The winner was agreed upon beforehand, and the second bidder was a dummy corporation. The trick had been used often in loans for shares. Frequently a serious second bidder would deliberately walk away, for a price. Gusinsky recalled that at one point Potanin came to his office and proposed to pay him several hundred million dollars to stay out of the auction. Potanin proposed that after he won, he would hire Gusinsky to run the company for him. "We will hire you because you are the only man who understands it," Potanin said, according to Gusinsky.[37]

But Gusinsky repeatedly refused to cooperate with Potanin. All he wanted was to get Potanin out. This was *his* deal! Both sides hardened as the deadline drew closer. Neither would walk away. They were getting locked in with foreign investors. Gusinsky warned Potanin: "If you participate, then everything that I know about your loans for shares auctions and all about your deals and relations will be made public after this!" It was an angry threat, typical of many that brought Gusinsky his share of enemies.

Potanin refused to back down. He suggested that they take the case to Chubais. Chubais was the arbiter they all trusted to be fair. Gusinsky agreed. Potanin told me the oligarchs were well aware that Chubais wanted "new rules of the game" in the Svyazinvest auction. "But I would say that, for different reasons, we were not sure this was serious."[38]

They also agreed to bring Berezovsky, then deputy secretary of the Kremlin Security Council, to the meeting with Chubais. Berezovsky had, in theory, given up his business interests while serving in government, but he was active in promoting the oligarchy and his own ambitions, both political and financial. At one point in June, Berezovsky tried, unsuccessfully, to recruit Soros into a bid to make Berezovsky chairman of the natural gas monopoly Gazprom. Berezovsky flew Soros to Sochi, the Black Sea resort, to see Chernomyrdin, the former chairman of Gazprom, and later Berezovsky lunched with Soros at the Logovaz Club. Soros recalled that Berezovsky grew terribly angry when Soros informed Nemtsov, a harsh critic of Gazprom, about Berezovsky's maneuvering to take over the company. Nemtsov vowed, "Over my dead body."[39] The deal never happened.

Berezovsky had become the coach of Team Tycoon and was constantly scrutinizing and guiding his players. "Berezovsky has to be number one everywhere," Gusinsky told me later. "He has to be the best man at every wedding, the grave digger at every funeral. If something happens somewhere without Berezovsky, he is full of anxiety." Berezovsky had no formal participation in Gusinsky's deal but had asked Gusinsky whether, in the event he won Svyazinvest, he could become a partner. "We'll discuss it later," Gusinsky said.

On July 23, 1997, the tycoons—Gusinsky, Potanin, and Berezovsky—secretly flew out of Moscow on Gusinsky's private business jet to Nice, and then on to Saint-Tropez. They took a boat to a seaside estate where Chubais was vacationing at the home of a friend. The mood was relaxed as they sat in a pleasant garden for six hours, replaying their arguments for Chubais. "They came with the same question," Chubais recalled. Was he serious about the new rules of the game? According to Chubais, the tycoons proposed a deal. They would carve up the forthcoming privatization riches among themselves. In this plan, Gusinsky would win Svyazinvest in a rigged auction, since he had made all the preparations. Then the next big company to come up would go to Potanin—Unified Energy Systems, the mighty nationwide electric power grid and generating company. Chubais remembered that they had all the details ready: the shares, the volumes, the conditions. "We came to an agreement," they said, turning to Chubais. "And do you agree?"

"No!" Chubais said. "I don't agree. Guys, there will be an auction!"

"He got stubborn," Gusinsky recalled. "He said, 'We took the decision that the one who pays more will be the winner.'"

Chubais recalled that the tycoons objected to the $1.2 billion starting price, set by the government, for Svyazinvest. "We will never jump over a rope set up by you," Chubais quoted one of them as saying. "I said, 'Dear Friends, what you call jumping over a rope is called competition and that's how it takes place everywhere, and that's how it is going to take place here. If you don't pay, you won't get it. The one who pays a ruble more will get it.'"[40]

Berezovsky recalled telling Chubais he was trying to change the rules too fast. "In the long run everybody wants to get to normal competition, but you can't change the situation in one day!" Berezovsky said.

"Don't dictate conditions to the state," Chubais replied, tersely.

What really angered Chubais was the way that Berezovsky and the others tried to force him to accept their cunning insider deals. At the memory of Berezovsky's statement to the *Financial Times* about the group of seven controlling half the Russian economy, Chubais flushed with anger. Who did they think they were? "What do you mean, giving this auction to Gusinsky and Berezovsky, and the next one to Potanin?" he asked. Later, he told me, he was thinking to himself, "This means that I was hired by them. They hired me and they are telling me that this goes here and that goes there." Chubais dug in his heels. No way! He would not be their puppet.

The talk turned sour. Gusinsky again blurted out that if Potanin was in the race, he would make a stink. "I promise that I will stir a scandal," he warned Chubais. He reminded Chubais that in recent months the "young reformers" had been treated warmly in Gusinsky's mass media. "We were saying that these men are making Russia good. We never wrote badly about them. We were always supporting them. This was editorial policy," Gusinsky said. But it could change overnight.

"I know that Kokh is playing on Potanin's side!" Gusinsky recalled protesting to Chubais in France. "And I'm going to prove it." There would be a big scandal unless Potanin quit the competition, he warned again.

The final warning came from Berezovsky. "In one day, you can't just break the system over your knee," Berezovsky said. "You are igniting a war. You don't want it, but it is going to happen."

Chubais walked the angry tycoons down to the waiting boat. Chubais could see trouble brewing. He knew what the big guns were capable of, because a year earlier, during the campaign, he had commanded those same guns. The television channels which had destroyed Korzhakov would now be aimed at him. His image would be smeared, his phones tapped, his movements followed, and the nasty *kompromat* flung in his face every day.

The flight back to Moscow was somber. The tycoons felt a sense of impending doom. The gambit to strike a deal with Chubais had failed. Now what? Gusinsky recalled that Potanin actively tried to find a compromise. Starting on the plane and continuing in three more meetings, Potanin suggested that they agree in advance on the price and the terms of a deal, according to Gusinsky. Potanin claimed he did not discuss the specific price. Chubais said he later discovered they had.

The first meeting was at Berezovsky's Logovaz Club. "Massive pressure was put on Potanin to step out of that auction," recalled Jordan, who was present and stood to reap big commissions in the deal.[41] "Potanin almost succumbed to the pressure, but I said, 'Vladimir, it's too late. I have brought in a consortium of Western investors, including George Soros, and they are not going to tolerate you stepping out now because of some political deal.'" Jordan recalled Berezovsky complained, "Potanin is breaking with us. He's breaking with the way we have run this country for a year and a half. And Potanin is going to destroy this place because of the way he is behaving. These are the rules of the game, and Potanin said no." Another meeting followed at Gusinsky's office. Still no resolution: Gusinsky wanted to win and Potanin refused to walk away.

The night before the auction, Potanin's plans suffered a setback. One of his investors, Kenneth Dart, the reclusive foam cup magnate who had also invested in Russian oil companies, withdrew his $300 million investment from the Potanin consortium. Jordan covered the gap, drawing funds from his own firm as well as Deutsche Morgan Grenfell. The deal was hot, and word on the street was that dozens of investors were lined up to put in even more money if Jordan needed them.

The minimum bid for Svyazinvest set by the government was $1.2 billion, but both sides guessed a winning bid would exceed $1.5 billion. The real question in the final days was whether the winner would need to go as high as $2 billion. How much was enough?

On the day of the auction, July 25, at about 3:00 P.M., Potanin and Gusinsky met alone in Gusinsky's office in the high-rise tower. Personally and politically, both oligarchs had staked their all—their reputations—on the deal. In this climactic final face-off, Gusinsky was the more emotional. He had never gotten a single brick or nail from the state, and now it was his turn. According to Gusinsky, Potanin said he was prepared to lose and named a figure he intended to bid.

Potanin denied that he named a figure while in Gusinsky's office. Potanin claimed that he just told Gusinsky to bid high if he really wanted to win. "Don't be relaxed," Potanin told Gusinsky. Chubais told me that he later learned that in the final Gusinsky-Potanin meeting, they discussed the price they would bid.

Right after Potanin left, Gusinsky recalled, all his partners converged on his office. "Potanin named the figure, but I think he is lying," Gusinsky told them. He added, "I think we must pay more." Gusinsky and Friedman were prepared to add another $100 million each of their own money to their bid, Gusinsky said, but with little time before the auction, they suddenly ran into a brick wall. For bureaucratic reasons, they could not get their partner, Telefonica, to approve a higher bid. The Spanish telephone company required board approval, and it would take time. Gusinsky was trapped.

Both Potanin and Gusinsky were also caught up in suspicion and doubt. They worried about leaks and spies. Did Potanin know that Gusinsky could not go higher because of Telefonica? Did Gusinsky know Potanin had lost Dart's $300 million? Did Gusinsky interpret the rumors about the Dart money pulling out as a ploy to lure him into making a lower bid? One of Gusinsky's major investors had his briefcase stolen just before the auction—had the other side grabbed the documents?

In the final hours, the Potanin side pondered the amount of their bid. As planned, the Soros organization and Jordan came to an agreement on the figure. At the sleek, glass-walled office building of Renaissance Capital, overlooking the Moscow River, managing director Leonid Rozhetskin spread twenty letters out on his desk. The letters were identical except for one number—the offering price for the Potanin-Soros bid. The purpose of the multiple letters was to avoid leaks right up to the last minute. Rozhetskin said he had studied the price Telefonica had paid for Latin American phone systems: $2,000 and even $3,000 a line. After a few phone calls, he picked up the letter with $1.87 billion written on it, which was the equivalent of $850 a line. He felt there was a good chance they would lose, given Telefonica's experience in Latin America.[42] But, he consoled himself—this was Russia; Telefonica was in a different market, out of the bounds of its own experience. He put the letter in a standard letter-sized envelope and slipped it into his suit pocket. He summoned a driver and headed to the Federal Property Fund building.

There he saw that Mikhail Friedman had brought Gusinsky's bid to the auction in a large, sealed envelope, inside of which were nested two other envelopes. The Gusinsky team had arranged a press conference and reception nearby to celebrate their anticipated victory. Zverev, the Gusinsky lobbyist, told me he had written a press release announcing that Gusinsky had won and would work together with Potanin. It was never issued.[43]

When the bids were opened at 5:00 P.M. for 25 percent plus one share of Svyazinvest, Gusinsky offered $1.71 billion to Potanin's $1.87 billion. Potanin had triumphed. Jordan was at home, wearing casual clothes and packing for a vacation, when Rozhetskin called him with the news. "I thought we had lost," Jordan recalled. "They had a strategic buyer, and I thought they were going to bid more than $2 billion." He called Potanin with the news they had won. "He thought it was a joke." Jordan threw on a suit and raced to his office.

With the loss, Gusinsky suffered a severe blow to his prestige, not to mention his dreams of becoming Russia's communications titan. For several days, urgent meetings were held at the White House and the Kremlin in an effort to avert all-out war among the oligarchs. The whole campaign team was thrown into the crisis: Dyachenko, Malashenko, Chernomyrdin, Chubais, and the other oligarchs. At stake was their insular, powerful club, their system, their whole experience.

"The solution was simple," Chubais recalled. "When I returned from vacation, we spent four or five nights in meetings. We were working day and night. Their main idea was to cancel the results of the auction and return the property, and then all would be in order." But, he added, "it was impossible." Chubais believed the new rules had worked: the Svyazinvest sale had brought in more money than any other sell-off in modern Russian history. Privately, Chubais was thrilled that the market had worked and that the highest bidder had won. Despite the threat of a war among the tycoons, he was not going to reverse the results now.

Perhaps they could not see it at the time, but the tight-knit oligarchy was breaking down and breaking up. Blinded by greed and wounded pride, they failed to listen to each other. Gusinsky and Berezovsky could not imagine that Chubais, once their ally, was serious about changing the rules of the game. Chubais underestimated how profoundly Gusinsky and Berezovsky refused to honor his new rules. Chubais calculated that—just as in Yeltsin's reelection campaign—they would have no choice but to go along in the end. He was wrong; the two offended tycoons went ballistic. They were infuriated that the winner was Potanin, who already had done quite well in loans for shares and was grabbing government cash faster than anyone. Malashenko later recalled that Chubais "started to pump resources into Potanin, you know, to make him the tallest guy of all. And it's like basketball, you cannot play basketball when there is a guy who is three meters tall. And from my point of view, that's what Chubais and Kokh were doing to create this monster out of Potanin."

The Svyazinvest auction was held on a languid Friday afternoon in Moscow, when traffic on the outbound highways was heavy with city dwellers fleeing for their cool country dachas. The summer news lull had set in. Over the weekend, when most people were hardly paying attention to television, and even as Gusinsky was madly trying to reverse the result of the auction, Berezovsky began firing off his big gun, the cannon of all cannons, Russia's most powerful television channel, ORT. His agent was Sergei Dorenko, a husky-voiced, handsome anchorman with a killer instinct for drama and propaganda. Dorenko had chiseled features, an extremely serious, even solemn look, and a deep, penetrating voice. He met Berezovsky after the 1994 bombing attack on Berezovsky's car, and he later became Berezovsky's most effective weapon on television. No subtle analysis, no cryptic between-the-lines hints were used in Dorenko's presentation. Perhaps because his manner was so brazen yet so self-assured, Dorenko cast a certain spell over viewers, especially those without a detailed knowledge of what he was talking about, and there were tens of millions of them. Dorenko did his attack-dog pieces not on the regular news but on a special prime-time "analytical" show called the *Sergei Dorenko Program,* which he anchored. The elite sniffed at Dorenko: How cheap! How crude! How opinionated! Kiselyov, while not universally admired, was the darling of the elite, but Dorenko was the master of the masses.

On Saturday, July 26, the day after the Svyazinvest auction, the history of Russian capitalism turned another corner. Up until this day, the oligarchs and reformers had been allies, working together against outside forces, such as Gennady Zyuganov or the "party of war." But when Dorenko's television show went on the air that summer Saturday evening, the club of tycoons and reformers began to fall apart. The oligarchs and reformers began to fight one another in what became known as the bankers' war. The destruction of the club left the Russian political and economic elite virtually paralyzed.

The first salvo was fired by Dorenko, agent of Berezovsky. His target was Potanin. Near the end of his Saturday show, Dorenko charged that Potanin used murky shell companies in the auction for Svyazinvest; the "profits are going to be siphoned off to an offshore zone." The investors in Potanin's deal, Dorenko intoned, were "pure speculators," in the unseemly Soviet sense of petty black marketeers, "people with a scandalous, tarnished-to-doubtful reputation," who "did not spend a single minute of their life dealing with communications." He attacked Jordan and Soros, saying the philanthropist was "one of the most famous speculators on the planet," and declared that Kokh, their patron, "writes the auction terms for his friends." Dorenko brought Nemtsov into the program too, saying he was "as active as a roach on the wall." Two days later, in an interview on Gusinsky's radio station, Echo of Moscow, Dorenko expanded on the metaphor. "Haven't you ever seen," he said, "that when you spray a cockroach with a special irritant it starts running around like mad?" Dorenko was asked whether there was a conspiracy between the government and Potanin. "I did not say conspiracy, but the whole thing smacks of it," he replied.[44]

Dorenko had lit the match, and it did not take long to ignite a full-scale media conflagration, just as Gusinsky and Berezovsky had promised. On the first day newspapers were published after the auction,

Monday, July 28, Gusinsky's broadsheet, *Sevodnya*, rendered a verdict in the headline: "The Money Stank." The article said Potanin and Kokh had become too friendly and that Potanin's money was of questionable origin. The young reformers were immediately thrown on the defensive, and the feisty Nemtsov wheeled out his favorite slogans to blast the losing oligarchs, Gusinsky and Berezovsky. "They don't need honest rules and democratic capitalism," he said. "They want bandit capitalism!" Nemtsov had never really defined his "bandit capitalism," and *Sevodnya* fired back with the obvious question: Who had been the father of it? Perhaps it was Chubais or Yeltsin? "It now transpires," the newspaper deadpanned, "that the guarantor of Russian democracy has presided over a sustained effort to build 'gangster capitalism.'"[45] The point was, If Russia had become a gangster state, weren't they all responsible?

Kokh, the privatization chief, resigned on August 13, announcing he wanted to go into private business. The initial Kremlin reaction was cordial; Yeltsin thanked Kokh for his services. Up to this point, Gusinsky had said nothing in public, as he tried to get Chubais to reverse the deal. But by mid-August it was evident Chubais would not budge. Gusinsky then attacked. In an August 14 interview on Echo of Moscow radio, Gusinsky said of Potanin's winning bid, "There is money, and there is money. As far as I am concerned, money has a smell." He recalled the discussion with Chubais about new rules of the game. "Honest rules of the game," he added, "presuppose that the seller and the buyer should not be in collusion." Gusinsky hinted that the government had been in cahoots with Potanin, but he was cautious. (The truth was that Gusinsky had expected that the government would be in cahoots with him, but he had lost.) The next day, Yeltsin unexpectedly weighed in, noting that both Svyazinvest and Norilsk Nickel auctions had been won by Potanin.[46] "The entire scandal," Yeltsin said, "is connected with the fact that certain banks are apparently closer to the soul of Alfred Kokh than others."

Kokh's role now came under closer scrutiny. Although no one paid much attention at the time, Kokh had earlier reported on his financial disclosure form that he had received a $100,000 advance to write a book about privatization. Alexander Minkin, the muckraking journalist who was close to Gusinsky since their theater days, wrote an article in the newspaper *Novaya Gazeta*, questioning why Kokh was given such a large advance from what he described as a tiny company,

Servina Trading, in Geneva. Minkin, using a Swiss reporter to make some checks, reported that the company had only a tiny room and two or three workers. He quoted a Servina official as saying they had not yet seen the manuscript. "Servina paid Kokh a hundred thousand dollars for hope only," Minkin said. "It's obvious that a tiny company cannot make such luxurious gestures. It was not Servina that paid. It was someone else paying through it. It is also clear that Kokh sold not the book, but something totally different."[47] Minkin was just getting warmed up.

Every day, the battle brought new headlines and new charges. The war consumed the "young reformers" and the tycoons. On Saturday morning, September 13, I grabbed a few newspapers and went to watch my sons play soccer. But once on the field, I stood riveted, not on the game but on *Nezavisimaya Gazeta*, the Berezovsky newspaper. The paper published a remarkable front-page ad hominem tirade against Chubais under the headline "Anatoly Chubais Seeks Control over Russia." What was interesting was that the attack was not the usual sleazy *kompromat* of secret documents or embarrassing wiretaps, but a thinking man's screed against Chubais. The byline was Ulyan Kerzonov, most likely a pen name for Berezovsky. The commentary was acid. Chubais, already a hated figure in Russian public opinion, was portrayed as darkly scheming and power hungry, "a cynical zealot," for whom "the ends justifies the means," whose mentality "resembles that of Lenin," a "ferocious pragmatist who has placed his faith solely in revolutionary expediency." The author complimented Chubais for creating, during the election campaign, "a closed-circuit oligarchic system, later nicknamed 'the seven banks.'" But now, the author said, Chubais was wrecking the group of seven bankers in order to build up Potanin alone as a "privately owned supermonopoly." The essay had all the markings of an angry personal letter from Berezovsky, furious that Chubais had ruined his cozy club of oligarchs, his *bolshoi kapital* operating system. "The 'seven banks' system could have become a normal market," the author said, "but Chubais decided otherwise."

The article was the talk of Moscow and reverberated the following evening on Kiselyov's widely watched Sunday television show, *Itogi*. "We haven't heard or read something like that for quite a long time," Kiselyov marveled. He was cautious and recalled later that he was distracted by negotiations for the release of a kidnapped NTV correspondent in Chechnya.[48] Dobrodeyev told me he felt trepidation and dismay when the bankers' war broke onto the airwaves. "I had doubts, and very big doubts," he said. It was one thing to use journalists and television for a fight against Zyuganov and the Communists, a cause that was "clear, explicable, and absolutely comprehensible to everyone." But Svyazinvest was an obscure commercial dispute. Should journalists risk their reputations on a war between avaricious business interests? "It was a shameful situation for the mass media as a whole," he recalled.

Yeltsin was furious at the growing discord, and he was also confused. He had given rise to the "young reformers" and the tycoons, and now they were at each other's throats. The vicious mudslinging every day in the newspapers "irritated me tremendously," Yeltsin recalled.[49] He summoned the oligarchs to the Kremlin on the Monday after the article appeared in *Nezavisimaya Gazeta*. Gusinsky, Potanin, Friedman, Khodorkovsky, Vinogradov, and Smolensky came, as did Yumashev, but Berezovsky, deputy secretary of the security council and theoretically a civil servant, was absent, as was Chubais. Smolensky told me that Chubais was "divorced from the banks, and it's hurting. . . . We shall have a hard life without him. Everybody feels it. We have been together a long time."[50]

It was the first time since the meeting after Davos that Yeltsin had seen the oligarchs as a group. Vinogradov recalled that Yeltsin appeared self-assured and was clear of voice. "I urged them, and they agreed, that banks cannot be, as it were, above the authorities," Yeltsin told reporters after the two-hour meeting. Yeltsin said the oligarchs agreed to stop attacking Chubais and Nemtsov, and "we achieved mutual understanding." Inside the meeting, Yeltsin also said that some bidders felt Kokh leaked information to one side during the Svyazinvest auction. Potanin came steeled for criticism: on the spot, in front of Yeltsin, he volunteered to give up his lucrative Customs Committee accounts and transfer the money to the Central Bank.[51]

Looking back, Yeltsin said he felt estranged from the tycoons. "Despite their assurances, I sensed that these men had not really become my allies. Potanin seemed to stick out from all the others. I couldn't rid myself of the hunch that he had his own agenda." Yeltsin said that behind their smiles and agreements, the tycoons left him cold. "It was as if I were dealing with a people of a different race," he said, "people made not of steel but of some kind of cosmic metal. Not a single side considered itself guilty. There was no area for compromise. There were no concrete concessions."

Indeed, Yeltsin at this critical moment was baffled. He remains confused in recalling the role of the oligarchs in his memoir. He vigorously defends how property was sold off cheaply to the oligarchs, welcomes approvingly their support for him in the 1996 campaign, and notes their interest in political stability, so their companies would grow. He insists they were not underworld figures. Yet, at the same time, Yeltsin decries the fact that the tycoons tried to influence the government and "tried to run the country behind the backs of the politicians." Yeltsin describes this as a "new and dangerous challenge." He calls the businessmen "new and illegitimate centers of power." He writes, ominously: "Our greatest threat came from the people with big money, who gobbled each other up and thus toppled the political edifice we had built with such difficulty." Yeltsin obviously both liked and disliked his oligarchs, the children of his capitalist revolution.[52]

Soros, who said he thought investing in the Svyazinvest deal was helping establish legitimate capitalism, found himself snared in the sleazy bankers' war. Alex Goldfarb, who had been the intermediary between Soros and Berezovsky earlier, told me that Soros expressed worry about the uproar. "Soros said it will all end very badly," Goldfarb told me. Goldfarb went to see Berezovsky in the middle of the bankers' war to appeal for a truce. He urged Berezovsky to stop the combat. "I said it will destroy everything," Goldfarb recalled. "Everyone was so ecstatic when they got rid of the party of war. They got the good side of Yeltsin, the reformist side, and then a few months later this ugly thing comes out."

"I am not an angel," Berezovsky told Goldfarb, "but those guys are worse."

Soros later recalled that he personally tried to dissuade Berezovsky from the onslaught, telling Berezovsky that he could be rich enough with the companies he already owned. "He told me I did not understand," Soros recalled. "It was not a question of how rich he was, but how he measured up against Chubais and against the other oligarchs. They had made a deal, and they must stick to it. He must destroy or be destroyed himself." Soros concluded that there was no way Berezovsky could be transformed from robber baron to legitimate capitalist.[53]

Jordan, who had brought Soros into the deal, suddenly found that his multiple-entry visa to Russia was yanked, just before he left Moscow for London in early October. Dorenko, sticking in the knife ever so smoothly, announced on his television show that Jordan, a U.S. citizen, was in possession of Russian government secrets, perhaps secret contracts about weapons sales. Jordan, he said, must "say 'God Bless America' every time his eyes fall on any sort of classified information." There was no secret who was behind the decision to pull Jordan's visa; it was Berezovsky. He said a few days later, "The case with Jordan is a matter of a U.S. citizen getting access to exclusive information about our financial and defense secrets."[54] Jordan's firm responded that the real issue was using the visa in a war of business competitors. Nemtsov stepped in and got Jordan a new visa.

In early October, London's *Financial Times* reported that the tiny company which paid Kokh's $100,000 book advance had ties to Potanin's Uneximbank: the link that Gusinsky had suspected. An official of Potanin's Swiss affiliate, Banque Unexim (Suisse), had previously been a director at Servina Trading and commissioned the book. The Moscow city prosecutor announced a criminal investigation into the book advance, saying it seemed to be unusually large given the potential subject. Potanin acknowledged that he and Kokh were friends but insisted it "does not affect the work." Chrystia Freeland, the *Financial Times* correspondent in Moscow who broke the story, later wrote that even more incriminating *kompromat* was waiting in the wings—the offended oligarchs obtained a shaky, handheld video of Kokh and Potanin on holiday at the Côte d'Azur one month after the Svyazinvest sale.[55] Kokh later told me he didn't see anything wrong vacationing with Potanin so soon after the Svyazinvest deal. "But what's wrong if I want to spend some time with my friends in France?" he asked curtly. He admitted, however, resentment over the investigation by the prosecutor. "I was nearly put in jail," he complained.[56] Chubais came to Kokh's defense again, saying Kokh had indeed written a book. "I have known Kokh for ten years and know that he is a man of integrity," Chubais told reporters. "Lavishly paid lies are reprinted from one newspaper owned by a banker to a newspaper owned by another, from a TV channel owned by one of them to a TV channel owned by another." Gusinsky had another view. He believed that Chubais was clean, but Kokh had taken money from Potanin and Chubais was trying to protect his friend.

Chubais decided it was time to strike back. With Nemtsov, he went to Yeltsin at his out-of-town retreat, Gorky 9, on November 4 and demanded that Yeltsin fire Berezovsky from the Security Council. Chubais argued that the war would subside if Berezovsky were dismissed. Yeltsin looked at Chubais and recalled that only a year before Chubais had asked him to appoint Berezovsky to the same post. Yeltsin later wrote in his memoir that he resented all the attention Berezovsky got as the supposed kingmaker, the power behind the throne of the Yeltsin years. "I never liked Boris Berezovsky and I still don't like him," Yeltsin wrote. He complained that Berezovsky always overstated his influence. "There weren't any mechanisms through which Berezovsky might have exercised influence over me, the president." Yeltsin did not address the book royalties that others said Berezovsky brought to the president's family.

Nor was it Berezovsky's style to whisper directly into Yeltsin's ear. Berezovsky operated through intermediaries and agents, through layers and indirection, including his friends in Yeltsin's inner circle.[57] For example, Yumashev invited Berezovsky to the Kremlin the day before he was sacked to show Berezovsky the presidential decree, Berezovsky said. Yumashev had advised Yeltsin against firing Berezovsky.

Yeltsin dismissed Berezovsky November 5. Berezovsky went to Echo of Moscow radio station to fire back at Chubais, saying he had a Bolshevik mentality. "He believes that ends justify means."

If Chubais thought that getting Berezovsky fired would be the end of it, he was mistaken. "I had a feeling," Yeltsin said, "that Chubais was about to get his head chopped off." He was right.

In late October, Chubais mentioned to a group of reporters traveling with him to London, at the end of an interview, that he and several of his deputies were writing a "monograph" about privatization. Chubais said 95 percent of the honorarium from the book would be given to charity, but he did not mention specifically how much they were being paid or by whom. Chubais said the book was originally designed to celebrate the fifth anniversary of the beginning of mass privatization. The interview was published on the front page of *Kommersant Daily*, the influential newspaper, on October 28 under the headline "Chubais Is Not a Reader; Chubais a Writer." The story hardly caused a ripple, but it set in motion a chain of events that would boomerang against Chubais.

Sergei Lisovsky, the advertising magnate who had worked on the 1996 campaign, recalled being invited to a strategy session by the

Berezovsky-Gusinsky camp to plan a counterattack on Chubais. The attack was to be based on new documents that the Berezovsky team had obtained about the Chubais monograph. The documents showed that Chubais and four members of his team received $90,000 each, or $450,000 altogether, for the book. The information could blow up into a scandal because it would reinforce the impression, created by the Kokh disclosures, that the young reformers were lining their own pockets. The amounts were relatively small compared to the gargantuan profits and payoffs in the years of easy money, but the symbolism was awful.

Lisovsky said there was a "detailed scenario" for the attack on Chubais, including "who was to start first, who was to pick it up." Lisovsky said he refused to participate. "You are committing suicide," he warned the Gusinsky-Berezovsky camp. "If you kill Chubais, you will eliminate yourself in several years' time, because in the long run, Chubais will never sink you, never jail you—he has created you as Russian capitalists. And anyone else in his place will treat you very cruelly."[58]

The plotters decided to make the material public through Minkin, the investigative journalist close to Gusinsky who earlier questioned the $100,000 book fee paid to Kokh. I knew Minkin from a few years earlier when he had told me a harrowing story of how he was attacked by pipe-wielding goons in the middle of the night for a story he had written. In the *perestroika* years, Minkin was known for some really penetrating stories about the Soviet Union. But there was another kind of investigative reporting that involved simply taking handouts of compromising materials from commercial interests or security services—the *kompromat*—and publicizing it. The use of *kompromat* was a sleazy business; it might be true, it might be forged, it might be half true, but it was always distributed to tarnish someone's reputation at the behest of a foe.

In this case, Minkin told me that the information about Chubais was given to him outright. He would not say who his source was, but he had no qualms disclosing the materials because he shared the same "principles." And, he said, he knew that Berezovsky and Gusinsky were behind it. The same documents were already on the desk of Anatoly Kulikov, the interior minister, Yeltsin recalled in his memoir. Minkin immediately went public in an interview on Gusinsky's radio station, Echo of Moscow, on November 12. Not by chance, Minkin's appearance on the radio station was covered by Berezovsky and Gusinsky's television stations. The fees for the book were "exorbitant," Minkin reported. "This is a veiled form of a bribe" and "a method of money laundering," he said.

Where had the money come from? Minkin said the publisher of the monograph was Sevodnya Press, which had been affiliated with the newspaper *Komsomolskaya Pravda* (and was not part of the newspaper *Sevodnya*). Sevodnya Press had been purchased that year by Potanin's Uneximbank, but it was not owned by Potanin until after the Chubais team had made the contracts to publish the book. Minkin correctly reported that money for the book had come from the fund that Chubais set up during the 1996 campaign, when he had received the $5 million from the tycoons. However, this accurate suggestion by Minkin, that Chubais was somehow laundering the campaign money, was totally overlooked in the ensuing uproar. The word "bribe" stuck out. So did the tenuous link to Potanin. Chubais and his team kept quiet about the true source of the money because they did not want to reopen the far more sensitive issue of the "black cash" and how Yeltsin's 1996 campaign was financed. A source close to Chubais told me that the book was actually a hastily conceived cover story for the planned transfer of the leftover 1996 campaign money to the team.

Minkin's words on the radio touched off a new storm. Chubais was defiant at first, insisting, "I do not see any crime against humanity here" and repeating that 95 percent of the money was being given to a "charity," which he described, puzzlingly, as a fund to protect private property rights headed by Yegor Gaidar. The promise to give the money to "charity" was rather vague, and Gaidar was furious that Chubais had roped him into the scandal when he had nothing to do with it. Two days after Minkin went public, Chubais said "the fee is high . . . and we must admit this." Chubais wrote Yeltsin a letter saying that although the book was real, he "considered himself guilty." Yeltsin immediately fired Alexander Kazakov, a Chubais ally, from his post in the Kremlin and then sacked Maxim Boiko, another Chubais protégé who headed the privatization agency, and Pyotr Mostovoi, head of the federal bankruptcy agency. All were Chubais men in the government and coauthors of the book. The fifth coauthor was Kokh. Finally, Chubais was relieved of his Finance Ministry portfolio, a major setback, although Yeltsin said he refused to give up on Chubais altogether and kept him in the government. "The book scandal was the banana peel on which the whole team of young reformers slipped," said Yeltsin. Chubais later sued Minkin for slander but lost.

The bankers' war was extraordinarily destructive for everyone. The young reformers and the tycoons squandered most of the year in their struggle. Chubais and Nemtsov never got back on track. Their reform agenda died. The irony was that outwardly Russia seemed to be on the comeback trail. "The year 1997 is one of missed opportunities," Vasiliev lamented. Arkady Yevstafiev, the Chubais aide, said the oligarchs were to blame. "They wanted to rule the country because they were greedy and wanted everything for themselves. There is a proverb: The appetite comes in the eating. And their appetite became huge. Berezovsky didn't need Chubais for one simple reason: he didn't give him an opportunity to grab everything in this hands. Chubais stood in his way."

"We lost 1995–1996—we can excuse that," said Steven Jennings, the investment banker who was Jordan's partner. "But we had a year of no change in 1997. That was when they should have gone for the jugular." Instead of aggressive reforms, the credibility of Chubais and Nemtsov was besmirched, their attention diverted, their energy sapped. If anything, the events served to etch oligarchic capitalism more deeply into the public consciousness—and demonstrated how powerful the tycoons and their television weapons had become.

Potanin also suffered. After he won the Svyazinvest auction, his plan for taking over the company and making a quick fortune fell apart. The government never let him in the door. The second stake was not sold off, and the value of the $1.87 billion investment collapsed. Soros later called Svyazinvest the worst investment he ever made. From a business standpoint, Gusinsky was lucky he lost, but he made lasting enemies in 1997. Kokh never forgot the wounds Gusinsky inflicted on him and later sought revenge. The rancor of Svyazinvest came back to haunt Gusinsky when he was in desperate trouble three years later. Gusinsky, who had doubts about the 1996 fling with Yeltsin, told me that he was also unsettled by the Svyazinvest debacle. "Exactly then, I realized that the further away I distance myself from the authorities," he recalled, "the safer my business is going to be and the more honestly I can look in the eyes of my children."

Even worse than the soiled reputations and bruised egos, the bankers' war crippled Russia's economic and political leadership. Chubias complained, "The major players on my team are being investigated. Enormous numbers of telephone calls are bugged. My closest relatives are being investigated. . . . My son is constantly being followed. And much else is happening nonstop. What has yet to be done? I haven't been shot at."[59] Casting worried glances over their shoulders every day, the Russian reformers were unprepared to look ahead at a critical time, a period when even the most experienced seaman would have had difficulty navigating the ship. A financial crisis broke out in East Asia while they were fighting over Svyazinvest. When Russia's economy began to slow in the autumn, Chubais and the reformers were so wrapped up in the Svyazinvest deal that they completely failed to see that Russia was vulnerable—and exposed—to nasty global trends.

The Russian Trading System index began the year at 213, and it reached a peak of 571 on October 6. In the midst of the good times, there was a sudden drop in temperature: the world's stock markets crashed on October 27. Russian markets went down with them, but the event was not seen as a catastrophe. Chubais was sanguine, even upbeat, about the year ahead: "This is the beginning of a turn," the beginning of a "long, ever more steep and powerful trajectory of growth, which will be clear and obvious . . . to every person's family. They will judge by his wages, his income, his ability to buy a modern car and have a proper vacation in summer."[60]

When I saw Chubais on December 2, he was still wounded and angry about the bankers' war. He said he was paying attention to East Asian financial statistics but predicted that the Asian crisis would be a small setback for Russia, perhaps a six-month postponement of economic recovery.[61] "Nothing can happen to the ruble," he insisted. Later in that month, Chubais said, "Today we really have every reason to say that the most dangerous point is behind us, that it occurred early in December."[62]

On December 10, Yeltsin was admitted to the hospital again.[63] The bear went back into his winter hibernation. A financial hurricane was bearing down on Moscow, and neither the father of Russian capitalism nor his quarrelsome children were ready for it.

Chapter 15

Roar of the Dragons

THE YEAR 1998 arrived with Mikhail Khodorkovsky riding high. Known for his modest personal tastes, Khodorkovsky preferred polo shirts and sport jackets to suits and ties, but he celebrated New Year's Eve in elegant style at Nostalgia, a Parisian eatery in the middle of Moscow. With an understated interior of antique furniture, the restaurant's pride was an unsurpassed cellar of six hundred exquisite French wines. On New Year's Eve, Eric Kraus, a stockbroker and loquacious Frenchman, caught sight of Khodorkovsky and his party of a dozen people at Nostalgia—and Kraus could not believe his eyes. On Khodorkovsky's table was a bottle of a prized Bordeaux, Château Haut-Brion. Curious, Kraus asked the waiter for the wine list. Château Haut-Brion was $4,000 a bottle. "Russia could do no wrong in 1997," Kraus remembered. "It was a country being reborn. Even the journalists were misty-eyed. We all felt like we were part of some grand social experiment."[1]

Khodorkovsky had reason for optimism. He was expanding by leaps and bounds.[2] In October he unabashedly told a business crowd in Washington that he wanted to be among the top ten world oil companies within a decade. Only thirty-four years old, he commanded

Yukos, with Russia's largest oil reserves, 100,000 workers, and a market capitalization of $9 billion. And his quest was not yet over.[3] In the next few months, he won control of another Russian oil trophy, Eastern Oil Company, at a government privatization sale. Unlike the bargain-basement purchase of Yukos, Khodorkovsky paid full price for Eastern, $1.2 billion for 45 percent of the company plus 9 percent bought on the open market, which gave him control. He planned to fold the company into Yukos.

Khodorkovsky got hooked on a new, alluring kind of easy money—loans from abroad. He borrowed heavily from the West to finance the acquisition of Eastern Oil Company. His ability to borrow was magnified many times over because he now controlled an ocean of oil in western Siberia. In October 1997 he took out a $300 million line of credit from Credit Suisse First Boston with no collateral. He took out three loans from Credit Lyonnais during the year, all based on a promise of future oil revenues, of which $299 million was still outstanding at year's end. Then on December 7, 1997, Khodorkovsky signed a megadeal with three major underwriters, Goldman Sachs, Merrill Lynch, and Credit Lyonnais, to borrow $500 million against future sales of oil. They paid Khodorkovsky upfront in exchange for revenues from 600,000 metric tons of oil each quarter to be sold through two French oil companies, Total and Elf Aquitaine.[4]

As he took these loans, Khodorkovsky was using transfer pricing to get the oil cheaply. He was demanding that the oilfield extraction companies, Yuganskneftegaz and Samaraneftegaz, sell the oil at dirt-cheap prices to his parent company, Yukos. Once he had purchased the cheap oil, Khodorkovsky pledged it, at much higher export prices, to secure the loans. He was using a clever means of stripping value out of the extraction companies, which were left with debts and expenses while he got the benefit of the new loans.

This was a risky game because Khodorkovsky did not own all of the oilfield extraction companies. They were still partially in the hands of Kenneth Dart, the foam cup magnate who had bought his shares in the early 1990s. Khodorkovsky's transfer pricing was pumping value away from Dart's holdings. Khodorkovsky's strategy demonstrated what became a fundamental rule of Russian capitalism in the late 1990s—control over a company was winner take all. Under Russian law, to control the key decisions, especially to put your people in management, you needed to own at least 51 percent of a company. If you owned less than that, you were vulnerable to losing the value of your holdings. Minority shareholders were at the mercy of the boss—their rights were often trampled and their profits stolen. Dart owned 12.85 percent of the shares of Yuganskneftegaz and 12.3 percent of Samaraneftegaz, the two big oilfield extraction companies that were the core of Yukos. He watched angrily as Khodorkovsky drained off the black gold and left him empty-handed.[5] Dart's representative, E. Michael Hunter, said that Yukos was "illegally looting its partially owned subsidiaries." Western lenders, anxious to court Khodorkovsky, didn't care. Goldman Sachs, Wall Street's biggest and richest partnership, was especially avid. When Dart complained that the lenders were making loans based on oil that was being wrongly taken from him, the lenders brushed aside the complaints.[6]

In search of still more cash to finance the purchase of Eastern Oil Company, Khodorkovsky borrowed $236 million from a consortium of three international banks, Daiwa of Japan, West Merchant, a subsidiary of WestLB of Germany, and Standard Chartered of London. This loan, also arranged by Goldman Sachs, later turned explosive. The loan was not secured by oil, but by shares of stock in Yukos itself. In this arrangement, known as a "repo" deal because the shares could be repossessed by the lender if the borrower defaulted, Khodorkovsky pledged about 30 percent of Yukos shares as security. The loan obligation was not taken directly by Yukos but by Menatep, the Khodorkovsky bank, and the money was used to help buy Eastern Oil Company.

Westerners were tripping over themselves to get money into the hands of Russian companies, often overlooking the pitfalls, lack of experience, poor management, corruption, and misleading or missing financial data. "People were throwing hundreds of millions of dollars at Menatep," a former Bank Menatep official told me. When the repo deal was being put together, this official was assigned to help with the "due diligence," in which the lenders carry out an investigation of the borrower in order to discover any hidden problems. A "due diligence" investigation is like a house inspection—you need to know whether there are any cracks in the walls before you close the deal. In Russia's speculative, booming economy, these investigations were often superficial. The lenders were so hungry for a piece of the action that they practically gave money away. In this case, the three lending banks sought to discover who owned Menatep. According to my source, who was present at the conversation, the lenders were given some absolutely uninformative piece of paper about the bank's shareholder structure, but *not* information about who really owned Menatep. "You don't need to know who owns this bank; it's not your business," a high-ranking Menatep official told them. "We need $200 million and we need it in forty-eight hours." My source added: "And you know what is amazing? They turned around and gave the money."

Who was at fault when the loan later blew up—the lenders or the borrowers? At the outset, the lenders failed to check for cracks in the house. But as long as the good times were rolling in Russia, neither lender nor borrower wanted to check anything. A crisis in East Asia? Lack of confidence in emerging markets? Declining oil prices? Why worry? For Khodorkovsky, another blockbuster deal was in the works.

On January 19, 1998, Khodorkovsky announced plans to combine Yukos, the second-largest Russian oil company, with Sibneft, a smaller but still formidable oil company Berezovsky had created for himself in the last days of loans for shares. The new oil giant, to be called Yuksi, would be Russia's largest vertically integrated oil company, with 22 percent of the country's production and the world's largest reserves. Khodorkovsky would head the new colossus, with the owners of Yukos controlling 60 percent and the Sibneft owners 40 percent. Yuksi would be "world-class," Khodorkovsky declared, and the announcement contained a hint of Khodorkovsky's motives: both he and Berezovsky wanted to compete for the upcoming privatization of the last major oil holding company not yet privatized, Rosneft. If they were together, their oil companies could pull in more Western lending and would stand a better chance of winning Rosneft than if they were apart. They faced possible competition from global energy firms such as British Petroleum and Royal Dutch/Shell. The lust for Western capital was palpable.

What was fascinating about the Yuksi announcement, however, was not the hype but the cast of characters who showed up that day at the dreary Foreign Ministry press center. Viktor Chernomyrdin blessed the merger with a short speech. Down in the front row, four tycoons who were almost never seen together in public were sitting shoulder to shoulder: Vladimir Gusinsky, Alexander Smolensky, Boris Berezovsky, and Mikhail Khodorkovsky. As I watched, it was hard to escape the conclusion that Berezovsky's vision had come true. The oligarchs had become a new "board of directors" of Russia, and they were beginning to divide up spheres of influence: Gusinsky as media magnate, Smolensky as banking king, Khodorkovsky as oil baron, and Berezovsky as their ever watchful coach. On the day of the Yuksi announcement, the tycoons were, tentatively, making still more ambitious plans. Gusinsky and Smolensky lent Khodorkovsky a hand to buy Eastern Oil Company, and discussions took place about a merger of their three banks. Gusinsky's Most and Khodorkovsky's Menatep would be folded into Smolensky's SBS-Agro, making Smolensky the banking king, while Khodorkovsky and Gusinsky could then devote time to their respective oil and media empires.

Gusinsky was also expanding rapidly and looking to the West for finance. His NTV-Plus satellite television service was already on the air, and he had placed an order for a high-powered digital satellite from Hughes Space and Communications International. The $143 million financing for the satellite, which was to be launched later in the year, came from abroad—a loan from the Exim Bank of the United States, guaranteed by the Russian Finance Ministry. Gusinsky also launched a new regional television network, TNT, to connect local stations with the flagship NTV and started a new international broadcasting service to carry NTV to Russian speakers in Israel. Most importantly, Gusinsky was intensively preparing an initial public offering of NTV stock in the United States in the summer. The offering would have valued NTV at between $1 billion and $1.5 billion. Gusinsky hoped to raise about $120 million in fresh capital at the outset, and more later. Gusinsky was expanding into movies too, founding a new movie production company and planning construction of an eleven-screen megaplex in the center of Moscow. He had high expectations that NTV-Plus would become the television of choice for the middle class, although the level of subscribers, about 130,000 at the turn of the year, was disappointing. He wanted millions.

Berezovsky's businesses were in the shadows; his holdings were a mysterious empire shielded by layers of shell companies and offshore havens. He was known to have obtained a major block of the oil company Sibneft created in loans for shares. Berezovsky never owned Aeroflot shares, but he reaped profits from millions of dollars in hard currency ticket sales. He acted as a middleman, making loans back to Aeroflot out of cash he had accumulated from the company's own revenues. He still owned the Logovaz car dealerships, and his media holdings were expanding beyond ORT television to include about a quarter ownership of TV-6, a Moscow channel, the newspaper *Nezavisimaya*

Gazeta, and the glossy magazine *Ogonyok.*[7] The publications and television gave Berezovsky an outlet for his views; his passion was politics, not business. After the bankers' war, when he lost his job at the Kremlin Security Council, Berezovsky remained an adviser to Valentin Yumashev, Yeltsin's chief of staff.

Smolensky was also addicted to Western loans. In 1997 he borrowed $55 million from West Merchant Bank Ltd. and $113 million from Chase Manhattan Corporation, and he floated his $250 million Eurobond.[8] Smolensky later admitted to me he was not really sure what to do with the money from the big Eurobond—he was borrowing because the lenders told him he could. "In retrospect, all experts say the bank should not have entered the international capital markets for another ten years. It was a strategic mistake, and I agree with that," Smolensky said. "We didn't need the capital."

Nonetheless, Smolensky and the others were gulping down Western money as fast as they could, and they constantly jetted to London and New York financial centers to make new deals. In 1997, for the first time, the loans taken out from foreign sources by Russian banks grew larger than the assets that the banks kept abroad. The banks were madly taking in overseas loans and using the money to buy high-flying stocks and bonds *inside* the country.[9]

The Yuksi merger itself was so hastily prepared that Khodorkovsky asked journalists not to inquire about too many details. One of Khodorkovsky's close associates later told me the real reason for the Yuksi merger was not to win Rosneft or borrow more money, although both would have been nice. "It was all about Khodorkovsky's ambition," he said, "to create the biggest oil company in Russia. The motives were not economic, but ambition."[10] The merger fell apart in five and a half months. Oil prices were falling because of dropping demand in East Asia. The tycoons sitting in the front row were smiling merrily, even as they floated down the river in a raft together—straight for a waterfall.

The ghost of the bankers' war still lingered in the spring. Angry and smarting from the autumn conflict, Berezovsky and Chubais faced off against each other. Their conflict paralyzed the political elite, undermined the confidence of investors, and left Russia unprepared for the approaching disaster. Both men gave a series of impassioned newspaper interviews in early March, savaging each other. The Chubais era "is over," Berezovsky declared. "Big capital is the Russian government's strongest mainstay now."[11] Chubais shot back: "We will have to drag ourselves away" from the tycoons, "literally by the hair."[12] Chubais taunted Berezovsky, saying the oligarchs' plan to destroy him after Svyazinvest "failed to produce the desired result." Chubais portrayed Berezovsky as an evil power broker who "with the snap of his fingers" can replace a vice prime minister. Berezovsky's entire business, Chubais said, is "political influence."[13]

In a remarkable performance, Chubais gave a resentment-filled interview to *Nezavisimaya Gazeta*, which Berezovsky had used to attack him the previous fall. "Lies, all lies," Chubais said. "It's a sold-out newspaper, sold-out journalists, and a sold-out chief editor." Chubais acknowledged that he was sick of work in the government. "Government service—I can't stand it," he complained. In Berezovsky's search for *kompromat* to use against him, Chubais reported, "My wife's friends were offered money—quite decent money—for any sleaze against me. They asked all my acquaintances in St. Petersburg—fifty or sixty people—if they could tell something about me."[14]

Berezovsky fell off a snowmobile racing at night at high speed on February 15, injured his spine, and was hospitalized in Switzerland in March.[15] Restless, he began an ambitious new political gambit, even more audacious than Chubais imagined with his comment about Berezovsky snapping the fingers to replace a vice premier. Berezovsky began plotting to choose Yeltsin's successor. The next elections were two years away, but Berezovsky did not want to wait until just a few months beforehand, as they had in 1996. He wanted to install his *bolshoi kapital* model in the Kremlin now, a model in which businessmen would call the shots and serve as the "board of directors" of Russia Inc. The prime minister would take orders, as a good chief executive officer should.

Berezovsky's insatiable ambition, his desire to set the bar as high as possible, was completely in character with his past, from his erstwhile visions of winning a Nobel Prize to his superdeals for the Zhiguli cars and his rescue mission for Yeltsin. But this time something was different. Russia was drifting toward an economic precipice. None of the oligarchs appeared to realize that danger lay ahead. Berezovsky did not grasp that his games would fuel instability when coolheaded stability was desperately needed. The bankers' war had already left a casualty-strewn battlefield. The constant infighting and mudslinging in the autumn of 1997 had made investors skittish about Russia, and the stock market declined. Now Berezovsky stirred up the chaos again.

His precise actions in this period are not completely clear. He loved intrigue and backroom maneuvering, and his public statements were often oblique. But what caught my ear was a phrase—typically indirect—that Berezovsky began to use over and over again. The oligarchs, he insisted, had to ensure the "continuity of power." What Berezovsky meant, but didn't dare say directly, was that they wanted a strong hand in determining Russia's next president. The voters? They would do what they were told, and they would be told on the oligarchs' television channels. More importantly, the tycoons wanted to install a leader who would broadly continue the same reform path as Yeltsin but would heed their demands, someone they could trust and manipulate. They needed a leader who would play by the rules of oligarchic capitalism.

What made this choice of a successor more urgent was Yeltsin's unsteadiness. He frequently appeared confused and remote in the early months of 1998. I heard constant rumors that he suffered periods of disorientation or blackouts. The oligarchs began to wonder, seriously, how long he would last as president. They knew that under Russian law, if Yeltsin stepped down for health reasons, the prime minister would automatically become the acting Russian president and would have a good chance to win the job permanently.

Thus choosing the next prime minister quite likely meant selecting Russia's next president. "I realized that the prime minister was going to be the next president," Berezovsky told me later. "This I understood well. That's why I was saying, the first criteria we had to evaluate was that this is the next president of Russia."[16]

Berezovsky thought it was imperative to replace the sitting prime minister, Viktor Chernomyrdin, who was tired and drifting. "Chernomyrdin had exhausted his potential," Berezovsky said later. "He was the prime minister for five years, in the most difficult time. Yeltsin was often out of shape, and Chernomyrdin was bearing a huge load. He was making promises to everybody—to the right, to the left, and over five years he gave so many promises that he became completely immobilized, like chains on his feet. I could see it was hard for him to move forward." Gusinsky, who participated in these discussions, told me he held a similar view.[17]

That Chernomyrdin was adrift was widely evident at the time. But Berezovsky may have had another motive. He wanted to install his own man. Berezovsky was always thinking about setting the bar as high as possible—and the idea that he would like to be kingmaker for the Russian presidency was not too high. Many politicians at the time speculated that Berezovsky's favorite was Ivan Rybkin, a former speaker of the Duma who had been chief of the Kremlin Security Council while Berezovsky was the deputy. Rybkin was an unassuming, quiet figure, completely uncharismatic, someone whom Berezovsky could trust. Rybkin could be manipulated too. However, when I spoke to Berezovsky about this several years later, he insisted that he had lobbied for a candidate who "would not be manipulated by anybody; these are my words." He said he wanted someone who would be independent from the oligarchs, or at least from any one of them. "I never named a candidate," he said. Gusinsky recalled that Berezovsky in fact advocated Rybkin.

What is not disputed is that the oligarchs were quietly working as a "board of directors" in the Kremlin. This included the same cast of characters that had come to the Yuksi announcement: Gusinsky, Khodorkovsky, Smolensky, and Berezovsky. It also included Yeltsin's daughter Tatyana Dyachenko and chief of staff Valentin Yumashev, who succeeded Chubais in the post. Yet another player was a quiet oil trader, Roman Abramovich, who was Berezovsky's partner in Sibneft and had become influential in Yeltsin's inner circle as well.

"We all spoke about this topic," Berezovsky acknowledged of the plotting to dump Chernomyrdin. "All the oligarchs when we would meet, Yumashev, Tatyana, Khodorkovsky—there was a club, and there was a conversation. About what? That Chernomyrdin had exhausted his potential."[18]

The group, Berezovsky claimed in a newspaper interview, was "more consolidated" than it had been before the 1996 election. Chubais and Potanin were absolutely excluded, however. Uneximbank was "beyond the pale" because of the bankers' war, and Chubais "should know his place—I hate to be that vulgar."[19]

The evidence suggests that Berezovsky and his allies in the Kremlin—chiefly Dyachenko and Yumashev—hatched the idea of dumping Chernomyrdin in February or March 1998. Berezovsky told me that although he did not speak to Yeltsin about it directly, "the question" of dumping Chernomyrdin "was debated for several months." Gusinsky recalled that the tycoons discussed it at a boardroom meeting at Khodorkovsky's oil company, Yukos.

One day in late February, Sergei Karaganov got a call to come to the Kremlin. The dapper, bald Karaganov was deputy director of the Institute of Europe, one of dozens of think tanks in the Russian Academy of Science. Karaganov was also chairman of a prestigious foreign policy council. Always tailored in elegant suits and bright ties, Karaganov had written the 1996 letter to Yeltsin warning of grave consequences if Yeltsin canceled the elections. Yeltsin read the letter and did not cancel the election. Karaganov was someone whom Yeltsin had listened to in the past.

Now Karaganov slipped into the Kremlin. In Yumashev's small Kremlin study, Karaganov also found Dyachenko and some of the oligarchs. They presented Karaganov with a plan. He would go to Yeltsin and urge him to dump the prime minister. They already had several possible candidates to replace Chernomyrdin. It was unspoken but immediately clear to Karaganov that this was no ordinary political maneuver.

The next day, Karaganov, brooding, returned to the Kremlin. He had lunch privately with Yumashev and Dyachenko. They offered him a high-level job in the Kremlin. But Karaganov was dubious. The plan to replace Chernomyrdin was an audacious power play by the tycoons. Karaganov nearly choked when he heard the words "corporate government." He then gave Yeltsin's daughter and his chief of staff a severe, angry soliloquy. Were the oligarchs out of their minds? Were they crazy? Were they trying to take over Russia? Perhaps, Karaganov said, he would simply tell Yeltsin that it was time to retire. Wasn't that really the implication?

"No!" Dyachenko insisted; this was going too far. Karaganov left the Kremlin and never heard about the plan again.[20] But the effort to dump Chernomyrdin accelerated.

In his memoirs, Yeltsin claimed that sacking Chernomyrdin was all his idea, that he was looking for a "someone younger and stronger" and had been searching for "three months" before he actually dismissed Chernomyrdin. Yeltsin's style was to be the power balancer, always scrambling and reassembling his court. But it is not known exactly how he came to the decision. It is possible Berezovsky succeeded in manipulating Yeltsin from behind the scenes. But it is also possible that Yeltsin had decided to move, and Berezovsky was trying to exploit the opening to his own ends.

The first specific action Yeltsin took, by his own account, was on Saturday, March 21, just two days before he fired Chernomyrdin. Yeltsin met the prime minister at his Gorky 9 residence outside Moscow. They talked about wage arrears, and Yeltsin told Chernomyrdin he was unhappy with his work. Chernomyrdin "looked at me with the doomed expression of an old, experienced apparatchik who understood everything," Yeltsin wrote. That evening, Saturday, Yeltsin summoned Yumashev and his press secretary, Sergei Yastrzhembsky, and told them to prepare a decree for Chernomyrdin's firing. Yeltsin recalled that Yumashev asked him to postpone the announcement until Monday, saying it would be a work day, and more businesslike. Yeltsin was reluctant but agreed to wait.

In fact, the brief delay allowed Berezovsky to waltz on stage. On Saturday, just as Yeltsin was telling aides of his plan to fire Chernomyrdin, Berezovsky taped an interview at his spacious country dacha for Yevgeny Kiselyov's television program, *Itogi.* His back was still hurting from the snowmobile accident and he was in discomfort during the taping, perched on a chair, packed all around with pillows. He also posed for the cameras with the snowmobile on which he suffered the accident. In the interview, Berezovsky foreshadowed the changes to come. He said he was focused on preparing for the elections in the year 2000, on ensuring "continuity of power." Then, with the self-assurance of a real power broker, he criticized virtually all the leading candidates in the polls to succeed Yeltsin, crisply rattling off his verdict on each one—"electable" or "not electable." It was the performance of a confident kingmaker. Berezovsky said he doubted whether the stodgy Chernomyrdin could be elected, and since there wasn't an obvious favorite, he hinted that there would be time for "new people." But he did not say who.[21]

On Sunday evening, Yeltsin told his aide, Yumashev, that his choice for prime minister was Sergei Kiriyenko, the thirty-five-year-old minister of fuel and energy. Kiriyenko was the banker from Nizhny Novgorod who in 1996 had said he wanted to cross the "raging river" to complete economic reforms with Yeltsin. Kiriyenko was progressive, earnest, and independent-minded, with short hair and wire-rim glasses that gave him a youthful, studious look. A protégé of Boris Nemtsov, Kiriyenko headed a bank and oil company in Nizhny, but he had limited experience in government and had served in Moscow less than a year.

Yeltsin arrived at the Kremlin on Monday, March 23, very early, to tape a television address about Chernomyrdin's dismissal. In the tape, however, Yeltsin did not mention Kiriyenko's name. He said that "for the time being, before the appointment of a new prime minister, I will myself perform his duties." He added, "In the near future I will nominate a candidate for this post." When he made the tape, Yeltsin clearly did not know who he was going to pick. I think a furious lobbying campaign was still under way that morning.

Kiriyenko said Yumashev called him at home late Sunday and asked him to be at the Kremlin early the next morning. Kiriyenko had no idea why he had been summoned to the Kremlin. He guessed that he had been called to a policy meeting about European Union trade policy. It was his daughter's birthday, and he promised her he would be home early. When the president offered him the job, Kiriyenko was stunned. It was a "total surprise." The Kremlin had to acknowledge that, contrary to what the president had said in his taped address, he could not serve as the acting prime minister. Kiriyenko got the job.

Kiriyenko was definitely not Berezovsky's cup of tea. Berezovsky later said the choice of Kiriyenko was "unpleasant" for him. Chubais could not conceal his glee that he had outfoxed Berezovsky. "Some oligarchs," he said, "woke up this morning in a cold sweat."[22] What happened? It is clear that Berezovsky and the other oligarchs started the process of replacing Chernomyrdin, but Berezovsky lost control of it. Kiriyenko zoomed in with the backing of Chubais, Yumashev, Dyachenko, and some of the other oligarchs. Perhaps Berezovsky mistakenly thought he had more time to manipulate Yeltsin. Or perhaps Yeltsin himself decided to bypass the wily oligarch. Who outfoxed whom? It was typical of Berezovsky and even more characteristic of Yeltsin that the answer is not clear. But the outcome was the same: Chernomyrdin was sacked.

Yeltsin said he wanted Chernomyrdin to prepare a presidential campaign—a lame excuse given that he had just removed Chernomyrdin from a high-profile position. The hapless Chernomyrdin went through the motions of starting the campaign, including a meeting with the "board of directors" of oligarchs at Berezovsky's Logovaz Club a few days later. Berezovsky said at the time he saw a different Chernomyrdin, with "tremendous potential." That was nonsense—Chernomyrdin's political future was actually quite bleak; his pro-Kremlin political party, Our Home Is Russia, was broke. Still, as became apparent later in the year, Berezovsky had not yet given up on him.

What everyone missed was that Yeltsin had just decapitated the government at the absolutely worst time. On March 27, Berezovsky met with a group of journalists over breakfast at the elegant Metropol Hotel in Moscow. His back still aching from the snowmobile injury, Berezovsky stood, immaculately tailored as always, as we listened to his soft, rapid-paced patter over croissants and orange juice. Berezovsky clearly felt that Kiriyenko was a political weakling and that Yeltsin was not in good shape. "I think it is bad because the president's health, his condition does not allow him to engage in active political work every day, which is undoubtedly necessary." He added, "It will take time to gain experience and strength, and who will fill the vacuum? I have no answer to this question."

Kiriyenko had no political base in Moscow, no clout in parliament, and he was doomed from the first day. His plight was aggravated by a five-week wait for confirmation in the Duma, the lower house of parliament. He was confirmed on the third and last ballot, having lost the first two votes.[23] Berezovsky spent most of April plotting against the Kremlin and trying to undermine Kiriyenko in his newspaper and on television, perhaps hoping Kiriyenko's nomination would fail. Yegor Gaidar told me at the time that Berezovsky was hungry for power, but his reach may have exceeded his grasp. "For Berezovsky, the essence of his business is politics, and intrigue, and that's the game he plays. He thinks he has the right to rule this country," complained Gaidar, no friend of the tycoon. "He has spoken openly. The government is too weak to rule, he says. Someone has to do it. They [the oligarchs] are strong and clever men, so they can do it, so they say. But I think he has overestimated himself."

"Berezovsky's biggest mistake was that he talked too much about his importance," Gaidar continued. "If and when you have a lot of influence, the best thing to do is keep quiet."

In mid-April, Yeltsin had his fill of Berezovsky's intrigues. He called Berezovsky and sternly demanded that the tycoon stop trying to undermine Kiriyenko in the parliament.[24] In a ceremony for Russian cosmonauts, Yeltsin said aloud what he had been thinking: if Berezovsky didn't stop the scheming he would send the tycoon on a long business trip outside of Russia—forever. It was an extraordinary moment, and the newspaper *Kommersant Daily*, which broke the story, said that Yumashev and Yastrzhembsky attempted afterward to hush up Yeltsin's outburst. It leaked anyway.[25] Two weeks later, Berezovsky got another appointment, as executive secretary of the Commonwealth of Independent States, the loose and largely ineffective organization of former Soviet republics except for the Baltics. The position was based in Minsk but gave Berezovsky the most important thing: a fresh power base and access to the Kremlin.

One of the most acid critics of the tycoons in this period was Andrei Piontkovski, a one-time mathematician and nuclear weapons strategist who wrote an entertaining newspaper commentary about the influence of the oligarchy. He told me that the maneuverings of Berezovsky in the spring had been extraordinarily costly and senseless. The oligarchs "have been destroying themselves before our eyes," he said. "I think there are no victors, only losers."[26] Piontkovsky was more correct than he realized.

The ruble was funny money. Russians did not trust their own currency, or the banks or government. They kept their money under a mattress—usually in dollars. Russia had an estimated $30 billion to $40 billion in American banknotes in circulation, the largest sum in any country outside the United States itself. Russians clung to their dollars because, both before and after the breakup of the Soviet Union, attempts to fiddle with the ruble had always led to chaos, and Gaidar's hyperinflation eroded any remaining public trust.[27]

So it was with some trepidation that the Russian government and Central Bank decided to make another ruble fix. On January 1, 1998, the Russian ruble was redenominated, which meant cutting three zeros off the end of the currency. What was six thousand rubles to the dollar became six, a strictly cosmetic change that was designed to wipe away the memory of hyperinflation and symbolize normalcy. Billions of new banknotes were printed months in advance. Fearing another panic, the government and Central Bank spent months preparing the population with advertising and soothing reassurances. "New zeros will never again appear on our banknotes," Yeltsin promised.

Nothing happened. The redenomination passed quietly, without panic. Another threshold was crossed on the road to normalcy, or so it seemed. The ghosts of past inflation had receded. Chubais proudly declared that Russia had tamed the ruble. "We have a stable currency which, incidentally, has the same exchange rate as the French franc," he boasted.[28] Chubais told Yeltsin in February that he wanted to leave the government; he had been desperate to leave for a long time.

Yeltsin asked Chubais, "What's with the economy?" Chubais recalled telling Yeltsin that he felt comfortable leaving the government because nothing bad would happen to the economy in the year ahead.

"The economy should grow this year. Nothing of any scale, positive or negative, will happen," Chubais said.

He was profoundly mistaken. It was the first of many errors in a troubled year for Chubais, who failed to see that Russia would suffer greatly from the changing winds of the global economy. He was in the raft with the tycoons as they blithely floated down the river. Russia was soon caught in the grip of two mighty dragons—writhing serpents of modern economics that tore the country apart. The first dragon was an explosion of debt. The second was a failure to recognize that the time had come for devaluation of the ruble. The dragons were creeping up together on Russia in the early spring. Many people saw the threat, but very few were certain that they would strike or when. Russia was in "crisis" so often that its leaders were paralyzed by crisis fatigue, numb to more alarmist warnings, and in this case the government contributed to the problem by reassuring everyone for too long that there would be no catastrophe. When it finally did hit—when the dragons attacked—it was too late to escape.

If you could have flown over Russia in early 1998 and viewed the economy in terms of topography, starkly different worlds would have appeared below. Spanning a landmass as large as the United States and Canada together, Russia had an economy that comprised several different realms. The timeless rural landscape remained rudimentary, isolated, and agrarian. Provincial urban Russia was a tableau of chaos and uncertainty. Industry functioned inefficiently; gargantuan factories churned out steel and automobiles but were forever plagued by losses. Workers, factories, and the government were all caught in a complex web of barter. Cash had almost disappeared from the economy. Large enterprises did 73 percent of their business in barter and paid only 8 percent of their taxes in cash. The swaps and trade-offs were a horribly distorting factor in everyday life, prompting two American scholars to conclude that Russia was becoming a "virtual economy" in which every important facet, such as prices, wages, and profits, were deceptive.[29]

Finally, if you flew over Moscow, you would have seen a world apart. Moscow was a throbbing boomtown before August 1998. The Moscow financial scene was cluttered with banks and exchanges, tycoons and stockbrokers, and trappings of wealth and power. Moscow was its own sort of virtual economy, awash in easy money. It was ruled by the oligarchs and their political patrons. Their battles and whims echoed loudly in the Moscow media, which they largely owned. It was here, in this Moscow boomtown, that the crisis of 1998 unfolded.

The trouble began with the chronically undisciplined Russian government. The country's public finances were a black hole. Simply put, Russia spent more money than it had, every day. Special-interest lobbies such as agriculture, the military-industrial complex, the banks, and the huge Soviet-era factories hauled away truckloads of subsidies, with hearty encouragement from the Communist-dominated parliament. At the same time, tax collection was abysmal.[30] When the government ran out of money, it simply stopped paying people. Russia was living beyond its means.

In the inflationary years of 1993 and 1994, one way to cover the deficit was to print more money, but that fueled hyperinflation. Chubais stopped that in 1995. Another way to cover the deficit was to obtain loans from the International Monetary Fund, which pledged a three-year, $10 billion loan starting in 1996 before Yeltsin's reelection.[31] Beginning in 1993, Russia found still another inflation-free way to finance the deficits—it borrowed the money on capital markets. At home, the borrowing was through the high-flying, short-term bonds known as GKOs. The acronym stood for the Russian words *gosudarstvenniye kratkosrochniye obligatzii,* or short-term government obligations. The GKO came to symbolize all that was crazy about the stock and bond market boom. The bonds were denominated in rubles and usually had a three- or six-month term. When they were first floated in May 1993, the market was small. At the end of 1994, only $3 billion in GKOs were outstanding. But at the end of the election year of 1996 the total zoomed to $42.7 billion. In 1997, the year of the "young reformers," the outstanding GKO debt went to $64.7 billion, and in mid-1998 it reached $70 billion. When risks seemed to be on the rise in Russia, especially before the 1996 election, the yields on GKOs soared, which meant the government had to pay even more to borrow even more. But the high yields also had a silver lining—the bonds were a wonderful source of easy money for Russian banks and anyone else who could get their hands on them. The GKOs sucked up capital that should have gone to productive investments. Victor

Huaco, the financier at Orion Capital Advisors Ltd. in Moscow, told me that a Russian company with $200 million would obviously rather put it in GKOs than invest in new equipment. "I can invest in new equipment and over a ten-year period get a return per year of 20 percent," he said. "Or, I can invest in GKOs, and in six months get 100 percent." The choice was easy money, once again.

Originally designed as a way for the government to raise money, the GKOs wound up costing money. The bonds took on a life of their own—they became an unsustainable pyramid scheme in which new investors were desperately needed to pay off the old ones, not unlike the MMM scam. In 1994, three-fourths of the proceeds from GKOs went to the Finance Ministry to help cover the deficit, but by 1997, a full 91 percent of the proceeds were being used *just to pay back earlier GKOs*, with only 9 percent going to the budget.[32]

After Yeltsin's 1996 reelection, global capital markets opened to Russia. Just as Khodorkovsky became hooked on Western finance, so too did the Russian federal government. Cities and regions also found borrowing irresistible.[33] With a green light from the financial ratings agencies like Standard & Poors, Fitch IBCA, and Moody's Investors Service, Russian government officials were soon jetting around the world on so-called road shows touting Eurobonds, which are bonds sold to foreigners denominated in hard currency, such as dollars or German marks or Italian lira. The proceeds from Eurobonds pumped cash into the Russian budget and masked the festering deficit mess at home. Russia floated a total of $14.9 billion in Eurobonds in 1997 and 1998.[34] The nagging, deepening budget deficit, and the borrowing to cover it, both at home and abroad, spawned the first dangerous dragon of 1998: debt. Russia was falling deeper and deeper into the maw.

The dangers took time to become apparent. In the feverish enthusiasm of the 1997 stock market boom, GKOs were seen as a hot investment. They were a government-backed Treasury bill, a sign of normalcy, a noninflationary way to pay for government spending. But as Russia soon discovered, an emerging market remained "hot" only as long as the suitors were ardent. Foreign investors could leave almost as soon as they came, for reasons entirely unrelated to Russia, and they did. Yeltsin courted prosperous South Korea in the 1990s at the expense of the decrepit North, and his diplomacy paid off as South Koreans helped fuel the portfolio investment boom. But when the financial storm hit East Asia in 1997, South Korean investors were the first to abandon Russia. They quickly evacuated the GKO market and took their money out of the country. Brazilian investors fled too. The Russian Central Bank tried in vain to compensate by buying GKOs on the open market. The Central Bank burned up an astounding amount of money in November 1997—its reserves plummeting from $22.9 billion to $16.8 billion in that month alone—trying to stabilize the GKO market. In one week, it lost $2 billion, a frightening drain.[35] It was a costly mistake, and the Central Bank decided it would no longer buck up the GKO market but use its precious reserves to support the ruble only. The Central Bank did not have enough reserves to do both jobs. Yeltsin approved the decision, and it went into effect December 1. Sergei Aleksashenko, then deputy head of the Central Bank, recalled watching nervously to see how investors would react. He was relieved when some investors returned to the GKO market and bought another $400 million of the bonds the next week. Aleksashenko recalled considering it "a serious sign that the hardest times were behind us."[36] He was wrong.

In order to keep luring investors and thus keep the budget deficit covered, on January 1, 1998, the Russian government liberalized the GKO market, making it much easier for foreign investors to buy GKOs and allowing them to get profits out. The casino doors were now fully open: new foreign investors took the place of the South Koreans and Brazilians. The GKO pyramid grew still larger. By the spring of 1998, foreigners held 28 percent of the GKOs.

Each Wednesday, the Finance Ministry paid off the GKOs that were coming due, but it was tricky to keep the pyramid from falling. The weekly game went like this: the government had to raise an average of 8 billion rubles to roll over existing debt as it matured. Each week it had to maintain the confidence of investors—about one-third of them foreigners—to reinvest enough money to pay off the bills coming due. With the oligarchs at war with each other, the budget hemorrhaging, and the Asian crisis bearing down on Moscow, investors had plenty to fear. As investors lost confidence and did not put their money back into GKOs, the government fell further behind, which caused investors to lose even more confidence, which caused the government to fall even further behind. A debt bomb was building up.

The crisis was aggravated by the decline in global oil prices. Oil was Russia's top export commodity; oil prices fell about 25 percent from 1997 to 1998, and tax revenues fell too. The government had to furiously borrow still more to cover the shortfalls. A turning point came on April 1, 1998, when the Finance Ministry held its regular weekly auction of new GKOs but suddenly found itself short: for the first time, money collected from the new issue was less than the government needed to pay off the maturing GKOs. The government had to cough up another $164 million just to pay off the earlier investors. The GKO market, which was supposed to be financing the federal budget, now had to be financed *by* the budget. The shortfall between what was raised at the weekly auctions and what was needed to redeem the maturing GKOs was 3.7 billion rubles in May, 12.8 billion in June, and 10 billion in the first two weeks of July.[37] The dragon roared.

Foreign investors liked the high-flying GKO market but demanded an insurance policy. The GKOs were denominated in rubles, so if the currency lost value during the three-month or six-month term of the bond, the investment would be a loss. The investors wanted protection against this risk, and Russia obliged because it needed them. The Central Bank approved a financial instrument known as a dollar-forward contract, in which the Russian commercial banks, for a fee, would cover any potential decline in the ruble—they would provide insurance against devaluation. These dollar-forwards were very lucrative as long as the ruble remained stable. The banks became a circus barker for the Russian state. "Come on in!" they shouted. "Big returns! Take it out safely in dollars when you leave!" The dollar-forwards business was snapped up by some of the tycoons, although it was risky. Later a Moscow court was considering a dispute between two banks over the dollar-forwards and ruled that they were not really financial contracts at all—but rather an unenforceable bet, a gamble, on the ruble rate. Vladimir Vinogradov's Inkombank was the biggest gambler, holding $1.8 billion worth of dollar-forwards, or about a third of the total, by July 1998. Potanin's Uneximbank had $1.4 billion, and Khodorkovsky's Menatep had $91 million. The Troika Dialog brokerage house estimated the total at $6.5 billion, based on bank reports, but the sum may have been higher. Brunswick Warburg, another brokerage, said the total was $9 billion.[38] The big gamble was that the ruble would remain stable in the next six months, and in fact the Central Bank had promised it would.

Chubais also believed in the rock-hard stability of the ruble. The "corridor" of 1995—in which the Central Bank pledged to keep the ruble exchange rate with the dollar within a narrow, defined limit and succeeded in doing so—led to his proudest accomplishment, the decline of inflation. This was more than an economic goal. For Chubais and a generation of young Russian politicians and businessmen, the stable ruble was an icon of their long quest for normalcy. They were criticized as harsh "monetarists" and "Chicago boys" in the mold of the University of Chicago's Milton Friedman, but they had no regrets—they had slain the awful inflation of the early 1990s.[39] The ruble corridor, which originally was an experiment, became a fact of life. In November 1997, the Central Bank went further and announced it would keep the ruble stable, within a 15 percent "band," until the year 2000. The average exchange rate for the coming years was to be 6.3 rubles to the dollar. This promise was a signal to the tycoons: the Central Bank would *not* devalue the ruble.

Even as the Central Bank pledged stability, the outside world was not standing still. The decline in oil prices began to be felt in Russia's balance of trade. Previously Russia had a strong trade surplus because, with massive reserves of oil and gas, it was exporting far more than it imported. The country could afford imports for many things it wanted but did not have—it was deluged with imported food, cosmetics, and electronics. The oil and gas went out, and Oreo cookies, L'Oreal shampoo, and Sony video recorders came in. In Moscow and other big cities, half the food supply was imported, much of it expensive and favored by the nascent middle class. As long as Russia had a strong trade surplus, the arrangement was fine and the ruble stable. However, when the value of oil exports fell, the trade surplus shrank. To defend the ruble at the same level, the Central Bank had to use up its reserves, week after week. Global sentiment was changing about emerging markets, of which Russia was one. Foreign investors were less willing to bring their money to Russia, so the Central Bank had to offer higher interest rates to attract it, which also drained its reserves. If the ruble were allowed to devalue, say, to seven or eight rubles per dollar, the pressure would ease. Russia could cope with the shifting winds of the global economy if it was flexible.

But for the economic and political elite in Russia in early 1998, the idea of ruble devaluation ran against everything they had worked for. Chubais and the Central Bank chairman, Sergei Dubinin, as well as his deputy, Aleksashenko, were deathly afraid that devaluation could lead to panic and political upheaval. A devaluation would probably cost them all their jobs. For some of the oligarchs who had oil and minerals to export, it would be salutary, since they could sell oil abroad for dollars, while their ruble costs at home, such as wages at the refinery, would drop. But a far more worrisome consideration was that devaluation would wreck the banks with big portfolios of Western loans and dollar-forward contracts. Their financial obligations were in dollars, but their assets were in rubles. If the ruble assets plunged in value, they would be hard-pressed to pay back the dollar debts.

Devaluation was the second dragon, and the elite—especially Chubais, the Central Bank, and some of the tycoons—were dead set against it. That is what they told Andrei Illarionov in early 1998.

Illarionov was a maverick economist, a radical free marketeer who had once been an adviser to Chernomyrdin. Director of a small think tank, the Institute of Economic Analysis, he worked out of a narrow, document-stuffed, two-room office in central Moscow. Illarionov had a reputation for being a prickly contrarian. He scolded Russian politicians, frequently lambasted the Central Bank, and was a thorn in the side of the reformers because of his constant harping that Russia had really not accomplished liberal reform; there was too much leftover socialism for his taste. As early as 1994, he declared there had never been "shock therapy." It was a reminder that the young reformers did not like to hear.

They also did not like to hear what Illarionov had to say in the spring of 1998. He studied the numbers: import and export statistics, the Central Bank's reserves, and the monetary base. He was especially alarmed by the decline in the Central Bank's currency reserves, made up of gold as well as foreign currency such as dollars. Illarionov used a simple criterion to judge whether the ruble would be stable. He compared the size of the Central Bank's reserves to the overall monetary base, a broad measure of the money supply. When the reserves declined, it was a warning, a flag, that the ruble could become unstable.[40] Illarionov first mentioned possible ruble instability in his institute's November 1997 newsletter; by spring, he was growing alarmed. He decided—in his own stubborn way—that devaluation was inevitable, and it would be easier to do it sooner, gradually, rather than later, abruptly. It was like letting the steam out of a pressure cooker—better to do it slowly than with a rush of explosive force.

Illarionov knew devaluation was a sensitive subject, given Russia's history of currency panic. He gingerly began trying to persuade government officials that they needed to consider it. He visited deputy finance ministers, bureaucrats, the Kremlin. He sometimes used charts but usually liked to just sketch his ideas on a sheet of blank white paper. "And the reaction, the first reaction was absolutely stupid, complete stupidity," he said. The officials all told him: there will be no devaluation. Why? "Because we decided that there will be no devaluation."

"It was so strange," Illarionov told me later, "because all these people are so young, advanced, so open to the new ideas, to the West—to everything. And there was such ignorance and pride; they felt that they knew everything." Illarionov was twenty minutes into his presentation when the officials interjected: but the Central Bank promised there would be no devaluation. After another twenty minutes, they would nod. Perhaps he was right.

"And they would be sitting there, saying okay, maybe, but we have only one request for you," Illarionov recalled. The request was always the same: "Please don't tell the journalists!" The Russian officials feared a panic. "Don't attract public attention," they warned him.[41]

The Central Bank was particularly loath to listen to Illarionov. Dubinin, the chairman, had presided over the end of hyperinflation, and he just finished the successful redenomination of the ruble, without panic. Why create unnecessary trouble? One Finance Ministry official told me that talk of devaluation left Dubinin paralyzed. "He was extremely scared of doing anything of this sort. He just couldn't do it."

Chubais generally trusted Dubinin and Aleksashenko, and he misjudged the economy completely in the first months of 1998. Illarionov gave a presentation calling for devaluation to a small club of liberal economists led by Gaidar. When Illarionov made his case, Pyotr Aven recalled, "Gaidar and Chubais just laughed."[42] (Chubais said he did not attend.)

Chubais was blinded by signs of growth in the economy. Growth meant a "qualitative" change for the better was coming. There would come "a different standard of living, a different relationship between rich and poor, a different dynamic of investment, a different foundation for growth, a different situation with nonpayment of taxes. Generally—everything is different."[43]

Chubais proudly surveyed what had already been accomplished: Russia was admitted to global financial markets; Russian companies were making deals with Goldman Sachs; inflation, the great threat of the last five years, was tamed. Chubais could hardly see a reason to throw it all away for devaluation. He simply did not believe devaluation was inevitable, and he feared the damage would be enormous—especially to the banks, to the oligarchs, and to Yeltsin. "At that time, what did it really mean to conduct devaluation?" Chubais told me later. "A devaluation of even 20 percent or 25 percent meant a total, mass bankruptcy of the country's banking system." What Chubais really feared was the political fallout. "We would have gotten mass discontent of the population," he said. "The protests, the lack of understanding, the lack of acceptance of that decision would have been absolutely terrible."

But the twin dragons—debt and devaluation—could not be wished away.

On taking office May 12, Kiriyenko vowed to keep his distance from the tycoons. He said his government would show them no favor. "There are interests of the state, and they will be ensured at all costs," he announced. Fastidiously, perhaps a little too enthusiastically, Kiriyenko refused to meet with the oligarchs. He refused to play by their rules.

But Kiriyenko was in trouble. On the day he finally named his cabinet, coal miners went on a nationwide strike, blocking key Siberian rail routes. They also came to Moscow and noisily banged their hats on the pavement outside the White House in protest. In another harbinger of difficulty, the parliament in May passed legislation to limit foreign investment in Unified Energy Systems, the huge Russian electricity monopoly, which was already a favorite of foreign portfolio investors. Chubais had just been appointed president of the company. The bill sent the worst possible message to skeptical overseas markets—foreign investment in Russia was not secure. On May 27, Khodorkovsky's megadeal, the proposed merger of Yukos and Sibneft, fell apart. On the same day came still more bad news. The government announced it could not find a bidder for Rosneft, one of the last big vertically integrated oil companies to be privatized. This blew a $2.1 billion hole in the budget. After months of political instability, investors saw that Russia would be that much further behind in the weekly race to pay off the GKOs. According to Aleksashenko, foreign investors were already fleeing and had yanked between $500 million and $700 million out of the government bond market in two weeks prior to the Rosneft disclosure. The stock market, which had been sliding all year, took a plunge on the Rosneft news, and the Central Bank was forced to raise interest rates to an extraordinary 150 percent. The Central Bank, which had reserves of $23.1 billion the previous October, was down to $14.6 billion. The bank spent about $900 million supporting the ruble on May 26 and May 27 alone.[44] Dubinin insisted the Central Bank would not devalue the ruble and said the high interest rates were intended as a "cold shower" to "prevent currency speculators from making quick money by playing games with the Russian ruble." Chubais quickly made a trip to Washington to meet with U.S. officials, including Deputy Secretary of State Strobe Talbott, Deputy Treasury Secretary Lawrence Summers, and Stanley Fischer, deputy managing director of the International Monetary Fund. President Clinton issued a written statement suggesting conditional support for further financial aid for Russia. The Chubais message to the administration in Washington was, Russia urgently needs help. But Clinton's statement contained no specific promises and no numbers, and no package was forthcoming. Kiriyenko was losing time but didn't seem to realize it.

On June 2, Yeltsin summoned the oligarchs to the Kremlin. The meeting was held in the same green room with a huge white marble table where Yeltsin had, the previous fall, implored them to stop quarreling over Svyazinvest. Smolensky looked thin and was chewing gum; Gusinsky was smartly outfitted in a double-breasted blazer. Chubais came, Berezovsky did not. At a time when foreign investors were fleeing, Yeltsin wagged his finger at the businessmen, insisting they not pull their money out of the Russian markets. "If you want foreign investors to invest, you should invest your own money as well," Yeltsin said. In fact, most of those at the table were rooted in Russia. They probably wished they could escape, but they could not. "All our money is in Russia," Gusinsky protested. After the meeting, Alexander Livshitz, Yeltsin's economic adviser, suggested that the market jitters could be calmed if a large sum were simply deposited for Russia at the IMF headquarters in Washington. Yeltsin sat quietly for a long time, then said, "No, we need to take the money. Otherwise we'll fail for sure."[45]

Back in Moscow after his visit to Washington, Chubais expressed hope for a calm GKO auction on June 4, the first after the market slump the previous week. But it was not to be. The debt dragon roared again—the Finance Ministry raised only 5.8 billion rubles in new securities, compared to the 8.4 billion that came due. The government had to dip into its accounts to pay off the rest. Kiriyenko was still sanguine. "I am absolutely certain the situation is under control," he said. Gaidar, who was working closely with Kiriyenko, said that "only illiterate half-wits" would want to see a controlled devaluation of the ruble. In fact, Russia was facing a crisis of confidence in the markets and pretending it did not exist. Chubais, the most experienced of the Russian economic reformers, missed the turning point. He was out of touch with the trading-floor sentiment, which was growing bearish day by day. This was not just another Russian government financial "crisis," like those of recent years. This was a storm. This was Meltdown.

Bernie Sucher was on that trading floor, and he felt like a prizefighter getting slugged every few minutes. Sucher, then thirty-eight, was a veteran of Wall Street who had spent a few years in Russia and took a long break before the peak of the speculative bubble in 1997. He returned to Moscow in March 1998 just in time to see the crisis unfolding. He was a tall, powerfully built man, who looked like a high school football lineman. When he came to Moscow, he couldn't get a decent steak, so he opened his own steak house. Later he opened a pair of popular American 1950s-style diners. One of them was a stone's throw from the statue of Lenin atop of the Oktyabrskaya Metro station. Milkshakes, hamburgers, equities, GKOs—Sucher knew them all. He was managing director of Troika Dialog, a stock brokerage that at the time was owned by Bank of Moscow, part of Luzhkov's empire.

Every day in the early summer of 1998, Sucher watched the stock markets slide. The quotations on his computer screens never reflected the real price of stocks; any genuine attempt to sell chased the prices down still further. The effect was punishing. "It was like being on the wrong end of a Rocky fight," he said. "It was like one of those idiotic sequences in the movie where there is just once punch after another landing on your chin and on your belly, and no human being can handle that punishment. Nobody could possibly throw that many punches and nobody could possibly take that many punches."[46]

"Every single day you had the stock market going down 3 percent, 5 percent, 7 percent, 10 percent! Every single day! You come in the morning, and you try and see if there is any possibility, if things will be better than they were last night." As an example, he said, for a hypothetical stock, he would see that the previous day's price was

$10. Sucher would offer $9.75 just to test the waters. No action. Also, he said, a client in New York who bought the stock at $15 might want to sell it at $10, but not at $9.75. Forced to hold deteriorating positions, clients and brokers grew increasingly frantic. "And the same thing happens the next night. And before you know it, the price has gone down to $9.50 or $9.40." A sickening pattern was taking shape.

The downward spiral was fueled by what the traders could easily understand—the Russian government was living beyond its means, and the ruble needed to be devalued. But the officials in government would have none of it. A dangerous gulf opened up between the perception of the markets and the view of the government. The markets heard the roar of the dragons, but the government did not.[47]

In June, Kiriyenko summoned private foreign investors to Moscow, including representatives of the major investment houses on Wall Street and in London. Kiriyenko and other officials all but begged the bankers not to flee, not to give up hope that Russia could straighten out the mess. But the jawboning betrayed a nervousness that had the opposite effect. "Foreign investors listened to the officials very attentively," recalled Illarionov. "They were amazed at the amount of attention devoted to them during the two weeks and drew what was a natural conclusion: the situation is serious and they should leave as soon as possible."[48] Augusto Lopez-Claros, a former IMF resident representative in Moscow and later an economist for Lehman Brothers in London, recalled that investors asked Kiriyenko whether the government needed a bailout package from the IMF. "No, we really don't need it," Kiriyenko said, promising that his government would get the budget deficit under control. "The fiscal measures are going to bear fruit and the market will rebound."

"They were slow in coming to the realization that Russia was the next domino," Lopez-Claros told me. "They were late."[49]

Kiriyenko faced a difficult choice. He very much wanted to avoid wrecking the banking system. He also wanted to keep his distance from the oligarchs. But at the same time, it became increasingly obvious that the tycoons and the banks were one. There was no separating them. Devaluation would wreck the banks, including the ones at the core of the oligarchs' empires. Gaidar recalled, "There was no easy way out." Yeltsin recalled that Kiriyenko "knew that a horrible financial crisis was bearing down on the country."[50]

Still, the Kremlin was sanguine. Yeltsin was getting optimistic reports from the government and the Central Bank that the worst scenarios could be avoided. He was told that July was the "peak" of their troubles and that in the autumn there would be more money, perhaps new sell-offs of both Gazprom, the natural gas monopoly, and Svyazinvest could be arranged to raise more cash.[51] It was nonsense.

The tycoons were hurting more every day as the price of their ruble assets dropped. The squeeze was excruciating for them all. Gusinsky suffered his own disappointment. After a long wait, he was prepared to float shares of NTV in the United States. But at the last minute, his financial advisers said the market was too uncertain. They urged him to wait until the fall—when conditions would surely be better. Gusinsky agreed to wait, but it was a fateful decision. He never made it to the stock market.[52]

Finally the oligarchs could remain on the sidelines no longer. After six months of drifting, they woke up. On June 16, the "board of directors" met at Berezovsky's Logovaz Club. They invited Chubais, who recently had taken on a major new job as chief of Unified Energy Systems, the electricity monopoly. Sensing danger, they implored Chubais to take on the added duties of Russia's special envoy to the IMF and World Bank. They wanted him to go Washington and come home with a multibillion dollar bailout. They realized that an international rescue package was the only hope. There was no other source of money to save Russia: not the markets, not the Central Bank.

Chubais had repeatedly denounced the cozy clubhouse of oligarchs and vowed to break their hold on power. Now the oligarchs, gathered under Berezovsky's roof, as well as a dozen of their top lieutenants, were begging him to save the country and save their necks. At the meeting, Chubais recalled, he insisted that someone else should take on the new responsibility, perhaps Gaidar or Boris Fyodorov, who was serving as tax minister, or Alexander Shokhin, a member of parliament who was close to the reformers. But the tycoons insisted on Chubais. They decided to take a secret ballot. Chubais got twenty votes, the others got one or two each. Chubais relented. "I accepted the rule that there would be a vote," he told me, "which means I accepted the result." It was his birthday, and the businessmen presented him with an expensive watch while Mikhail Friedman played "Happy Birthday" on a piano and they all joined in singing to him, in English.[53]

Even Berezovsky was willing to extend his hand to Chubais, reluctantly. Berezovsky recalled later, "At the time, I believed Chubais was the best negotiator. No one could solve this problem better than Chubais, so I thought."[54] Badri Patarkatsishvili, Berezovsky's deputy, turned to him in amazement. "Listen, like idiots we spent two years destroying this man, and now we ask him to rescue us?"[55]

The tycoons then went to the Kremlin and got Yumashev to sign off on the deal. Yumashev got Yeltsin to sign the decree, and the oligarchs headed out to see Kiriyenko at an old government rest home in Volynskoye, in western Moscow. "Kiriyenko was forced to back off from his vow never to deal with the oligarchs or depend on them in any way," Yeltsin recalled. "Kiriyenko told them bluntly that he needed help." He realized he had no choice.

Chubais announced that he would seek a $10 billion to $15 billion loan from the IMF. Chubais thought that just a show of force—a big credit to boost the Central Bank reserves—would be sufficient to calm the markets. He was still not prepared to think about devaluation. Grigory Glazkov, the friend of Chubais who had argued with him at the collective farm in 1979, had become a deputy finance minister at the time. He recalled talking to Chubais just after he was appointed special envoy.

"You have to devalue," Glazkov told Chubais.

"No!" Chubais responded. "Can you imagine the consequences of what will happen?"

Glazkov replied, "You have no choice. You will devalue anyway, but it will be much worse than if you do it now." Chubais stuck by his position—there would be no devaluation.[56] He stubbornly told journalists, "The rumors about a devaluation of the ruble are absolutely the reverse of the truth."[57]

As Chubais spoke, things were beginning to unravel. On June 17, the Central Bank returned to the practice of the previous year and began to give rubles to the Finance Ministry to pay for the GKOs coming due; on that day, the "credit" was more than $1 billion worth of rubles.[58] The Central Bank was under fierce pressure to prop up the ruble and to prevent the GKO pyramid from crashing. But the reserves had shrunk even lower than the previous November, when the bank gave up trying to do both.

In these critical weeks, Russia's addiction to borrowing deepened further. On June 18, Goldman Sachs celebrated the opening of a new Moscow office, flying in former President George H. W. Bush and paying him more than $100,000. "I am optimistic," Bush, having just come from a meeting with Yeltsin, told the city's financial elite at a reception in the elegant baroque House of Unions in central Moscow. "I believe Russia is going to thrive." The boys at Goldman Sachs were feeding Russia's debt addiction. Goldman had pulled out of Russia in 1994 but came rushing back three years later, arranging its loan to Yukos in 1997 and arranging Eurobonds for the cash-strapped Russian government in the summer of 1998.

The Eurobonds were essentially loans from overseas investors to Russia. The first that Goldman Sachs arranged was a $1.25 billion Eurobond on June 3. Two weeks later, in a surprise move, Russia went back to global capital markets and borrowed $2.5 billion, with Deutsche Bank as the underwriter. Although it was not known at the time, the Finance Ministry had secretly taken out $500 million "bridge loans" from Goldman Sachs and Deutsche Bank. When the proceeds of the Eurobonds came through, some of the cash was turned right around to pay back the banks.

In July, Goldman Sachs came through with the biggest deal of the year, a $6.4 billion Eurobond. This transaction was a swap in which Russia said to investors, Give us back your short-term, high-yielding GKOs, and we'll pay you back later on, in dollars. The holders of the short-term, ruble-denominated GKOs would be offered seven-year and ten-year dollar-denominated bonds with lower interest rates. The GKOs were paying about 50 percent while the Eurobonds paid 8.75 percent and 11 percent. The deal promised to temporarily relieve pressure on the Finance Ministry's weekly GKO squeeze; about $4.4 billion in GKOs were retired. But in other ways, it was a fateful mistake for Russia. If devaluation was coming—and the dragon was roaring ever louder—then those Eurobonds would be much more expensive for Russia to pay back in the future in dollars than to pay back the same amount of GKOs in devalued rubles. Russia was mortgaging itself down the line for a possible short-term fix. Goldman Sachs was walking away with a handsome commission as a reward—about $56 million for the June and July bond issues. Goldman Sachs did not want to take any risks in Russia and just skimmed the profits.[59] Yeltsin's advisers later concluded that the deal "failed to rescue" the government, and several economists also concluded that the swap failed to achieve its advertised goals.[60]

At the same time Goldman Sachs was sponsoring its glittering coming-out party, the firm stonewalled the Russian Securities Commission, which was looking into charges that Yukos had hurt minority investors. Goldman Sachs, which surely would not have been so cavalier with the U.S. Securities and Exchange Commission, essentially told the Russian regulator, "Forget it." When Dmitry Vasiliev, the Securities Commission chairman, wrote to Goldman and the other loan arrangers asking for information about the Yukos loan, he got back a curt reply. Although they would like to help, the bankers said, "we are unable to provide you with any of the information requested." Goldman, which *Fortune* magazine described that month as "the most powerful investment bank in the world," was more than willing to enjoy the juicy commissions from Russia's Eurobonds, but when it came to answering a basic question from the Russian Securities Commission, the response was silence.[61]

Chubais finally succeeded in winning approval for an IMF rescue package in mid-July. The total was $22.6 billion in loans from a variety of international sources, but the critical first installment would be $5.6 billion. The idea was that the money would bolster the Central Bank's currency reserves and persuade the markets that Russia could weather the storm. At the last minute, the IMF cut $800 million off the planned first installment of its package because the Kiriyenko government had been unable to get promised tax legislation enacted. Kiriyenko struggled valiantly to cut spending and push a legislative package through the Duma, but the bills were only partially adopted. Nonetheless, Chubais was relieved when the IMF board approval was made final on July 21. He told one of his aides, Leonid Gozman, after the negotiations with the IMF, "Now we are safe." He added, "If it hadn't been for this, we were several days away from catastrophe." Gozman recalled, "He was really happy."[62] But Chubais had miscalculated again.

The rescue package had the desired effect for a week or so. The markets calmed down. Chubais concluded that the bailout was working. "So, what is a crisis? A crisis is a matter of trust," Chubais told me later. "The financial markets' trust of the government's policy. We hadn't been able to create that trust, but the IMF enabled us to create it. After that decision, the interest rates went down, the market went up a little bit." Chubais went on a vacation to Ireland.

But then the twin dragons began to roar again. Illarionov, who had at first predicted devaluation quietly in his conversations with bureaucrats and politicians, spoke out more loudly in newspaper articles, especially in *Nezavisimaya Gazeta*, Berezovsky's paper. Illarionov gave a press conference July 29, saying devaluation was "inevitable." Illarionov said it would be dangerous to wait, just as he had argued in the spring that it was better to let off the pressure at the outset than all at once. "It is better to accept the inevitable," he said, "and it will be less painful than the subsequent devaluation."

As the government continued to insist there would be no devaluation, Russian and global financial markets concluded it was coming. Lopez-Claros, the Lehman Brothers economist, recalled meeting with Finance Ministry officials in early August. The government showed private bankers its assumptions, including the wildly optimistic hope that investors—Russian and foreign—would not exit the GKO market. The same assumptions were built into the IMF deal, and they were dreadfully wrong. "We were aghast," Lopez-Claros said. "They didn't realize the foreign investors were getting out." The departures turned into a stampede. "By the time the IMF package had come down," Boris Jordan told me, "most of investor sentiment was—great, we are going to get liquidity and we'll try and get what we can out." In other words, investors were not reassured about anything except the prospect that they might be able to cash in their stocks and bonds for dollars and then run for the exits. The issue of "liquidity"—the ability to switch the ruble assets to dollars—was key. The banking system was increasingly illiquid. Not everyone could make it to the exits. Why some investors got liquidity and others did not was a combination of factors—connections, luck, rumors, bribery, and sheer timing. The Central Bank spent $3.5 billion between July 20 and August 19 trying to support the ruble. The ratings agencies, Moody's Investors Service and Standard & Poors, lowered the credit ratings of Russia and its leading banks. Smolensky's SBS-Agro tried to unload truckloads of government securities, desperate to raise cash. The Russian banking system sank into a full-blown liquidity crisis, and banks stopped making loans to one another. One worrisome sign to the markets was that Sberbank, the state-owned savings bank that held a total of $17 billion in government debt, refused to roll over, or reinvest, its maturing GKOs one week when they came due in late July. The cash-strapped government was forced to dig deeper to pay off the maturing bonds. Sberbank was controlled by the Central Bank. Why did they suddenly stop playing the game? Were they fleeing their own market? If so, that was very bad news indeed.[63] "Russia gets the $4.8 billion from the IMF, and it gets blown out the window because nobody rolls over their GKOs," Jordan said. "Everybody is exiting the market, including the Russians!"

Chubais admitted that he lost touch with market sentiment. "We were sure we could break out of the situation with this package" from the IMF, he said. "I was mistaken. It didn't break the situation." Gaidar said they failed to realize how profoundly the markets had lost confidence in the government. "A lot of people, including myself, thought that the July package would change the attitudes of the market," he recalled. They were wrong, but Gaidar was so preoccupied by the day-to-day financial firestorm that he didn't even contemplate the possibility that they were fighting a losing battle.

Yeltsin was also restless and feeling helpless. According to his aides' memoir, "When the Central Bank said everything was under control, worse things had happened, we'll make it, he was nervous and tormented by doubts but still believed it." Yeltsin did not understand economics, but he was haunted by fears he had erred with the one currency that he profoundly understood, political power. He wondered—to whom had he not given enough authority? Whom had he failed to support?[64]

The doomed Kiriyenko could do little to salve the wrath of the markets. He had tried to draw up responsible, long-term plans, but they were useless in the face of a brutal, immediate crisis, and no amount of promises could soothe the panic. "The markets proclaimed their own verdict," he lamented later. "They can read our balance sheet as well as we can."

Kiriyenko was clobbered on the morning of August 13 by a letter that was published in the *Financial Times* from Soros. Known to all as the man who broke the Bank of England for his bet against the British pound in 1992, Soros wrote, "The meltdown in Russian financial markets has reached the terminal phase." Soros called for an immediate injection of $15 billion by the Western industrial democracies, a devaluation of the ruble by 15 to 25 percent, and creation of a currency board, a complex mechanism in which a troubled currency is backed up by a more solid one such as the dollar. Soros said he intended his letter to be a "wake-up call" to Western governments and was not trying to profit from the situation. Ironically, Soros had written the letter in part because the Russian government had quietly come to him seeking another "bridge loan" prior to the planned sale of the next packet of shares in Svyazinvest.[65] His letter hit like a thunderclap. The Russian stock exchange took a nosedive and trading was stopped; soon the first signs of disquiet appeared on the streets. Modest lines began to form at currency exchange points—the Russian Everyman was once again fleeing his own currency and trying to buy dollars.

On the morning of Friday, August 14, Yeltsin flew to Novgorod to begin a vacation. As soon as his helicopter landed at 10:00 A.M., journalists shouted questions to him. Would there be a devaluation? Yeltsin: "There will be no devaluation, I state this loudly and clearly."

Yeltsin added, "It's not that I am making it up, or it's a fantasy." No, he reassured the journalists, "We'll keep control." Yeltsin said he would not cut his vacation short and return to Moscow. "If I am back, they'll be saying this means things are in a real mess, that a disaster has started, and that things are really going to pieces. . . . No, on the contrary, everything's going the way it ought to."[66]

But by this time the dragons were roaring louder than Yeltsin. During the week, several banks, including Smolensky's SBS-Agro, had failed to meet margin calls. Tokobank, once considered a model Russian bank, which had been in trouble since May, defaulted on a $60 million loan on Wednesday. Then on Friday, Imperial Bank defaulted on a $50 million syndicated loan. Menatep was next—on Monday, Khodorkovsky's bank had a payment on an $80 million loan coming due that it could not possibly make. Jordan told *Kommersant Daily* in an interview published August 12, "Today all our great oligarchs are bankrupt. Why, for example, is Menatep fighting for Tokobank, which is in the hole for $250 million? Why do they need this bank? Because for the reconstruction of Tokobank, the Central Bank is giving $100 million, and Menatep hopes to solve their problem, make payments on their credit this way." Menatep executives were furious at Jordan.

On August 14, the same day that Yeltsin insisted there would be no devaluation, the Russian government and Central Bank faced the reality that devaluation was inevitable. Aleksashenko recalled that at a meeting at Kiriyenko's office in the Russian White House, "the final diagnosis" was acknowledged. "Long lines of people appeared at currency exchanges in all the big cities of Russia," he said. "The Central Bank took it as a sign that people had lost faith in the ruble." The bank might be able to fight off market psychology, but not mass psychology, he said. Moreover, it became clear that the debt dragon was also on the verge of attack: there were no more sources of money to pay off the GKOs coming due the following week. The Central Bank reserves were low. Foreign countries and investors refused to help. No one would lend money to Russia under any circumstances.[67]

Chubais was trying to enjoy his summer vacation, driving around Ireland on that Friday, when his mobile telephone kept ringing. He abandoned the vacation and flew back to Moscow, arriving at 5:00 A.M. on Saturday morning. The government's brain trust assembled at Kiriyenko's government dacha, including Chubais, Gaidar, Dubinin, Aleksashenko, the finance minister, Mikhail Zadornov, and others. They acknowledged that devaluation was "inevitable," Aleksashenko said, but the real debate was over the GKOs. Should the government walk away from its obligations? They decided to "restructure" the GKOs, issuing new bonds at a later date. (That plan was never implemented; the government effectively defaulted and stopped paying GKOs altogether.) Were there alternatives? Yes. They could force the Central Bank to use its reserves to pay off the GKO debts, but no one knew how long the bank could hold out. They could print money to pay off the debts and risk hyperinflation. No one wanted to even contemplate that, haunted by the inflation disaster of the early 1990s.

The Saturday meeting did not settle the most sensitive issue—what to do about the banks. The fear of a banking crisis was real. On Sunday, under pressure from some of the oligarchs, in circumstances that have never been fully clear, Kiriyenko agreed to protect the banks. He consented to a "moratorium" under which Russian banks and companies would not have to pay back any foreign debts for three months. It was an invitation for the tycoons to run away from their obligations forever, more than $16 billion in loans, according to an estimate made soon thereafter by Chubais.[68] It meant that the Russian state was participating in the rape of foreign investors.

It was an extraordinary measure—a gift for the tycoons. Aven recalled that Berezovsky called him in Italy, where Aven was vacationing, urging him to fly back to Moscow immediately. Berezovsky told me he urged Aven to return to Moscow to help Chubais with the impending difficulties of devaluation. Berezovsky said he felt Chubais and his aides "didn't understand what they were doing." Khodorkovsky also sought the moratorium, Aven recalled. Menatep faced the Monday deadline for a loan payment it could not make.[69]

Aven had expected a ruble devaluation, and his bank carefully avoided the dollar-forward contracts, but he was stunned that Chubais and Kiriyenko had decided on both devaluation and default at the same time. "It was an absolute surprise," he said. "We had $100 million of GKOs, so we figured with a devaluation we might lose 20 percent of their value. We had no idea about a default—absolutely no idea."

Malashenko, who was the political eyes and ears for Gusinsky, had heard rumors but recalled that he also did not think that the government would carry out default and devaluation at the same time. "I didn't take it seriously," he told me, "because it was incredible. What the hell—you are going to have default and devaluation simultaneously? Every expert was just laughing at this because it never happens. So I thought that maybe it was not actually going to be that bad. I can tell you only one thing: there are probably some insiders who simply knew what was going to happen, but nobody else understood. And that's why so many Russian companies and oligarchs found themselves in such deep shit after August 17."

On Sunday, August 16, Kiriyenko and Chubais flew by helicopter to Yeltsin, who was at Rus, a hunting lodge about sixty miles northwest of Moscow. They outlined their plan and offered their resignations, but Yeltsin refused to accept them. Two days after he promised the country there would be no devaluation, Yeltsin agreed to the twin measures of default and devaluation, without even waiting for Kiriyenko to explain the details. "Go ahead," Yeltsin cut off Kiriyenko, "Take the emergency measures necessary."[70]

When Kiriyenko and Chubais returned to Moscow, they went directly to the White House. It was late, nearly midnight, and the parking lot outside the imposing white stone tower was filled with the black monster jeeps that the tycoons used as security chase vehicles. The oligarchs' own limos had been allowed inside the perimeter gates, but their thick-necked, black-jacketed bodyguards waited outside. The rest of the country slept—as the oligarchs and the government gave each other one last, hearty embrace.

Across Russia, the millions of people who would feel the impact of devaluation and default got no warning, while a handful of businessmen, who had once gathered at the villa on Sparrow Hills, were invited to witness the final act and even shape it to save their own skins. Their very presence at such a delicate moment—the onset of Russia's biggest economic crisis since the Soviet collapse—was testimony to the bonds between wealth and power. For the oligarchs, it marked the peak of their authority, the zenith of their collective might, but in many ways it was a crisis of their own making. Their noisy quarreling over Svyazinvest, their kingmaker games in the Kremlin, their addiction to easy money and foreign loans—all this brought them and Russia to the precipice. In the broad carpeted hallways on the fourth and fifth floors of the White House, the oligarchs lingered into the early morning hours and wondered what was in store. The world they had built was about to change with a ferocity they had not foreseen. Could their system survive? Could they?

At midnight, a weary Chubais retired to an office on the fourth floor. Gaidar was with him. Dubinin, the Central Bank chairman, drifted in and out. Coffee and tea were served; Chubais still wore a tie from the meeting with Yeltsin and opened his laptop computer. In a file named Meeting, Chubais had made notes the day before, reconstructing what happened the previous week. He wrote:

> Deterioration of situation during the whole week and an abrupt slide on Friday:
>
> 1. Rates at exchange points—with the official rate of 6.18, it is 7 at exchange points, and on Monday it can be 7.2 or 7.3—that is, the upper boundary of the corridor set for three years will be breached!
>
> 2. Beginning with Thursday—margin calls have not been paid, that is, mandatory bank payments on borrowed credits. There were two of them by Friday; there will be another four beginning Monday.
>
> 3. A slowdown of payments in the banking system begins to turn into a complete halt. Receipts of revenue from taxation to the budget drops sharply. If margin call payments are not postponed beginning Monday, the halt may happen already by the middle of the week.
>
> 4. Declining Central Bank reserves—in the course of the week about $1.5 billion was spent, which is almost twice more than the previous week. And $1 billion was spent on Friday alone. It is obvious that without taking tough decisions the unfolding panic at the currency market can fully drain the Central Bank of reserves in less than a week.

Chubais knew they could not go on like this, but he dreaded what was coming. He looked defeated, felt at rock bottom. The default meant that Russia cheated foreign investors out of billions of dollars they had brought to Russia's boisterous new markets for debt and equity. True, they had come out of greed, seeking obscene profits, collecting handsome fees, and overlooking the serious risks. But they also had come because Chubais made it possible; indeed, he beckoned them to a promised land. In his own mind, Chubais often replayed this landscape, where he had seen only great promise. The GKOs, Eurobonds, stocks, and dollar-forwards were all signs of how far they had traveled in so few years. They were crazy about markets and the markets were crazy about Russia. Then the romance fell apart. "Financial markets are very neurotic creatures," Chubais mused later. "Like a young lady, they respond sharply to doubtful news—they faint." Chubais also insisted that the government had no choice, at the end, but to lie to investors about impending devaluation.[71]

Late Sunday night, a new difficulty arose. Earlier in the day, Chubais believed he had received a green light from the IMF for Russia's default and devaluation plans, and he told this to Yeltsin while they were at the hunting lodge. On his return to the White House, however, the IMF began to object. Chubais telephoned Michel Camdessus, managing director of the fund, Fischer, Summers, and the undersecretary of the Treasury for international affairs, David A. Lipton. The IMF officials said, Don't do it. They suggested asking the Duma for new tax increases and appealing to parliament for a special session. Chubais said it was impossible. Tense hours of phone negotiations followed. The IMF threatened a "divorce" from Russia if the plan went ahead. Finally, the steely Chubais just exploded. "Do you realize what might happen here?" he shouted over the phone. "We will have Indonesia here. It's not just the miners banging their hats outside the White House. There will be a collapse of the banking system of Russia. A real collapse!" Chubais was emotional, severe, uncompromising. Chubais said the plan could not be stopped and would be announced the next morning, August 17. The long night of phone calls ended. Before hanging up, one of the Westerners said simply to Chubais, "Good luck."[72]

During the long night, Chubais called in the oligarchs—Berezovsky, Khodorkovsky, Aven, Friedman, and Potanin. He explained the plan. The ruble would be allowed to sink to 9.5 to the dollar. More painfully, their GKOs would become worthless paper. The tycoons just sat there, in dreadful silence.[73] The consequences were clear: they were about to be hit hard, especially the banks. "They are all bankrupt," Jordan recalled of the scene. "All they wanted to do was protect themselves for as long as they could."

Berezovsky had supported the idea of a gradual devaluation earlier in the year; his newspaper, *Nezavisimaya Gazeta*, provided a platform for Illarionov's warnings. But at this late hour, Berezovsky was alarmed that Chubais was acting against the advice of the IMF. Vinogradov, the most vulnerable, recalled he was furious about the devaluation, since his dollar-forward contracts, now up to $2.5 billion, would crush him. He had gambled on a stable ruble and lost. "Why do you have to conduct devaluation now and so drastically?" he pleaded. "This will lead to windows of banks being broken, stores being robbed!"[74] But some of the others were spared from utter destruction. Those who had natural resources—Khodorkovsky and Berezovsky had oil, while Potanin had metals and oil—would still enjoy ample cash flow from hard-currency exports. However, the banks would go up in smoke; both Khodorkovsky and Potanin had large banks.

The three-month moratorium was a lifeline thrown to the tycoons by their creator, Chubais. It gave them enough time to protect at least some of their assets. Chubais recalled the oligarchs pointing to the wrecked banking system and imploring him to "make at least some reciprocal step, help us at least in some way to escape the obligations that we have." Chubais agreed. That reciprocal step was the moratorium. It was supposed to be ninety days protection from their creditors, but in fact the tycoons got more. Some loans were never repaid, just forgotten; others paid just pennies on the dollar.

"It is a gift to the people whose arms and legs you have just cut off," Chubais recalled. "Then you give them crutches."

The default, devaluation, and moratorium were announced the next morning, August 17. The crutches were just what Khodorkovsky needed to walk away from loans he had taken on earlier, and that is what he did. According to a former Menatep official, the bank's leadership anxiously watched on Friday, August 14, to see if Imperial Bank would fail to make its payments. A default by Imperial could trigger a crisis and relieve them of a loan payment due Monday. Khodorkovsky still had Yukos, and he still had the ocean of oil in western Siberia. But for the loans, his answer was, Too bad—*force majeure*—and good-bye.[75]

"Menatep treated the West as they had always treated the Russian government, as a free source of funds," the Menatep banker told me. "We can get all the money we want by saying the right things. They presold the oil and pledged the oil, and borrowed from all sorts of programs, and played off the heated competition from the foreign banks that wanted to establish a client base here. They simply overleveraged themselves. They were thirty-four-year-olds who suddenly had hundreds of millions of dollars thrown at them and they overborrowed."

The glittering, go-go days of the Moscow boom were over, for a while. In the first few weeks, the Central Bank tried to hold the ruble at about 9.5 to the dollar but on September 2 let the currency float freely. It eventually settled at more than twenty to the dollar. An eerie mood settled over the city in those first days, a sense of opportunity lost. The autumn billboard advertising campaigns were all launched in late August, as if nothing had happened. The Italian designer Ermigildo Zenga opened a fancy boutique as if there might still be customers. In *Kommersant Daily*, ads beckoned for Gucci, DeBeers, Luis Vitton, as if the party would still go on. The neon lights in the city kept flashing in the month after the ruble devaluation, but on the streets was an emptiness, a stillness, like a commercial neutron bomb had gone off. It left all the symbols of prosperity but destroyed the people, and their money.

Summer vacations were still winding down, but in early September, when people dragged themselves back into the city from their dachas, panic began to set in. The banking system was locked up tight and payrolls were stalled. The automatic teller machines turned cold and silent; the most common sign in store doorways was "closed for technical reasons," which meant, no money today. The city felt aimless, in free fall, especially as the supply of imports began to dwindle and prices rose suddenly.[76] Shoppers panicked over shampoo, raiding store shelves as if they would never see L'Oreal again. The memories of the old brown soap of Soviet times—one chunk for a family of four—suddenly flooded back. Crazy buy-anything moods gripped people for weeks. In the outdoor markets, simple things like salt, sugar, flour, and matches disappeared. Every hour, currency exchange points posted new ruble-dollar exchange rates. The gyrations took on an otherworldly dimension in September. When some of the dollar-forward contracts came due, the ruble suddenly and strongly appreciated in value and then just as mysteriously fell back again. Living standards took a tumble, falling by 40 percent. The economic shock wave hurt everyone, but it was especially cruel to the middle class, which had just barely put down roots in the new market economy. They were people who had given up their state jobs to work for themselves, who traveled to Paris and bought jeans and cosmetics and dined out late at Moscow's fancy restaurants. They were part of a hardworking entrepreneurial class that tasted the fruits of the first prosperity, mostly in Moscow, and contributed to it. "It's really been very shaky," sighed Natalya Toumashkova, an advertising and personnel consultant who saw her business collapse almost overnight after the devaluation. "I remember in the first coup, in 1991, we were really scared. We felt it could go back. But the second time, in 1993, we already felt things were irreversible. Now we are in shock—that things could change back so fast!" We were talking in the almost empty cavernous dining hall of Le Gastronome, a restaurant of marble pillars and tinkling chandeliers that was once filled shoulder to shoulder with designer-suited business executives. Marina Boroditskaya, a writer and translator who was a longtime friend of Toumashkova, sadly surveyed the immaculate white tablecloths, shining crystal wine goblets, and empty chairs, as the sun glinted in through the massive arched windows. "I went out and bought fifteen rolls of toilet paper," she said, "just in case." The crash hit especially hard at small businesses like Toumashkova's that were built from scratch and prospered on the energy of the financial community—banks, advertising, the exchanges, and all that went with them. In the year of the dragons, the trade and catering business in Russia fell 46 percent, while entrepreneurial small businesses declined 31 percent from the boom year of 1997.[77]

The oligarchs were restive in the days after the crash. On August 20, Kiriyenko recalled, Berezovsky, Gusinsky, Smolensky, and some other bankers came to him seeking a bailout for Smolensky's SBS-Agro bank. Berezovsky wanted the bailout without changing the ownership of the bank, Kiriyenko said. Kiriyenko refused. "We will make sure you are dismissed," Berezovsky replied. "Just try," Kiriyenko said.[78] Berezovsky later denied that this meeting took place. "Absolute stupidity," he said of Kiriyenko's claim.

On August 23, Yeltsin dismissed Kiriyenko, setting off a strange free-for-all in which Berezovsky again rushed in to play his hand at power broker. Yeltsin reappointed Chernomyrdin as acting prime minister, a proposal that Berezovsky said he made to Yeltsin through Yumashev.[79] Months earlier, Berezovsky helped engineer Chernomyrdin's firing, but now he brought Chernomyrdin back. On the day of the appointment, according to an eyewitness, when Chernomyrdin arrived and walked down the long carpeted corridor at the Russian White House, he paused before entering the prime minister's office. There Berezovsky was waiting for him. It was fitting that Berezovsky went in first—and Chernomyrdin followed. Berezovsky was still thinking about the 2000 election, which would pick Yeltsin's successor. "Our interests for 2000 are to ensure the continuity of power," he said. Yeltsin, in language that suggested Berezovsky was pulling the strings, repeated what the tycoon had said, almost word for word, in appointing Chernomyrdin. "One important consideration" favoring Chernomyrdin, Yeltsin said, is "to support the continuity of power." Berezovsky was back in business, snapping his fingers and choosing who would run the country.

Rumors swept Moscow that Yeltsin was being urged by members of his own family and by the tycoons to step down once Chernomyrdin was confirmed by parliament. Looking terribly weak and vulnerable, Yeltsin appeared on television on August 28 seated at a small round table in the Kremlin. "I want to say that I'm not going anywhere, I'm not going anywhere," he said, speaking slowly but clearly. "I'm not going to resign." A few days later, Berezovsky openly broached the idea of Yeltsin's resignation in a radio interview. "If there is no strong authority, Boris Nikolayevich will have to resign before his term expires to clear the field for the creation of such strong authority."

Yet Berezovsky again lost the initiative. Yeltsin's authority was at a nadir, and parliament voted Chernomyrdin down after nearly two weeks of bickering. The economy slid further. Markets and banks were paralyzed. Luzhkov denounced the State Duma for inaction. "I am terribly upset that for two weeks they can't make one concrete decision," he said. "As two mice might say, why do we need cheese? Right now, we need to get out of this mousetrap." Facing a recalcitrant parliament, Yeltsin abandoned Chernomyrdin on September 10 and nominated Yevgeny Primakov, the foreign minister and staid symbol of the old school, who was confirmed. Berezovsky's latest fling with power politics was over—for a while.

Smolensky did not have an ocean of oil, just a sea of depositors, and they turned angry at the doors to the SBS-Agro branch on Pushkin

Square in the center of Moscow. In early September a mob besieged the office, demanding their deposits. Smolensky's dream of becoming the Russian equivalent of the Bank of America was going up in smoke; his hopes of winning over the trust of millions of depositors was vanishing before his eyes. Two weeks after the crash, I saw him at the bank's offices, and he bore the baleful look of a man under stress, nervously folding a small sheet of white paper in his hands, ever tighter and tighter. "At the moment," he acknowledged, "I do not know what can make people keep their money in banks. I do not see what can motivate people to do it."

After the crash, Smolensky's bank, SBS-Agro, with its 1,200 branches, 5.7 million depositors, automatic tellers, credit cards, and aspirations to become a commercial retail banking giant, became the symbol of all that went wrong. It was hit by a classic bank run as panicky depositors begged for their money back. The tycoons may have won protection from foreign creditors with the moratorium, but they didn't have protection from their own people. In August, Russians pulled 17 billion rubles out of the thirty largest banks, or about 10 percent of all deposits, compared to just 2 billion the month before.[80] By mid-September, Kiriyenko's fears were realized: the banking system was crashing. Payments just stopped, even though the Central Bank tried furiously to inject more rubles into the system. Crowds of cheated depositors angrily spat epithets at Smolensky from the streets. He had fooled them. "Banks cannot expect depositors back in the near future," Smolensky sighed, "and they are right, because they were deceived."

Inside, Smolensky's bank was also a strange house of funny money. In the first week of September, Smolensky told me that SBS-Agro held $1 billion in GKOs that had been frozen. It also had $1 billion in obligations to foreign investors, including the Eurobond, syndicated loans, and credits. Smolensky said payments of $162 million were overdue. He was ruined, he said, by the GKO default. "Like Bolsheviks, they just took away this money. We saw this in 1917." But when I saw Smolensky a year after the crash, he told me a different story. He said that SBS-Agro really had only kopeks in GKOs, and it was the Western loans that wrecked him. Smolensky was always secretive, and the truth was impossible to find out. He took a $100 million stabilization loan from the Central Bank on August 14, three days before the crash.

Dubinin said that Smolensky came to him after August 17 and demanded 2 billion rubles immediately and "afterward maybe 8 or 10 billion more."[81] Other banks were also demanding liquidity, and the Central Bank made a series of mysterious "stabilization loans," the fate of which was never clear. The Central Bank dished out a $345 million loan to SBS-Agro, guaranteed by 40 regional governments, in October 1998. But when the Central Bank attempted to impose a temporary administration on SBS-Agro, trying to take it over, Smolensky barred the door, just as he had done to Central Bank auditors in 1993. He simply refused to let the Central Bank come in.

Dubinin claimed Berezovsky rose to the defense of Smolensky, warning the Central Bank not to try and take over SBS-Agro. "We will not let you do it," Berezovsky said.[82] Dubinin could not get a fix on what SBS-Agro assets could be seized, if any. "The holding company is built in such a way that it looks as if nothing belongs to the bank," he said. "So if we bankrupt, roughly speaking, the bank, then we can't legally get near this property."[83] Smolensky had deliberately built his empire that way, and the murky structure would bedevil those chasing Smolensky's wealth in the months and years ahead. Dubinin failed to get in the door, and he resigned on September 7, accusing Smolensky of "sabotage." He was replaced with Viktor Gerashchenko, the former Central Bank chief who had been Smolensky's arch foe in the early 1990s.

Like Khodorkovsky, Smolensky made good use of the crutch to avoid repaying his debts to foreigners, during the moratorium and afterward. The Russian depositors who entrusted him with their savings were also left out in the cold. After the crash, thousands of SBS-Agro depositors met regularly to vent their rage. They passed around leaflets that described how the bank's assets had been mysteriously spirited away, leaving just an empty shell. They shared their misery with each other. Lyudmila Isayeva, a trim, elderly woman with a very upright posture, came to one of the meetings in a neat gray blazer, her hair pulled back in a ballerina bun. She wore pink lipstick and carried a clutch of documents. A professional translator, Isayeva was a pensioner who had deposited $10,000 in SBS-Agro, money she had saved for years in hopes of buying a bigger apartment. She withdrew her money from the state bank after the hyperinflation of the early 1990s, which eroded her savings until they were worth "just bread, milk, and sausage." In the boom of 1997, she went looking for a commercial bank to deposit her life savings. "One that was reliable," she said, repeating the word over and over again. "Reliable."

She pored over the magazines to see which commercial bank was the most reliable. "There were banks with A, A1, A2 ratings. B was less good. SBS-Agro was constantly in the A1 position," she said. "It was constantly among the best of the commercial banks." Her deposit in SBS-Agro paid monthly interest, which she collected at the local branch. She authorized the deposit to remain, month after month. "Eventually, since I came every month, the people working there started to know me. Finally, they convinced me to put my money in for one year. The one-year term ended in July 1998, and I prepared to take out my money. I wanted to finally pay for that apartment."

It was early August when she asked for the withdrawal. "They said their cash registers didn't have that much money in them and to come back in five days." They gave her the same excuse several times, each time providing a written promise to pay.

On Friday evening, August 14, she recalled seeing the television broadcasts of Yeltsin in Novgorod promising that the situation was "under control." On Monday came the crash, and she never saw the $10,000 again. "I just wasn't lucky," she recalled a year after the crash, standing in a crowd of the cheated depositors at a press conference.

Tatyana Kazantseva, fifty, an economist who worked at another bank, said she lost $20,000 in SBS-Agro. Her salary had been automatically deposited in the doomed bank. "I blame the government, but I also blame Smolensky," she said after two years of failed attempts to recover her money. "We trusted him. We wanted to be like civilized people. We didn't put our money under the pillow. We trusted." When I heard these sad stories, I was reminded that only two years earlier the $250 million Eurobond was arranged for Smolensky on the premise that he would be able to persuade Russians to trust their banks. In October 2000 Andrew Higgins of the *Wall Street Journal* asked Smolensky about the foreign creditors who lost more than $1 billion in SBS-Agro. Smolensky replied that they deserve only "dead donkey ears."[84]

It was the year of dead donkey ears. Berezovsky stumbled in his aspiration to become a power broker, and his political gamesmanship stirred up a costly distraction just as an economic crisis was bearing down on Russia. From the early days, the oligarchs had manipulated political power to their ends, but this time it backfired. Chubais, whose stubborn determination had served him so well before, this time was blinded by it—he had worked so long to create a stable ruble that he could not let go until it was too late. Chubais also suffered a costly lesson in how suddenly markets can render their own, harsh verdicts. Foreign investors, who had plied the Russians with easy money, found that they had been deceived. They had deceived themselves too by failing to look more closely at their borrowers. After the crash, the oligarchs were in various stages of agony, escape, and recovery, and the coming months would be among the most difficult in their young careers. They would never be together again, as they had been on the Sparrow Hills and during the Davos Pact. Their backs were to the wall, but their brand of wild capitalism endured. It did not perish with the roar of the dragons.

Chapter 16

Hardball and Silver Bullets

VLADIMIR GUSINSKY'S dream machine was launched on November 22, 1998, at Cape Canaveral, just five years after he and two discouraged television journalists came up with an improbable plan to start their own channel from scratch. On the Florida coast, Gusinsky watched anxiously as a Delta II rocket launched into orbit his new 3,141-pound satellite, Bonum-1, which could broadcast dozens of television channels directly to homes across European Russia. As he gazed skyward, Gusinsky felt enormous pride: his satellite was the first ever built by an American firm for a customer in the former Soviet Union.[1] After launch, the Hughes 376 high-powered satellite spread out its round, two-meter wide antenna and began an eleven-year flight, sending streams of digital news and entertainment down to the waiting trademark-green NTV-Plus receiver dishes below.

Gusinsky's dream was that a carpet of NTV-Plus receivers would spread across the Russian landscape, linking millions of viewers with his satellite. But the dream was inexorably linked with the fate of the Russian economy. Gusinsky gambled that a new middle class would take hold, including millions of families who would want—and could afford—to pay $299 for the satellite dish to receive around-the-clock movies, sports, news, children's programming, and other channels that he hoped to offer them someday. Both technically and financially, Gusinsky's expansion goals were extraordinarily ambitious. The satellite was controlled from a new ground station Gusinsky built outside Moscow. He planned a sprawling new production facility for NTV. He was making three hundred hours a year of television soap operas. Just five years after starting NTV, he already thought of himself as one of Europe's largest media companies. He was trying to cover three different levels of television in Russia all at once: by satellite, direct to people's homes, with NTV-Plus; by traditional terrestrial signal, from a broadcasting tower, with his flagship NTV channel; and with TNT, the fledgling affiliate network that was beginning to snake across Russia's regions.

But the August 17, 1998, ruble crash came at the worst possible moment for Gusinsky. The first shock wave of devaluation prompted the nascent middle class to reduce all discretionary spending—for restaurants, for electronics, and for entertainment. For Gusinsky, the result was like a slow-motion car wreck; the disaster took some time to sink in, but it was inevitable. NTV-Plus had reached 180,000 subscribers at the end of 1998, but a year later it had only 109,000. The original plan had been for half a million or more. Even worse, many of Gusinsky's current subscribers could not afford to pay their bills. Then the television advertising market collapsed in late 1998 in a way that was particularly painful for Gusinsky. The devaluation made imported products suddenly more expensive, and imports were the mainstay of his advertising—commercials pushing American toothpaste and Japanese electronics. After August 17, NTV advertising revenues fell by two-thirds.[2]

Gusinsky scaled back. He scrubbed plans for the expanded NTV studios, gave up his dream to build movie theaters, and abandoned hope of floating the company's stock on Wall Street, the most important part of his expansion strategy. "The crisis came and everything died," he told me a few years later. Gusinsky was a victim of bad timing, outsized dreams, and a sudden reversal in the fortunes of his longed-for middle class. He was a product of his own impulsive expansion in the early years. His philosophy had been, Build it and they will come. The whole satellite business had been based on European and Asian models in which the first five years were investment intensive. Profits came later, in the seventh or eighth year. Gusinsky had not yet made it to the profit years. Now, like a tide, the money flows changed direction; Gusinsky's costs were high and his revenues dwindled. He would have to pay off the expensive satellite, for which he still owed $123.7 million to the Export-Import Bank of the United States, without the expected profits. "What is a business, particularly one you have built?" Gusinsky asked me, rhetorically, looking back on his plight. "It is like a bicycle racer who races very fast. He leans forward and pedals so fast . . . because if he doesn't keep pedaling, he'll fall down and break his head and hands. You have to run fast if you want to be first."

Gusinsky fell. The economic crisis was like a patch of gravel that caused his bike to skid out from under him. The satellite turned out to be a financial albatross. Igor Malashenko, the NTV president, asserted later that it was Gusinsky's single biggest business mistake. He and others close to Gusinsky saw the satellite as a symbol of Gusinsky's early style—to dream the impossible dream and hope it would come true. In this case, the economy tumbled and the dream was no longer viable. Gusinsky didn't shift his vision fast enough.

"My partners said to me that I was a fool for trying to build an empire," Gusinsky said. They wanted Gusinsky to set aside his profits as a cushion rather than plow them back into the business. Gusinsky told them the satellite was the best way to deliver television in a country with decrepit infrastructure. He told me he invested $1.2 billion in retained earnings and loans into NTV-Plus. But he didn't count on the ruble crash. "The mistake was, we thought Russia was stable enough to invest in the business, and growth."[3]

Gusinsky wasn't alone in his troubles after the crash. Berezovsky, still anxious to play the role of wheeler-dealer, was threatened with arrest and political exile by an openly hostile prime minister, Yevgeny Primakov. Khodorkovsky, failing to pay off his loans, waged a dirty campaign to get rid of his Western creditors and minority shareholders. Smolensky's bank closed and he slipped out of public view. Luzhkov weathered the economic crisis, and for a while he was considered a potential successor to Yeltsin. But his political aspirations were quickly, and crudely, destroyed. The happy days were over.

For the oligarchs, events took a particularly ominous turn in late autumn. The Russian people were resentful and confused by the economic collapse, and a search for scapegoats began. There were plenty of potential targets. A poll taken in Moscow two weeks after the crash showed that Viktor Chernomyrdin, Boris Yeltsin, and Sergei Kiriyenko were the first three names mentioned when people were asked, Who is to blame? Then came the oligarchs, bankers, and financiers, followed by parliament, the reformers, and the Central Bank.[4]

But the most ominous threats came from an outspoken Communist extremist in parliament, Albert Makashov, a crude, vengeful man who had been jailed in 1993 for his part in an armed attempt to storm the Ostankino television station during Yeltsin's violent confrontation with parliament. As far back as 1996, the tycoons had feared an anti-Semitic backlash; now Makashov tried to ignite it. On November 11, he attacked Berezovsky. "Don't behave as a Yid," he said, using a slur for Jew. "Give this country, this nation . . . a billion or two of your green money and this nation will calm down." Communist leader Gennady Zyuganov refused to denounce Makashov in public, saying that it was enough that Makashov had received an internal party reprimand. Then Zyuganov joined the attacks on the Jewish bankers, reviving anti-Semitic rhetoric of the Soviet era. "Our people are not blind," Zyuganov said. "They cannot turn a blind eye to the aggressive, destructive role of Zionist capital in ruining Russia's economy and plundering her property owned by all. There is a growing understanding among the people that the origin of all the current troubles is the criminal course of an antipeople, supranational oligarchy that seized power."[5]

After a while it became evident that Makashov and Zyuganov were out of touch. Their attempt to incite hatred seemed menacing in the aftermath of the ruble collapse, but within a few months it disappeared, and the public did not take up their battle cry against the Jewish bankers. Anti-Semitism remained a latent force in some parts of Russian society, and the oligarchs were unpopular in many quarters, but the spark did not ignite. Perhaps anti-Semitism was fading since it no longer had the official backing of the state; or perhaps the urge to survive in hard times was stronger than the urge to hate.

What hurt the oligarchs was not public opinion but internecine battles with outside investors, with each other, and with the Kremlin. In the two and a half years after the ruble crash, the oligarchs fought costly, self-destructive conflicts motivated by a raw hunger for power and greed. This chapter is the story of four of those conflicts. It does not mark the end of the oligarchs, but it does mark the sunset of the roaring 1990s and the Yeltsin epoch in which they played such a prominent role.

Hard times meant hardball, and Mikhail Khodorkovsky was a master of the game. When he first won Yukos, Khodorkovsky sent three hundred of his best security men to Siberia to physically take over the company's wells and refineries, according to a former Menatep official. Oil towns like Nefteyugansk were notoriously filled with gangsters who sucked money out of the industry. Khodorkovsky paid special attention to the accountants and financial controllers at his new properties. "He personally went to every single financial controller and head accountant in all the daughter companies and said, 'This is who you work for now, don't screw around,'" the former Menatep official told me. The rules of this game were winner take all.[6]

After the crash, Khodorkovsky took a scorched earth approach to his Western creditors and minority shareholders. He wanted to shake them from his tail and reclaim ownership of all, or at least most, of Yukos. When the ninety-day moratorium had expired, Menatep defaulted on the $236 million loan from Daiwa of Japan, West Merchant of Germany, and Standard Chartered of London, for which Menatep had pledged about 30 percent of the shares in Yukos as collateral.[7]

At the time, Khodorkovsky was also nose to nose in an increasingly tense confrontation with Dart, the minority shareholder in the Yukos extraction subsidiaries. For more than a year, Dart, a reclusive billionaire, seethed as Khodorkovsky drained away the value of his investments. Now Khodorkovsky was ready for war. He didn't need to coddle investors any longer because Russia had the world's worst credit rating as a country, and the Western lenders would not be back for a while. Khodorkovsky struck against both his Western creditors and his minority shareholders by hijacking the oil company away from them. Even more audaciously, he tried to take it out of Russia altogether.

In the early turbulent years of his banking career, Khodorkovsky built an offshore financial network. Menatep branched out to offshore havens in Switzerland, Gibraltar, the Caribbean, and other secretive locations where hundreds of millions of dollars could easily be hidden. When he obtained Yukos, Khodorkovsky moved his money into this offshore financial network. This was a common practice in the oil industry; oil was one of the most surefire methods to move wealth out of Russia. Whenever Yukos oil left Russia for abroad, it was sold through offshore trading companies that Khodorkovsky controlled. The oil wealth then accumulated outside Russia, avoiding taxes and other risks inside the country. The offshore network was an ever rotating menu of odd names and places. One key component, for a while, was Jurby Lake Ltd. on the Isle of Man, a well-known offshore tax haven in the United Kingdom. Jurby Lake was a group of oil trading companies that handled the Yukos exports and then deposited the earnings to other select companies controlled by Khodorkovsky and his partners, according to documents describing the structure and a former Menatep official who spoke to me about it. Menatep Bank had its own web of offshore links, such as Menatep Ltd. Gibraltar and Menatep Finance SA of Switzerland. Moreover, Khodorkovsky in 1994 purchased 20 percent of Valmet Group, a Geneva-based global investment management company with offices in Gibraltar, Cyprus, the Isle of Man, and other financial centers catering to clients who wanted to avoid taxes and detection.[8]

Khodorkovsky's far-reaching offshore network was typical for Russian big business. All the other oligarchs—indeed, thousands of Russian businessmen—did the same thing, although many on a scale less grand. Every month, by very rough calculations, up to $2 billion slipped out of Russia in wire transfers, phony import-export documents, oil shipments, and other means. The leakage was known as capital flight, and it became one of Russia's most debilitating sicknesses in the 1990s. Over the decade, perhaps $100 to $150 billion flowed out of Russia, money that was needed for investment at home, to rebuild factories and start businesses. Instead, Russian capital found its way to overseas bank accounts, real estate, luxury resorts, and offshore tax havens. The money was on the run for many reasons: to hide it from taxes, shareholders, investors, and creditors; to conceal the pillage of natural resources or stripped factory assets; or just to skirt political and economic upheaval.

Sadly, capital flight was a sickness that no one in the Russian elite was willing to cure. A midlevel banker once told me that getting capital out of the country was so easy because no one wanted to stop it. Although Russia had some Central Bank rules against exporting capital, they were widely ignored and almost never enforced. Too many people benefited by the leakage—politicians, tycoons, and even small-time factory directors who stashed their rake-off abroad.[9] Stopping capital flight really meant changing the entire operating system of the country, creating a stable, rule-of-law state, and that task was too big for Yeltsin and his generation in the first decade of post-Soviet Russia. Occasionally the Russian government machine would rouse itself to attempt halfhearted police state methods to stanch the leakage. Departing airport passengers were asked by Customs Service officers to open their wallets to show how much cash they were carrying out of Russia. I saw this happen many times at Sheremetyevo Airport as I waited impatiently in line. It was a pathetic and silly exercise, when everyone knew that $1 billion could fly out by wire transfers, undetected. Capital flight did not have a departure gate.

Stunning evidence of the full extent of the phenomenon of capital flight came in the aftermath of the ruble crash when it was disclosed that the Russian Central Bank had sent billions of dollars out of the country through a tiny offshore company, the Financial Management Company in Jersey, a favorite tax haven in the United Kingdom. The full story of this obscure company, FIMACO, was never disclosed, but the obvious message was that even the government was taking advantage of offshore havens. If the Central Bank, paragon of stability, guardian of Russia's treasure, could divert its currency reserves to a tiny offshore company, then there was no telling what others might dare.[10]

To wrest Yukos out of the grip of its creditors and minority shareholders, Khodorkovsky created an elaborate plan to move the oil company offshore. A complex transfer of shares would scatter Yukos and its daughter companies to the winds, making it impossible for others to find where he was hiding them. The plan was even more audacious than moving oil profits abroad. Khodorkovsky was taking the whole company offshore. The plan was to leave the minority shareholders and the Western creditors with an empty shell, while he took the company's shares to small, remote islands in the Atlantic and Pacific Oceans.

Khodorkovsky began with a scheme to issue millions of new shares in the subsidiaries. The new shares would dilute the value of those held by Dart. Dart's shares in the subsidiaries were relatively small—12.85 percent of Yuganskneftegaz, 12.3 percent of Samaraneftegaz, and 13 percent of Tomskneft, which gave him little leverage in how the companies were run. Even so, Khodorkovsky resorted to battleship tactics against Dart, just to make sure there was no question about victory. For example, at the time there were 40 million shares of Yuganskneftegaz outstanding. Khodorkovsky laid plans to issue 77.8 million new shares. This meant that Dart's share of the overall company would drop from 12.85 percent to less than 5 percent. The story was the same with the other subsidiaries. For Samaraneftegaz, Khodorkovsky planned to add 67.4 million shares to the existing 37.6 million. At Tomskneft, he planned to add 135 million shares to the existing 45 million. In short, Dart's holdings were becoming the incredible shrinking oil company. This onerous tactic was the same as the transfer pricing that had originally drawn Dart's anger in 1998. Hundreds of millions of dollars were at stake.[11]

For his next sleight of hand, Khodorkovsky decided to sell all these millions of new shares in the oil extraction subsidiaries to obscure, distant offshore companies. For example, Yuganskneftegaz shares would be sold to Asbury International Inc. of the Bahamas, Rennington International Associates Ltd. of Ireland, Thornton Services Ltd. of the Isle of Man, and Brahma Ltd. of the Isle of Man. Who were these mysterious new buyers? Khodorkovsky-affiliated shell companies, most probably. Khodorkovsky could not admit that he controlled these offshore companies, since the whole gambit would be illegal under Russian law, but he was surely not selling his oil company to strangers.[12]

In yet another brazen twist, Khodorkovsky proposed that the additional millions of shares would be purchased not with cash but with *veksels*, or promissory notes, issued by the other Yukos extraction subsidiaries. How the mysterious buyers would obtain the *veksels* in the first place is just one of the many mysteries about Khodorkovsky's plan that I could never fathom. The whole transaction was a circular, deceptive paper chase: one company issues millions of new shares, sells them to distant offshore companies, and collects a promissory note for the shares. The loser was going to be Dart.

To ratify the share dilution gambit, three emergency shareholder meetings, one for each oil extraction subsidiary, were called on March 16, 23, and 30, 1999. The meetings were held at a palatial prerevolutionary castle in the center of Moscow at 5 Kolpachny Lane, once a Komsomol building and later Menatep headquarters. Outside the gate, shareholders of Yuganskneftegaz presented their papers to a clerk for admittance. Some were allowed to enter, but one of Dart's representatives, John J. Papesh, was not. He asked for a pass but was refused. He was presented with a court order signed by a provincial judge just a few days earlier. The order froze Dart's shares on a technicality. Papesh was left out in the cold. Inside the meeting, the 77 million new shares were quickly issued, dramatically shrinking Dart's holding. "This is the Russian version of theft in the executive suite," Papesh fumed afterward. "It is red-collar crime." The huge share emissions were approved at the other two meetings as well. An even more bizarre dodge occurred in June at a subsequent scheduled meeting of Tomskneft shareholders. When the minority shareholders arrived at 5 Kolpachny Lane, they saw a sign saying the meeting had been moved to a small town south of Moscow, and it would start in two hours. They jumped in their car and raced off; the address turned out to be an old building under reconstruction. Inside, up a makeshift stairway without handrails, they found a room with seven chairs, a table, and two copies of the meeting agenda. The construction workers said the "meeting" had concluded twenty minutes earlier. They were out of luck.

Yet the battle was not over. When it came to business in offshore zones, Dart was no neophyte, being heir to a $3 billion fortune created when his father and grandfather invented a way to mass-produce foam cups. Dart renounced his U.S. citizenship to become a citizen of Belize, a tiny country known as an offshore tax haven. He was a hard-nosed player in global investments, once facing down the government of Brazil over a bond issue, and he was prepared for tough battles with Khodorkovsky. In the early 1990s, Dart sunk hundreds of millions of dollars into Russia during mass privatization, buying up stakes in many of the oil extraction companies and other properties. Like many other foreign investors, he was a speculator, buying low and hoping to sell high.[13] While Dart sought profit, Khodorkovsky, who bought Yukos cheaply in loans for shares, did not want Dart's profit to come out of his own pocket. He wanted Dart to go away. A collision was inevitable.

The two magnates had been thrown together in a shotgun wedding: Dart as minority shareholder in the extraction subsidiaries and Khodorkovsky as the winner of the Yukos holding company. It was always expected that, sooner or later, they would have to settle. But first they were making war. Each side threw lawyers, public relations companies, and private detectives into the battle. Yukos issued statements calling Dart a "green mailer" (someone who practices pressure tactics in hopes of reaping a fat profit) and a "vulture." Dart said Khodorkovsky was "looting" the subsidiaries.

When Dart got wind of Khodorkovsky's offshore gambit with the Yukos subsidiaries, he began to chase the shares around the globe. Dart's lawyers filed suit in such offshore jurisdictions as the Marshall Islands, the British Virgin Islands, and the Isle of Man to try and stop Khodorkovsky. In a remarkable piece of detective work, Dart lawyers and private investigators compiled a dense, complex flow chart, showing what they believed to be Khodorkovsky's far-flung corporate structure. The chart was a jungle of arrows and boxes illustrating shell companies, ownership ties, and share transfers stretching from Cyprus in the Mediterranean to Nuie in the Pacific Ocean. Across the bottom it included, in small boxes marked with a star, the names and locations of offshore zones that Khodorkovsky intended to use as the new "home" base for his oil subsidiaries. The chart, while impressive in its detail, was still not complete; in fact, Khodorkovsky's offshore empire stretched even further than the document suggested. For example, the chart did not mention the Jurby Lake structure of oil-exporting companies.

While fighting Dart with one hand, Khodorkovsky tried to shake off Western creditors with the other. The three banks that had loaned Khodorkovsky's Bank Menatep $236 million could, under terms of the deal, claim a total of about 30 percent of Yukos when Menatep defaulted on the loan. The 30 percent was a sizable chunk of the oil company. If Khodorkovsky relinquished it, he could, at some point in the future, be vulnerable to losing control of Yukos. This he did not want to do, at any cost.

Khodorkovsky's game with the banks was partly psychological warfare. If he made a strong enough case that he was not going to pay back the money, he calculated, maybe the Westerners would eventually give up and just write off the debt as a loss at the end of the fiscal year. This was not an unreasonable expectation: the big Western banks and investment funds knew there were huge risks in emerging markets like Russia. They had reaped fortunes in the last few years as the Russian stock market skyrocketed. So what if they had a bad year? They might try and squeeze the debtor a little, but they knew they had little leverage inside Russia because the courts were weak. The Western banks had both a limited attention span and a diffuse chain of command. The managers were not making decisions with their own money; it was other people's money. They would not suffer just because of some bad loans in Russia. But Khodorkovsky, by contrast, had everything at stake. He was playing for his own survival. He used ruthless tactics to make sure his foes got the point. He took the Yukos-owned shares in the oil-extraction subsidiaries and sent them offshore along with the new, diluted shares. (This action only came to light when one of the small minority shareholders looked at the register, the book in which share ownership is recorded.) The bottom line was that the banks were being left with 30 percent of an empty shell. Daiwa Europe Ltd., which held about 13 percent of Yukos, issued a statement expressing concern that its assets would be "irretrievably lost."[14] That was putting it mildly.

James Fenkner, the Troika Dialog analyst I had met during the boom years, wrote a note to clients about Khodorkovsky's gambit entitled "How to Steal an Oil Company." Fenkner told me he was stunned at Khodorkovsky's nerve. "It's incredibly brazen," Fenkner said. "A couple of years ago, people said Russian managers will steal, but only a little and it will improve over time. What this case shows is that it is all or nothing. It's kind of shocking. The second-largest oil company in Russia is no longer held under Russia's jurisdiction."

Perhaps no one in Moscow watched these developments with more foreboding than Dmitri Vasiliev, the chairman of the Russian Federal Securities Commission. The lively, diminutive Vasiliev, who was Anatoly Chubais's deputy during mass privatization, had argued that the greatest mistake in Russian capitalism was the failure to build institutions that would create rules and laws to regulate the market after the first wave of reforms. His own Securities Commission was an example—its enforcement powers were extremely weak. I often thought of Vasiliev as the referee at a soccer match, blowing his whistle and waving his arms around wildly as the big, muscular players ran roughshod over anything in their way and ignored him. Vasiliev was a small hero of Russian capitalism at a time when it needed a big hero. He believed in the rules and tried to make them stick, but he was overwhelmed by a system that operated on a level that was beyond the official rules.

Vasiliev chose his fights very carefully. He was especially fearful of the tycoons because they could strike back against him personally. Investigating the tycoons was risky and sometimes impossible. For example, a truck carrying 607 boxes of Menatep Bank documents mysteriously plunged into the Dubna River on May 24, 1999.[15] That was how things were done in Russia, a state where the rule of law had yet to be established and enforcing the securities law was a distant dream. Vasiliev held a long talk with Chubais about the best way to investigate one of the oligarchs. For tactical reasons, Vasiliev liked to strike first and settle later. But it could be risky to take the oligarchs by surprise; they had legions of spies, guards, and guns. Chubais urged Vasiliev to be more cautious. Better to warn the sleeping bear before you poke him in the eye, Chubais suggested.

Vasiliev scored an important victory in 1998 in his first test case, forcing Vladimir Potanin and Boris Jordan to back down from a planned dilution of minority shareholders in the oil company Sidanco.[16] At the time, Vasiliev raised concerns about a similar share dilution at Yukos, but he told me later that including Yukos was a tactic to show that he was not picking on Potanin alone. Vasiliev recalled that he got a written pledge in 1998 from Yukos that they would follow the rules. But in early 1999, after the ruble crash, investors' complaints, chiefly from Dart, continued to pile up about Yukos.

In the spring Khodorkovsky launched his brazen plan to hijack the entire oil company. Vasiliev announced in April that he would conduct a full-fledged investigation into whether Yukos had violated minority shareholder rights. It was a risk he had to take, but how? At first, he tried to get the minority shareholders to do the hard work—he loudly and publicly insisted they should go to the courts. Dart did so and was able to persuade six courts in offshore zones to temporarily block the share transfers. At the Securities Commission, Vasiliev had little real power and only one option: to decide whether to formally register, or approve, the millions of new shares that were being issued. The only legal grounds for rejecting the shares would be a determination that the offshore havens were in fact controlled by Khodorkovsky; then the issuance of the shares might be illegal. But penetrating the offshore havens was way beyond Vasiliev's ability. The commission had a small budget and could not send lawyers globe-trotting in search of the elusive Yukos shares.

In the next few weeks, Khodorkovsky sent a message to Vasiliev: Get out of my way! A vice president of the oil company warned him privately, in a personal meeting, that Yukos would do everything it could to block the Federal Securities Commission. Yukos was a big oil company backed up by a powerful oligarch, and the Securities Commission was a weak agency. Vasiliev took the threat seriously, recalling what Chubais had said about going on the attack against the tycoons.

Vasiliev had precious few weapons at his disposal. His feeling of helplessness was deepened by a problem within his own commission, unknown to all but a few people at the time. The Securities Commission had benefited from an $89 million loan by the World Bank to help Russia improve its capital markets. Vasiliev used some money from the project to pay for the commission's press office and computers that allowed outsiders to read reports about its regulatory decisions on the Internet. The press office was run under a contract with Burson-Marsteller, a global public relations company. The key official at the public relations company was Mark D'Anastasio, managing director of the international development practice, who was based in Washington. D'Anastasio was a public relations man who specialized in building up a long-term image for his client. He told me that he had worked hard for several years to build a "squeaky-clean good guy" image abroad for Vasiliev. The goal of the World Bank program, which paid the bill for Burson-Marsteller's work, was to improve "transparency" and to provide more "complete and reliable" information about companies in the stock market.[17]

But Vasiliev discovered in 1999 that D'Anastasio and Burson-Marsteller were also, at the same time, representing Yukos and Khodorkovsky, whom the commission was investigating. With the World Bank money, the PR company was supposedly building "transparency," but with Yukos they were actively defending an oligarch who was hiding shares of an oil company in offshore zones. Vasiliev concluded that it was a direct conflict of interest. But Vasiliev was afraid to fire Burson-Marsteller because he desperately needed the press office and the computer support—he had little to work with as it was. If he threw out Burson-Marsteller, he told me, he probably would lose the badly needed World Bank money. "They had me by the throat," he recalled.

D'Anastasio acknowledged to me later that he was representing both sides. After Vasiliev protested privately to him, the public relations company wrote a letter promising there would be no contact between the two clients. But in fact, D'Anastasio continued to deal with both of them. According to both Vasiliev and D'Anastasio, the public relations man at one point even proposed to Vasiliev that he might be an interlocutor with Yukos, a peacemaker. Furious, Vasiliev wondered what kind of peace would that be. How could he represent the interests of the regulator and the regulated at the same time?

When I asked D'Anastasio about the conflict of interest a few years later, he said it might have been a problem had the hostility continued for a long time, but he did not think it would go on. Besides, the rules in Russia were not as clear as rules in a developed market economy, he said. D'Anastasio also had his own preferences: he admired Khodorkovsky, whom he called "a figure of historic proportions." Khodorkovsky complained frequently to D'Anastasio that Vasiliev was going too far. D'Anastasio agreed.[18]

My own view was that Burson-Marsteller was playing a direct role in weakening the very capital markets they were being paid to improve. What is amazing is that it didn't seem to bother them—they played by Russian rules. It is not hard to see why Vasiliev felt vulnerable. His friends were his enemies.

In late June, as a result of a complaint from the trade association of stockbrokers, all trading in Yukos and the oil extraction companies was halted on Russia's chief stock exchange, the Russian Trading System.[19] This was a setback for Yukos, but Vasiliev admitted at a press conference on June 29 that his probe of Yukos was running into a brick wall. The securities commission lacked investigative powers—all it could do was ask for information. No one, not even the Russian government agencies, came forward with any answers or help for his investigation. The Fuel and Energy Ministry and the State Tax Service ignored his requests. Even so, Vasiliev insisted, "The investigation will not be stopped." Then, on July 21, Vasiliev announced that he was turning the files over to the law enforcement authorities for a criminal investigation—the Interior Ministry, the Federal Tax Police, and the Federal Security Service. On the same day, Yukos fired back with an angry statement, accusing Vasiliev of taking sides with the "famous speculator" Kenneth Dart.[20] More pressure followed. On August 18, the Yukos vice president who had warned Vasiliev earlier that Yukos would fight him took action against Vasiliev. He quietly filed a complaint against Vasiliev in the general prosecutor's office on the grounds of slander, based on the July 21 news conference. Under Russian law, slander was a criminal offense. I was appalled when I heard about this. I had been at the press conference, and it was clear that Vasiliev had not slandered Khodorkovsky or Yukos, since investigating the oil company was clearly part of his official responsibilities. But Vasiliev saw the criminal complaint for what it really was, a message. He would face interminable difficulties, interrogations, and who knows what else they could come up with. The prosecutor's office was notoriously on the take. It was common at the time for all different kinds of law enforcement bodies to take bribes to frame someone in a dispute. I knew a young man involved in a commercial dispute who was framed; the police had planted a bomb in his trunk and then arrested him. In the lawless state, anything was possible. Poke the bear between the eyes, and you took enormous risks.

Rather than fight, a frustrated and discouraged Vasiliev resigned from the commission on October 17. "The system here doesn't protect investors," Vasiliev lamented. A few days before his departure, the Samaraneftegaz share dilution—the proposed issuance of 67 million new shares—came before the commission. Although the application was in order, Vasiliev said he voted against it on principle. "It was all legal, but from a moral point of view, I understood it was theft." He was outnumbered. The commission voted its approval.[21]

Khodorkovsky had won. Eight weeks after Vasiliev quit, Dart settled with Khodorkovsky and sold his shares for an undisclosed sum. It is not known whether Dart suffered a loss or made a profit on his investment in Russian oil. But it is clear that Khodorkovsky achieved his main goal: getting control of his oil company and getting rid of the minority shareholder. The scorched earth plan had worked.

Khodorkovsky defeated the creditors too. The three banks that loaned money to Khodorkovsky did not have infinite patience, and Khodorkovsky outlasted them. West Merchant, which had suffered heavy losses in the Russian crash, had originally loaned Khodorkovsky's Menatep $135 million. According to one well-informed insider, Khodorkovsky went to Germany and told top officials of West LB, the parent bank, that he could not possibly pay back the Menatep debt because of the Russian economic crisis. Menatep Bank had collapsed in the crash. But one German bank official threw up his arms in exasperation, noting that Khodorkovsky's oil company, Yukos, was still going strong. What did he mean, he could not pay them back?

But Khodorkovsky put on a very persuasive show, and the Western banks lost their nerve in dealing with the wily Russian. "Khodorkovsky said he was hard-hit," said the insider at the German bank. "He got sympathy and understanding, when he should have been hit with a hammer." As a result, rather than press Khodorkovsky to pay back the money, the German bank sold off the assets for $67.5 million, or half what the bank had originally loaned Khodorkovsky. A similar thing happened to Daiwa, the Japanese bank which had been part of the deal. Daiwa sold out its share for $40 million. The lenders had given up and taken a loss. Next, Khodorkovsky quietly bought back his shares at bargain-basement prices. Of the approximately 30 percent of Yukos he had pledged for the original $236 million loan, he managed to buy back 23.7 percent after the lenders threw in the towel.[22] It was a good deal: his reward for defaulting on the loan was that Khodorkovsky got most of his shares back, and for less than half the cash he had originally borrowed.

Although Khodorkovsky told the German bank that he had been badly hurt by the crash, the condition of Yukos soon improved dramatically. Oil prices went back up, and Yukos amassed an estimated $2.8 billion in cash by the end of the year 2000. If the banks had been willing to wait a little longer, they might have recovered their $236 million loan. But the Western lenders proved to be weak-kneed. Khodorkovsky had tried to hijack the oil company out from under them.

For Khodorkovsky, hardball paid dividends.[23]

The shattered landscape of the Russian economy left no one who had participated in the events of recent years unscathed—not Anatoly Chubais and the young reformers, not Boris Berezovsky and the oligarchs, not the ailing Boris Yeltsin. They were all tarnished by the upheaval; the Russian people, resentful and bewildered, regarded them with suspicion. The economic crisis left a political vacuum in its wake. The question of "continuity of power," as Berezovsky had put it, remained unresolved. There was no obvious successor to Yeltsin.

But Yuri Luzhkov was still on his feet. No one could blame the Moscow mayor for the nationwide flirtation with easy money and GKOs. Luzhkov's reputation was not damaged by the crash, although the shock wave hit the city hard, especially the new middle class.

While visiting London on September 30, Luzhkov hinted for the first time that he would run for president. Speaking to journalists at a press conference held at the Russian embassy, Luzhkov said he wanted to remain mayor for the time being. But, he added cautiously, "If I see that presidential hopefuls do not possess the necessary statesmanlike views to ensure Russia's stability and progress, I will join the race." On hearing these words, I immediately realized that Luzhkov had made the decision to run. Perhaps he had concluded that the other contenders had been crippled by the crash. Behind the scenes, Vladimir Yevtushenkov, chief of the Systema conglomerate, the most influential businessman in city affairs, encouraged Luzhkov in his ambition. Yevtushenkov was a prime mover behind the creation of Center TV, the channel of the Luzhkov empire, which could become a key building block for a presidential campaign. Although Center TV suffered from a miserably dull programming schedule, it quickly acquired some of the most modern broadcasting equipment and technology in the country and devoted generous hours of airtime to uncritical interviews of Luzhkov. Another sign of Luzhkov's ambition was the formation of a political movement, Otechestvo (Fatherland), with Luzhkov at the head. Political consultants were being lined up. Yevtushenkov told me he believed Luzhkov could succeed by campaigning on the slogan that he would transform Russia as he had changed Moscow. "I believed that he had a chance, an historic chance, and he had to take advantage of it," Yevtushenkov said.

Luzhkov considered running at a time when a great power vacuum opened up in Russian politics. Yeltsin was in ill health, his authority badly eroded by the economic crisis, and he had not handpicked a successor. The oligarchs, especially Berezovsky, were worried that the spoils they had won, the fantastic wealth and property, could be taken away. They worried that Luzhkov might saunter right into the Kremlin in the next election, given the lack of other alternatives, and impose his Moscow model on Russia. They did not like Luzhkov's model, in which he was the boss and they were the supplicants. But the Kremlin—Yeltsin, his staff, and the oligarchs who were close to them—did not know what to do about the power vacuum. The months after the ruble crash found them insecure, paranoid, and at sea.

Luzhkov had weaknesses too. Running for president in Russia required a certain all-out competitive character, such as Yeltsin, who was a politician down to his very core and thought about power and politics *all the time.* Luzhkov was not this sort of politician. He saw himself as a *khozyain* who, to succeed, for tactical advantage, had to engage in politics. Luzhkov had tailored a system in Moscow to serve his own ends, a political machine that did not tolerate competition to his rule. He was acclaimed at the polls and praised in the newspapers. There is no doubt he was a genuinely popular figure, but his was a very protected life. Jumping into the national political scene meant that Luzhkov was stepping outside Moscow, leaving the playing field he controlled for new and uncertain territory.

Luzhkov attempted to make the leap, but his steps were plagued with difficulty from the very beginning. If he had thought about it, Luzhkov might have sought Yeltsin's blessing or at least tried to steer clear of the erratic president and his inner circle. Instead, Luzhkov immediately pointed his guns at Yeltsin and opened fire, criticizing Yeltsin as unfit to remain president. When Yeltsin was reported by the

Kremlin to be suffering from bronchitis at his country residence outside Moscow in October, Luzhkov said, "A short ailment is one thing, but if the man cannot work and fulfill his duties, then it is necessary to find the will and courage to say so." Luzhkov and Yeltsin had been allies in the past—Yeltsin had picked Luzhkov out of the sea of bureaucrats during the *perestroika* years in Moscow; Luzhkov was on Yeltsin's side in the 1993 confrontation with parliament; they had campaigned together in 1996. But now Luzhkov was plunging headlong into conflict not only with Yeltsin personally but with the president's coterie, a group that included Berezovsky. It was a battle that would be far more destructive than Luzhkov realized. In a climate of uncertainty, the early months of 1999 brought a series of events that frightened Yeltsin's inner circle, including Berezovsky. The result was that Luzhkov was put on the Kremlin enemies list. The people around Yeltsin decided to destroy Luzhkov's chances of becoming Yeltsin's successor.

In this period, Berezovsky was again thrown on the defensive, this time by Yevgeny Primakov, the prime minister. Primakov was an old warhorse of the late Soviet years. His economic policy in early 1999 was to hold the status quo, leading to a period of relative calm after the tumult of the crash. But Primakov was less reticent about Berezovsky. He actively went after the oligarch. After the Duma approved an amnesty freeing 94,000 prisoners, Primakov told a cabinet meeting on January 28, 1999, that "we are freeing up space for those who are about to be jailed—people who commit economic crimes." Within days, prosecutors and gun-toting men in camouflage and black masks raided Berezovsky's companies in Moscow, the Sibneft headquarters and Aeroflot. The message was unmistakable: Berezovsky was a target.

At the Sibneft building, the masked men seized boxes of materials from a small company, Atoll, which was reportedly a Berezovsky security service. One of Luzhkov's most loyal newspapers, the popular broadsheet *Moskovsky Komsomolets,* said investigators believed Berezovsky used Atoll to spy on the Yeltsin family, including Yeltsin's daughter Dyachenko. Berezovsky believed that Primakov had personally ordered the investigations and arrest warrants against him. Sometime later, Berezovsky went to see Primakov, who denied that he had harassed the oligarch. In a moment of high tension and drama in Primakov's office, Berezovsky told me he took a document from his coat pocket and confronted Primakov with evidence that he had personally ordered the probe. According to Berezovsky, the former prime minister, Chernomyrdin, was also present at this moment and was so stunned and embarrassed that he got up from the table and left the room in a hurry. Chernomyrdin's discomfit was understandable: Berezovsky had managed to obtain a copy of the prime minister's own secret order.[24]

While Primakov pursued Berezovsky from one side, a fresh scandal broke to further deepen the sense of paranoia in Yeltsin's circle. The new controversy involved the general prosecutor, Yuri Skuratov, who was probing Kremlin corruption. Some of the allegations pointed to payoffs made by a Swiss engineering company, Mabetex, which had carried out Kremlin remodeling work, to people in the tight-knit Yeltsin clan.

Skuratov, a colorless figure, had broad powers, yet he was singularly ineffective as chief law enforcement officer in Russia's years of crazy capitalism. He had not brought any major figures to account for corruption or solved any of the highly publicized contract killings. Moreover, Skuratov had personal problems. He had been secretly set up with some prostitutes and videotaped. The tape was being used to blackmail him.

On the same day as the raids against Sibneft, Yeltsin abruptly asked Skuratov to quit. A copy of the tape was leaked to state television. At first Skuratov agreed to quit but then changed his mind and decided to fight. In a desperate attempt to save himself, Skuratov began to publicize his half-finished investigations, including the probe into Kremlin building contracts. Skuratov was a contradictory and maddening figure whose hints of corruption were never followed by concrete prosecutions. Still, the mere mention of Skuratov and his investigation into Mabetex was enough to panic the Kremlin team.

The Skuratov affair, the raids on Berezovsky firms, the fallout from the ruble crash, Primakov's vow to put the tycoons in jail, and the launch of Luzhkov's presidential campaign all came in the same few months. In retrospect, a chain of events was set in motion. Skuratov threw out the dirt on the Kremlin family, alarming Yeltsin's inner circle. Luzhkov picked up on the allegations, saying the prosecutor should be allowed to continue his investigations, which antagonized Yeltsin and his aides. Then, fighting back, Berezovsky and the Kremlin set out to wreck Luzhkov.[25]

The Skuratov affair was followed by an arrest warrant issued by the prosecutor's office on April 5 for Berezovsky on grounds that he had misused cash from Aeroflot foreign ticket sales. Berezovsky's reply was that he "never worked a day at Aeroflot." This was literally true, but beside the point. Berezovsky never needed to work at Aeroflot to rake off the company's foreign currency earnings. The announcement was a major blow to Berezovsky, who was in France at the time. The raids, investigations, and arrest warrants were unprecedented for a man who had so often—and so effortlessly—strolled through the corridors of power. Berezovsky also lost his post as executive secretary of the Commonwealth of Independent States on March 4.

Spring was a time of trouble for the Yeltsin inner circle. Skuratov threatened new disclosures. Berezovsky faced arrest. Then in May the Communists in the Duma tried to impeach Yeltsin. The impeachment failed, but there were rumors that the Kremlin, or its corporate allies, paid $30,000 each for votes to support the ailing president.

Luzhkov opposed Yeltsin's impeachment, but he became more vocal in his attacks on the Yeltsin camp. Russia was not being run by Yeltsin, Luzhkov declared, but by a cabal, a "regime" in the Kremlin. His use of this word "regime" over and over again particularly riled the Yeltsin circle. Luzhkov singled out Berezovsky as part of the "regime," along with Alexander Voloshin, a bearded, balding onetime railway worker and economist who had worked with Berezovsky during the All-Russian Automobile Alliance project. Voloshin, who entered the Kremlin as an economics specialist, rose to become Yeltsin's chief of staff, succeeding Valentin Yumashev. Voloshin was a figure in the shadows who relished hardball tactics. Like Berezovsky, he was determined not to let Luzhkov become the next president of Russia. Berezovsky knew that if Luzhkov came to power, the tycoons could be at risk of having their property taken away. The rules of the game would be changed, and they would no longer run the country.

Berezovsky began to ponder how to attack Luzhkov. One of Berezovsky's most effective spear carriers was Sergei Dorenko, the television commentator who had participated in the bankers' war. With a husky voice, manly good looks, and a mischievous sense of showmanship, Dorenko was the television personality that politicians loved to hate. To a Westerner, Dorenko's television style might seem crude, unpolished, even down-market, but time and again Dorenko scored in

Russia as a television ringmaster who gleefully put the politicians in their place.

Berezovsky thought Dorenko was a magnificent talent. He told me that he first recalled seeing Dorenko on television after his Mercedes had been blown up. He was watching television and Dorenko was using a snide tone, saying another moneybags was hit by a bomb today, too bad. Berezovsky was not offended and called his secretary immediately. "Would you please find Dorenko?" he asked. "It seems to me he is a very talented guy." He added, "I have never taken the content seriously. But the form that he creates, I take very seriously; I like it."

Dorenko remembered that they met much later. When Berezovsky wanted to see him, Dorenko at first refused. "I said I was busy," Dorenko told me. Berezovsky persisted. He showed up and waited in Dorenko's outer office. And waited. This was Berezovsky's trademark style: he was always willing to wait, never too humble. It was summer and there was sliced watermelon in the office. "My assistants were asking me what to do with Berezovsky; he sits there and doesn't go away." Dorenko added, "And I said I didn't know. I said, 'Give him some watermelon.' He sat there for forty minutes eating watermelon and then went away." Later they agreed to meet over lunch at a Japanese restaurant and found that there was a chemistry between them. Within an hour that day, Berezovsky signed up Dorenko for his ORT television channel.

Dorenko's particular style of television was what the Russians called an "author's program," which is a mixture of video footage of news events and commentary. The format gives the anchor wide latitude to express himself. NTV's Yevgeny Kiselyov had a similar show, the popular *Itogi* on Sunday evenings, but Kiselyov was a high-brow presence. Dorenko was different—blunt, sarcastic, flamboyant.

Berezovsky was at work behind the scenes, trying to ease out Primakov. On May 12, 1999, Yeltsin fired Primakov. Yeltsin appeared to be increasingly remote and eccentric. He may have been jealous of Primakov's popularity or persuaded that Primakov could not cope with the economy. Yeltsin replaced Primakov with Sergei Stepashin, a one-time interior minister with the demeanor of a loyal police captain. He was as obedient as a man could be but not strong-willed. One of Stepashin's first acts was to announce that he would not prosecute Berezovsky.

Stepashin had hardly settled in when the Kremlin began discussing his dismissal. Berezovsky later recalled that Stepashin was viewed as "weak" by the Kremlin inner circle.[26] Stepashin was a legal expert, but he seemed paralyzed when it came to politics. Every day, support was draining away from Yeltsin and toward Luzhkov. The Kremlin circle decided they had to find someone else. They had to solve the problem of "continuity of power." On August 10, Yeltsin fired Stepashin, the fourth premier Yeltsin had dumped in a year and a half. In Stepashin's place, Yeltsin appointed Vladimir Putin, a spry man with cold eyes and sandy hair who was the little-known chief of the Federal Security Service. Putin was initially viewed as a caretaker, but he became much, much more.

That summer the political vacuum, the palpable lack of leadership, settled on Moscow like a fog. Berezovsky, no longer being hounded by Primakov, was anxious to play kingmaker once more. He came to Dorenko and proposed a new program tailored to Dorenko, a pure author's delight: *The Sergei Dorenko Show.*

Then came another bolt of alarming news for the Kremlin circle. Two of Berezovsky's arch foes, Luzhkov and Primakov, were teaming up, announcing a political alliance, and setting their sights on the Kremlin. They were attracting support from key governors and mayors around the country, and when they made the announcement, it was clear they were becoming a force to be reckoned with. They had what is called momentum in American politics—a sense of inevitability hung over them. They were not very charismatic, but that didn't matter. What counted was a perception that they would be heirs to the Kremlin. There wasn't another obvious successor to Yeltsin. Luzhkov knew they were in trouble for just that reason. He sensed that the Kremlin staff was already gunning for them. There was "powerful pressure and opposition to formation of our bloc," he said. "But we are not afraid of it. We are strong."[27]

The Kremlin inner circle was distressed. Three days after the Luzhkov-Primakov press conference, several Western journalists and I were invited to the Kremlin to speak to Voloshin, Yeltsin's chief of staff. It was a rare opportunity to hear directly from the Yeltsin "family," the embattled Kremlin circle that included Berezovsky, Voloshin, Dyachenko, and Yumashev. Voloshin, dressed casually on a Saturday, spoke very softly in a room of gleaming white marble. He was surprisingly candid. He made it clear that the Kremlin could not tolerate the thought of Primakov and Luzhkov becoming Yeltsin's successors. Primakov was a wily old Soviet spy, he said. Luzhkov brought no more sympathy. "His surrounding is semicriminal," he said. "It is not a secret to anyone. The whole of Russia is talking about it." But he admitted that Luzhkov had achieved some results. "Of course Moscow could afford to build a lot of things, for example, the Ring Road. Luzhkov is known as a builder. He built a lot. Some economists calculated that the money that was spent on the road would be enough to pave it with silver—three or five centimeters thick!"

I left with a feeling the Kremlin was lashing out at Luzhkov because they lacked a successor to Yeltsin and didn't know what to do. It was a hot, breezy August afternoon as I walked across the cobblestones of Red Square after the meeting—the autumn political season seemed distant, the intrigues and backbiting so senseless. I should have known that the clues from the Kremlin were not accidental. Berezovsky never rested. Only a few months before, thrown on the defensive by Primakov, he had been on the run from prosecutors and masked men breaking into his businesses. Now the compressed ball of energy was back—and preparing to strike.

Dorenko also watched the Luzhkov-Primakov alliance with disdain and decided to make Luzhkov the "star" of his autumn television program. He had often been at loggerheads with both Primakov and Luzhkov, so the attack on Luzhkov would dovetail perfectly with his personal feelings. He relished the idea. Berezovsky and Dorenko spoke by telephone about how to carry out the onslaught.

Berezovsky: "Seryozha, this is Boris. Hello dear. How are things?"

Dorenko: "The clerks are writing."

Berezovsky: "Think—what kind of scheme. Think!" Berezovsky used a Russian slang word, *razvodka,* which means a scheme in the sense of a setting one partner against the other. Then Dorenko and Berezovsky brainstormed how to smear Luzhkov's reputation and destroy his political viability. Their conversations were wiretapped and later printed in a newspaper.[28]

Dorenko's programs always included a bit of truth to keep his commentary plausible, but then he tried to twist the facts to make a point. Often Dorenko took his show to the absurd. To highlight Primakov's ill health after his hip operation, Dorenko showed the gory details of surgeons cutting away at legs and thighs. "Oh, that was a piece of work!" Dorenko laughed at the memory. Another part of Dorenko's power was the creative side of the show, presented with no apologies, no hesitation, and more than a little tabloid embellishment. Dorenko would have been perfectly in his element announcing a UFO sighting.

Throughout the autumn, Dorenko toyed with the powerful mayor of Moscow, not in a slugfest but in a teasing, wicked series of broadcasts that always portrayed the mayor in a terrible light. Dorenko waited for Luzhkov to react and then used the reaction to repeat the smear. "These programs weren't done solely by me of course," Dorenko commented facetiously. "Luzhkov and Primakov were helping me; the three of us were making those programs. We were working as a team."

For Luzhkov, the televised assault by Dorenko came at an awful time in Moscow. A series of bomb blasts terrorized the city's population. In September, explosions ripped apart three Moscow apartment complexes, killing more than three hundred people in their sleep. Luzhkov rushed to the scene each time. He struggled to maintain calm and oversee the rescue operation as hysteria and anger spread.

Putin, the new prime minister, was catapulted to leadership at this moment. Putin had an ultracool demeanor; a voter once remarked to me that Putin looked like a cheetah ready to strike. Putin blamed the bombings on Chechens, and, in the climate of fear, his public approval ratings skyrocketed as he prepared to launch a new large-scale military offensive in Chechnya. At the same time, Luzhkov saw his own political rating collapse, his city aflame and crazed with fear, and his reputation torn to shreds every Sunday on television. It all happened at once.

Dorenko was more interested in destroying Luzhkov than the brewing war in Chechnya. On October 17, Dorenko devoted most of his program to portraying Luzhkov as a hypocrite. Dorenko described how a hospital was rebuilt in the southern Russian city of Budyonovsk. The hospital was wrecked during a terrorist raid in the first Chechen war. Dorenko said Luzhkov took credit for rebuilding the hospital but never thanked the donor of the money. Dorenko repeated the point several times, saying Luzhkov hogged all the credit for the hospital. "Darlings!" Dorenko said, figuratively, to the Moscow mayor's office. "What are you doing? Why don't you just thank" the donor.[29]

In the next segment Dorenko hinted at mysterious money transfers from Moscow to foreign banks. Dorenko noted recent articles in the *New York Times* about the Bank of New York channeling Russian money out of the country.[30] A document flashed on the screen: a bank transfer to the Bank of New York. Forty million dollars! Another! A third! No one who saw the show—myself included—could quite figure out what was going on, but Dorenko was all about form, not substance. He closed with a killer line impugning Luzhkov. "I suppose that Luzhkov is not going to share the details with the public," he said, "but perhaps he will have to share the peculiarities of his economic activity with the investigating teams working on the theme of Russian money laundering in the Bank of New York."

At the end of the show, Dorenko dropped another video bomb on Luzhkov's head. He showed a series of fast-paced, alternating video clips. First, Luzhkov at the mayor's office, attacking the Kremlin "regime," and the ill Yeltsin; then Luzhkov at the climactic rally of the Yeltsin 1996 campaign, supporting Yeltsin. "I say, Russia, Yeltsin, freedom!" Luzhkov bellowed at the rally. "Russia, Yeltsin, victory!" The crowd roared. "Russia! Yeltsin! Our future!"

Dorenko said nothing—he didn't need to. He had savaged Luzhkov. There was nothing inconsistent in what Luzhkov had really said. Yeltsin was his choice in 1996, and Yeltsin was sick two years later. But Dorenko flashed the two scenes back and forth in a way that made Luzhkov look silly, and the tactic was damaging. "I think this is hypocrisy," Dorenko recalled, relishing the memory of his handiwork. "Hy-poc-ri-sy!"

Luzhkov was stunned at the Dorenko show. He had been mayor of Moscow for more than five years and was the boss of his city. Luzhkov sputtered angry denunciations at Dorenko and took him to court for slander, a tactic that he had always used in Moscow politics. But it had not been very effective against Dorenko. "It's madness," Luzhkov said. "It's a kind of psychotic attack, in the sense that it is usually mentally unstable people who do this sort of thing," he declared.[31] "It is shocking for Russia. It includes lies and slander, floods of dirt poured on politicians and statesmen."[32]

Luzhkov got so caught up in the Dorenko television torture chamber that he did not break out to make a case for himself. He never launched the one slogan that Yevtushenkov thought might be the basis for a presidential bid—that he could rebuild Russia. His wife, Yelena Baturina, told me at the time that "politics from my point of view is a very hard choice for Yuri Mikhailovich now. Politics doesn't always use proper methods. He finds himself at a loss. He has a lot of principles, and very often his opponents do not have any at all."[33] When I talked to Yevtushenkov, he also recalled that Luzhkov was not prepared for what hit him. "For long years," he said, "Yuri Mikhailovich lived in an environment, in an atmosphere of being everybody's favorite. And on a large scale, he was a sacred cow whom nobody dared criticize much. . . . He was not prepared, morally, for what would happen. He just wasn't prepared."

The relentless drumbeat of negative broadcasts took their toll on Luzhkov. Dorenko had enormous reach on ORT, since the signal covered the whole of Russia. In October, the Public Opinion Foundation, a leading private polling company that also worked for the Kremlin, reported that Luzhkov's standing in the polls was beginning to collapse. It was common for presidential front-runners in a crowded field to have only 20 percent or slightly more in weekly polls. In January, 15 percent of those questioned said they would vote for Luzhkov as president. In October it had fallen to only 5 percent. The percentage of those saying they mistrusted Luzhkov went from 35 percent in late 1998 to 51 percent a year later.

Dorenko reached the apogee of his smear campaign on November 7, 1999. Again he reached for a topic that was connected to real events—the murder of Paul Tatum, the U.S. businessman gunned down in 1996 after a dispute over the Radisson-Slavyanskaya Hotel. No one was ever apprehended or even charged for the murder.

Dorenko told me that the Tatum show fell into his lap. Ever since he began the on-air smear campaign, his office was deluged with people bringing him complaints about Luzhkov. "Dozens of people asked to meet with me and were bringing documents on Luzhkov," he recalled. "And among all those people, a guy comes to me and tells me, 'Look, two months ago I was in Florida and I taped an interview with some crazy American. . . . He is kind of disturbed.'" The crazy American claimed that Luzhkov was to blame for Tatum's murder. The crazy American was about to become Dorenko's video Gatling gun. Dorenko spoke to Berezovsky about how to cast the Tatum program for maximum effect to smear Luzhkov. Berezovsky suggested a convoluted, bizarre story line that involved the Federal Security Service. But he was careful to instruct that Putin, the former FSB head, be left out of the show.

Dorenko went on the air. He said at the opening of the program, "Luzhkov is guilty of Tatum's death, as Tatum said the instant before he died. So testifies Jeff Olson, friend of the dead man." Olson was the "crazy American."

Olson was then shown sitting in an enormous leather chair, a can of Dr Pepper™ on a stand next to him. Olson made a surprising claim that was difficult to believe: He was a Tatum friend who was the first to be called about the murder. "Paul, when he was shot, was still alive for several minutes after he was hit by the bullets. He was communicating a little bit with the bodyguards, the bodyguards were communicating with the office, the office was communicating to me. His last words to the office, to me, were: 'Luzhkov is responsible, he did this to me.'"

Dorenko then plunged into a long, twisted narrative, following Berezovsky's cues. The raw thrust of Dorenko's point was to blame Luzhkov for the murder. The rest of the facts, conspiracies, and testimony passed in a blur. To top it off, Dorenko closed the evening with a piece attempting to link Luzhkov with the head of the Aum Shumriko, the Japanese sect that poisoned the Tokyo subway, and the Church of Scientology. No bit of guilt by association, no scrap of ammunition escaped Dorenko. It was all a show.

Berezovsky loved it. That autumn, he was campaigning for a seat in the Duma from Karachayevo-Cherkessia, an ethnically divided republic in southern Russia. Berezovsky was also actively organizing the new parliamentary party to support Putin. The gathering storm of a military offensive in Chechnya was highly popular, and Putin was riding a wave of acclaim. Berezovsky was also serving as kingmaker to Putin. He let Dorenko handle the assault on Luzhkov, a serious potential rival to Putin, who needed to be pushed out of the way.

When I asked Berezovsky at the time what he thought of the Dorenko show, he answered, "The voters watch it with pleasure. And the answer to whether it is good or bad can only be the democratic tradition: if you don't like it, turn your TV off. If you like it, go ahead and watch it. From my point of view, it is a brilliant show."

"I absolutely don't attempt to analyze the content," he added. "I am an admirer of his talent: from my point of view, the form is amazing. That is, the level of influence that he achieves. It is real talent."[34] In other words, Berezovsky loved the smear and didn't care if it was far from the truth.

At the end of the parliamentary campaign, Luzhkov, wounded and bitter, held one last rally in Moscow on the edge of Red Square at Vasilyevsky Slope. It was dark as the crowd gathered. In the background, St. Basil's Cathedral was brightly illuminated by spotlights. The moment was filled with distress for Luzhkov. Near the same spot, three and a half years earlier, Luzhkov delivered his rousing endorsement of Yeltsin. Now he was reduced to shouting at Yeltsin, shouting in vain into the cold night air, shouting so his voice reverberated against the Kremlin walls just beyond. Luzhkov, wearing his trademark cap, rattled off his critique of the ruling powers, recalling the GKO pyramids, the ruble crash, mass privatization. "They are afraid of us!" he declared. "They are afraid of us because we say it is necessary to bring to justice all those who allowed this lawlessness, and this theft of the country's property and money!" The crowd was wooden, mostly city workers and trade union supporters who were bused in and marched to their preassigned spot on the cobblestone slope. They left immediately after it was over. They carried placards such as "Dorenko Is Berezovsky's Puppy," and "Hands Off Our Mayor!" It seemed to me that Luzhkov made a huge mistake in devoting his final energy to shadowboxing with Dorenko. He could have run a powerful political campaign based on Moscow as a showcase city, but he never did. I wrote in my notebook that Luzhkov "is a *khozyain* at heart, who's made some effort to be a politician, but he's been mowed down by Dorenko and the rest, and he surely doesn't know how to respond to it." Luzhkov was still fuming about the "regime" at the end of the rally. He said bitterly, "We had to show those scoundrels that we are a real force, that we won't give in. We had to show that we can stand up to a flood of lies and slander. We are against the ways in which the regime is starting to rule in the country."

Luzhkov won his libel suits against Dorenko, but he lost the larger political war. His hopes of running for president were dashed, although he was reelected Moscow mayor in December 1999 by 70 percent. Luzhkov continued to rule Moscow, but the chance that he might lead Russia after Yeltsin was destroyed.

When I asked Luzhkov about the events of that autumn more than a year later, he was still furious. He blamed Yeltsin, Yeltsin's inner circle, Berezovsky, and "parasitic capital." When I suggested he had not fought back vigorously enough, Luzhkov grew quite animated. He recalled the lawsuits he filed and insisted that he had tried to respond. "Were we supposed to drive tanks in the direction of the Ostankino TV center?" he asked. "It is absolutely well-known that in all his episodes, Dorenko was slandering me, and he knows it. He received huge money from Berezovsky, a fee, huge money. By court decision he was ordered to pay $4,500. He is laughing at justice. We don't have effective justice."

Dorenko was proud of his work. He created fifteen shows that decimated Luzhkov's hopes of becoming president of Russia. He called them "fifteen silver bullets."

The ruble crash hit all three television channels very hard, but Gusinsky was particularly vulnerable because his ambitions had once soared so high. For ORT, still 51 percent owned by the state but controlled by Berezovsky, the government provided a lifeline, a $100 million loan from a state bank. Kiselyov told me that NTV was anxious for a loan from the state as well. Even though the channel took pride in the fact it was outside control of the state, even though it freely criticized Yeltsin and the government, Kiselyov said NTV would have gladly accepted a government loan too, and went so far in these desperate times as to broach the idea. He believed the government had caused the crisis, so the government should help the television industry as a whole survive. The financial health of Gusinsky's companies began to deteriorate. The Russian television advertising market fell 47.5 percent from 1998, and it was down 77 percent from precrash projections.[35] Meanwhile, the cost of servicing his debts was large. The government remained silent about a loan. "So, ORT got a government loan of $100 million, and we got nothing," Kiselyov said. "That was one of the most worrying things that happened to us." NTV carried increasingly critical coverage of the Yeltsin circle—including unflattering reports about Voloshin, the chief of staff, who was depicted in one Kiselyov broadcast as Lenin. Viewers were clumsily reminded of Voloshin's past working with Berezovsky on the AVVA scheme. The show was poorly produced and not very persuasive. The deposed prosecutor, Skuratov, who so infuriated the Kremlin, also got a generous amount of airtime on NTV to spread his charges against the Yeltsin family and inner circle.

In midsummer 1999, Gusinsky met with Voloshin. In this period, Gusinsky and Berezovsky were at loggerheads. There may have been other reasons, but the obvious source of tension was politics. Gusinsky was betting on Luzhkov, and Berezovsky was determined to destroy the mayor. At the time, the Kremlin still did not have a successor to Yeltsin. The problem of "continuity of power" remained. Voloshin had the coming election on his mind when he met Gusinsky.

At this point, Gusinsky might have pulled back and thus avoided a potentially catastrophic collision with Yeltsin and his team. He might have focused on building up his media empire and avoided taking sides in the coming campaign. But he did not take this route. He was an oligarch, and oligarchs played for the big stakes. They ruled the country. Remaining on the sidelines was not an option. Gusinsky pushed ahead—backing Luzhkov—and made a mistake that led to the destruction of all he had built.

At the meeting with Voloshin, Gusinsky later recalled, "Voloshin said, as if he was joking, 'Let's pay you $100 million so that you won't be in our way while the election is on. You could go on a vacation.'" Gusinsky said he told Voloshin that he could not repeat the experience of 1996, when the news media lined up behind Yeltsin.[36]

Voloshin was not in the mood to help Gusinsky, and the Kremlin instead began to turn the screws on him. Voloshin accused Gusinsky of running up big debts to Gazprom and "resorting to the tried-and-tested method of information racketeering," pressuring the Kremlin for loans. Voloshin told Gusinsky to forget about any assistance from the government. "Since the management of the holding company and specifically NTV television channel have such an unfriendly attitude toward the authorities, it is not entirely clear why these authorities should be helping Media-Most resolve its problems," Voloshin said.[37] Kiselyov, the popular television anchorman, later recalled the dialog with the Kremlin that summer in blunter terms. The Kremlin demanded NTV support for whoever was handpicked to be Yeltsin's successor; little choice was offered. "Join us or rot in hell," Kiselyov said they were told.[38]

When the Chechen war reignited in August 1999, Gusinsky's troubles deepened. A band of Chechen rebels led a cross-border incursion into neighboring Dagestan, an internal Russian republic that is a patchwork of nationalities. The attack came in a remote mountainous zone. The Chechens were led by Shamil Basayev, a bearded, ruthless Chechen warrior who had also, over the years, been on speaking terms with Berezovsky. Berezovsky said he warned the Kremlin that the incursion was coming. Despite the advance signals, the Kremlin did not make a serious attempt to stop it.[39]

The fresh hostilities propelled Putin to prominence. He wasted no time ordering the Russian military to attack the Chechen rebels. His ratings went through the roof to levels of approval not seen since Yeltsin's early days. As prime minister, he was also in the line of succession should Yeltsin resign or become incapacitated. He came out of nowhere in an atmosphere of fear and uncertainty, a time of hysteria, when thirteen-floor prefabricated concrete buildings in Moscow imploded violently and randomly in the middle of the night; sleeping children, mothers, and fathers were crushed instantly by a nightmare of falling stone, steel, and glass. Without any debate, with nary a critical question asked, the political environment was transformed from a vacuum to a one-man regime. With Putin, the Kremlin had solved the problem of "continuity of power" in one fell swoop. No one knew what Putin stood for or what he had done during his career as a KGB spy. He appeared to be standing up, decisively, to defend them against the Chechens, after Yeltsin's years of weakness and vacillation. Putin embodied and articulated the Russian hatred for the Chechens. Putin vowed to wipe out the Chechens "in the outhouse."

The onset of new hostilities put NTV outside the Kremlin circle, just as it had in the first war, but this time the circumstances were markedly different. In the first conflict, the Russian military made only lame efforts to control the flow of information, and journalists from NTV made their mark bringing home the gruesome, vivid images of battle that often contradicted the official version. But in late 1999, the Kremlin and the military attempted to bottle up the television channels. The scenes on television were not of combat but of Russian generals reading official statements. Battlefield information was strictly censored. In a major setback for Gusinsky, one of his first partners in NTV, Oleg Dobrodeyev, who championed the groundbreaking coverage of the first war in 1995, left the channel in a disagreement over how to cover the second war. This time Dobrodeyev was sympathetic to the army. "When you see everything with your own eyes," he told *Krasnaya Zvezda*, the military newspaper, "when in real time the Defense Ministry generals are giving you information, you don't have to ask anyone for anything else."[40]

The first Chechen war had become intensely unpopular at home, but the second offensive, carried out in an atmosphere of public fear after the Moscow explosions, was hugely popular. This too put Gusinsky and NTV in a difficult position; the public did not want to hear criticism of the war. Yet another difference was that NTV journalists did not have as much access to the Chechen side because of the threat of kidnapping. An NTV star correspondent, Yelena Masyuk, and two members of her crew had been ransomed from Chechen kidnappers in 1997. After this, many journalists had less sympathy for the Chechens. Still, NTV correspondents attempted to cover the war as best they could under extremely difficult conditions.

Berezovsky was hospitalized in the fall for hepatitis, but even from his hospital bed, he was in hyperspeed. He organized and bankrolled the creation of a new political party, Unity, which he hoped would later support Putin's agenda in the State Duma, the lower house of parliament. For those who had watched the labored, difficult work of party building in Russia, the rise of Unity in such a short period was nothing short of stupendous, since the party had no discernible ideology, platform, or charismatic leaders—but it had Putin. His popularity, combined with Berezovsky's money, was sufficient to win enough seats to make Unity the second largest bloc in the next parliament.[41] Berezovsky simultaneously won his own seat from District 15 in Karachayevo-Cherkessia.[42]

Berezovsky did more than anyone to set the stage for Putin to become the next leader of Russia, but the final act came from Yeltsin himself. Ailing and isolated, Yeltsin resigned on a snowy New Year's Eve in 1999 and appointed Putin acting president. It was a surprise announcement delivered with a certain inevitability, given Yeltsin's long absences and ill health. "Russia must enter the new millennium with new politicians, new faces, new intelligent, strong, and energetic people," Yeltsin said in a television address. "And for those of us who have been in power for many years, we must go."

Yeltsin had informed Putin that he would turn the reins over to him about two weeks earlier. Yeltsin told his family just that afternoon that he was stepping down. Moscow was amazingly calm. There had been weeks of speculation about some kind of techno-catastrophe as computer clocks turned over to the year 2000, and perhaps that was one reason for the quiet. On New Year's Eve, I found people shopping and thinking of themselves and their families, and politics was simply drowned out. The streets were empty and fireworks split the air throughout the night.

What was worrisome that night was the speed and suddenness with which Putin was forced on Russia. When he was appointed acting president by Yeltsin, he had less than a year's experience in leadership of the grinding, tortured machine that was Russia's protodemocracy and newborn market economy. Former Soviet President Mikhail Gorbachev, who had been close to Primakov, spoke for many when he said, "Putin is holding on, thanks to his mystery. Mysterious appearance, mysterious glance, mysterious phrases. But it so happens the man opens his mouth and has nothing to say."

Putin had previously thrived in closed worlds, spending seventeen years as a KGB agent and several years after that as a behind-the-scenes deputy to Anatoly Sobchak, the first elected mayor of St. Petersburg. Until handpicked by Yeltsin to be prime minister, Putin had never been a public figure. When he was named acting president, he had no idea what it was like to campaign for office. He had never been forced to deal with angry voters or critical news media. He agonized over giving interviews to the press. He found campaigns distasteful. "You have to be insincere and promise something that you cannot fulfill," he said. "So you either have to be a fool who does not understand what you are promising or deliberately lie." Oddly, Putin did not think there was an honest way—to make promises and try to fulfill them.

My own impression is that Putin knew, from his KGB years, that economic modernization was the only way forward for Russia, but he did not understand how to build a democracy, or even how it functioned. His own rapid rise to power offered him few, if any, useful lessons about democracy. He was elevated to the presidency on the updraft of a military campaign, while his chief opponents, Luzhkov and Primakov, were destroyed on television by his backroom team. He never had to go through the experience of being defeated at the polls. He never had to engage in real political competition. He rarely subjected himself to the give-and-take of press conferences and never took part in a debate.

During his five years as a Soviet KGB spy in East Germany, Putin missed the critically important political and economic upheavals in Moscow. He missed the period when journalists were considered beacons of freedom; he missed the triumph of public associations, like the human rights group Memorial, which became powerful forces for change in society; and he missed the early experiments in electoral politics such as the Congress of People's Deputies. Putin simply missed the birth of civil society. When he became acting president, he was light-years away from the open, rambunctious media that Gusinsky had created. Putin was a closed man who did not see the need, for example, to explain himself to the public. He told journalists that he saw them as belonging to his "command," an us-or-them, suspicious mentality. He paid lip service to freedom of speech, but his own view was entirely Soviet, that television should be an organ of the state.

Putin told Dorenko once that television shaped reality. "You understand," Putin said, "there are certain cases when if you don't tell about something, it didn't happen." Dorenko, who knew as well as anyone in Russia the power of television, said of Putin: "As a politician, he believes himself to be a product of television. And he thinks that only television can destroy him. Not newspapers—he is not afraid of newspapers because people don't read newspapers."

In Putin's world, Gusinsky was a marked man. His television channel, with its open criticism of the Kremlin and Putin, ran counter to all of Putin's instincts and desires. "He hates Gusinsky," Dorenko told me. "First of all, he believed Gusinsky was working for Luzhkov and he wanted to take revenge. Second, with Luzhkov defeated, Putin thought Gusinsky had rebuilt himself to serve American political interests. And third, Gusinsky cannot be controlled. He is strong and not a Putin man. That is, Putin cannot stand beside anybody whose opinion differs from his own, especially publicly. You can try and argue with him privately; I have done that. But publicly you cannot."

Gusinsky was a marked man in another way too. Putin, who was stationed by the KGB in Dresden during the Gorbachev period, not only missed the political upheaval in the late 1980s but also the wild, crazy economic explosion of the final Soviet years, the period of the cooperatives and early banks when Gusinsky, Berezovsky, Smolensky, and Khodorkovsky had all made their leap from the old system to the new one. Throughout most of the Yeltsin period, when the oligarchs were gaining power and influence, Putin's perch was as a second-tier municipal official, then an obscure Kremlin aide, and finally head of the Security Service for one year. Rushed to the seat of power as Yeltsin's successor, he took a suspicious view of the tycoons. When asked in a radio interview what the future held for the oligarchs, Putin said, if one meant "those people who fuse, or help fusion of power and capital—there will be no oligarchs of this kind as a class."[43]

At the time, this comment unleashed a torrent of speculation about what Putin really meant. My own view was that Putin understood full well the distortions that oligarchic capitalism had brought to Russia. That was not really the issue; the question was what Putin intended to do about it. Did he want to change the system? Many Westerners, especially those in the financial markets, rejoiced at Putin's words because they believed he would carry out an assault on the system of opaque, dirty deals, clean up the mess, and make Russia safe for foreign investment. If Putin had really been serious about systemic change, about building a competitive, market-oriented, rule-of-law approach, then it would have been welcome news indeed.

But Putin did not begin with an assault on the system. He began with an attack on one of the oligarchs: Gusinsky. Starting soon after the March 2000 election, which Putin won, the Kremlin intensified a relentless campaign, through surrogates, to destroy Gusinsky's media business and largely succeeded over the following year. Putin's backroom team had already ruined Luzhkov's presidential hopes. Then they turned on Gusinsky and, amazingly, they eventually turned on their own creator, Berezovsky. Putin's approach to oligarchic capitalism during his first year was not to change the system. He just wanted to get control of it.

Gusinsky recalled with some pride how he had once taken the chairman of Gazprom, Rem Vyakhirev, to see the ground station that Gusinsky's conglomerate, Media-Most, had built to operate the satellites for NTV-Plus. Ever since it bought 30 percent of NTV in 1996, Gazprom had been a friendly investor in the television company. Gazprom, a gargantuan, hidebound monopoly that operated by its own secretive methods, was a pillar of the Russian economy. The company earned billions of dollars from lucrative gas exports to Europe. It was a cushion of capital for Gusinsky after the 1996 election. Gazprom was there for Gusinsky again after he failed to float his shares on Wall Street. It agreed to guarantee a $211 million loan for Gusinsky through Credit Suisse First Boston and paid off the loan when Gusinsky could not. Gusinsky now had a debt to Gazprom. A deal was struck to boost Gazprom's stake in the holding company, Media-Most, in exchange for paying off the debt. Under the terms, Gazprom would get 25 percent plus one share of Media-Most. Gazprom agreed to the deal, but details were still being worked out early in the year 2000, when Putin was elected.

Then everything changed. The Kremlin entered the picture, and Gusinsky felt a noose tightening around his neck. Gazprom would no longer be his friend.

A disturbing sign of trouble came in early May 2000. Gusinsky was negotiating to sell his Most Bank to a Central Bank subsidiary. The plan had been drawn up and was ready to be signed when the chairman of the Central Bank, Viktor Gerashchenko, received a phone call from the Kremlin. The caller was Putin's chief of staff, Voloshin, and he told the central banker not to go ahead with the deal. According to several accounts I heard at the time, Gerashchenko told Voloshin to go to hell and hung up the phone.

The next call came ten minutes later from Putin, who also instructed Gerashchenko not to sign the deal. This time, Gerashchenko obeyed.

On the morning of May 11, three minibuses of armed, masked men identifying themselves as tax police pulled up at the headquarters building of Gusinsky's holding company, Media-Most, in the center of Moscow. The building was lavishly appointed by Russian standards, with fountains, marble floors, and a luxurious amphitheater. The raiders, wearing black masks with only their eyes showing and wielding semiautomatic rifles, ordered the employees to leave their offices and remain in the cafeteria while they searched the building. What were they searching for? Who were they? All day the authorities gave conflicting accounts: they were tax police; no, they were searching for bugging equipment; no, they were investigating Gusinsky's debts. The raid was just the first hint of what was to come.

To Gusinsky's surprise, Gazprom turned hostile. Gazprom appointed Alfred Kokh, the salty former privatization chief who had overseen loans for shares and Svyazinvest, to manage its share of Media-Most. Kokh was still angry at Gusinsky three years after the Svyazinvest fiasco. He knew Gusinsky was behind the disclosure that he had received the $100,000 book advance from a company linked to Potanin. He was still seething at the way Gusinsky had used his media to disclose the book advance. This was no casual decision by Gazprom; it was tantamount to putting Gusinsky's most hateful enemy in charge of his business. I ran into Kokh during this period at his office in central Moscow. He was extremely agitated at something he had seen about himself on one of the proliferating Internet sites that carried *kompromat* from anonymous sources. Kokh invited me to look at the computer screen in his office. I don't remember what it was that so agitated him, but I well remember his shouting that it was all Gusinsky's fault. "Bandit!" he said over and over again of Gusinsky. The wounds of Svyazinvest still festered, and Kokh was in a position to extract his revenge.

On the day of the raid against his headquarters, Gusinsky flew back to Russia from a business trip to Israel. Speaking to reporters at the airport, he denounced the show of force as "political pressure." Still, Gusinsky could not help but feel that he had been through all this before, when Korzhakov's goons had chased his car into the center of Moscow in 1994. The Kremlin had pressured him then too, and he had been forced to flee the country for six months until things cooled down. But he survived that, and NTV had thrived. "History repeats itself somehow," he said, rather philosophically. "If you remember 1994, all this has happened already."

More worrisome was the changed attitude of Gazprom. The mammoth company was run like a private fiefdom in which Vyakhirev could do as he pleased. This worked to Gusinsky's advantage from 1996 until 2000, when Gazprom was his ally. Gusinsky said that, as a major shareholder in NTV, "Gazprom never attempted to interfere." Only a few months earlier, Vyakhirev agreed to take the larger share of Media-Most in exchange for the unpaid debt. It was a debt-for-equity swap, a transaction hardly unusual in the West. Gazprom was a "partner," Gusinsky told me, "and I had no reason not to trust the deal."

But after Putin took office, Gazprom was no longer willing to take Gusinsky's equity. Gazprom demanded that Gusinsky pay cash, which the Kremlin knew Gusinsky did not have. Gusinsky said he believed that Vyakhirev was personally pressured by the Kremlin into the about-face. Moreover, Gusinsky, who had wide contacts in the West, found it much harder to raise new capital abroad. The masked men raiding his offices had taken care of that. Just the news photos of a police investigation were enough to scare away investors. "You understand, investors are afraid of scandals," Gusinsky told me. His attempts to borrow from abroad were effectively blocked by the Kremlin. Gusinsky, stubborn, emotional and vain, concluded that Putin was personally out to get him. "If the president of such a big country as Russia, who has internal problems, problems with governing, problems with Chechnya, problems with the government, finds time to call up Gerashchenko—I think it is clear who is dealing with Gazprom, and why."[44]

The next blow fell on Gusinsky personally. He openly criticized Putin. "The myth of Putin as a president who advocates reforms, democracy, free speech, and so on, is history now," Gusinsky said defiantly the first week of June. "His real actions unmask him, revealing his true face, you know."[45] A week later, Gusinsky was asked to come answer questions at the general prosecutor's office. At issue was the origin of several bullets for a decorative pistol belonging to a Gusinsky aide that had been confiscated in the May 11 raid. For reasons that were not clear, Gusinsky was not alarmed by the summons and went to answer the questions without a lawyer, taking only a bodyguard. He was originally scheduled to answer questions at 2:00 P.M. but was delayed and arrived at 5:00 P.M. Then, at 6:15 P.M., his lawyers received a note from the prosecutor's office that Gusinsky was under arrest. Later in the evening, the prosecutors announced that Gusinsky was being held as a suspect in an old fraud case involving privatization of a St. Petersburg television company, Russian Video. The whole arrest was carried out with haste; the original documents said that Gusinsky was to be taken to Lefortovo, the large federal prison, but instead he was thrown in Moscow's most notorious prison, Butyrskaya, an overcrowded, eighteenth-century jail, and denied access to a lawyer.

Putin, who was on a state visit to Spain, pretended that he had no idea what was happening and claimed that he could not even get the general prosecutor, Vladimir Ustinov, on the telephone. But Putin displayed a surprisingly detailed knowledge of the case. He clearly had been briefed about Gusinsky's financial plight. Putin claimed that Gusinsky had taken $1.3 billion in loans for Media-Most but "returned almost nothing," including debts to Gazprom. "Several days ago Gusinsky did not pay back another $200 million loan," Putin added, "and Gazprom again paid the outstanding debt. I wonder why Gazprom should spend money on this." Putin's words revealed the Kremlin's crude tactics: to force Gusinsky to pay all his debts at once, effectively to bankrupt him.[46] Although Putin claimed he was not involved in Gusinsky's arrest, it was a lie. He had his hands on the hangman's noose now being strung around Gusinsky's neck.

When he heard about the arrest, Sergei Dorenko grew angry. Dorenko had indirectly helped Putin come to power with his fifteen silver bullets, but he did not like what he saw unfolding. That evening, NTV was broadcasting an edition of its popular talk show,

Glas Naroda (Vox Populi). The subject was Gusinsky's arrest. The show was broadcast from an amphitheater-like studio and encouraged participation by a large audience. Dorenko was Berezovsky's man, but he rushed to Gusinsky's defense. Wearing jeans and a sweatshirt, Dorenko drove madly to the studio. Halfway there, his beeper went off. It was Kiselyov, inviting him to appear on the air immediately. Berezovsky called on his mobile phone, seeming a bit confused about what was happening. "Oh Borya!" Dorenko replied. "They are simply idiots!" he said of the arrest of Gusinsky. "And you know I am on my way to the studio." Berezovsky was surprised but silent.

The show was filled with passion. Politicians, lawyers, and journalists from Gusinsky's publications, and others who were just his friends, appeared with emotions flashing in their eyes, their anger searing and deep. The imprisonment of Gusinsky was nothing other than an assault on Russia's fragile freedoms, they said, an arbitrary reversion to the old authoritarianism. "This is an action of threat and revenge," said Andrei Cherkizov, an acerbic radio commentator on Gusinsky's Echo of Moscow station. "It's a threatening action—if you misbehave, this will happen to you also," said Boris Nemtsov, the young reformer who was now a progressive member of parliament.

Dorenko was hardly a beacon of idealism when it came to defending a free press. He was a showman, and he had personally carried out a debilitating smear campaign against Luzhkov. But he had guts, and on this night he was not afraid to say what he saw happening. Dorenko's comments were the most memorable of the entire evening. He declared that Putin had given the green light for the "robots" of the old regime, the security services, to return to the fore. Dorenko had disliked Primakov as a symbol of this old regime. Now, Dorenko realized, Putin was turning out to be just a continuation of the old school—arbitrary attacks, total control. Just six weeks after Putin had taken office, and at a time when he was still being hailed in the West as a young, post-Yeltsin remedy for Russia's ailments, Dorenko punctured the image with just as much energy as he had smashed Luzhkov.

"We thought something happened over these last ten years," he said, referring to the rise of Russian democracy since the collapse of the Soviet Union. "We thought that the old system broke over these ten years. We dumped the robots. They have been lying there. And they stirred and started moving again, as if they heard some music. They got up and started moving. Today the security structures throughout the whole country are taking a message from Putin's rise to power.... They hear music that we do not hear, and they get up like zombies and walk. They surround us. And they will go far if there is silence.... We need to bash them over the head every day."

More amazing than Dorenko's eloquent and revealing speech that night was the phone call he got a few days later, after Putin returned to Moscow. Putin invited Dorenko to the Kremlin, urgently. Putin behaved like a KGB man, always seeking control, even over his enemies. Putin offered Dorenko tea and pastry and then said, "Sergei, something has happened with our relationship."

Dorenko replied that was not the point. "You have sent a very important message to everyone in this country, to everyone," Dorenko said. "To all the policemen, to all the FSB people. You told them to try and catch journalists, businessmen, and Jews. This is what you said. Because Gusinsky is a Jew connected with the press and a businessman. And now you can issue any kinds of decrees or laws, but people will know what you really want: to catch journalists, businessmen, and Jews."[47]

Dorenko recalled that, at the mention of Jews, Putin told him that Israeli Prime Minister Ehud Barak had called Putin and asked why he was attacking Gusinsky. Putin then recounted how he had told Barak that Gusinsky "isn't paying taxes in Israel" or Russia. Dorenko was appalled.

"I told him, 'Vladimir Vladimirovich, that has nothing to do with you. You are not an investigator, are you? You are a politician. It's not your level; there are other people whose job it is to deal with that. It's absolutely not your level where he is paying his taxes. And second, in Russia, it is ridiculous. The policeman who will tomorrow smash Jews, journalists, and businessmen... doesn't even know the word 'taxes.'"

Putin seemed uneasy. He tried to change the subject. "You and I are on the same team," he appealed to Dorenko.

Dorenko replied, "I am not on anyone's team."

Gusinsky was formally charged with fraud and released late on Friday evening, June 16, on a pledge not to leave Moscow. A few days later, Gusinsky sat awkwardly in a chair on a pedestal for a live broadcast interview on *Glas Naroda,* questioned by his partner Kiselyov. Gusinsky was never an easy interview; his emotions seemed to creep up on him, and he would change his thoughts in midsentence. He was surrounded by sympathetic journalists, and he appeared uneasy as the center of attention. But he was very clear and lucid about Putin. The Russian president, he said, knew everything about his arrest and imprisonment. "More than that," he added, "the decision was taken personally by Mr. President." The Kremlin, Gusinsky declared, had divided the tycoons into "friends" and "foes," and he was one of the foes. Gusinsky also acknowledged that the oligarchs had given the Kremlin plenty of reason to think they could command the news media—the 1996 campaign for Yeltsin was the precedent. "A very big and grave mistake," Gusinsky said. "It was in 1996 that we gave birth to a small monster. . . . Today the authorities are really using the instruments that we presented to them in 1996."[48]

The next six weeks underscored that Putin was playing hardball. He wanted to break Gusinsky. The raids on Gusinsky's corporate headquarters, the charges of fraud, and the jail episode were just the beginning of the end. The Kremlin intensified the pressure in June and July. The point man behind the scenes was Mikhail Lesin, founder of the advertising agency Video International, who had been named press minister by Putin. Lesin once did a flourishing business with Gusinsky. His advertising agency had been the exclusive broker for airtime on NTV, and both men prospered in the mid-1990s. But Video International pulled up stakes and terminated the relationship in late 1999. Soon thereafter, Lesin joined the campaign against Gusinsky. A close associate of Lesin told me that Lesin harbored personal animosity toward Gusinsky, feeling that he had never shown him enough respect. Lesin had quite willingly thrown himself into the attack on Gusinsky and was joined by Kokh.[49]

A long, secret negotiation began between Gusinsky and his tormentors. Gusinsky was in a financially vulnerable position. In addition to the $211 million loan that Gazprom had guaranteed, the next loan, also guaranteed by Gazprom, of $262 million, was coming due in July 2001. The total debt of Gusinsky's company to Gazprom was $473 million. In the old days, Gusinsky could count on strong television revenues to carry the burden of debt service, but after the ruble crash, his financial situation was strained.

In the talks, the Kremlin's goal, working through Kokh and Lesin, was to wrest NTV away from Gusinsky, who was still facing criminal prosecution. Malashenko told me that Lesin presented Gusinsky with an ultimatum. If he sold the business to Gazprom, he could go free.

The deal offered was this: $300 million in cash for the whole of Gusinsky's empire, Media-Most and NTV, as well as forgiveness of the outstanding $473 million in debts. Gusinsky recalled that NTV alone had been valued at more than $1 billion overall when he was thinking of selling shares in New York before the crash—now they were offering him nickels and dimes for his company! Still, he felt pressured. He did not want to go back to jail and there were continuing raids against his companies. On July 7, investigators carted off more documents from NTV. Gusinsky later told me, "They said it more than once. There were constant threats to put me in jail cells with tubercular prisoners and people with AIDS. . . . I was indeed a hostage. When you have a gun to your head, you have two options: to meet the condition of the bandits or take a bullet in your head."

On July 18 Gusinsky signed a written statement, secret at the time, witnessed by two of his lawyers. The statement said he was being forced against his will to sell his business, in exchange for a promise to drop the criminal charges and permission to go abroad. Gusinsky said Lesin, the press minister, was the one "forcing me to conclude this transaction." Two days later, on July 20, again acting secretly, he signed the agreement to sell out for $300 million. A document attached to the sale called for the criminal charges against Gusinsky to be dropped.[50] A few days later, Putin returned from a summit meeting at Okinawa, where he had been lavishly praised by leaders of the Western industrial democracies. On July 27 Russian prosecutors abruptly and without explanation announced they were dropping all charges against Gusinsky. The secret agreement to sell out was not mentioned. Gusinsky immediately boarded his private jet and flew out of Russia to visit his family in Spain. He did not come back again.

Over the next several weeks, negotiations were quietly held in London to iron out the deal. But in September, Gusinsky was having second thoughts, even though some of his partners and his wife urged him to take the $300 million. Gusinsky said he felt that NTV was like a home he had grown up in, and he feared Putin wanted to turn it into a "brothel." He decided not to sell out and tore up the deal. It was another turning point for Gusinsky, where he might have avoided more trouble. But he was still feeling the drive and ambition of an oligarch—he would not let them push him around.

I met Gusinsky one rainy September afternoon in London. He was defiant and energized. He wanted to resist the Kremlin and stand up for NTV, as he had successfully done under fire in 1995. His cellular telephone rang incessantly with calls from Moscow. His four top journalists and editors—Kiselyov, Sergei Parkhomenko of *Itogi* magazine, Mikhail Berger of the newspaper *Sevodnya*, and Alexei Venediktov of Echo of Moscow Radio—flew back and forth to London and Gusinsky's home in Spain for conferences. Malashenko went to Soros seeking help. Soros told Malashenko that he had found an investor willing to take the risks: CNN founder Ted Turner. But all the wrangling came to naught. Putin wanted Gusinsky out, and Putin was stronger. The prosecutor issued new warrants for Gusinsky's arrest through Interpol. Gusinsky was detained in Spain and twice jailed there, before the Spanish high court threw out the case, saying there was no evidence Gusinsky had committed a crime. Gusinsky's executives, including Malashenko, fled Russia, fearing they would be arrested. Kiselyov fought on. In the year of pressure tactics, there were more than thirty raids by the prosecutor and other law enforcement agencies against Gusinsky's businesses.

"There is nothing I can do," Putin lamely told journalists from NTV on January 29 at a Kremlin meeting. This was just nonsense, and untrue. Putin was actually quite deeply involved in the case. He took Kiselyov aside on the day of the Kremlin meeting. "I know everything about your hours and hours of phone conversations with Gusinsky," he said, revealing that he was reading transcripts of the wiretaps.

"So what, we have been partners since 1993!" Kiselyov protested.

"I know all the *instructions* you get from Gusinsky," Putin said coldly.

Putin was the driving force behind the entire affair, and he, as well as his backroom boys, were intent on victory. Kiselyov told me there were two groups around Putin helping crush Gusinsky. One was the "grudge" group—Lesin and Kokh, who had their own reasons for taking revenge on the oligarch. The other were the security services, Putin's friends and power base. Ustinov, the general prosecutor, twice summoned Kiselyov for secret meetings at the headquarters of the prosecutor's office. To avoid detection, Kiselyov was brought into the building in central Moscow in an unmarked car through a backdoor. Kiselyov thought the meetings were strange, and Ustinov stilted, as if he were talking to hidden microphones. Ustinov wanted to know what it would take to resolve the crisis. Kiselyov demanded that charges against Gusinsky be dropped. The talks came to nothing.

Gusinsky finally lost control of the television station in April. Gazprom, in a hastily assembled board meeting, got control of 25 percent plus one share and moved to seize control over NTV. The old management was removed. Kokh appointed a new general director, Boris Jordan, the young hustler who had been Potanin's fast-talking partner in the Svyazinvest auction. Jordan had promised not to use force to take over the station, but at 4:00 A.M. on April 14 he arrived at NTV with his own security guards and assumed control. The arrival of Kokh and Jordan at NTV was met by hissing and moans from the staff. Kiselyov and many other journalists walked out. Gazprom also took control of *Sevodnya*, Gusinsky's first newspaper, and closed it. Then came the news magazine *Itogi*. The magazine's staff, arriving for work one morning, was ignominiously fired and locked out of their offices, including the founders, chief editor Parkhomenko, and his deputy, Masha Lipman.

The age of dreams was over.

For several years, Berezovsky had doggedly pursued his goal of maintaining the "continuity of power" after Yeltsin. He finally found his preferred successor to Yeltsin in Putin. With slavish coverage of ORT television, Berezovsky helped Putin get elected president for a four-year term on March 27, 2000. Once he had made the ultimate power play in delivering a new Russian president, I assumed Berezovsky would feel secure and powerful. I was wrong.

Little more than a year after Primakov had frightened Berezovsky, the oligarch was on the run again. Had Berezovsky misjudged Putin? Or did Putin toss him aside, no longer wanting a reminder that he too was a creation of Russia's most ambitious kingmaker? Just as Gusinsky was being ground down by the Kremlin, Putin and Berezovsky had their own falling out.

At first Berezovsky seemed to have little to worry about. He told me approvingly that Putin was loyal to his friends. To make the point, Berezovsky offered a personal anecdote. He said Putin, at some risk, had come to a birthday party for Berezovsky's wife at the Logovaz Club during the time of tension with Primakov the previous spring. Putin was then head of the Federal Security Service, and it could not have been easy to show up at Berezovsky's famous club. But Putin took the risk, Berezovsky boasted, to show that personal feelings of loyalty were above politics.

"I realize it would be very interesting for the public if Putin, after becoming the president, would jail Berezovsky," the oligarch told me, referring to himself in the third person. We were sitting at the same large table at the Logovaz mansion where I had often talked with Berezovsky, although this time he seemed more serene than in the past. He took off his sport coat and savored red wine from a tall glass. "To be honest, I am not expecting this, neither tomorrow nor in the nearest future." That was March 22, 2000.

But then came the unexpected. First, Putin and Berezovsky had a disagreement over Chechnya. Putin was vigorously prosecuting the war against Chechen separatists, while Berezovsky began calling for peace talks. Putin asked Berezovsky to cut off all ties with the Chechen warlords. Berezovsky said he agreed to Putin's request but told the new Russian president there was no military solution in Chechnya.

Next, Berezovsky grew alarmed at Putin's proposal for stronger Kremlin control over Russia's independent-minded regional governors. In a major power play, Putin announced a plan to impose seven new unelected supergovernors on the existing eighty-nine regional chiefs. Five of the seven Putin appointees were former KGB men or military men. Putin also sought legislation allowing him to fire governors. Berezovsky saw it as an autocratic move. He liked the idea of a loose collection of independent governors, even though he realized that the Russian Federation under Yeltsin had become a crazy-quilt mix of both strong and weak regional powers, and that governors often defied the Kremlin. Berezovsky also knew governors were extremely important in decisions about heavy industry—such as aluminum and automobiles—and he clearly did not relish the thought of all power in the country being controlled by the Kremlin. Berezovsky, for example, had tried to play power broker in more than one Russian region and had succeeded in getting the former general Alexander Lebed elected in Krasnoyarsk.

Berezovsky made an appeal to Putin that the Russian Federation should be loosened, perhaps even turned into a confederation of more autonomous, independent states. But Putin was not listening. Putin did exactly the opposite of what Berezovsky recommended. They had a long talk, Berezovsky recalled, and he realized that his fears about Putin's autocratic streak were well-founded. "He said he still believed that we had to build a liberal democratic state in Russia," Berezovsky said later, "but we had to do it by force, because people were not ready for it." He added, "Putin believes everything has to be governed from above, so it is necessary to concentrate power, concentrate the mass media, and to rule business."

Berezovsky wrote Putin a lengthy private letter, but the Russian president brushed him aside. On May 30 Berezovsky publicly broke with Putin for the first time and issued an open letter attacking him. I spoke to him on that steamy afternoon at the Logovaz mansion, where he seemed frazzled. The serenity I had noticed in March was gone. Berezovsky accused Putin of "demolishing some democratic institutions" in moves that would "cheat" Russia's voters of their elected local leaders and destroy the regional political elites. The criticism cannot have gone down very well with Putin. On July 17 Berezovsky surprised me again by resigning his seat in the State Duma, which he had held only six months. "I do not want to take part in this spectacle," he told reporters, "I do not want to participate in Russia's collapse and the establishment of an authoritarian regime."

When a nuclear-powered submarine, the *Kursk,* sank in August, taking with it the lives of all 118 on board, Putin reacted awkwardly. Television, including Berezovsky's ORT, showed the Russian president riding a jet ski in the Black Sea while vacationing at the southern Russian resort at Sochi. Putin seemed uninformed, hesitated to accept calls for international aid, and repeatedly lied about the fate of the sailors trapped in the submarine.

Putin erupted in anger at the news coverage. He said the oligarchs and their television channels had been destroying the state, and the army and navy too. Dorenko was ordered taken off the air immediately. Putin called Berezovsky to complain that ORT had compared the sunken submarine to the Chernobyl nuclear accident. Berezovsky suggested a meeting. Putin said fine. The next day, Berezovsky arrived at the Kremlin to find Voloshin waiting for him instead of Putin.

"Listen," Voloshin told Berezovsky, "either you give up ORT within two weeks or you will follow Gusinsky."

"This is not the way to talk to me," Berezovsky replied. "You are forgetting something. I am not Gusinsky."

Berezovsky asked Voloshin to set up the meeting with Putin. Voloshin agreed. He called Berezovsky the next day at 2:00 P.M. and asked the tycoon to show up at the Kremlin in an hour. Berezovsky came. Voloshin was again waiting in his office. Putin arrived, tense, and

Berezovsky launched into a defense of how ORT had covered the *Kursk* disaster, including its interviews with bereaved widows of the lost sailors.

"This is helping you, it's not obstructing you," Berezovsky said, "because only openness can help you, nothing else."

"Is that all?" Putin asked.

"Yes, that's all, the main thing," Berezovsky replied.

"And now, I have something to tell you," Putin said. He opened a file. He began to read in a monotone. Berezovsky did not recall the exact words, but the gist of it was that ORT was corrupt and managed by just one person, Berezovsky, who took all the money under his control.

Berezovsky had a flashback to his nemesis, Primakov. The document was right out of Primakov's campaign against him the previous year. This was really galling to Berezovsky. "The signature down there, is it Yevgeny Maximovich Primakov?" Berezovsky asked Putin. "Why are you reading it to me?"

"I want to run ORT," Putin said. "I personally am going to run ORT."

Berezovsky was stunned. Dorenko had said that Putin viewed himself as a creature of television, and now it was clear that he wanted to control every minute on the air. "Listen, Volod," Berezovsky replied, using a friendly, shortened form of Vladimir. "This is ridiculous, at a minimum. And second, it is unrealizable."

"ORT covers 98 percent of Russian territory, of Russian households," Putin replied, coldly.

"Don't tell me the statistics!" Berezovsky answered. "I know them all. Do you understand what you are talking about? In fact, you want to control all the mass media in Russia—yourself!"[51]

Putin stood up and left. Berezovsky went back to his office and dashed off a short letter to Putin. He wrote that Putin was committing the same mistakes over and over again, first by escalating the conflict in Chechnya, then by imposing his will on the governors, and finally in taking over the mass media. Berezovsky lamented that the president was trying to "find solutions to complex problems by simple means." Putin was trying to become an autocrat. It wouldn't work. He gave the letter to Voloshin.

The letter marked Berezovsky's bailout from the Kremlin inner circle. The power broker had reached a dead end. He had given up on his own creation. Berezovsky concluded there was no point in fighting Putin over his television station. He sold his interest in ORT to Roman Abramovich, who was his partner in Sibneft, and one of the younger, new generation of oligarchs willing to cooperate with the Kremlin. Berezovsky then left the country.

When I saw Berezovsky a few months later in New York City, he recalled one final scene from his encounter with Putin. In their last conversation in the Kremlin, Putin had turned to him plaintively, fixing his cold stare on Berezovsky, the short, hyperactive man with the soft rat-a-tat voice who would wait on your doorstep for hours. Putin looked at him, the power broker extraordinaire who had, with his own hands and tireless ambition and dreams of great wealth, done more than anyone to shape the age of the oligarchs. Now their days of glory were over. New players were coming, new fortunes being made. And a new Russian leader sat in the Kremlin.

"You," Putin said, "you were one of those who asked me to be president. So, how can you complain?"

Berezovsky had no answer.

Epilogue

THE SOUND AND FURY of the Yeltsin era came to a muffled end. Yeltsin was a sad figure on the last night of his presidency. His televised farewell speech from the Kremlin on December 31, 1999, was laced with words of regret. "Many of our hopes have not come true," he acknowledged, asking the Russian people to forgive him. "What we thought would be easy turned out to be painfully difficult."

The oligarchs, the sons of Yeltsin's unruly capitalism, took different paths.

Of the six, Mikhail Khodorkovsky ended up the wealthiest. After the dark days of 1999, when he played hardball with lenders and investors, Khodorkovsky demonstrated once again his shrewd judgment. He switched from tough guy to gentleman, realizing that his fortune could be multiplied if he played by more open and honest Western rules. He paid dividends to shareholders for the first time, published accounts by international standards, and reinvested profits into his oil business. Yukos shares resumed trading on the Russian stock market and soared from $0.20 a share to $3.60 a share. Khodorkovsky became much wealthier, since he and his partners controlled 69 percent of the company. His coffers overflowed with cash after world oil prices rose suddenly in 1999 and 2000. In the annual *Forbes* magazine list of the world's five hundred wealthiest men in 2001, Khodorkovsky was the richest Russian on the list, with a net worth estimated at $2.4 billion.

Anatoly Chubais, who led the reformers in the Yeltsin years, was no longer at center stage. Gone were the days when his every word made headlines. In 1999, he threw himself into fixing Russia's decrepit electricity monopoly, and he became just one among many Russian industrial barons. Chubais enthusiastically backed Vladimir Putin at the outset of the second Chechen war. Chubais did not see Putin as a threat to Russian democracy or a free press, but rather as a strong-willed leader who would throw his weight behind Russia's modernization. When Putin crushed Vladimir Gusinsky and wrested NTV away from him, Chubais expressed regret but did not defend Gusinsky. He had only bad memories of the bankers war and Gusinsky's role in it.

After the presidential campaign, Yuri Luzhkov went back to his familiar role as *khozyain* of Moscow. He no longer harbored ambitions for the presidency. Chastened, he paid deference to Putin and returned to his own protected realm, as builder and boss of the capital city.

Alexander Smolensky dropped out of sight. For a while he worked on establishing a new bank, using some of the offices of the bankrupt SBS-Agro, but then sold it.

Gusinsky's media empire fell apart under the relentless pressure of Putin's Kremlin, but the journalists who worked for Gusinsky were not destroyed. Many of them stuck together and attempted to rebuild. With Gusinsky's blessing, Yevgeny Kiselyov took a core group of the NTV staff and set up shop at a smaller Moscow television station, TV-6. Boris Berezovsky, who owned the station, now shared it with Gusinsky's journalists. But starting over was hard work, and the NTV dream was difficult to rekindle. Gusinsky owned part of the Israeli newspaper *Ma'ariv* and often visited the United States. But he could not go home again to Russia.

Berezovsky was as restless as ever, but his days as power broker were over. He felt it was risky to return to Russia and did not go back, although his predominant business and political interests were inside the country. Berezovsky still controlled two influential daily newspapers and the TV-6 television station, but he was forced by the Kremlin to sell the larger ORT television channel, which had been his most influential tool. Berezovsky concluded that he had made a mistake bringing Putin to power, but he could do little about it from abroad. Berezovsky, who once epitomized the insider, who championed the embrace of wealth and power, was now on the outside looking in.

On July 18, 2001, after more than a year in office, Putin held a news conference. A reporter asked him about Berezovsky. He sighed and responded, "Boris Berezovsky—who's that?"

Afterword to the Paperback Edition

Of all the oligarchs, none survived and thrived quite as well as Mikhail Khodorkovsky in the years 2000 to 2003. World oil prices remained high, and Yukos became the largest company in Russia, as measured by market capitalization. Khodorkovsky and his core partners reaped billions of dollars in dividends. In 2002, for the first time, Khodorkovsky disclosed the ownership structure of Yukos. With this decision, he became the first owner of a major company to break with the climate of secrecy in which Russian capitalism was born in the 1990s, and this pioneering step forward was even more surprising because of Khodorkovsky's own history of murky deals. The disclosure revealed that the oil company was controlled by Group Menatep, a Gibraltar company owned by Khodorkovsky and a handful of close friends. Khodorkovsky's share of Yukos was worth about $8 billion. Leonid Nevzlin, the computer programmer who had been an early recruit to Khodorkovsky's youth science center, was also a billionaire shareholder. So was Vasily Shakhnovsky, the onetime engineer who thought up the idea for the Club on Sparrow Hills and later become a Yukos executive.

When I finished writing *The Oligarchs* in 2001, Khodorkovsky's shift in approach toward more openness and toward Western business practices was already evident. In the subsequent two years, as he sought to turn Yukos into a global oil giant, the change deepened. He proposed building a pipeline to China and, in a demonstration of how Russia could support American energy needs, shipped a tanker full of crude oil to Texas.

Khodorkovsky also talked about becoming a major force behind the development of philanthropy and civil society in Russia. These ambitions went well beyond the status he had already achieved as the wealthiest oligarch of his generation. He supported a widening circle of charitable activities inside Russia. When American financier George Soros pulled out, saying that his work was finished after donating billions of dollars to Russia in the 1990s, Khodorkovsky became the largest single private philanthropist in the country. He began a foundation, Open Russia, to advocate expanded ties between Russia and the West, especially Britain and the United States. His initial investment was $16 million—a fraction of the billions of dollars in profits and dividends generated by the oil company.

The launch of Open Russia in Washington was a businesslike affair and spoke volumes about how far Khodorkovsky had come. The event was held in the historic Thomas Jefferson Building of the Library of Congress. About one hundred lobbyists and government officials dined in the Members Room, an ornate chamber with painted silk panels in the high ceilings where the House of Representatives once met. The host was James H. Billington, the Librarian of Congress and one of the leading scholars of Russian history in the United States. Billington's classic work *The Icon and the Axe*, an interpretive history of Russian thought and culture, was published in 1966, when Khodorkovsky was just three years old. The scholar told his dinner guests that Khodorkovsky was a "visionary" and added, "It's not often you get someone who has done well and wants to do good." Khodorkovsky made a $1 million donation to the Open World exchange program, inspired by Billington, which brought young Russian leaders to the United States for short-term visits. Khodorkovsky also donated money to the National Book Festival, sponsored by Billington. At that event he was photographed with President Bush and First Lady Laura Bush, a potent reminder of how much things had changed for Khodorkovsky since the dark days of 1999.

Khodorkovsky's ambitions, however, were not yet satisfied. On April 22, 2003, Yukos announced plans to merge with Sibneft, the oil company originally created by Boris Berezovsky. The reader may recall that a proposed merger of these two oil companies fell apart in 1998. Now the combined company, to be called YukosSibneft, would be the fourth-largest oil company in the world by production. Once combined, the colossus would be a tempting target for a merger with—or sale to—another international oil company. This was Khodorkovsky's intent, and his most ambitious goal ever: to build up his empire and then sell it off to ExxonMobil or ChevronTexaco. The rewards would be fantastic. His vast oil reserves would be turned into cash worth tens of billions of dollars. And the dream was not implausible: the Russian oil companies were still cheap by international standards, and earlier in the year British Petroleum had made a $6.7 billion investment in another Russian oil company. A study by United Financial Group showed that the enterprise value of Yukos, per barrel of oil, was the equivalent of only about 10 percent of Exxon. It was not hard to see why Yukos would be a tempting catch.

Khodorkovsky was never comfortable in public, but as his fortunes improved he became a public figure and found himself spotlighted with great intensity as the richest man in Russia. Still fresh in my own mind were the nasty corporate disputes of the late 1990s. I wondered whether the same businessman who had championed such shady transactions a few years earlier could become the new standard-bearer for corporate governance and transparency in Russia. But Khodorkovsky's new direction was tangible, and impossible to dismiss.

After Putin had forced Gusinsky and Berezovsky to leave Russia, he came to an understanding with the oligarchs who remained: don't interfere in Kremlin affairs, and you can keep your gains from the crazy capitalism of the 1990s. For Khodorkovsky and some of the other businessmen, these gains were the huge natural resource companies, such as Yukos, that they had obtained cheaply in the privatization of state assets and that now produced mountains of cash for them. As his wealth and prominence steadily grew, it seemed to me that Khodorkovsky was careful to toe the Kremlin line. When it came to political support for parties in parliament, Khodorkovsky told me that he made the expected donations of tens of millions of dollars, including big contributions to the progressive parties Yabloko and the Union of Right Forces, but he did so with Kremlin supervision, like most of the other businessmen.

Khodorkovsky stirred quiet speculation that he might have a political future in mind for himself when he announced he would leave Yukos in 2007, a year before a presidential election. But his activities seemed natural for a rich and powerful tycoon and did not appear to be crossing the line Putin had drawn.

Then suddenly, something snapped in the Kremlin. The big screen of Khodorkovsky's dreams went dark.

The trouble began on February 20, 2003, when Khodorkovsky and other businessmen gathered in the Kremlin for one of their periodic formal meetings with Putin. When his turn came to speak, Khodorkovsky complained about the continuing scourge of corruption in government, and then he singled out a recent murky oil deal. A small company, Severnaya Neft, had been sold to a larger, state-owned oil company, Rosneft, for a wildly inflated price, hundreds of millions of dollars more than it was worth. What was going on? After Khodorkovsky mentioned this, Putin responded sharply, in a threatening tone. "Yukos has excess reserves," he asked, "and how did it get them?"

Soon, Khodorkovsky was the target of a Kremlin campaign to intimidate him. A small, relatively unknown Moscow think tank published a report warning ominously of a "creeping oligarchic coup" in Russia in which the tycoons supposedly were planning to take over parliament and push around the Russian president. Next, a glossy magazine, *Kompromat.Ru*, which published *kompromat*, the mixture of fact and fiction that was often used in Russia for smear campaigns devoted an entire issue to Khodorkovsky. The Yukos team was no stranger to kompromat, but it looked at the article with a sense of foreboding. It was another warning.

Then, on July 2, 2003, one of Khodorkovsky's key lieutenants, Platon Lebedev, was arrested by the Russian authorities on charges of embezzlement in connection with the privatization of a fertilizer company in 1994. It was a flimsy charge, since the privatization had been litigated and settled in court the previous year. The arrest stunned Khodorkovsky. Lebedev was director of Group Menatep and one of the billionaire shareholders of Yukos.

The day of Lebedev's arrest, the market capitalization of Yukos had reached $31 billion.

The arrest was followed by more police raids on company buildings, and investigations were launched against other core partners of Khodorkovsky, who was personally interrogated. Agents from the Federal

Security Service showed up at his daughter's school and asked the principal for a list of all the students. The pattern was exactly the same as that used against Gusinsky earlier. Khodorkovsky was suddenly thrust on the defensive.

Khodorkovsky said the campaign against him was being directed by a group of security service men around Putin who wanted to drive him out of Russia. Their motivations were not clear. Khodorkovsky had tripped over something big when he raised the oil company deal during the February meeting with Putin. The security services retaliated. It was not hard to see that Khodorkovsky was one of the big winners of the age. Among the losers were the former KGB men who had been left behind by the collapse of the Soviet Union and the ensuing decade of turmoil. They had not managed to grab large corporate assets in the Yeltsin years, and they were envious of the oligarchs. With Putin in power, they saw a chance to enrich themselves. Putin told reporters he would not interfere with their investigations.

Khodorkovsky, the epitome of self-confidence for so many years, was unsettled. He told me that he would not give in to the security services. He vowed not to flee Russia. He pondered putting up a public fight but he knew it would be difficult. Khodorkovsky realized that Putin had certain core beliefs that were shaped in his years in the KGB. Putin looked with disdain on the brash tycoons. In an interview with the *New York Times*, Putin gave voice to this resentment. "We have a category of people who have become billionaires, as we say, overnight," he said. "The state appointed them as billionaires. It simply gave out a huge amount of property, practically for free. They said it themselves. 'I was appointed a billionaire.' Then...they got the impression that the gods themselves slept on their heads, that everything is permitted to them."

Khodorkovsky celebrated his fortieth birthday in June 2003 at a time of deepening gloom. The Kremlin permitted the merger of Yukos and Sibneft, but at the same time intensified the campaign of intimidation aimed at Khodorkovsky and his partners.

Events took a dramatic turn on October 25, 2003. Khodorkovsky's private plane touched down in the Siberian city of Novosibirsk, where he was met by armed commandos. He was arrested, flown to Moscow and jailed on charges of fraud and tax evasion. "I'm not sorry about anything I've done," Khodorkovsky said in a statement released by his lawyer, "Nor am I sorry about what's happened today."

The attack on Khodorkovsky underscored yet again that the oligarchs and the system they had built remained a potent force in Putin's Russia. It was true that Putin set a different tone than Yeltsin. He talked about reestablishing the power of the state, and he prohibited the oligarchs from openly pulling strings in the Kremlin. Indeed, Putin showed little tolerance for political competition of any kind. He pushed for the creation of parties in the lower house of parliament that would rubber-stamp Kremlin decisions. He sought to limit the powers of the elected governors, weakened the upper house of parliament, and by mid-2003 had eliminated all of the independent national television networks remaining in Russia.

But oligarchic capitalism was entrenched. Two researchers in Moscow, Peter Boone and Denis Rodionov, prepared a study of Russia's sixty-four largest companies in August 2002—all firms in which the government no longer had a controlling stake. They found that 85 percent of the sales of these companies were controlled by just eight large financial-industrial groups.

The bigger companies thrived, but one consequence of the age of the oligarchs was that small and medium-size enterprises were stunted and did not expand. A huge obstacle for these firms was lack of access to capital. The banking system was still largely dysfunctional, a legacy of the 1990s. It was hard for entrepreneurs to get loans to start new businesses, while the oligarchs had plenty of capital and could easily finance their own needs.

As Khodorkovsky showed in these years, the nature of oligarchic capitalism was evolving. Khodorkovsky's transformation raised a very important question for Russia: Would the other oligarchs also eventually mend their ways? Would they become more like the American tycoons such as Carnegie and Rockefeller? And what were the forces of change that caused such an evolution?

One answer was that as the oligarchs gained more and more control over their companies, they became better stewards out of sheer self-interest. In the 1990s they fought bitter fights to gain majority ownership; now that it was all theirs, they were more inclined to treat the company nicely. The Boone and Rodionov study found that big tycoons stopped corporate abuse because now they were the uncontested owners. "The new property owners," they wrote, "have now turned from promoting lawlessness and low transparency to supporting the rule of law and property rights."

Another sign of change seen at Yukos and other companies was that once the oligarchs gained control, they began to focus on bringing in good managers, often from abroad. They found that better corporate behavior tended to drive up the market value of each company. This argument suggested that, over time, others would also see the riches that flowed from Khodorkovsky's example and they would follow it.

But the attack on Khodorkovsky also offered a stark reminder of the darker side of Russian capitalism. When Khodorkovsky opened up his books and ownership structure, few other major companies followed his example, and almost no one among the businessmen was willing to defend him in public. Khodorkovsky's transparency seemed to have backfired; others were frightened, and secure in the old ways of secrecy and coercion. Nasty corporate battles continued under Putin, much as they had under Yeltsin. New oligarchs, hungry for property, continued to use the same shady methods—coercion and subterfuge—that the Yeltsin generation had used. The economist Joel Hellman described this continuing battle for property as "permanent redistribution": as long as a tycoon could get property cheaply by using force or bribery, and as long as the state remained weak and without the rule of law, there would continue to be unseemly contests for wealth and power.

Boris Berezovsky remained in self-imposed exile in London. He continued to attack Putin and sponsored a parliamentary party, Liberal Russia. The Russian authorities pressed new charges against Berezovsky, stemming from a business deal with Avtovaz in the 1990s, and sought to extradite him. Berezovsky denied the charges. In September 2003 he won political asylum from Britain and a London court threw out the extradition request.

Vladimir Gusinsky was unbowed. He sold his remaining shares in NTV to Gazprom for $50 million. He continued to show a flair for entrepreneurship and laid plans for new businesses. He controlled part of the Israeli newspaper *Maariv* and a Russian-language satellite television channel in New York, where he lived. He did not return to Russia. In August 2003 Gusinsky flew to Greece for a vacation on his yacht. The Greek authorities arrested him based on an old extradition request from the year 2000, issued by Russia. Gusinsky thought the request had lapsed. He was released on bail, and on October 14, 2003, a Greek appeals court threw out the Russian extradition request. Gusinsky was free again.

Alexander Smolensky did not reappear on the business scene in

Russia. He had established a small bank, but later he turned it over to his son and busied himself with a small jewelry boutique. Yuri Luzhkov was enthusiastically building bridges, office towers, and highways as mayor of Moscow, but he kept a low profile in national politics. Anatoly Chubais remained an important business and political figure as the head of the electricity monopoly. He had devoted years to trying to overhaul the mammoth company, and a major reform of the system was coming close to reality in 2003.

David E. Hoffman
Washington, D.C.
October 27, 2003

Notes

Author's Note on Sources

In the 1990s the new Russia was often obscure, impenetrable, and deceptive. Many of those who made the fortunes described in this book sought to keep their stories secret. Yet, compared with earlier periods in Russian history, my impression as a correspondent in Moscow from 1995 to 2001 was that Russia had become a relatively open place. The financial empires and tycoons were often at war with one another—and that was good for openness. The cacophony of voices was confusing but also revealing.

In order to assemble the portraits and chronicle the rise of the oligarchs, I relied on many different sources of information. The most important source was more than two hundred interviews I conducted with participants in these events. All six subjects—Boris Berezovsky, Anatoly Chubais, Vladimir Gusinsky, Mikhail Khodorkovsky, Yuri Luzhkov, and Alexander Smolensky—granted me interviews.

I also relied on a number of memoirs that offered valuable first-person accounts of important events, verbatim transcripts of press conferences, several academic studies of the period by American and Russian scholars, and the rich literature about the collapse of the Soviet Union.

The documentary trail is sketchy on the successes and failures of the early banks and cooperatives mentioned here. For this period, I relied heavily on the personal recollections of the participants.

When Western investors began to scrutinize the factories and refineries being sold off during the privatization of state property in the 1990s, more information became available. Western brokerage firms published a large number of research reports on Russian businesses and industries. Also, as the Russians began to borrow on global capital markets and trade shares on Russia's own stock exchange, they were required to issue more detailed financial statements. I have pored over many of these documents. Some of the early reporting on the Russian oil and banking industries was especially useful. But all these sources required caution. The financial reports rarely acknowledged such abuses as asset stripping and transfer pricing, and research reports were sometimes little more than glossy advertisements from stock brokers trying to sell shares.

I also viewed many stories in the Russian press with caution. As a journalist, I admired the pioneering work of a few Russian colleagues. But all too often the press was a tool that the oligarchs used in their wars, and news reports had to be weighed in light of which financial group or tycoon was the underlying sponsor. I have relied, as much as possible, on published interviews in which the subject is quoted directly in question-and-answer format. In some cases, I have returned to the journalists or the subjects of the articles for a better explanation of who was doing what to whom.

A serious problem for any understanding of Russia in the 1990s is *kompromat*—the materials used by businessmen, politicians, and others to smear their enemies. Often *kompromat* is a mixture of genuine information and falsified materials, impossible to sort out. An enormous amount of *kompromat* found its way into the press and onto the Internet, and I have sought to avoid it as a source for this book.

Even the most aggressive research on my part often ended in disappointment. The reader will notice moments when the inexplicable happens—when a bank suddenly inherits a windfall, when a factory is given away for nothing, when a tiny company explodes from zero to $1 billion. What occurred at these critical junctures was often impossible to reconstruct, and it remains part of the mystery of the new Russia. I hope this book begins to unravel the mystery, but I acknowledge that many secrets of the oligarchs remain untold.

SHADOWS AND SHORTAGES

1. Andrei Sinyavsky, *Soviet Civilization: A Cultural History* (New York: Arcade, 1990), p. 181.
2. Lev Timofeyev, "A New Theory of Socialism," *Moscow News*, December 10, 1996.
3. Alena V. Ledeneva, *Russia's Economy of Favors: Blat, Networking, and Informal Exchange* (Cambridge: Cambridge University Press, 1998).
4. Igor Primakov and Masha Volkenstein, interview by author, December 11, 1999.
5. This account is based on many interviews with Irina Makarova, who retraced the train ride with me on December 2, 1999. The train ride out of Kursky Station is also the setting for a book that was hugely popular among young people who, like Irina, had come of age in the 1970s era of stagnation. Venedict Erofeyev, a maverick, rebellious writer, captured the meaning of escape in *Moskva-Petushki.* The work was published in *samizdat,* books outlawed by the state but self-published, often as carbon copy manuscripts, and passed from hand to hand. *Moskva-Putushki* was a tragic, satirical work. Erofeyev was a rebel against the system. He wrote in slang-filled prose about the train ride from Kursky Station to his own town, Petushki, a paradise of jasmine and singing birds. Erofeyev drinks during the entire train ride to Petushki, and in a cruel parody he never reaches his paradise. He comes full circle back to Moscow and perishes. Erofeyev came across to Irina's generation as the antisystem hero. Instead of the bold, optimistic, modern, utopian Soviet man who changes the future through supreme effort, he is capable of changing nothing and is just carried along. Ultimately, the system breaks its teeth on him because he does not care. He neither fears nor conforms; he drifts.
6. John Kenneth Galbraith, *A History of Economics: The Past as the Present* (London: Hamish Hamilton, 1987).
7. At the time Marx wrote, there was vivid evidence to support his views. The industrializing European economies imposed great hardships on workers and gave rise to huge inequalities between the rich and poor.
8. Alec Nove, *An Economic History of the USSR, 1917–1991,* 3d ed. (London: Penguin, 1992).
9. Vitaly Naishul, interview by author, October 7 and December 9, 1999. Naishul's work, *Drugaya Zhizn,* or *Another Life,* is available in Russian at www.inme.ru and www.libertarium.ru. Among his many publications I found especially useful was *The Supreme and Last Stage of Socialism* (London: Center for Research into Communist Economies, 1991).
10. Moisei Eydelman, "Monopolized Statistics under a Totalitarian Regime," in *The Destruction of the Soviet Economic System: An Insiders' History,* ed. Michael Ellman and Vladimir Kontorovich (New York: Sharpe, 1998), p. 75.
11. Sergei Ermakov, a demographer and professor at the International Institute of Economics and Law, told me that information on mortality was kept secret well into Gorbachev's *glasnost* reforms. Thus Soviet citizens were not told that their life expectancy was falling below that of Western Europeans. Ermakov said his own work was long confined to theoretical models. Ermakov, interview by author, November 27, 1999.

ALEXANDER SMOLENSKY

1. The lyrics were written by Alexander Galich.
2. Alexander Smolensky, interview by author, October 10, 1997, and August 30, 1999.
3. Eduard Krasnyansky, interview by author, September 2, 1999, and March 17, 2000.
4. This was a modest salary at the time. The Soviet ruble was not convertible. Its value in dollars is hard to measure because consumer goods were in such shortage that having money was often less important than having access to goods. In the late Soviet period, black market rates were about five rubles per dollar and rose by 1990 to between twenty and thirty rubles per dollar. After the Soviet Union collapsed, the ruble could be exchanged for dollars. Anders Åslund, *Gorbachev's Struggle for Economic Reform* (Ithaca: Cornell University Press, 1991), p. 184.
5. Alex Goldfarb, interview by author, February 27, 2000, and May 27, 2000.
6. "Report, based on operational data, in regards to Stolichny Savings Bank," undated, in Russian. I received this twelve-page law enforcement dossier on Smolensky in 1997 from the organization of a rival banker. Portions of it concerning Smolensky's biography, including the 1981 arrest, I have confirmed from other sources and from Smolensky himself. However, some of it is unconfirmed and appears to be police speculation, which I have omitted. Smolensky claimed he reported to the construction brigade but did not serve out the term.
7. Timothy J. Colton, *Moscow: Governing the Socialist Metropolis* (Cambridge: Harvard University Press, Belknap Press, 1995), p. 494.
8. Mikhail Gorbachev, *Memoirs* (New York: Doubleday, 1995). Gorbachev recalls, "We felt that we could fix things, pull ourselves out of this hole by the old methods, and then begin significant reforms. This was probably a mistake that wasted time, but that was our thinking then" (p. 218).
9. Åslund, *Gorbachev's Struggle,* p. 161.
10. Åslund, *Gorbachev's Struggle*, pp. 167–181; Dimenico Mario Nuti, "The New Soviet Cooperatives: Advances and Limitations" (European University Institute, Florence, Italy, July 1988).
11. Viktor Loshak, interview by author, March 18, 1999.
12. Yelena Baturina, interview by author, August 23, 1999.
13. Alexander Panin, interview by author, March 11, 1999.
14. Joel S. Hellman, "Breaking the Bank: Bureaucrats and the Creation of Markets in a Transitional Economy" (Ph.D. diss., Columbia University, 1993).
15. Alexander Bekker, interview by author, October 3, 1997.
16. Hellman, "Breaking the Bank," p. 150.
17. Ron Chernow, *The Death of the Banker* (New York: Vintage, 1997). Chernow's major work on Morgan is *The House of Morgan: An American Banking Dynasty and the Rise of Modern Finance* (New York: Touchstone, 1990).
18. Hellman, "Breaking the Bank," p. 166.
19. Hellman, "Breaking the Bank," p. 162.
20. Hellman, "Breaking the Bank," p. 163.
21. Joel Hellman, interview by author, June 4, 1998.
22. "Offering Circular," SBS-Agro, $250 million notes, July 18, 1987.
23. Anonymous source, interview by author, October 3, 1998.

24. Sergei Pluzhnikov, Sergei Sokolov, "Operation SBS," *Sovershenno Sekretno* 6 (1999).

YURI LUZHKOV

1. Yuri Luzhkov, *We Are Your Children, Moscow* (Moscow: Vagrius, 1996) in Russian. In English, revised as: *Moscow Does Not Believe in Tears: Reflections of a Moscow Mayor*, trans. Mark Davidov (Chicago: Martin, 1996).
2. Leon Aron, *Yeltsin: A Revolutionary Life* (New York: St. Martin's, 2000), p. 153.
3. Alexander Vladislavlev, interview by author, April 15, 1999.
4. Vice Rector Vladimir Koshelev, interview by researcher Anne Nivat, April 28, 1999; and Rector Albert Vladimirov, interview by author, May 7, 1999, at the Russian State University of Oil and Gas in the name of I. M. Gubkin. Also, "Information for Entering Students in Moscow," Gubkin Institute, 1954.
5. Luzhkov, interview by author, February 5, 2001. Luzhkov recalled that the meeting ended with a dramatic confrontation. The hall was emptied of the audience, so only the top managers remained. One by one, they roundly denounced Luzhkov. The party man suggested that he be fired. "I am ready to leave," Luzhkov recalled saying. But he was not fired. He received a reprimand, still protesting that his idea was a good one.
6. Timothy J. Colton, "Understanding Yuri Luzhkov," *Problems of Post-Communism*, September-October 1999, pp. 14–26.
7. Colton, "Understanding Yuri Luzhkov," pp. 14–26.
8. Alexander Panin, interview by author, March 18, 1999, and April 9, 1999.
9. Yelena Baturina, interview by author, August 23, 1999.
10. Viktor Loshak, interview by author, March 18, 1999.
11. Yuri Bortsov, *Yuri Luzhkov* (Rostov-on-Don: Feniks, 1999), p. 148. The quotation originally appeared in *Vechernaya Moskva*, February 20–27, 1997.
12. David Remnick, "Hundreds of Co-Ops Lead a Soviet Revolution," *Washington Post*, February 4, 1988, p. A25.
13. Luzhkov, *Seventy-Two Hours of Agony* (Moscow: Magisterium, 1991), pp. 79–80. In Russian.
14. Vladimir Bokser, interview by author, November 13, 1999.
15. Colton, *Moscow*, p. 615.
16. Francis X. Clines, *New York Times*, March 22, 1990, p. 1; April 16, 1999, p. 1.
17. James Blitz, "Moscow Is 'Close to Catastrophe,'" *London Sunday Times*, May 27, 1990.
18. Benjamin B. Fischer, ed., *At Cold War's End: U.S. Intelligence on the Soviet Union and Eastern Europe, 1989–1991* (Washington: Central Intelligence Agency, 1999). See National Intelligence Estimate (NIE) 11–18–90, November 1990, "The Deepening Crisis in the USSR: Prospects for the Next Year."
19. Vasily Shakhnovsky, interview by author, November 26, 1999.
20. Another popular perception at the time was that Popov was tolerant of corruption. Popov had once said that bureaucrats should list their preferred payoffs like items on a restaurant menu.

21. I am in debt to Margaret L. Paxson for this definition.
22. Mikhail Shneider, interview by author, March 26, 1999.
23. Gavriil Popov, interview by author, February 13, 1997.
24. Alexander Osovtsov, interview by author, March 29, 1999.
25. Michael Dobbs, "Soviet Price Hikes Draw Anger, Pessimism," *Washington Post*, April 3, 1991, p. A19.
26. Elizabeth Shogren, "Reformer to Face Three Communists in Moscow Vote," *Los Angeles Times*, June 6, 1991, p. 8.
27. Colton, *Moscow*, p. 651.
28. Luzhkov, *Seventy-Two Hours*, p. 38.
29. Alexei Venediktov, interview by author, August 28, 1999.
30. Luzhkov was appointed to a four-man commission that ran the Soviet economy in the final months before the Soviet Union collapsed. He appeared frequently on television, touring construction sites, bus stops, and food lines.

Anatoly Chubais

1. Nina Oding, interview by author, October 23, 1999.
2. For a description of the library at this time, I am indebted to Alexei Yurchak, letter to the author, June 9, 2000.
3. Grigory Glazkov, interview by author, December 1, 1999; and Yuri Yarmagaev, interview by author, October 22, 1999.
4. Anatoly Chubais, interview by author, May 13, 2000.
5. *Obshchaya Gazeta*, interview with Chubais, February 22–28, 1996. In Russian.
6. Igor Chubais, interview by author, May 25, 2000.
7. Vladimir Korabelnikov, interview by author, October 21, 1999.
8. Chubais résumé, provided by RAO Unified Energy Systems, October 25, 1999.
9. Sergei Vasiliev, interview by author, August 24, 1999.
10. Janos Kornai, *Economics of Shortage* (Amsterdam: North Holland, 1980).
11. Friedrich A. Hayek, *The Road to Serfdom* (Chicago: University of Chicago Press, 1944).
12. Friedrich A. Hayek, "The Use of Knowledge in Society," *American Economic Review*, September 1945, pp. 519–530.
13. Gaidar's thesis was entitled "Indicators for Evaluating Activity in Self-Financing Enterprises (Based on a Study of the Electrical Engineering Industry)."
14. Pyotr Aven, interview by author, October 22, 1999; July 11, 2000.
15. Yegor Gaidar, *Days of Defeat and Victory* (Seattle: University of Washington Press, 1999), p. 29. Originally published in Russian (Moscow: Vagrius, 1996).
16. Chubais, interview by author, February 20, 2001.
17. Gaidar recalled in his memoir that "I should point out I was right on the mark in casting Chubais in a key role." He does not say which role. Nina Oding told me, "Chubais took the role of public relations. He was in PR because he knew how to talk about ideas, to simplify them, better than anyone. They didn't think he would do privatization. They thought he would be entirely responsible for PR."
18. Dmitriev told me that their institute, the Institute of Economics and Finance,

held a treasure of economics works, a library from the Imperial Russian Central Bank with a large number of books about capitalism, some dating back to prerevolutionary days, which the authorities had never bothered to lock up. Dmitriev said he also read contemporary Western texts through a progressive supervisor who gave him access to the *spetzkhran*. Finally, Dmitriev pointed out that his institute emphasized systems analysis and mathematics, a more technical approach to economics that minimized ideology.

19. Naishul, *Another Life.*
20. This account of the seminar is based on my interviews with Naishul, Chubais, Glazkov, Gaidar, Dmitriev, and Dmitry Vasiliev.
21. Anatoly B. Chubais and Sergei A. Vasiliev, "Economic Reform and Structural Change in the USSR," in *Ten Years of Russian Economic Reform* (London: Center for Research into Post-Communist Economies, 1999).
22. Sergei Belyaev, interview by author, October 18, 1999. Belyaev was then a member of the council and recalls that Chubais, "very sure of himself," delivered a speech on how shock therapy could be applied to Russia.

MIKHAIL KHODORKOVSKY

1. Peter Slevin, then a reporter for the *Miami Herald*, gave the author notes from an interview with Khodorkovsky in the first week of August 1991 before the coup attempt. See also Slevin, "The New Soviet Up-and-Comers Trade Party Line for Bottom Lines," *Miami Herald*, August 18, 1991.
2. Alexei Yurchak, letter to the author, February 17, 2000; Yurchak, interview by author, October 9, 1999, January 3, 2000. Yurchak's doctoral dissertation, "The Cynical Reason of Late Socialism: Language, Ideology, and the Culture of the Last Soviet Generation" (Duke University, 1997) is a compelling work that I found immensely helpful.
3. Steven L. Solnick, *Stealing the State: Control and Collapse in Soviet Institutions* (Cambridge: Harvard University Press, 1998), p. 60. Chapter 4 describes the Komsomol's troubles and collapse.
4. Earlier, the Komomsol had officially sponsored many youth activities such as concerts, and there had been a youth underground as well. But Komsomol's role declined in Gorbachev's years while the informal associations rapidly expanded.
5. Solnick, *Stealing the State,* p. 288 n. 168.
6. Olga Kryshtanovskaya, interview by author, November 3, 1999. According to Solnick and others, self-financing had another side: huge central budget accounts of the Komsomol were spirited away into private hands and commercial banks, including one, Finistbank, which was founded by funds from the Komsomol central committee. At the same time, the party and the KGB also transferred enormous riches to their own front companies and bank accounts, many overseas. The full extent of this process has never been revealed, but it was undoubtedly quite substantial.
7. Konstantin Zatulin, interview by author, March 22, 1999.
8. Alexander Khachaturov, interview by author, November 19, 1998.

9. Mikhail Khodorkovsky, interview by author, June 19, 2000.
10. Sheindlin recalled that Khodorkovsky was accompanied by Leonid Nevzlin, who later became a close associate. However, Nevzlin said he was not there. It could have been another Khodorkovsky associate. Sheindlin was also uncertain of the date.
11. Khodorkovsky gave a different account: "I found a group of young specialists in my institute who could make a special device to measure a high temperature in an alloy. After that, together with them, we found an institute that could order such work from us. It was the Institute of High Temperatures of the Academy of Science. And we asked them if they would like to order this work from us." He said the answer was affirmative. (Khodorkovsky, interview by author). In his remarks to Igor Bunin in 1994, Khodorkovsky said his "first credit" was 164,000 rubles and that he used the money for investment. He told author Rose Brady that he "hired students to do research" for the Institute of High Temperature and, Brady says, the "job pulled in 169,000 rubles." Rose Brady, *Kapitalizm* (New Haven: Yale University Press, 1999), p. 55.
12. According to the decision of the Komsomol central committee, local groups were "given an opportunity to determine for themselves a form of expenditure of Komsomol funds—in cash or noncash." *Komsomol i Molodezh' Rossii* (Moscow: Komsomol, 1990), p. 33. In Russian.
13. Although the Komsomol played a role in his success, Khodorkovsky expressed disdain for it. He told me he had been passed over for a higher-level job and had become disenchanted with the organization. "I had bad relations with the Komsomol," he said.
14. The connection was his friend Sergei Monakhov, who was leader of the local Komsomol organization and remained a member of Khodorkovsky's team.
15. Leonid Nevzlin, interview by author, March 16, 2000.
16. Andrei Gorodetsky, interview by author, November 24, 1998.
17. Peter Slevin, notes from interview with Khodorkovsky, August 1991, given to author.
18. Igor Bunin, *Forty Stories of Success* (Moscow: Center for Political Technology, 1994), pp. 169–178.
19. Slevin, notes from Khodorkovsky interview; and Slevin, "New Soviet Up-and-Comers."
20. Yelena Baturina, who was then an assistant to Luzhkov, said that Khodorkovsky was refused because it was unclear whether one of the youth science centers could be turned into a purely commercial organization, a cooperative. But she added that there was great concern about mixing noncash and cash together, that it would do "big damage" to the Soviet economy. Baturina, interview by author, August 23, 1999, Moscow. Panin said that Luzhkov was so worried about this that he testified on the subject before parliament.
21. Igor Primakov, interview by author, December 11, 1999.
22. Anonymous source, interview by author.
23. Bunin, *Forty Stories*, p. 172.
24. Khodorkovsky, in the Bunin interview, gave a slightly different account of why

he was pressed, saying it was the result of a new government rule that barred him from paying people in advance, upsetting the chain of cash conversions, trade, and payments. He did not say precisely when this took place.

25. Yulia Latynina, "Mikhail Khodorkovsky: Chemistry and Life: Unknown Pages from the Life of a Superoligarch," *Sovershenno Sekretno*, August 1, 1999, pp. 3–5.
26. In his remarks to Slevin in 1991, Khodorkovsky offered a clue about the deal with Zhiltsotsbank. "We went to get a loan and we ended up paying *them* to write a set of rules for us," he said.
27. The name was derived from the Russian acronym for Inter-branch Center for Scientific and Technological Programs.
28. Bunin, *Forty Stories*, p. 171.
29. Joel Hellman, interview by author, June 4, 1999.
30. Mikhail Berger, "Conversation with the President on Reform," *Izvestiya*, July 28, 1990.
31. Daniel Sneider, "The Soviet Economy: Commercial Banking Is Off and Running," *Christian Science Monitor*, December 31, 1991, p. 5.
32. Mikhail Khodorkovsky and Leonid Nevzlin, *Chelovek c Rublyom* (Moscow: Menatep-Inform, 1992).
33. Vladislav Surkov, interview by author, October 18, 1999. Surkov had become a top Kremlin political adviser by this time. He ended our interview saying he had to rush off to attend a meeting with Khodorkovsky and the Kremlin chief of staff.
34. Latynina, *Sovershenno Sekretno*.
35. Hellman, "Breaking the Bank." Hellman wrote, "Several commercial banks maintained covert correspondent relations with foreign banks, well before they were granted a license to conduct hard currency operations. Menatep even set up affiliates in Budapest, Switzerland, and Gibraltar for transferring and maintaining hard currency accounts abroad for Soviet clients." Hellman said his information was based on an interview with Alexander Golubovich, a vice president of Menatep (p. 163). He also said, "Though virtually all commercial banks were officially prohibited from dealing with hard currency, this restriction was routinely ignored. From the very beginning, commercial banks were engaged in a wide range of illegal hard currency transactions" (pp. 162–163).
36. Kathleen Day, "Riggs Had Ties to Firms in Probe," *Washington Post*, September 18, 1999, p. E1.
37. Sneider, "Soviet Economy."
38. Bunin, *Forty Stories*, p. 174.
39. Gaidar wrote in his memoir that the issue came up because two high-ranking former Soviet intelligence officials had written to Yeltsin about the matter, and Yeltsin asked Gaidar to look into it.
40. Fritz W. Ermarth, "Seeing Russia Plain: The Russian Crisis and American Intelligence," *National Interest*, Spring 1999.

BORIS BEREZOVSKY

1. Leonid Boguslavsky, interview by author, April 26, 2000; May 16, 2000.
2. Vladimir Grodsky, interview by author, June 30, 2000.
3. Boris Berezovsky, interview, *Novoye Russkoye Slovo* (New York), March 11–12, 2000, pp. 10–11.
4. Boris Berezovsky, interview by author, March 22, 2000.
5. Alexander Oslon, interview by author, May 29, 2000. Oslon became one of Russia's leading political pollsters: head of the Public Opinion Foundation.
6. Berezovsky's publications include a candidate of science dissertation, "Dispatching by Vector Criteria of Queues of Requests in Computer Systems," which he defended in 1975, when he was twenty-nine years old. In 1981 he cowrote *Binary Relations in Multicriteria Optimization*, with V. I. Borzenko and L. M. Kempner (Moscow: Nauka). In 1983 he defended a doctor of technical science dissertation, "Working Out the Theoretical Foundations for the Algorithimization of Preproject Decisionmaking and Its Application." In 1984 he wrote, with A. V. Gnedin, *Problem of the Best Choice* (Moscow: Nauka). In 1989 he wrote, with Y. Barishnikov, Borzenko, and Kempner, *Multicriteria Optimization: Mathematical Aspects* (Moscow: Nauka). All these publications are in Russian.
7. Mark Levin, interview by author, June 9, 2000.
8. This kind of trade-off is described in *Bolshaya Paika*, by Yuli Dubov (Moscow: Vagrius, 2000) In Russian. The book is described by Dubov as fiction but appears to be a thinly disguised memoir of Berezovsky's early years in business. On page 40, Dubov describes how the Berezovsky character helps a scientist at the institute buy his first car in exchange for reading a dissertation and agreeing to be the "opponent" at the defense.
9. Pyotr Aven, whose father, Oleg, was a founder and leading scientist at the institute, told me that many of the mathematicians whom Berezovsky brought into his laboratory were Jews who could not get work elsewhere.
10. Levin, interview by author.
11. Berezovsky's final academic quest was to become a corresponding member of the Russian Academy of Sciences, which he achieved.
12. "Berezovsky: The Most Reliable System Is Me," *Obshchaya Gazeta*, December 3–9, 1998, p. 8.
13. For connections, Avtovaz was a gold mine. Berezovsky used his *svyazi* there to get spare parts for friends. Berezovsky earned a respectable professor's salary of five hundred rubles a month, but he was always scrounging for money, Grodsky recalled. "I just recall that Borya was used to borrowing money. And he always lacked money. He borrowed from me, from other colleagues. Borya spent a lot, and he never had enough money."
14. The statistics are taken from a display on the history of the factory at the official museum in Togliatti.
15. Alexander Zibarev, a deputy director of the factory, told a reporter the Russian car market "is like a hungry dog; you throw it a new car and it gobbles it up." *New York Times*, June 30, 1992, p. D2.
16. It may have helped Berezovsky that his mentor, and director of the institute, Alexander Trapeznikov, was a deputy head of the State Committee on Science

and Technology. Still, it is not clear why the state committee would have paid such a large sum.

17. National Intelligence Estimate (NIE) 11–23–88, reprinted in Benjamin B. Fischer, ed., *At Cold War's End: U.S. Intelligence on the Soviet Union and Eastern Europe, 1989–1991* (Washington, D.C.: Central Intelligence Agency, 1999), p. 1.
18. Yuli Dubov, *Bolshaya Paika* (Moscow: Vagrius, 2000). The word *paika* here is prison slang for the ration an inmate receives in a prison or labor camp, when food is divided among members of a group. The title means "big piece," and to explain it, Dubov refers to another author who wrote that "in a camp it's not the small *paika* that gets you, but the big one." The point is that you die not when you don't have enough food but when you have more than others and they start envying you. Dubov's comment that he painted what he saw was made in a *Novaya Gazeta* interview (February 28, 2000). I also interviewed Dubov about the book and Berezovsky's early years on May 3, 2000. Many people I spoke with said *Bolshaya Paika* contains accurate descriptions of specific events, such as Berezovsky's dealings with the factory. However, the book's bias toward Berezovsky is plain—he is portrayed as a business genius.
19. Berezovsky later became the exclusive dealer for Mercedes in Russia. He told me how fascinated he was to discover German efficiency. The Germans planned six months in advance to stage a banquet to mark the opening of a dealership, and they carried out the plan. "I thought I had fallen into a crazy house," Berezovsky told me, recalling the day that the Mercedes representative told him of the plan. "A *half year beforehand*," he was given a card that said "this table and that table, these people are sitting here, how many sausages, how much beer. And everything went off exactly as they had planned it." The example suggests how tumultuous life was in Russia at the time—six months' time was considered an eternity.
20. Once Berezovsky recalled how he stopped at a German gas station and forgot to pay after fueling up. "I forgot!" he said. "And I drove off. I hear some kind of horrifying scream behind me. I look in the mirror and I see that a person is running after me and is screaming something in German. I stopped and right away understood what happened. That I hadn't paid the money. "I go backward, drive up to the person, and he is screaming, 'POLITSA! POLITSA! RUSSIAN!' I don't know what to do, now that I'm going to have to deal with the police. I don't know how to stop him. He's a grown, middle-aged man. And suddenly, you know, again, it's that intuition, suddenly I realized that I could stop him only in one way. I started cursing at him. Really. With Russian curses. And he suddenly stopped. Was silent. He schlumped over like a dog with a tail between its legs and said, 'Enough, enough.' I went, paid my money, and drove away!"
21. Yuri Tselikov, interview by author, March 31, 2000.
22. Valery Ivanov, interview by my researcher Margaret Paxson, February 16, 2000. We were deeply saddened to learn Ivanov was murdered in Togliatti on April 29, 2002.
23. Anatoly Ivanov, interview by author, March 29, 2000.
24. By one account, there were four major criminal wars in Togliatti in the 1990s. Vladimir Ovchinsky described them in *Moscow News*, June 18–24, 2000. The first occurred when criminal groups took over businesses in the city in the late

1980s and began blackmailing citizens buying Zhigulis; they also took control of the assembly line. The first war climaxed with a fight involving seventy gang members near the Hotel Zhiguli. The second war was fought in 1994–1996; sixty-six people were killed. After the war the city and factory were divided into zones of influence controlled by powerful clans. A third criminal war broke out in 1996 and was followed by Operation Cyclone, an effort by the federal Interior Ministry to clean up the factory. "Avtovaz was literally in the hands of bandits," Ovchinsky wrote. In the first half of the year 2000, the fourth war broke out: sixteen contract murders. Ovchinsky said 500 million rubles a year were being siphoned off by criminal groups in 1999. "One can conclude that Togliatti is still an epicenter of the Russian criminal world. The Mafia structures have an ability to imitate, adjust themselves, and live separately, apart from any economic or political transformations. The murder of leaders of criminal groups hardly influences the situation because new leaders appear."

25. "Changes in the Free Delivery Price, on the Basis of Models Manufactured by VAZ," a chart (in Russian).
26. Logovaz official price list as of January 1, 1993.
27. Exchange rate table, Central Bank of Russia.
28. "Volga Automobile Works, Descriptive Memorandum," Bear Stearns, 1991.
29. *Bolshaya Paika*, p. 247.

VLADIMIR GUSINSKY

1. Vladimir Gusinsky, interview by author, September 22, 2000.
2. Valery Belyakovich, interview by author, September 12, 2000.
3. J. A. E. Curtis, *Manuscripts Don't Burn: Mikhail Bulgakov, A Life in Letters and Dairies* (London: Bloomsbury, 1991).
4. Alexander Minkin, interview by author, July 12, 2000.
5. Tatyana Volodina, actress, Tula Academic Drama Theater, telephone interview by author from Tula, September 27, 2000. Volodina provided details from the program of the performance. Also "Youth of an Oligarch," *Moscow News*, July 4–10, 2000, p. 13.
6. Gusinsky later said of Bobkov, "When the Communists had a lot of clout, he helped us a lot because he had some influence over them. . . . Bobkov had considerable clout with old-timers in the Communist Party. . . . As for me, this is what I think happened. Dissidents were harassed by the state machine in which Bobkov used to be a cog. But I never fought the regime; I studied at the GITIS [state theater institute], an ideological institute of higher education, one might say. I was a person absolutely loyal to the authorities. It is another thing that I was an unruly character, and a Jew. I didn't have much of a future then. You can condemn me as you like, but I, personally, don't have the right to judge and punish Bobkov. Dissidents, fighters against that regime—they have various rights." *Obshchaya Gazeta*, June 8–14, 2000, pp. 1–3.
7. Margery Kraus, interview by author, July 13, 2001; "U.S. Firm, Soviets Establish Joint Venture to Venture Jointly," Associated Press, December 13, 1988.
8. Boris Khait, interview by author, September 14, 2000.

9. Yuri Schekochikhin, "Fear," *Literaturnaya Gazeta*, June 10, 1992, p. 11.
10. Lloyd Grove, "Russky Business: The Mogul in Exile Who's Got Moscow Up in Arms," *Washington Post*, April 7, 1995, p. D1.
11. Oleg Dobrodeyev, interview by author, July 20, 2000.
12. Mikhail Leontiev, interview by author, July 4, 2000.
13. Sergei Zverev, interview by author, June 23, 2000.
14. Lee Hockstader, "Brave New World: Moscow Anchor Leads Bold, Bloody Experiment in Press Freedom," *Washington Post*, March 29, 1995, p. B1.
15. Yevgeny Kiselyov, interview by author, August 2, 2000.
16. Igor Malashenko, interview by author, July 25, 2000.
17. Chrystia Freeland, *Sale of the Century* (New York: Crown Business, 2000), p. 155.

UNLOCKING THE TREASURE

1. In his memoir, Gaidar recalls that he broke party taboos in the journal and wrote about such topics as inflation, unemployment, poverty, social stratification, the budget deficit, and military spending. Moreover, "we tried to explain to the ruling elite how ruinous its course was." Yegor Gaidar, *Days of Defeat and Victory* (Seattle: University of Washington Press, 1999), p. 35. Gaidar hailed from a well-known family of the intelligentsia. His grandfather, Arkady Petrovich Gaidar, was author of famous Soviet-era children's stories. His father, Timur, was a foreign correspondent for *Pravda*.
2. Boris Yeltsin, *The Struggle for Russia* (New York: Times Books, 1994), pp. 125–126.
3. Pyotr Aven, interview by author, July 11, 2000.
4. Mikhail Berger, interview by author, October 10, 2000.
5. Mikhail Dmitriev, interview by author, November 19, 1999.
6. Yeltsin had a similar conception. He recalled, "Gaidar's ministers and Gaidar himself basically took this position with us: Your business is political leadership; ours is economics. Don't interfere with us as we do our work, and we won't butt in on your exalted councils, your cunning behind-the-scenes intrigue, which we don't understand anyway." Yeltsin, *Struggle for Russia*, pp. 156–157.
7. Maxim Boycko [Boiko], Andrei Shleifer, and Robert Vishny, *Privatizing Russia* (Cambridge: MIT Press, 1995). According to the authors, who participated on the Chubais team, privatizers believed that "political influence over economic life was the fundamental cause of economic inefficiency, and that the principal objective of reform was, therefore, to *depoliticize* economic life" (pp. 10–11).
8. Yegor Gaidar, interview by author, September 29, 2000.
9. Chubais press conference, April 21, 1993.
10. Gaidar, *Days*, p. 129.
11. Gaidar, *Days*, p. 66.
12. Jeffery Sachs, *Poland's Jump to the Market Economy* (Cambridge: MIT Press, 1993).
13. Gaidar, *Days*, p. 86.
14. Anatoly Chubais, ed., *Privatizatzia Po-Rossiiski* (Moscow: Vagrius, 1999), p. 20. In Russian.

15. Chubais interview, *Literaturnaya Gazeta*, October 12, 1994, p. 10.
16. Chubais, *Privatizatzia*, p. 28.
17. Chubais, *Privatizatzia*, pp. 29–31. The Kolo story was originally reported by the newspaper *Kuranty* in late February, and the scheme was also described by Berger in *Izvestia*. Chubais denounced the scheme at a press conference on February 28, 1992. See Francis X. Clines, "Russian to Fight Private Sell-offs by Ex-Officials," *New York Times*, February 29, 1992, p. 5; and John-Thor Dahlburg, "Russia's Neo-Capitalists Learning Art of Rip-Off," *Los Angeles Times*, March 1, 1992, p. 1.
18. Dmitri Vasiliev, interview by author, September 16, 1999; November 20, 1999; and September 18, 2000.
19. Gaidar, interview by author, September 29, 2000; Chubais recollections from *Privatizatzia*. The auction was described by Fred Hiatt, "Russia Auctions Off State-owned Firms," *Washington Post*, April 5, 1992, p. A1.
20. Gaidar, interview by author, September 29, 2000.
21. Gaidar, *Days*, p. 131
22. Vasiliev, interview by author.
23. Sachs had recommended Andrei Shleifer, a professor of economics at Harvard University. Along with Jonathan Hay, he played a key role in organizing Western help to support Chubais and Vasiliev. Among other activities, the Westerners helped design the Russian privatization vouchers, helped write the laws and decrees, and helped set up and carry out the great sell-off. Some criticism has subsequently been aimed at these efforts. The author acknowledges that this issue is beyond the scope of this book. However, the author believes it is mistaken to criticize the Westerners alone for what occurred in Russia. Many of the most fateful choices were made by the Russians, such as the decision to free prices, property, and trade before building the institutions of a free market. The Westerners often advised and encouraged them in the direction they took, but Yeltsin, Gaidar, and Chubais led the way.
24. Anatoly Chubais, interview by author, May 13, 2000.
25. Chubais, *Privatizatzia*, p. 34.
26. In the end there were three options. The first, proposed by Chubais, distributed 25 percent to the workers, who could then buy an additional 10 percent of the shares at 70 percent of the (low) book value of the enterprise, and management could buy 5 percent at the book value. This was effectively 40 percent to insiders. Option 2, proposed by the industrialists, allowed workers and managers to buy 51 percent of the enterprise at 1.7 times the book value. A third option for medium-sized companies allowed managers to buy up to 40 percent if employees agreed, but with restrictions. In the end, studies showed the overwhelming majority of enterprises were privatized using option 2, the one proposed by the factory directors. Anders Åslund, *How Russia Became a Market Economy* (Washington, DC: Brookings Institution, 1995), pp. 233–235.
27. There was a major debate within the privatization team on whether to model Russia's privatization after the Czech or the Polish models, both of which were getting under way at the time. The Polish model involved large mutual funds in which people would obtain shares. The Czech variant was more open, using

vouchers that people could dispose of as they wished. "From the political viewpoint, the signals coming from Poland and Czechoslovakia in 1992 made it clear that the Czechs were excited about privatization and involved with it, while the Poles were not. Choice made all the difference. Since popular involvement was deemed absolutely essential for the sustainability of Russian privatization, vouchers were a clear choice" (Boycko [Boiko], Shleifer, and Vishny, *Privatizing Russia*, p. 83).

28. Chubais made the claim at an August 21, 1992, press conference introducing the vouchers. He said he figured that the price of a secondhand Volga was only 2,000 or 3,000 rubles—this was the so-called residual price, after depreciation, which was sometimes used for selling off state property such as ten-year-old taxis to their drivers. It was not a real price. Since the face value of a voucher was 10,000 rubles, a voucher "could be sufficient to buy two or even three, and with luck even more Volga cars," Chubais claimed. In fact, Chubais later acknowledged "errors" in his public relations pitch for vouchers. He said he was thinking at the time that a voucher might buy a share that would appreciate significantly. The two Volgas claim was one of Chubais's biggest goofs and the butt of jokes for many years. Chubais, *Privatizatzia*, p. 191; Chubais press conference, August 21, 1992.
29. Celestine Bohlen, "Citizens of Russia to Be Given a Share of State's Wealth," *New York Times*, October 1, 1992, p. 1.
30. Chubais, *Privatizatzia*, p. 157.
31. Vasiliev, interview by author, November 20, 1999.
32. Paul Bograd, interview by author, March 26, 1999.
33. In *Privatizatzia*, Chubais recalled, "We had to make hundreds of thousands of people do something they had never done before. We had to fundamentally change their attitude to property.... I remember sitting with Gaidar at some regional meeting. There are, maybe, a thousand people in the audience. And I feel with my skin that we are like two Martians for them. Completely alien.... You had to adjust to their own way of thinking. You had to realize that you cannot make dozens of thousands of people all of a sudden understand the Martian language you are talking. You must speak their language" (pp. 144–145).
34. Boycko [Boiko], Shleifer, and Vishny, *Privatizing Russia*, p. 86.
35. Leonid Rozhetskin, interview by author, March 10, 1999.
36. Chubais, speech to the State Duma, April 12, 1994.
37. Chubais, *Privatizatzia*, p. 187.
38. Boycko [Boiko], Shleifer, and Vishny, *Privatizing Russia*, pp. 100–101.
39. Dmitry Vasiliev, press conference, July 13, 1999.
40. The voucher funds suffered from a crucial design error as well. Because Chubais and Vasiliev feared they could become too powerful, the funds were limited to owning 10 percent of any one company. This meant the funds were a weak voice in the boardrooms of the companies they owned. "The voucher funds failed because people feared they would become too powerful—and as a result we ended up with nothing," one of the designers told me.
41. Hans-Joerg Rudloff, interview by author, September 7, 2000; November 10, 2000.
42. Boris Jordan, interview by author, October 1, 2000.

43. Rudloff, interview by author, November 10, 2000.
44. Steven Jennings, interview by author, March 3, 2000.
45. Chernomyrdin, press conference, *Rossiiskie Vesti*, December 16, 1992, p. 1.
46. Anders Åslund, "Why Has Russia's Economic Transformation Been So Arduous?" (paper delivered at the World Bank Annual Bank Conference on Development Economics, April 28–30, 1999); Åslund, *"How Russia Became a Market Economy,"* (Washington, DC: Brookings Institution, 1995), pp. 191–193.
47. Mikhail Berger, interview by author, October 10, 2000.
48. Arkady Yevstafiev, interview by author, March 7, 2000.
49. "Anatoly Chubais: Up to 80 percent of State Property for Vouchers," *Literaturnaya Gazeta*, November 18, 1992, p. 10.
50. Chubais, interview by author, May 13, 2000.
51. Chubais, *Privatizatzia*, pp. 160–161.
52. I personally interviewed the intermediary, who asked to remain anonymous. When I asked Chubais about the contribution, he said, "Soros back then really played a positive role" but refused to discuss details.
53. *Literaturnaya Gazeta*, November 18, 1992, p. 10.
54. William Browder, interview by author, March 21, 2000.
55. Yulia Latynina, *Sovershenno Sekretno*, Moscow, August 1, 1999. Latynina added of Khodorkovsky's buying binge: "No public funds would have been sufficient for so extensive a program, but, fortunately, a large part of the enterprises were purchased at investment competitions, at which the winner was the one that promised to invest more money in the enterprise. As a consequence of Menatep's extreme attentiveness in regard to the government officials that organized the competition, and also to the 'red directors' in command of the enterprises, its promises were believed more often than those of others. Menatep was, generally, invariably courteous to the directors and would invariably toss them onto the garbage heap after the shares had been purchased."
56. Boycko [Boiko], Shleifer, and Vishny, *Privatizing Russia*, pp. 109, 119.
57. Chrystia Freeland, *Sale of the Century* (New York: Crown Business, 2000).
58. "Sale of the Century," *Economist*, May 14, 1994, p. 67. The article pointed out that the book value of Russian companies was fixed once, in January 1992, and was not adjusted even though Russian prices had risen 10,500 percent since then. The book value, which is based on the depreciated value of an enterprise's capital stock and takes no account of property or intangible assets, was still being used as the basis for the voucher auctions. Jordan was quoted as saying that there were still big risks. "These are extraordinarily low asset values, but you must be careful about using the word cheap," he said.
59. Chubais, interview by author, May 13, 2000.

EASY MONEY

1. Kadannikov interview, *Profil*, October 23, 2000, pp. 22–27. In Russian.
2. Bryan Brumley, "Factory Managers Back Privatization Plans, Criticize Financial Policy," Associated Press, October 26, 1992. Kadannikov opened a one-day meeting with Gaidar and cabinet ministers in Togliatti, praising privatization but criticizing the Gaidar government on financial and tax issues.

3. Bella Zlatkis, interview by author, October 18, 2000.
4. International Monetary Fund, "International Financial Statistics," quoted in *Evolution of Monetary Policy Instruments in Russia*, IMF Working Paper, December 1997, p. 17.
5. International Monetary Fund, *Relative Price Convergence in Russia*, IMF Working Paper, May 1995, p. 1.
6. Yegor Gaidar, *Days of Defeat and Victory* (Seattle: University of Washington Press, 1999), p. 80.
7. Yevgeny Myslovsky, *Beware: Swindle Invest, A Guide for Law Enforcement Agencies* (Moscow: Spas, 1996), p. 21.
8. Alexander Oslon, interview by author, May 29, 2000.
9. "Russian Car Alliance Starts Sales of Registered Stocks," *Business-Tass* (Moscow), December 14, 1993.
10. The founders, according to Leonid Valdman, deputy general director of AVVA, were Avtovaz, 25 percent; Logovaz, 15 percent; Forus Holding, a Swiss firm of Berezovsky's, 15 percent; the Russian Federal Property Fund, 15 percent; Obedinennie Bank (close to Berezovsky), 10 percent; Kuibyshevneft, an oil company, 10 percent; Samara Oblast administration, 5 percent; and Avtovazbank, 5 percent. The data accompanied a Valdman interview that was published November 4, 1994, in the magazine *Kommersant Vlast*.
11. "Car Consortium to Run Lottery," *Moscow Times*, February 18, 1994.
12. Yuri Zektser, interview by author, October 30, 2000.
13. Avtovaz was privatized by option 2, which meant 51 percent for workers and managers, 27 percent in voucher auctions, and 22 percent in an investment tender.
14. Yuli Dubov, *Bolshaya Paika* (Moscow: Vagrius, 2000), pp. 247–275. Many details described by Dubov are corroborated by other evidence, including news reports and AVVA annual reports.
15. Translations of the MMM commercials are from my own tape. However, I benefited from a superb analysis of the MMM advertising campaign as soap opera in *Consuming Russia: Popular Culture, Sex, and Society Since Gorbachev* (Durham, N.C.: Duke University Press, 1999). See chapter 3, Eliot Borenstein, "Public Offerings, MMM, and the Marketing of Melodrama" (pp. 49–75).
16. James Meek, "Russian Investment Firms Head for the Rocks," *Guardian* (London), April 28, 1994, p. 12.
17. Mary Darby, "In Ponzi We Trust," *Smithsonian Magazine*, December 1998.
18. Mikhail Dubik, "MMM: Is Seeing Success Believing?" *Moscow Times*, May 19, 1994.
19. Carey Goldberg, "It's Risky Business in Russia," *Los Angeles Times*, June 9, 1994, p. 1.
20. Golubkov was played by an actor, Vladimir Permyakov, who related his own rags-to-riches story. "I came from Siberia and dragged out a miserable existence playing occasionally at a small Moscow theater. I had no money and very little hope to succeed as an actor, but my work with MMM turned everything around." Mikhail Dubik, "Lyonya in the Flesh: A Tale of Rags to Riches," *Moscow Times*, August 25, 1994.
21. Depositor's information sheet, provided by Yevgeny Kovrov, director, Federal Fund for the Defense of the Rights of Depositors and Shareholders.

22. Goldberg, "Risky Business."
23. Yevgeny Kovrov, interview by author, April 28, 2000.
24. Helen Womack, "Gamblers Push MMM's Share Price Up Again," *Independent* (London), July 29, 1994, p. 12.
25. Russia's Itar-Tass news agency reported September 26, 2000, that investigators were still seeking Mavrodi's whereabouts.
26. Goldberg, "Risky Business."
27. Yevgeny Myslovsky, interview by author, October 10, 2000.
28. His comments were made on an NTV documentary, *Independent Investigation*, produced by Nilcolai Nikolayev, broadcast March 16, 2000.
29. Zektser, interview by author. He said AVVA had fulfilled the obligations of the investment tender, which called for $111 million to be invested in the factory by the end of 1995, but it is hard to see how AVVA accomplished this.
30. "Interview with the President of AO Avtovaz: V. Kadannikov," *Trud*, November 2, 1994. In Russian.
31. "Information Report about the General Meeting of Shareholders of the AOO All-Russian Automobile Alliance," *Ekonomika i Zhizen*, May 20, 1995. In Russian.
32. Kadannikov continued to mask the events years later. In an interview in April 2000, when asked whether he had used AVVA to seize Avtovaz, he replied, "I cannot quite understand why anybody would need a plant; why seize it? It's hard work, low profit. And what's the use in just making do with the turnover? You can do it for a couple of months, and then what?" He also blamed the government, saying it had "eaten up the people's money very fast." *Vedomosti*, April 5, 2000, p. A5.
33. Berezovsky interview, *Moscow News*, May 16, 1996.
34. Speculation finally came to an end in mid-1995 when the government and Central Bank announced a ruble-dollar "corridor" that limited currency movement and thus crimped the superprofits of traders.
35. Smolensky, interview by author, August 30, 1999.
36. Yegorov made the comments to the seventh congress of the Association of Russian Banks. "Chubais Tells Banks to Focus on Industry," *Moscow Times*, April 23, 1997.
37. "Learning to Lend," CentreInvest Securities, October 24, 1997, p 7.
38. Bank Menatep (Group), *Independent Auditors Report*, Arthur Andersen, 1995.
39. Former Menatep vice president, interview by author.
40. Vladimir Vinogradov, interview by author, June 28, 2000.
41. Yulia Latynina, "Mikhail Khodorkovsky: Chemistry and Life: Unknown Pages from the Life of a Superoligarch," *Sovershenno Sekretno*, August 1, 1999, pp. 3–5.
42. Victor Huaco, interview by author, April 14, 1999.
43. "MMM Deflates Shares, Russia Weighs Action on Stock Scandal," *Agence France Press*, July 29, 1994.
44. Grigory Satarov, a one-time adviser to Boris Yeltsin and president of INDEM, the Information for Democracy Fund, Mark Levin, an economics professor, and M. L. Tsirik, a graduate student, lay out this argument in their analytical study, "Russia and Corruption: Who Is Doing What to Whom?" prepared for the Council on Foreign and Defense Policy, Moscow, 1998. They concluded that among

the most important reasons for corruption in the new Russia, aside from historical ones, were "the rapid transition to a new economic system that was not supported by the necessary legal base and legal culture; the absence during Soviet times of a normal legal system and the corresponding cultural tradition; the collapse of the party control system."

45. "Diagnosis: Corruption: Is It Possible to Kill the Illness of Russia?" *Vechernaya Moskva*, October 18, 1999, p. 3. A roundtable discussion, in Russian.

THE MAN WHO REBUILT MOSCOW

1. Ryszard Kapuscinski, "The Temple and the Palace," *The New Yorker*, May 23, 1994.
2. Vladimir Mokrousov and Valentina Mokrousova, interview by author, November 3, 2000. In another sign of his caution, Makrousov submitted the mock-up twinned with another, the St. Georges Cathedral.
3. Flore Martinant de Preneuf, "The Historical and Political Significance of the Reconstruction of the Cathedral of Christ the Savior in Moscow" (M.Phil. thesis, Oxford, 1997), an excellent recounting of how the cathedral was rebuilt in the early 1990s.
4. De Prenuef, "Historical," p. 29.
5. Vasily Shakhnovsky, interview by author, November 26, 1999.
6. Mokrousova interview, November 3, 2000.
7. When I interviewed Luzhkov on February 5, 2001, he handed me a thirty-four-page response to questions I had posed in advance. Of the cathedral, he said, "I always believed that the revival of Russia must not begin with demagoguery on macroeconomic subjects but with spiritual revival. I thought the restoration of the cathedral—barbarically destroyed—was a symbol of this revival."
8. Andrei Zolotov Jr., "Resurrecting the Past," *Moscow Times*, August 19, 2000, p. iv; Mikhail Ogorodnikov, interview by author, November 2, 2000. Ogorodnikov is spokesman for the Fund for the Restoration of the Cathedral of Christ the Savior.
9. De Preneuf. This story is attributed to an engineer-metalworker interviewed on the site.
10. Ogorodnikov interview. In his written answers to my questions about the Cathedral, Luzhkov said, "Investments in the construction of the cathedral are voluntary contributions. Do you really think that people would have invested so much money for construction of more down-to-earth projects?" He claimed neither the city nor the federal government suffered "losses" as a result of the reconstruction. The project created thousands of jobs and boosted Moscow tourism, he noted.
11. Larisa Piyasheva, interview by author, March 23, 1999.
12. Popov news conference, December 19, 1991.
13. Luzhkov, interview, *Komsomolskaya Pravda*, November 26, 1997.
14. Luzhkov, interview, *Komsomolskaya Pravda*.
15. Valery Simonov, "Moscow Does Not Believe in Rubles?" *Komsomolskaya Pravda*, November 24, 1993, p. 1.
16. Luzhkov, written answers.

17. Luzhkov, interview, *Komsomolskaya Pravda.*
18. Chubais press conference, March 23, 1994.
19. Yeltsin news conference, June 10, 1994.
20. John Lloyd, "Russian Investment 'To Surge,'" *Financial Times*, July 5, 1994.
21. Andrei Shatalov, interview by author, February 14, 1997.
22. Luzhkov, interview by author, February 5, 2001.
23. Yaroslav Skvortsov, *Kommersant Vlast*, April 29, 1997.
24. Obid Jasinov, deputy general director, and other officials of Moscow Mechanized Construction no. 5, interview by author, February 12, 1997;"Moscow Construction: Together on the Path of Creation," *Moskovskaya Pravda*, January 29, 1997, p. 9.
25. Mikhail Moskvin-Tarkhanov, interview by author, November 2, 2000.
26. Tatyana Tsyba, "Why Do the Russians So Dislike Moscovites?" *Komsomolskaya Pravda*, February 12, 1997.
27. Pavel Bunich, interview by author, February 18, 1997.
28. Lee Hockstader, "Moscow Is a Haven of Haves amid Russia's Sea of Have-Nots," *Washington Post*, December 27, 1996, p. A1.
29. Donald Jensen, "The Boss: How Yuri Luzhkov Runs Moscow," *Demokratizatsiya*, Winter 2000, pp. 83–122.
30. Yegor Gaidar, "Why the Living Is Good in Moscow" (speech to the Moscow branch of the Democratic Choice of Russia Party, published in *Moscow News*, February 26, 1998); Gaidar press conference, February 6, 1998.
31. Luzhkov, written answers.
32. Vladimir Yevtushenkov, interview by author, April 9, 2000.
33. Yelena Baturina, interview by author, August 23, 1999.
34. Baturina interview.
35. Luzhkov, interview by author, February 5, 2001.
36. Baturina told me the Luzhniki contract was "my great luck and success," since her firm went on to win dozens more such contracts in Moscow and other Russian cities, as well as abroad. The stadium was 49 percent owned by the city. Baturina said she won a tender for the seats with a low bid, but, just as important, she said she was the only bidder with the correct specifications to meet the European standards.
37. Yuri Minkovski, "The First Underground Shopping Mall in the Heart of Moscow," *Cost Engineering*, February 1998, pp. 15–17. *Cost Engineering* is published by the American Association of Cost Engineers.
38. Natalya Shulyakovskaya, "Defining the Moscow Style," *Moscow Times Business Journal* 2 (1998): 6. Dozens of these useless spires could be seen in Moscow atop new glass-and-steel office buildings.
39. Leonid Filatyev, head of the coordination group for decoration of the cathedral, interview by author, December 6, 2000. "Take, for instance, the text inscribed on the dome at the top," he said. "How do you put the text in place so that it would exactly fit the length of the sphere? If you do it manually, it will take a long time. The computer can deal with this quickly and produce a print from which the painters can copy the drawing onto the wall. But the technique of painting was the original one from the nineteenth century."
40. "Moscow Celebrates," *Time*, September 8, 1997, p. 38.

41. Lee Hockstader, "Puttin' on the Ritz in Russia," *Washington Post*, August 3, 1995, p. 22.
42. Hockstader, "Moscow Is a Haven."
43. A long battle against the *propiska* was carried out by Veronika Kutsillo, a journalist who wanted to live in Moscow. She had grown up in Kazakhstan. As a student at Moscow State University, she had a permit, but when she graduated and got a job at the newspaper *Kommersant Daily*, she needed another to live permanently in the capital and to buy an apartment. The Moscow police said they would only give her the permit if she paid the "fee" for city services, then set at five hundred times the minimum wage, or about $2,000. "In my view this was completely groundless," Kutsillo told me. "They could not explain what the money was being taken for. They tried to explain it was for the metro, for using roads, movie theaters, and so forth. But any person who comes here pays to take the metro, pays for all of this." Kutsillo wanted the permit because she did not want to live as a second-class citizen; she wanted to be legal. "What does it mean not to have a *propiska*?" she asked. "A person can't get a license for a car without it, can't register a car in their name, can't go to the local health clinic, and you can't even call an ambulance without huge problems. I couldn't get married. If there are children, you can't send them to school, to nursery school, and you can't get a passport for travel abroad." Kutsillo had read all the federal laws on residency, which were clear that the only restrictions on freedom of movement could be war or catastrophe. There was neither in Moscow. Kutsillo appeared before the Russian Constitution Court to present her case personally and won a major decision on April 4, 1996. The court declared that although requiring people to register was permissible, the process could not be used as a "foundation for limiting a person's rights or freedoms." The court declared that every citizen "has a right for free movement, a right to choose a place of residence," and that paying a residency fee, as Moscow had required, "contradicts the right of citizens to freely choose a place of residence." The city government quickly responded. The mayor's press office issued a statement warning the news media not to portray Moscow as a "city without borders" or to say that people were free to come live in the city. The statement declared that "an endless inflow of people to reside here may be the end of Moscow, and this would be true for any other big city as well." Luzhkov formally canceled the *propiska.* But the mayor decided to try and implement it by another means—to demand a fee, slightly lower than before, from anyone who purchased an apartment in the city. A top city official said at the time, "The ruling of the Constitutional Court is mandatory for Moscow, but the life of the city will be determined by its own rules." Kutsillo had won a round, but the fight was not over. Two years later, on February 2, 1998, the Constitutional Court again upheld the principle of the Kutsillo case, that a city may register people only to "certify the act of the free expression of will of a citizen" to live there. The city cannot be "granting permission" or limiting where people choose to live, nor can it dictate how long a person can live in a particular place, the court said. Luzhkov's defiance of the court was clearly irritating the justices. One of them, Vladimir Yaroslavtsev, read a statement to Kutsillo's newspaper, *Kommersant Daily*, which had campaigned

against the *propiska*, saying, "We would like to warn Luzhkov and other regional heads: there will be no closed cities!" Eventually, a fee was created, of a thousand dollars or more, for transfer of real estate, so that the cost of getting residence was built into the purchase price of an apartment. Although Kutsillo had won in principle, the great wall around Moscow remained.

44. Chrystia Freeland, "Moscow: Mayor Says Nyet to Foreign Words," *Financial Times*, March 1, 1997.
45. Chrystia Freeland et al., "A Mayor with Attitude," *Financial Times*, November 4, 1996, p. 22.
46. Luzhkov, written answers. He added: "I also deal a lot with the problems of corruption. And not just every day, but every morning and every evening, and sometimes at night. To my deep belief, the increased criminalization of the economy and of life is the consequence of the economic system that was built by our liberal reformers, one more consequence of privatization." He also said, "In my view, the level of corruption in Moscow is relatively quite modest, by Russian standards." Although the situation in Moscow is not ideal, Luzhkov argued, the enormous investment in Moscow would not have come had corruption actually been so severe.
47. Julia Rubin, "U.S. Businessman Slain amid Russian Rivalry," Associated Press, November 28, 1996.
48. The U.S. embassy said the decision to revoke the visa was based on a provision of the law prohibiting entrance to "any alien who the Consular Officer or the Attorney General knows or has reason to believe seeks to enter the United States to engage solely, principally or incidentally in unlawful activity." Dzhabrailov angrily replied, "This is a disgrace for America. Have they any proof of this?" Nick Allen, "U.S. Revokes Radisson TV Chief's Visa," *Moscow Times*, November 30, 1996.
49. In the March 26, 2000, election, Dzhabrailov took last place, receiving 78,498 votes out of 75 million cast. He later boasted about the result with a new set of billboard advertisements.
50. Alessandra Stanley, "The Power Broker," *New York Times Magazine*, August 31, 1997, p. 44.
51. Luzhkov, written answers.
52. Andrew Kramer, "Detectives Fight Odds in Contract Hit Cases," *Moscow Times*, November 27, 1996.
53. Vladimir Yevtushenkov, interview by author, April 9, 2000.
54. Gaidar, "Why the Living Is Good."
55. Marina Rassafonova, "Yuri Luzhkov Failed to Defend His Honor and Dignity," *Kommersant Daily*, May 20, 1998; Anna Ostapchuk, "Luzhkov Against Gaidar," *Moscow News*, May 26, 1998; Alexander Fedorov, "Yuri Luzhkov Won in Court Claim to Yegor Gaidar," *Moskovska Pravda*, October 29, 1998.
56. Ana Uzelac, "Police: Moscow Official Put $700K in Switzerland," *Moscow Times*, November 25, 2000.
57. Adi Ignatius, "Mayor Yuri Luzhkov Leads a Capital City Rife with Corruption," *Wall Sreet Journal*, February 13, 1995, p. 1.
58. Mark Whitehouse, "Moscow Mayor Steals Political Spotlight," *Wall Street Journal*, May 20, 1999, p. 14.

59. Vladimir Yevtushenkov, interview by author, December 1, 1997; April 9, 2000. Yevtushenkov told me that, among his early business ventures, he helped Vladimir Vinogradov set up Inkombank, which became one of the largest commercial banks. My story on the rise of Systema appeared in the *Washington Post,* December 19, 1997, p. 1.
60. Natalya Shulyakovskaya, "A Family of Born Leaders," *Moscow Times*, February 9, 1999.
61. *Interfax Telecommunications Report,* February 4–10, 1998. The old exchange was removed in 1998.
62. Matt Bivens, "The Meteoric Rise of Luzhkov's System," *Moscow Times Business Review*, February 1999, p. 11.
63. Russian law stipulates that any auction must have a minimum of two bidders. Yevtushenkov said there were several bidders in this tender, but according to newspaper reports there was only one besides the Moscow Committee on Science and Technology, and the second bidder also had ties to Systema.
64. Perhaps one reason for their secrecy was a provision in the deal, not apparent at the time, that eventually allowed Yevtushenkov to take control of the phone company. Once he satisfied the investment requirements in the initial tender, the provision granted Yevtushenkov the right to issue new shares in the telephone giant. The phone company issued 638,634 new shares in addition to the 1.2 million already outstanding. This had the effect of allowing him to take control, increasing Systema's share to 59.9 percent of the voting shares of the phone company, a solid majority. When I heard about this provision in 1998, I was dumbfounded. I went back to the original 1995 fax I had received from the Moscow property committee describing the conditions of the tender. It said nothing about the right to issue new shares. The key provision in the privatization—which allowed Systema to bootstrap itself into control of Russia's largest city phone company—had been kept out of the public eye. The biggest loser was Svyazinvest, the largely state-owned national telephone holding company, which went from owning 46.6 percent of voting shares in the Moscow phone company to 27.9 percent.
65. Speaking to diplomats, journalists, and businessmen March 4, 1999, Luzhkov said, "I can officially tell you that all those myths that are spread around have nothing to do with reality. As far as Systema is concerned, attention to it is very high today, but many have tried to view Systema as some sort of extra pocket of the Moscow government, or a spare pocket for the mayor who has some sort of political motivations before the elections. Drop all these thoughts. We work honestly. We are not using what you suggest. And the suggestions themselves—when we read them—speak only to the bad taste of those who make them." Natalya Shulyakovskaya, "Luzhkov: I Don't Funnel City Deals to Wife," *Moscow Times*, March 5, 1999.
66. Alexei Ulyukaev, interview by author, October 31, 1997; Ulyukaev's essay on Moscow published October 13, 1997 in *Expert* magazine; and an unpublished, undated paper by Ulyukaev, "The Moscow Mayor's Appetite," p. 38. The prospectus was for the city's $500 million 1997 Eurobond.
67. Luzhkov press conference, March 10, 1995.

THE CLUB ON SPARROW HILL

1. The location was renamed Lenin Hills in 1935 but is still known by many as Sparrow Hills.
2. Vasily Shakhnovsky, interview by author, November 26, 1999; December 18, 2000.
3. Shakhnovsky, interview by author, and Leonid Nevzlin, interview by author, March 16, 2000; Mikhail Khodorkovsky, interview by author, June 19, 2000; Vladimir Vinogradov, interview by author, June 28, 2000; Alexander Smolensky, interview by author, August 30, 1999.
4. Anonymous source, notes of conversation with participant in the club meetings.
5. *Report of the Department for Public Relations of AO Logovaz,* undated, but prepared for a meeting in summer 1994.
6. He told me he did not stay there long. Boris Berezovsky, interview by author, December 20, 1996.
7. This gang warfare is described by Paul Klebnikov in *Godfather of the Kremlin: Boris Berezovsky and the Looting of Russia* (New York: Harcourt, 2000). However, much about this conflict remains unknown. It is not clear to what extent Berezovsky was a victim or a cause of the gang violence. It later became evident, during the Russian war in Chechnya, that Berezovsky enjoyed excellent connections with the Chechens.
8. Berezovsky, interview by author, February 28, 2001.
9. Leonid Boguslavsky, interview by author, May 16, 2000.
10. Ellen Mickiewicz, *Changing Channels: Television and the Struggle for Power in Russia* (Oxford: Oxford University Press, 1997), p. 238.
11. Igor Malashenko, interview by author, July 25, 2000.
12. For the channel, this was supposedly an improvement. Alexander Yakovlev, then chairman of Ostankino, said that when Reklama Holding was formed, the channel's revenues went from 5 billion rubles a month to 35 billion. Jean MacKenzie, "Listyev Killing Linked to TV Shakeup," *Moscow Times,* March 3, 1995. A lengthy, unsigned story in the magazine *Kommersant Weekly* on March 28, 1995, said that Channel 1 received 16 billion rubles in the first half of 1994. After the creation of Reklama Holding, the amount rose to 104 billion in the second half. Still others said that Reklama Holding was simply centralizing the same process of ripping off Channel 1 that had been carried out by the independent producers.
13. *Report of the Department for Public Relations of AO Logovaz.*
14. Stephanie Baker-Said, "TV Advertising Sales, Ad Time Up in 1996," *Moscow Times,* March 4, 1997, p. 3.
15. Berezovsky had both money and politics in mind. He was willing to take early losses in exchange for immediate political influence and big profits later. In our 1996 interview, Berezovsky told me that he invested in media for "influence on the political process. And at the same time, at the first stage, I understood it wasn't going to give profits. I don't want to talk about exact numbers, but I can say that ORT today is for me not a source of profits but a source of *enormous* expenditures." However, he said it could be "made *very* profitable," with the right investment. "These investments aren't enough today. But already today it is possible to attract big money." He summed up both reasons. "One is political:

the protection of my interests. And the second reason: it is business." He told me in 2001 that he lost control of ORT before ever realizing the big profits, but all of his hopes for political influence were fulfilled. "All the political tasks that I formulated for ORT were fulfilled."

16. On March 27, 1998, Berezovsky told a group of journalists that Aven introduced him to Yumashev.
17. Alexander Korzhakov's recollections are contained in his memoir, *Boris Yeltsin: From Dawn to Sunset* (Moscow: Interbook, 1997). Despite their once close relationship, Yeltsin and Korzhakov displayed great animosity toward each other after Korzhakov's 1996 dismissal. In his memoir, Yeltsin said he had not read Korzhakov's book, but "I am told it contains much untruth and sleaze. I decided not to read it because I couldn't contain my revulsion." He says Korzhakov was overpromoted and had "concentrated more power into his hands than he could handle." Yeltsin said Korzhakov's influence—appointing people in government, for example—is "entirely my fault." Yeltsin, *Midnight Diaries* (New York: PublicAffairs, 2000), p. 69.
18. Korzhakov made this comment on the television program *Sovershenno Sekretno*, November 21, 1999.
19. Korzhakov, *Boris Yeltsin*, p. 283.
20. Berezovsky recalled in the meeting with reporters in 1998, "Earlier than others, we started thinking about what was going to happen in 1996, and together we lobbied the idea of creating ORT."
21. The agreement between the new company, ORT, and Ostankino was published in *Rossiiskaya Gazeta*, February 16, 1995.
22. Berezovsky also gave Korzhakov power of attorney, turning all the shares over to Yeltsin in case there was any doubt about Berezovsky's loyalty. But this appears to have been more a gambit to reassure Korzhakov than anything else. Korzhakov said at a November 30, 1998, press conference that he never showed the documents to Yeltsin. Details of the authorization were first published in "Yeltsin Is Shareholder," *Kommersant Daily*, November 19, 1998.
23. Ivan Franko, "A Man Capable of Resolving Questions," *Kommersant Daily*, November 2, 1996, p. 15.
24. Berezovsky, interview by author, February 28, 2001.
25. Text of Yeltsin's remarks to Ostankino journalists, March 2, 1995, *BBC Summary of World Broadcasts*.
26. The killing was surrounded by a number of still unexplained events. I offer a summary here to give the reader a sense of the unanswered questions that followed the murder.

    The day before the murder, February 28, Berezovsky met with a man he has identified as Nikolai Plekhanov, a member of an underworld gang. According to Berezovsky, he was told by police who came with Plekhanov that the gangster knew who had planted the bomb attack against Berezovsky the previous year, and that Plekhanov had once again been ordered to assassinate him. Berezovsky said he gave Plekhanov $100,000 that day, in the presence of the militiamen. Berezovsky also videotaped the encounter. The money was intended to forestall another assassination attempt, Berezovsky said.

Berezovsky then flew off to London on an official trip with Chernomyrdin. Upon hearing about Listyev's murder, Berezovsky returned immediately by private jet to Moscow.

Two days after the murder, Berezovsky and one of the independent Channel 1 producers, Irena Lesnevskaya, recorded a videotaped appeal to Yeltsin. Berezovsky told me the tape was Lesnevskaya's idea. They had sought a meeting with Yeltsin, but Korzhakov insisted they make the tape instead. The tape was recorded in Korzhakov's office in the Kremlin. (Korzhakov said he never actually showed the tape to Yeltsin.) On the tape, they nervously pointed the finger at some vague, power-mad, spooky Moscow organization that included Gusinsky and Luzhkov. Lesnevskaya said, "I have no doubt that this logical scheme was built up by the Most group, by Mr. Gusinsky, Mr. Luzhkov, and the structure under him, a huge pyramid with islands; the former KGB came up with this [devious] plan to assassinate Vlad." A twenty-three-minute segment of the Berezovsky-Lesnevskaya tape was played by Korzhakov at a Moscow press conference November 30, 1998; a longer version is reproduced in Klebnikov, *Godfather.*

On the tape with Lesnevskaya, Berezovsky also complained at length about a long standoff with armed antiriot police outside the Logovaz mansion in the aftermath of Listyev's murder. They came wanting to search the club. Berezovsky refused to let them in but eventually, after phone calls to the general prosecutor (among others), agreed to be questioned. The investigators wanted a copy of the ORT charter, he said, and he gave it to them.

Three days after the killing, Berezovsky said, "I believe that reasons for the assassination of Vladislav Listyev are political, although many now speak about his commercial activities." In 1999, Berezovsky went further and accused Korzhakov and his circle of responsibility for the killing. Berezovsky said that Listyev's murder was linked to Korzhakov and former Federal Security Service director Mikhail Barsukov. The murder "was committed by this group of people," he said. Berezovsky told me that he believes Korzhakov attempted to frame him for the Listyev murder.

Lisovsky's offices were also searched after the murder. When I asked Lisovsky about it five and a half years later, he showed a flash of emotion and described bitter memories about what he called Listyev's arrogance. Lisovsky claimed the murder stemmed from Listyev's personal life or may have been an attempt to frame Lisovsky and others in the television business. "Naturally, this death made all of us who were members of the television community accomplices and witnesses," Lisovsky said. Lisovsky, interview by author, December 15, 2000.

27. Anonymous source, interview by author.
28. Berzovsky, interview by author, February 28, 2001.
29. Franko, "Man."
30. Julie Tolkacheva, "Moscow's Capitalist Elite: Wealthy and Wary," *Moscow Times*, July 22, 1994.
31. "Nikolai Glushkov: The Mass Media Should Know the Facts Earlier Than the Investigators," *Kommersant Daily,* November 23, 2000, p. 1. This article is an interview with Glushkov.
32. Sergei Zverev, interview by author, June 23, 2000.

33. Vladimir Gusinsky, interview by author, September 22, 2000.
34. John Lloyd, "The General with a Hot Line to Yeltsin," *Financial Times*, December 22, 1994, p. 3.
35. Korzhakov said in a 1999 television interview, "This was my decision, I did not let him out. I locked the plane and told Soskovyets, 'On you go.'" *Sovershenno Sekretno*, November 21, 1999.
36. "The Snow Is Falling," *Rossiyskaya Gazeta*, November 19, 1994.
37. Carlotta Gall and Thomas de Waal, *Chechnya: Calamity in the Caucasus* (New York: New York University Press, 1998). This book contains the best account of the origins of the war.
38. According to the account Gusinsky gave Chrystia Freeland in *Sale of the Century*, Rogozin also demanded that Gusinsky cough up some *kompromat* against Luzhkov.
39. Savostyanov was then head of the Moscow branch of the Federal Counterintelligence Service, which was a successor to the KGB and was later folded into the Federal Security Service (FSB), the main domestic federal security service.
40. Gusinsky, interview by author, September 22, 2000.
41. Yegveny Kiselyov, interview by author, August 2, 2000.
42. The Soviet war in Afghanistan, 1979–1989, had been hidden and propagandized.
43. Yuri Bogomolov, "News Battles Mirror 'Hot War,'" *Moscow News*, January 13, 1995.
44. Mickiewicz, *Changing Channels*, p. 256.

THE EMBRACE OF WEALTH AND POWER

1. Charles Ryan, interview by author, March 16, 1999; January 30, 2001.
2. The Russian government and Central Bank announced on August 24, 1995, that they would maintain the corridor, which had begun on July 5, until the end of the year. The outer limits were set at 4,300 and 4,900 rubles to the dollar. The ruble closed that day at 4,428 to the dollar. Chubais claimed that the first two months of the corridor had chilled speculation; before the limits were introduced, he said, about $1 billion a week was passing through exchange markets, which fell to $400 million.
3. The annual interest rates on these bonds was 262.9 percent in January 1995 and 236 percent in February, and it remained above 100 percent for eight months of that year, according to the Russian Central Bank, "Interest Rates in 1995," available at www.cbr.ru/eng/statistics/credit_statistics/print.asp/file=interest rates_95_e.htm.
4. Bank Menatep (Group) *Independent Auditor's Report,* Arthur Andersen, International Accounting Methods, 1995.
5. Mikhail Khodorkovsky, interview by author, June 19, 2000.
6. *Almanac of Russian Petroleum 1999* (New York: Energy Intelligence Group, 1999), p. 65.
7. Nat Moser and Peter Oppenheimer, "The Oil Industry: Structural Transformation and Corporate Governance," in Brigitte Granville and Peter Oppenheimer, eds., *Russia's Post-Communist Economy* (Oxford: Oxford University Press, 2001).
8. Khodorkovsky wrote an article in a Russian newspaper at the time describing

the "radical changes" in the old state-run structure of the oil industry, and its needs for new investment credits. Mikhail Khodorkovsky, "Investment Activity Is Vital for Russia's Fuel and Energy Sector," *Finansovye Izvestia*, November 19, 1992, p. 7. Menatep Bank also announced in 1992 that it was seeking outside credits to help the oil industry. In 1992 Khodorkovsky told Thane Gustafson, a long-time specialist in Soviet and Russian energy issues, that he was providing credits to the oil industry. Thane Gustafson, *Capitalism Russian-Style* (Cambridge: Cambridge University Press, 1999), p. 121.

9. Priobskoye field, discovered in 1992, occupies an area of 5,466 square kilometers along the Ob River, one hundred kilometers west of Nefteyugansk, with about 4.5 billion barrels of oil. Yuganskneftegaz has a license for about 72 percent of the field, the Northern Territory, according to a Yukos press release, October 28, 1999, on passage of production-sharing legislation for the field.
10. Stephen O'Sullivan, *Russian Oil: Financial Analysis*, MC Securities Ltd., London, February 26, 1997; "Yuganskneftegaz," MN-Fund, Moscow, undated; *Annual Report*, Yuganskneftegaz, May 1997.
11. Salomon Brothers, *Yuganskneftegaz*, June 25, 1996, p. 24.
12. One important reason why foreign investors bought stock in many of these oil extraction companies was availability. In the early 1990s it was not yet possible to buy shares in the big holding companies, which were just being created. Investors also thought the oil field extraction company stocks were cheap.
13. Dart bought other oil field stocks as well, but these two were the core of Yukos.
14. Alexei Mitrofanov, telephone interview by author, October 29, 1998.
15. Nina Yermakova and other teachers at School 58, interview by author, November 12, 1998.
16. Oleg Churilov, interview by author, March 1, 1999.
17. Oleg Klimov, interview by author, February 25, 1999.
18. Norilsk was a major player in global metals markets too. By 2001 Norilsk was producing 20 percent of the world's nickel, 20 percent of the platinum, and 40 percent of the palladium, according to company estimates.
19. Dun & Bradstreet Russia, *Unexim Group: Report on Financial-Industrial Group*, updated May 1997; Thompson Bankwatch, *Unexim Bank: Company Report*, September 27, 1996; Uneximbank annual reports and publications. The $300 million is Potanin's own estimate. The letter urging clients to join Potanin was quoted in *Kommersant Weekly*, June 1, 1992, and in *Kommersant Daily*, October 15, 1992, by reporter Dmitry Simonov, and again by Yaroslav Skvortsov and Mikhail Loginov in *Kommersant Daily*, November 16, 1995.
20. Thomson Bankwatch, *Unexim Bank: Company Report*, September 27, 1996. The bank's assets reached $3 billion by the end of 1995.
21. Boris Jordan, interview by author, October 1, 2000; Steven Jennings, interview by author, March 3, 2000.
22. "Who Will Buy Russia?" *Economist*, September 9, 1995, p. 73.
23. Dmitri Vasiliev, interview by author, September 16, 1999.
24. Anatoly Chubais, ed., *Privatizatzia Po-Rossiiski* (Moscow: Vagrius, 1999), p. 183.
25. Sergei Belyaev, interview by author, October 18, 1999.
26. Chubais, interview by author, May 13, 2000.

27. Vladmir Potanin, interview by Patricia Kranz of *Business Week,* September 8, 1997. Her article on Potanin, "Russia's Most Powerful Man," appeared in *Business Week,* November 24, 1997.
28. Paul Bograd, interview by author, March 26, 1999.
29. Khodorkovsky, interview by author, June 19, 2000.
30. Gaidar, interview by author, September 29, 2000.
31. William Flemming, "Business-State Relations in Post-Soviet Russia: The Politics of Second Phase Privatization, 1995–1997" (M.Phil. thesis, Oxford University, 1998). I am indebted to Flemming for his excellent research and thoughtful assistance on loans for shares, especially the important link with the 1996 election.
32. *Transition Report 1999* (London: European Bank for Reconstruction and Development), chap. 6, "Governance in Transition," p. 115.
33. Chubais later acknowledged, after the auctions were nearly over, that allowing the auctioneer to bid on the properties was a mistake. "Not for legal but rather for ethical reasons it can be said we made a mistake here," he told journalists December 15, 1995, promising it would not happen again. But in fact it did.
34. Alfred Kokh, *The Selling of the Soviet Empire* (New York: SPI, 1998), p. 121.
35. Alexander Vorobyev, "Amnesty's Effect on Corruption Case Prosecution Noted," *Rossiyskaya Gazeta,* January 18, 2000. Vorobyev was press secretary of the Interior Ministry unit, which investigated the deals and said the probe was dropped at the end of 1999 because of an amnesty statute approved by parliament.
36. The Khodorkovsky lieutenant told me this story.
37. The bankers, in a statement published November 26, accused Menatep of reneging on its earlier promised investments. They said Khodorkovsky won dozens of auctions with promises to invest $600 million in the factories that he took over but then failed to invest. "Practically not a single obligation was fulfilled by the bank," the bankers declared, mentioning Khodorkovsky's voracious appetite for factories: phosphates, aluminum, food, and steel, among others. Similar charges were made against Khodorkovsky in later years as well, that he scooped up companies at investment tenders without making the promised investments. Replying on December 10 in an interview published in *Kommersant Daily,* Khodorkovsky said he had not given absolute guarantees for the privatization tenders but instead had issued letters *promising* to make the other investments. A footnote in Menatep's 1995 audit said the banking group "has participated throughout 1995 in investment tenders and loan-for-shares auctions which resulted in drawing comfort letters with an expected value of investments up to Rbm 1,047,359. The comfort letters do not contain any obligation."
38. Chubais said in his December 15 press conference, "I wouldn't like to offend anybody, but some banks are known to have chosen such tactics for themselves: they needed these auctions, in which they had no funds to take part, in order to raise a hue and cry over rejection of their applications and then, relying on those scandals, to try and negotiate with the winners in a bid to get their share. Unfortunately, these tactics are quite well known and some banks pursued them in exactly this way. Such things did happen."
39. Menatep at the time held a 12 percent take in Smolensky's bank, the audit shows.
40. Chrystia Freeland, "Bidders Claim Exclusion from Russian Oil Sell-off," *Finan-*

cial Times, November 1, 1995, p. 3, and Freeland, "War of Words in the Reform Club: Protests are Growing over Russia's Privatization Program," *Financial Times*, December 2, 1995, p. 7.

41. Yuli Dubov, interview by author, May 3, 2000.
42. "Korzhakov Says Berezovsky Stole ORT," *Komsomolskaya Pravda*, January 28, 1999.
43. Leonid Krutalov, "Alexander Korzhakov: Sleeping with the Enemy," *Moskovsky Komsomolets*, November 3, 1999, p. 2.
44. Berezovsky, interview by author, February 28, 2001.
45. Berezovsky disclosed this in an interview published in *Nezavisimaya Gazeta*, February 3, 1998, p. 1.
46. Smolensky, who eschewed Russian industry, told me he knew of Potanin's efforts to organize loans for shares, but he didn't want any factories. He recalled that Potanin had organized meetings at his bank to choose the properties that would be included in loans for shares, but "I didn't visit a single time." However, he participated in raising the money for Berezovsky's investment in Sibneft, which he said was not budget money from the state but "real money."
47. Boiko's comments were made in an interview in *Kommersant Daily*, March 14, 1995, p. 3.
48. "Russia's Financial-Industrial Elite," a cable by Waller, May 26, 1995; Waller, multiple interviews by author, 1996–2000.
49. Thomas E. Graham, interview by author, June 22, 2000. Graham said that he originally wrote the essay for publication by the Moscow Center of the Carnegie Endowment for International Peace, but the text languished there and was picked up by Tretyakov instead.
50. Gusinsky took no chances. He came back just as President Clinton was visiting for a summit with Yeltsin to celebrate the fiftieth anniversary of the end of World War II. Gusinsky figured that no one would cause trouble while the U.S. president was in town, and he was right.

Saving Boris Yeltsin

1. Mikhail Berger, "Two Zyuganovs: One for West, One for Home?" *Izvestiya*, February 6, 1996, pp. 1–2; Berger, interview by author, January 17, 2001.
2. Anatoly Chubais, interview by author, May 13, 2000.
3. Arkady Yevstafiev, interview by author, March 7, 2000.
4. Chubais press conference, February 5, 1996.
5. Vladimir Gusinsky, interview by author, September 22, 2000.
6. Boris Berezovsky, interview by author, July 5, 1996.
7. Natalya Gevorkyan, "Young Russian Capital Helped the President Win the Election," *Kommersant Daily*, June 17, 1997, p. 4.
8. George Soros, *Open Society: Reforming Global Capitalism* (New York: PublicAffairs, 2000), p. 242.
9. Berezovsky, interview by author, February 28, 2001.
10. Berger told me that the two men discussed hiring Chubais for the campaign at that moment.

11. Chubais discussed the $5 million arrangement with a group of reporters on December 2, 1997. Earlier news reports stated that Smolensky gave an interest-free, five-year loan to Chubais of 14 billion rubles, then worth about $3 million, which was paid over three installments in March 1996 to the Chubais fund. This may have been just part of the sum which the tycoons paid Chubais. The newspaper *Izvestia* published the story of the $3 million interest-free loan on July 1, 1997, and Smolensky told me a similar story in a 1997 interview. Chubais, without mentioning the precise total, also said in a response to *Izvestia* on July 5, 1997, that he had created the center. "The foundation indeed conducted financial activity: we received an interest-free loan—which is absolutely normal in relations between social organizations, of which the fund was one, and commercial structures, both for Russia and any democratic country." Chubais said he paid 515 million rubles, or about $95,000, in taxes on his income of 1.7 billion rubles or $300,000 which he said was earned between his firing in January and his return to government service when appointed chief of Yeltsin's administration after the election. "The major part came from my truly well paid lectures and consulting services and for my work in the Center for Protection of Private Property, from which I came to the presidential administration." *Interfax*, January 21, 1997; Associated Press, "Lawmakers Accuse Chubais of Violating Civil Service Law," February 5, 1997.
12. Chubais, interview by author, May 13, 2000.
13. Boris Yeltsin, *Midnight Diaries* (New York: PublicAffairs, 2000), p. 17
14. Lee Hockstader and David Hoffman, "Yeltsin Campaign Rose from Tears to Triumph," *Washington Post*, July 7, 1996, p. 1.
15. Yevstafiev, interview by author, March 7, 2000.
16. Yeltsin, *Midnight Diaries*, p. 19
17. Berezovsky, interview by author, July 5, 1996.
18. Yeltsin, *Midnight Diaries*, p. 21
19. Alexander Oslon, interview by author, May 16, 1996.
20. Michael Kramer, "Rescuing Boris," *Time*, July 15, 1996, p. 28.
21. Korzhakov, appearance on *Sovershenno Sekretno*, November 21, 1999.
22. Vladimir Chernov, "If Papa Hadn't Become President," interview of Dyachenko, *Ogonyok*, October 23, 2000, p. 5.
23. Gevorkyan, "Young Russian Capital."
24. Anatoly Kulikov, "I Will Not Participate in Adventures," interview, *Nezavisimaya Gazeta*, July 23, 1999, p. 8.
25. Chernov, "Papa."
26. Karaganov, interview by author, November 9, 2000.
27. Yeltsin, *Midnight Diaries*, p. 25.
28. Yevgeny Kiselyov, *President of All Russia*, April 2000. Four-part NTV documentary.
29. Yeltsin, *Midnight Diaries*, p. 27.
30. Yavlinsky said Yeltsin once asked him to pull out before the first round. He refused. Kiselyov, *President of All Russia*.
31. Paul Bograd, "Summary of Electoral Strategy," memo to Chubais, April 25, 1996; Bograd, "Second Round Strategy," memo to Yevstafiev, May 7, 1996; Bograd,

"The 30 Percent Target: A Strategy for an Electoral Majority Based upon Economic Reform, Democratic Principles, and Strong Leadership," undated; Bograd, interview by author, March 26, 1999.

32. Mikhail Margelov, interview by author, November 2, 2000.
33. Alexei Levinson, interview by author, June 1996. Levinson is with the All-Russian Center for the Study of Public Opinion.
34. Hockstader, "Yeltsin Paying Top Ruble for Positive News Coverage," *Washington Post*, June 30, 1996, p. 1. The European Institute for the Media in Dusseldorf, which monitored the Russian elections and came up with the estimates, also said it counted 300 positive references to Yeltsin compared to 150 for Zyuganov.
35. Vladimir Vinogradov, interview by author, June 28, 2000.
36. Plenty of crisp $100 bills were available at the time too. In the spring of 1996, the U.S. Treasury replaced the old $100 bill with a new one that was better protected against counterfeiting. A very large supply of the new bills—millions of dollars worth—was shipped to Russia and kept for a while in the U.S. embassy in Moscow before being swapped for the old bills through the Russian banking system. The United States carried out a public relations campaign in Russia to reassure people that the new bill was legal tender.
37. Kiselyov, *President of All Russia.*
38. The newspaper *Novaya Gazeta* published a lengthy article on the subject in March 2000, stating that it had thirty-seven pages of documents, including the list of oligarchs and their structures that paid for the Yeltsin campaign. The article contained many tantalizing conclusions, including a similar description of the scheme of reprocessing the MinFin bonds. However, I was told by an informed source that the article was not produced by the newspaper but was received from an outside source and published verbatim. The identity of the outside source is not known.
39. Konstantin Kagalovsky, "Corruption in Defense of Democracy," *Sevodnya*, July 6, 1999, p. 1.
40. Victoria Clark, "Yeltsin's Man Stills His Master's Voice," *Observer*, May 5, 1996, p. 20.
41. Korzhakov, *Sovershenno Sekretno.*
42. Streletsky claims his men carried out a secret operation, late at night on June 18, to open the safe in the office of German Kuznetsov, deputy finance minister for international financial settlements. It was room 2–17 in the Russian White House, headquarters of the Chernomyrdin government. Streletsky said he suspected the room was at the core of the Chubais campaign finance operation. According to Streletsky's account, during the nighttime incursion, his men found $1.5 million in cash wrapped in plastic and blank forms for money transfers of $5 million each for printing services and advertising. The blanks showed that money was being transferred to the Bahamas and to Baltic divisions of American banks. The five blanks in the safe were numbers 19–23. If there were eighteen previous ones, he concluded, that meant a total of $115 million. Streletsky's men bugged the room, he said, listening to everything from the floor above, hoping to catch whoever drew cash from the safe. Streletsky is not a neutral source. He was attempting to disrupt the Chubais team, and his account should be read in that light. It seems strange that the Kremlin's own security service

had to bug the government's own building to gather information on Yeltsin's own campaign operatives. Streletsky's version of how the trap was set appeared in his book, *Obscurantism* (Moscow: Detektiv-Press, 1998).

43. Sergei Lisovsky, interview by author, December 15, 2000.
44. A tape of Lavrov's comments was made public on June 26, 1999, by Viktor Ilyukhin, chairman of the Duma security committee, a Soviet-era prosecutor who was close to Korzhakov.
45. Sergei Zverev, interview by author, June 23, 2000.
46. Chubais said in an NTV interview that Barsukov at first reacted to the call "like an astonished child," saying he did not even know Yevstafiev or Lisovsky. *Hero of the Day*, June 20, 1996.
47. Tape of Kiselyov bulletin; Christophe Beadufe, "Yeltsin Election Aides Arrested, Cancellation of Vote Feared," Agence France Presse, June 20, 1996.
48. Yevgeny Kiselyov, interview by author, August 2, 2000.
49. The real source of the $538,850 was never determined. Yevstafiev said he did not touch the box. When I asked Lisovsky about it four years later, he said, "It is altogether unclear" if there was a box of money. I replied, "It's not clear that there wasn't." Lisovsky retorted, "Let us stop here; that it's unclear if there was, and unclear if there wasn't." In December 1996, the popular broadsheet newspaper *Moskovsky Komsomolets*, which is part of Luzhkov's empire, published what it described as a transcript of a conversation between Chubais, Ilyushin, and a third man, identified as Sergei Krasavchenko. The conversation was supposedly secretly tape-recorded June 22 by the Russian "special services," two days after the detention of Yevstafiev and Lisovsky.

    Chubais expresses fear for the fate of his aides and suggests the documents in the case be hushed up. All three men called the transcript a fake, denying the meeting had taken place. The veracity of the transcript is not known. On April 7, 1997, the general prosecutor closed the investigation without finding out where the money came from. No one was charged with wrongdoing. An audit of the 1996 campaign said of the money: "There are no official documents confirming ownership of this sum by the federal budget or by a private or legal entity." The money was turned over to the government on April 17, 1997.
50. Berezovsky addressed the issue November 17 on NTV. His explanation included the statement that "I simply exercised the right of any Jew to formalize my relations with Israel. You know, Israel is a unique country. Any Jew, wherever he lives, has the right to be a citizen of Israel." He was describing the 1950 Law of Return: "Every Jew has the right to come to this country as an *oleh*" (a Jew immigrating to Israel) and that a visa for an *oleh* should be granted to "every Jew who has expressed his desire to settle in Israel." Many Israeli Jews also retain citizenship in other countries.
51. Berezovsky's desire for respect was severely dented by a highly critical article in *Forbes*, published in December 1996, headlined, "Godfather of the Kremlin?" He sued the magazine for libel in Britain. On March 6, 2003, prior to a trial, *Forbes* acknowledged in a British court that it did not have evidence to support some allegations in the article, and that "it was wrong to characterize Mr. Berezovsky as a mafia boss." Berezovsky dropped the libel suit.

52. A later estimate was that Gazprom loaned Gusinsky $130 million and the debt was converted to equity, giving Gazprom the 30 percent share in NTV.
53. Andrei Richter, interview by author, October 1996.

THE BANKERS' WAR

1. Anatoly Chubais interview, *New Times*, December 1996.
2. Boris Yeltsin, *Midnight Diaries* (New York: PublicAffairs, 2000), p. 80.
3. Boris Nemtsov, interview by author, November 1995.
4. "Man of Power," Chaubais interview, *Obshchaya Gazeta*, January 9–15, 1997, p. 9.
5. Dmitri Vasiliev, interview by author, September 16, 1999; November 20, 1999.
6. Nemtsov, interview by author, September 20, 1997.
7. Chubais recalled that on a visit to London, he and Nemtsov asked Prime Minister Tony Blair, "What do you think is better, Communism or bandit capitalism?" According to Chubais, Blair thought for a minute and said, "Bandit capitalism is better." Chubais added, "Absolutely right. And then the question arises, Bandit capitalism or normal capitalism? When this dilemma arises, you have to solve it." Chubais, remarks to reporters, December 2, 1997. Author's transcript.
8. Chubais later gave what I thought was a cogent description of the three competing models of capitalism in the late 1990s in Russia. "Position of Berezovsky: businessmen must control the *vlast*" (a word that means the authorities, the political powers). "Luzhkov's position: the *vlast* must control business." The young reformers, he said, wanted to "separate business from *vlast*—separate ownership from *vlast*." Chubais, remarks to reporters. Author's transcript.
9. Chubais, interview by author, May 13, 2000.

   Chubais also said at the time: "Imagine a situation in which a person who has earned a lot of money, who regards himself as the master of the country, reasons as follows: I got the president elected, I got the government appointed, and now it is the time for me to collect my dividends. Such an attitude is repulsive and unacceptable to me." Chubais, interview by V. Bazhenov, *Argumenty & Fakty*, November 20, 1997, p. 1.
10. Yeltsin, *Midnight Diaries*, p. 90.
11. Chubais, interview by author, May 13, 2000.
12. Steven Mufson and David Hoffman, "Russian Crash Shows Risks of Globalization; Speculators Ignored Economy's Realities," *Washington Post*, November 8, 1998, p. 1.
13. Anders Åslund, "Why Has Russia's Economic Transformation Been So Arduous?" (paper presented to the World Bank Annual Bank Conference on Development Economics, April 29–30, 1999). Åslund points out that another factor, in addition to Yeltsin's reelection, was the 1996 agreement for a three-year extended fund facility with the International Monetary Fund. These loans were conditioned on performance benchmarks by Russia, which were often not met. The "soft" agreement, Åslund says, "convinced foreigners and Russians alike that Russia was too big—or too nuclear—to fail, and that anything goes in Russia" (p. 12).
14. James Fenkner, interview by author, September 26, 1998.

15. I have heard many stories about these abuses. They were nicely summarized by Mark Whitehouse in the *Moscow Times*, "Dirty Dealing," April 7, 1998, p. 1.
16. Smolensky, interview by author, October 10, 1997; August 31, 1999.
17. Standard & Poor press release, July 14, 1997. The agency's "speculative grade long-term counterparty rating" for SBS-Agro was single-B and the outlook was "plus/positive," the best of the four banks rated.
18. Offering circular, SBS-Agro Finance B.V., prospectus, July 18, 1997.
19. Xavier Jordan, interview by author, July 1997; Jordan, telephone interview by author, October 6, 1997.
20. Had he been offered, Gusinsky confessed that he might have grabbed an oil company too. Gusinsky told me, "Had they invited me, it would have been a difficult decision for me to make. I think I would probably have participated if I had been invited."
21. The magazine was published in association with *Newsweek*, which is owned by the Washington Post Company. *Itogi* was typical of Gusinsky's start-ups: smart, entertaining and provocative. If you were exhausted from the political tedium all week long in the newspapers, you could look forward to reading *Itogi*, which was aimed at an intelligent, middle-class audience. Travel, leisure, and consumer goods were featured prominently, as well as thoughtful coverage of the arts.
22. Gusinsky had sought foreign investors for the stake, but it was still too early; he did not want to give up control, and they did not want to take the risks.
23. Alexei Mukhin, *Special Services and Their Representatives in Russian Society* (Moscow, 1999), pp. 35–36. Pamphlet. In Russian.
24. Gusinsky said the Italians wanted the stake, but "the military blocked the selling." Chubais said, "Gusinsky was helping to convince the special services that were categorically against the auction."
25. Gusinsky and Potanin confirmed this in October 1997 interviews, as did Andrei Trapeznikov, Chubais's press secretary. Gusinsky, interview by author, October 15, 1997; Potanin, interview by author, October 14, 1997; Trapeznikov, telephone interview by author, October 25, 1997.
26. Igor Malashenko, interview by author, March 7, 1997.
27. Gusinsky, interview by author, September 22, 2000.
28. Jordan and Potanin announced on July 9 that they were merging Jordan's Renaissance Capital with Potanin's International Financial Company. The merger did not go through until after the Svyazinvest auction, but the two were already working closely together.
29. Jordan, interview by author, October 1, 2000.
30. Soros, interview by author, June 1997.
31. Jordan, interview by author, May 22, 1998. The story of the loan was first disclosed by Chrystia Freeland, "Soros 'Lent Millions' to Bail Out Kremlin," *Financial Times*, March 5, 1998.
32. John Thornhill, "Robber Capitalism to Shareholder Rights: George Soros Has Overcome His Misgivings About Investing in Russia," *Financial Times*, July 30, 1997, p. 38.
33. Subscription agreement, July 24, 1997: "Subscription Agreement. Deutsche Bank AG and Open Joint Stock Company and 'United Export Import Bank' and

Renaissance Capital International Limited and Svyaz Finance Ltd. and Mustcom Limited and ICFI (Cyprus) Limited and The Investors and Renaissance Subscribers." Draft, July 23, 1997, in possession of the author.

34. This investor, who asked to remain anonymous, told me he bought into both Potanin's and Gusinsky's investment consortiums for Svyazinvest—it was so hot he wanted to be certain of winning something.

35. Potanin's strategy is described in official documents and internal memos on the deal, which I obtained from a potential investor.

36. Yeltsin, *Midnight Diaries*, p. 95.

37. Gusinsky, interview by author, October 15, 1997.

Potanin also confirmed that discussions about a merger or deal took place beforehand. In Potanin's version, "I proposed from the very beginning our participation in his consortium, where he is the leader. If we win together he can do whatever he wants." But Gusinsky refused.

38. Potanin, interview by author, October 14, 1997.

39. George Soros, *Open Society: Reforming Global Capitalism* (New York: PublicAffairs, 2000), p. 259.

40. Chubais, remarks to reporters, December 2, 1997, author's transcript.

41. Jordan's Renaissance Capital contributed about $200 million of the offered price. But he had brought in outside investors for the consortium, and if they won the auction, he stood to reap about $39 million in commissions, according to internal memos. The commissions would be even higher if the winning bid was over $1.5 billion.

42. Credinstalt investment bank estimated at the time the average value for telecommunications companies in emerging markets was $2,500 per line. "State Nets $1.9 Bln from Svyazinvest Sale," *Moscow Times*, July 26, 1997, p. 1.

43. Leonid Rozhetskin, interview by author, October 8, 1997; Sergei Zverev, interview by author, June 23, 2000.

44. Except where otherwise indicated, all quotations from broadcasts have been taken from verbatim transcripts.

45. Anton Zvyagilsky, "The Money Stank," *Sevodnya*, July 28, 1997, p. 1.

46. The second sale of Norilsk, the last chapter in loans for shares, had come just ten days after Svyazinvest. Potanin sold it to himself, as expected.

47. The context for this scandal had been set earlier. Minkin disclosed on August 4, 1997, in *Novaya Gazeta* the transcript of a conversation between Nemtsov and the advertising mogul Lisovsky. Nemtsov was quoted as saying he was owed $100,000 for an autobiographical book, *Provincial*, and he wanted the money urgently in order to declare it on his disclosure form. The financial disclosure forms were Nemtsov's own idea. Nemtsov says he is in a tight spot because Yeltsin is about to sign the decree requiring the disclosures, and he is afraid that if he leaves the money off his form, there will be criticism later. The public reaction to the disclosure was negative: $100,000 seemed like a huge sum for a book. Minkin's story on Kokh appeared soon thereafter. "Kokh Left His Chair to Avoid Going to Jail," *Novaya Gazeta*, August 18, 1997, p. 1.

48. Correspondent Yelena Masyuk and her NTV crew were kidnapped May 10, 1997, in Chechnya. They were released August 18 after Berezovsky paid a $1 million ransom.

49. Yeltsin, *Midnight Diaries*, p. 91.
50. Smolensky, interview by author, October 10, 1997.
51. The Yeltsin comments about Kokh and Potanin's offer were disclosed that evening by Khodorkovsky in a television interview by Kiselyov. *Hero of the Day*, NTV, September 16, 1997.
52. Yeltsin, *Midnight Diaries*, pp. 88–101.
53. Soros, *Open Society*, p. 245.
54. "Berezovsky Backs Revocation of Visa for Financier Jordan," *Moscow Times*, October 11, 1997.
55. Chrystia Freeland, *Sale of the Century* (New York: Crown Business, 2000), p. 288.
56. Kokh, interview by author, May 14, 2000. An investigation by the Moscow prosecutor was closed in December 1999 because the Duma passed a broad amnesty for minor offenses that precluded prosecution.
57. These included Yumashev, who was Yeltsin's chief of staff, and later Alexander Voloshin, who succeeded him. Both had worked with or had been close to Berezovsky, not to mention Berezovsky's ties to Dyachenko from the 1996 campaign onward.
58. Lisovsky, interview by author, December 15, 2000.
59. Chubais, remarks to reporters, December 2, 1997, author's transcript.
60. Chubais, interview by V. Bazhenov, *Argumenty & Fakty*, November 20, 1997, p. 1.
61. Chubais, remarks to reporters, December 2, 1997, author's transcript.
62. Chubais interview, *Moskovsky Komsomolets*, December 19, 1997, p. 2.
63. Yeltsin's press secretary, Sergei Yastrzhembsky, said at the time that Yeltsin was taken to Barvikha, but later it was disclosed he had also been taken to the hospital where he had his heart operation.

ROAR OF THE DRAGONS

1. Eric Kraus, interview by author, January 22, 2001.
2. In one sign of this expansion, Khodorkovsky was poised to gain full control of a giant Siberian oil field. In 1993 Amoco won an international tender for 50 percent of the huge Priobskoye field, which was then held by Yuganskneftegaz. When Khodorkovsky took over Yuganskneftegaz and its holding company, Yukos, in 1995, he proposed new terms. Amoco refused to accept the new terms and the deal was paralyzed for several years. In 1998 Amoco was merged into BP, and the joint company abandoned the Priobskoye field on March 19, 1999, after investing more than $100 million.
3. Andrei Sheatov, "Russian Oil Tycoon Plans to Place Among Ten World Oil Firms," Itar-Tass dispatch from Khodorkovsky's appearance before the Russian-American Business Council in Washington, October 23, 1997.
4. Yukos consolidated financial statements for the year ending December 31, 1997, published June 26, 1998, by Price Waterhouse; "Preliminary Information Memorandum," Yukos Oil Corporation, Five-Year Export Secured Credit Facility, March 1998.
5. This practice, transfer pricing, was controversial yet widespread in the Russian oil industry at the time. According to analysts Nat Moser and Peter Oppenheimer, Yukos recorded an after-tax profit in 1996 of $91.5 million while the oil

extraction companies Yuganskneftegaz and Samaraneftegaz lost $345 million. In 1996 Yuganskneftegaz lost $195 million alone through transfer pricing. Moser and Oppenheimer, "The Oil Industry: Structural Transformation and Corporate Governance," in Brigitte Granville and Peter Oppenheimer, eds., *Russia's Post-Communist Economy* (Oxford: Oxford University Press, 2001.)

6. Hunter of Arrowhead Enterprises Ltd., an investment company of Dart, made the "looting" comment to the *Financial Times*, March 11, 1998. Hunter further detailed the allegations in two letters to Jon S. Corzine, chairman and chief executive officer, Goldman Sachs, January 28 and February 17, 1998. The three banks replied perfunctorily that they could not disclose "any information" about the loan.
7. *Nezavisimaya Gazeta*, a broadsheet newspaper written for the intelligentsia,the first truly independent paper born in *perestroika*, fell on hard times in the mid-1990s. After an internal staff dispute, the paper locked its doors and stopped publishing. Editor Vitaly Tretyakov went to a tiny Greek island for a holiday. Berezovsky flew a helicopter to the island, flew him back to Moscow on a chartered plane, paid for guards to break open the doors, and took over as financial sponsor of the paper, which had virtually no advertising. Vitaly Tretyakov, interview by author, March 10, 1997.
8. Andrew Higgins, "Insufficient Funds: How a Russian Banker Outfoxed Creditors to Rebuild an Empire," *Wall Street Journal*, October 4, 2000, p. 1.
9. Foreign liabilities of the Russian banking system—money raised abroad—rose from 11 percent to 17.5 percent of total liabilities during 1997. "Ruble Crisis Again," *Russian Economic Trends*, June 1998.
10. Credit Suisse First Boston, in a research note on the merger, made a similar point: "In our view, the main benefits of the merger to the group are greater political clout and greater visibility. The combination of the political clout of Mr. Khodorkovsky and Mr. Berezovsky will make Yuksi a powerful lobbyist within Russia."
11. *Trud*, March 4, 1998, p. 2.
12. Anatoly Chubais, "I Am Against the Board of Directors of Russia," interview by Yevgenia Albats, *Kommersant Daily*, March 5, 1998, p. 1.
13. Alexander Budberg, "Chicago Boys Never Give Up," *Moskovsky Komsomolets*, March 5, 1998, p. 2.
14. *Nezavisimaya Gazeta*, "Venal Newspaper, Venal Journalists, Venal Chief Editor!" March 8, 1998, p. 1.
15. Berezovsky said on *Itogi* (NTV) on March 22 that he suffered a broken spine and underwent surgery in Switzerland. He was discharged from the hospital March 13, 1998, but continued to undergo rehabilitation until returning to Moscow.
16. Boris Berezovsky, interview by author, February 28, 2001.
17. Vladimir Gusinsky, interview by author, June 7, 2001.
18. Berezovsky, interview by author, February 28, 2001.
19. *Moscow News*, February 26-March 4, 1998, pp. 1–4.
20. Sergei Karaganov, interview by author, November 9, 2000.
21. *Itogi*, March 22, 1998. Berezovsky later told me that when he taped the interview, he did not know Yeltsin would announce the decision to fire Chernomyr-

din on Monday. Kiselyov, who conducted the interview, recalled that Berezovsky flew back to Switzerland for more back treatments—which he might not have done had he known Yeltsin was about to act.

22. Alessandra Stanley, "Shake-up in Russia: The Meaning; The Reformers Did It. No, Blame the Bankers," *New York Times*, March 24, 1998, p. 8.
23. Kiriyenko was confirmed on April 24 in a secret ballot by a vote of 251 to 25 in the 450-member chamber.
24. Berezovsky said in an interview on NTV's *Hero of the Day*, April 16, that Yeltsin had called him and they had had a "friendly and constructive conversation."
25. Andrei Bagrov, "Yeltsin Threatens Berezovsky with Deportation," *Kommersant Daily*, April 15, 1998, p. 1.
26. Andrei Piontkovsky, interview by author, May 1998.
27. Repeated attempts to fiddle with the currency led to panic and public distrust. The Soviet government decreed on January 22, 1991, that all fifty- and one hundred-ruble banknotes would have to be exchanged in three days in order to reduce the money supply, setting off a panic. Many people could not change their money in time. In 1993 Yeltsin's government stumbled badly over a plan to force everyone to change their Soviet-era rubles into new Russian banknotes. In addition, hyperinflation during the early 1990s wiped out the savings of millions of people. And on "Black Tuesday," October 11, 1994, the ruble plunged 27 percent against the dollar. The lesson many Russians took from this period was, Keep your money in dollars.
28. Chubais interview, *Interfax-AiF*, March 23–29, 1998, pp. 2–3.
29. Glifford G. Gaddy and Barry W. Ickes, "Russia's Virtual Economy," *Foreign Affairs*, September-October 1998, p. 53. This important article called attention to the powerful distortions caused by barter and nonpayments.
30. Tax dodging was endemic, in part because the taxes were punitive and the code unreformed. However, economist Al Breach pointed out an additional factor. In an economy that was awash in barter transactions—a factory would trade its refrigerators for a two-month supply of electricity or swap metal pipe for a truckload of socks—it was extremely difficult to collect taxes in cash. Breach calculated that cash made up only 60 percent of the tax revenues in 1997, and trying to extract more in the barter economy was like "trying to suck water out of a stone." It was impossible in this environment to raise enough taxes to balance the budget, he said; the only thing to do was slash spending further, which is the one thing Russian politicians refused to do. Kiriyenko tried, but it was too late. Al Breach, *Russia: Now a Competitive Exchange Rate—The Revival of the Real Economy*, Global Economics Paper no. 22, Goldman Sachs, July 23, 1999. The problem of demonetization of the economy, the disappearance of cash, was severe and plagued enterprises as well as the government. Chubais said in Washington on July 21, 1998, that Unified Energy Systems, the electricity monopoly that he headed, collected only 14 percent of its payments in cash and 86 percent in barter, "which is awful."
31. The IMF loans were supposed to be linked to conditions that Russia would make key reforms, but the conditions were often softened or bent when Russian reforms fell short. Between the admittance of Russian to the IMF on June 1,

1992, and September 1, 1998, the International Monetary Fund provided Russia with about $18.8 billion. The loans approved in approximate dollar terms were as follows: a standby arrangement, August 5, 1992, to January 4, 1993, $1.1 billion; systemic transformation facility, July 6, 1993, to April 10, 1995, $2.9 billion; standby arrangements, April 11, 1995, to March 26, 1996, $6.8 billion; extended fund facility, March 26, 1996, to March 25, 1999, $10 billion (not including the rescue package approved by the IMF in 1998, which was only partially disbursed). Andrei Illarionov, director, Institute of Economic Analysis, testimony before the House Banking and Financial Services Committee, General Oversight and Investigations Subcommittee, September 10, 1998.

32. Gary Peach, "Pyramid Crash Began on Fool's Day," *Moscow Times*, August 17, 1999.
33. More than twenty regions issued their own bonds. One of the more bizarre debt schemes was the agro-bond, a short-term debt paper that represented restructured federal agricultural loans to the regions. By some estimates $830 million in these bonds was outstanding at 1998 precrash exchange rates, and 90 percent of them later went into default. Sujata Rao, *Moscow Times*, April 27, 1999, p. 15.
34. *The Crisis of the Russian Financial System: Key Factors, Economic Policies, and Initial Results*, Institute for the Economy in Transition, 2000, p. 26.
35. International Reserves in 1997, Central Bank of Russia.
36. Sergei Aleksashenko, *Fight for the Ruble* (Moscow: AlmaMater, 1999), p. 129.
37. "T-Bill Market Suffers Biggest Crisis in Its History," *Interfax*, July 29, 1998.
38. *Forwards Are Not the Way Forward*, Troika Dialog Research, November 1998. An indication that the sum was higher came from Vinogradov, who told me he held $2.5 billion as of the August 17 crash. Reporting requirements for banks were skimpy, and information remains incomplete. The $9 billion estimate is from *Surviving Devaluation*, a research report by Brunswick Warburg, June 8, 1998, p. 9.
39. Budberg, "Chicago Boys." Chubais recalled Luzhkov declaring that "the age of monetarism is over." But Chubais answered that monetarism had worked. "The sole reason we can seriously talk about economic growth today is that it was preceded by six years of tough monetarism." Monetarism generally refers to an economic policy in which the money supply is tightly restricted in order to control inflation. The ruble corridor was the mechanism for controlling the money supply, and it meant that the Central Bank dramatically reduced the massive subsidies and cheap credits issued in earlier years. This approach was never really understood by the Soviet-era red directors, who were accustomed to receiving enormous infusions of subsidies.
40. Illarionov later said he also watched the reserves as compared to the total foreign investment in Russian bonds: if all the overseas investors pulled out, would the Central Bank have enough currency to pay off the bonds? As of January 1, 1998, the bank held $12.9 billion in currency reserves and $4.8 billion in illiquid gold reserves. Foreigners held about $18 billion of outstanding Russian treasury bills.
41. Andrei Illarionov, interview by author, October 14, 1999.
42. Pyotr Aven, interview by author, October 22, 1999.
43. Chubais, interview by author, May 13, 2000.

44. Yuri Baturin et al, *Epokha Yeltsina* (The Yeltsin Epoch) (Moscow: Vagrius, 2001), pp. 727–750. This work is a collective memoir by a group of Yeltsin's Kremlin aides.
45. Baturin et al., *Epokha Yeltsina.*
46. Bernie Sucher, interview by author, October 8 and 29, 1999.
47. The situation was never black and white, however. Some market participants also failed to see the devaluation coming until it was too late. Brunswick Warburg's June 8 report stated, "We believe a collapse in the ruble can now be avoided."
48. Illarionov, testimony before the House committee.
49. Augusto Lopez-Claros, interview by author, September 17, 1999; April 13, 2000.
50. Yeltsin, *Midnight Diaries,* p. 169.
51. Baturin et al., *Epokha Yeltsina.*
52. Malashenko, interview by author, July 25, 2000.
53. Chubais, interview by author, February 20, 2001; Bill Powell and Yevgenia Albats, "Summer of Discontent," *Newsweek*, January 18, 1999; Chrystia Freeland, *Sale of the Century* (New York: Crown Business, 2000), pp. 308–309.
54. Berezovsky, interview by author, February 28, 2001.
55. Chubais, interview by author, February 20, 2001.
56. Grigory Glazkov, interview by author, December 1, 1999.
57. Itar-Tass, June 19, 1998.
58. Aleksashenko, *Fight*, pp. 169–171.
59. Joseph Kahn and Timothy O'Brien, "For Russia and Its U.S. Bankers, Match Wasn't Made in Heaven," *New York Times*, October 18, 1998, p. 1.
60. Baturin et al., *Epokha Yeltsina*; Charles Wyplosz and Ksenia Yudaeva, "The Costs of Debt Conversion: Russia and Mexico Compared," *Russian Economic Trends Quarterly*, October-December, 1998; Homi Kharas, Brian Pinto, Sergei Ulatov, Lawrence H. Summers, and John Williamson, "An Analysis of Russia's 1998 Meltdown: Fundamentals and Market Signals/Comments and Discussion," Brookings Papers on Economic Activity, Brookings Institution, Washington, DC, 2001. The latter study concluded that Russia made a mistake taking on so much debt in the summer of 1998. The country took on $16 billion in external debt between June 1 and July 24, 1998. This, combined with the exposure of Russian banks, "was what triggered the August crisis," the authors concluded.
61. Letter from Credit Lionnais S.A., Goldman Sachs International Bank, and Merrill Lynch Capital Markets Bank Ltd., to Dmitry Vasiliev, August 14, 1998.
62. Leonid Gozman, interview by author, October 27, 1999.
63. Illarionov told me that Sberbank was the largest player to withdraw from the GKO market in the two weeks before August 14, and he questioned whether the Central Bank had influenced this decision. Illarionov said he believed the Central Bank was playing political games, trying to undermine the Kiriyenko government, perhaps to deflect the blame for any crisis over a coming devaluation. The Central Bank in late July mysteriously froze the Finance Ministry accounts for several days, paralyzing its ability to make routine payments. Yeltsin had to intervene, according to the memoir by Baturin and colleagues. Dmitri Vasiliev, a frequent critic of the Central Bank, also mentioned this episode as an example of how the bank was playing a dangerous political game with the government. "It

was a complete, 100 percent provocation," Vasiliev said of the freeze on the accounts. "I think they wanted to either overturn the government or make the government do something—to have them be the first to do it."

64. Baturin et al., *Epokha Yeltsina.*
65. Soros said he offered some ideas for a public-private fund but was overtaken by events. George Soros, *Open Society: Reforming Global Capitalism* (New York: PublicAffairs, 2000), pp. 247–250.
66. "Yeltsin Denies Plans to Devalue Ruble, Says Markets Under Control," *Interfax*, August 14, 1998.
67. Aleksashenko, *Fight*, p. 199.
68. Yevgenia Albats, "Anatoly Chubais: We Await a Difficult Year and a Half or Two Years," *Kommersant Daily*, September 8, 1998, p. 1.
69. Aven, interview by author, October 22, 1999.
70. Yeltsin, *Midnight Diaries*, p. 175.
71. Albats, "Anatoly Chubais." Chubais read from the computer file to Albats in this interview. Chubais also addressed the issue of deception of investors. A devaluation or default on GKOs earlier in the year "would have been perceived in an extremely negative way around the world," he said. "By not doing it back then, we demonstrated that the government was struggling to the end. It undertook all the possible thinkable and unthinkable efforts not to fail the expectations of our partners both inside the country and abroad.... Right, it did not work. Right, we failed. It was impossible to wait longer to take the decisions that were made on August 17. The abyss was next." Chubais defended Yeltsin for lying about the coming devaluation on August 14. "This is exactly what needed to be said," Chubais insisted. "Any sober-minded politician will tell you that unfortunately this is exactly how the authorities must behave in such extreme situations.... authorities have no right to announce in a difficult financial situation, 'We don't know if we are going to cope or not,' [people] will start running away at once." Chubais was then asked if the authorities have a right to lie. "In such a situation, it is the duty of the authorities to do it. They are o-b-l-i-g-e-d to. Hence now, the international financial institutions, despite everything we did to them—and we cheated them for $20 billion—there is an understanding that we had no other way out any longer, and had we done it the way suggested by Illarionov, they would have stopped doing business with us forever. That is, that catastrophe would have been the same as now, but any hope that investors would return would have been lost." This remark caused a stir when the *Los Angeles Times* quoted Chubais as saying Russia had "conned" the IMF out of $20 billion. Chubais replied in a letter to the newspaper that he meant the $20 billion was "cheated" from foreign creditors by Russian banks taking advantage of the moratorium. Albats told me that Chubais in the interview was referring to foreign investors, not the IMF.
72. Chubais did not know how the IMF would react until a statement was released the morning of the decision, in which Camdessus reiterated the view that it was important for Russia to carry out reforms. He went on, "It is important that the international community as a whole, both public and private sectors, show solidarity for Russia at this difficult time." Chubais was relieved.

73. Andrei Trapeznikov and Leonid Gozman, interview by author, August 20, 1998.
74. Vinogradov, interview by author, June 28, 2000.
75. Former Menatep Bank official who asked to remain anonymous.
76. Monthly consumer inflation shot up 38 percent in September, but the hyperinflation that some predicted would follow devaluation never appeared.
77. Organization of Economic Cooperation and Development, *Russian Federation Report*, March 2000, p. 44.
78. Natalya Gridneva, "Former Prime Minister Sergei Kiriyenko Tells All About Dismissal," *Kommersant Daily*, January 19, 1999.
79. Berezovsky, interview by author, February 28, 2001.
80. "Resolving the Banking Crisis," *Russian Economic Trends*, November 1998, pp. 1–8.
81. Dubinin press conference, September 7, 1998.
82. Dubinin press conference, September 7, 1998.
83. Jeanne Whalen, "SBS-Agro Chief Faces Fall of Empire," *Moscow Times*, September 12, 1998.
84. Higgins, "Insufficient Funds."

HARDBALL AND SILVER BULLETS

1. Vladimir Gusinsky, interview by author, May 4, 2001. Gusinsky also was proud of the fact that the satellite would make his television truly independent, as his signal would be outside the control of the state.
2. By one estimate, annual NTV revenues prior to the crash exceeded $100 million. *Kommersant Vlast*, January 27, 1998. The station was Russia's most profitable major television broadcaster before the crash, but it suffered a net loss of $25 million in the following year. Chris Renaud, letter to the editor, *Wall Street Journal Europe*, April 30, 2001.
3. Gusinsky's enterprise experienced other troubles as well. The global shift from analog to digital signals for satellite television came just as NTV-Plus was taking off. The Bonum-1 satellite was digital, but Gusinsky had trouble managing it. One NTV official told me that NTV-Plus went through five different managers in this period.
4. In late August, 936 Moscow residents were polled by the All-Russian Center for the Study of Public Opinion, one of Russia's leading pollsters. The results were published in *Moskovskaya Pravda* on September 4, 1998. The question was: "Who in your opinion is guilty first of all for the present financial crisis in Russia?" The former government of Chernomyrdin received 38 percent; Yeltsin, 36 percent; the government of Kiriyenko, 15 percent; oligarchs, bankers, and financiers, 9 percent; the State Duma, 8 percent; policies of the reformers-democrats, 8 percent; Central Bank (Sergei Dubinin), 6 percent; global financial crisis, 2 percent; foreign banks and financiers, 1 percent; those who do not pay taxes, 1 percent; others, 10 percent; difficult to say, 14 percent. (Respondents were allowed to choose more than one item, so the results exceed 100 percent.) A similar poll of 1,862 people nationwide taken at the same time showed that a far larger number of people in the nationwide sample—56 percent—blamed Yeltsin.

5. Zyuganov circulated an open letter including these remarks, *Washington Post*, December 25, 1998, p. A42.
6. In the summer of 1998, before the crash, workers in Nefteyugansk held a rally to denounce Yukos for months of unpaid wages. The rally was led by Mayor Vladimir Petrukhov. The mayor had sent telegrams to Yeltsin, Kiriyenko, and others in June denouncing Khodorkovsky and Yukos, saying they were "suffocating" the town. At the rally one protester held a sign reading "Bring Khodorkovsky to Justice." On June 26, Petrukhov was shot and killed as he walked to work. The murderer was never found. Yukos said it had nothing to do with the crime.
7. West Merchant was a London-based subsidiary of West LB, a huge German bank based in Dusseldorf.
8. Kathleen Day, "Riggs Had Ties to Firms in Probe," *Washington Post*, September 18, 1999, p. E1.
9. The reformers and liberals acknowledged that capital flight was a problem, but they took a classic free market view: that capital flight could only be stopped when the conditions were created inside Russia to attract capital into the country, namely, stability, rule of law, and protection of property rights. In theory they were right, but practically those conditions did not exist in the lawless, chaotic years of the 1990s. Waiting for the right conditions meant watching capital flee at a debilitating pace.
10. It is not unusual for countries to park their currency reserves abroad in safe securities or bonds of other countries. But it is highly unusual for a country to turn over its reserves to a small, little-known management company like this one. The Central Bank claimed it was trying to shield reserves from threat of legal seizure. However, Eric Kraus pointed out, "If you are going to shelter Central Bank assets, you don't set up a Jersey shell company which any bright divorce lawyer could crack open in an afternoon." Moreover, many of the transactions remain unexplained and look suspicious. For example, the Central Bank used the offshore shell company to make secret backdoor investments in high-yielding Russian government bonds known as GKOs, according to my own research and a letter from PricewaterhouseCoopers to Gerashchenko, August 4, 1999.
11. Dart was also angry at Khodorkovsky's ridiculously low offer to buy out his shares. According to a worksheet from AB Image, a public relations agency representing Dart Management, Khodorkovsky offered to pay fifty-four cents a share. That valued Yuganskneftegaz at $22 million. However, the subsidiary's annual production of 25 million tons of oil was worth $2 billion in global export prices at the time. Khodorkovsky offered thirty-two cents per share for Samaraneftegaz, or a valuation of the subsidiary at $11 million, when its annual production was worth $840 million on global markets. His offer was eleven cents per share for Tomskneft, for a valuation of $3.1 million, compared to annual production worth $640 million.
12. The Russian Joint Stock Company law had a provision on so-called interested party transactions. The idea was to avoid a conflict of interest in which the people who control decisions to sell assets or shares, the "interested party," could sell the assets to themselves or companies they controlled. If Khodorkovsky controlled the offshore companies, then voting to sell the subsidiaries to them could break the law. However, enforcement was weak.

13. It is impossible to estimate what price Dart paid initially. Shares in Yuganskneftegaz, for example, traded from $5 a share at the outset in mid–1994 to as much as $40 a share when the market reached its peak later in the year, and later fell again to below $5 a share. Dart may have been one of the two or three largest private investors in Russia in the mid 1990s, although he was very secretive about his holdings.
14. Telephone statement by Daiwa Europe Ltd. to the author, undated.
15. Gleb Pyanikh, *Kommersant Daily*, May 29, 1999, p. 1.
16. One reason Potanin and Jordan were forced to back down was a public campaign against the dilution waged by William Browder, the successful fund manager, who had a $100 million stake in Sidanco and was furious at their plans to reduce his stake.
17. World Bank, *Capital Development Project, Technical Annex*, May 6, 1996, pp. 9, 28.
18. Mark D'Anastasio, interview by author, May 29, 2001. Burson-Marsteller's work for Khodorkovsky included the use of press interviews to improve his image during a visit to the United States in the spring of 1999, just as Vasiliev was conducting his investigation. Khodorkovsky spoke for eight hours to a *New York Times* reporter on this trip. But the result was not what Khodorkovsky had intended. The article was not published until September, and it came just as new allegations about Russian money laundering were being raised. Timothy L. O'Brien, "Follow the Money, If You Can," *New York Times*, September 5, 1999.
19. Alexei Tsyganok, vice president, Russian Trading System, letter to the author, November 16, 1999; National Association of Participants in the Stock Market, letter to the council of directors of the Russian Trading System, June 19, 1999.
20. Yukos, press release, July 21, 1999: "The position of Dmitry Vasiliev in the conflict of Yukos with the Dart group has become tendentious."
21. The criminal case against Vasiliev was quietly dropped a month after his resignation.
22. "Yukos, Rising to the First Tier," Credit Suisse First Boston (Europe) Ltd., March 8, 2001, p. 27.
23. Khodorkovsky later disclosed that two of the three lenders in the 1998 $500 million loan, Merrill Lynch and Goldman Sachs, had panicked after the crash and sold their paper for as little as eighteen cents on the dollar. They sold because they thought Yukos might default. Khodorkovsky said the two lost about $150 million "needlessly" (Khodorkovsky to reporters and editors at the *Washington Post*, May 18, 2000). Yukos later canceled all the planned share emissions and transfers to offshore zones—the threat had sufficed.
24. Berezovsky, interview by author, February 28, 2001.
25. Luzhkov said Skuratov had been subject to "blackmail" with the video, which he said was made a year earlier. The upper chamber of parliament, the Federation Council, was responsible for overseeing the prosecutor. When the matter arose, Luzhkov, a leading member of the chamber, joined his fellow regional leaders in voting to keep Skuratov on the job. Yeltsin was furious.
26. Berezovsky, comments to reporters and editors of the *Washington Post*, September 19, 2000.

27. As a precaution, Luzhkov requested, and won, approval from the city council to advance the date of the next mayoral election from June 2000 to December 1999. Luzhkov won reelection by 70 percent of the vote.
28. Some of the Berezovsky-Dorenko calls were published in the newspaper *Novaya Gazeta* on December 16, 1999. The newspaper often published materials from shady special services. Dorenko told me that the transcript was accurate but may have included several calls between him and Berezovsky as they planned the attack. Dorenko called the tycoon "Bor" instead of Boris, and Berezovsky called Dorenko "dear." Berezovsky confirmed the accuracy of the transcripts and also said they may have been a compilation.
29. The donor was Behjget Pacolli, the Swiss businessman who was reportedly at the center of the Kremlin reconstruction scandal. Pacolli, whose firms restored the Kremlin halls, complained rather piously that he spent $870,000 to rebuild the hospital at Luzhkov's request but never received so much as a thank-you note.
30. The *New York Times* reported in mid-August 1999 that U.S. investigators were probing a "money laundering" scheme in which billions of dollars was spirited out of Russia. In February 2000, a former bank vice president, Lucy Edwards, and her husband, Peter Berlin, pleaded guilty to running the scheme through a company, Benex International, that channeled money from Russia through the Bank of New York and on to other destinations. However, they were just couriers, and the people who ordered the money sent out of Russia were not identified. Most of it appeared to be capital flight: money avoiding taxes, duties, and risks inside Russia.
31. *Komsomolskaya Pravda*, October 5, 1999, p. 2.
32. Luzhkov interview, broadcast on TV6, a Moscow-based channel, October 31, 1999.
33. Yelena Baturina, interview by author, August 23, 1999.
34. Berezovsky, meeting with correspondents, November 26, 1999.
35. Renaud, letter to the editor.
36. Robyn Dixon, "Pushing the Boundaries of a Free Press; Russia: Media Tycoon's Struggle with the Kremlin Is Seen as a Litmus Test of What President Putin Will Allow," *Los Angeles Times*, June 1, 2000. Gusinsky repeated his version of the meeting at a briefing for correspondents, including the author, on June 2, 2000.
37. Andrei Vandenko, "The Kremlin Will Be Paying Back with Interest," *Komsomolskaya Pravda*, August 3, 1999, pp. 3–5. Interview with Voloshin.
38. Susan B. Glasser and Peter Baker, "Kremlin Wages War of Nerves: TV Network Struggles with Outside Pressures and Internal Tension," *Washington Post*, January 29, 2001, p. A13.
39. Berezovsky's role in the onset of the Chechen hostilities has been the subject of much speculation. Berezovsky had good connections among some Chechen groups, but I think he was more of an intermediary than an instigator. The origins of the second war lie primarily in disorder inside Chechnya and weariness with the conflict in Moscow. The first factor, internal disorder, was caused by a split between Aslan Maskhadov, the Chechen president, and Basayev. Maskhadov, who had been Moscow's interlocutor, lost control of the disparate Chechen fighting groups. The second factor was Kremlin indecision. Anton Surikov, a former Russian military intelligence officer who later became a staff

director of a Russian parliamentary committee, told me Russian officials had indications that Basayev was planning something on the Dagestani border that summer. "It was not being hidden," he said. "There was a certain panic here. There was a feeling of complete helplessness." Likewise, Voloshin said in August, "The dates [of the Basayev assault] were definitely known several days before." But, he added, the "area is hilly and difficult to guard. There are hundreds of different paths, plenty of canyons, mountain paths. There is no border, actually. . . . That is why it is not possible just to line up soldiers to guard the border." Berezovsky told me that he began warning the Kremlin in May and June 1999 that Chechen commanders were telling him that things were getting out of control and "there may be trouble in Dagestan." Berezovsky added, "I passed it all on to Stepashin, who was the prime minister then. I had a meeting with him and told him. He said, 'Boris, don't worry. We know everything, all is under control.'" Separately, Stepashin told me the planning for a crackdown on Chechnya was under way earlier in the year after a Russian Interior Ministry general was kidnapped. He said the Russian authorities had intelligence in June of a possible attack, and "we were planning to implement" a cordon around Chechnya "irrespective of Basayev's assault." Stepashin said he chaired a meeting of the Kremlin Security Council in July, and "we all came to the conclusion that there was a huge hole on our border that won't be closed if we don't [advance] to the Terek [River inside Chechnya]. It was a purely military decision." Stepashin said that after his dismissal, Putin picked up the plans he had put in place and continued with them. Basayev's reasons for staging the dramatic cross-border incursion, and his reading of how Russia would respond, are not clear. He declared at the time that he hoped to trigger an uprising in Dagestan, rallying support for the creation of an Islamic state. But it was a futile effort. The raid triggered alarms in Dagestan, which is a mosaic of ethnic groups, and many villages began arming themselves to fight the Chechens. Eventually Russian troops beat them back to the border, and Putin launched the larger offensive. Another unanswered question is who was responsible for the apartment house bombings that triggered the war. Putin and his government blamed Chechens. Inside Russia, some have speculated that the blasts were carried out by shadowy groups possibly linked to security services as a way to propel Putin to power. When Berezovsky was asked about this on September 19, 2000, during a meeting with *Washington Post* editors and reporters, he said that at first he could not believe the security services would have done it; he was sure it was the Chechens. But, he added, "I have more and more doubts that it was done by Chechens."

40. "Oleg Dobrodeyev: The Army: These Are Our Brothers and Sons," *Krasnaya Zvezda*, September 29, 1999. Dobrodeyev left NTV in January 2000 and was appointed head of the government-owned channel, RTR.
41. Berezovsky took credit for the creation of Unity in the May interview and again in a meeting with *Washington Post* reporters and editors, September 19, 2000.
42. As a member of parliament, Berezovsky would also enjoy automatic immunity from prosecution, unless revoked by a majority of the chamber. However, he denied running for this reason.
43. Radio Mayak, March 18, 2000.

44. Gusinsky, remarks to reporters at Media-Most headquarters building, June 2, 2000.
45. Gusinsky interview, *Obshchaya Gazeta*, June 8–14, 2000, pp. 1–3.
46. Putin and his representatives repeatedly used this $1.3 billion figure to suggest that Gusinsky owed all the money at once. In fact, the debts were spread out over the coming years, according to a schedule prepared by Gusinsky in July 2000. The $211 million CSFB loan guaranteed by Gazprom came due in March 2000. Then NTV had a $40 million loan from Gazprom bank due in November. A $262 million loan from CSFB to Media-Most was due in July 2001. A $223 million loan from the city of Moscow to Media-Most was due in February 2003, and a $40 million loan to Media-Most from Vneshtorg Bank in May 2003. The Gusinsky companies also had $222 million in loans from the state savings bank, Sberbank, which was collateralized by Russian government dollar-denominated bonds which, on maturity in 2003, will be $72.3 million in excess of the loans. By 2009 Gusinsky must pay off the $123.7 million balance on the U.S. ExIm Bank loan for the satellite. The Russian Finance Ministry also guaranteed a $32.5 million loan for purchase of a Russian satellite. Gusinsky and his top officials often said that although the company had large debts, it was growing rapidly and NTV was profitable before the 1998 crash.
47. Dorenko, interview by author, February 16, 2001.
48. Gusinsky, in appearance on *Glas Naroda,* June 20, 2000.
49. I once attended a "background" briefing by Lesin for a group of journalists. Lesin told journalists he was only trying to serve as an intermediary between the Kremlin and Gusinsky. But numerous other sources said Lesin played a key role in bringing pressure to bear on Gusinsky.
50. This part, protocol 6, of the agreement was controversial. It said that the case against Gusinsky would be dropped and that Gusinsky and members of his companies could stay in Russia or leave as they pleased, as long as they did not damage the Russian state. The document is initialed by Lesin and Kokh. Lesin clearly did not have the power to drop the case against Gusinsky. Kokh later claimed the document was Gusinsky's idea.
51. Berezovsky's longtime confidant and deputy, Badri Patarkatsishvili, added details about the Kremlin's intentions in an interview published July 4, 2001, in *Kommersant Daily*, Berezovsky's newspaper. He said that another Berezovsky aide, Nikolai Glushkov, had been arrested to pressure Berezovsky. In order to get Glushkov out of jail, Patarkatsishvili said, the Kremlin insisted that Berezovsky "sell the media empire and . . . end his political activity." He said the conditions were set by Voloshin. After Berezovsky gave up his shares in ORT, the Kremlin refused to have Glushkov released from jail. Voloshin "deceived" them, he charged.

Bibliography

Aganbegyan, Abel. *The Economic Challenge of Perestroika.* Bloomington: Indiana University Press, 1988.

———. *Inside Perestroika: The Future of the Soviet Economy.* New York: Harper & Row, 1989.

Aganbegyan, Abel, ed. *Perestroika Annual: Two.* New York: Brassey's, 1989.

———. *Perestroika, 1989.* New York: Scribner's, 1988.

Aksyonov, Vassily. *The Island of Crimea.* New York: Random House, 1983.

Albats, Yevgenia. *The State Within a State.* New York: Farrar Straus Giroux, 1994.

Aron, Leon. *Yeltsin: A Revolutionary Life.* New York: St. Martin's, 2000.

Åslund, Anders. *Building Capitalism.* Cambridge: Cambridge University Press, 2001.

———. *Gorbachev's Struggle for Economic Reform.* Ithaca: Cornell University Press, 1991.

———. *How Russia Became a Market Economy.* Washington, DC: Brookings Institution, 1995.

Åslund, Anders, ed. *Economic Transformation in Russia.* London: Pinter, 1994.

Barker, Adele Marie, ed. *Consuming Russia: Popular Culture, Sex, and Society Since Gorbachev.* Durham, N.C.: Duke University Press, 1999.

Baturin, Yuri, et al. *Epokha Yeltsina* (The Yeltsin Epoch). Moscow: Vagrius, 2001.

Bergson, Abram, and Herbet S. Levine, eds. *The Soviet Economy: Toward the Year 2000.* London: George Allen & Unwin, 1983.

Berlin, Isaiah. *Karl Marx.* Oxford: Oxford University Press, 1996.

Blasi, Joseph R., Maya Kroumova, and Douglas Kruse. *Kremlin Capitalism: Privatizing the Russian Economy.* Ithaca: Cornell University Press, 1997.

Bortsov, Yuri. *Yuri Luzhkov.* Rostov-on-Don: Feniks, 1999.

Boycko [Boiko], Maxim, Andrei Shleifer, and Robert Vishny. *Privatizing Russia.* Cambridge: MIT Press, 1995.

Brady, Rose. *Kapitalizm.* New Haven: Yale University Press, 1999.

Brown, Archie. *The Gorbachev Factor.* Oxford: Oxford University Press, 1996.

Bunin, Igor. *Biznesmeni Rossii* (Businessmen of Russia). Moscow: OKO, 1994.

Chernow, Ron. *The Death of the Banker.* New York: Vintage, 1997.

———. *The House of Morgan: An American Banking Dynasty and the Rise of Modern Finance.* New York: Simon & Schuster, 1990.

Chubais, Anatoly, ed. *Privatizatzia Po-Rossiiski* (Privatization in the Russian way). Moscow: Vagrius, 1999.

Coase, R. H. *The Firm, the Market, and the Law.* Chicago: University of Chicago Press, 1988.

Colton, Timothy. *Moscow.* Cambridge: Harvard University Press, Belknap Press, 1995.

Dallin, Alexander, and Gail W. Lapidus, eds. *The Soviet System: From Crisis to Collapse.* Boulder: Westview, 1995.

De Préneuf, Flore Martinant. "The Historical and Political Significance of the Reconstruction of the Cathedral of Christ the Saviour in Moscow." M.Phil. thesis, Oxford University, 1997.

Dobbs, Michael. *Down with Big Brother.* New York: Knopf, 1997.

Dreiser, Theodore. *An American Tragedy.* 1925.

———. *The Financier.* 1912.

Dubov, Yuli. *Bolshaya Paika.* Moscow: Vagrius, 2000.

Ellman, Michael, and Vladimir Kontorovich, eds. *The Destruction of the Soviet Economic System: An Insider's History.* New York: Sharpe, 1998.

Erofeyev, Venedict. *Moskva-Petushki.* Paris: Albin Michel, 1979. In English: *Moscow Circles.* London: Writers and Readers Publishing Cooperative, 1981. Originally *samizdat* (early 1970s).

European Bank for Reconstruction and Development. *Transition Report 1998: Financial Sector in Transition.* London: EBRD, 1998.

———. *Transition Report 1999: Ten Years of Transition.* London: EBRD, 1999.

Fischer, Benjamin B., ed. *At Cold War's End: U.S. Intelligence on the Soviet Union and Eastern Europe, 1989–1991.* Washington, D.C.: Center for the Study of Intelligence, CIA, 1999.

Fitzpatrick, Shelia, Alexander Rabinowitch, and Richard Stites, eds. *Russia in the Era of NEP.* Bloomington: Indiana University Press, 1991.

Freeland, Chrystia. *Sale of the Century.* New York: Crown Business, 2000.

Gaidar, Yegor. *Days of Defeat and Victory.* Seattle: University of Washington Press, 1999.

Gaidar, Yegor, ed. *Ekonomika Perekhodnova Perioda* (Economics of the transition period). Moscow: Institute for the Economy in Transition, 1998.

Galbraith, John Kenneth. *A History of Economics: The Past as the Present.* London: Hamish Hamilton, 1987.

Gall, Carlotta, and Thomas de Waal. *Chechnya: Calamity in the Caucasus.* New York: New York University Press, 1998.

Goltsov, C., A. Myakenky, and C. Shoiko. *Surrogaty Tsennikh Bumag: Teoriya, Praktika, Dokumenty* (Surrogate money: Theory, practice, and documents). Moscow, 1998. A guide for law enforcement bodies.

Gorbachev, Mikhail. *Memoirs.* New York: Doubleday, 1995.

Gregory, Paul R. *Before Command: An Economic History of Russia from Emancipation to the First Five-Year Plan.* Princeton: Princeton University Press, 1994.

Gustafson, Thane. *Capitalism Russian-Style.* Cambridge: Cambridge University Press, 1999.

———. *Crisis Amid Plenty: The Politics of Soviet Energy under Brezhnev and Gorbachev.* Princeton: Princeton University Press, 1989.

Haines, Gerald K., and Robert E. Leggett. *CIA's Analysis of the Soviet Union, 1947–1991.* Washington, DC: Center for the Study of Intelligence, CIA, 2001.

Handelman, Stephen. *Comrade Criminal.* London: Michael Joseph, 1994.

Haupt, Robert. *Last Boat to Astrakhan: A Russian Memoir, 1990–1996.* Milsons Point, N.S.W.: Random House Australia, 1996.

Hayek, Friedrich A. *The Fatal Conceit: The Errors of Socialism.* Chicago: University of Chicago Press. 1988.

———. *Individualism and Economic Order.* Chicago: University of Chicago Press. 1948.

———. *The Road to Serfdom.* Chicago: University of Chicago Press, 1944.

Hellman, Joel Scott. "Breaking the Bank: Bureaucrats and the Creation of Markets in a Transitional Economy." Ph.D. diss., Columbia University, 1993.

Helsinki Watch. *Nyeformalny: Civil Society in the USSR.* A Helsinki Watch Report, February 1990.

Hewett, Ed A. *Reforming the Soviet Economy.* Washington: Brookings Institution, 1988.

Hewett, Ed A., and Victor H. Winston, eds. *Milestones in Glasnost and Perestroyka: Politics and People.* Washington: Brookings Institution, 1991.

Hosking, Geoffrey. *A History of the Soviet Union, 1917–1991.* London: Fontana, 1992.

Johnson, Juliet. *A Fistful of Rubles: The Rise and Fall of the Russian Banking System.* Ithaca: Cornell University Press, 2000.

Josephson, Matthew. *The Robber Barons.* New York: Harcourt Brace, 1934.

Kaiser, Robert G. *Russia: The People and the Power.* London: Secker & Warburg, 1976.

———. *Why Gorbachev Happened.* New York: Simon & Schuster, 1991.

Kaufman, Richard F., and John P. Hardt, eds. *The Former Soviet Union in Transition.* Armonk, N.Y.: Sharpe, 1993. Joint Economic Committee, U.S. Congress.

Khodorkovsky, Mikhail, and Leonid Nevzlin. *Chelovek C Rublyom* (Man with a ruble). Moscow: Mentep-Inform, 1992.

Kirichenko, E. *Khram Khrista Spasitelya B Moskve* (Cathedral of Christ the Savior in Moscow). Moscow: Planeta, 1992.

Klebnikov, Paul. *Godfather of the Kremlin: Boris Berezovsky and the Looting of Russia.* New York: Harcourt, 2000.

Knight, Amy W. *The KGB: Police and Politics in the Soviet Union.* Winchester, Mass.: Allen & Unwin, 1988.

Kokh, Alfred. *The Selling of the Soviet Empire.* New York: SPI Books, 1998.

Kornai, János. *Economics of Shortage.* Amsterdam: North Holland Publishing, 1980.

———. *The Socialist System: The Political Economy of Communism.* Oxford: Oxford University Press, 1992.

Korzhakov, Alexander. *Boris Yeltsin: Ot Rassveta Do Zakata* (Boris Yeltsin: From dawn till dusk). Moscow: Interbuk, 1997.

Lane, David. *The Political Economy of Russian Oil.* Lanham, Md.: Rowman & Littlefield, 1999.

Layard, Richard, and John Parker. *The Coming Russian Boom: A Guide to New Markets and Politics.* New York: Free Press, 1996.

Ledeneva, Alena V. *Russia's Economy of Favors: Blat, Networking, and Informal Exchange.* Cambridge: Cambridge University Press, 1998.

Lloyd, John. *Rebirth of a Nation: An Anatomy of Russia.* London: Michael Joseph, 1998.

Luzhkov, Yuri. *My Deti Tvoi, Moskva* (We are your children, Moscow). Moscow: Vagrius, 1996. In English, revised: Moscow *Does Not Believe in Tears.* Chicago: Martin, 1996.

Malia, Martin. *The Soviet Tragedy: A History of Socialism in Russia, 1917–1991.* New York: Free Press, 1994.

Marx, Karl, and Friedrich Engels. *The Communist Manifesto.* London, 1848.

Marx, Karl, and Friedrich Engels, eds. *Capital.* Vol. 1. 100th anniversary edition of the original 1867 German edition. New York: International Publishers, 1967.

McFaul, Michael. *Russia's 1996 Presidential Election: The End of Polarized Politics.* Stanford, Calif.: Hoover Institution Press, 1997.

———. *Russia's Unfinished Revolution: Political Change from Gorbachev to Putin.* Ithaca: Cornell University Press, 2001.

Mickiewicz, Ellen. *Changing Channels: Television and the Struggle for Power in Russia.* Oxford: Oxford University Press, 1997.

Mukhin, Alexei. *"Oligarkhi" Rossii* ("Oligarchs" of Russia). Moscow: CPIK-Tsenter, 1999.

Myslovsky, Yevgeny. *Vnimaniye: "Kidal-Invest"* (Beware: "Swindle-invest"). Moscow: Spas, 1996.

Naishul, Vitaly. *Another Life.* Moscow. Available at www.inme.ru/d1 and www.libertarium.ru. Originally samizdat, 1985.

Nove, Alec. *An Economic History of the USSR.* London: Penguin, 1992.

Oberdorfer, Don. *The Turn.* New York: Simon & Schuster, 1991.

Organization for Economic Cooperation and Development. *Russian Federation: Economic Survey, 1999–2000.* Paris: OECD, 2000.

Palazchenko, Pavel. *My Years with Gorbachev and Shevardnadze.* University Park: Pennsylvania State University Press, 1997.

Pelevin, Victor. *Babylon.* London: Faber & Faber, 2000.

Popov, Gavriil. *Ot i Do: Rossiya Put' K Sotsial-demokratii* (From and 'til: Russia, the path to social democracy). Moscow: Galactica, 1996.

Randolph, Eleanor. *Waking the Tempests: Ordinary Life in the New Russia.* New York: Simon & Schuster, 1996.

Remnick, David. *Lenin's Tomb.* New York: Random House, 1993.

———. *Resurrection: The Struggle for a New Russia.* New York: Random House, 1997.

Ries, Nancy. *Russian Talk: Culture and Conversation During Perestroika.* Ithaca: Cornell University Press, 1997.

Roxburgh, Angus. *The Second Russian Revolution.* London: BBC Books, 1991.

Ryback, Timothy. *Rock Around the Bloc.* Oxford: Oxford University Press, 1990.

Sachs, Jeffrey. *Poland's Jump to the Market Economy.* Cambridge: MIT Press, 1993.

Sachs, Jeffrey D., and Katharina Pistor. *The Rule of Law and Economic Reform in Russia.* Boulder: Westview, 1997.

Shane, Scott. *Dismantling Utopia: How Information Ended the Soviet Union.* Chicago: Ivan R. Dee, 1994.

Shevtsova, Lilia. *Yeltsin's Russia: Myths and Reality.* Washington: Carnegie Endowment for International Peace, 1999.

Shleifer, Andrei, and Daniel Treisman. *Without a Map: Political Tactics and Economic Reform in Russia.* Cambridge: MIT Press, 2000.

Sinyavsky, Andrei. *Soviet Civilization: A Cultural History.* New York: Arcade, 1990.

Smith, Adam. *The Wealth of Nations.* Edited by Edwin Cannan. Chicago: University of Chicago Press, 1976.

Smith, Gordon B. *Soviet Politics: Struggling with Change.* London: Macmillan, 1992.

Solnick, Steven L. *Stealing the State: Control and Collapse in Soviet Institutions.* Cambridge: Harvard University Press, 1998.

Soros, George. *The Crisis of Global Capitalism: Open Society Endangered.* New York: PublicAffairs, 1998.

———. *Open Society: Reforming Global Capitalism.* New York: PublicAffairs, 2000.

Smith, Hedrick. *The Russians.* New York: Quadrangle/New York Times Book, 1976.

Steele, Jonathan. *Eternal Russia.* London: Faber & Faber, 1994.

Streletsky, Valery. *Obscurantism.* Moscow: Detektiv Press, 1999.

Taranovski, Theodore. *Reform in Modern Russian History: Progress or Cycle?* Washington, DC: Woodrow Wilson Center Press; Cambridge: Cambridge University Press, 1995.

Tarkhanov, Alexei, and Sergei Kavtaradze. *Architecture of the Stalin Era.* New York: Rizzoli International, 1992.

Troitsky, Artemy. *Back in the USSR.* London: Omnibus, 1987.

Tucker, Robert C. *The Marx-Engels Reader.* New York: Norton, 1972.

Ulyukaev, Alexei. *B Ozhidanii Krizisa* (In expectation of crisis). Moscow: Strelets, 1999.

Vaksberg, Arkady. *The Soviet Mafia.* New York: St. Martin's, 1991.

Vasiliev, Sergei. *Ten Years of Russian Economic Reform: A Collection of Papers.* London: Center for Research into Post-Communist Economies, 1999.

West, James L., and Iurii A. Petrov, eds. *Merchant Moscow: Images of Russia's Vanished Bourgeoisie.* Princeton: Princeton University Press, 1998.

White, Stephen. *Russia Goes Dry.* Cambridge: Cambridge University Press, 1996.

Williams, Phil, ed. "Russian Organized Crime: The New Threat?" *Transnational Organized Crime* 2, nos. 2–3 (1996). Special double issue.

Wilson, David, and Geoffrey Dayton. *Soviet Oil and Gas to 1990: The Market for LPG.* Cambridge, Mass.: Abt Associates, 1982.

Wolfe, Bertram D. *Three Who Made a Revolution.* New York: Time-Life Books, 1964.

Woodruff, David. *Money Unmade: Barter and the Fate of Russian Capitalism.* Ithaca: Cornell University Press, 1999.

Yeltsin, Boris. *Midnight Diaries.* New York: PublicAffairs, 2000.

———. *The Struggle for Russia.* New York: Times Books, 1994.

Yurchak, Alexei. "The Cynical Reason of Late Socialism: Language, Ideology, and Culture of the Last Soviet Generation." Ph.D. diss., Duke University, 1997.

Zaslavskaya, Tatyana. *The Second Socialist Revolution: An Alternative Soviet Strategy.* Bloomington: Indiana University Press, 1990.

Acknowledgments

I benefited from the generous assistance of many people who offered recollections, documents, and comments on this book. Masha Lipman, the most skilled and insightful of a new generation of Russian journalists, guided me for more than five years through contemporary Russia, and brilliantly scrutinized every chapter. Natalia Alexandrova was a tireless translator, an inspiring critic, and a friend dedicated to telling this story as well as it could be told. Irina Makarova not only took me on a train ride to the past, described in Chapter 1, but devoted great energy and talent to translating and research.

Glenn Waller, one of the most astute observers of Russia in the 1990s, shared his experiences and thoughts over many hours of conversation. Michael McFaul provided a spark of inspiration and years of valuable counsel. Olga Kryshtanovskaya patiently tutored me on the structure, history, and habits of the oligarchy. Chrystia Freeland, the *Financial Times* bureau chief in Moscow during the 1990s, often scooped me but never failed me as friend, colleague, and traveling companion in these tumultuous years, which took us through decaying factories, ghostly coal mines, and mysterious Russian corporate boardrooms. Anders Åslund chronicled the economic history of the Gorbachev and Yeltsin years in his own works, and in many conversations enhanced my understanding of the unfolding story. Steven L. Solnick provided encouragement and key materials on the collapse of the Komsomol. Thomas E. Graham helped me sort through countless riddles of the oligarchy. Joel Hellman had the good fortune to see the tycoons in action during the early years, and he provided sharp analysis of the later period in many of our meetings in Moscow. William Browder was a wise tutor in how to penetrate the obscure business empires of the oligarchs.

At the *Washington Post*, I am especially indebted to the late Katharine Graham, for her early faith in me, and Donald Graham, for both his personal encouragement and his profound commitment to journalism. With rare vision, Jackson Diehl saw the oligarchs as a story for the *Post* and encouraged me to write this book. I owe a special debt to Robert Kaiser, who led the way with his long-standing interest in Russia and his leadership as an editor; he provided constant support and valued criticism. Benjamin C.

Bradlee, Leonard Downie Jr., and Steve Coll built a great reporting enterprise that devoted time, space, and resources to the story of Russia in the 1990s. Glenn Frankel was a terrific writing coach. Phil Bennett taught me about elegant editing. Lou Cannon was a mentor and partner from my first days at the *Post*. Michael Getler launched me into the world of foreign correspondence. Michael Dobbs and David Remnick showed the way with great Moscow correspondence during perestroika and after. I also received help and contributions from *Post* colleagues Peter Baker, Paul Blustein, Alan Cooperman, Douglas Farah, Mary Lou Foy, Susan Glasser, Virginia Hamill, Fred Hiatt, Jim Hoagland, Lee Hockstader, Sharon LaFraniere, Robert McCartney, Steven Mufson, Don Oberdorfer, Lucian Perkins, Gene Robinson, Margaret Shapiro, Peter Slevin, and Daniel Williams.

In Moscow, Jörg Eigendorf was gracious and unstinting with his experiences and archives. Patricia Kranz of *Business Week* shared important material from her interviews. Flore de Preneuf made available her fine research on the Cathedral of Christ the Savior, and William Flemming shared his careful study of the loans-for-shares transactions.

I am deeply indebted to Margaret Paxson, an anthropologist, who devoted a year to research on the oligarchy, and to Masha Danilova, who translated with curiosity and enthusiasm. Jeff Kahn, Anna Masterova, Marlena Hurley, and Anne Nivat also contributed. I thank my friend Sergei Belyakov, navigator of life; Volodya Alexandrov, manager of all things; and Nadia Avinerious, patient teacher.

I am grateful to St Antony's College, Oxford, and Professor Archie Brown for an enriching year of study there.

Esther Newberg found this book a home. Peter Osnos of PublicAffairs was an enthusiast from the beginning, when it was a distant dream, and made it a reality. Kate Darnton was a splendid editor.

A large number of people granted interviews, offered documents, and freely gave advice. They include Tom Adshead, Yevgenia Albats, Pyotr Aven, Vasily Babikov, Oleg Babinov, Mikhail Baev, Yelena Baturina, Alexander Bekker, Sergei Belyaev, Valery Belyakovich, Mikhail Berger, Bernard Black, Andrei Bogolubov, Paul Bograd, Leonid Boguslavsky, Maxim Boiko, Vladimir Bokser, Mark Bond, Artyom Borovik, Konstantin Borovoi, Al Breach, Pavel Bunich, Igor Bunin, Michael Caputo, Nikolai Chetverikov, Igor Chubais, Oleg Churilov, Timothy Colton, Mark D'Anastasio, Mikhail Dmitriev, Tamara Dobretsova, Oleg Dobrodeyev, Mikhail Dodonov, Sergei Dorenko, Yuli Dubov, Sergei Ermakov, James Fenkner, Murray Feshbach, David Filipov, Andrew Fox, Yegor Gaidar, Natalya Gevorkyan, Martin Gilman, Grigory Glazkov, Alex Goldfarb, Andrei Gorodetsky, Leonid Gozman, Vladimir Grodsky, Peter Halloran, Jonathan Hay, Victor Huaco, Andrei Illarionov, Valery Ivanov, Sergei Ivanov, Anatoly Ivanov, Steven Jennings, Donald Jensen, Boris Jordan, Xavier Jordan, Konstantin Kagalovsky, Jan Kalicki, Sergei Karaganov, Alexei Kara-Murza, Irina Karelina, Alexander Khachaturov, Boris Khait, Alexander Khandruyev, Sergei Kiriyenko, Yevgeny Kiselyov, Sonia Kishkovsky, Oleg Klimov, Alfred Kokh, Anatoly Kolosov, Vladimir Korabelnikov, Vladimir Koshelev, Yevgeny Kovrov, Andrew Kramer, Yelena Krasnitskaya, Eduard Krasnyansky, Eric Kraus, Margery Kraus, Veronika Kutsillo, Viktor Kuvaldin, Mikhail Larkin, Yulia Latynina, Mikhail Leontiev, Mark Levin, Tatyana Likhonova, Ruslan Linkov, Sergei Lisovsky, Alexander Livshitz, John Lloyd, Augusto Lopez-Claros, Vladimir Lopukhin, Viktor Loshak, Vladimir Lototsky, Igor Malashenko, Mikhail Margelov, Sergei Markov, Andrew Meier, Andrei Melnichenko, Alexander Minkin, Vladimir Mokrousov, Valentina Mokrousova, Sergei Monakhov, Nat Moser, Mikhail Moskvin-Tarkhanov, Alexei Mukhin, Arkady Murashev, Alexander Muzykantsky, Yevgeny Myslovsky, Vitaly Naishul, Boris Nemtsov, Leonid Nevzlin, Leonid Nikitinsky, Vyacheslav Nikonov, Kemer Norkin, Stephen O'Sullivan, Nina Oding, Mikhail Ogorodnikov, John

Ordway, Alexander Oslon, Alexander Osovtsov, Dmitri Ostalsky, Alexander Panin, Sergei Parkhomenko, Sergei Pashin, Masha Pavkenko, Boris Pavlov, Gary Peach, Brian Pinto, Andrei Piontkovsky, Larisa Piyasheva, Dzhokhan Pollyeva, Dmitri Ponomarev, Gavriil Popov, Vladimir Potanin, Igor Primakov, Thomas Reed, Yuri Reva, Andrei Richter, Sergei Rogov, Leonid Rozhetskin, Hans-Joerg Rudloff, Charles Ryan, Yevgeny Savostyanov, Vasily Shakhnovsky, Akexander Sheindlin, Lilia Shevtsova, Mikhail Shneider, Yuri Skuratov, Dmitri Sliko, Tim Smith, Galina Starovoitova, Olga Starovoitova, Sergei Stupar, Bernard Sucher, Vladislav Surkov, Ludmila Telen, John Thornhill, Gary Titarenko, Andrei Trapeznikov, Vitaly Tretyakov, Yuri Tselikov, Alexei Uluykaev, Chris Van Riet, Levan Vasadze, Dmitri Vasiliev, Sergei Vasiliev, Alexei Venediktov, Vladimir Vinogradov, Alexander Vladislavlev, Masha Volkenstein, James Wallar, Brian Whitmore, Richard Wirthlin, Alexei Yablokov, Yuri Yarmagayev, Nina Yermakova, Yevgeny Yasin, Arkady Yevstafiev, Vladimir Yevtushenkov, Alexei Yurchak, Konstantin Zatulin, Yuri Zektser, Larisa Zelkova, Bella Zlatkis, Andrei Zorin, Alexander Zurabov, and Sergei Zverev.

Most of all, I am forever indebted to my wife, Carole, for her care and support of the whole project, from the first files to the final sentences, and I thank my sons Daniel and Benjamin, and my parents, for their forbearance during my long absences.

Index

PublicAffairs is a nonfiction publishing house founded in 1997. It is a tribute to the standards, values, and flair of three persons who have served as mentors to countless reporters, writers, editors, and book people of all kinds, including me.

I.F. STONE, proprietor of *I. F. Stone's Weekly*, combined a commitment to the First Amendment with entrepreneurial zeal and reporting skill and became one of the great independent journalists in American history. At the age of eighty, Izzy published *The Trial of Socrates,* which was a national bestseller. He wrote the book after he taught himself ancient Greek.

BENJAMIN C. BRADLEE was for nearly thirty years the charismatic editorial leader of *The Washington Post.* It was Ben who gave the *Post* the range and courage to pursue such historic issues as Watergate. He supported his reporters with a tenacity that made them fearless and it is no accident that so many became authors of influential, best-selling books.

ROBERT L. BERNSTEIN, the chief executive of Random House for more than a quarter century, guided one of the nation's premier publishing houses. Bob was personally responsible for many books of political dissent and argument that challenged tyranny around the globe. He is also the founder and longtime chair of Human Rights Watch, one of the most respected human rights organizations in the world.

For fifty years, the banner of Public Affairs Press was carried by its owner Morris B. Schnapper, who published Gandhi, Nasser, Toynbee, Truman and about 1,500 other authors. In 1983, Schnapper was described by *The Washington Post* as "a redoubtable gadfly." His legacy will endure in the books to come.

Peter Osnos, *Publisher*